PRAISE FOR *WRITE GREAT CODE, VOLUME 1: UNDERSTANDING THE MACHINE*

"If you are programming without benefit of formal training, or if you lack the aegis of a mentor, Randall Hyde's Write Great Code series should rouse your interest . . . The first five chapters and the Boolean Logic chapter are worth the price of the book."
—UNIX REVIEW

"The book explains in detail what most programmers take for granted."
–COMPUTER SHOPPER (UK)

"Great fun to read."
—VSJ MAGAZINE

"Not for the novice, this book details the innermost workings of the machine at a very complex level. Programmers who are interested in working at that level will the find the book most helpful."
—SECURITYITWORLD.COM

"It fills in the blanks nicely and really could be part of a Computer Science degree required reading set. . . . Once this book is read, you will have a greater understanding and appreciation for code that is written efficiently—and you may just know enough to do that yourself."
—MACCOMPANION, AFTER GIVING IT A 5 OUT OF 5 STARS RATING

"*Write Great Code: Understanding the Machine* should be on the required reading list for anyone who wants to develop terrific code in any language without having to learn assembly language."
—WEBSERVERTALK

"Hyde is taking on a topic that continues to lie at the core of all development, the foundations of computer architecture."
—PRACTICAL APPLICATIONS

"Isn't your typical 'teach yourself to program' bo͙ ͙ ͙ relevant to all languages, and all levels of programming experie ͙ and read this book."
—BAY AREA LARGE INSTALLATION SYSTEM ADMINIS

D1379361

WRITE GREAT CODE

Volume 2: Thinking Low-Level, Writing High-Level

by Randall Hyde

NO STARCH
PRESS
San Francisco

Publisher: William Pollock
Managing Editor: Elizabeth Campbell
Cover and Interior Design: Octopod Studios
Developmental Editor: Jim Compton
Technical Reviewer: Benjamin David Lunt
Copyeditor: Kathy Grider-Carlyle
Compositor: Riley Hoffman
Proofreader: Stephanie Provines

For information on book distributors or translations, please contact No Starch Press, Inc. directly:

No Starch Press, Inc.
555 De Haro Street, Suite 250, San Francisco, CA 94107
phone: 415.863.9900; fax: 415.863.9950; info@nostarch.com; www.nostarch.com

Library of Congress Cataloging-in-Publication Data (Volume 1)

Hyde, Randall.
  Write great code : understanding the machine / Randall Hyde.
      p. cm.
  ISBN 1-59327-003-8
1. Computer programming. 2. Computer architecture. I. Title.
    QA76.6.H94 2004
    005.1--dc22
                                            2003017502

BRIEF CONTENTS

CONTENTS IN DETAIL

5
COMPILER OPERATION AND CODE GENERATION 61

6
TOOLS FOR ANALYZING COMPILER OUTPUT 115

7
CONSTANTS AND HIGH-LEVEL LANGUAGES 165

8
VARIABLES IN A HIGH-LEVEL LANGUAGE 189

9
ARRAY DATA TYPES   241

10
STRING DATA TYPES   281

11
POINTER DATA TYPES   315

14
CONTROL STRUCTURES AND
PROGRAMMATIC DECISIONS

439

15
ITERATIVE CONTROL STRUCTURES

489

16
FUNCTIONS AND PROCEDURES   521

ENGINEERING SOFTWARE   579

APPENDIX
A BRIEF COMPARISON OF THE 80X86 AND
POWERPC CPU FAMILIES   581

ONLINE APPENDICES   589

INDEX   591

ACKNOWLEDGMENTS

Originally, the material in this book was intended to appear as the last chapter of *Write Great Code, Volume 1*. Hillel Heinstein, the developmental editor for Volume 1, was concerned that the chapter was way too long and, despite its length, did not do the topic justice. We decided to expand the material and turn it into a separate volume, so Hillel is the first person I must acknowledge for this book's existence.

Of course, turning a 200-page chapter into a complete book is a major undertaking, and there have been a large number of people involved with the production of this book. I'd like to take a few moments to mention their names and the contributions they've made.

Mary Philips, a dear friend who helped me clean up *The Art of Assembly Language*, including some material that found its way into this book.

Bill Pollock, the publisher, who believes in the value of this series and has offered guidance and moral support.

Elizabeth Campbell, production manager and my major contact at No Starch, who has shepherded this project and made it a reality.

Kathy Grider-Carlyle, the editor, who lent her eyes to the grammar.

Jim Compton, the developmental editor, who spent considerable time improving the readability of this book.

Stephanie Provines, whose proofreading caught several typographical and layout errors.

Riley Hoffman, who handled the page layout chores and helped ensure that the book (especially the code listings) was readable.

Christina Samuell, who also worked on the book's layout and provided lots of general production help.

Benjamin David Lunt, the technical reviewer, who helped ensure the technical quality of this book.

Leigh Poehler and Patricia Witkin, who'll handle the sales and marketing of this book.

I would also like to acknowledge Susan Berge and Rachel Gunn, former editors at No Starch Press. Although they moved on to other positions before getting to see the final product, their input on this project was still valuable.

Finally, I would like to dedicate this book to my nieces and nephews: Gary, Courtney (Kiki), Cassidy, Vincent, Sarah Dawn, David, and Nicholas. I figure they will get a kick out of seeing their names in print.

INTRODUCTION

There are many aspects of great code—far too many to describe properly in a single book. Therefore, this second volume of the Write Great Code series concentrates on one important part of great code: performance. As computer systems have increased in performance from MHz, to hundreds of MHz, to GHz, the performance of computer software has taken a back seat to other concerns. Today, it is not at all uncommon for software engineers to exclaim, "You should never optimize your code!" Funny, you don't hear too many computer application users making such statements.

Although this book describes how to write efficient code, it is not a book about optimization. Optimization is a phase near the end of the software development cycle in which software engineers determine why their code does not meet performance specifications and then massage the code to achieve those specifications. But unfortunately, if no thought is put into the performance of the application until the optimization phase, it's unlikely that optimization will prove practical. The time to ensure that an application has reasonable performance characteristics is at the beginning, during the design and implementation phases. Optimization can fine-tune the performance of a system, but it can rarely deliver a miracle.

Although the quote is often attributed to Donald Knuth, who popularized it, it was Tony Hoare who originally said, "Premature optimization is the root of all evil." This statement has long been the rallying cry of software engineers who avoid any thought of application performance until the very end of the software-development cycle—at which point the optimization phase is typically ignored for economic or time-to-market reasons. However, Hoare did not say, "Concern about application performance during the early stages of an application's development is the root of all evil." He specifically said *premature optimization*, which, back then, meant counting cycles and instructions in assembly language code—not the type of coding you want to do during initial program design, when the code base is rather fluid. So, Hoare's comments were on the mark. The following excerpt from a short essay by Charles Cook (www.cookcomputing.com/blog/archives/000084.html) describes the problem with reading too much into this statement:

> I've always thought this quote has all too often led software designers into serious mistakes because it has been applied to a different problem domain to what was intended.
>
> The full version of the quote is "We should forget about small efficiencies, say about 97% of the time: premature optimization is the root of all evil." and I agree with this. It's usually not worth spending a lot of time micro-optimizing code before it's obvious where the performance bottlenecks are. But, conversely, when designing software at a system level, performance issues should always be considered from the beginning. A good software developer will do this automatically, having developed a feel for where performance issues will cause problems. An inexperienced developer will not bother, misguidedly believing that a bit of fine tuning at a later stage will fix any problems.

Hoare was really saying that software engineers should worry about other issues, like good algorithm design and good implementations of those algorithms, before they worry about traditional optimizations, like how many CPU cycles a particular statement requires for execution.

Although you could certainly apply many of this book's concepts during an optimization phase, most of the techniques here really need to be done during initial coding. If you put them off until you reach "code complete," it's unlikely they will ever find their way into your software. It's just too much work to implement these ideas after the fact.

This book will teach you how to choose appropriate high-level language (HLL) statements that translate into efficient machine code with a modern optimizing compiler. With most HLLs, using different statements provides many ways to achieve a given result; and, at the machine level, some of these ways are naturally more efficient than others. Though there may be a very good reason for choosing a less-efficient statement sequence over a more efficient one (e.g., for readability purposes), the truth is that most software engineers have no idea about the runtime costs of HLL statements. Without such knowledge, they are unable to make an educated choice concerning statement selection. The goal of this book is to change that.

An experienced software engineer may argue that the implementation of these individual techniques produces only minor improvements in performance. In some cases, this evaluation is correct; but we must keep in mind that these minor effects accumulate. While one can certainly abuse the techniques this book suggests, producing less readable and less maintainable code, it only makes sense that, when presented with two otherwise equivalent code sequences (from a system design point of view), you should choose the more efficient one. Unfortunately, many of today's software engineers don't know which of two implementations actually produces the more efficient code.

Though you don't need to be an expert assembly language programmer in order to write efficient code, if you're going to study compiler output (as you will do in this book), you'll need at least a reading knowledge of it. Chapters 3 and 4 provide a quick primer for 80x86 and PowerPC assembly language.

In Chapters 5 and 6, you'll learn about determining the quality of your HLL statements by examining compiler output. These chapters describe disassemblers, object code dump tools, debuggers, various HLL compiler options for displaying assembly language code, and other useful software tools.

The remainder of the book, Chapters 7 through 15, describes how compilers generate machine code for different HLL statements and data types. Armed with this knowledge, you will be able to choose the most appropriate data types, constants, variables, and control structures to produce efficient applications.

While you read, keep Dr. Hoare's quote in mind: "Premature optimization is the root of all evil." It is certainly possible to misapply the information in this book and produce code that is difficult to read and maintain. This would be especially disastrous during the early stages of your project's design and implementation, when the code is fluid and subject to change. But remember: This book is not about choosing the most efficient statement sequence, regardless of the consequences; it is about understanding the cost of various HLL constructs so that, when you have a choice, you can make an educated decision concerning which sequence to use. Sometimes, there are legitimate reasons to choose a less efficient sequence. However, if you do not understand the cost of a given statement, there is no way for you to choose a more efficient alternative.

Those interested in reading some additional essays about "the root of all evil" might want to check out the following web pages (my apologies if these URLs have become inactive since publication):

http://blogs.msdn.com/ricom/archive/2003/12/12/43245.aspx

http://en.widipedia.org/wiki/Software_optimization

1

THINKING LOW-LEVEL, WRITING HIGH-LEVEL

"If you want to write the best high-level language code, learn assembly language."
—Common programming advice

This book doesn't teach anything revolutionary. It describes a time-tested, well-proven approach to writing great code—to make sure you understand how the code you write will actually execute on a real machine. Programmers with a few decades of experience will probably find themselves nodding in recognition as they read this book. If they haven't seen a lot of code written by younger programmers who've never really mastered this material, they might even write it off. This book (and Volume 1 of this series) attempts to fill the gaps in the education of the current generation of programmers, so they can write quality code, too.

This particular volume of the Write Great Code series will teach you the following concepts:

- Why it's important to consider the low-level execution of your high-level programs

- How compilers generate machine code from high-level language (HLL) statements

- How compilers represent various data types using low-level, primitive, data types
- How to write your HLL code to help the compiler produce better machine code
- How to take advantage of a compiler's optimization facilities
- How to "think" in assembly language (low-level terms) while writing HLL code

The journey to understanding begins with this chapter. In it, we'll explore the following topics:

- Misconceptions programmers have about the code quality produced by typical compilers
- Why learning assembly language is still a good idea
- How to think in low-level terms while writing HLL code
- What you should know before reading this book
- How this book is organized
- And last, but not least, what constitutes great code

So without further ado, let's begin!

1.1 Misconceptions About Compiler Quality

In the early days of the personal computer revolution, high-performance software was written in assembly language. As time passed, optimizing compilers for high-level languages were improved, and their authors began claiming that the performance of compiler-generated code was within 10 to 50 percent of hand-optimized assembly code. Such proclamations ushered the ascent of high-level languages for PC application development, sounding the death knell for assembly language. Many programmers began quoting numbers like "my compiler achieves 90 percent of assembly's speed, so it's insane to use assembly language." The problem is that they never bothered to write hand-optimized assembly versions of their applications to check their claims. Often, their assumptions about their compiler's performance are wrong.

The authors of optimizing compilers weren't lying. Under the right conditions, an optimizing compiler can produce code that is almost as good as hand-optimized assembly language. However, the HLL code has to be written in an appropriate fashion to achieve these performance levels. To write HLL code in this manner requires a firm understanding of how computers operate and execute software.

1.2 Why Learning Assembly Language Is Still a Good Idea

When programmers first began giving up assembly language in favor of using HLLs, they generally understood the low-level ramifications of the HLL statements they were using and could choose their HLL statements appropriately. Unfortunately, the generation of computer programmers that followed them did not have the benefit of mastering assembly language. As such, they were not in a position to wisely choose statements and data structures that HLLs could efficiently translate into machine code. Their applications, if they were measured against the performance of a comparable hand-optimized assembly language program, would surely embarrass whoever wrote the compiler.

Vetran programmers who recognized this problem offered a sagely piece of advice to the new programmers: "If you want to learn how to write good HLL code, you need to learn assembly language." By learning assembly language, a programmer will be able to consider the low-level implications of their code and can make informed decisions concerning the best way to write applications in a high-level language.

1.3 Why Learning Assembly Language Isn't Absolutely Necessary

While it's probably a good idea for any well-rounded programmer to learn to program in assembly language, the truth is that learning assembly isn't a necessary condition for writing great, efficient code. The important thing is to understand how HLLs translate statements into machine code so that you can choose appropriate HLL statements.

One way to learn how to do this is to become an expert assembly language programmer, but that takes considerable time and effort—and it requires writing a lot of assembly code.

A good question to ask is, "Can a programmer just study the low-level nature of the machine and improve the HLL code they write without becoming an expert assembly programmer in the process?" The answer is a qualified yes. The purpose of this book, the second in a series, is to teach you what you need to know to write great code without having to become an expert assembly language programmer.

1.4 Thinking Low-Level

When the Java language was first becoming popular in the late 1990s, complaints like the following were heard:

> Java's interpreted code is forcing me to take a lot more care when writing software; I can't get away with using linear searches the way I could in C/C++. I have to use good (and more difficult to implement) algorithms like binary search.

Statements like that truly demonstrate the major problem with using optimizing compilers: They allow programmers to get lazy. Although optimizing compilers have made tremendous strides over the past several decades, no optimizing compiler can make up for poorly written HLL source code.

Of course, many naive HLL programmers read about how marvelous the optimization algorithms are in modern compilers and assume that the compiler will produce efficient code regardless of what they feed their compilers. But there is one problem with this attitude: although compilers can do a great job of translating well-written HLL code into efficient machine code, it is easy to feed the compiler poorly written source code that stymies the optimization algorithms. In fact, it is not uncommon to see C/C++ programmers bragging about how great their compiler is, never realizing how poor a job the compiler is doing because of how they've written their programs. The problem is that they've never actually looked at the machine code the compiler produces from their HLL source code. They blindly assume that the compiler is doing a good job because they've been told that "compilers produce code that is almost as good as what an expert assembly language programmer can produce."

1.4.1   Compilers Are Only as Good as the Source Code You Feed Them

It goes without saying that a compiler won't change your algorithms in order to improve the performance of your software. For example, if you use a linear search rather than a binary search, you cannot expect the compiler to substitute a better algorithm for you. Certainly, the optimizer may improve the speed of your linear search by a constant factor (e.g., double or triple the speed of your code), but this improvement may be nothing compared with using a better algorithm. In fact, it's very easy to show that, given a sufficiently large database, a binary search processed by an interpreter with no optimization will run faster than a linear search algorithm processed by the best compiler.

1.4.2   Helping the Compiler Produce Better Machine Code

Let's assume that you've chosen the best possible algorithm(s) for your application and you've spent the extra money to get the best compiler available. Is there something you can do to write HLL code that is more efficient than you would otherwise produce? Generally, the answer is, yes, there is.

One of the best-kept secrets in the compiler world is that most compiler benchmarks are rigged. Most real-world compiler benchmarks specify an algorithm to use, but they leave it up to the compiler vendors to actually implement the algorithm in their particular language. These compiler vendors generally know how their compilers behave when fed certain code sequences, so they will write the code sequence that produces the best possible executable.

Some may feel that this is cheating, but it's really not. If a compiler is capable of producing that same code sequence under normal circumstances (that is, the code generation trick wasn't developed specifically for the benchmark), then there is nothing wrong with showing off the compiler's performance. And if the compiler vendor can pull little tricks like this, so can you. By carefully choosing the statements you use in your HLL source code, you can "manually optimize" the machine code the compiler produces.

Several levels of manual optimization are possible. At the most abstract level, you can optimize a program by selecting a better algorithm for the software. This technique is independent of the compiler and the language.

Dropping down a level of abstraction, the next step is to manually optimize your code based on the HLL that you're using while keeping the optimizations independent of the particular implementation of that language. While such optimizations may not apply to other languages, they should apply across different compilers for the same language.

Dropping down yet another level, you can start thinking about structuring the code so that the optimizations are only applicable to a certain vendor or perhaps only a specific version of a compiler from some vendor.

At perhaps the lowest level, you begin to consider the machine code that the compiler emits and adjust how you write statements in an HLL to force the generation of some desirable sequence of machine instructions. The Linux kernel is an example of this latter approach. Legend has it that the kernel developers were constantly tweaking the C code they wrote in the Linux kernel in order to control the 80x86 machine code that the GCC compiler was producing.

Although this development process may be a bit overstated, one thing is for sure: Programmers employing this process will produce the best possible machine code. This is the type of code that is comparable to that produced by decent assembly language programmers, and it is the kind of compiler output that HLL programmers like to brag about when arguing that compilers produce code that is comparable to handwritten assembly. The fact that most people do not go to these extremes to write their HLL code never enters into the argument. Nevertheless, the fact remains that carefully written HLL code can be nearly as efficient as decent assembly code.

Will compilers ever produce code that is as good as what an expert assembly language programmer can write? The correct answer is no. However, careful programmers writing code in high-level languages like C can come close if they write their HLL code in a manner that allows the compiler to easily translate the program into efficient machine code. So, the real question is "How do I write my HLL code so that the compiler can translate it most efficiently?" Well, answering that question is the subject of this book. But the short answer is "Think in assembly; write in a high-level language." Let's take a quick look at how to do this.

1.4.3   How to Think in Assembly While Writing HLL Code

HLL compilers translate statements in that language to a sequence of one or more machine language (or assembly language) instructions. The amount of space in memory that an application consumes and the amount of time that an application spends in execution are directly related to the number of machine instructions and the type of machine instructions that the compiler emits.

However, the fact that you can achieve the same result with two different code sequences in an HLL does not imply that the compiler generates the same sequence of machine instructions for each approach. The HLL if and switch/case statements are classic examples. Most introductory programming texts suggest that a chain of if-elseif-else statements is equivalent to a switch/case statement. Let's examine the following trivial C example:

```
switch( x )
    {
        case 1:
            printf( "X=1\n" );
            break;

        case 2:
            printf( "X=2\n" );
            break;

        case 3:
            printf( "X=3\n" );
            break;

        case 4:
            printf( "X=4\n" );
            break;

        default:
            printf( "X does not equal 1, 2, 3, or 4\n" );
    }

/* equivalent IF statement */

    if( x == 1 )
            printf( "X=1\n" );
    else if( x == 2 )
            printf( "X=2\n" );
    else if( x == 3 )
            printf( "X=3\n" );
    else if( x == 4 )
            printf( "X=4\n" );
    else
            printf( "X does not equal 1, 2, 3, or 4\n" );
```

Although these two code sequences might be semantically equivalent (that is, they compute the same result), there is no guarantee whatsoever at all that the compiler will generate the same sequence of machine instructions for these two examples.

Which one will be better? Unless you understand how the compiler translates statements like these into machine code, and you have a basic understanding of the different efficiencies between various machine instructions, you can't evaluate and choose one sequence over the other. Programmers who fully understand how a compiler will translate these two sequences can judiciously choose one or the other of these two sequences based on the quality of the code they expect the compiler to produce.

By thinking in low-level terms when writing HLL code, a programmer can help an optimizing compiler approach the code quality level achieved by hand-optimized assembly language code. Sadly, the converse is usually True as well: if a programmer does not consider the low-level ramifications of his HLL code, the compiler will rarely generate the best possible machine code.

1.5 Writing High-Level

One problem with thinking in low-level terms while writing high-level code is that it is almost as much work to write HLL code in this fashion as it is to write assembly code. This negates many of the familiar benefits of writing programs in HLLs such as faster development time, better readability, easier maintenance, and so on. If you're sacrificing the benefits of writing applications in an HLL, why not simply write them in assembly language to begin with?

As it turns out, thinking in low-level terms won't lengthen your overall project schedule as much as you would expect. Although it does slow down the initial coding, the resulting HLL code will still be readable and portable, and it will still maintain the other attributes of well-written, great code. But more importantly, it will also possess some efficiency that it wouldn't otherwise have. Once the code is written, you won't have to constantly think about it in low-level terms during the maintenance and enhancement phases of the software life cycle. Therefore, thinking in low-level terms during the initial software development stage will retain the advantages of both low-level and high-level coding (efficiency plus ease of maintenance) without the corresponding disadvantages.

1.6 Assumptions

This book was written with certain assumptions about the reader's prior knowledge. You'll receive the greatest benefit from this material if your personal skill set matches these assumptions:

- You should be reasonably competent in at least one imperative (procedural) programming language. This includes C and C++, Pascal, BASIC, and assembly, as well as languages like Ada, Modula-2, and FORTRAN.

- You should be capable of taking a small problem description and working through the design and implementation of a software solution for that problem. A typical semester or quarter course at a college or university (or several months of experience on your own) should be sufficient preparation.

- You should have a basic grasp of machine organization and data representation. You should know about the hexadecimal and binary numbering systems. You should understand how computers represent various high-level data types such as signed integers, characters, and strings in memory. Although the next couple of chapters provide a primer on machine language, it would help considerably if you've picked up this information along the way. *Write Great Code, Volume 1* fully covers the subject of machine organization if you feel your knowledge in this area is a little weak.

1.7 Language-Neutral Approach

Although this book assumes you are conversant in at least one imperative language, it is not entirely language specific; its concepts transcend whatever programming language(s) you're using. To help make the examples more accessible to readers, the programming examples we'll use will rotate among several languages such as C/C++, Pascal, BASIC, and assembly. When presenting examples, I'll explain exactly how the code operates so that even if you are unfamiliar with the specific programming language, you will be able to understand its operation by reading the accompanying description.

This book uses the following languages and compilers in various examples:

- C/C++: GCC, Microsoft's Visual C++, and Borland C++
- Pascal: Borland's Delphi/Kylix
- Assembly Language: Microsoft's MASM, Borland's TASM, HLA (the High-Level Assembler), and the GNU assembler, Gas
- BASIC: Microsoft's Visual Basic

If you're not comfortable working with assembly language, don't worry; the two-chapter primer on assembly language and the online reference (www.writegreatcode.com) will allow you to read compiler output. If you would like to extend your knowledge of assembly language, you might want to check out my book *The Art of Assembly Language* (No Starch Press, 2003).

1.8 Characteristics of Great Code

What do we mean by *great code*? In Volume 1 of this series I presented several attributes of good code. It's worth repeating that discussion here to set the goals for this book.

Different programmers will have different definitions for great code. Therefore, it is impossible to provide an all-encompassing definition that will satisfy everyone. However, there are certain attributes of great code that nearly everyone will agree on, and we'll use some of these common characteristics to form our definition. For our purposes, here are some attributes of great code:

- Great code uses the CPU efficiently (that is, the code is fast).
- Great code uses memory efficiently (that is, the code is small).
- Great code uses system resources efficiently.
- Great code is easy to read and maintain.
- Great code follows a consistent set of style guidelines.

- Great code uses an explicit design that follows established software engineering conventions.
- Great code is easy to enhance.
- Great code is well tested and robust (that is, it works).
- Great code is well documented.

We could easily add dozens of items to this list. Some programmers, for example, may feel that great code must be portable, must follow a given set of programming style guidelines, must be written in a certain language, or must *not* be written in a certain language. Some may feel that great code must be written as simply as possible while others may feel that great code is written quickly. Still others may feel that great code is created on time and under budget. And you can think of additional characteristics.

So what is great code? Here is a reasonable definition:

> Great code is software that is written using a consistent and prioritized set of good software characteristics. In particular, great code follows a set of rules that guide the decisions a programmer makes when implementing an algorithm as source code.

This book will concentrate on some of the efficiency aspects of writing great code. Although efficiency might not always be the primary goal of a software development effort, most people will generally agree that inefficient code is *not* great code. This does not suggest that code isn't great if it isn't as efficient as possible. However, code that is grossly inefficient (that is, noticeably inefficient) never qualifies as great code. And inefficiency is one of the major problems with modern applications, so it's an important topic to emphasize.

1.9 The Environment for This Text

Although this text presents generic information, parts of the discussion will necessarily be system specific. Because the Intel Architecture PCs are, by far, the most common in use today, I will use that platform when discussing specific system-dependent concepts in this book. However, those concepts will still apply to other systems and CPUs (e.g., the PowerPC CPU in the older Power Macintosh systems or some other RISC CPU in a Unix box), although you may need to research the particular solution for an example on your specific platform.

Most of the examples in this book run under both Windows and Linux. When creating the examples, I tried to stick with standard library interfaces to the OS wherever possible and makes OS-specific calls only when the alternative was to write "less than great" code.

Most of the specific examples in this text will run on a late-model Intel-Architecture (including AMD) CPU under Windows or Linux, with a reasonable amount of RAM and other system peripherals normally found on a modern PC.[1] The concepts, if not the software itself, will apply to Macs, Unix boxes, embedded systems, and even mainframes.

---

[1] A few examples, such as a demonstration of PowerPC assembly language, do not run on Intel machines, but this is rare.

1.10 For More Information

No single book can completely cover everything you need to know in order to write great code. This book, therefore, concentrates on the areas that are most pertinent for writing great software, providing the 90 percent solution for those who are interested in writing the best possible code. To get that last 10 percent you're going to need additional resources. Here are some suggestions:

- Become an expert assembly language programmer. Fluency in at least one assembly language will fill in many missing details that you just won't get from this book. The purpose of this book is to teach you how to write the best possible code without actually becoming an assembly language programmer. However, the extra effort will improve your ability to think in low-level terms. An excellent choice for learning assembly language is my book *The Art of Assembly Language* (No Starch Press, 2003).

- Study compiler construction theory. Although this is an advanced topic in computer science, there is no better way to understand how compilers generate code than to study the theory behind compilers. While there is a wide variety of textbooks available covering this subject, there is considerable prerequisite material. You should carefully review any book before you purchase it in order to determine if it was written at an appropriate level for your skill set. You can also use a search engine to find some excellent tutorials on the Internet.

- Study advanced computer architecture. Machine organization and assembly language programming is a subset of the study of computer architecture. While you may not need to know how to design your own CPUs, studying computer architecture may help you discover additional ways to improve the HLL code that you write. *Computer Architecture, A Quantitative Approach* by Patterson, Hennessy, and Goldberg (Morgan Kaufmann, 2002) is a well-respected textbook that covers this subject matter.

2

SHOULDN'T YOU LEARN ASSEMBLY LANGUAGE?

Although this book will teach you how to write better code without mastering assembly language, the absolute best HLL programmers do know assembly, and that knowledge is one of the reasons they write great code. Though this book can provide a 90 percent solution for those who just want to write great HLL code, learning assembly language is the only way to fill in that last 10 percent. Though teaching you to master assembly language is beyond the scope of this book, it is still important to discuss this subject and point you in the direction of other resources if you want to pursue the 100 percent solution after reading this book. In this chapter we'll explore the following concepts:

- The problem with learning assembly language
- High-Level Assemblers (HLAs) and how they can make learning assembly language easier
- How you can use real-world products like Microsoft Macro Assembler (MASM), Borland Turbo Assembler (TASM), and HLA to easily learn assembly language programming

- How an assembly language programmer *thinks* (the assembly language programming paradigm)
- Resources available to help you learn assembly language programming

2.1 Roadblocks to Learning Assembly Language

Learning assembly language, *really* learning assembly language, will offer two benefits: First, you will gain a *complete* understanding of the machine code that a compiler can generate. By mastering assembly language, you'll achieve the 100 percent solution that the previous section describes and you will be able to write better HLL code. Second, you'll be able to drop down into assembly language and code critical parts of your application in assembly language when your HLL compiler is incapable, even with your help, of producing the best possible code. So once you've absorbed the lessons of the following chapters to hone your HLL skills, moving on to learn assembly language is a very good idea.

There is only one catch to learning assembly language: In the past, learning assembly language has been a long, difficult, and frustrating task. The assembly language programming paradigm is sufficiently different from HLL programming that most people feel like they're starting over from square one when learning assembly language. It's very frustrating when you know how to achieve something in a programming language like C/C++, Java, Pascal, or Visual Basic, and you cannot figure out the solution in assembly language while learning assembly.

Most programmers prefer being able to apply what they've learned in the past when learning something new. Unfortunately, traditional approaches to learning assembly language programming tend to force HLL programmers to forget what they've learned in the past. This, obviously, isn't a very efficient use of existing knowledge. What was needed was a way to leverage existing knowledge while learning assembly language.

2.2 *Write Great Code, Volume 2*, to the Rescue

Once you've read through this book, there are three reasons you'll find it much easier to learn assembly language:

- You will be better motivated to learn assembly language, as you'll understand why mastering assembly language can help you write better code.
- This book provides two brief primers on assembly language (one on 80x86 assembly language, on one PowerPC assembly language), so even if you've never seen assembly language before, you'll learn some assembly language by the time you finish this book.
- You will have already seen how compilers emit machine code for all the common control and data structures, so you will have learned one of the most difficult lessons a beginning assembly programmer faces—how to achieve things in assembly language that they already know how to do in an HLL.

Though this book will not teach you how to become an expert assembly language programmer, the large number of example programs that demonstrate how compilers translate HLLs into machine code will aquaint you with many assembly language programming techniques. You will find these useful should you decide to learn assembly language after reading this book.

Certainly, you'll find this book easier to read if you already know assembly language. The important thing to note, however, is that you'll also find assembly language easier to master once you've read this book. And as learning assembly language is probably the more time consuming of these two tasks (learning assembly or reading this book), the most efficient approach is probably going to be to read this book first.

2.3 High-Level Assemblers to the Rescue

Way back in 1995, I had a discussion with the UC Riverside Computer Science department chair. I lamented the fact that students had to start all over when taking the assembly course and how much time it took for them to relearn so many things. As the discussion progressed, it became clear that the problem wasn't with assembly language, per se, but with the syntax of existing assemblers (like Microsoft's Macro Assembler, MASM). Learning assembly language entailed a whole lot more than learning a few machine instructions. First of all, you have to learn a new programming style. Mastering assembly language doesn't consist of learning the semantics of a few machine instructions; you also have to learn how to put those instructions together to solve real-world problems. And *that's* the hard part to mastering assembly language.

Second, *pure* assembly language is not something you can efficiently pick up a few instructions at a time. Writing even the simplest programs requires considerable knowledge and a repertoire of a couple dozen or more machine instructions. When you add that repertoire to all the other machine organization topics students must learn in a typical assembly course, it's often several weeks before they are prepared to write anything other than "spoon-fed" trivial applications in assembly language.

One important feature that MASM had back in 1995 was support for HLL-like control statements such as .if, .while, and so on. While these statements are not true machine instructions, they do allow students to use familiar programming constructs early in the course, until they've had time to learn enough machine instructions so they can write their applications using low-level machine instructions. By using these high-level constructs early on in the term, students can concentrate on other aspects of assembly language programming and not have to assimilate everything all at once. This allows students to start writing code much sooner in the course and, as a result, they wind up covering more material by the time the term is complete.

An assembler that provides control statements similar to those found in HLLs (in additional to the traditional low-level machine instructions that do the same thing) is called a *high-level assembler.* Microsoft's MASM (v6.0 and later) and Borland's TASM (v5.0 and later) are good examples of high-level assemblers. In theory, with an appropriate textbook that teaches assembly language programming using these high-level assemblers, students could begin writing simple programs during the very first week of the course.

The only problem with high-level assemblers like MASM and TASM is that they provide just a few HLL control statements and data types. Almost everything else is foreign to someone who is familiar with HLL programming. For example, data declarations in MASM and TASM are completely different than data declarations in most HLLs. Beginning assembly programmers still have to relearn a considerable amount of information, despite the presence of HLL-like control statements.

2.4 The High-Level Assembler (HLA)

Shortly after the discussion with my department chair, it occurred to me that there is no reason an assembler couldn't adopt a more high-level syntax without changing the semantics of assembly language. For example, consider the following statements in C/C++ and Pascal that declare an integer array variable:

```
int intVar[8]; // C/C++
```

```
var intVar: array[0..7] of integer; (* Pascal *)
```

Now consider the MASM declaration for the same object:

```
intVar sdword 8 dup (?) ;MASM
```

While the C/C++ and Pascal declarations differ from each other, the assembly language version is radically different from either. A C/C++ programmer will probably be able to figure out the Pascal declaration even if she's never seen Pascal code before. The converse is also true. However, the Pascal and C/C++ programmers probably won't be able to make heads or tails of the assembly language declaration. This is but one example of the problems HLL programmers face when first learning assembly language.

The sad part is that there really is no reason a variable declaration in assembly language has to be so radically different from declarations found in HLLs. It will make absolutely no difference in the final executable file which syntax an assembler uses for variable declarations. Given that, why shouldn't an assembler use a more high-level-like syntax so people switching over from HLLs will find the assembler easier to learn? This was the question I was pondering back in 1996 when discussing the assembly language course with my department chair. And that led me to develop a new assembler specifically geared toward teaching assembly language programming to students who had already mastered a high-level programming language: the *High-Level Assembler*, or HLA. In HLA, for example, the aforementioned array declaration looks like this:

```
var intVar:int32[8]; // HLA
```

Though the syntax is slightly different from C/C++ and Pascal (actually, it's a combination of the two), most HLL programmers will probably be able to figure out the meaning of this declaration.

The whole purpose of HLA's design is to create an assembly language programming environment that is as familiar as possible to traditional (imperative) high-level programming languages, without sacrificing the ability to write *real* assembly language programs. Those components of the language that have nothing to do with machine instructions use a familiar high-level language syntax while the machine instructions still map on a one-to-one basis to the underlying 80x86 machine instructions.

By making HLA as similar as possible to various HLLs, students learning assembly language programming don't have to spend as much time assimilating a radically different syntax. Instead, they can apply their existing HLL knowledge, thus making the process of learning assembly language easier and faster.

A comfortable syntax for declarations and a few high-level-like control statements aren't all you need to make learning assembly language as efficient as possible. One very common complaint about learning assembly language is that it provides very little support for the programmer—programmers have to constantly reinvent the wheel while writing assembly code. For example, when learning assembly language programming using MASM or TASM, we quickly discover that assembly language doesn't provide useful I/O facilities such as the ability to print integer values as strings to the user's console. Assembly programmers are responsible for writing such code themselves. Unfortunately, writing a decent set of I/O routines requires sophisticated knowledge of assembly language programming. Yet the only way to gain that knowledge is by writing a fair amount of code first, and writing such code without having any I/O routines is difficult. Therefore, another facility a good assembly language educational tool needs to provide is a set of I/O routines that allow beginning assembly programmers to do simple I/O tasks, like reading and writing integer values, before they have the sophistication to write such routines themselves. HLA provides this facility in the guise of the *HLA Standard Library*. This is a collection of subroutines and macros that make it very easy to write complex applications by simply calling those routines.

Because of the ever-increasing popularity of the HLA assembler, and the fact that HLA is a free, open-source, and public domain product available for Windows and Linux, this book uses HLA syntax for compiler-neutral examples involving assembly language.

2.5   Thinking High-Level, Writing Low-Level

The goal of HLA is to allow a beginning assembly programmer to think in HLL terms while writing low-level code (in other words, the exact opposite of what this book is trying to teach). Ultimately, of course, an assembly programmer needs to think in low-level terms. But for the student first approaching assembly language, being able to think in high-level terms is a Godsend—the student can apply techniques he's already learned in other languages when faced with a particular assembly language programming problem.

Eventually, the student of assembly language needs to set aside the high-level control structures and use their low-level equivalents. But early on in the process, having those high-level statements available allows the student to concentrate on (and assimilate) other low-level programming concepts. By controlling the rate at which a student has to learn new concepts, the educational process can be made more efficient.

Ultimately, of course, the goal is to learn the low-level programming paradigm. And that means giving up HLL-like control structures and writing pure low-level code. That is, "thinking low-level and writing low-level." Nevertheless, starting out by "thinking high-level while writing low-level" is a great way to learn assembly language programming. It's much like stop smoking programs that use patches with various levels of nicotine in them—the patch wearer is gradually weaned off the need for nicotine. Similarly, a high-level assembler allows a programmer to be gradually weaned away from thinking in high-level terms. This approach is just as effective for learning assembly language as it is when you're trying to stop smoking.

2.6 The Assembly Programming Paradigm (Thinking Low-Level)

Programming in assembly language is quite different from programming in common HLLs. For this reason, many programmers find it difficult to learn how to write programs in assembly language. Fortunately, for this book, you need only a reading knowledge of assembly language to analyze compiler output; you don't need to be able to write assembly language programs from scratch. This means that you don't have to master the hard part of assembly language programming. Nevertheless, if you understand how assembly programs are written you will be able to understand why a compiler emits certain code sequences. To that end, we'll spend time here to describe how assembly language programmers (and compilers) "think."

The most fundamental aspect of the assembly language programming paradigm[1] is that tasks you want to accomplish are broken up into tiny pieces that the machine can handle. Fundamentally, a CPU can only do a single, tiny, task at once (this is true even for CISC processors). Therefore, complex operations, like statements you'll find in an HLL, have to be broken down into smaller components that the machine can execute directly. As an example, consider the following Visual Basic assignment statement:

```
profits = sales - costOfGoods - overhead - commissions
```

No practical CPU is going to allow you to execute this entire VB statement as a single machine instruction. Instead, you're going to have to break this down to a sequence of machine instructions that compute individual components of this assignment statement. For example, many CPUs provide a *subtract* instruction that lets you subtract one value from a machine register. Because the assignment statement in this example consists of three subtractions, you're

---

[1] *Paradigm* means model. A programming paradigm is a model of how programming is done, so the assembly language programming paradigm is a description of the ways assembly programming is accomplished.

going to have to break the assignment operation down into at least three different subtract instructions.

The 80x86 CPU family provides a fairly flexible subtract instruction: sub. This particular instruction allows the following forms (in HLA syntax):

```
sub( constant, reg );        // reg = reg - constant
sub( constant, memory );     // memory = memory - constant
sub( reg1, reg2 );           // reg2 = reg2 - reg1
sub( memory, reg );          // reg = reg - memory
sub( reg, memory );          // memory = memory - reg
```

Assuming that all of the identifiers in the original Visual Basic code represent variables, we can use the 80x86 sub and mov instructions to implement the same operation with the following HLA code sequence:

```
// Get sales value into EAX register:

mov( sales, eax );

// Compute sales-costOfGoods (EAX := EAX - costOfGoods)

sub( costOfGoods, eax );

// Compute (sales-costOfGoods) - overhead
// (note: EAX contains sales-costOfGoods)

sub( overhead, eax );

// Compute (sales-costOfGoods-overhead) - commissions
// (note: EAX contains sales-costOfGoods-overhead)

sub( commissions, eax );

// Store result (in EAX) into profits:

mov( eax, profits );
```

The important thing to notice here is that a single Visual Basic statement has been broken down into five different HLA statements, each of which does a small part of the total calculation. The secret behind the assembly language programming paradigm is knowing how to break down complex operations into a simple sequence of machine instructions as was done in this example. We'll take another look at this process in Chapter 13.

HLL control structures are another big area where complex operations are broken down into simpler statement sequences. For example, consider the following Pascal if statement:

```
if( i = j ) then begin

    writeln( "i is equal to j" );

end;
```

CPUs do not support an if machine instruction. Instead, you compare two values that set *condition-code flags* and then test the result of these condition codes by using *conditional jump* instructions. A common way to translate an HLL if statement into assembly language is to test the opposite condition (i <> j) and then jump over the statements that would be executed if the original condition (i = j) evaluates to True. For example, here is a translation of the former Pascal if statement into HLA (using *pure* assembly language, that is, no HLL-like constructs):

```
mov( i, eax );        // Get i's value
cmp( eax, j );        // Compare to j's value
jne skipIfBody;       // Skip body of if statement if i <> j

<< code to print string >>

skipIfBody:
```

As the Boolean expressions in the HLL language control structures become more complex, the number of corresponding machine instructions also increases. But the process remains the same. Later, we'll take a look at how compilers translate high-level control structures into assembly language (see Chapters 14 and 15).

Passing parameters to a procedure or function, accessing those parameters within the procedure or function, and accessing other data local to that procedure or function is another area where assembly language is quite a bit more complex than typical HLLs. We don't have the prerequisites to go into how this is done here (or even make sense of a simple example), but rest assured that we will get around to covering this important subject a little later in this book (see Chapter 16).

The bottom line is that when converting some algorithm from a high-level language, you have to break the problem into much smaller pieces in order to code it in assembly language. As noted earlier, the good news is that you don't have to figure out which machine instructions to use when all you're doing is reading assembly code—the compiler (or assembly programmer) that originally created the code will have already done this for you. All you've got to do is draw a correspondence between the HLL code and the assembly code. And how you accomplish that will be the subject of much of the rest of this book.

2.7   *The Art of Assembly Language* and Other Resources

While HLA is a great tool for learning assembly language, by itself it isn't sufficient. A good set of educational materials that use HLA are absolutely necessary to learn assembly language using HLA. Fortunately, such material exists; in fact, HLA was written specifically to support those educational materials (rather than the educational materials being created to support HLA). The number one resource you'll find for learning assembly programming with HLA is *The Art of Assembly Language* (No Starch Press, 2003).

This book was specifically written to teach assembly language in the gradual manner this chapter describes. Experience with thousands and thousands of students and others who've read *The Art of Assembly Language* attests to the success of this approach. If you're someone who knows an HLL and wants to learn assembly language programming, you should seriously consider taking a look at *The Art of Assembly Language.*

The Art of Assembly Language certainly isn't the only resource available on assembly language programming. Jeff Duntemann's *Assembly Language Step-by-Step* (Wiley, 2000) is geared toward programmers who are learning assembly language programming as their first programming language (that is, they do not have any high-level programming language experience). Though readers of *Write Great Code* generally don't fall into this category, this different approach to teaching assembly may work better for some people.

Programming from the Ground Up by Jonathon Barlett (Bartlett Publishing, 2004) teaches assembly language programming using GNU's Gas assembler. This book is especially useful to those who need to analyze GCC's 80x86 output. An older, free version of this book can be found online on Webster at http://webster.cs.ucr.edu/AsmTools/Gas/index.html.

Professional Assembly Language (Programmer to Programmer) by Richard Blum (Wrox, 2005) is another book that uses the GNU assembler on the 80x86 and should be of interest to those wanting to read GCC's Gas output.

Dr. Paul Carter also has an interesting online tutorial on assembly language programming. You can find links to Dr. Carter's current version of the book on the links page on Webster at http://webster.cs.ucr.edu/links.htm.

Of course, Webster has lots of assembly language programming resources available, including several online e-texts. If you're interested in learning more about assembly language programming, you'll definitely want to visit the Webster site, at http://webster.cs.ucr.edu.

These are not the only sources of information about assembly language programming available. In particular, a quick search on the Internet using your favorite search engine will turn up thousands of pages of information about assembly language programming. There are also a couple of Usenet newsgroups, alt.lang.asm and comp.lang.asm.x86, where you can ask lots of questions concerning assembly language programming. There are several web-based forums for assembly language, as well. Once again, a search of the Internet via Google or some other Internet search engine will turn up more information than you'll be able to digest any time soon.

3

8 0 X 8 6 ASSEMBLY FOR THE HLL PROGRAMMER

Throughout this book, you'll examine high-level language code and compare it to the machine code that a compiler generates for the high-level code. Making sense of a compiler's output requires some knowledge of assembly language. Becoming an expert assembly programmer takes time and experience. Fortunately, such skill isn't necessary for our purposes. All you really need is the ability to read code generated by compilers and other assembly language programmers; you don't need to be able to write assembly language programs from scratch. This chapter

- Describes the basic 80x86 machine architecture
- Provides a basic overview of 80x86 assembly language so that you will be able to read the 80x86 output produced by various compilers
- Describes the addressing modes that the 32-bit 80x86 CPUs support
- Describes the syntax that several common 80x86 assemblers use (HLA, MASM/TASM, and Gas)

- Describes how to use constants and declare data in assembly language programs

In addition to this chapter, you will also want to take a look at the online resources (www.writegreatcode.com), which present a minimal 80x86 instruction set that you'll need when examining compiler output.

3.1 Learning One Assembly Language Is Good, Learning More Is Better

If you intend to write code for a processor other than the 80x86, you should really learn how to read at least two different assembly languages. By doing so, you'll avoid the pitfall of coding for the 80x86 in an HLL and then finding that your "optimizations" only work on the 80x86 CPU. For this reason, Chapter 4 is an equivalent primer on the PowerPC CPU. You'll see that both processor families rely on many of the same concepts, but that there are some important differences (summarized in the appendix).

Perhaps the main difference between complex instruction set computer (CISC) architectures such as the 80x86 and reduced instruction set computer (RISC) architectures like the PowerPC is the way they use memory. RISC architectures provide a relatively clumsy memory access, and applications go to great lengths to avoid accessing memory. The 80x86 architecture, on the other hand, can access memory in many different ways, and applications generally take advantage of this facility. While there are advantages and disadvantages to both approaches, the bottom line is that code running on an 80x86 has some fundamental differences from comparable code running on a RISC architecture such as the PowerPC.

3.2 80x86 Assembly Syntaxes

While 80x86 programmers can choose from a wide variety of program development tools, this abundance has a minor drawback: syntactical incompatibility. Different compilers and debuggers for the 80x86 family output different assembly language listings for the exact same program. This is because those tools emit code for different assemblers. For example, Microsoft's Visual C++ package generates assembly code compatible with Microsoft Macro Assembler (MASM). Borland's C++ compiler generates code compatible with Borland's Turbo Assembler (TASM). The GNU Compiler Suite (GCC) generates Gas-compatible source code (Gas is the GNU Assembler from the Free Software Foundation). In addition to the code that compilers emit, you'll find tons of assembly programming examples written with assemblers like FASM, NASM, GoAsm, HLA, and more.

It would be nice to use just a single assembler's syntax throughout this book, but because our approach is not compiler specific, we must consider the syntaxes for several different common assemblers. This book will generally present non–compiler-specific examples using the High-Level Assembler (HLA). Therefore, this chapter will discuss the syntaxes for four assemblers: MASM, TASM, Gas, and HLA. Fortunately, once you master the syntax for one assembler, learning the syntax of other assemblers is very easy. It's like switching from one dialect of BASIC to another.

3.3 Basic 80x86 Architecture

The Intel CPU is generally classified as a *Von Neumann machine.* Von Neumann computer systems contain three main building blocks: the *central processing unit (CPU), memory,* and *input/output (I/O) devices.* These three components are connected together using the *system bus* (consisting of the address, data, and control buses). The block diagram in Figure 3-1 shows this relationship.

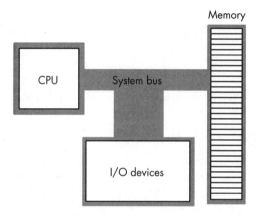

Figure 3-1: Block diagram of a Von Neumann system

The CPU communicates with memory and I/O devices by placing a numeric value on the address bus to select one of the memory locations or I/O device port locations, each of which has a unique binary numeric *address.* Then the CPU, I/O, and memory devices pass data among themselves by placing the data on the data bus. The control bus contains signals that determine the direction of the data transfer (to or from memory, and to or from an I/O device).

3.3.1 Registers

The register set is the most prominent feature within the CPU. Almost all calculations on the 80x86 CPU involve at least one register. For example, to add the value of two variables and store their sum into a third variable, you must load one of the variables into a register, add the second operand to the register, and then store the register's value into the destination variable. Registers are middlemen in almost every calculation. Therefore, registers are very important in 80x86 assembly language programs.

The 80x86 CPU registers can be broken down into four categories: general-purpose registers, special-purpose application-accessible registers, segment registers, and special-purpose kernel-mode registers. We will not consider the last two sets of registers, because the segment registers are not used very much in modern 32-bit operating systems (e.g., Windows, BSD, BeOS, and Linux), and the special-purpose kernel-mode registers are intended for writing operating systems, debuggers, and other system-level tools. Such software construction is well beyond the scope of this text.

3.3.2 80x86 General-Purpose Registers

The 80x86 (Intel family) CPUs provide several general-purpose registers for application use. These include eight 32-bit registers that have the following names:

EAX, EBX, ECX, EDX, ESI, EDI, EBP, and ESP

The E prefix on each name stands for *extended.* This prefix differentiates the 32-bit registers from the eight 16-bit registers that have the following names:

AX, BX, CX, DX, SI, DI, BP, and SP

Finally, the 80x86 CPUs provide eight 8-bit registers that have the following names:

AL, AH, BL, BH, CL, CH, DL, and DH

The most important thing to note about the general-purpose registers is that they are not independent. That is, the 80x86 does not provide 24 separate registers. Instead, it overlaps the 32-bit registers with the 16-bit registers, and it overlaps the 16-bit registers with the 8-bit registers. Figure 3-2 shows this relationship.

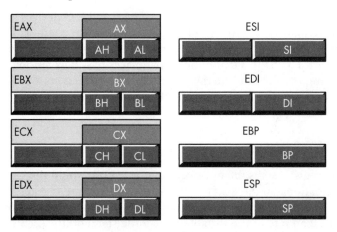

Figure 3-2: Intel 80x86 CPU general-purpose registers

The fact that modifying one register may modify as many as three other registers cannot be overemphasized. For example, modifying the EAX register may also modify the AL, AH, and AX registers. You will often see compiler-generated code using this feature of the 80x86. For example, a compiler may clear (set to zero) all the bits in the EAX register and then load AL with a one or zero in order to produce a 32-bit True (1) or False (0) value. Some machine instructions manipulate only the AL register, yet the program may need to return those instructions' results in EAX. By taking advantage of the register overlap, the compiler-generated code can use an instruction that manipulates AL to return that value in all of EAX.

Although Intel calls these registers *general purpose*, you should not infer that you can use any register for any purpose. The SP/ESP register pair for example, has a very special purpose that effectively prevents you from using it for any other purpose (it's the *stack pointer*). Likewise, the BP/EBP register has a special purpose that limits its usefulness as a general-purpose register. All the 80x86 registers have their own special purposes that limit their use in certain contexts; we will consider these special uses as we discuss the machine instructions that use them (see the online resources).

3.3.3   The 80x86 EFLAGS Register

The 32-bit EFLAGS register encapsulates numerous single-bit Boolean (True/False) values (or *flags*). Most of these bits are either reserved for kernel mode (operating system) functions or are of little interest to application programmers. Eight of these bits are of interest to application programmers reading (or writing) assembly language code: the overflow, direction, interrupt disable,[1] sign, zero, auxiliary carry, parity, and carry flags. Figure 3-3 shows their layout within the low-order (LO) 16 bits of the EFLAGS register.

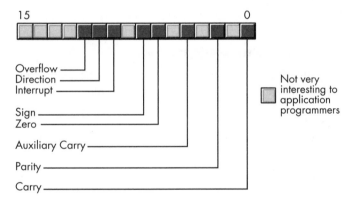

Figure 3-3: Layout of the 80x86 flags register (LO 16 bits)

Of the eight flags that application programmers can use, four flags in particular are extremely valuable: the overflow, carry, sign, and zero flags. We call these four flags the *condition codes*. Each flag has a state—set or cleared—that you can use to test the result of previous computations. For example, after comparing two values, the condition-code flags will tell you if one value is less than, equal to, or greater than a second value.

---

[1] Applications programs cannot modify the interrupt flag, but we'll look at this flag later in this text, hence the discussion of this flag here.

3.4   Literal Constants

Most assemblers support literal numeric, character, and string constants. Unfortunately, just about every assembler out there uses a different syntax for literal constants. The following subsections describe the syntax for the assemblers we'll be using in this book.

3.4.1   Binary Literal Constants

All assemblers provide the ability to specify base-2 (binary) literal constants. Few compilers emit binary constants, so you probably won't see these values in the output a compiler produces, but you may see them in handwritten assembly code.

3.4.1.1   Binary Literal Constants in HLA

Binary literal constants in HLA begin with the special percent character (%) followed by one or more binary digits (0 or 1). Underscore characters may appear between any two digits in a binary number. By convention, HLA programmers separate each group of four digits with an underscore. For example:

```
%1011
%1010_1111
%0011_1111_0001_1001
%1011001010010101
```

3.4.1.2   Binary Literal Constants in Gas

Binary literal constants in Gas begin with the special 0b prefix followed by one or more binary digits (0 or 1). For example:

```
0b1011
0b10101111
0b0011111100011001
0b1011001010010101
```

3.4.1.3   Binary Literal Constants in MASM and TASM

Binary literal constants in MASM/TASM consist of one or more binary digits (0 or 1) followed by the special b suffix. For example:

```
1011b
10101111b
0011111100011001b
1011001010010101b
```

3.4.2 Decimal Literal Constants

Decimal constants in most assemblers take the standard form—a sequence of one or more decimal digits without any special prefix or suffix. This is one of the two common numeric formats that compilers emit, so you will often see decimal literal constants when reading compiler output.

3.4.2.1 Decimal Literal Constants in HLA

HLA allows you to optionally insert underscores between any two digits in a decimal number. HLA programmers generally use underscores to separate groups of three digits in a decimal number. For example, take the following numbers:

```
123
1209345
```

In HLA a programmer could insert underscores as shown here:

```
1_024
1_021_567
```

3.4.2.2 Decimal Literal Constants in Gas, MASM, and TASM

Gas, MASM, and TASM use a string of decimal digits (the standard "computer" format for decimal values). For example:

```
123
1209345
```

MASM, TASM, and Gas (unlike HLA) do not allow embedded underscores in decimal literal constants.

3.4.3 Hexadecimal Literal Constants

Hexadecimal (base-16) literal constants are the other common numeric format you'll find in assembly language programs (especially those that compilers emit).

3.4.3.1 Hexadecimal Literal Constants in HLA

Hexadecimal literal constants in HLA consist of a string of hexadecimal digits (0..9, a..f, or A..F) with a $ prefix. Underscores may optionally appear between any two hexadecimal digits in the number. By convention, HLA programmers separate sequences of four digits with underscores.
For example:

```
$1AB0
$1234_ABCD
$dead
```

3.4.3.2 Hexadecimal Literal Constants in Gas

Hexadecimal literal constants in Gas consist of a string of hexadecimal digits (0..9, a..f, or A..F) with a 0x prefix. For example:

```
0x1AB0
0x1234ABCD
0xdead
```

3.4.3.3 Hexadecimal Literal Constants in MASM and TASM

Hexadecimal literal constants in MASM/TASM consist of a string of hexadecimal digits (0..9, a..f, or A..F) with an h suffix. The values must begin with a decimal digit (0 if the constant would normally begin with a digit in the range a..f). For example:

```
1AB0h
1234ABCDh
0deadh
```

3.4.4 Character and String Literal Constants

Character and string data are also common data types that you'll find in assembly programs. MASM and TASM do not differentiate between literal character or string constants. HLA and Gas, however, use a different internal representation for characters and strings, so the distinction between the two literal constant forms is very important in those assemblers.

3.4.4.1 Character and String Literal Constants in HLA

Literal character constants in HLA take a couple of different forms. The most common form is a single printable character surrounded by a pair of apostrophes, such as 'A'. To specify an apostrophe as a literal character constant, HLA requires that you surround a pair of apostrophes by apostrophes (''''). Finally, you may also specify a character constant using the # symbol followed by a binary, decimal, or hexadecimal numeric value that specifies the ASCII code of the character you want to use. For example:

```
'a'
''''
' '
#$d
#10
#%0000_1000
```

String literal constants in HLA consist of a sequence of zero or more characters surrounded by quotes. If a quote must appear within a string constant, the string constant will contain two adjacent quotes to represent a quote character within the string.

For example:

```
"Hello World"
"" -- The empty string
"He said ""Hello"" to them"
"""" -- string containing one quote character
```

3.4.4.2   Character and String Literal Constants in Gas

Character literal constants in Gas consist of an apostrophe followed by a single character. For example:

```
'a
' '
'!
```

String literal constants in Gas consist of a sequence of zero or more characters surrounded by quotes. String literal constants in Gas use the same syntax as C strings. You use the \ escape sequence to embed special characters in a Gas string. For example:

```
"Hello World"
"" -- The empty string
"He said \"Hello\" to them"
"\"" -- string containing one quote character
```

3.4.4.3   Character/String Literal Constants in MASM and TASM

Character and string literal constants in MASM/TASM take the same form: a sequence of one or more characters surrounded by either apostrophes or quotes. These assemblers do not differentiate character constants and string constants. For example:

```
'a'
"'" - An apostrophe character
'"' - A quote character
"Hello World"
"" -- The empty string
'He said "Hello" to them'
```

3.4.5   Floating-Point Literal Constants

Floating-point literal constants in assembly language typically take the same form you'll find in HLLs (a sequence of digits, possibly containing a decimal point, optionally followed by a signed exponent). For example:

```
3.14159
2.71e+2
1.0e-5
5e2
```

3.5   Manifest (Symbolic) Constants in Assembly Language

Almost every assembler provides a mechanism for declaring symbolic (named) constants. In fact, most assemblers provide several ways to associate a value with an identifier in the source file.

3.5.1   Manifest Constants in HLA

The HLA assembler, true to its name, uses a high-level syntax for declaring named constants in the source file. You may define constants in one of three ways: in a const section, in a val section, or with the ? compile-time operator. The const and val sections appear in the declaration section of an HLA program and their syntax is very similar. The difference between them is that you may reassign values to identifiers you define in the val section and you may not reassign values to identifiers appearing in a const section. Although HLA supports a wide range of options in these declaration sections, the basic declaration takes the following form:

```
const
    someIdentifier := someValue;
```

Wherever *someIdentifier* appears in the source file (after this declaration), HLA will substitute the value *someValue* in the identifier's place. For example:

```
const
    aCharConst := 'a';
    anIntConst := 12345;
    aStrConst := "String Const";
    aFltConst := 3.12365e-2;

val
    anotherCharConst := 'A';
    aSignedConst := -1;
```

In HLA, the ? statement allows you to embed val declarations anywhere whitespace is allowed in the source file. This is sometimes useful because it isn't always convenient to declare constants in a declaration section. For example:

```
?aValConst := 0;
```

3.5.2   Manifest Constants in Gas

Gas uses the .equ statement to define a symbolic constant in the source file. This statement has the following syntax:

```
.equ        symbolName, value
```

Here are some examples of "equates" within a Gas source file:

```
.equ        false, 0
.equ        true, 1
.equ        anIntConst, 12345
```

3.5.3   Manifest Constants in MASM and TASM

MASM and TASM also provide a couple of different ways to define manifest constants within a source file. One way is with the equ directive:

```
false       equ   0
true        equ   1
anIntConst  equ   12345
```

Another way is with the = operator:

```
false      =    0
true       =    1
anIntConst =    12345
```

The difference between the two is minor; see the MASM and TASM documentation for details.

NOTE   *For the most part, compilers tend to emit the equ form rather than the = form.*

3.6   80x86 Addressing Modes

An *addressing mode* is a hardware-specific mechanism for accessing instruction operands. The 80x86 family provides three different classes of operands: register operands, immediate operands, and memory operands. The following subsections discuss each of these addressing modes.

3.6.1   80x86 Register Addressing Modes

Most 80x86 instructions can operate on the 80x86's general-purpose register set. You access a register by specifying its name as an instruction operand.

Let's consider some examples of how our assemblers implement this strategy, using the 80x86 mov (move) instruction.

3.6.1.1   Register Access in HLA

The HLA mov instruction looks like this:

```
mov( source, destination );
```

This instruction copies the data from the *source* operand to the *destination* operand. The 8-bit, 16-bit, and 32-bit registers are certainly valid operands for this instruction. The only restriction is that both operands must be the same size.

Now let's look at some actual 80x86 mov instructions:

```
mov( bx, ax );      // Copies the value from BX into AX
mov( al, dl );      // Copies the value from AL into DL
mov( edx, esi );    // Copies the value from EDX into ESI
```

3.6.1.2 Register Access in Gas

Gas prepends each register name with percent sign (%). For example:

```
%al, %ah, %bl, %bh, %cl, %ch, %dl, %dh
%ax, %bx, %cx, %dx, %si, %di, %bp, %sp
%eax, %ebx, %ecx, %edx, %esi, %edi, %ebp, %esp
```

The Gas syntax for the mov instruction is similar to HLA's, except that it drops the parentheses and semicolons and requires the assembly language statements to fit completely on one physical line of source code. For example:

```
mov %bx, %ax     // Copies the value from BX into AX
mov %al, %dl     // Copies the value from AL into DL
mov %edx, %esi   // Copies the value from EDX into ESI
```

3.6.1.3 Register Access in MASM and TASM

The MASM and TASM assemblers use the same register names as HLA, and a basic syntax that is similar to Gas, except that these two assemblers reverse the operands. That is, a typical instruction like mov takes the form:

```
mov destination, source
```

Here are some examples of the mov instruction in MASM/TASM syntax:

```
mov ax, bx       ; Copies the value from BX into AX
mov dl, al       ; Copies the value from AL into DL
mov esi, edx     ; Copies the value from EDX into ESI
```

3.6.2 Immediate Addressing Mode

Most instructions that allow register and memory operands also allow immediate, or constant, operands. The following HLA mov instructions, for example, load appropriate values into the corresponding destination registers.

```
mov( 0, al );
mov( 12345, bx );
mov( 123_456_789, ecx );
```

Most assemblers allow you to specify a wide variety of literal constant types when using the immediate addressing mode. For example, you can supply numbers in hexadecimal, decimal, or binary form. You can also supply character constants as operands. The rule is that the constant must fit in the size specified for the destination operand. Here are some additional examples involving HLA, MASM/TASM, and Gas:

```
mov( 'a', ch );  // HLA
mov 'a, %ch      // Gas
mov ch, 'a'      ;MASM/TASM

mov( $1234, ax ); // HLA
mov 0x1234, ax    // Gas
mov ax, 1234h     ; MASM/TASM

mov( 4_012_345_678, eax ); // HLA
mov 4012345678, eax        // Gas
mov eax, 4012345678        ; MASM/TASM
```

Almost every assembler lets you create symbolic constant names and supply those names as source operands. For example, HLA predefines the two Boolean constants true and false so you may supply those names as mov instruction operands:

```
mov( true, al );
mov( false, ah );
```

Some assemblers even allow pointer constants and other abstract data type constants. (See the reference manual for your assembler for all the details.)

3.6.3 Displacement-Only Memory Addressing Mode

The most common addressing mode, and the one that's the easiest to understand, is the *displacement-only* (or *direct*) addressing mode, in which a 32-bit constant specifies the address of the memory location, which may be either the source or the destination operand.

For example, assuming that variable J is a byte variable appearing at address $8088, the HLA instruction mov(J, al); loads the AL register with a copy of the byte at memory location $8088. Likewise, if the byte variable K is at address $1234 in memory, then the instruction mov(dl, K); writes the value in the DL register to memory location $1234 (see Figure 3-4).

The displacement-only addressing mode is perfect for accessing simple scalar variables. It is the addressing mode you would normally use to access static or global variables in an HLL program.

NOTE *Intel named this addressing mode "displacement-only" because a 32-bit constant (displacement) follows the mov opcode in memory. On the 80x86 processors, this displacement is an offset from the beginning of memory (that is, address zero).*

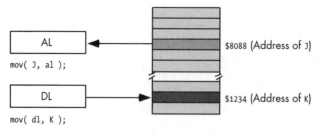

Figure 3-4: Displacement-only (direct) addressing mode

The examples in this chapter will often access byte-sized objects in memory. Don't forget, however, that you can also access words and double words on the 80x86 processors by specifying the address of their first byte (see Figure 3-5).

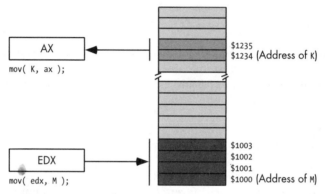

Figure 3-5: Accessing a word or double word using the direct addressing mode

MASM, TASM, and Gas use the same syntax for the displacement addressing mode as HLA. That is, for the operand you simply specify the name of the object you want to access. Some MASM and TASM programmers put brackets around the variable names, although this is not strictly necessary with those assemblers.

Here are several examples using HLA, Gas, and MASM/TASM syntax:

```
mov( byteVar, ch );  // HLA
movb byteVar, %ch // Gas
mov ch, byteVar      ;MASM/TASM

mov( wordVar, ax );  // HLA
movw wordVar, ax    // Gas
mov ax, wordVar     ; MASM/TASM

mov( dwordVar, eax );   // HLA
movl dwordVar, eax      // Gas
mov eax, dwordVar       ; MASM/TASM
```

3.6.4   Register Indirect Addressing Mode

The 80x86 CPUs let you access memory indirectly through a register using the register indirect addressing modes. We call these modes indirect because the operand is not the actual address. Instead, the operand's value specifies the memory address to use. In the case of the register indirect addressing modes, the register's value is the address to access. For example, the HLA instruction mov(eax, [ebx]); tells the CPU to store EAX's value at the location whose address is in EBX.

3.6.4.1   Register Indirect Modes in HLA

There are eight forms of this addressing mode on the 80x86. Using HLA syntax they look like this:

```
mov( [eax], al );
mov( [ebx], al );
mov( [ecx], al );
mov( [edx], al );
mov( [edi], al );
mov( [esi], al );
mov( [ebp], al );
mov( [esp], al );
```

These eight addressing modes reference the memory location at the offset found in the register enclosed by brackets (EAX, EBX, ECX, EDX, EDI, ESI, EBP, or ESP, respectively).

NOTE   *The register indirect addressing modes require a 32-bit register. You cannot specify a 16-bit or 8-bit register when using an indirect addressing mode.*

3.6.4.2   Register Indirect Modes in MASM and TASM

MASM and TASM use exactly the same syntax as HLA for the register indirect addressing modes—a pair of brackets around a register name—although the operand order is reversed in instructions like mov.

Here are the MASM/TASM equivalents of the instructions given earlier:

```
mov al, [eax]
mov al, [ebx]
mov al, [ecx]
mov al, [edx]
mov al, [edi]
mov al, [esi]
mov al, [ebp]
mov al, [esp]
```

3.6.4.3 Register Indirect Modes in Gas

Gas, on the other hand, uses parentheses around the register names. Here are Gas variants of the previous HLA mov instructions:

```
movb (%eax), %al
movb (%ebx), %al
movb (%ecx), %al
movb (%edx), %al
movb (%edi), %al
movb (%esi), %al
movb (%ebp), %al
movb (%esp), %al
```

3.6.5 Indexed Addressing Mode

The effective address is the ultimate address in memory that an instruction will access once all the address calculations are complete. The indexed addressing mode computes an *effective address*[2] by adding the address (also called the *displacement* or *offset*) of the variable to the value held in the 32-bit register appearing inside the square brackets. Their sum provides the memory address that the instruction accesses. So if VarName is at address $1100 in memory and EBX contains 8, then mov(VarName [ebx], al); loads the byte at address $1108 into the AL register (see Figure 3-6).

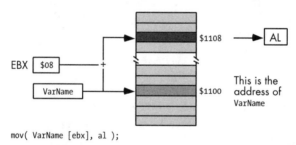

```
mov( VarName [ebx], al );
```

Figure 3-6: Indexed addressing mode

3.6.5.1 Indexed Addressing Mode in HLA

The indexed addressing modes use the following HLA syntax, where VarName is the name of some static variable in your program:

```
mov( VarName[ eax ], al );
mov( VarName[ ebx ], al );
mov( VarName[ ecx ], al );
mov( VarName[ edx ], al );
mov( VarName[ edi ], al );
mov( VarName[ esi ], al );
mov( VarName[ ebp ], al );
mov( VarName[ esp ], al );
```

---

[2] The effective address is the ultimate address in memory that an instruction will access, once all the address calculations are complete.

3.6.5.2 Indexed Addressing Mode in MASM and TASM

MASM and TASM support the same syntax as HLA, but they also allow several variations of this syntax for specifying the indexed addressing mode. The following are equivalent formats, and they demonstrate some of the variations MASM and TASM support:

```
varName[reg₃₂]
[reg₃₂+varName]
[varName][reg₃₂]
[varName+reg₃₂]
[reg₃₂][varName]
varName[reg₃₂+const]
[reg₃₂+varName+const]
[varName][reg₃₂][const]
varName[const+reg₃₂]
[const+reg₃₂+varName]
[const][reg₃₂][varName]
varName[reg₃₂-const]
[reg₃₂+varName-const]
[varName][reg₃₂][-const]
```

MASM and TASM also allow many other combinations. These assemblers treat two juxtaposed items within brackets as though they were separated by the + operator. The multitude of combinations arises because of the commutative nature of addition.

Here are the MASM/TASM equivalents to HLA example given in Section 3.6.5.1, "Indexed Addressing Mode in HLA":

```
mov   al, VarName[ eax ]
mov   al, VarName[ ebx ]
mov   al, VarName[ ecx ]
mov   al, VarName[ edx ]
mov   al, VarName[ edi ]
mov   al, VarName[ esi ]
mov   al, VarName[ ebp ]
mov   al, VarName[ esp ]
```

3.6.5.3 Indexed Addressing Mode in Gas

As with the register indirect addressing mode, Gas uses parentheses rather than brackets. Here is the syntax that Gas allows for the indexed addressing mode:

```
varName(%reg₃₂)
const(%reg₃₂)
varName+const(%reg₃₂)
```

Here are the Gas equivalents to the HLA instructions given earlier:

```
movb VarName( %eax ), al
movb VarName( %ebx ), al
```

```
movb VarName( %ecx ), al
movb VarName( %edx ), al
movb VarName( %edi ), al
movb VarName( %esi ), al
movb VarName( %ebp ), al
movb VarName( %esp ), al
```

3.6.6   Scaled-Indexed Addressing Modes

The scaled-indexed addressing modes are similar to the indexed addressing modes with two differences. The scaled-indexed addressing modes allow you to:

- Combine two registers plus a displacement
- Multiply the index register by a (scaling) factor of 1, 2, 4, or 8

To see what makes this possible, consider the following HLA example:

```
mov( eax, VarName[ ebx + esi * 4 ] );
```

The primary difference between the scaled-indexed addressing mode and the indexed addressing mode is the inclusion of the esi * 4 component. This example computes the effective address by adding in the value of ESI multiplied by 4 (see Figure 3-7).

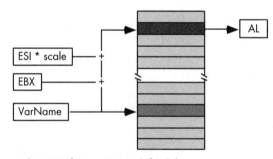

```
mov( VarName [ebx + esi * scale], al );
```

Figure 3-7: Scaled-indexed addressing mode

3.6.6.1   Scaled-Indexed Addressing in HLA

HLA's syntax provides several different ways to specify the scaled-indexed addressing mode. Here are the various syntactical forms:

```
VarName[ IndexReg₃₂ * scale ]
VarName[ IndexReg₃₂ * scale + displacement ]
VarName[ IndexReg₃₂ * scale - displacement ]

[ BaseReg₃₂ + IndexReg₃₂ * scale ]
[ BaseReg₃₂ + IndexReg₃₂ * scale + displacement ]
[ BaseReg₃₂ + IndexReg₃₂ * scale - displacement ]
```

```
VarName[ BaseReg₃₂ + IndexReg₃₂ * scale ]
VarName[ BaseReg₃₂ + IndexReg₃₂ * scale + displacement ]
VarName[ BaseReg₃₂ + IndexReg₃₂ * scale - displacement ]
```

In these examples, BaseReg₃₂ represents any general-purpose 32-bit register; IndexReg₃₂ represents any general-purpose 32-bit register except ESP; scale must be one of the constants: 1, 2, 4, or 8; and VarName represents a static variable name.

3.6.6.2   Scaled-Indexed Addressing in MASM and TASM

MASM and TASM support the same syntax for these addressing modes as HLA, but with additional forms comparable to those presented for the indexed addressing mode. Those forms are just syntactical variants based on the commutativity of the + operator.

3.6.6.3   Scaled-Indexed Addressing in Gas

As usual, Gas uses parentheses rather than brackets to surround scaled-indexed operands. Gas also uses a three-operand syntax to specify the *base register*, the *index register*, and the *scale value*, rather than the arithmetic expression syntax that the other assemblers employ. The generic syntax for the Gas scaled-indexed addressing mode is

```
expression( baseReg₃₂, indexReg₃₂, scaleFactor )
```

More specifically:

```
VarName( ,IndexReg₃₂, scale )
VarName + displacement( ,IndexReg₃₂, scale )
VarName - displacement( ,IndexReg₃₂, scale )

( BaseReg₃₂, IndexReg₃₂, scale )
displacement( BaseReg₃₂, IndexReg₃₂, scale )

VarName( BaseReg₃₂, IndexReg₃₂, scale )
VarName + displacement( BaseReg₃₂, IndexReg₃₂, scale )
VarName - displacement( BaseReg₃₂, IndexReg₃₂, scale )
```

3.7   Declaring Data in Assembly Language

The 80x86 provides only a few low-level machine data types on which individual machine instructions operate. Those data types are listed here:

- *Bytes* hold arbitrary 8-bit values.
- *Words* hold arbitrary 16-bit values.
- *Double words*, or *dwords*, hold arbitrary 32-bit values.

- *Real32 objects* (also called *Real4 objects*) hold 32-bit single-precision floating-point values.

- *Real64 objects* (also called *Real8 objects*) hold 64-bit double-precision floating-point values.

NOTE *80x86 assemblers typically support TByte (ten-byte) and Real80/Real10 data types, but we won't consider using those types here because most HLL compilers don't use these data types. (However, certain C/C++ compilers support Real80 values using the long double data type.)*

3.7.1 Data Declarations in HLA

The HLA assembler, true to its high-level nature, provides a wide variety of single-byte data types including character, signed integer, unsigned integer, Boolean, and enumerated types. Were you to actually write an application in assembly language, having all these different data types (along with the type checking that HLA provides) would be quite useful. For our purposes, however, all we really need is to allocate storage for byte variables and set aside a block of bytes for larger data structures. The HLA byte type is all we really need for 8-bit and array objects.

You can declare byte objects in an HLA static section as follows:

```
static
    variableName : byte;
```

To allocate storage for a block of bytes, you'd use the following HLA syntax:

```
static
    blockOfBytes : byte[ sizeOfBlock ];
```

These HLA declarations create *uninitialized* variables. Technically speaking, HLA always initializes static objects with zeros, so they aren't truly uninitialized. The main thing here is that this code does not explicitly initialize these byte objects with a value. You can, however, tell HLA to initialize your byte variables with a value when the operating system loads the program into memory using statements like the following:

```
static
    // InitializedByte has the initial value 5:

    InitializedByte : byte := 5;

    // InitializedArray is initialized with 0, 1, 2, and 3;

    InitializedArray : byte[4] := [0,1,2,3];
```

3.7.2 Data Declarations in MASM and TASM

In MASM or TASM, you would normally use the db or byte directives within a .data section to reserved storage for a byte object or an array of byte objects. The syntax for a single declaration would take one of these equivalent forms:

```
variableName    db      ?
variableName    byte    ?
```

The preceding declarations create uninitialized objects (which are actually initalized with zeros, just as with HLA). The ? in the operand field of the db/byte directive informs the assembler that you don't want to explicitly attach a value to the declaration.

To declare a variable that is a block of bytes, you'd use syntax like the following:

```
variableName    db      sizeOfBlock dup (?)
variableName    byte    sizeOfBlock dup (?)
```

To create objects with an initial value other than zero, you could use syntax like the following:

```
                    .data
InitializedByte     db      5
InitializedByte2    byte    6
InitializedArray0   db      4 dup (5)    ;array is 5,5,5,5
InitializedArray1   db      5 dup (6)    ;array is 6,6,6,6,6
```

To create an initialized array of bytes whose values are not all the same, you simply specify a comma-delimited list of values in the operand field of the MASM and TASM db/byte directive:

```
                    .data
InitializedArray2   byte    0,1,2,3
InitializedArray3   byte    4,5,6,7,8
```

3.7.3 Data Declarations in Gas

The GNU Gas assembler uses the .byte directive in a .data section to declare a byte variable. The generic form of this directive is

```
variableName: .byte 0
```

Gas doesn't provide an explicit form for creating uninitialized variables; instead, you just supply a zero operand for uninitialized variables. Here are two actual byte variable declarations in Gas:

```
InitializedByte: .byte    5
ZeroedByte       .byte    0  // Zeroed value
```

The GNU assembler does not provide an explicit directive for declaring an array of byte objects, but you may use the `.rept/.endr` directives to create multiple copies of the `.byte` directive as follows:

```
variableName:
        .rept   sizeOfBlock
        .byte   0
        .endr
```

NOTE   *You can also supply a comma-delimited list of values if you want to initialize the array with different values.*

Here are a couple of array declaration examples in Gas:

```
        .section    .data
InitializedArray0: // Creates an array with elements 5,5,5,5
        .rept       4
        .byte       5
        .endr

InitializedArray1:
        .byte       0,1,2,3,4,5
```

3.7.3.1   Accessing Byte Variables in Assembly Language

When accessing byte variables, you simply use the variable's declared name in one of the 80x86 addressing modes. For example, given a byte object named byteVar and an array of bytes named byteArray, you could use any of the following instructions to load that variable into the AL register using the mov instruction:

```
// HLA's mov instruction uses "src, dest" syntax:

mov( byteVar, al );
mov( byteArray[ebx], al ); // EBX is the index into byteArray

// Gas' movb instruction also uses a "src, dest" syntax:

movb byteVar, %al
movb byteArray(%ebx), %al

; MASM's & TASM's mov instructions use "dest, src" syntax

mov al, byteVar
mov al, byteArray[ebx]
```

For 16-bit objects, HLA uses the word data type, MASM and TASM use either the dw or word directives, and Gas uses the `.int` directive. Other than the size of the object these directives declare, their use is identical to the byte declarations.

For example:

```
// HLA example:

static

    // HLAwordVar: two bytes, initialized with zeros:

    HLAwordVar : word;

    // HLAwordArray: eight bytes, initialized with zeros:

    HLAwordArray : word[4];

    // HLAwordArray2: 10 bytes, initialized with 0, ..., 5:

    HLAwordArray2 : word[5] := [0,1,2,3,4];

; MASM/TASM example:

                    .data
MASMwordVar         word    ?
TASMwordArray       word    4 dup (?)
MTASMwordArray2     word    0,1,2,3,4

// Gas example:

                    .section    .data
GasWordVar:         .int    0
GasWordArray:

                    .rept   4
                    .int    0
                    .endr

GasWordArray2:      .int    0,1,2,3,4
```

For 32-bit objects, HLA uses the dword data type, MASM and TASM use the dd or dword directives, and Gas uses the .long directive. For example:

```
// HLA example:

static
    // HLAdwordVar: 4 bytes, initialized with zeros:

    HLAdwordVar : dword;

    // HLAdwordArray: 16 bytes, initialized with zeros.

    HLAdwordArray : dword[4];

    // HLAdwordArray: 20 bytes, initialized with 0, ..., 4:

    HLAdwordArray2 : dword[5] := [0,1,2,3,4];
```

```
; MASM/TASM example:

                        .data
MASMdwordVar            dword   ?
TASMdwordArray          dword   4 dup (?)
MTASMdwordArray2        dword   0,1,2,3,4

// Gas example:

                        .section    .data
GasDWordVar:            .long   0
GasDWordArray:

                        .rept   4
                        .long   0
                        .endr

GasDWordArray2:         .long   0,1,2,3,4
```

3.8   Specifying Operand Sizes in Assembly Language

80x86 assemblers use two mechanisms to specify their operand sizes:

- The operands specify the size using type checking (most assemblers do this).

- The instructions themselves specify the size (in the case of Gas).

  For example, consider the following three HLA mov instructions:

```
mov( 0, al );
mov( 0, ax );
mov( 0, eax );
```

In each case, the register operand specifies the size of the data that the mov instruction copies into that register. MASM/TASM use a similar syntax (though the operands are reversed):

```
mov al, 0 ;8-bit data movement
mov ax, 0 ;16-bit data movement
mov eax, 0 ;32-bit data movement
```

The important thing to note in each of these six cases is that the instruction mnemonic (mov) is exactly the same. The operand, not the instruction mnemonic, specifies the size of the data transfer.

3.8.1   Type Coercion in HLA

However, there is one problem with this approach. Consider the following HLA example:

```
mov( 0, [ebx] );  // Copy zero to the memory location
                  // pointed at by EBX.
```

This instruction is ambiguous. The memory location to which EBX points could be a byte, a word, or a double word. Nothing in the instruction tells the assembler the size of the operand. Faced with an instruction like this, the assembler will report an error and you will have to explicitly tell it the size of the memory operand. In HLA's case, this is done with a type coercion operator as follows:

```
mov( 0, (type word [ebx]) );  // 16-bit data movement.
```

In general, you can coerce any memory operand to an appropriate size using the HLA syntax:

```
(type new_type memory)
```

where new_type represents a data type (such as byte, word, or dword) and memory represents the memory address whose type you would like to override.

3.8.2 Type Coercion in MASM and TASM

MASM and TASM suffer from this same problem. You will need to coerce the memory location using a coercion operator like the following:

```
mov  word ptr [ebx], 0   ; 16-bit data movement.
```

Of course, you can substitute byte or dword in these two examples to coerce the memory location to a byte or double word size.

3.8.3 Type Coercion in Gas

The Gas assembler doesn't require type coercion operators because it uses a different technique to specify the size of its operands: the instruction mnemonic explicitly specifies the size. Rather than using a single mnemonic like mov, Gas uses three mnemonics that consist of mov with a single character suffix that specifies the size. The Gas mov mnemonics are:

> **movb**   Copy an 8-bit (byte) value
>
> **movw**   Copy a 16-bit (word) value
>
> **movl**   Copy a 32-bit (long) value

There is never any ambiguity when using these mnemonics, even if their operands don't have an explicit size. For example:

```
movb 0, (%ebx) // 8-bit data copy
movw 0, (%ebx) // 16-bit data copy
movl 0, (%ebx) // 32-bit data copy
```

3.9 The Minimal 80x86 Instruction Set

Although the 80x86 CPU family supports hundreds of instructions, few compilers actually use more than a couple dozen of these instructions. If you're wondering why compilers don't use more of the available instructions, the answer is because many of the instructions have become obsolete over time as newer instructions reduced the need for older instructions. Some instructions, such as the Pentium's MMX and SSE instructions, simply do not correspond to functions you'd normally perform in an HLL. Therefore, compilers rarely generate these types of machine instructions (such instructions generally appear only in handwritten assembly language programs). Therefore, you don't need to learn the entire 80x86 instruction set in order to study compiler output. Instead, you need only learn the handful of instructions that compilers actually emit for the 80x86. The online resources (www.writegreatcode.com) provide a reasonable subset of the 80x86 instructions that you will commonly encounter when examining the output of an 80x86-based compiler.

3.10 For More Information

This chapter and the online resources present only a small subset of the 80x86 instruction set. Some compilers will, undoubtedly, use some instructions not present in this book. The Intel Pentium manual set, available online at www.intel.com, provides the complete reference for the 80x86 instruction set. Another excellent 80x86 reference is my book *The Art of Assembly Language* (No Starch Press, 2003). Jonathon Bartlett's *Programming from the Ground Up* (Bartlett Publishing, 2004) and Richard Blum's *Professional Assembly Language* (Wrox, 2005) provide a treatment of the Gas assembler for those who are working with GNU tools.

4

POWERPC ASSEMBLY FOR THE HLL PROGRAMMER

Throughout this book you'll be examining high-level language code and comparing it against the machine code that the compiler generates for the high-level code. Making sense of the compiler's output requires some knowledge of assembly language programming. Though becoming an expert assembly language programmer takes time and experience, such a skill level isn't necessary for our purposes. All you really need is the ability to read code that compilers and other assembly language programmers have produced; you don't need the ability to write assembly language programs from scratch. The purpose of this chapter is to provide a basic overview of PowerPC assembly language so that you will be able to read the PowerPC output produced by compilers on machines like the older Power Macintosh or for game consoles such as the Sony PlayStation 3 or the Xbox 2. This chapter

- Describes the basic PowerPC machine architecture
- Provides a basic overview of PowerPC assembly language so that you will be able to read the PowerPC output produced by the GCC compiler

- Describes the memory addressing modes of the PowerPC CPU
- Describes the syntax that the PowerPC Gas assembler uses
- Describes how to use constants and declare data in assembly language programs

In addition to this chapter, you will also want to take a look at the online resources (www.writegreatcode.com), which describe a minimal PowerPC instruction set that you'll need when examining compiler output.

4.1 Learning One Assembly Language Is Good; More Is Better

If you intend to write code for a processor other than the PowerPC, then you should really learn how to read at least two different assembly languages. By doing so, you'll avoid the pitfall of coding for the PowerPC in an HLL and then finding that your "optimizations" only work on the PowerPC CPU. A good second instruction set to learn is the Intel 80x86 instruction set, which Chapter 3 describes (in fact, the 80x86 instruction set is often the *first* instruction set and the PowerPC is the second instruction set that people learn). Other possible processors to consider include the ARM processor family, the SPARC processor family, the MIPS processor family, the 680x0 processor family, or the IA-64 processor. As a general rule, you should familiarize yourself with the instruction sets of at least one RISC CPU and one CISC CPU. The 80x86 and 680x0 processor families are good examples of CISC CPUs; the PowerPC, SPARC, MIPS, and ARM processor families provide good examples of RISC CPUs. The IA-64 processor is actually what is known as a VLIW (very large instruction word) processor, though it's closer in design to a RISC than a CISC CPU. This book chooses to cover the 80x86 and PowerPC families because they are the most popular CPUs in use on contemporary machines.

This chapter and the online resources provide more of a reference than a tutorial on PowerPC assembly language. You'll reap the greatest benefit from this chapter if you skim it rapidly and then refer back to it whenever you have a question about the assembly code you'll be seeing throughout the rest of this book.

4.2 Assembly Syntaxes

In Chapter 3 you saw that there are signficant syntax differences in the code generated by various assembles for the 80x86. With the PowerPC, by contrast, the various assemblers use a much more uniform syntax, so this book uses the syntax employed by the Gas assembler as provided with (the PowerPC version of) Mac OS X. As GNU's Gas assembler for the PowerPC uses a relatively standard PowerPC assembly language syntax, you should have no trouble reading PowerPC assembly listings produced for other assemblers (such as the Code Warrior assembler) if you learn the Gas syntax.

4.3 Basic PowerPC Architecture

The IBM/Motorola PowerPC CPU family is generally classified as a *Von Neumann machine.* Von Neumann computer systems contain three main building blocks: the *central processing unit (CPU), memory,* and *input/output (I/O) devices.* These three components are connected together using the *system bus* (consisting of the address, data, and control buses). The block diagram in Figure 3-1 shows this relationship.

The CPU communicates with memory and I/O devices by placing a numeric value on the address bus to select one of the memory locations or I/O device port locations, each of which has a unique binary numeric *address.* Then the CPU, I/O, and memory devices pass data between themselves by placing the data on the data bus. The control bus provides signals that determine the direction of the data transfer (to/from memory and to/from an I/O device).

Within the CPU the registers are the most prominent feature. The PowerPC CPU registers can be broken down into several categories: general-purpose integer registers, floating-point registers, special-purpose application-accessible registers, and special-purpose kernel-mode registers. This text will not consider the last set of registers. The special-purpose kernel-mode registers are intended for writing operating systems, debuggers, and other system-level tools. Such software construction is well beyond the scope of this text, so there is little need to discuss the special-purpose kernel-mode registers.

4.3.1 General-Purpose Integer Registers

The PowerPC CPUs provide 32 general-purpose integer registers for application use. Most compilers refer to these registers via the names R0..R31. On most PowerPC processors (circa 2005) these registers are 32 bits wide. On higher-end PowerPC processors these registers are 64 bits wide.

4.3.2 General-Purpose Floating-Point Registers

The PowerPC processor also provides a set of 32 64-bit floating-point registers. Assemblers and compilers generally refer to these registers using the register names F0..F31 (or FPR0..FPR31). These registers can hold single- or double-precision floating-point values.

4.3.3 User-Mode-Accessible Special-Purpose Registers

The user-mode-accessible special-purpose registers include the condition-code register(s), the floating-point status and control register, the XER register, the LINK register, the COUNT register (CTR), and the time base registers (TBRs).

4.3.3.1   Condition-Code Registers

The condition-code register is 32 bits wide, but it is actually a collection of eight 4-bit registers (named CR0, CR1, ..., CR7) that hold the status of a previous computation (e.g., the result of a comparison). The PowerPC uses CR0 to hold the condition codes after an integer operation, and it uses CR1 to hold the condition codes after a floating-point operation. Programs typically use the remaining condition-code registers to save the status of some operation while other operations take place.

The individual bits in the CR0 condition-code register are

- The LT bit (CR0: bit 0). Set if an operation produces a negative result. Also indicates a "less than" condition.

- The GT bit (CR0: bit 1). Set if the result is positive (and nonzero) after an operation. Also indicates a "greater than" condition.

- The zero bit (CR0: bit 2). This bit is set when the result of an operation is zero. This also indicates the "equality" condition.

- The summary overflow bit (CR0: bit 3). This indicates a signed integer overflow during a chain of operations (see the XER register description in Section 4.3.3.3, "XER Register").

The individual bits in the CR1 condition-code register hold the following values:

- Floating-point exception bit (CR1:bit 0)

- Common-point enable exception bit (CR1: bit1)

- Floating-point invalid exception bit (CR1: bit 2)

- Floating-point overflow exception bit (CR1: bit 3)

Table 4-1 describes how the PowerPC sets the CR*n* bits after a comparison instruction.

Table 4-1: CR*n* Field Bit Settings for Comparisons

CR*n* Bit	Meaning	Description
0	Less than (integer or floating-point)	For integer registers, this bit is set if one register is less than another (or a small immediate constant). Unsigned and signed comparisons are possible using different instructions. For floating-point registers, this bit is set if the value in one floating-point register is less than the value in another after a floating-point comparison (which is always a signed comparison).
1	Greater than (integer or floating-point)	For integer registers, this bit is set if one register is greater than another (or a small immediate constant). Unsigned and signed comparisons are possible using different instructions. For floating-point registers, this bit is set if the value in one floating-point register is greater than the value in another after a floating-point comparison (which is always a signed comparison).

Table 4-1: CRn Field Bit Settings for Comparisons (continued)

CRn Bit	Meaning	Description
2	Equal (integer or floating-point)	For integer registers, this bit is set if one register is equal to another (or a small immediate constant). Unsigned and signed comparisons are the same when comparing for equality. For floating-point registers, this bit is set if the value in one floating-point register is equal to the value in another after a floating-point comparison.
3	Summary overflow (integer) Not A Number, NaN (floating-point)	After an integer operation, this bit indicates whether an overflow has occurred. This bit is sticky insofar as you can only clear it, once set, by explicitly clearing the SO bit in the XER register. After a floating-point operation, this bit indicates whether one of the two floating-point operands is NaN.

4.3.3.2 Floating-Point Status and Control Register

The floating-point status and control register is a 32-bit register containing 24 status bits and 8 control bits. The status bits appear in bit positions 0..23, and the control bits consume bit positions 24..31. The PowerPC CPU updates the status bits at the completion of each floating-point instruction; the program is responsible for initializing and manipulating the control bits.

Most of the status bits in the floating-point status and control register are *sticky*. This means that once a bit is set, it remains set until explicitly cleared by software. This allows the CPU to execute a sequence of floating-point operations and test for an invalid result at the end of the sequence of operations rather than having to test for an invalid operation after each instruction. This reduces the number of tests an application must do and, therefore, increases the performance (and reduces the size) of the application.

The exact nature of the floating-point status bits are not important here (the PowerPC code we'll be looking at in this book rarely checks the floating-point status), so we'll skip their complete discussion. For more details, please consult the PowerPC documentation available from IBM (www.ibm.com).

4.3.3.3 XER Register

The PowerPC XER register collects several disparate values that don't have a home elsewhere. The low-order (LO) three bits maintain the summary overflow (bit 0), overflow (bit 1), and carry (bit 2) conditions. The high-order (HO) eight bits contain a byte count for some PowerPC string operations.

The overflow and summary overflow bits are set by instructions that produce a signed integer result that cannot be represented in 32 or 64 bits (depending on the instruction). The summary overflow bit is a sticky bit that, once set, remains set until the program explicitly clears the bit. The overflow bit, on the other hand, simply reflects the status (overflow/no overflow) of the last arithmetic operation; in particular, if an arithmetic operation does not produce an overflow, then that operation clears the overflow bit.

The carry flag is set whenever an arithmetic instruction produces an unsigned integer result that cannot be held in 32 or 64 bits (depending on the instruction); this bit also holds the bits shifted out of a register operand in a shift left or right operation.

4.3.3.4 The LINK Register

The PowerPC LINK register holds a *return address* after the execution of a *branch and link (bl)* instruction. The execution of a branch and link instruction leaves the address of the instruction following the branch in the LINK register. PowerPC applications use this register to implement return from subroutine operations as well as compute program-counter relative addresses for various operations. The PowerPC can also use the LINK register for indirect jumps (e.g., for implementing switch statements).

4.3.3.5 The COUNT Register

The COUNT register (also called CTR) has two purposes: as a loop-control register and to hold the target address for an indirect jump. Most compilers use the COUNT register for this latter purpose; you'll see the COUNT register used for implementing indirect jumps throughout code in this book.

4.3.3.6 The Time Base Registers (TBL and TBU)

These two registers, Time Base Lower (TBL) and Time Base Upper (TBU), are read-only in user mode. Applications can use these two registers (which actually concatenate to form a single 64-bit register) to compute the execution time of an instruction sequence. However, as few compilers consider the values in these registers, we'll ignore them in this book.

4.4   Literal Constants

Like most assemblers, Gas supports literal numeric, character, and string constants. This section describes the syntax for the various constants that Gas supports and various compilers emit.

4.4.1   Binary Literal Constants

Binary literal constants in Gas begin with the special 0b prefix followed by one or more binary digits (0 or 1). Examples:

```
0b1011
0b10101111
0b0011111100011001
0b1011001010010101
```

4.4.2 Decimal Literal Constants

Decimal literal constants in Gas take the standard form—a sequence of one or more decimal digits without any special prefix or suffix. Examples:

```
123
1209345
```

4.4.3 Hexadecimal Literal Constants

Hexadecimal literal constants in Gas consist of a string of hexadecimal digits (0..9, a..f, or A..F) with a 0x prefix. Examples:

```
0x1AB0
0x1234ABCD
0xdead
```

4.4.4 Character and String Literal Constants

Character literal constants in Gas consist of an apostrophe followed by a single character. Examples:

```
'a
' '
'!
```

String literal constants in Gas consist of a sequence of zero or more characters surrounded by quotes. String literal constants in Gas use the same syntax as C strings. You use the \ escape sequence to embed special characters in a Gas string. Examples:

```
"Hello World"
"" -- The empty string
"He said \"Hello\" to them"
"\"" -- string containing a single quote character
```

4.4.5 Floating-Point Literal Constants

Floating-point literal constants in assembly language typically take the same form you'll find in HLLs—a sequence of digits, possibly containing a decimal point, optionally followed by a signed exponent. Examples:

```
3.14159
2.71e+2
1.0e-5
5e1
```

4.5 Manifest (Symbolic) Constants in Assembly Language

Almost every assembler provides a mechanism for declaring symbolic (named) constants. Gas uses the .equ statement to define a symbolic constant in the source file. This statement uses the following syntax:

```
.equ        symbolName, value
```

Here are some examples of "equates" within a Gas source file:

```
.equ        false, 0
.equ        true, 1
.equ        anIntConst, 12345
```

4.6 PowerPC Addressing Modes

PowerPC instructions can access three types of operands: register operands, immediate constants, and memory operands.

4.6.1   PowerPC Register Access

Gas allows assembly programmers (or compiler writers) to access the PowerPC general-purpose integer registers by name or number: R0, R1, ..., R31.

Floating-point instructions access the floating-point registers by their name (F0..F31). Note that floating-point registers are only legal as floating-point instruction operands (just as integer instructions are accessible only within integer instructions).

4.6.2   The Immediate Addressing Mode

Many integer instructions allow a programmer to specify an immediate constant as a source operand. However, as all PowerPC instructions are exactly 32 bits in size, a single instruction cannot load a 32-bit (or larger) constant into a PowerPC register. The PowerPC's instruction set does support immediate constants that are 16 bits in size (or smaller). The PowerPC encodes those constants into the opcode and sign extends their values to 32 bits (or 64 bits) prior to using them.

For immediate values outside the range −32,768..+32,767, the PowerPC requires that you load the constant into a register using a couple of instructions and then use the value in that register. The most obvious downside to this is that the code is larger and slower, but another problem is that you wind up using a (precious) register to hold the immediate value. Fortunately, the PowerPC has 32 general-purpose registers available, so using a register for this purpose isn't quite as bad as on a CPU with fewer registers (like the 80x86).

4.6.3 PowerPC Memory Addressing Modes

The PowerPC CPU is a load/store architecture, meaning that it can only access (data) memory using load and store instructions. All other instructions operate on registers (or small immediate constants). With a load/store architecture, for example, you cannot directly add the contents of some memory location to a register value—you must first load the memory data into a register and then add that register to the destination register's value.

RISC CPUs generally eschew complex addressing modes, instead relying upon sequences of machine instructions using simple addressing modes to achieve the same effect. The PowerPC, true to its RISC heritage, supports only three memory addressing modes. One of those is a special addressing mode used only by the load string and store string instructions. So for all practical purposes, the PowerPC only supports two memory addressing modes. They are *register plus displacement* and *register plus register* (base plus index).

4.6.3.1 Register Plus Displacement Addressing Mode

The PowerPC register plus displacement addressing mode adds a signed 16-bit displacement value, signed extended to 32 bits, with the value from a general-purpose integer register to compute the effective memory address. The Gas syntax for this addressing mode is the following:

```
displacementValue( Rn )
```

where *displacementValue* is a signed 16-bit expression and Rn represents one of the PowerPC's 32-bit general-purpose integer registers (R0..R31). R0 is a special case in this addressing mode, however. If you specify R0, then the PowerPC CPU substitutes the value zero in place of the value in the R0 register. This provides an *absolute* or *displacement-only* addressing mode that accesses memory locations 0..32,767 (and also the final 32KB at the end of the address space).

The lbz (load byte with zero extension) instruction is a typical load instruction that uses the register plus displacement addressing mode. This instruction fetches a byte from memory, zero extends it to 32 bits (64 bits on the 64-bit variants of the PowerPC), and then copies the result into a destination register. An example of this instruction is

```
lbz R3, 4(R5)
```

This particular instruction loads the LO byte of R3 with the byte found in memory at the address held in R5 plus four. It zeros out the HO bytes of R3.

Most load and store instructions (like lbz) on the PowerPC support a special *update* form. When using the register plus displacement addressing mode, these instructions work just like the standard load instructions except that they update the base address register with the final effective address. That is, they add the displacement to the base register's value after loading the value from memory. The `lbzu` instruction is a good example of this form:

```
lbzu R3, 4(R5)
```

This instruction not only copies the value from memory location [R5+4][1] into R3, but it also adds four to R5. Note that you may not specify R0 as a base register when using the update form (remember, the PowerPC substitutes the value zero for R0, and you cannot store a value into a constant).

4.6.3.2 Register Plus Register (Indexed) Addressing Mode

The PowerPC also supports an indexed addressing mode that uses one general-purpose register to hold a base address and a second general-purpose register to hold an index from that base address. This addressing mode is specified as part of the instruction mnemonic. For example, to use the indexed addressing mode with the `lbz` instruction, you'd use the `lbzx` mnemonic. Instructions using this addressing mode typically have three operands: a destination operation (for loads) or a source operand (for store operations), a base register (R*b*), and an index register (R*x*). The `lbzx` instruction, for example, uses the following syntax:

```
lbzx Rd, Rb, Rx
```

Example:

```
lbzx R3, R5, R6
```

This example loads R3 with the zero-extended byte found at the memory address [R5 + R6].

An update form of the indexed addressing mode also exists (e.g., `lbzux`). This form updates the base register with the sum of the base and index registers after computing the effective memory address. The index register's value is unaffected by the update form of the instruction.

4.7 Declaring Data in Assembly Language

The PowerPC CPU provides only a few low-level machine data types on which individual machine instructions can operate.

These data types are the following:

- Bytes that hold arbitrary 8-bit values

- Words that hold arbitrary 16-bit values (these are called *halfwords* in PowerPC terminology)

- Double words that hold arbitrary 32-bit values (these are called *words* in PowerPC terminology)

---

[1] The brackets ([]) denote indirection. That is, [R5+4] represents the memory at the address specified by the contents of R5 plus four.

- Quad words that hold 64-bit values (these are called *double words* in PowerPC terminology)
- Single-precision floating-point values (32-bit single floating-point values)
- Double-precision, 64-bit, floating-point values

NOTE   *Although the standard PowerPC terminology is byte, halfword, word, and double word for 8-, 16-, 32-, and 64-bit integer values, outside of this chapter this book will use the x86 terminology to avoid confusion with the 80x86 code that also appears herein.*

The GNU Gas assembler uses the .byte directive in a .data section to declare a byte variable. The generic form of this directive is

```
variableName: .byte 0
```

Gas doesn't provide an explicit form for creating uninitialized variables; just supply a zero operand for uninitialized variables. Here is an actual byte variable declaration in Gas:

```
IntializedByte: .byte    5
```

The GNU assembler does not provide an explicit directive for declaring an array of byte objects, but you may use the .rept/.endr directives to create multiple copies of the .byte directive as follows:

```
variableName:
        .rept    sizeOfBlock
        .byte    0
        .endr
```

Note that you may also supply a comma-delimited list of values if you want to initialize the array with different values.

Here are a couple of array declaration examples in Gas:

```
        .section    .data ;Variables go in this section
InitializedArray0: ; Creates an array with elements 5,5,5,5
        .rept    4
        .byte    5
        .endr

InitializedArray1:
        .byte    0,1,2,3,4,5
```

For 16-bit objects Gas uses the .int directive. Other than the size of the object these directives declare, their use is identical to the byte declarations, for example:

```
        .section    .data
GasWordVar:     .int    0
```

```
; Create an array of four words, all initialized to zero:

GasWordArray:
                .rept   4
                .int    0
                .endr

; Create an array of 16-bit words, initialized with
; the value 0, 1, 2, 3, and 4:

GasWordArray2:      .int    0,1,2,3,4
```

For 32-bit objects, Gas uses the .long directive:

```
                .section    .data
GasDWordVar:        .long   0

; Create an array with four double-word values
; initialized to zero:

GasDWordArray:
                .rept   4
                .long   0
                .endr

; Create an array of double words initialized with
; the values 0, 1, 2, 3, 4:

GasDWordArray2:     .long   0,1,2,3,4
```

For floating-point values, Gas uses the .single and .double directives to reserve storage for an IEEE-format floating-point value (32 or 64 bits, respectively). Because the PowerPC CPU does not support immediate floating-point constants, if you need to reference a floating-point constant from a machine instruction, you will need to place that constant in a memory variable and access the memory variable in place of the imediate constant. Here are some examples of their use:

```
                .section    .data
GasSingleVar:       .single 0.0
GasDoubleVar:       .double 1.0

; Create an array with four single-precision values
; initialized to 2.0:

GasSingleArray:
                .rept   4
                .single 2.0
                .endr
```

```
; Create an array of double-precision values initialized with
; the values 0.0, 1.1, 2.2, 3.3, and 4.4:

GasDWordArray2:    .double 0.0,1.1,2.2,3.3,4.4
```

4.8 Specifying Operand Sizes in Assembly Language

PowerPC instructions generally operate only upon 32-bit or 64-bit data. Unlike CISC processors, individual PowerPC instructions don't operate on differing data types. The add instruction, for example, operates only on 32-bit values (except on 64-bit implementations of the PowerPC, where it operates on 64-bit values when in 64-bit mode). Generally, this isn't a problem. If two PowerPC registers contain 8-bit values, you'll get the same result by adding those two 32-bit registers together that you'd get if they were 8-bit registers, if you only consider the LO 8 bits of the sum.

Memory accesses, however, are a different matter. When reading and (especially when) writing data in memory, it's important that the CPU access only the desired data size. Therefore, the PowerPC provides some size-specific load and store instructions that specify byte, 16-bit halfword, and 32-bit word sizes.

4.9 The Minimal Instruction Set

Although the PowerPC CPU family supports hundreds of instructions, few compilers actually use all of these instructions. If you're wondering why compilers don't use more of the available instructions, the answer is because many of the instructions have become obsolete over time as newer instructions reduced the need for older instructions. Some instructions, such as the PowerPC's AltiVec instructions, simply do not correspond to operations you'd normally perform in an HLL. Therefore, compilers rarely generate these types of machine instructions (such instructions generally appear only in handwritten assembly language programs). Therefore, you don't need to learn the entire PowerPC instruction set in order to study compiler output. Instead, you need only learn the handful of instructions that the compiler actually emits on the PowerPC. The online resources present the subset of the PowerPC instruction set that this book uses.

4.10 For More Information

This chapter and the online resources (www.writegreatcode.com) contain descriptions of the more common PowerPC instructions. They do not, by any means, provide a complete description of the PowerPC instruction set. Those who are interested in additional details about the instruction set should consult IBM's document *PowerPC Microprocessor Family: The Programming Environments for 32-bit Processors.* You can find this on IBM's website at www.ibm.com.

5

COMPILER OPERATION AND CODE GENERATION

In order to write HLL code that produces efficient machine code, you really need to understand how compilers and linkers translate high-level source statements into executable machine code. A complete presentation of compiler theory is beyond the scope of this book; however, in this chapter I do explain the basics of the translation process so you can understand the limitations of HLL compilers, and you'll be able to work within those limitations.

This chapter

- Teaches you about the different types of input files programming languages use
- Explores the differences between various language implementations such as compilers and interpreters
- Shows how typical compilers process source files to produce executable programs

- Discusses the process of optimization and why compilers cannot produce the best possible code for a given source file
- Describes the different types of output files that compilers produce
- Provides an in-depth look at some common object-file formats, such as COFF and ELF
- Covers memory organization and alignment issues that affect the size and efficiency of executable files a compiler produces
- Explains how linker options can affect the efficiency of your code

This material provides the basis for all the chapters that follow, and the information this chapter presents is crucial if you want to help a compiler produce the best possible code. I will begin with the discussion of compiler file formats.

5.1   File Types That Programming Languages Use

A typical program can take many forms. A *source file* is a human-readable form that a programmer creates and supplies to a language translator (e.g., a compiler). A typical compiler translates the source file or files into an *object code* file. A linker program combines separate object modules to produce a relocatable or executable file. Finally, a loader (usually the operating system) loads the executable file into memory and makes the final modifications to the object code prior to execution. Please note that the modifications are to the object code that is now in memory. The actual file on the disk does not get modified. These are not the only types of files that language-processing systems manipulate, but they are typical. To fully understand compiler limitations, understanding how the language processor deals with each of these file types is important. I'll begin with a discussion of source code.

5.2   Programming Language Source Files

Traditionally, source files contain pure ASCII (or some other character set) text that a programmer has created with a text editor. One advantage to using pure text files is that a programmer can manipulate a source file using any program that processes text files. For example, a program that counts the number of lines in an arbitrary text file will also count the number of source lines in a program. Because there are hundreds of little filter programs that manipulate text files, maintaining source files in a pure text format is a good approach. This format is sometimes called plain vanilla text.

5.2.1   Tokenized Source Files

Some language processing systems (especially interpreters) maintain their source files in a special *tokenized* form. Tokenized source files generally use special single-byte *token* values to represent reserved words and other lexical elements in the source language. Tokenized source files are often smaller than text source files because they compress multicharacter reserved words and values to single byte tokens. Furthermore, maintaining the source file in a tokenized form can help an interpreter run faster because processing strings of 1-byte tokens is far more efficient than recognizing reserved word strings; interpreters that operate on tokenized code are generally an order of magnitude faster than interpreters that operate on pure text.

Reconstructing the original source file (or a close resemblance) from the tokenized form of a program is easy. Generally, the tokenized form consists of a sequence of bytes that map directly to strings such as if and print in the original source file. By using a table of strings and a little extra logic, deciphering a tokenized program to obtain the original source file is easy. (Usually, you lose any extra whitespace you inserted into the source file, but that's about the only difference.) Many of the original BASIC interpreters found on early PC systems worked this way. You'd type a line of BASIC source code into the interpreter and the interpreter would immediately tokenize that line and store the tokenized form in memory. Later, when you executed the LIST command, the interpreter would *detokenize* the source code in memory to produce the listing.

On the flip side, tokenized source files often use a proprietary format and, therefore, cannot take advantage of general-purpose tools that manipulate text files. This includes programs like word count (*wc*), entab, and detab. (Word count counts the number of lines, words, and characters in a text file, entab replaces spaces with tabs, and detab replaces tabs with spaces.)

To overcome this limitation, most languages that operate on tokenized files provide the ability to *detokenize* a source file and produce a standard text file from the tokenized data. Such language translators also provide the ability to retokenize a source file, given an ASCII text file. To run such a language's source file through a standard text-based filter program, a programmer would first detokenize the source file to produce a text file, run the resulting text file through some filter program, and then retokenize the output of the filter program to produce a new tokenized source file. Although this is a considerable amount of work, it does allow language translators that work with tokenized files to take advantage of various text-based utility programs.

5.2.2 Specialized Source File Formats

Some programming languages do not use a traditional text-based file format at all. They often use graphical elements (such as flowcharts or forms) to represent the instructions the program is to perform. Borland's Delphi programming language provides an example of this. The "form designer" component of the Delphi programming language provides a good example of a nontextual source format.

5.3 Types of Computer Language Processors

We can generally place computer language systems into one of four categories: pure interpreters, interpreters, incremental compilers, and compilers. These systems differ in how they process the source program and execute the result, which affects the efficiency of the execution process.

5.3.1 Pure Interpreters

Pure interpreters operate directly on a text source file and tend to be very inefficient. An interpreter continuously scans the source file (usually an ASCII text file), processing it as string data. Recognizing *lexemes* (language components such as reserved words, literal constants, and the like) consumes time. Indeed, many interpreters spend more time processing the lexemes (that is, performing *lexical analysis*) than they do actually executing the program. Pure interpreters tend to be the smallest of the computer language processing programs. This is because every language translator has to do lexical analysis, and the actual on-the-fly execution of the lexeme takes only a little additional effort. For this reason, pure interpreters are popular where a very compact language processor is desirable. Pure interpreters are also popular for scripting languages and very high-level languages that let you manipulate the language's source code as string data during program execution.

5.3.2 Interpreters

An *interpreter* executes some representation of a program's source file at runtime. This representation isn't necessarily a text file in human-readable form. As noted in the previous section, many interpreters operate on tokenized source files in order to avoid lexical analysis during execution. Some interpreters read a text source file as input and translate the input file to a tokenized form prior to execution. This allows programmers to work with text files in their favorite editor while enjoying fast execution using a tokenized format. The only costs are an initial delay to tokenize the source file (which is unnoticeable on most modern machines) and the fact that it may not be possible to execute strings as program statements.

5.3.3 Compilers

A *compiler* translates a source program in text form into executable machine code. This is a complex process, particularly in optimizing compilers. There are a couple of things to note about the code a compiler produces. First, a compiler produces machine instructions that the underlying CPU can directly execute. Therefore, the CPU doesn't waste any cycles decoding the source file while executing the program—all of the CPU's resources are dedicated to executing the machine code. As such, the resulting program generally runs many times faster than an interpreted version does. Of course, some compilers do a better job of translating HLL source code into machine code than other compilers, but even low-quality compilers do a better job than most interpreters.

A compiler's translation from source code to machine code is a one-way function. It is very difficult, if not impossible, to reconstruct the original source file if you're given only the machine code output from a program. (By contrast, interpreters either operate directly on source files or work with tokenized files from which it's easy to reconstruct some semblance of the source file.)

5.3.4 Incremental Compilers

An *incremental compiler* is a cross between a compiler and an interpreter.[1] There is no single definition of an incremental compiler because there are many different types of incremental compilers. In general, though, like an interpreter, an incremental compiler does not compile the source file into machine code. Instead, it translates the source code into an intermediate form. Unlike interpreters, however, this intermediate form does not usually exhibit a strong relationship to the original source file. This intermediate form is generally the machine code for a *virtual (hypothetical) machine language*. That is, there is no real CPU that can execute this code. However, it is easy to write an interpreter for such a virtual machine, and that interpreter does the actual execution. Because interpreters for virtual machines are usually much more efficient than interpreters for tokenized code, the execution of this virtual machine code is usually much faster than the execution of a list of tokens in an interpreter. Languages like Java use this compilation technique, along with a *Java byte code engine* (an interpreter program, see Figure 5-1) that interpretively executes the Java "machine code." The big advantage to virtual machine execution is that the virtual machine code is portable; that is, programs running on the virtual machine can execute anywhere there is an interpreter available. True machine code, by contrast, only executes on the CPU (family) for which it was written. Generally, interpreted virtual machine code runs about two to ten times faster than interpreted code, and pure machine code generally runs anywhere from two to ten times faster than interpreted virtual machine code.

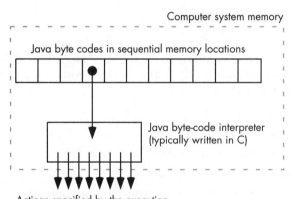

Figure 5-1: The Java byte-code interpreter

In an attempt to improve the performance of programs compiled via an incremental compiler, many vendors (particularly Java systems vendors) have resorted to a technique known as *just-in-time compilation*. The concept is based

---

[1] Actually, in recent years the term *incremental compiler* has taken on another meaning as well— the ability to compile pieces of the program and recompile them as necessary (given changes in the source file). We will not consider such systems here.

on the fact that the time spent in interpretation is largely consumed by fetching and deciphering the virtual machine code at runtime. This interpretation occurs repeatedly as the program executes. Just-in-time compilation translates the virtual machine code to actual machine code whenever it encounters a virtual machine instruction for the first time. By doing so, the interpreter is spared the interpretation process the next time it encounters the same statement in the program (e.g., in a loop). Although just in time compilation is nowhere near as good as a true compiler, it can typically improve the performance of a program by a factor of two to five times.

An interesting note about older compilers and some freely available compilers is that they would compile the source code to assembly language and then you would have to have a separate compiler, known as an assembler, to assemble this output to the machine code wanted. Most modern and high efficient compilers, skip this step altogether. See Section 5.5, "Compiler Output," for more on this subject.

This chapter describes how compilers generate machine code. By understanding how a compiler generates machine code, you can choose appropriate HLL statements to generate better, more efficient machine code. If you want to improve the performance of programs written with an interpreter or incremental compiler, the best advice you can follow is to use an optimizing compiler to process your application. For example, GNU provides a compiler for Java that produces optimized machine code rather than interpreted Java byte code; the resulting executable files run much faster than interpreted Java byte code.

5.4 The Translation Process

A typical compiler is broken down into several logical components that compiler writers call *phases*. Although the number and names of these phases may change somewhat among different compilers, common phases you'll find in many compilers include:

- The *lexical analysis* phase
- The *syntax analysis* phase
- The *intermediate code generation* phase
- The *native code generation* phase
- The *optimization* phase for compilers that support it

Figure 5-2 shows how the compiler logically arranges these phases to translate source code in the HLL into machine (object) code.

Although Figure 5-2 suggests that the compiler executes these phases sequentially, most compilers do not execute in this order. Instead, the phases tend to execute in parallel, with each phase doing a small amount of work, passing its output on to the next phase, and then waiting for input from the previous phase. In a typical compiler, the *parser* (the syntax analysis phase) is probably the closest thing you will find to the main program or the master process. The parser usually drives the compilation process, insofar as it calls the *scanner* (lexical analysis phase) to obtain input and calls the intermediate code generator to process the parser's output. The intermediate code generator may (optionally) call the optimizer and then call the native code generator. The native code generator may (optionally) call the optimizer as well. The output from the native code generation phase is the executable code. After the native code generator/optimizer emits some code, it returns to the intermediate code generator, which returns to the parser, which requests more input from the scanner, and the process repeats. Note that other compiler organizations are possible. Some compilers, for example, don't have an optimization phase; others allow the user to choose whether the compiler runs this phase. Similarly, some compilers dispense with intermediate code generation and directly call a native code generator. Some compilers include additional phases that process object modules compiled at different times. The details often vary by compiler, but these phases are the ones you will find in a typical optimizing compiler.

Although Figure 5-2 doesn't correctly show the execution path of a typical compiler, it does correctly show the *data flow* through the compiler. That is, the scanner reads the source file, translates it to a different form, and then passes this translated data on to the parser. The parser accepts its input from the scanner, translates that input to a different form, and then passes this new data to the intermediate code generator. Similarly, the remaining phases read their input from the previous phase, translate the input to a (possibly) different form, and then pass that input on to the next phase. The compiler writes the output of its last phase to the executable object file.

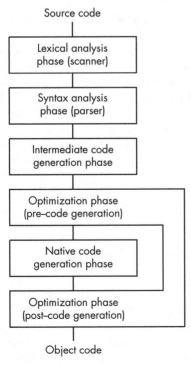

Figure 5-2: Phases of compilation

5.4.1 Lexical Analysis and Tokens

The scanner is responsible for reading the character/string data found in the source file and breaking this data up into tokens that represent the *lexical items* present in the source file. These lexical items, or *lexemes*, are the character sequences found in the source file that we would recognize as atomic components of the language. For example, a lexical analyzer (*lexer*) for the C language would recognize substrings like if and while as C reserved words. The lexer would not, however, pick out the "if" within the identifier ifReady and treat that as a reserved word. Instead, the scanner considers the context in which a reserved word is used so that it can differentiate between reserved words and identifiers. For each lexeme, the scanner creates a small data package known as a *token* and passes this data package on to the parser. The token typically contains several values:

- A small integer that uniquely identifies the token's class (whether it's a reserved word, identifier, integer constant, operator, or character string literal).

- Another value that differentiates the token within a class (for example, this value would indicate which reserved word the scanner has processed).

- Any other attributes the scanner might associate with the lexeme.

NOTE　*Do not confuse this reference to a token with the compressed-style tokens in an interpreter discussed previously. Tokens are simply a variable-sized block of memory that describes a different item or block of memory to the interpreter/compiler.*

When the scanner sees the character string 12345 in the source file, for example, the token's class might be literal constant, the second value might identify this as an integer constant, and an attribute for this token might be the numeric equivalent of this string (i.e., twelve thousand, three hundred, and forty-five). Figure 5-3 demonstrates what this token package might look like in memory. The value 345 is used as the token value (to indicate a numeric constant), the value 5 is used as the token class (indicating a literal constant), the attribute value is 12345 (the numeric form of the lexeme), and the lexeme string is "12345" as scanned by the lexer. Different code sequences in the compiler can refer to this token data structure as appropriate.

345	"Token" value
5	Token class
12345	Token attribute
"12345"	Lexeme

Figure 5-3: A token for the lexeme "12345"

Strictly speaking, the lexical analysis phase is optional. A parser could work directly with the source file. However, the parser often refers to a token (or lexeme if there is no scanner) several times while processing a source file. By preprocessing a source file and breaking it up into a sequence of tokens, the compilation process can be more efficient. Processing the string data in a source file is one of the more time-consuming operations. By converting string lexemes into small token packets, the scanner allows the parser to deal with tokens as integer values rather than via string manipulation. Because most CPUs can handle small integer values much more efficiently than string data, and because the parser has to refer to the token data multiple times, this preprocessing by the scanner saves considerable time during compilation. Generally, pure interpreters are the only language systems that rescan each token during parsing, and this is one of the major reasons pure interpreters are so slow (compared to, say, an interpreter that stores the source file in a tokenized form to avoid constantly processing a pure-text source file).

5.4.2 Parsing (Syntax Analysis)

The parser is the part of the compiler that is responsible for checking whether the source program is syntactically (and semantically) correct.[2] If the compiler discovers an error in the source file, it is usually the parser that discovers and reports the error. The parser is also responsible for reorganizing the token stream (that is, the source code) into a more complex data structure that represents the meaning or semantics of the program. The scanner and parser generally process the source file in a linear fashion from the beginning to the end of the file, and the compiler usually reads the source file only once. Later phases, however, will need to refer to the body of the source program in a random-access fashion. By building up a data structure representation of the source code (often called an *abstract syntax tree* or AST), the parser makes it possible for the code generation and optimization phases to easily reference different parts of the program.

By organizing this data structure according to the semantics of the source file, the parser simplifies the translation task faced by the code generation and optimization phases. Figure 5-4 shows how a compiler might represent the expression "12345+6" using three nodes in an abstract syntax tree.

5.4.3 Intermediate Code Generation

The intermediate code generation phase is responsible for translating the AST representation of the source file into a quasi-machine code form. There are two reasons compilers typically translate a program into an intermediate form rather than converting it directly to native machine code.

First, the compiler's optimization phase can do certain types of optimizations, such as common subexpression elimination, much more easily on this intermediate form.

Second, many compilers, known as cross-compilers, generate executable machine code for several different CPUs. By breaking the code generation

---

[2] Some compilers actually have separate syntax and semantic analysis phases. Many compilers, however, combine both of these activities into the parser.

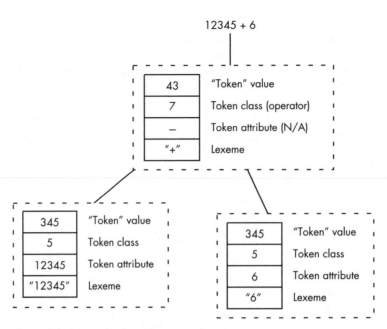

12345 + 6

43	"Token" value
7	Token class (operator)
—	Token attribute (N/A)
"+"	Lexeme

345	"Token" value
5	Token class
12345	Token attribute
"12345"	Lexeme

345	"Token" value
5	Token class
6	Token attribute
"6"	Lexeme

Figure 5-4: A portion of an abstract syntax tree

phase into two pieces—the intermediate code generator and the native code generator—the compiler writer can move all the CPU-independent activities into the intermediate code generation phase and write this code only once. This simplifies the native code generation phase. Because the compiler only needs one intermediate code generation phase but may need separate native code generation phases for each CPU the compiler supports, it's wise to move as much of the CPU-independent code as possible into the intermediate code generator to reduce the size of the native code generators. For the same reason, the optimization phase is often broken into two components (see Figure 5-2): a CPU-independent component (the part following the intermediate code generator) and a CPU-dependent component.

5.4.4   Optimization

The optimization phase, which follows intermediate code generation, translates the intermediate code into a more efficient form. This generally involves eliminating unnecessary entries from the AST. For example, this optimizer might transform the following intermediate code:

```
move the constant 5 into the variable i
move a copy of i into j
move a copy of j into k
add k to m
```

to something like:

```
move the constant 5 into k
add k to m
```

If there are no more references to i and j, the optimizer can eliminate all references to them. Indeed, if k is never used again, the optimizer can replace these two instructions with the single instruction add 5 to m. Note that this type of transformation is valid on nearly all CPUs. Therefore, this type of transformation/optimization is perfect for first optimization phase.

5.4.4.1 The Problem with Optimization

However, transforming intermediate code "into a more efficient form" is not a well-defined process. What makes one form of a program more efficient than another? The primary definition of efficiency in a program is that the program minimizes the use of some system resource. The two primary system resources that programmers consider are memory (space) and CPU cycles (speed). A compiler's optimizer could manage other resources, but space and speed are the principal ones. Even if we consider only these two facets of optimization, describing the "optimal" result is difficult. The problem is that optimizing for one goal (say, better performance) may create conflicts when attempting to simultaneously optimize for another goal (such as reduced memory usage). For this reason, the optimization process is usually a case of compromise management, where you make tradeoffs and sacrifice certain subgoals (for example, running certain sections of the code a little slower) in order to create a reasonable result (for example, creating a program that doesn't consume too much memory).

5.4.4.2 Optimization's Effect on Compile Time

You might think that it's possible to choose a single goal (for example, highest possible performance) and optimize strictly for that. However, the compiler must also be capable of producing an executable result in a reasonable amount of time. The optimization process is an example of what complexity theory calls an *NP-complete problem*. These are problems that are, as far as we know, *intractable*. That is, a guaranteed correct result cannot be produced (for example, an optimal version of a program) without computing all possibilities and choosing the best result from those possibilities. Unfortunately, the time generally required to solve an NP-complete problem increases exponentially with the size of the input, which in the case of compiler optimization means roughly the number of lines of source code.

This means that in the *worst case*, producing a truly optimal program would take longer than it was worth. Adding one line of source code could approximately *double* the amount of time it takes to compile and optimize the code. Adding two lines could *quadruple* the amount of time. In fact, a full guaranteed optimization of a modern application could take longer than the known lifetime of the universe.[3]

---

[3] Yes, you read that correctly. Imagine that compiling an n-line program takes 100 years. Adding only 40 lines of code to this program will increase the compilation time by about a trillion years if the time required by the optimization increases exponentially with the number of lines of source code. Now you can change the exponents around and play other games (meaning you could add a few more lines of code to the project), but the end result is the same—by adding a small number of lines to your code you can increase the compilation time to the point that it will never complete, because the machine will die long before the program finishes compilation.

For all but the smallest source files (a few dozen lines), a perfect optimizer would take far too long to be of any practical value (note that such optimizers have been written, search for "superoptimizers" using your favorite Internet search engine for all the details). For this reason, compiler optimizers rarely produce a truly optimal program. They simply produce the best result they can given the limited amount of CPU time the user is willing to allow for the process.

Rather than trying all possibilities and choosing the best result, modern optimizers use *heuristics* and *case-based algorithms* to determine the transformations they will apply to the machine code they produce. If you want to produce the best possible machine code from your HLL programs, you need to be aware of the heuristics and algorithms that typical compilers use during optimization. By writing your code in a manner that allows an optimizer to easily process your code, you can help guide the compiler to produce better machine code. In the following subsections, I'll discuss the techniques you'll need to know in order to help a compiler produce better machine code.

5.4.4.3   Basic Blocks, Reducible Code, and Optimization

Writing great code that works synergistically with your compiler's optimizer requires a basic understanding of the optimization process. In this section I will discuss how a compiler organizes the intermediate code it produces in order to do a good job during the later optimization phases. The way you write your HLL source code has a profound effect on the compiler's ability to organize the intermediate code (to produce better machine code), so understanding how the compiler does this is very important if you want to be able to help control the operation of the compiler's optimizer.

When it analyzes code, a compiler's optimizer will keep track of variable values as control flows through the program. The process of tracking this information is known as *data flow analysis*. After careful data flow analysis, a compiler can determine where a variable is uninitialized, when the variable contains certain values, when the program no longer uses the variable, and (just as importantly) when the compiler simply doesn't know anything about the variable's value. For example, consider the following Pascal code:

```
path := 5;
if( i = 2 ) then begin

    writeln( 'Path = ', path );

end;
i := path + 1;
if( i < 20 ) then begin

    path := path + 1;
    i := 0;

end;
```

A good optimizer will replace this code with something like the following:

```
if( i = 2 ) then begin

    (* Because the compiler knows that path = 5 *)

    writeln( 'path = ', 5 );

end;
i := 0;      (* Because the compiler knows that path < 20 *)
path := 6;   (* Because the compiler knows that path < 20 *)
```

In fact, the compiler probably would not generate code for the last two statements; instead, it would substitute the value 0 for i and 6 for path in later references. If this seems impressive to you, just note that some compilers can track constant assignments and expressions through nested function calls and complex expressions.

Although a complete description of how a compiler achieves this is beyond the scope of this book, you should have a basic understanding of how compilers keep track of variables during the optimization phase because a sloppily written program can thwart the compiler's optimization abilities. Great code works synergistically with the compiler, not against it.

Some compilers can do some truly amazing things when it comes to optimizing high-level code. However, you should note one thing: optimization is an inherently slow process. As noted earlier, optimization is provably an intractable problem. Fortunately, most programs don't require full optimization. A good approximation of the optimal program, even if it runs a little slower than the optimal program, is an acceptable compromise when compared to intractable compilation times.

The major concession to compilation time that compilers make during optimization is that they search for only so many possible improvements to a section of code before they move on. Therefore, if your programming style tends to confuse the compiler, it may not be able to generate an optimal (or even close to optimal) executable because the compiler has too many possibilities to consider. The trick is to learn how compilers optimize the source file so you can accommodate the compiler.

To analyze data flow, compilers divide the source code into sequences known as *basic blocks*. A basic block is a sequence of sequential machine instructions into and out of which there are no branches except at the beginning and end of the basic block. For example, consider the following C code:

```
x = 2;            // Basic Block 1
j = 5;
i = f( &x, j );
j = i * 2 + j;
if( j < 10 )      // End of Basic Block 1
{
    j = 0;        // Basic Block 2
    i = i + 10;
    x = x + i;    // End of Basic Block 2
```

```
}
else
{
    temp = i;        // Basic Block 3
    i = j;
    j = j + x;
    x = temp;        // End of Basic Block 3
}
x = x * 2;           // Basic Block 4
++i;
--j;

// End of Basic Block 4

printf( "i=%d, j=%d, x=%d\n", i, j, x );

// Basic Block 5 begins here
```

This code snippet contains four basic blocks. Basic block 1 starts with the beginning of the source code. A basic block ends at the point where there is a jump into or out of the sequence of instructions. Basic block 1 ends at the beginning of the if statement because the if can transfer control to either of two locations. The else clause terminates basic block 2. It also marks the beginning of basic block 3 because there is a jump (from the if's then clause) to the first statement following the else clause. Basic block 3 ends, not because the code transfers control somewhere else, but because there is a jump from basic block 2 to the first statement that begins basic block 4 (from the if's then section). Basic block 4 ends with a call to the C printf function.

The easiest way to determine where the basic blocks begin and end is to consider the assembly code that the compiler will generate for that code. Wherever there is a conditional branch/jump, unconditional jump, or call instruction, a basic block will end. Note, however, that the basic block includes the instruction that transfers control to a new location. A new basic block begins immediately after the instruction that transfers control to a new location. Also, note that the target label of any conditional branch, unconditional jump, or call instruction begins a basic block.

The nice thing about basic blocks is that it is easy for the compiler to track what is happening to variables and other program objects in a basic block. As the compiler processes each statement, it can (symbolically) track the values that a variable will hold based upon their initial values and the computations on them within the basic block.

A problem occurs when the paths from two basic blocks join into a single code stream. For example, at the end of basic block 2 in the current example, the compiler could easily determine that the variable j contains zero because code in the basic block assigns the value zero to j and then makes no other assignments to j. Similarly, at the end of basic block 3, the program knows that j contains the value j0+x (assuming j0 represents the initial value of j upon entry into the basic block). But when the paths merge at the beginning of basic block 4, the compiler probably can't determine whether j will contain zero or the value j0+x. So, the compiler has to note that j's value could be either of two different values at this point. While keeping track of two possible values that a variable might contain at a given point is easy for a decent optimizer, it's not hard to imagine a situation where the compiler would have to keep track of many different possible values. In fact, if you have several if statements that the code executes in a sequential fashion, and each of the paths through these if statements modifies a given variable, then the number of possible values for each variable doubles with each if statement. In other words, the number of possibilities increases exponentially with the number of if statements in a code sequence. At some point, the compiler cannot keep track of all the possible values a variable might contain, so it has to stop keeping track of that information for the given variable. When this happens, there are fewer optimization possibilities that the compiler can consider.

Fortunately, although loops, conditional statements, switch/case statements, and procedure/function calls can increase the number of possible paths through the code exponentially, in practice compilers have few problems with typical well-written programs. This is because as paths from basic blocks converge, programs often make new assignments to their variables (thereby eliminating the old information the compiler was tracking). Compilers generally assume that programs rarely assign a different value to a variable along every distinct path in the program, and their internal data structures reflect this. So keep in mind that if you violate this assumption, the compiler may lose track of variable values and generate inferior code as a result.

Compiler optimizers are generally written to handle well-written programs in the source language. Poorly structured programs, however, can create control flow paths that confuse the compiler, reducing the opportunities for optimization.

Good programs produce *reducible flow graphs*. A flow graph is a pictorial depiction of the control flow through the program. Figure 5-5 is a flow graph for the previous code fragment.

As you can see, arrows connect the end of each basic block with the beginning of the basic block into which they transfer control. In this particular example, all of the arrows flow downward, but this isn't always the case. Loops, for example, transfer control backward in the flow graph. As another example, consider the following Pascal code:

```
write( "Input a value for i:" );
readln( i );
j := 0;
while( j < i and i > 0 ) do begin

    a[j] := i;
    b[i] := 0;
    j := j + 1;
    i := i - 1;

end; (* while *)
k := i + j;
writeln( 'i = ', i, 'j = ', j, 'k = ', k );
```

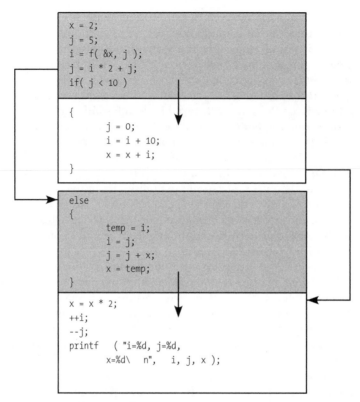

```
x = 2;
j = 5;
i = f( &x, j );
j = i * 2 + j;
if( j < 10 )

    {
            j = 0;
            i = i + 10;
            x = x + i;
    }

else
    {
            temp = i;
            i = j;
            j = j + x;
            x = temp;
    }

x = x * 2;
++i;
--j;
printf    ( "i=%d, j=%d,
        x=%d\    n",    i, j, x );
```

Figure 5-5: An example flow graph

Figure 5-6 shows the flow graph for this simple code fragment.[4]

Well-structured programs have flow graphs that are *reducible*. Although a complete description of what a reducible flow graph consists of is beyond the scope of this book, any program that consists only of structured control statements (if, while, repeat..until, etc.) and avoids gotos will be reducible (actually, the presence of a goto statement won't necessarily produce a program that is not reducible, but programs that are not reducible generally have goto statements in them). This is an important issue because compiler optimizers can generally do a much better job when working on reducible programs. In contrast, programs that are not reducible tend to confuse optimizers.

What makes reducible programs easier for optimizers to deal with is that the basic blocks in such a program can be collapsed in an outline fashion with enclosing blocks inheriting properties (for example, which variables the block modifies) from the enclosed blocks. By processing the source file in an outline fashion, the optimizer can deal with a small number of basic blocks, rather than a large number of statements. This hierarchical approach to optimization is more efficient and allows the optimizer to maintain more information about the state of a program. Furthermore, the exponential

---

[4] This flow graph has been somewhat simplified for purposes of clarity. This simplification does not affect the discussion of basic blocks.

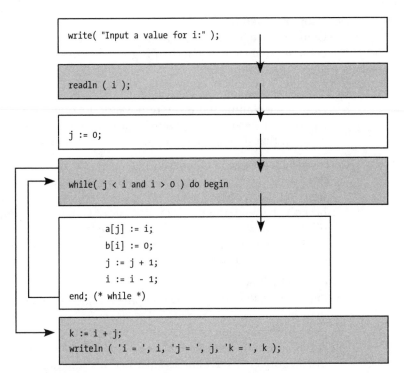

```
write( "Input a value for i:" );

readln ( i );

j := 0;

while( j < i and i > 0 ) do begin

        a[j] := i;
        b[i] := 0;
        j := j + 1;
        i := i - 1;
end; (* while *)

k := i + j;
writeln ( 'i = ', i, 'j = ', j, 'k = ', k );
```

Figure 5-6: Flow graph for a while loop

time complexity of the optimization problem works for us in this case. By reducing the number of blocks the code has to deal with (using reduction), you dramatically reduce the amount of work the optimizer must do. Again, the exact details of how the compiler achieves this are not important here. The important thing to note is that if you avoid goto statements and other bizarre control transfer algorithms in your programs, your programs will usually be reducible, and the optimizer will be able to do a better job of optimizing your code.

Attempts to "optimize" your code by sticking in lots of goto statements to avoid code duplication and to avoid the execution of unnecessary tests may actually work against you. While you may save a few bytes or a few cycles in the immediate area you're working on, the end result might also sufficiently confuse the compiler so that it cannot do a good job of global optimization, producing an overall loss of efficiency.

5.4.4.4 Common Compiler Optimizations

Later chapters will provide complete definitions and examples of common compiler optimizations in programming contexts where compilers typically use them. But for now, here's a quick preview of the basic types:

Constant folding

Constant folding computes the value of constant expressions or subexpressions at compile time rather than emitting code to compute the result at runtime.

Constant propagation

Constant propagation replaces a variable access by a constant value if the compiler determines that the program assigned that constant to the variable earlier in the code.

Dead code elimination

Dead code elimination is the removal of the object code associated with a particular source code statement when the program will never use the result of that statement, or when a conditional block will never be true.

Common subexpression elimination

Frequently, part of an expression will appear elsewhere in the current function. If the values of the variables appearing in this subexpression haven't changed, the program does not need to recompute the value of the expression. The program can save the value of the subexpression on the first evaluation and then use that value everywhere else that the subexpression appears.

Strength reduction

Often, the CPU can directly compute a value using a different operator than the source code specifies. For example, a shift operation can implement multiplication or division by a constant that is a power of 2, and certain modulo (remainder) operations are possible using bitwise and instructions (the shift and and instructions generally execute much faster than the multiply and divide instructions). Most compiler optimizers are good at recognizing such operations and replacing the more expensive computation with a less expensive sequence of machine instructions.

Induction

In many expressions, particularly those appearing within a loop, the value of one variable in the expression is completely dependent upon some other variable. Frequently, the compiler can eliminate the computation of the new value or merge the two computations into one for the duration of that loop.

Loop invariants

The optimizations so far have all been techniques a compiler can use to improve code that is already well written. Handling loop invariants, by contrast, is a compiler optimization for fixing bad code. A loop invariant is an expression that does not change on each iteration of some loop. An optimizer can compute the result of such a calculation just once, outside the loop, and then use the computed value within the loop's body. Many optimizers are smart enough to discover loop invariant calculations and can use *code motion* to move the invariant calculation outside the loop.

Good compilers can perform many other optimizations. However, there are the standard optimizations that you should expect any decent compiler to do.

5.4.4.5 Controlling Compiler Optimization

By default most compilers do very little optimization: You must explicitly tell the compiler to perform any optimization. This might seem counterintuitive; after all, we generally want compilers to produce the best possible code for us. However there are many definitions of "optimal," and no single compiler output is going to satisfy every possible definition for this term. Therefore, most compilers enable optimization only when you explicitly tell them to.

You might still question why the typical default condition for most compilers is *no optimization at all.* You might argue that some sort of optimization, even if it's not the particular type you're interested in, is better than no optimization at all. However, no optimization is the default state for a few reasons:

- Optimization is a slow process. You get quicker turnaround times on compiles when you have the optimizer turned off. This can be a big help when going through rapid edit-compile-test cycles.

- Many debuggers don't work properly with optimized code, and you have to turn off optimization in order to use a debugger on your application.

- Most compiler defects occur in the optimizer. By emitting unoptimized code, you're less likely to encounter defects in the compiler (then again, the compiler's author is less likely to be notified about defects in the compiler, too).

Most compilers provide command-line options that let you control the types of optimization the compiler performs. Early C compilers under Unix used command-line arguments like -0, -01, and -02 to control the optimization phases of the compiler. Many later compilers (C and otherwise) have adopted this same strategy, if not exactly the same command-line options. The bottom line is that you've generally got some control over the type of optimizations the compiler performs.

If you're wondering why a compiler might offer multiple options to control optimization rather than just having a single option (optimization or no optimization), remember that "optimization" means different things to different people. Some people might want code that is optimized for space; others might want code that is optimized for speed (and the two optimizations could be mutually exclusive in a given situation). Some people might want a small amount of optimization, but won't want the compiler to take forever to process their files, so they'd be willing to live with a small set of fast optimizations. Others might want to control optimization for a specific member of a CPU family (such as the Pentium 4 processor in the 80x86 family). Furthermore, some optimizations are "safe" (that is, they always produce correct code) only if the program is written in a certain way. You certainly don't want to enable such optimizations unless the programmer guarantees that they've written their code in an appropriate fashion. Finally, for programmers who are carefully writing their HLL code, some optimizations the compiler performs may actually produce inferior code, so the ability to choose specific optimizations can be very handy to the programmer who wants to produce the best possible code. Therefore, most modern compilers provide considerable flexibility over the types of optimizations they perform.

Consider the Microsoft Visual C++ compiler. Here is a list of the command-line options that MSVC++ provides to control optimization:

-OPTIMIZATION-

```
/O1 minimize space
/Op[-] improve floating-pt consistency
/O2 maximize speed
/Os favor code space
/Oa assume no aliasing
/Ot favor code speed
/Ob<n> inline expansion (default n=0)
/Ow assume cross-function aliasing
/Od disable optimizations (default)
/Ox maximum opts. (/Ogityb1 /Gs)
/Og enable global optimization
/Oy[-] enable frame pointer omission
/Oi enable intrinsic functions
```

-CODE GENERATION-

```
/G3 optimize for 80386
/Gy separate functions for linker
/G4 optimize for 80486
/Ge force stack checking for all funcs
/G5 optimize for Pentium
/Gs[num] disable stack checking calls
/G6 optimize for Pentium Pro
/Gh enable hook function call
/GB optimize for blended model (default)
/GR[-] enable C++ RTTI
/Gd __cdecl calling convention
/GX[-] enable C++ EH (same as /EHsc)
/Gr __fastcall calling convention
/Gi[-] enable incremental compilation
/Gz __stdcall calling convention
/Gm[-] enable minimal rebuild
/GA optimize for Windows application
/EHs enable synchronous C++ EH
/GD optimize for Windows DLL
/EHa enable asynchronous C++ EH
/Gf enable string pooling
/EHc extern "C" defaults to nothrow
/GF enable read-only string pooling
/QIfdiv[-] enable Pentium FDIV fix
/GZ enable runtime debug checks
/QIOf[-] enable Pentium 0x0f fix
```

GCC has a comparable, though much longer list, that you can view by specifying -v --help on the GCC command line. Most of the individual optimization flags begin with -f. You can also use -On, where *n* is a single digit integer value, to specify different levels of optimization. You should take care when using -03 (or higher), as this may perform some unsafe optimizations in certain cases.

5.4.5 Comparing Different Compilers' Optimizations

One real-world constraint on our ability to produce great code is that different compilers provide a wildly varying set of optimizations. Even when two different compilers perform the same optimizations, they differ greatly in the effectiveness of their optimizations.

Fortunately, you can visit several websites that have benchmarked various compilers. Using your favorite search engine, just search for a topic like "compiler benchmarks" or "compiler comparisons" and have fun. A very good website that compares several modern compilers is www.willus.com. (Click the *Compiler Benchmarks* link.)

5.4.6 Native Code Generation

The native code generation phase is responsible for translating the intermediate code into machine code for the target CPU. An 80x86 native code generator, for example, might translate the intermediate code sequence just given into something like the following:

```
mov( 5, eax ); // move the constant 5 into the EAX register.
mov( eax, k ); // Store the value in EAX (5) into k.
add( eax, m ); // Add the value in EAX to variable m.
```

The second optimization phase, which takes place after native code generation, handles machine idiosyncrasies that don't exist on all machines. For example, an optimizer for a Pentium II processor might replace an instruction of the form add(1, eax); with the instruction inc(eax);. Optimizers for certain 80x86 processors might arrange the sequence of instructions one way to maximize parallel execution of the instructions in a superscalar CPU while an optimizer targeting a different (80x86) CPU might arrange the instructions differently.

5.5 Compiler Output

In the previous section, I said that compilers typically produce machine code as their output. Strictly, this is neither necessary nor even that common. Most compiler output is not code that a given CPU can directly execute. Some compilers emit assembly language source code, which requires further processing by an assembler prior to execution. Some compilers produce an object file, which is similar to executable code but is not directly executable, and some compilers actually produce source code output that requires further processing by a different HLL compiler. I'll discuss these different output formats and their advantages and disadvantages in this section.

5.5.1 Emitting HLL Code as Compiler Output

Some compilers actually emit output that is source code for a different high-level programming language (see Figure 5-7). For example, many compilers (including the original C++ compiler) emit C code as their output. Indeed, compiler writers who emit some high-level source code from their compiler frequently choose the C programming language.

Emitting HLL code as compiler output offers several advantages. The output is human readable and is generally easy to verify. The HLL code emitted is often portable across various platforms; for example, if a compiler emits C code, you can usually compile that output on several different machines because C compilers exist for most platforms. By emitting HLL code, a translator can rely on the optimizer of the target language's compiler, thereby saving the effort of writing an optimizer. Emitting HLL code is usually much easier than emitting other types of code output. This allows a compiler writer to create a less complex code generator module and rely on the robustness of some other compiler for the most complex part of the compilation process.

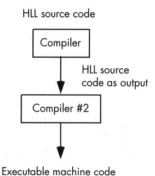

Figure 5-7: Emission of HLL code by a compiler

Of course, emitting HLL code has several disadvantages. First and foremost, this technique usually takes more processing time than directly generating executable code. To produce an executable file a second, otherwise unnecessary, compiler might need to be utilized. Worse, the output of that second compiler might need to be further processed by another compiler or assembler, exacerbating the problem. Another disadvantage to this approach is that embedding debugging information that a debugger program can use is difficult. Perhaps the most fundamental problem with this approach, however, is that HLLs are usually an abstraction of the underlying machine. Therefore, it could be quite difficult for a compiler to emit statements in an HLL that efficiently map to low-level machine code.

Generally, compilers that emit HLL statements as their output translate a very high-level language (VHLL) into a lower-level language. For example, C is often considered to be a fairly low-level HLL. That is one of the reasons C is a popular output format for many compilers. Attempts have been made to create a special, portable, low-level language specifically for this purpose, but such projects have never been enormously popular. Check out any of the "C--" projects on the Internet for examples of such systems (www.cminusminus.org).

If you want to write efficient code by analyzing compiler output, you'll probably find it more difficult to work with compilers that output HLL code. With a standard compiler, all you have to learn is the particular machine code statements that your compiler produces. However, when a compiler emits HLL statements as its output, learning to write great code with that compiler is more difficult. You need to understand how the main language emits the HLL statements and how the second compiler translates the code into machine code.

Generally, compilers that produce HLL code as their output are either experimental compilers or compilers for VHLLs. As such, expecting those compilers to emit efficient code is generally asking too much. If you're interested in writing great code that is efficient, you'd probably be wise to avoid a compiler that emits HLL statements. A compiler that directly generates machine code (or assembly language code) is more likely to produce smaller and faster running executables.

5.5.2 Emitting Assembly Language as Compiler Output

Many compilers will emit human-readable assembly language source files rather than binary machine code files (see Figure 5-8). Probably the most famous example of this is the FSF/GNU GCC compiler suite, which emits assembly language output for the FSF/GNU Gas assembler. Like compilers that emit HLL source code, emitting assembly language has some advantages and disadvantages.

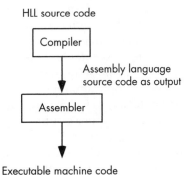

Figure 5-8: Emission of assembly code by a compiler

The principal disadvantage to emitting assembly output is similar to the disadvantages of emitting HLL source output—you have to run a second language translator (namely the assembler) to produce the actual object code for execution. Another possible disadvantage is that some assemblers may not allow the embedding of debug meta-information that allows a debugger to work with the original source code (though many assemblers do support the ability to embed this information). These two disadvantages turn out to be minimal if a compiler emits code for an appropriate assembler. For example, FSF/GNU's Gas assembler is very fast and supports the insertion of debug information for use by source level debuggers. Therefore, the FSF/GNU compilers don't suffer as a result of emitting Gas output.

The advantage of assembly language output, particularly for our purposes, is that it is easy to read the compiler's output and determine which machine instructions the compiler emits. Indeed, this compiler facility is one I'll use throughout this book to analyze compiler output. From a compiler writer's perspective, emitting assembly code frees the compiler writer from having to worry about several different object code output formats—the underlying assembler handles those problems. This allows the compiler writer to create a more portable compiler, and if they want to have their compiler generate code for different operating systems, they won't have to incorporate several different object output formats into their compiler. True, the assembler has to be capable of this, but you only need to repeat this exercise once for each object file format, rather than once for each format multiplied by the number of compilers you write. The FSF/GNU compiler suite has taken good advantage of this.

Another advantage of compilers that can emit assembly language output is that they generally allow you to embed *inline assembly language* statements in the HLL code. This allows you to insert a few machine instructions directly into time-critical sections of your code when there is a benefit to using assembly language, without the hassle of having to create a separate assembly language program and link its output to your HLL program.

5.5.3 Emitting Object Files as Compiler Output

Most compilers translate the source language into an object file format. An object file format is an intermediate file format that contains machine instructions and binary runtime data along with certain meta-information. This meta-information allows a linker/loader program to combine various object modules to produce a complete executable. This allows programmers to link *library modules* and other object modules that they've written and compiled separately from their main application module.

The advantage of object module output is that you don't need a separate compiler or assembler to convert the compiler's output to object code form. This saves a small amount of time when running the compiler. Note, however, that a linker program must still process the object file output, which consumes a small amount of time once compilation is complete. Nevertheless, linkers are usually quite fast, so it's usually more cost-effective to compile a single module and link it with several previously compiled modules than it is to compile all the modules together to form an executable file.

Object modules are binary files and do not contain human-readable data. For this very reason, analyzing compiler output is a bit more difficult using object modules. Fortunately, there are utility programs that will disassemble the output of an object module into a human-readable form. Even though the result isn't as easy to read as straight assembly output from a compiler, you can still do a reasonably good job by studying compiler output when the compiler emits object files. Section 5.6, "Object File Formats," provides a detailed look at the elements of an object file, focusing on the COFF format.

Because object files are often difficult to analyze, many compiler writers provide an option to emit assembly code instead of object code. This handy feature makes it much easier to analyze compiler output, a trick I'll use with various compilers throughout this book.

5.5.4 Emitting Executable Files as Compiler Output

Some compilers directly emit an executable output file. Such compilers are often very fast, producing almost instantaneous turnaround during the edit-compile-run-test-debug cycle. Unfortunately, the output from such compilers is often the most difficult to analyze, requiring the use of a debugger or disassembler program and a lot of manual work to read the machine instructions the compiler emits. Nevertheless, the fast turnaround offered by such compilers tends to make them popular. Later in this book, we'll look at how to analyze executable files that such compilers produce.

5.6 Object File Formats

As previously noted, object files are among the most popular output mechanisms that compilers use. Even though it is possible to create a proprietary object file format, one that only a single compiler and its associated tools can use, most compilers emit code using one or more standardized object file formats. This allows different compilers to share the same set of object file utilities, including linkers, librarians, dump utilities, disassemblers, and so on. Examples of common object module formats include: OMF (Object Module Format), COFF (Common Object File Format), PE/COFF (Microsoft's variant on COFF), and ELF (Executable and Linkable Format). Many other object file formats exist, and there are several variants of these file formats.

COFF is an attempt to create a universal object file format and, in fact, many object file formats are simply an extension of the COFF format (e.g., ELF, like PE/COFF has its roots in the COFF file format). Although most programmers understand that object files contain a representation of the machine code that an application executes, they generally don't realize the impact that the organization of the object file has on their application. In this section I'll discuss the internal organization of object files and how they can impact the performance and size of an application. Although detailed knowledge of the internal representation of an object file isn't absolutely needed to write great code, having a basic understanding of object file formats can help you organize your source files to better take advantage of the way compilers and assemblers generate code for your applications.

An object file usually begins with a header that comprises the first few bytes of the file. This header contains certain *signature information* that identifies the file as a valid object file along with several other values that define the location of various data structures in the file. Beyond the header, an object file is usually divided into several sections, each containing application data, machine instructions, symbol table entries, relocation data, and other metadata (data about the program). In some cases, the actual code and data represent only a small part of the entire object code file. To get a feeling for how object files are structured, it's worthwhile to look at a specific object file format in detail. I'll use the COFF format in the following discussion because most object file formats are based on, or very similar to, the COFF format. The basic layout of a COFF file is shown in Figure 5-9. The following sections describe the difference sections of this format in more detail.

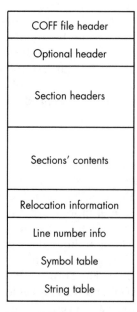

Figure 5-9: Layout of a COFF file

5.6.1   The COFF File Header

At the beginning of every COFF file is a *COFF file header*. Here are the definitions that Microsoft Windows and Linux use for the COFF header structure:

```
// Microsoft Windows winnt.h version:

typedef struct _IMAGE_FILE_HEADER {
```

```
        WORD        Machine;
        WORD        NumberOfSections;
        DWORD       TimeDateStamp;
        DWORD       PointerToSymbolTable;
        DWORD       NumberOfSymbols;
        WORD        SizeOfOptionalHeader;
        WORD        Characteristics;
} IMAGE_FILE_HEADER, *PIMAGE_FILE_HEADER;

// Linux coff.h version:

struct COFF_filehdr {
        char f_magic[2];            /* magic number */
        char f_nscns[2];            /* number of sections */
        char f_timdat[4];           /* time & date stamp */
        char f_symptr[4];           /* file pointer to symtab */
        char f_nsyms[4];            /* number of symtab entries */
        char f_opthdr[2];           /* sizeof(optional hdr) */
        char f_flags[2];            /* flags */
};
```

The Linux coff.h header file uses traditional Unix names for these fields; the Microsoft winnt.h header file uses (arguably) more readable names. Despite the differences in field names and declarations, both of these definitions describe the same object—a COFF header file. Here's a summary of each field in the header:

f_magic/Machine

Identifies the system for which this COFF file was created. In the original Unix definition, this value identified the particular port of Unix for which the code was created. Today's operating systems define this value somewhat differently, but the bottom line is that this value is a signature that specifies whether the COFF file contains data or machine instructions that are appropriate for the current operating system and CPU.

f_nscns/NumberOfSections

Specifies how many segments (sections) are present in the COFF file. A linker program can iterate through a set of section headers (described a little later) using this value.

f_timdat/TimeDateStamp

Contains a Unix-style timestamp (number of seconds since January 1, 1970) value specifying the file's create date and time.

f_symptr/PointerToSymbolTable

Contains a file offset value (that is, the number of bytes from the beginning of the file) that specifies where the *symbol table* begins in the file. The symbol table is a data structure that specifies the names and other information about all external, global, and other symbols used by the code in the COFF file. Linkers use the symbol table to resolve external references. This symbol table information may also appear in the final executable file for use by a symbolic debugger.

f_opthdr/SizeOfOptionalHeader

Specifies the size of the optional header that immediately follows the file header in the file (that is, the first byte of the optional header immediately follows the f_flags/Characteristics field in the file header structure). A linker or other object code manipulation program would use the value in this field to determine where the optional header ends and the section headers begin in the file. The section headers immediately follow the optional header, but the optional header's size isn't fixed. Different implementations of a COFF file can have different optional header structures. If the optional header is not present in a COFF file, the f_opthdr/SizeOfOptionalHeader field will contain zero, and the first section header will immediately follow the file header.

f_flags/Characteristics

A small bitmap that specifies certain Boolean flags, such as whether the file is executable, whether it contains symbol information, whether it contains line number information (for use by debuggers), and so on.

5.6.2 The COFF Optional Header

The COFF optional header contains information pertinent to executable files. This header may not be present if the file contains object code that is not executable (because of unresolved references). Note, however, that this optional header is always present in Linux COFF and Microsoft PE/COFF files, even when the file is not executable. The Windows and Linux structures for this optional file header take the following forms in C:

```
// Microsoft PE/COFF Optional Header (from winnt.h)

typedef struct _IMAGE_OPTIONAL_HEADER {
    //
    // Standard fields.
    //

    WORD    Magic;
    BYTE    MajorLinkerVersion;
    BYTE    MinorLinkerVersion;
    DWORD   SizeOfCode;
    DWORD   SizeOfInitializedData;
    DWORD   SizeOfUninitializedData;
    DWORD   AddressOfEntryPoint;
    DWORD   BaseOfCode;
    DWORD   BaseOfData;

    //
    // NT additional fields.
    //

    DWORD   ImageBase;
    DWORD   SectionAlignment;
    DWORD   FileAlignment;
```

```
WORD    MajorOperatingSystemVersion;
WORD    MinorOperatingSystemVersion;
WORD    MajorImageVersion;
WORD    MinorImageVersion;
WORD    MajorSubsystemVersion;
WORD    MinorSubsystemVersion;
DWORD   Win32VersionValue;
DWORD   SizeOfImage;
DWORD   SizeOfHeaders;
DWORD   CheckSum;
WORD    Subsystem;
WORD    DllCharacteristics;
DWORD   SizeOfStackReserve;
DWORD   SizeOfStackCommit;
DWORD   SizeOfHeapReserve;
DWORD   SizeOfHeapCommit;
DWORD   LoaderFlags;
DWORD   NumberOfRvaAndSizes;
IMAGE_DATA_DIRECTORY DataDirectory[IMAGE_NUMBEROF_DIRECTORY_ENTRIES];
} IMAGE_OPTIONAL_HEADER32, *PIMAGE_OPTIONAL_HEADER32;


// Linux/COFF Optional Header format (from coff.h)

typedef struct
{
  char  magic[2];  /* type of file */
  char  vstamp[2]; /* version stamp */
  char  tsize[4];  /* text size in bytes, padded to
                       FW bdry */
  char  dsize[4]; /* initialized   data "   " */
  char  bsize[4]; /* uninitialized data "   " */
  char  entry[4]; /* entry pt. */
  char  text_start[4]; /* base of text used for this file */
  char  data_start[4]; /* base of data used for this file */
} COFF_AOUTHDR;
```

The first thing you will notice is that these structures are not identical.
The Microsoft version has considerably more information than the Linux
version. The f_opthdr/SizeOfOptionalHeader field exists in the file header to
determine the actual size of the optional header.

magic/Magic

Provides yet another signature value for the COFF file. This signature
value identifies the file type (i.e., COFF) rather than the system under
which it was created. Linkers use the value of this field to determine if
they are truly operating on a COFF file (instead of some arbitrary file
that would confuse the linker).

vstamp/MajorLinkerVersion/MinorLinkerVersion

Specifies the version number of the COFF format so that a linker
written for an older version of the file format won't try to process
files intended for newer linkers.

tsize/SizeOfCode

Attempts to specify the size of the code section found in the file. If the COFF file contains more than one code section, the value of this field is undefined, although it usually specifies the size of the first code/text section in the COFF file.

dsize/SizeOfInitializedData

Specifies the size of the data segment appearing in this COFF file. Once again, this field is undefined if there are two or more data sections in the file. Usually, this field specifies the size of the first data section if there are multiple data sections.

bsize/SizeOfUninitializedData

Specifies the size of the BSS section (the uninitialized data section) in the COFF file. As for the text and data sections, this field is undefined if there are two or more BSS sections; in such cases this field usually specifies the size of the first BSS section in the file.

Entry/AddressOfEntryPoint

Contains the starting address of the executable program. Like other pointers in the COFF file header, this field is actually an offset into the file; it is not an actual memory address.

text_start/BaseOfCode

Specifies a file offset into the COFF file where the code section begins. If there are two or more code sections, this field is undefined, but it generally specifies the offset to the first code section in the COFF file.

data_start/BaseOfData

Specifies a file offset into the COFF file where the data section begins. If there are two or more data sections, this field is undefined, but it generally specifies the offset to the first data section in the COFF file.

There is no need for a bss_start/StartOfUninitializedData field. The COFF file format assumes that the operating system's program loader will automatically allocate storage for a BSS section when the program loads into memory. There is no need to consume space in the COFF file for uninitialized data (however, Section 5.7, "Executable File Formats," describes how some compilers actually merge BSS and DATA sections together for performance reasons).

The optional file header structure is actually a throwback to the *a.out* format, an older object file format used in Unix systems. This is why it doesn't handle multiple text/code and data sections, even though COFF allows them.

The remaining fields in the Windows variant of the optional header hold values that Windows' linkers allow programmers to specify. The purpose of most of these should be fairly clear to anyone who has manually run Microsoft's linker from a command line; in any case, their particular purposes are not important here. What is important to note is that COFF does not require a specific data structure for the optional header. Different implementations of COFF (such as Microsoft's) may freely extend the definition of the optional header.

5.6.3   COFF Section Headers

The section headers follow the optional header in a COFF file. Unlike the file and optional headers, a COFF file may contain multiple section headers. The f_nscns/NumberOfSections field in the file header specifies the exact number of section headers (and, therefore, sections) found in the COFF file. Keep in mind that the first section header does not begin at a fixed offset in the file. Because the optional header's size is variable (and, in fact, could even be zero if it is not present), you have to add the f_opthdr/SizeOfOptionalHeader field in the file header to the size of the file header to get the starting offset of the first section header in the file. Section headers are a fixed size, so once you obtain the address of the first section header you can easily compute the address of any other section header by multiplying the desired section header number by the section header size and adding this to the base offset of the first section header.

Here are the C struct definitions for Windows and Linux section headers:

```
// Windows section header structure (from winnt.h)

typedef struct _IMAGE_SECTION_HEADER {
    BYTE    Name[IMAGE_SIZEOF_SHORT_NAME];
    union {
            DWORD    PhysicalAddress;
            DWORD    VirtualSize;
    } Misc;
    DWORD    VirtualAddress;
    DWORD    SizeOfRawData;
    DWORD    PointerToRawData;
    DWORD    PointerToRelocations;
    DWORD    PointerToLinenumbers;
    WORD     NumberOfRelocations;
    WORD     NumberOfLinenumbers;
    DWORD    Characteristics;
} IMAGE_SECTION_HEADER, *PIMAGE_SECTION_HEADER;
```

```
// Linux section header definition (from coff.h)

struct COFF_scnhdr
{
  char s_name[8]; /* section name */
  char s_paddr[4]; /* physical address, aliased s_nlib */
  char s_vaddr[4]; /* virtual address */
  char s_size[4]; /* section size */
  char s_scnptr[4]; /* file ptr to raw data */
  char s_relptr[4]; /* file ptr to relocation */
  char s_lnnoptr[4]; /* file ptr to line numbers */
  char s_nreloc[2]; /* number of relocation entries */
```

```
    char s_nlnno[2]; /* number of line number entries */
    char s_flags[4]; /* flags */
};
```

If you inspect these two structures closely you'll find that they are roughly equivalent (the only structural difference is that Windows overloads the physical address field, which in Linux is always equivalent to the VirtualAddress field, to hold a VirtualSize field).

Here's a summary of each field:

s_name/Name

Specifies the name of the section. As is apparent in the Linux definition, this field is limited to eight characters and, as such, section names will be a maximum of eight characters long. (Usually, if a source file specifies a longer name, the compiler/assembler will truncate it to eight characters when creating the COFF file.) If the section name is exactly eight characters long, those eight characters will consume all eight bytes of this field and there will be no zero-terminating byte. If the section name is shorter than eight characters, a zero-terminating byte will follow the name. The value of this field is often something like .text, CODE, .data, or DATA. Note, however, that the name does not define the segment's type. You could create a code/text section and name it DATA; you could also create a data section and name it .text or CODE. The s_flags/Characteristics field determines the actual type of this section.

s_paddr/PhysicalAddress/VirtualSize

Not used by most tools. Under Unix-like operating systems (e.g., Linux), this field is usually set to the same value as the VirtualAddress field. Different Windows tools set this field to different values (including zero); the linker/loader seems to ignore whatever value appears here.

s_vaddr/VirtualAddress

Specifies the section's loading address in memory (i.e., its virtual memory address). Note that this is a runtime memory address, not an offset into the file. The program loader uses this value to determine where to load the section into memory.

s_size/SizeOfRawData

Specifies the size, in bytes, of the section.

s_scnptr/PointerToRawData

Provides the file offset to the start of the section's data in the COFF file.

s_relptr/PointerToRelocations

Provides a file offset to the relocation list for this particular section.

s_nreloc/NumberOfRelocations

Specifies the number of relocation entries found at that file offset. Relocation entries are small structures that provide file offsets to address data in the section's data area that must be patched when the file is loaded into memory. We won't discuss these relocation entries in this book because of the space limitations. If you're interested in more details, check out one of the references appearing at the end of this chapter.

`s_lnnoptr/PointerToLinenumbers`

Contains a file offset to the line number records for the current section.

`s_nlnno/NumberOfLinenumbers`

Specifies how many line number records can be found at that offset. Line number information is used by debuggers and is beyond the scope of this chapter. Again, see the references at the end of this chapter if you're interested in more information about the line number entries.

`s_flags/Characteristics`

A bitmap that specifies the characteristics of this section. In particular, this field will tell you whether the section requires relocation, whether it contains code, whether it is read-only, and so on.

5.6.4 COFF Sections

The section headers provide a directory that describes the actual data and code found in the object file. The `s_scnptr/PointerToRawData` field contains a file offset to where the raw binary data or code is sitting in the file, and the `s_size/SizeOfRawData` field specifies the length of the section's data. Due to relocation requirements, the data actually appearing in the section block may not be an exact representation of the data that the operating system loads into memory. This is because many instruction operand addresses and pointer values appearing in the section may need to be *patched* to relocate the file based on where the operating system loads it into memory. The relocation list (which is separate from the section's data) contains offsets into the section where the operating system must patch the relocatable addresses. The operating system performs this patching when loading the section's data from disk.

Although the bytes in a COFF section may not be an exact representation of the data that appears in memory at runtime (due to relocation), the COFF format requires that all of the bytes in the section *map* to the corresponding address in memory. This allows the loader to copy the section's data directly from the file into sequential memory locations. The relocation operation never inserts or deletes bytes in a section; it only changes the values of certain bytes appearing in the section. This requirement helps simplify the system loader and improves the performance of the application because the operating system doesn't have to move large blocks of memory around when loading the application into memory. The drawback to this scheme is that the COFF format misses the opportunity to compress redundant data appearing in the section's data area. However, the designers of the COFF format felt it was more important to emphasize performance over space in their design.

5.6.5   The Relocation Section

The relocation section in the COFF file contains the offsets to the pointers in the COFF sections that must be relocated when the system loads those sections' code or data into memory.

5.6.6   Debugging and Symbolic Information

The last three sections shown in Figure 5-9 contain information that debuggers and linkers use. One section contains line number information that a debugger uses to correlate lines of source code with the executable machine code instructions. The symbol table and string table sections hold the public and external symbols for the COFF file. Linkers use this information to resolve external references between object modules; debuggers use this information to display symbolic variable and function names during debugging.

5.6.7   Learning More About Object File Formats

This book doesn't provide a complete description of the COFF file format. However, understanding the basics of an object file format, such as COFF, is important if you want to understand how compilers and linkers work and how the organization of your source code impacts the final executable file. If you're interested in writing a great linker program, you'll definitely want to dig deeper into the various object code formats (COFF, ELF, OMF, etc.). If you aren't writing applications such as assemblers, compilers, and linkers, you really don't need to know that much about COFF file formats. If for some reason you do need to study this area further, see the references at the end of this chapter.

5.7   Executable File Formats

Most operating systems use a special file format for executable files. Often, the executable file format is similar to the object file format, the principal difference being that there are usually no unresolved external references in the executable file. For example, the Microsoft Windows Portable Executable (PE) format is a slightly modified version of the COFF file format (consisting of the same elements shown in Figure 5-9).

In addition to machine code and binary data, executable files contain other metadata, including debugging information, linkage information for dynamically linked libraries, and information that defines how the operating system should load different sections of the file into memory. Depending on the CPU and operating system, the executable files may also contain relocation information so that the operating system (OS) can patch absolute addresses when it loads the file into memory. Object code files contain the same information, so it's not surprising to find that the executable file formats used by many operating systems are similar to their object file formats.

The ELF format, employed by Linux, QNX, and other Unix-like operating systems, is very typical of a combined "object module format" and executable format. Indeed, the name of the format (ELF stands for Executable and Linkable Format) suggests the dual nature of this file format. Microsoft's PE file format is a straightforward modification of the COFF format. Most modern operating systems use an executable format that is similar to their object file format which allows the OS designer to share code between the loader (responsible for executing the program) and linker applications. As such, there is little reason to discuss the specific data structures found in an executable file. Doing so would largely repeat the information found in the previous sections (assuming, of course, we were to discuss a COFF-based executable file format like PE/COFF).

Although the file structure, internal data structures, and metadata appearing in an executable file are very similar to those appearing in an object code file, some very practical differences in the layout of these two types of files are worth mentioning. In particular, object code files are usually designed to be as small as possible while executable files are usually designed to load into memory as fast as possible, even if this means that the file is larger than absolutely necessary. It may seem paradoxical that a larger file could load into memory faster than a smaller file; however, the OS might load only a small part of the executable file into memory at one time if it supports virtual memory. A well-designed executable file format can take advantage of this fact by laying out the data and machine instructions in the file to reduce virtual memory overhead.

5.7.1 Pages, Segments, and File Size

As you may recall from *Write Great Code, Volume 1: Understanding the Machine*, virtual-memory subsystems and memory-protection schemes generally operate on *pages* in memory. A page on a typical processor is usually between 1KB and 64KB in size. Whatever the size, a page is the smallest unit of memory to which you can apply discrete protection features (such as whether the data in that page is read-only, read/write, or executable). In particular, you cannot mix read-only/executable code with read/write data in the same page—the two must appear in separate pages in memory. Using the 80x86 CPU family as our example, we see that pages in memory are 4KB each. Therefore, the minimum amount of code space and the minimum amount of data space we can allocate to a process is 8KB if we have read/write data and we want to place the machine instructions in read-only memory. In fact, most programs contain several *segments* or *sections*[5] to which we can apply individual protection rights, and each of these sections is going to require a unique set of one or more pages in memory that are not shared with any of the other sections. A typical program has four or more sections in memory: code or text, static data, uninitialized data, and stack are the most common sections. In addition, many compilers also generate heap segments, linkage segments, read-only segments, constant data segments, and application-named data segments (see Figure 5-10).

---

[5] The terms *section* and *segments* are synonymous and this book will use them interchangeably.

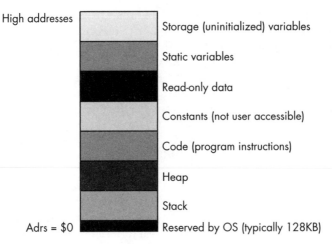

High addresses — Storage (uninitialized) variables

Static variables

Read-only data

Constants (not user accessible)

Code (program instructions)

Heap

Stack

Adrs = $0 — Reserved by OS (typically 128KB)

Figure 5-10: Typical segments found in memory

Because operating systems map segments to pages, a segment will always require some number of bytes that are a multiple of the page size. For example, if a program has a segment that contains only a single byte of data, that segment will still consume 4,096 bytes on an 80x86 processor. Similarly, if an 80x86 application consists of six different segments (or sections), then that application will consume at least 24KB in memory, regardless of the number of machine instructions and data bytes that the program uses and regardless of the executable file's size.

Many executable file formats (e.g., ELF and PE/COFF) provide an option for a *block started by symbol*[6] (BSS) section in memory. The BSS section is where a programmer can place uninitialized static variables. As their values are uninitialized, there is no need to clutter the executable file with random data values for each of these variables. Therefore, the BSS section in some executable file formats is just a small stub that tells the OS loader the size of the BSS section. With such a BSS section in the executable file, you can add new uninitialized static variables to your application without affecting the executable file's size. When you increase the amount of BSS data, the compiler simply adjusts a value to tell the loader how many bytes to reserve for the uninitialized variables. Were you to add those same variables to an initialized data section, the size of the executable file would grow with each byte of data that you added. Obviously, saving space on your mass storage device is a good thing to do, so using BSS sections to reduce your executable file sizes is a useful optimization.

The one thing that many people tend to forget, however, is that a BSS section still requires main memory at runtime. Even though the executable file size may be smaller, each byte of data you declare in your program translates to one byte of data in memory. Some programmers get the mistaken impression that the executable's file size is indicative of the amount of memory that the program consumes. This, however, isn't necessarily true, as our BSS example shows. A given application's executable file might consist of only

---

[6] This is an old assembly language term.

600 bytes, but if that program uses four different sections, with each section consuming a 4KB page in memory, the program will require 16,384 bytes of memory when the OS loads it into memory. This is because the underlying memory protection hardware requires the OS to allocate whole pages of memory to a given process.

5.7.2 Internal Fragmentation

Another reason an executable file might be smaller than an application's *execution memory footprint* (the amount of memory the application consumes at runtime) is *internal fragmentation.* Internal fragmentation occurs when you must allocate sections of memory in fixed-sized chunks even though you might need only a portion of each chunk (see Figure 5-11).

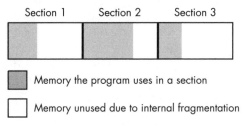

Figure 5-11: Internal fragmentation

Remember that each section in memory consumes an integral number of pages, even if that section's data size is not a multiple of the page size. All bytes from the last data/code byte in a section to the end of the page holding that byte are wasted; this is internal fragmentation. Some executable file formats allow you to pack each section without padding it to some multiple of the page size. However, as you'll soon see, there may be a performance penalty for packing sections together in this fashion, so some executable formats don't pack the sections in the executable file.

Finally, don't forget that an executable file's size does not include any data (including data objects on the heap and values placed on the CPU's stack) allocated dynamically at runtime. As you can see, an application can actually consume much more memory than the executable file's size.

Hackers commonly compete to see who can write the smallest "Hello World" program using their favorite language. Assembly language programmers are especially guilty of bragging about how much smaller they can write this program in assembly than they can in C or some other HLL language. There is something to be said for the exercise as a mental challenge. However, whether the program's executable file is 600 or 16,000 bytes long, the chances are pretty good that the program will consume exactly the same amount of memory at runtime once the operating system allocates four or five pages for the program's different sections. While writing the world's shortest "Hello World" application might afford someone certain bragging rights because of the accomplishment, in real-world terms such an application saves almost nothing at runtime. Due to internal fragmentation, the program still consumes as much memory at runtime as a less-optimized version of the application.

5.7.3 So Why Optimize for Space?

This is not to suggest that optimizing for space isn't worthwhile. Programmers who write great code consider all the machine resources their application uses, and they avoid wasting those resources. However, attempting to take this process to an extreme is a waste of effort. Once you've gotten a given section below 4,096 bytes (on an 80x86 or other CPU with a 4KB page size), additional optimizations save you nothing. Of course, if a given section is already larger than 4,096 bytes, and it is possible to shrink the section below this threshold, an optimization attempt might be worthwhile. Remember, the *allocation granularity*, that is, the minimum allocation block size, is 4,096 bytes. If you have a section with 4,097 bytes of data, it's going to consume 8,192 bytes at runtime. It would behoove you to reduce that section by 1 byte (thereby saving 4,096 bytes at runtime). However, if you have a data section that consumes 16,380 bytes, attempting to reduce its size by 4,092 bytes in order to reduce the file size is going to be difficult unless the data organization was very bad to begin with.

You should note that most operating systems allocate disk space in clusters (or blocks) that are often comparable to (or even larger than) the page size for the memory management unit in the CPU. Therefore, if you shrink an executable's file size down to 700 bytes in an attempt to save disk space (an admirable goal, even given the gargantuan size of modern disk drive subsystems) the savings won't be as great as you'd expect. That 700-byte application, for example, is still going to consume a minimum of one block on the disk's surface. All you achieve by reducing your application's code or data size is to waste that much more space in the disk file—subject, of course, to section/block allocation granularity.

For larger executable files, those larger than the disk block size, internal fragmentation has less impact with respect to wasted space. If an executable file packs the data and code sections without any wasted space between the sections, then internal fragmentation only occurs at the end of the file, in the very last disk block. Assuming that file sizes are random (even distribution), then internal fragmentation will waste approximately one-half of a disk block per file (that is, an average of 2KB per file when the disk block size is 4KB). For a very small file, one that is less than 4KB in size, this might represent a significant amount of the file's space. For larger applications, however, the wasted space becomes insignificant. So it would seem that as long as an executable file packs all the sections of the program sequentially in the file, the file will be as small as possible. But is this really desirable?

Assuming all things are equal, having smaller executable files is a good thing. However, as is often the case, all things aren't always equal. Therefore, sometimes creating the smallest possible executable file isn't really best. To understand why, recall the earlier discussion of the operating system's virtual memory subsystem. When an operating system loads an application into memory for execution, it doesn't actually have to read the entire file. Instead, the operating system's paging system can load only those pages needed to start the application. This usually consists of the first page of executable code, a page of memory to hold stack-based data, and, possibly, some data pages.

In theory, an application could begin execution with as few as two or three pages of memory and bring in the remaining pages of code and data *on demand* (as the application requests the data or code found in those pages). This is known as *demand-paged memory management*. In practice, most operating systems actually preload pages for efficiency reasons (maintaining a *working set* of pages in memory). However, the bottom line is that operating systems generally don't load the entire executable file into memory. Instead, they load various blocks as the application requires them. As a result, the effort needed to load a page of memory from a file can dramatically affect a program's performance. So one might ask if there is some way to organize the executable file to improve performance when the operating system uses demand-paged memory management. The answer is yes, if you make the file a little larger.

The trick to improving performance is to organize the executable file's blocks to match the memory page layout. This means that sections (segments) in memory should be aligned on page-sized boundaries in the executable file. It also means that disk blocks should be the size of, or a multiple of the size of, a disk sector or block. This being the case, the virtual memory management system can rapidly copy a single block on the disk into a single page of memory, update any necessary relocation values, and continue program execution. On the other hand, if a page of data is spread across two blocks on the disk and is not aligned on a disk block boundary, the operating system has to read two blocks (rather than one) from disk into an internal buffer and then copy the page of data from that buffer to the destination page where it belongs. This extra work can be very time-consuming and have a negative impact on application performance.

For this reason, some compilers will actually pad the executable file to ensure that each section in the executable file begins on a block boundary that the virtual memory management subsystem can map directly to a page in memory. Compilers that produce such files often produce much larger executable file sizes than compilers that don't employ this technique. This is especially true if the executable file contains a large amount of BSS (uninitialized) data that a packed file format can represent very compactly.

Because some compilers produce packed files at the expense of execution time, while others produce expanded files that load and run faster, it's dangerous to attempt to compare compiler quality by comparing the size of the executable files they produce. The best way to determine the quality of a compiler's output is by directly analyzing that output, not by using a weak metric such as output file size. Analyzing compiler output is the subject of the very next chapter, so if you're interested in the topic, keep on reading.

5.8   Data and Code Alignment in an Object File

As I pointed out in *Write Great Code, Volume 1*, aligning data objects on an address boundary that is "natural" for that object's size can improve performance. It's also true that aligning the start of a procedure's code or the starting instruction of a loop on some nice boundary can also improve performance. Compiler writers are well aware of this fact and they will often emit *padding bytes* in the data or code stream to properly align data or code sequences on an appropriate boundary. However, note that the linker is free to move sections of code around when linking two object files to produce a single executable result. You may wonder "How does the linker respect the wishes of the code generator with respect to data alignment?"

Sections are generally aligned to a page boundary in memory. For a typical application, the text/code section will begin on a page boundary, the data section will begin on a different page boundary, the BSS section (if it exists) will begin on its own page boundary, and so on. However, this does not imply that each and every section associated with a section header in the object files starts on its own page in memory. The linker program will combine sections that have the same name into a single section in the executable file. So, for example, if two different object files both contain a .text segment, the linker will combine the two into a single .text section in the final executable file. By combining sections that have the same name, the linker avoids wasting a large amount of memory to internal fragmentation.[7] How does the linker respect the alignment requirements of each of the sections it combines? The answer, of course, depends on exactly what object file format and operating system you're using, but the answer is usually found in the object file format itself. For example, in Windows' PE/COFF file the IMAGE_OPTIONAL_HEADER32 structure contains a field named SectionAlignment. This field specifies the address boundary that the linker and operating system must respect when combining sections and when loading the section into memory. Under Windows, the SectionAlignment field in the PE/COFF optional header will usually contain 32 or 4,096. The 4KB value, of course, will align a section to a 4KB page boundary in memory. The alignment value of 32 was probably chosen because this is a reasonable cache line value (see *Write Great Code, Volume 1,* for a discussion of cache lines). Other values are certainly possible—an application programmer can usually specify section alignment values by using linker (or compiler) command-line parameters.

5.8.1   Choosing a Section Alignment Size

Within a section, a compiler, assembler, or other code-generation tool can guarantee any alignment that is a submultiple of the section's alignment. For example, if the section's alignment value is 32, then alignments of 1, 2, 4, 8, 16, and 32 are possible within that section. It should be obvious that larger alignment values are not possible. If a section's alignment value is 32 bytes, you cannot guarantee alignment within that section on a 64-byte boundary, because the operating system or linker will only respect the section's alignment value and it can place that section on any boundary that is a multiple of 32 bytes. And about half of those will not be 64-byte boundaries.

---

[7] Imagine combining 20 object files, each containing a short library routine, into an executable file. If each routine averaged about 100 bytes of code and the linker was forced to align each .text (or code) section on a page boundary, the library routines would wind up requiring 20×4KB, or 80KB of space when only about 20×100, or 2KB, of space is really necessary.

Perhaps less obvious, but just as true, is the fact that you cannot align an object within a section on a boundary that is not a submultiple of the section's alignment. For example, a section with a 32-byte alignment value will not allow an alignment of 5 bytes. True, you could guarantee that the offset of some object within the section would be a multiple of 5; however, if the starting memory address of the section is not a multiple of 5, then the address of the object you attempted to align might not fall on a multiple of 5 bytes. The only solution is to pick a section alignment value that is some multiple of 5.

Because memory addresses are binary values, most language translators and linkers limit alignment values to a power of 2 that is less than or equal to some maximum value, usually the memory management unit's page size. Many languages restrict the alignment value to a small power of 2 (such as 32, 64, or 256).

5.8.2   Combining Sections

When a linker combines two sections, it has to respect the alignment values associated with each section because the application may depend on that alignment for correct operation. Therefore, a linker or other program that combines sections in object files must not simply concatenate the data for the two sections when building the combined section.

When combining two sections, a linker might have to add padding bytes between the sections if one or both of the their lengths is not a multiple of the sections' alignment. For example, if two sections have an alignment value of 32, and one section is 37 bytes long and the other section is 50 bytes long, the linker will have to add 27 bytes of padding between the first and second sections, or it will have to add 14 bytes of padding between the second section and the first (the linker usually gets to choose in which order it places the sections in the combined file).

The situation gets a bit more complicated if the alignment values are not the same for the two sections. When a linker combines two sections, it has to ensure that the alignment requests are met for the data in both sections. If the alignment value of one section is a multiple of the other section's alignment value, then the linker can simply choose the larger of the two alignment values. For example, if the alignment values are always powers of 2 (which most linkers require), then the linker can simply choose the larger of the two alignment values for the combined section.

If one section's alignment value is not a multiple of the other's, then the only way to guarantee the alignment requirements of both sections when combining them is to use an alignment value that is product of the two values (or, better yet, the *least common multiple* of the two values). For example, combining a section aligned on a 32-byte boundary with one aligned on a 5-byte boundary requires an alignment value of 160 bytes (5×32). Because of the complexities of combining two such sections, most linkers require section sizes to be small powers of 2, which guarantees that the larger segment align value is always a multiple of the smaller alignment value.

5.8.3 Controlling the Section Alignment

You typically use linker options to control the section alignment within your programs. For example, with the Microsoft LINK.EXE program, the /ALIGN:value command-line parameter tells the linker to align all sections in the output file to the specified boundary (which must be a power of 2). GNU's ld linker program lets you specify a section alignment by using the BLOCK(value) option in a linker script file. The Mac OS X linker (ld) provides a -segalign value command-line option you can use to specify section alignment. The exact command and possible values are specific to the linker; however, almost every modern linker allows you to specify the section alignment properties. Please see your linker's documentation for details.

Note one thing about setting the section alignment: more often than not a linker will require that all sections in a given file be aligned on the same boundary (which is a power of 2). Therefore, if you have different alignment requirements for all your sections, then you'll need to choose the largest alignment value for all the sections in your object file.

5.8.4 Section Alignment and Library Modules

Section alignment can have a very big impact on the size of your executable files if you use a lot of short library routines. Suppose, for example, that you've specified an alignment size of 16 bytes for the sections associated with the object files appearing in a library. Each library function that the linker processes will be placed on a 16-byte boundary. If the functions are small (fewer than 16 bytes in length), the space between the functions will be unused when the linker creates the final executable. This is another form of internal fragmentation.

To understand why you would want to align the code (or data) in a section on a given boundary, just remember how cache lines work (see *Write Great Code, Volume 1*). By aligning the start of a function on a cache line, you may be able to slightly increase the execution speed of that function as it may generate fewer cache misses during execution. For this reason, many programmers like to align all their functions at the start of a cache line. Although the size of a cache line varies from CPU to CPU, a typical cache line is 16 to 64 bytes long, so many compilers, assemblers, and linkers will attempt to align code and data to one of these boundaries. On the 80x86 processor, there are some other benefits to 16-byte alignment, so many 80x86-based tools default to a 16-byte section alignment for object files.

Consider, for example, the following short HLA (High-Level Assembler) program, processed by Microsoft tools, that calls two relative small library routines:

```
program t;
#include( "bits.hhf" )

begin t;

    bits.cnt( 5 );
```

```
        bits.reverse32( 10 );

end t;
```

Here is the source code to the bits.cnt library module:

```
unit bitsUnit;

#includeonce( "bits.hhf" );


    // bitCount-
    //
    //   Counts the number of "1" bits in a dword value.
    //   This function returns the dword count value in EAX.

    procedure bits.cnt( BitsToCnt:dword ); @nodisplay;

    const
        EveryOtherBit       := $5555_5555;
        EveryAlternatePair  := $3333_3333;
        EvenNibbles         := $0f0f_0f0f;

    begin cnt;

        push( edx );
        mov( BitsToCnt, eax );
        mov( eax, edx );

        // Compute sum of each pair of bits
        // in EAX. The algorithm treats
        // each pair of bits in EAX as a two
        // bit number and calculates the
        // number of bits as follows (description
        // is for bits zero and one, but it generalizes
        // to each pair):
        //
        //   EDX =    BIT1  BIT0
        //   EAX =       0  BIT1
        //
        //   EDX-EAX =   00 if both bits were zero.
        //               01 if Bit0=1 and Bit1=0.
        //               01 if Bit0=0 and Bit1=1.
        //               10 if Bit0=1 and Bit1=1.
        //
        // Note that the result is left in EDX.

        shr( 1, eax );
        and( EveryOtherBit, eax );
        sub( eax, edx );

        // Now sum up the groups of two bits to
        // produces sums of four bits.  This works
        // as follows:
```

```
//
// EDX = bits 2,3, 6,7, 10,11, 14,15, ..., 30,31
//       in bit positions 0,1, 4,5, ..., 28,29 with
//       zeros in the other positions.
//
// EAX = bits 0,1, 4,5, 8,9, ... 28,29 with zeros
//       in the other positions.
//
// EDX + EAX produces the sums of these pairs of bits.
// The sums consume bits 0,1,2, 4,5,6, 8,9,10, ...
//                                        28,29,30
// in EAX with the remaining bits all containing zero.

mov( edx, eax );
shr( 2, edx );
and( EveryAlternatePair, eax );
and( EveryAlternatePair, edx );
add( edx, eax );


// Now compute the sums of the even and odd nibbles in
// the number.  Since bits 3, 7, 11, etc. in EAX all
// contain zero from the above calculation, we don't need
// to AND anything first, just shift and add the two
// values.
// This computes the sum of the bits in the four bytes
// as four separate value in EAX (AL contains number of
// bits in original AL, AH contains number of bits in
// original AH, etc.)

mov( eax, edx );
shr( 4, eax );
add( edx, eax );
and( EvenNibbles, eax );


// Now for the tricky part.
// We want to compute the sum of the four bytes
// and return the result in EAX.  The following
// multiplication achieves this.  It works
// as follows:
// (1) the $01 component leaves bits 24..31
//     in bits 24..31.
//
// (2) the $100 component adds bits 17..23
//     into bits 24..31.
//
// (3) the $1_0000 component adds bits 8..15
//     into bits 24..31.
//
// (4) the $1000_0000 component adds bits 0..7
//     into bits 24..31.
//
// Bits 0..23 are filled with garbage, but bits
// 24..31 contain the actual sum of the bits
```

```
    //  in EAX's original value.  The SHR instruction
    //  moves this value into bits 0..7 and zeroes
    //  out the HO bits of EAX.

    intmul( $0101_0101, eax );
    shr( 24, eax );

    pop( edx );

  end cnt;

end bitsUnit;
```

Here is the source code for the bits.reverse32 library function. Note that this source file also includes the bits.reverse16 and bits.reverse8 functions (to conserve space, the bodies of these functions do not appear below). Although the operation of these functions is not pertinent to our discussion, note that these functions swap the values in the HO and LO bit positions. Because these three functions appear in a single source file, any program that includes one of these functions will automatically include all three (because of the way compilers, assemblers, and linkers work).

```
unit bitsUnit;

#include( "bits.hhf" );


    procedure bits.reverse32( BitsToReverse:dword ); @nodisplay; @noframe;
    begin reverse32;

        push( ebx );
        mov( [esp+8], eax );

        // Swap the bytes in the numbers:

        bswap( eax );

        // Swap the nibbles in the numbers

        mov( $f0f0_f0f0, ebx );
        and( eax, ebx );
        and( $0f0f_0f0f, eax );
        shr( 4, ebx );
        shl( 4, eax );
        or( ebx, eax );

        // Swap each pair of two bits in the numbers:

        mov( eax, ebx );
        shr( 2, eax );
        shl( 2, ebx );
        and( $3333_3333, eax );
```

```
        and( $cccc_cccc, ebx );
        or( ebx, eax );

        // Swap every other bit in the number:

        lea( ebx, [eax + eax] );
        shr( 1, eax );
        and( $5555_5555, eax );
        and( $aaaa_aaaa, ebx );
        or( ebx, eax );
        pop( ebx );
        ret( 4 );

    end reverse32;


    procedure bits.reverse16( BitsToReverse:word );
        @nodisplay; @noframe;
    begin reverse16;

        // Uninteresting code that is very similar to
        // that appearing in reverse32 has been snipped...

    end reverse16;


    procedure bits.reverse8( BitsToReverse:byte );
        @nodisplay; @noframe;
    begin reverse8;

        // Uninteresting code snipped...

    end reverse8;


end bitsUnit;
```

The Microsoft dumpbin.exe tool allows you to examine the various
fields of an OBJ or EXE file. Running dumpbin with the /headers command-
line option on the bitcnt.obj and reverse.obj files (produced for the HLA
standard library) tells us that each of the sections are aligned to a 16-byte
boundary. Therefore, when the linker combines the bitcnt.obj and
reverse.obj data with the sample program given earlier, it will align the
bits.cnt function in the bitcnt.obj file on a 16-bit boundary, and it will
align the three functions in the reverse.obj file on a 16-byte boundary
(note that it will not align each function in the file on a 16-byte boundary.
That task is the responsibility of the tool that created the object file, if
such alignment is desired). By using the dumpbin.exe program with the
/disasm command-line option on the executable file, you can see that the

linker has honored these alignment requests (note that an address that is aligned on a 16-byte boundary will have a 0 in the LO hexadecimal digit):

```
Address    opcodes              Assembly Instructions
---------  ------------------   ----------------------------
04001000: E9 EB 00 00 00        jmp        040010F0
04001005: E9 57 01 00 00        jmp        04001161
0400100A: E8 F1 00 00 00        call       04001100

; Here's where the main program starts.

0400100F: 6A 00                 push       0
04001011: 8B EC                 mov        ebp,esp
04001013: 55                    push       ebp
04001014: 6A 05                 push       5
04001016: E8 65 01 00 00        call       04001180
0400101B: 6A 0A                 push       0Ah
0400101D: E8 0E 00 00 00        call       04001030
04001022: 6A 00                 push       0
04001024: FF 15 00 20 00 04     call       dword ptr ds:[04002000h]

;The following INT3 instructions are used as padding in order
;to align the bits.reverse32 function (which immediately follows)
;to a 16-byte boundary:

0400102A: CC                    int        3
0400102B: CC                    int        3
0400102C: CC                    int        3
0400102D: CC                    int        3
0400102E: CC                    int        3
0400102F: CC                    int        3

; Here's where bits.reverse32 starts. Note that this address
; is rounded up to a 16-byte boundary.

04001030: 53                    push       ebx
04001031: 8B 44 24 08           mov        eax,dword ptr [esp+8]
04001035: 0F C8                 bswap      eax
04001037: BB F0 F0 F0 F0        mov        ebx,0F0F0F0F0h
0400103C: 23 D8                 and        ebx,eax
0400103E: 25 0F 0F 0F 0F        and        eax,0F0F0F0Fh
04001043: C1 EB 04              shr        ebx,4
04001046: C1 E0 04              shl        eax,4
04001049: 0B C3                 or         eax,ebx
0400104B: 8B D8                 mov        ebx,eax
0400104D: C1 E8 02              shr        eax,2
04001050: C1 E3 02              shl        ebx,2
04001053: 25 33 33 33 33        and        eax,33333333h
04001058: 81 E3 CC CC CC CC     and        ebx,0CCCCCCCCh
0400105E: 0B C3                 or         eax,ebx
04001060: 8D 1C 00              lea        ebx,[eax+eax]
04001063: D1 E8                 shr        eax,1
```

```
04001065: 25 55 55 55 55       and         eax,55555555h
0400106A: 81 E3 AA AA AA AA    and         ebx,0AAAAAAAAh
04001070: 0B C3                or          eax,ebx
04001072: 5B                   pop         ebx
04001073: C2 04 00             ret         4
```

; Here's where bits.reverse16 begins. As this function appeared
; in the same file as bits.reverse32, and no alignment option
; was specified in the source file, HLA and the linker won't
; bother aligning this to any particular boundary. Instead, the
; code immediately follows the bits.reverse32 function
; in memory.

```
04001076: 53                   push        ebx
04001077: 50                   push        eax
04001078: 8B 44 24 0C          mov         eax,dword ptr [esp+0Ch]

        .
        .    ;uninteresting code for bits.reverse16 and
        .    ; bits.reverse8 was snipped
```

; end of bits.reverse8 code

```
040010E6: 88 04 24             mov         byte ptr [esp],al
040010E9: 58                   pop         eax
040010EA: C2 04 00             ret         4
```

; More padding bytes to align the following function (used by
; HLA exception handling) to a 16-byte boundary:

```
040010ED: CC                   int         3
040010EE: CC                   int         3
040010EF: CC                   int         3
```

; Default exception return function (automatically generated
; by HLA):

```
040010F0: B8 01 00 00 00       mov         eax,1
040010F5: C3                   ret
```

; More padding bytes to align the internal HLA BuildExcepts
; function to a 16-byte boundary:

```
040010F6: CC                   int         3
040010F7: CC                   int         3
040010F8: CC                   int         3
040010F9: CC                   int         3
040010FA: CC                   int         3
040010FB: CC                   int         3
040010FC: CC                   int         3
040010FD: CC                   int         3
040010FE: CC                   int         3
040010FF: CC                   int         3
```

```
; HLA BuildExcepts code (automatically generated by the
; compiler):

    04001100: 58                      pop       eax
    04001101: 68 05 10 00 04          push      4001005h
    04001106: 55                      push      ebp


            .
            .     ; Remainder of BuildExcepts code goes here
            .     ; along with some other code and data
            .

; Padding bytes to ensure that bits.cnt is aligned
; on a 16-byte boundary:

    0400117D: CC                      int       3
    0400117E: CC                      int       3
    0400117F: CC                      int       3

; Here's the low-level machine code for the bits.cnt function:

    04001180: 55                      push      ebp
    04001181: 8B EC                   mov       ebp,esp
    04001183: 83 E4 FC                and       esp,0FFFFFFFCh
    04001186: 52                      push      edx
    04001187: 8B 45 08                mov       eax,dword ptr [ebp+8]
    0400118A: 8B D0                   mov       edx,eax
    0400118C: D1 E8                   shr       eax,1
    0400118E: 25 55 55 55 55          and       eax,55555555h
    04001193: 2B D0                   sub       edx,eax
    04001195: 8B C2                   mov       eax,edx
    04001197: C1 EA 02                shr       edx,2
    0400119A: 25 33 33 33 33          and       eax,33333333h
    0400119F: 81 E2 33 33 33 33       and       edx,33333333h
    040011A5: 03 C2                   add       eax,edx
    040011A7: 8B D0                   mov       edx,eax
    040011A9: C1 E8 04                shr       eax,4
    040011AC: 03 C2                   add       eax,edx
    040011AE: 25 0F 0F 0F 0F          and       eax,0F0F0F0Fh
    040011B3: 69 C0 01 01 01 01       imul      eax,eax,1010101h
    040011B9: C1 E8 18                shr       eax,18h
    040011BC: 5A                      pop       edx
    040011BD: 8B E5                   mov       esp,ebp
    040011BF: 5D                      pop       ebp
    040011C0: C2 04 00                ret       4
```

The exact operation of this program really isn't important (after all, it doesn't actually do anything useful). What is important to note is how the linker inserts extra bytes ($cc, the int 3 instruction) before a group of one or more functions appearing in a source file to ensure that they are aligned on the specified boundary.

In this particular example, the bits.cnt function is actually 64 bytes long, and the linker inserted only 3 bytes in order to align it to a 16-byte boundary. This percentage of waste—the number of padding bytes compared to the size of the function—is quite low. However, if you have a large number of small functions, the wasted space can become significant (as with the default exception handler in this example that has only two instructions). When creating your own library modules, you will need to weigh the inefficiencies of extra space for padding against the small performance gains you'll obtain by using aligned code.

Object code dump utilities (like dumpbin.exe) are quite useful for analyzing object code and executable files in order to determine attributes such as section size and alignment. Linux (and most Unix-like systems) provide the objdump utility that is comparable. I'll discuss using these tools in the next chapter, as they are great tools for analyzing compiler output.

5.9 Linkers and Their Effect on Code

The limitations of object file formats such as COFF and ELF have a big impact on the quality of code that compilers can generate. Because of the design of object file formats, linkers and compilers often have to inject extra code into an executable file that wouldn't be otherwise necessary. In the following sections I'll explore some of the problems that generic object code formats like COFF and ELF inflict on the executable code.

One problem with generic object file formats like COFF and ELF is that they were not designed to produce efficient executable files for specific CPUs. Instead, they were created to support a wide variety of different CPUs and to make it easy to link together object modules. Unfortunately, their versatility often prevents them from creating the best possible object files. In this section I'll explore some of the problems associated with generic object file formats and why they force compilers to generate code that is somewhat less than great.

Perhaps the biggest problem with the COFF and ELF formats is that relocation values in the object file must apply to 32-bit pointers in the object code. This creates problems, for example, when an instruction encodes a displacement or address value with less than 32 bits. On some processors, such as the 80x86, displacements smaller than 32 bits are so small (e.g., the 80x86's 8-bit displacement) that you would never use them to refer to code outside the current object module. However, on some RISC processors, such as the PowerPC, displacements are much larger (26 bits in the case of the PowerPC branch instruction). This can lead to code kludges like the function stub generation that GCC produces for external function calls. Consider the following C program and the PowerPC code that GCC emits for it:

```
#include <stdio.h>
int main( int argc )
{
```

```
        .
        .
        .
    printf
    (
        "%d %d %d %d %d ",
        .
        .
        .
    );
    return( 0 );
}

; PowerPC assembly output from GCC:

            .
            .
            .

        ;The following sets up the
        ; call to printf and calls printf:

        addis r3,r31,ha16(LC0-L1$pb)
        la r3,lo16(LC0-L1$pb)(r3)
        lwz r4,64(r30)
        lwz r5,80(r30)
        lwz r6,1104(r30)
        lwz r7,1120(r30)
        lis r0,0x400
        ori r0,r0,1120
        lwzx r8,r30,r0
        bl L_printf$stub ; Call to printf "stub" routine.

        ;Return from main program:

        li r0,0
        mr r3,r0
        lwz r1,0(r1)
        lwz r0,8(r1)
        mtlr r0
        lmw r30,-8(r1)
        blr

; Stub, to call the external printf function.
; This code does an indirect jump to the printf
; function using the 32-bit L_printf$lazy_ptr
; pointer that the linker can modify.

        .data
        .picsymbol_stub
L_printf$stub:
        .indirect_symbol _printf
        mflr r0
        bcl 20,31,L0$_printf
```

```
LO$_printf:
        mflr r11
        addis r11,r11,ha16(L_printf$lazy_ptr-LO$_printf)
        mtlr r0
        lwz r12,lo16(L_printf$lazy_ptr-LO$_printf)(r11)
        mtctr r12
        addi r11,r11,lo16(L_printf$lazy_ptr-LO$_printf)
        bctr
.data
.lazy_symbol_pointer
L_printf$lazy_ptr:
        .indirect_symbol _printf

; The following is where the compiler places a 32-bit
; pointer that the linker can fill in with the address
; of the actual printf function:

        .long dyld_stub_binding_helper
```

The compiler must generate the L_printf$stub stub because it doesn't know how far away the actual printf routine will be when the linker adds it to the final executable file. It's unlikely that printf would be sitting outside the plus or minus 32MB range that the PowerPC's 24-bit branch displacement supports (extended to 26 bits); however, the compiler doesn't know for a fact that this is the case. If printf is part of a shared library that is dynamically linked in at runtime, it very well could be outside this range. Therefore, the compiler has to make the safe choice and use a 32-bit displacement for the address of the printf function. Unfortunately, PowerPC instructions don't support a 32-bit displacement because all PowerPC instructions are 32 bits long. A 32-bit displacement would leave no room for the instruction's opcode. Therefore, the compiler has to store a 32-bit pointer to the printf routine in a variable and jump indirect through that variable. Unfortunately, accessing a 32-bit memory pointer on the PowerPC takes quite a bit of code if you don't already have the address of that pointer in a register. Hence all the extra code following the L_printf$stub label.

If the linker were able to adjust 26-bit displacements rather than just 32-bit values, there would be no need for the L_printf$stub routine or the L_printf$lazy_ptr pointer variable. Instead, the bl L_printf$stub instruction would be able to branch directly to the printf routine (assuming it's not more than plus or minus 32MB away). Because single program files generally don't contain more than 32MB of machine instructions, there would rarely be the need to go through the gymnastics this code does in order to call an external routine.

Unfortunately, there is nothing you can do about the object file format; you're stuck with whatever format the operating system specifies (which is usually a variant of COFF or ELF on modern 32-bit machines). However, you can work within the limitations of the object file format your operating system and CPU imposes.

If you expect your code to run on a CPU like the PowerPC (or some other RISC processor) that cannot encode 32-bit displacements directly within instructions, you can optimize by avoiding cross-module calls as much as possible. While it's not good programming practice to create monolithic applications, where all the source code appears in one source file (or is processed by a single compilation), there really is no need to place all of your own functions in separate source modules and compile each of them separately from the others—particularly if these routines make calls to one another. By placing a set of common routines your code uses into a single compilation unit (source file), you allow the compiler to optimize the calls among these functions and avoid all the stub generation on processors like the PowerPC. Note that this is not a suggestion to simply move all of your external functions into a single source file. The code is better only if the functions in a module call one another or share other global objects. If the functions are completely independent of one another and are called only by code external to the compilation unit, then you've saved nothing because the compiler may still need to generate stub routines in the external code.

5.10 For More Information

This chapter barely touches on the subject of compiler theory. For more information on this subject, you'll probably want to look at one of the many compiler construction textbooks available. The seminal work is Aho, Sethi, and Ullman's *Compilers: Principles, Techniques, and Tools* (Addison-Wesley, 1986). Even though this book is a bit old, it still contains a good discussion of general compiler theory that you may find useful. There are, of course, dozens of books on this subject.

Object file formats and executable file formats vary by operating system and compiler. Your operating system vendor will probably provide the specifications for the file formats they use. For common object file formats, such as COFF and ELF, you will also find books available from various publishers— for example, *Understanding and Using COFF* by Gintaras R. Gircys (O'Reilly & Associates, 1988) and *Linkers and Loaders* by John Levine (Morgan Kaufmann/ Academic Press, 2000), which covers various object file formats. The Windows PE/COFF and OMF (object module format) file formats are documented in various papers you can find on the Internet.

NOTE   *You can also find various versions of these documents on my Webster webpage at http://webster.cs.ucr.edu/Page_TechDocs/index.html. A quick search with Google or some other Internet search engine will turn up dozens of additional documents you can reference.*

6

TOOLS FOR ANALYZING COMPILER OUTPUT

In order to write great code, you've got to recognize the difference between programming language sequences that just do their job and those that do a great job. In the context of our discussion, great code sequences use fewer instructions, fewer machine cycles, or less memory than mediocre code sequences. If you're working in assembly language, the CPU manufacturers' data sheets and a bit of experimentation are all you need to determine which code sequences are great and which are not. When working with HLLs, however, you need some way to map the high-level language statements in a program to the corresponding machine code, so that you can determine the quality of those HLL statements. In this chapter, I'll discuss the following:

- How to view and analyze a compiler's machine-language output so you can use that information to write better HLL code
- How to tell certain compilers to produce a human-readable assembly language output file

- How to analyze binary object output files using various tools such as dumpbin.exe and objdump.exe
- How to use a disassembler to examine the machine-code output that a compiler produces
- How to use a debugger to analyze compiler output
- How to compare two different assembly language listings for the same HLL source file to determine which version is better

Analyzing compiler output is one of the principal skills you'll need to develop in order to determine the quality of the code your compiler produces for a given input source file. In this chapter, you'll learn how to obtain the output that you can use for such analysis.

6.1 Background

Most compilers available today emit object-code output that a linker program reads and processes in order to produce an executable program. Because the object-code file generally consists of binary data that is not human-readable, many compilers also provide an option to produce an assembly language listing of the code the compiler generates. By activating this option, you can observe the compiler's output and, possibly, adjust your HLL source code in order to produce better output. Indeed, with a specific compiler and a thorough knowledge of its optimizations, you can write HLL source code that compiles to machine code that is almost as good as the best handwritten assembly language code. Although you can't expect such optimizations to work with a different compiler, this trick will let you write good code with one compiler that is still be able to run your code (possibly less efficiently) on other processors. This is an excellent solution for code that needs to run as efficiently as possible on a certain class of machines but still needs to run on other CPUs.

NOTE   *Keep in mind that examining compiler output can lead you to implement nonportable optimizations. That is, when you examine your compiler's output you might decide to modify your HLL source code to produce better output from your compiler; however, those optimizations might not carry over to a different compiler.*

The ability to emit assembly language output is compiler specific. Some compilers do this by default. GCC, for example, always emits an assembly language file. Most compilers, however, must be explicitly told to produce an assembly language listing. Some compilers produce an assembly listing that can be run through an assembler to produce object code. Some compilers may only produce assembly annotation in a listing file and that "assembly code" is not syntax compatible with any existing assembler. For your purposes, it doesn't matter if a real-world assembler is capable of processing the compiler's assembly output; you're only going to read that output to determine how to tweak the HLL code to produce better object code.

For those compilers that can produce assembly language output, the readability of the assembly code varies considerably. Some compilers insert the original HLL source code into the assembly output as comments which makes it easy to correlate the assembly instructions with the HLL code. Other compilers (such as GCC) emit pure assembly language code, so unless you're well versed in that particular CPU's assembly language, analyzing the output can be difficult.

Another problem that may affect the readability of the compiler output is the optimization level you choose. If you disable all optimizations, it is often easier to determine which assembly instructions correspond to the HLL statements. Unfortunately, with the optimizations turned off, most compilers generate low-quality code. If you are viewing assembly output from a compiler in order to choose better HLL sequences, then you must specify the same optimization level that you will use for the production version of your application. You should never tweak your high-level code to produce better assembly code at one optimization level and then change the optimization level for your production code. If you do this, you might wind up doing extra work that the optimizer would normally do for you. Worse, those hand optimizations could actually prevent the compiler from doing a decent job when you increase its optimization level.

When you specify a higher level of optimization for a compiler, the compiler will often move code around in the assembly output file, eliminate code entirely, and do other code transformations that obfuscate the correspondence between the high-level code and the assembly output. Still, with a bit of practice, it is possible to determine which machine instructions correspond to a given statement in the HLL code.

To analyze compiler output, you'll need to learn a couple of things. First, you'll need to learn enough assembly language programming so that you can effectively read compiler output. Second, you'll need to learn how to tell a compiler (or some other tool) to produce human-readable assembly language output. Finally, you'll have to learn how to correlate the assembly instructions with the HLL code. Chapters 2 and 3 taught you how to read some basic assembly code. This chapter discusses how to translate compiler output into a human-readable form. And the rest of this book deals with analyzing that assembly code so you can generate better machine code by wisely choosing your HLL statements.

6.2 Telling a Compiler to Produce Assembly Output

How you tell a compiler to emit an assembly language output file is specific to the compiler. For that information, you'll need to consult the documentation for your particular compiler. This section will look at four commonly used C/C++ compilers: GCC, Borland's C/C++ v5.0, Borland's C/C++ v5.0 with the Intel backend, and Microsoft's Visual C++.

6.2.1 Assembly Output from GNU and Borland Compilers

To emit assembly output with the Borland and GCC compilers, specify the -S option on the command line when invoking the compiler. Here are three sample command lines for these compilers:

```
gcc -O2 -S t1.c // -O2 option is for optimization
bcc32 -O2 -S t1.c
bcc32i -O2 -S t1.c // Borland C++ with Intel backend
```

The -S option, when supplied to GCC, doesn't actually tell the compiler to produce an assembly output file. GCC always produces an assembly output file. The -S simply tells GCC to stop all processing after it has produced an assembly file. GCC will produce an assembly output file whose root name is the same as the original C file (t1 in these examples) with a .s suffix.

When supplied to the Borland compilers, the -S option will cause the compiler to emit an assembly language source file (with a .asm suffix) rather than an object file. This assembly output file is compatible only with Borland's TASM (the Turbo Assembler). You will not be able to assemble this file with MASM or any other assembler (not that you care, because all you're going to do is read the assembly source file).

6.2.2 Assembly Output from Visual C++

The Visual C++ compiler (VC++) uses the -FAs command-line option to specify MASM-compatible assembly language output. The following is a typical command line to VC++ to tell it to produce an assembly listing:

```
cc -O2 -FAs t1.c
```

6.2.3 Example Assembly Language Output

As an example of producing assembly language output from a compiler, consider the following (arbitrary) C program:

```
#include <stdio.h>
int main( int argc, char **argv )
{
    int i;
    int j;

    i = argc;
    j = **argv;

    if( i == 2 )
    {
        ++j;
    }
    else
```

```
    {
        --j;
    }

    printf( "i=%d, j=%d\n", i, j );
    return 0;
}
```

The following subsections provide the compiler output for Visual C++, Borland C++, and GCC from this code sequence in order to get a feeling for the differences between the assembly language listings produced for this C code sequence.

6.2.3.1   Visual C++ Assembly Language Output

Compiling this file with VC++ using the command line

```
cc -FAs -O1 t1.c
```

produces the following (MASM) assembly language output.

The exact meaning of each assembly language statement appearing in this output isn't important—yet! What is important is seeing the difference between the syntax in this listing and the listings for Borland C++ and Gas that appear in the following sections.

```
TITLE   t1.c
        .386P
include listing.inc
if @Version gt 510
.model FLAT
else
_TEXT   SEGMENT PARA USE32 PUBLIC 'CODE'
_TEXT   ENDS
_DATA   SEGMENT DWORD USE32 PUBLIC 'DATA'
_DATA   ENDS
CONST   SEGMENT DWORD USE32 PUBLIC 'CONST'
CONST   ENDS
_BSS    SEGMENT DWORD USE32 PUBLIC 'BSS'
_BSS    ENDS
_TLS    SEGMENT DWORD USE32 PUBLIC 'TLS'
_TLS    ENDS
;       COMDAT ??_C@_0M@NHID@i?$DN?$CFd?0?5j?$DN?$CFd?6?$AA@
_DATA   SEGMENT DWORD USE32 PUBLIC 'DATA'
_DATA   ENDS
;       COMDAT _main
_TEXT   SEGMENT PARA USE32 PUBLIC 'CODE'
_TEXT   ENDS
FLAT    GROUP _DATA, CONST, _BSS
        ASSUME  CS: FLAT, DS: FLAT, SS: FLAT
endif
PUBLIC  _main
PUBLIC  ??_C@_0M@NHID@i?$DN?$CFd?0?5j?$DN?$CFd?6?$AA@   ; `string'
EXTRN   _printf:NEAR
```

```
;        COMDAT ??_C@_OM@NHID@i?$DN?$CFd?o?5j?$DN?$CFd?6?$AA@
; File t1.c
_DATA   SEGMENT
??_C@_OM@NHID@i?$DN?$CFd?o?5j?$DN?$CFd?6?$AA@ DB 'i=%d, j=%d', OaH, OOH ;
`string'
_DATA   ENDS
;        COMDAT _main
_TEXT   SEGMENT
_argc$ = 8
_argv$ = 12
_main   PROC NEAR                                            ; COMDAT
```

```
; 4    :        int i;
; 5    :        int j;
; 6    :
; 7    :        i = argc;
; 8    :        j = **argv;

        mov     eax, DWORD PTR _argv$[esp-4]

; 9    :
; 10   :        if( i == 2 )

        cmp     DWORD PTR _argc$[esp-4], 2
        mov     eax, DWORD PTR [eax]
        movsx   eax, BYTE PTR [eax]
        jne     SHORT $L776

; 11   :        {
; 12   :                ++j;

        inc     eax

; 13   :        }
; 14   :        else

        jmp     SHORT $L777
$L776:

; 15   :        {
; 16   :                --j;

        dec     eax
$L777:

; 17   :        }
; 18   :
; 19   :        printf( "i=%d, j=%d\n", i, j );

        push    eax
        push    DWORD PTR _argc$[esp]
        push    OFFSET FLAT:??_C@_OM@NHID@i?$DN?$CFd?o?5j?$DN?$CFd?6?$AA@ ;
`string'
        call    _printf
        add     esp, 12                                      ; 0000000cH
```

```
; 20    :         return 0;

        xor     eax, eax

; 21    : }

        ret     0
_main   ENDP
_TEXT   ENDS
END
```

As you can see by reading through this listing, VC++ emits comments containing the original C code (as well as line numbers in the original source file).

6.2.3.2 Borland C++ Assembly Language Output

Now consider the output that the Borland C++ compiler produces from the same C source file with the command line bcc32 -4 -S -O1 t1.c:

```
.386p
        model flat
        ifndef  ??version
        ?debug  macro
        endm
        endif
        ?debug  S "t1.c"
        ?debug  T "t1.c"
_TEXT   segment dword public use32 'CODE'
_TEXT   ends
_DATA   segment dword public use32 'DATA'
_DATA   ends
_BSS    segment dword public use32 'BSS'
_BSS    ends
DGROUP  group   _BSS,_DATA
_TEXT   segment dword public use32 'CODE'
_main   proc    near
?live1@0:
    ;
    ;   int main( int argc, char **argv )
    ;
@1:
        push    ebp
        mov     ebp,esp
    ;
    ;   {
    ;           int i;
    ;           int j;
    ;
    ;           i = argc;
    ;
        mov     edx,dword ptr [ebp+8]
```

```
;
;              j = **argv;
;
?live1@32: ; EDX = i
        mov       eax,dword ptr [ebp+12]
        mov       ecx,dword ptr [eax]
        movsx     eax,byte ptr [ecx]

;
;
;              if( i == 2 )
;
?live1@48: ; EAX = j, EDX = i
        cmp       edx,2
        jne       short @2

;
;              {
;                      ++j;
;
        inc       eax

;
;              }
;
        jmp       short @3

;
;              else
;              {
;                      --j;
;
@2:
        dec       eax

;
;              }
;
;              printf( "i=%d, j=%d\n", i, j );
;
@3:
        push      eax
        push      edx
        push      offset s@
        call      _printf
        add       esp,12

;
;              return 0;
;
?live1@128: ;
        xor       eax,eax

;
;      }
;
@5:
@4:
        pop       ebp
        ret
_main   endp
_TEXT   ends
```

```
_DATA    segment dword public use32 'DATA'
s@       label   byte
         ;       s@+0:
         db      "i=%d, j=%d",10,0
         align   4
_DATA    ends
_TEXT    segment dword public use32 'CODE'
_TEXT    ends
         extrn   _printf:near
         public  _main
         extrn   __setargv__:near
         ?debug  D "F:\BC5\INCLUDE\_null.h" 8277 8192
         ?debug  D "F:\BC5\INCLUDE\_nfile.h" 8277 8192
         ?debug  D "F:\BC5\INCLUDE\_defs.h" 8277 8192
         ?debug  D "F:\BC5\INCLUDE\stdio.h" 8277 8192
         ?debug  D "t1.c" 11825 25587
         end
```

Although the Borland code output is not radically different from that produced by the Microsoft VC++ compiler, you can see that the two are not identical. The differences include some segment definitions (which don't affect the executable code these compilers generate), the emission of debug directives by bcc32, label names, and the like. In spite of these differences between the machine-code sequences produced by these two compilers, an experienced assembly language programmer can easily determine that they achieve the same results.

One important similarity you'll notice between the Borland and Visual C++ output is that both compilers insert the original C code into the assembly output file. This is handy because it's easier to read the compiler's output when the compiler annotates the assembly output in this fashion.

6.2.3.3 Borland C++/Intel Backend Assembly Output

Borland actually supplies two versions of its compiler with the Borland C++ v5.0 package. Both compilers share the same *frontend* but have different *backends.* The frontend of the compiler processes the source language while the backend of the compiler generates native code and optimizes it. The bcc32 compiler uses a Borland-written backend to the compiler and the bcc32i compiler uses an Intel-written backend. Although both compilers produce TASM-compatible assembly output, their output is quite a bit different. Consider the following output file produced with the command line bcc32i -O1 -S t1.c:

```
; -- Machine type P
; mark_description "Intel Reference C Compiler Release 5 Version x";
; mark_description "Built Feb 20 1996 16:27:57";
;ident "Intel Reference C Compiler Release 5 Version x"
         .386P
         .387
         ifndef  ??version
?debug   macro
         endm
```

```
                endif
                ?debug   S "t1.c"
                ?debug   T "t1.c"
DGROUP   group   _DATA,_BSS
                ASSUME   cs:_TEXT,ds:DGROUP,ss:DGROUP
_TEXT SEGMENT PARA PUBLIC USE32  'CODE'
_TEXT ENDS
_DATA SEGMENT PARA PUBLIC USE32  'DATA'
                ALIGN  010H
_DATA ENDS
_BSS SEGMENT PARA PUBLIC USE32  'BSS'
                ALIGN  010H
_BSS ENDS
                ?debug   D "t1.c" 11825 25587
                ?debug   D "F:\BC5\INCLUDE\stdio.h" 8277 8192
                ?debug   D "F:\BC5\INCLUDE\_defs.h" 8277 8192
                ?debug   D "F:\BC5\INCLUDE\_nfile.h" 8277 8192
                ?debug   D "F:\BC5\INCLUDE\_null.h" 8277 8192
_DATA SEGMENT PARA PUBLIC USE32  'DATA'
@p_3@type@template EQU 0
__1BSCTMPLPCK@SI8 EQU 0
_DATA ENDS
_TEXT SEGMENT PARA PUBLIC USE32  'CODE'
; -- Begin _main
; mark_begin;
                ALIGN    4                                    ; 0
                PUBLIC   _main
_main   PROC NEAR
@B1@3:                           ; preds: B1.2

                push     ebp                                  ; 2
                mov      ebp, esp                             ; 2
                sub      esp, 3                               ; 2
                and      esp, -8                              ; 2
                add      esp, 4                               ; 2
                mov      eax, DWORD PTR 12[ebp]               ; 2
                mov      edx, eax                             ; 2
                mov      eax, DWORD PTR 8[ebp]                ; 2

                sub      esp, 20                              ; 2
                mov      edx, DWORD PTR [edx]                 ; 8
                cmp      eax, 2                               ; 10
                movsx    ecx, BYTE PTR [edx]                  ; 8
                je       @B1@1        ; PROB 5%               ; 10
                                 ; LOE:%eax%ecx%ebx%ebp%esi%edi%esp%al%ah%cl%ch
@B1@4:                           ; preds: B1.3

                lea      edx, DWORD PTR -1[ecx]                    ; 16
                                 ; LOE:%eax%edx%ebx%ebp%esi%edi%esp%al%ah%dl%dh
@B1@5:                           ; preds: B1.4 B1.1

                add      esp, 12                              ; 19
                push     edx                                  ; 19
                push     eax                                  ; 19
                push     OFFSET @p_1@s                        ; 19
```

```
        call    _printf                                    ; 19
                        ; LOE:%ebx%ebp%esi%edi%esp
@B1@6:                  ; preds: B1.5

        xor     eax, eax                                   ; 20
        add     esp, 20                                    ; 20
        mov     esp, ebp                                   ; 20
        pop     ebp                                        ; 20
        ret                                                ; 20
            ; LOE:%ebx%ebp%esi%edi%esp
@B1@1:      ; Infrequent ; preds: B1.3

        lea     edx, DWORD PTR 1[ecx]                       ; 12
        jmp     @B1@5           ; PROB 100%                 ; 12
        ALIGN   4                                          ; 0
                    ; LOE:%eax%edx%ebx%ebp%esi%edi%esp%al%ah%dl%dh
; mark_end;
_main ENDP
_TEXT ENDS
_DATA SEGMENT PARA PUBLIC USE32 'DATA'
@2@1_2ab_p@1 EQU 0
@2@1_2pab_p@1 EQU 0
_DATA ENDS
_TEXT SEGMENT PARA PUBLIC USE32 'CODE'
_2@1_2auto_size EQU 20
; -- End _main
_TEXT ENDS
_DATA SEGMENT PARA PUBLIC USE32 'DATA'
@p_1@s  DB      "i=%d, j=%d",10,0
EXTRN    __setargv__ :BYTE
_DATA ENDS
_TEXT SEGMENT PARA PUBLIC USE32 'CODE'
EXTRN   _printf:NEAR
EXTRN   __chkstk:NEAR
_TEXT ENDS
        END
```

Note that the Intel backend does not insert the original C source code into the output assembly file. As a result, correlating the assembly and original C source files is more difficult when using the Intel backend for the Borland C++ compiler. Beyond this, the bcc32i compiler's assembly language output differs from Visual C++ and bcc32 in many of the same ways that bcc32 and VC++ differ: the directives are slightly different, the labels are different, and so on. However, for the simple C program in these examples, their outputs are more similar than different (for more complex source input files you would begin to see some significant differences between the compilers).

6.2.3.4 GCC Assembly Language Output (PowerPC)

GCC is another compiler that doesn't insert the C source code into the assembly output file. In GCC's case, it's somewhat understandable; producing assembly output is something the compiler always does (rather than something it does because of a user request). By not inserting the C source code into the output file, GCC can cut down compilation times by a small amount (because the compiler won't have to write the data and the assembler won't have to read this data). Here's the output of GCC for a PowerPC processor when using the command line gcc -O1 -S t1.c:

```
.data
.cstring
        .align 2
LC0:
        .ascii "i=%d, j=%d\12\0"
.text
        .align 2
        .globl _main
_main:
LFB1:
        mflr r0
        stw r31,-4(r1)
LCFI0:
        stw r0,8(r1)
LCFI1:
        stwu r1,-80(r1)
LCFI2:
        bcl 20,31,L1$pb
L1$pb:
        mflr r31
        mr r11,r3
        lwz r9,0(r4)
        lbz r0,0(r9)
        extsb r5,r0
        cmpwi cr0,r3,2
        bne+ cr0,L2
        addi r5,r5,1
        b L3
L2:
        addi r5,r5,-1
L3:
        addis r3,r31,ha16(LC0-L1$pb)
        la r3,lo16(LC0-L1$pb)(r3)
        mr r4,r11
        bl L_printf$stub
        li r3,0
        lwz r0,88(r1)
        addi r1,r1,80
        mtlr r0
        lwz r31,-4(r1)
        blr
LFE1:
.data
.picsymbol_stub
L_printf$stub:
        .indirect_symbol _printf
```

```
        mflr r0
        bcl 20,31,LO$_printf
LO$_printf:
        mflr r11
        addis r11,r11,ha16(L_printf$lazy_ptr-LO$_printf)
        mtlr r0
        lwz r12,lo16(L_printf$lazy_ptr-LO$_printf)(r11)
        mtctr r12
        addi r11,r11,lo16(L_printf$lazy_ptr-LO$_printf)
        bctr
.data
.lazy_symbol_pointer
L_printf$lazy_ptr:
        .indirect_symbol _printf
        .long dyld_stub_binding_helper
.data
.constructor
.data
.destructor
        .align 1
```

As you can see, the output of GCC is quite sparse. Of course, as this is PowerPC assembly language comparing this assembly output to the 80x86 output from the Visual C++ and Borland compilers isn't really practical.

6.2.3.5   GCC Assembly Language Output (80x86)

The following code provides the GCC compilation to 80x86 assembly code for the t1.c source file:

```
.file   "t1.c"
        .version        "01.01"
gcc2_compiled.:
.section        .rodata
.LC0:
        .string "i=%d, j=%d\n"
.text
        .align 4
.globl main
        .type   main,@function
main:
        pushl %ebp
        movl %esp,%ebp
        subl $8,%esp
        movl 12(%ebp),%eax
        movl 8(%ebp),%edx
        movl (%eax),%eax
        movsbl (%eax),%eax
        cmpl $2,%edx
        jne .L3
        incl %eax
        jmp .L4
        .align 4
.L3:
```

```
        decl %eax
.L4:
        addl $-4,%esp
        pushl %eax
        pushl %edx
        pushl $.LC0
        call printf
        xorl %eax,%eax
        leave
        ret
.Lfe1:
        .size   main,.Lfe1-main
        .ident  "GCC: (GNU) 2.95.2 19991024 (release)"
```

This example should help demonstrate that the massive amount of code that GCC emitted for the PowerPC is more a function of the machine's architecture rather than the compiler. If you compare this to the code that other compilers emit, you'll discover that it is roughly equivalent.

6.2.4   Analyzing Assembly Output from a Compiler

Unless you're well versed in assembly language programming, analyzing assembly output can be tricky. If you're not an assembly language programmer, about the best you can do is count instructions and assume that if a compiler option (or reorganization of your HLL source code) produces fewer instructions, the result is better. In reality, this assumption isn't always correct. Some machine instructions (particularly on CISC processors such as the 80x86) require substantially more time to execute than other instructions. A sequence of three or more instructions on a processor such as the 80x86 *could* execute faster than a single instruction that does the same operation. Fortunately, a compiler is not likely to produce both of these sequences based on a reorganization of your high-level source code. Therefore, you don't usually have to worry about such issues when examining the assembly output.

Note that some compilers *will* produce two different sequences if you change the optimization level. This is because certain optimization settings tell the compiler to favor shorter programs while other optimization settings tell the compiler to favor faster executing code. The optimization setting that favors smaller executable files will probably pick the single instruction over the three instructions that do the same work (assuming those three instructions compile into more code); the optimization setting that favors speed will probably pick the faster instruction sequence.

This section uses various C/C++ compilers in its examples, but you should remember that compilers for other languages also provide the ability to emit assembly code. You'll have to check your compiler's documentation to see if this is possible and what options you use to produce the assembly output. Some compilers (Visual C++ and Borland's C++ Builder, for example) provide an integrated development environment (IDE) that you may use in place of a command-line tool. Even though most compilers that work through an IDE also work from the command line, you can usually specify assembly output from within an IDE as well as from the command line. Once again, see your compiler vendor's documentation for details on doing this.

6.3   Using Object-Code Utilities to Analyze Compiler Output

Although many compilers provide an option to emit assembly language rather than object code, a large number of compilers do not provide this facility—they can only emit binary machine code to an object code file. Because of this, analyzing such compiler output is going to be a bit more work and it's going to require some specialized tools. If your compiler emits object-code files (such as PE/COFF or ELF files) to be fed into a linker, you can probably find an "object code dump" utility that will help you analyze the compiler's output. For example, Microsoft's dumpbin.exe program does this, and the FSF/GNU dumpobj program provides similar capabilities for ELF files under Linux and other operating systems. The following subsections discuss using these two tools when analyzing compiler output.

One benefit of working with object files is that they usually contain symbolic information. That is, in addition to binary machine code the object file contains strings specifying identfier names appearing in the source file (such information does not normally appear in an executable file). Object-code utilities can usually display these source-code symbolic names within the machine instructions that reference the memory locations associated with these symbols. Although these object-code utilities can't automatically correlate the HLL source code with the machine instructions, you can use the symbolic information when you're studying the output of one of these object-code dumping utilities—names like *JumpTable* are much easier to understand than memory addresses like $401_1000.

6.3.1   *The Microsoft dumpbin.exe Utility*

Microsoft provides a small tool, dumpbin.exe, which allows you to examine the contents of a Microsoft PE/COFF file.[1] This program is a command-line tool that you run as follows:

```
dumpbin <options> <filename>
```

The *<filename>* command-line parameter is the name of the object file that you want to examine, and the *<options>* parameter is a set of optional command-line arguments that specify the type of information you want to display. Both of these options each begin with a slash (/). Here is a listing of the possible options (obtained via the /? command-line option):

```
Microsoft (R) COFF Binary File Dumper Version 6.00.8447
Copyright (C) Microsoft Corp 1992-1998. All rights reserved.

usage: DUMPBIN [options] [files]
```

---

[1] Actually, dumpbin.exe is just a *wrapper* program for link.exe; that is, it processes its own command-line parameters and builds a link.exe command line and runs the linker.

```
options:

      /ALL
      /ARCH
      /ARCHIVEMEMBERS
      /DEPENDENTS
      /DIRECTIVES
      /DISASM
      /EXPORTS
      /FPO
      /HEADERS
      /IMPORTS
      /LINENUMBERS
      /LINKERMEMBER[:{1|2}]
      /LOADCONFIG
      /OUT:filename
      /PDATA
      /RAWDATA[:{NONE|BYTES|SHORTS|LONGS}[,#]]
      /RELOCATIONS
      /SECTION:name
      /SUMMARY
/SYMBOLS
```

Though the primary use of dumpbin is to look at the object code a compiler produces, it will also display a considerable amount of interesting information about a PE/COFF file. For information on the meaning of many of the dumpbin.exe command-line options, you may want to review Section 5.6, "Object File Formats," or Section 5.7, "Executable File Formats."

The following subsections describe several of the possible dumpbin.exe command-line options and provide example output for a simple "Hello World" program written in C:

```
#include <stdio.h>

int main( int argc, char **argv)
{
    printf( "Hello World\n" );
}
```

6.3.1.1   The dumpbin.exe /all Command-Line Option

The /all command-line option instructs dumpbin.exe to display all the information it can *except* for a disassembly of the code found in the object file. Here is the (shortened) output that dumpbin.exe produces for the "Hello World" example (most of the raw data output has been cut to save space):

```
G:\>dumpbin /all hw.exe
Microsoft (R) COFF Binary File Dumper Version 6.00.8168
Copyright (C) Microsoft Corp 1992-1998. All rights reserved.
```

```
Dump of file hw.exe

PE signature found

File Type: EXECUTABLE IMAGE

FILE HEADER VALUES
             14C machine (i386)
               3 number of sections
        4105413F time date stamp Mon Jul 26 10:37:03 2004
               0 file pointer to symbol table
               0 number of symbols
              E0 size of optional header
             10F characteristics
                   Relocations stripped
                   Executable
                   Line numbers stripped
                   Symbols stripped
                   32 bit word machine

OPTIONAL HEADER VALUES
             10B magic #
            6.00 linker version
            4000 size of code
            3000 size of initialized data
               0 size of uninitialized data
            1043 RVA of entry point
            1000 base of code
            5000 base of data
          400000 image base
            1000 section alignment
            1000 file alignment
            4.00 operating system version
            0.00 image version
            4.00 subsystem version
               0 Win32 version
            8000 size of image
            1000 size of headers
               0 checksum
               3 subsystem (Windows CUI)
               0 DLL characteristics
          100000 size of stack reserve
            1000 size of stack commit
          100000 size of heap reserve
            1000 size of heap commit
               0 loader flags
              10 number of directories
               0 [        0] RVA [size] of Export Directory
            5484 [       28] RVA [size] of Import Directory
               0 [        0] RVA [size] of Resource Directory
               0 [        0] RVA [size] of Exception Directory
               0 [        0] RVA [size] of Certificates Directory
               0 [        0] RVA [size] of Base Relocation Directory
               0 [        0] RVA [size] of Debug Directory
               0 [        0] RVA [size] of Architecture Directory
```

```
        0 [         0] RVA [size] of Special Directory
        0 [         0] RVA [size] of Thread Storage Directory
        0 [         0] RVA [size] of Load Configuration Directory
        0 [         0] RVA [size] of Bound Import Directory
     5000 [        A4] RVA [size] of Import Address Table Directory
        0 [         0] RVA [size] of Delay Import Directory
        0 [         0] RVA [size] of Reserved Directory
        0 [         0] RVA [size] of Reserved Directory


SECTION HEADER #1
      .text name
     3B56 virtual size
     1000 virtual address
     4000 size of raw data
     1000 file pointer to raw data
        0 file pointer to relocation table
        0 file pointer to line numbers
        0 number of relocations
        0 number of line numbers
 60000020 flags
          Code
          Execute Read

RAW DATA #1
  00401000: 55 8B EC 68 30 60 40 00 E8 05 00 00 00 83 C4 04  UÔ8h0`@.F....,-.
  00401010: 5D C3 53 56 BE 70 60 40 00 57 56 E8 4B 01 00 00  ]+SV+p`@.WVFK...

                        .
                        .
                        .

  00404B50: FF 25 50 50 40 00                                †%PP@.

SECTION HEADER #2
     .rdata name
      80E virtual size
     5000 virtual address
     1000 size of raw data
     5000 file pointer to raw data
        0 file pointer to relocation table
        0 file pointer to line numbers
        0 number of relocations
        0 number of line numbers
 40000040 flags
          Initialized Data
          Read Only

RAW DATA #2
  00405000: D8 56 00 00 62 55 00 00 70 55 00 00 7E 55 00 00  +V..bU..pU..~U..
  00405010: 92 55 00 00 A6 55 00 00 C2 55 00 00 D8 55 00 00  ýU..™U..-U..+U..

                        .
                        .
                        .
```

```
004057F0: 00 00 1B 00 43 6C 6F 73 65 48 61 6E 64 6C 65 00    ....CloseHandle.
00405800: 4B 45 52 4E 45 4C 33 32 2E 64 6C 6C 00 00          KERNEL32.dll..
```

Section contains the following imports:

```
    KERNEL32.dll
                    405000 Import Address Table
                    4054AC Import Name Table
                         0 time date stamp
                         0 Index of first forwarder reference

                   2DF   WriteFile
                   174   GetVersion
                    7D   ExitProcess
                   29E   TerminateProcess
                    F7   GetCurrentProcess
                   2AD   UnhandledExceptionFilter
                   124   GetModuleFileNameA
                    B2   FreeEnvironmentStringsA
                    B3   FreeEnvironmentStringsW
                   2D2   WideCharToMultiByte
                   106   GetEnvironmentStrings
                   108   GetEnvironmentStringsW
                   26D   SetHandleCount
                   152   GetStdHandle
                   115   GetFileType
                   150   GetStartupInfoA
                   19D   HeapDestroy
                   19B   HeapCreate
                   2BF   VirtualFree
                   19F   HeapFree
                   22F   RtlUnwind
                    CA   GetCommandLineA
                   199   HeapAlloc
                    BF   GetCPInfo
                    B9   GetACP
                   131   GetOEMCP
                   2BB   VirtualAlloc
                   1A2   HeapReAlloc
                   13E   GetProcAddress
                   1C2   LoadLibraryA
                   11A   GetLastError
                    AA   FlushFileBuffers
                   26A   SetFilePointer
                   1E4   MultiByteToWideChar
                   1BF   LCMapStringA
                   1C0   LCMapStringW
                   153   GetStringTypeA
                   156   GetStringTypeW
                   27C   SetStdHandle
                    1B   CloseHandle

SECTION HEADER #3
   .data name
   1E08 virtual size
```

```
       6000 virtual address
       1000 size of raw data
       6000 file pointer to raw data
          0 file pointer to relocation table
          0 file pointer to line numbers
          0 number of relocations
          0 number of line numbers
   C0000040 flags
              Initialized Data
              Read Write

RAW DATA #3
  00406000: 00 00 00 00 00 00 00 00 00 00 00 00 3F 1A 40 00   ............?.@.

                      .
                      .
                      .


  00406FE0: 00 00 00 00 00 00 00 00 00 00 00 00 00 00 00 00   ................
  00406FF0: 00 00 00 00 00 00 00 00 00 00 00 00 00 00 00 00   ................

Summary

       2000 .data
       1000 .rdata
       4000 .text
```

As you can see, running dumpbin.exe on a Microsoft EXE file produces considerable output. The problem with this approach is that an EXE file contains all the routines from the language's standard library (e.g., the C Standard Library) that the linker has merged into the application. When analyzing compiler output in order to improve your application's code, wading through all this extra information pertaining to code outside your program can be tedious. Fortunately, there is an easy way to pare down the unnecessary information—run dumpbin on your object (OBJ) files rather than your executable (EXE) files. For example, here is the output of dumpbin with the /all option when you supply hw.obj rather than the hw.exe filename as the command-line parameter:

```
G:\>dumpbin /all hw.obj
Microsoft (R) COFF Binary File Dumper Version 6.00.8168
Copyright (C) Microsoft Corp 1992-1998. All rights reserved.


Dump of file hw.obj

File Type: COFF OBJECT

FILE HEADER VALUES
             14C machine (i386)
               3 number of sections
        4105413E time date stamp Mon Jul 26 10:37:02 2004
              E5 file pointer to symbol table
```

```
                   C number of symbols
                   0 size of optional header
                   0 characteristics

SECTION HEADER #1
  .drectve name
           0 physical address
           0 virtual address
          26 size of raw data
          8C file pointer to raw data
           0 file pointer to relocation table
           0 file pointer to line numbers
           0 number of relocations
           0 number of line numbers
      100A00 flags
             Info
             Remove
             1 byte align

RAW DATA #1
    00000000: 2D 64 65 66 61 75 6C 74 6C 69 62 3A 4C 49 42 43  -defaultlib:LIBC
    00000010: 20 2D 64 65 66 61 75 6C 74 6C 69 62 3A 4F 4C 44   -defaultlib:OLD
    00000020: 4E 41 4D 45 53 20                                NAMES

    Linker Directives
    -----------------
    -defaultlib:LIBC
    -defaultlib:OLDNAMES

SECTION HEADER #2
    .text name
           0 physical address
           0 virtual address
          12 size of raw data
          B2 file pointer to raw data
          C4 file pointer to relocation table
           0 file pointer to line numbers
           2 number of relocations
           0 number of line numbers
    60500020 flags
             Code
             16 byte align
             Execute Read

RAW DATA #2
    00000000: 55 8B EC 68 00 00 00 00 E8 00 00 00 00 83 C4 04  UÔ8h....F....,-.
    00000010: 5D C3                                            ]+

RELOCATIONS #2
                                            Symbol    Symbol
    Offset    Type              Applied To  Index     Name
    --------  ----------------  ----------------  --------  ------
    00000004  DIR32                  00000000         B  $SG340
    00000009  REL32                  00000000         8  _printf
```

```
SECTION HEADER #3
   .data name
        0 physical address
        0 virtual address
        D size of raw data
       D8 file pointer to raw data
        0 file pointer to relocation table
        0 file pointer to line numbers
        0 number of relocations
        0 number of line numbers
C0300040 flags
          Initialized Data
          4 byte align
          Read Write

RAW DATA #3
  00000000: 48 65 6C 6C 6F 20 57 6F 72 6C 64 0A 00          Hello World..

COFF SYMBOL TABLE
000 00000000 DEBUG  notype        Filename    | .file
    t.c
002 000A1FE8 ABS    notype        Static      | @comp.id
003 00000000 SECT1  notype        Static      | .drectve
    Section length   26, #relocs    0, #linenums    0, checksum        0
005 00000000 SECT2  notype        Static      | .text
    Section length   12, #relocs    2, #linenums    0, checksum 11D64EEB
007 00000000 SECT2  notype ()     External    | _main
008 00000000 UNDEF  notype ()     External    | _printf
009 00000000 SECT3  notype        Static      | .data
    Section length    D, #relocs    0, #linenums    0, checksum E4C58F28
00B 00000000 SECT3  notype        Static      | $SG340

String Table Size = 0x0 bytes

  Summary

        D .data
       26 .drectve
       12 .text
```

This example clearly demonstrates the quantity of output you get when using the /all command-line option. Use this option with care!

6.3.1.2   The dumpbin.exe /disasm Command-Line Option

The /disasm command-line option is the one of greatest interest. It produces a disassembled listing of the object file. As for the /all option, you shouldn't try to disassemble an EXE file using the dumpbin.exe program. The disassembled listing you'll get will be quite long and the vast majority of the code will probably be the listings of all the library routines your application calls. For example, the simple "Hello World" application generates over 5,000 lines of disassembled code. All but a small handful of those statements correspond to library routines. Wading through that amount of code will prove overwhelming to most people.

However, if you disassemble the `hw.obj` file rather than the executable file, here's the output you will typically get:

```
Microsoft (R) COFF Binary File Dumper Version 6.00.8168
Copyright (C) Microsoft Corp 1992-1998. All rights reserved.


Dump of file hw.obj

File Type: COFF OBJECT

_main:
  00000000: 55                    push        ebp
  00000001: 8B EC                 mov         ebp,esp
  00000003: 68 00 00 00 00        push        offset _main
  00000008: E8 00 00 00 00        call        0000000D
  0000000D: 83 C4 04              add         esp,4
  00000010: 5D                    pop         ebp
  00000011: C3                    ret

  Summary

        D .data
       26 .drectve
       12 .text
```

If you look closely at this disassembled code, you'll find the major problem with disassembling object files rather than executable files—most addresses in the code are relocatable addresses, which appear as $00000000 in the object code listing. As a result, you will probably have a hard time figuring out what the various assembly statements are doing. For example, in the `hw.obj`'s disassembled listing you see the following two statements:

```
00000003: 68 00 00 00 00        push        offset _main
00000008: E8 00 00 00 00        call        0000000D
```

In fact, this code is not pushing the offset of the _main label onto the stack, and it is not calling the procedure at address $d. As you can see by looking at the object code emitted for these two instructions, the address field contains all zeros. If you run `dumpbin` on `hw.obj` and supply a /all command-line parameter, you'll notice that this file has two relocation entries:

Offset	Type	Applied To	Symbol Index	Symbol Name
00000004	DIR32	00000000	B	$SG340
00000009	REL32	00000000	8	_printf

RELOCATIONS #2

The Offset column tells you the byte offset into the file where the relocations are to be applied. Note, in the disassembly above, that the push instruction starts at offset $3, so the actual immediate constant is at offset $4. Similarly, the call instruction begins at offset $8, so the address of the actual routine that needs to be patched is 1 byte later, at offset $9. From the relocation information that dumpbin.exe outputs, you can discern the symbols associated with these relocations ($SG340 is an internal symbol that the C compiler generates for the "Hello World" string. _printf is, obviously, the name associated with the C printf function).

Cross-referencing every call and memory reference against the relocation list may seem like a pain, but at least you get symbolic names when you do this.

Consider the first few lines of the disassembled code when you apply the /disasm option to the hw.exe file:

```
File Type: EXECUTABLE IMAGE

  00401000: 55                   push      ebp
  00401001: 8B EC                mov       ebp,esp
  00401003: 68 30 60 40 00       push      406030h
  00401008: E8 05 00 00 00       call      00401012
  0040100D: 83 C4 04             add       esp,4
  00401010: 5D                   pop       ebp
  00401011: C3                   ret
                                   .
                                   .
                                   .
```

Notice that the linker has filled in the addresses (relative to the load address for the file) of the offset $SG360 and _print labels. This may seem somewhat convenient, however, you should note that these labels (especially the _printf label) are no longer present in the file. When you are reading the disassembled output, the lack of these labels can make it very difficult to figure out which machine instructions correspond to HLL statements. This is yet another reason why you should use object files rather than executable files when running dumpbin.exe.

If you think it's going to be a major pain to read the disassembled output of the dumpbin.exe utility, don't get too upset. For optimization purposes, you're often more interested in the code differences between two versions of an HLL program than you are in figuring out what each machine instruction does. Therefore, you can easily determine which machine instructions are affected by a change in your code by running dumpbin.exe on two versions of your object files (once before the change to the HLL code and one created afterward). For example, consider the following modification to the "Hello World" program:

```
#include <stdio.h>

int main( int argc, char **argv )
{
```

```
        char *hwstr = "Hello World\n";

        printf( hwstr );
}
```

Here's the disassembly output that dumpbin.exe produces:

```
Microsoft (R) COFF Binary File Dumper Version 6.00.8168
Copyright (C) Microsoft Corp 1992-1998. All rights reserved.


Dump of file hw.obj

File Type: COFF OBJECT

_main:
  00000000: 55                       push        ebp
  00000001: 8B EC                    mov         ebp,esp
  00000003: 51                       push        ecx
  00000004: C7 45 FC 00 00 00        mov         dword ptr [ebp-4],offset _main
            00
  0000000B: FF 75 FC                 push        dword ptr [ebp-4]
  0000000E: E8 00 00 00 00           call        00000013
  00000013: 59                       pop         ecx
  00000014: 33 C0                    xor         eax,eax
  00000016: C9                       leave
  00000017: C3                       ret

  Summary

        D .data
       54 .debug$S
       2A .drectve
       18 .text
```

By comparing this output with the previous assembly output (either
manually or by running one of the programs based on the Unix diff
utility), you can see the effects the changes to your HLL source code have
had on the emitted machine code. Section 6.6, "Comparing Output from
Two Compilations," discusses the merits of both methods.

6.3.1.3 The dumpbin.exe /headers Command-Line Option

The /headers option instructs dumpbin.exe to display the COFF header files
and section header files. The /all option also prints this information, but
the /header option displays only the header information without all the other
information. Here's the sample output for the "Hello World" executable file:

```
G:\WGC>dumpbin /headers hw.exe
Microsoft (R) COFF Binary File Dumper Version 6.00.8168
Copyright (C) Microsoft Corp 1992-1998. All rights reserved.
```

Dump of file hw.exe

PE signature found

File Type: EXECUTABLE IMAGE

FILE HEADER VALUES
            14C machine (i386)
              3 number of sections
       41055ABA time date stamp Mon Jul 26 12:25:46 2004
              0 file pointer to symbol table
              0 number of symbols
             E0 size of optional header
            10F characteristics
                   Relocations stripped
                   Executable
                   Line numbers stripped
                   Symbols stripped
                   32 bit word machine

OPTIONAL HEADER VALUES
            10B magic #
           7.00 linker version
           5000 size of code
           4000 size of initialized data
              0 size of uninitialized data
           106E RVA of entry point
           1000 base of code
           6000 base of data
         400000 image base
           1000 section alignment
           1000 file alignment
           4.00 operating system version
           0.00 image version
           4.00 subsystem version
              0 Win32 version
           A000 size of image
           1000 size of headers
              0 checksum
              3 subsystem (Windows CUI)
              0 DLL characteristics
         100000 size of stack reserve
           1000 size of stack commit
         100000 size of heap reserve
           1000 size of heap commit
              0 loader flags
             10 number of directories
              0 [0] RVA [size] of Export Directory
           6B8C [28] RVA [size] of Import Directory
              0 [0] RVA [size] of Resource Directory
              0 [0] RVA [size] of Exception Directory
              0 [0] RVA [size] of Certificates Directory
              0 [0] RVA [size] of Base Relocation Directory
              0 [0] RVA [size] of Debug Directory
              0 [0] RVA [size] of Architecture Directory

```
           0 [         0] RVA [size] of Special Directory
           0 [         0] RVA [size] of Thread Storage Directory
           0 [         0] RVA [size] of Load Configuration Directory
           0 [         0] RVA [size] of Bound Import Directory
        6000 [        D0] RVA [size] of Import Address Table Directory
           0 [         0] RVA [size] of Delay Import Directory
           0 [         0] RVA [size] of Reserved Directory
           0 [         0] RVA [size] of Reserved Directory


SECTION HEADER #1
   .text name
   4C38 virtual size
   1000 virtual address
   5000 size of raw data
   1000 file pointer to raw data
      0 file pointer to relocation table
      0 file pointer to line numbers
      0 number of relocations
      0 number of line numbers
60000020 flags
         Code
         Execute Read

SECTION HEADER #2
  .rdata name
   1018 virtual size
   6000 virtual address
   2000 size of raw data
   6000 file pointer to raw data
      0 file pointer to relocation table
      0 file pointer to line numbers
      0 number of relocations
      0 number of line numbers
40000040 flags
         Initialized Data
         Read Only

SECTION HEADER #3
   .data name
   1C48 virtual size
   8000 virtual address
   1000 size of raw data
   8000 file pointer to raw data
      0 file pointer to relocation table
      0 file pointer to line numbers
      0 number of relocations
      0 number of line numbers
C0000040 flags
         Initialized Data
         Read Write

   Summary

      2000 .data
```

```
2000 .rdata
5000 .text
```

If you look back at the discussion of object file formats in Chapter 5 (see Section 5.6, "Object File Formats"), you'll be able to make sense of the information that dumpbin.exe outputs when you specify the /headers option.

6.3.1.4 The dumpbin.exe /imports Command-Line Option

dumpbin.exe's /imports option lists all of the dynamic-link symbols that the operating system must supply when the program loads into memory. This information isn't particularly useful for analyzing code emitted for HLL statements, so this chapter will not consider this option beyond this brief mention.

6.3.1.5 The dumpbin.exe /relocations Command-Line Option

The /relocations option displays all the relocation objects in the file. This command is quite useful because it provides a list of all the symbols for the program and the offsets of their use in the disassembly listing. Of course, the /all option also presents this information, but the /relocations option provides just this information without all the other output.

6.3.1.6 Other dumpbin.exe Command-Line Options

The dumpbin.exe utility supports many more command-line options beyond those this chapter describes. You can get a list of the possible options by specifying /? on the command line when running dumpbin.exe. You can also read more about dumpbin.exe online at www.msdn.com. Just search for "dumpbin.exe," and click the DUMPBIN Reference link.

6.3.2 The FSF/GNU objdump.exe Utility

If you're running the GNU toolset on your operating system (for example, under Linux or BSD), you can use the FSF/GNU objdump.exe utility to examine the object files produced by GCC and other GNU-compliant tools. Here are the command-line options that objdump.exe supports:

```
Usage: objdump <option(s)> <file(s)>
 Display information from object <file(s)>.
 At least one of the following switches must be given:
  -a, --archive-headers    Display archive header information
  -f, --file-headers       Display the contents of the overall file header
  -p, --private-headers    Display object format specific file header contents
  -h, --[section-]headers  Display the contents of the section headers
  -x, --all-headers        Display the contents of all headers
  -d, --disassemble        Display assembler contents of executable sections
  -D, --disassemble-all    Display assembler contents of all sections
  -S, --source             Intermix source code with disassembly
  -s, --full-contents      Display the full contents of all sections requested
  -g, --debugging          Display debug information in object file
  -G, --stabs              Display (in raw form) any STABS info in the file
```

```
-t, --syms                   Display the contents of the symbol table(s)
-T, --dynamic-syms           Display the contents of the dynamic symbol table
-r, --reloc                  Display the relocation entries in the file
-R, --dynamic-reloc          Display the dynamic relocation entries in the file
-v, --version                Display this program's version number
-i, --info                   List object formats and architectures supported
-H, --help                   Display this information
```

Given the following m.hla source code fragment:

```
begin t;

        // test mem.alloc and mem.free:

        for( mov( 0, ebx ); ebx < 16; inc( ebx )) do

                // Allocate lots of storage:

                for( mov( 0, ecx ); ecx < 65536; inc( ecx )) do

                        rand.range( 1, 256 );
                        malloc( eax );
                        mov( eax, ptrs[ ecx*4 ] );

                endfor;

        endfor;
                .
                .
                .
```

here is some sample output produced on the 80x86, created with the Linux command line objdump -S m:

```
08048246 <_HLAMain>:
        .
        . // Some deleted code here,
        . // that HLA automatically generated.
        .
 8048274:       bb 00 00 00 00          mov    $0x0,%ebx
 8048279:       e9 d5 00 00 00          jmp    8048353 <L1021_StartFor__hla_>

0804827e <L1021_for__hla_>:
 804827e:       b9 00 00 00 00          mov    $0x0,%ecx
 8048283:       eb 1a                   jmp    804829f <L1022_StartFor__hla_>

08048285 <L1022_for__hla_>:
 8048285:       6a 01                   push   $0x1
 8048287:       68 00 01 00 00          push   $0x100
 804828c:       e8 db 15 00 00          call   804986c <RAND_RANGE>
 8048291:       50                      push   %eax
 8048292:       e8 63 0f 00 00          call   80491fa <MEM_ALLOC>
 8048297:       89 04 8d 60 ae 04 08    mov    %eax,0x804ae60(,%ecx,4)
```

```
0804829e <L1022_continue__hla_>:
 804829e:       41                      inc     %ecx

0804829f <L1022_StartFor__hla_>:
 804829f:       81 f9 00 00 01 00       cmp     $0x10000,%ecx
 80482a5:       72 de                   jb      8048285 <L1022_for__hla_>

080482a7 <L1022_exitloop__hla_>:
 80482a7:       b9 00 00 00 00          mov     $0x0,%ecx
 80482ac:       eb 0d                   jmp     80482bb <L1023_StartFor__hla_>
```

These listings are only a fragment of the total code (which is why certain labels are not present). Nevertheless, you can see how the objdump can be useful for analyzing compiler output as this short example demonstrates how you can disassemble the object code for a code fragment in question.

As with the Microsoft dumpbin.exe tool, the FSF/GNU objdump utility can display additional information beyond the machine code disassembly that may prove useful when you're analyzing compiler output. For most purposes, however, the GCC -S (assembly output) is the most useful option. Here is an example of a disassembly of some C code using the objdump.exe utility. First, the original C code:

```
#include <stdio.h>
int main( int argc, char **argv )
{
    int i,j,k;

    j = **argv;
    k = argc;
    i = j && k;
    printf( "%d\n", i );
    return 0;
}
```

Here's the Gas output from GCC for the C code:

```
.file   "t.c"
        .section        .rodata
.LC0:
        .string "%d\n"
        .text
.globl main
        .type   main,@function
main:
        pushl   %ebp
        movl    %esp, %ebp
        subl    $24, %esp
        andl    $-16, %esp
        movl    $0, %eax
        subl    %eax, %esp
```

```
        movl    12(%ebp), %eax
        movl    (%eax), %eax
        movsbl  (%eax),%eax
        movl    %eax, -8(%ebp)
        movl    8(%ebp), %eax
        movl    %eax, -12(%ebp)
        movl    $0, -4(%ebp)
        cmpl    $0, -8(%ebp)
        je      .L2
        cmpl    $0, -12(%ebp)
        je      .L2
        movl    $1, -4(%ebp)
.L2:
        subl    $8, %esp
        pushl   -4(%ebp)
        pushl   $.LC0
        call    printf
        addl    $16, %esp
        movl    $0, %eax
        leave
        ret
.Lfe1:
```

Now here's the objdump.exe disassembly of the main function:

```
.file   "t.c"
        .section        .rodata
.LC0:
        .string "%d\n"
        .text
.globl main
        .type   main,@function
main:
        pushl   %ebp
        movl    %esp, %ebp
        subl    $24, %esp
        andl    $-16, %esp
        movl    $0, %eax
        subl    %eax, %esp
        movl    12(%ebp), %eax
        movl    (%eax), %eax
        movsbl  (%eax),%eax
        movl    %eax, -8(%ebp)
        movl    8(%ebp), %eax
        movl    %eax, -12(%ebp)
        movl    $0, -4(%ebp)
        cmpl    $0, -8(%ebp)
        je      .L2
        cmpl    $0, -12(%ebp)
        je      .L2
        movl    $1, -4(%ebp)
```

```
.L2:
        subl    $8, %esp
        pushl   -4(%ebp)
        pushl   $.LC0
        call    printf
        addl    $16, %esp
        movl    $0, %eax
        leave
        ret
.Lfe1:
```

As you can see, the assembly code output is somewhat easier to read than objdump.exe's output.

6.4 Using a Disassembler to Analyze Compiler Output

Although using an object-code dump tool is one way to analyze compiler output, another possible solution is to run a *disassembler* on the executable file. A disassembler is a utility that translates binary machine code into human-readable assembly language statements (the phrase "human-readable" is debatable, but that's the idea, anyway). As such, disassemblers are another tool you can use to analyze compiler output.

There is a subtle, but important, difference between an object-code dump utility (which contains a simple disassembler) and a sophisticated disassembler program. Object-code dump utilities are automatic, but they get easily confused if the object code contains funny constructs (such as buried data in the instruction stream). An *automatic disassembler* is very convenient to use, requiring little expertise on the part of the user, but such programs rarely disassemble the machine code correctly. A full-blown *interactive disassembler*, on the other hand, requires more training to use properly, but it is capable of disassembling tricky machine-code sequences with a little help from its user. As such, decent disassemblers will work in situations where a simplistic object-code dump utility will fail. Fortunately, most compilers do not always emit the kind of tricky code that confuses object-code dump utilities, so you can sometimes get by without having to learn how to use a full-blown disassembler program. Nevertheless, having a disassembler handy can be useful in situations where a simplistic approach doesn't work.

Several "free" disassemblers are available, I'm going to describe the use of the IDA disassembler in this section. IDA is a very powerful disassembler, based on a commercial product (IDA is the free version of IDA Pro, a very capable and powerful disassembler system). The IDA Pro disassembler is available from www.datarescue.com. A trial version is also available from this same address. The free version is available at several software repository sites on the Internet. Just search for "IDA Pro disassembler" with your favorite search engine to locate a copy of the free version. This chapter will describe how to use IDAFRE4.1 (the 4.1 version of the IDA free disassembler).

When you first run IDA, the window appearing in Figure 6-1 is displayed.

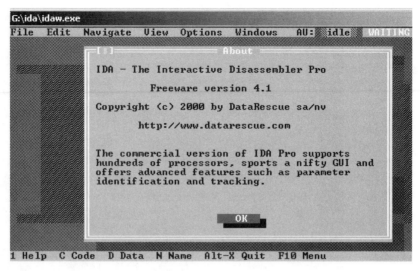

Figure 6-1: IDA opening window

Pressing the ENTER key clears the splash screen and opens up a file dialog box, as shown in Figure 6-2.

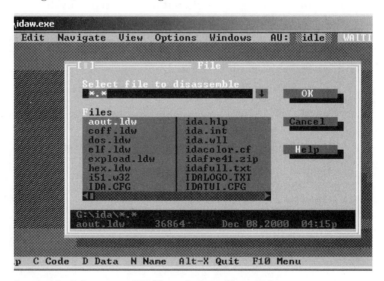

Figure 6-2: Selecting an EXE file to disassemble in IDA

Enter the filename of the EXE file you want to disassemble (press the Tab key to get to the filename entry box if it's not already selected). Once you enter a filename, IDA brings up the format dialog box as shown in Figure 6-3. In this dialog box, you can select the binary file type (e.g., MS-DOS EXE file, PE/COFF executable file, or pure binary) and the options to use when disassembling the file. IDA Pro does a good job of choosing reasonable default values for these options, so most of the time you'll just accept the defaults unless you're working with some weird binary files.

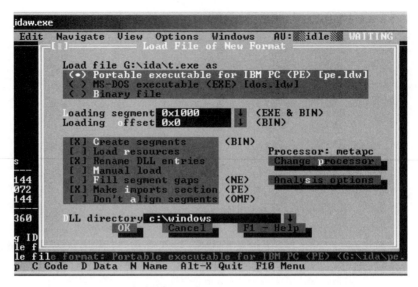

Figure 6-3: IDA executable file format box

Generally, IDA will figure out the appropriate file type information for a standard disassembly and then it will automatically disassemble the file. To produce an assembly language output file, press ALT+F to open the file menu, and select **Produce Output File**. From the resulting submenu, select **Produce ASM file**. Here are the first few lines of the disassembly of the t.c file given in the earlier section:

```
; File Name    : G:\t.exe
; Format       : Portable executable for IBM PC (PE)
; Section 1. (virtual address 00001000)
; Virtual size                 : 00003B56 (   15190.)
; Section size in file         : 00004000 (   16384.)
; Offset to raw data for section: 00001000
; Flags 60000020: Text Executable Readable
; Alignment     : 16 bytes ?
; OS type        : MS Windows
; Application type: Executable 32bit


            model flat

; -------------------------------------------------------------

; Segment type: Pure code
_text           segment para public 'CODE' use32
                assume cs:_text
                ;org 401000h
                assume es:nothing, ss:nothing, ds:_data, fs:nothing,
gs:nothing
```

```
; ----------- S U B R O U T I N E -------------------------

sub_0_401000    proc near                   ; CODE XREF: start+AF?p

arg_0           = dword ptr  4

                mov     eax, [esp+arg_0]
                mov     ecx, [esp+arg_0]
                and     eax, ecx
                push    eax
                push    offset unk_0_406030
                call    sub_0_401020
                add     esp, 8
                xor     eax, eax
                retn
sub_0_401000    endp
```

Just note that sub_0_401000 turns out to be the body of the main function in the C program.

IDA is an *interactive* disassembler. This means that it provides lots of complex features that you can use to guide the disassembly to produce a more reasonable assembly language output file. However, the "automatic" mode of operation is generally all you will need in order to example compiler output files in order to determine the quality of the code that your compiler generates. For more details on IDA or IDA Pro, see its user's manual.

6.5   Using a Debugger to Analyze Compiler Output

Another option you can use to analyze compiler output is a debugger program, which usually incorporates a disassembler that you can use to view machine instructions. Using a debugger to view the code your compiler emits can either be an arduous task or a breeze—depending on the debugger you use. Typically, if you use a stand-alone debugger, you'll find that it takes considerably more effort to analyze your compiler's output than if you use a debugger built into a compiler's integrated development environment. This section looks at both approaches.

6.5.1   Using an IDE's Debugger

The Microsoft Visual C++ environment provides excellent tools for observing the code produced by a compilation (of course, the compiler also produces assembly output, but that can be ignored here). To view the output using the Visual Studio debugger, first compile your C/C++ program to an executable file and then select **Build ▸ Start Debug ▸ Step Into** from the Visual Studio Build menu. When the debug palette comes up, click the disassembly view button (see Figure 6-4).

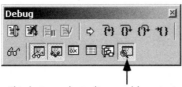

This button selects disassembly output

Figure 6-4: Visual Studio disassembly view button

Pressing the disassembly view button brings up a window with text similar to the following:

```
19:     {
00401010   push      ebp
00401011   mov       ebp,esp
00401013   sub       esp,48h
00401016   push      ebx
00401017   push      esi
00401018   push      edi
00401019   lea       edi,[ebp-48h]
0040101C   mov       ecx,12h
00401021   mov       eax,0CCCCCCCCh
00401026   rep stos  dword ptr [edi]
20:     int i,j;
21:
22:     i = argc & j;
00401028   mov       eax,dword ptr [ebp+8]
0040102B   and       eax,dword ptr [ebp-8]
0040102E   mov       dword ptr [ebp-4],eax
23:     printf( "%d", i );
00401031   mov       ecx,dword ptr [ebp-4]
00401034   push      ecx
00401035   push      offset string "%d" (0042001c)
0040103A   call      printf (00401070)
0040103F   add       esp,8
24:     return 0;
00401042   xor       eax,eax
25:     }
00401044   pop       edi
00401045   pop       esi
00401046   pop       ebx
00401047   add       esp,48h
0040104A   cmp       ebp,esp
0040104C   call      __chkesp (004010f0)
00401051   mov       esp,ebp
00401053   pop       ebp
00401054   ret
```

Of course, because Microsoft's Visual C++ package is already capable of outputting an assembly language file during compilation, using the Visual Studio integrated debugger in this manner isn't necessary. However, some compilers do not provide assembly output, and debugger output may be the easiest way to view the machine code the compiler produces. For example,

Borland's Delphi compiler does not provide an option to produce assembly language output. Given the massive amount of class library code that Delphi links into an application, attempting to view the code for a small section of your program by using a disassembler would be like trying to find a needle in a haystack. A better solution is to use the debugger built into the Delphi environment.

To view the machine code that Delphi (or Kylix under Linux) generates, set a breakpoint in your code where you wish to view the machine code, and then compile and run your application. When the breakpoint triggers, select **View ▶ Debug Windows ▶ CPU**. This brings up a CPU window like the one appearing in Figure 6-5. From this window you can examine the compiler's output and adjust your HLL code to produce better output.

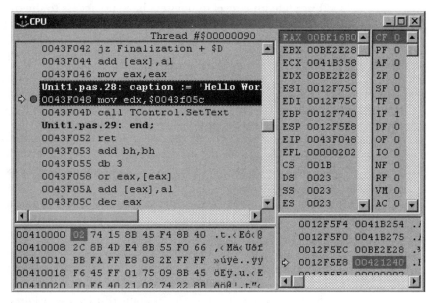

Figure 6-5: Delphi CPU window

6.5.2   Using a Stand-Alone Debugger

If your compiler doesn't provide its own debugger as part of an integrated development system, another alternative is to use a separate debugger such as OllyDbg, DDD, or GDB to disassemble your compiler's output. Simply load the executable file into the debugger for normal debugging operations.

Most debuggers that are not associated with a particular programming language are machine-level debuggers that disassemble the binary machine code into machine instructions for viewing during the debugging operation. One problem with using machine-level debuggers is that locating a particular section of code to disassemble can be difficult. Remember, when you load the entire executable file into a debugger, you also load all the statically linked library routines and other runtime support code that don't normally appear in the application's source file. Searching through all this extraneous code to find out how the compiler translates a particular sequence of statements to machine code can be time-consuming. Some serious code sleuthing may be necessary. Fortunately, most linkers collect all the library routines together and place them either at the beginning or end of the executable file. Therefore, the code associated with your application will generally appear near the beginning or end of the executable file. Nevertheless, if the application is large, finding a particular function or code sequence among all the code in that application can be difficult.

Debuggers generally come in one of three different flavors: pure machine-level debuggers, symbolic debuggers, and source-level debuggers. Symbolic debuggers and source-level debuggers require executable files to contain special debugging information[2] and, therefore, the compiler must specifically include this extra information.

Pure machine-level debuggers have no access to the original source code or symbols in the application. A pure machine-level debugger simply disassembles the machine code found in the application and displays the listing using literal numeric constants and machine addresses. Reading through such code is difficult, but if you understand how compilers generate code for the HLL statements (as this book will teach you), then locating the machine code is easier. Nevertheless, without any symbolic information to provide a "root point" in the code, analysis can be difficult.

Symbolic debuggers use special symbol table information found in the executable file (or a separate debugging file, in some instances) to associate labels with functions and, possibly, variable names in your executable file. This feature makes locating sections of code within the disassembly listing much easier. When symbolic labels identify calls to functions, it's much easier to see the correspondence between the disassembled code and your original HLL source code. One thing to keep in mind, however, is that symbolic information is only available if the application was compiled with debugging mode enabled. Check your compiler's documentation to determine how to activate this feature for use with your debugger.

Source-level debuggers will actually display the original source code associated with the file the debugger is processing. In order to see the actual machine code the compiler produced, you often have to activate a special machine-level view of the program. As with symbolic debuggers, your compiler must produce special executable files (or auxiliary files) containing debug information that a source-level debugger can use. Clearly, source-level debuggers are much easier to work with because they show the correspondence between the original HLL source code and the disassembled machine code.

6.6 Comparing Output from Two Compilations

If you are an expert assembly language programmer and you're well versed in compiler design, it should be pretty easy for you to determine what changes you'll need to make to your HLL source code to improve the quality of the output machine code. However, most programmers (especially those who

---

[2] Some debuggers keep the debug information in a separate file rather than the executable file.

do not have considerable experience studying compiler output) can't just read a compiler's assembly language output. They have to compare the two sets of outputs (before and after a change) to determine which code is better. After all, not every change you make to your HLL source files will result in better code. Some changes will leave the machine code unaffected (in which case, you should use the more readable and maintainable version of the HLL source code). In other cases, you could actually make the output machine code worse. Therefore, unless you know exactly what a compiler is going to do when you make changes to your HLL source file, you should do a before-and-after comparison of the compiler's output machine code before accepting any modifications you make.

6.6.1   Before-and-After Comparisons with diff

Of course, the first thought any experienced software developer is going to have is, "Well, if we have to compare files, we'll just use diff!" As it turns out, a typical diff (compute file differences) program will be useful for certain purposes, but it will not be universally applicable when comparing two different output files from a compiler. The problem with a program like diff is that it works great when there are only a few differences between two files. Alas, diff will not prove very useful when comparing two wildly different machine language output files. For example, consider the following C program (t.c) and two different outputs produced by the Microsoft VC++ compiler:

```c
extern void f( void );
int main( int argc, char **argv )
{
    int boolResult;

    switch( argc )
    {
        case 1:
            f();
            break;

        case 10:
            f();
            break;

        case 100:
            f();
            break;

        case 1000:
            f();
            break;

        case 10000:
            f();
            break;
```

```
        case 100000:
            f();
            break;

        case 1000000:
            f();
            break;

        case 10000000:
            f();
            break;

        case 100000000:
            f();
            break;

        case 1000000000:
            f();
            break;

    }
    return 0;
}
```

Here's the assembly language output MSVC++ produces when using the command line cl /Fa t.c (that is, when compiling without optimization):

```
TITLE   t.c
    .386P
include listing.inc
if @Version gt 510
.model FLAT
else
_TEXT       SEGMENT PARA USE32 PUBLIC 'CODE'
_TEXT       ENDS
_DATA       SEGMENT DWORD USE32 PUBLIC 'DATA'
_DATA       ENDS
CONST       SEGMENT DWORD USE32 PUBLIC 'CONST'
CONST       ENDS
_BSS        SEGMENT DWORD USE32 PUBLIC 'BSS'
_BSS        ENDS
_TLS        SEGMENT DWORD USE32 PUBLIC 'TLS'
_TLS        ENDS
FLAT        GROUP _DATA, CONST, _BSS
    ASSUME CS: FLAT, DS: FLAT, SS: FLAT
endif
PUBLIC      _main
EXTRN       _f:NEAR
_TEXT       SEGMENT
_argc$ = 8
_main       PROC NEAR
; File t.c
```

```
; Line 7
    push    ebp
    mov     ebp, esp
    sub     esp, 8
; Line 11
    mov     eax, DWORD PTR _argc$[ebp]
    mov     DWORD PTR -8+[ebp], eax
    cmp     DWORD PTR -8+[ebp], 100000
    jg      SHORT $L1207
    cmp     DWORD PTR -8+[ebp], 100000
    je      $L1199
    cmp     DWORD PTR -8+[ebp], 100
    jg      SHORT $L1208
    cmp     DWORD PTR -8+[ebp], 100
    je      SHORT $L1196
    cmp     DWORD PTR -8+[ebp], 1
    je      SHORT $L1194
    cmp     DWORD PTR -8+[ebp], 10
    je      SHORT $L1195
    jmp     $L1191
$L1208:
    cmp     DWORD PTR -8+[ebp], 1000
    je      SHORT $L1197
    cmp     DWORD PTR -8+[ebp], 10000
    je      SHORT $L1198
    jmp     SHORT $L1191
$L1207:
    cmp     DWORD PTR -8+[ebp], 100000000
    jg      SHORT $L1209
    cmp     DWORD PTR -8+[ebp], 100000000
    je      SHORT $L1202
    cmp     DWORD PTR -8+[ebp], 1000000
    je      SHORT $L1200
    cmp     DWORD PTR -8+[ebp], 10000000
    je      SHORT $L1201
    jmp     SHORT $L1191
$L1209:
    cmp     DWORD PTR -8+[ebp], 1000000000
    je      SHORT $L1203
    jmp     SHORT $L1191
$L1194:
; Line 13
    call    _f
; Line 14
    jmp     SHORT $L1191
$L1195:
; Line 17
    call    _f
; Line 18
    jmp     SHORT $L1191
$L1196:
; Line 21
    call    _f
```

```
; Line 22
    jmp    SHORT $L1191
$L1197:
; Line 25
    call   _f
; Line 26
    jmp    SHORT $L1191
$L1198:
; Line 29
    call   _f
; Line 30
    jmp    SHORT $L1191
$L1199:
; Line 33
    call   _f
; Line 34
    jmp    SHORT $L1191
$L1200:
; Line 37
    call   _f
; Line 38
    jmp    SHORT $L1191
$L1201:
; Line 41
    call   _f
; Line 42
    jmp    SHORT $L1191
$L1202:
; Line 45
    call   _f
; Line 46
    jmp    SHORT $L1191
$L1203:
; Line 49
    call   _f
$L1191:
; Line 53
    xor    eax, eax
; Line 54
    mov    esp, ebp
    pop    ebp
    ret    0
_main   ENDP
_TEXT   ENDS
END
```

Here's the assembly listing VC++ produces when using the command line cl /02 /Fa t.c (/02 enables optimization for speed in Visual C++; see Section 5.4.4.5, "Controlling Compiler Optimization"):

```
TITLE  t.c
    .386P
include listing.inc
```

```
if @Version gt 510
.model FLAT
else
_TEXT      SEGMENT PARA USE32 PUBLIC 'CODE'
_TEXT      ENDS
_DATA      SEGMENT DWORD USE32 PUBLIC 'DATA'
_DATA      ENDS
CONST      SEGMENT DWORD USE32 PUBLIC 'CONST'
CONST      ENDS
_BSS       SEGMENT DWORD USE32 PUBLIC 'BSS'
_BSS       ENDS
_TLS       SEGMENT DWORD USE32 PUBLIC 'TLS'
_TLS       ENDS
;   COMDAT _main
_TEXT      SEGMENT PARA USE32 PUBLIC 'CODE'
_TEXT      ENDS
FLAT       GROUP _DATA, CONST, _BSS
    ASSUME CS: FLAT, DS: FLAT, SS: FLAT
endif
PUBLIC     _main
EXTRN      _f:NEAR
;   COMDAT _main
_TEXT      SEGMENT
_argc$ = 8
_main      PROC NEAR
; File t.c
; Line 7
    mov     eax, DWORD PTR _argc$[esp-4]
    cmp     eax, 100000
    jg      SHORT $L548
    je      SHORT $L534
    cmp     eax, 100
    jg      SHORT $L549
    je      SHORT $L534
    dec     eax
    je      SHORT $L534
    sub     eax, 9
    jne     SHORT $L531
; Line 45
    call    _f
; Line 49
    xor     eax, eax
; Line 50
    ret     0
$L549:
; Line 7
    cmp     eax, 1000
    je      SHORT $L534
    cmp     eax, 10000
    jne     SHORT $L531
; Line 45
    call    _f
; Line 49
    xor     eax, eax
```

```
; Line 50
    ret    0
$L548:
; Line 7
    cmp    eax, 100000000
    jg     SHORT $L550
    je     SHORT $L534
    cmp    eax, 1000000
    je     SHORT $L534
    cmp    eax, 10000000
    jne    SHORT $L531
; Line 45
    call   _f
; Line 49
    xor    eax, eax
; Line 50
    ret    0
$L550:
; Line 7
    cmp    eax, 1000000000
    jne    SHORT $L531
$L534:
; Line 45
    call   _f
$L531:
; Line 49
    xor    eax, eax
; Line 50
    ret    0
_main   ENDP
_TEXT   ENDS
END
```

It doesn't take a very sharp eye to notice that the two assembly language output files are radically different. Running them through diff simply produces a lot of noise:[3]

```
17,19d16
< ; COMDAT _main
< _TEXT SEGMENT PARA USE32 PUBLIC 'CODE'
< _TEXT ENDS
25d21
< ; COMDAT _main
28c24
< _main PROC NEAR
---
```

---

[3] For those unfamiliar with the output of a Unix diff program, just note that those lines beginning with "<" are coming from one file, and those beginning with ">" come from the other file you specify. The exact meaning of all these lines is not important; what is important is that if there is a lot of output from the diff program, there are a lot of differences between the two files. If the two files are identical, diff produces no output at all. So we can use the amount of output from diff as a rough metric of the number of differences.

```
>  _main PROC NEAR
29a26,29
>  ; Line 7
>      push    ebp
>      mov ebp, esp
>      sub esp, 8
31,42c31,67
<      mov eax, DWORD PTR _argc$[esp-4]
<      cmp eax, 100000
<      jg  SHORT $L1242
<      je  SHORT $L1228
<      cmp eax, 100
<      jg  SHORT $L1243
<      je  SHORT $L1228
<      dec eax
<      je  SHORT $L1228
<      sub eax, 9
<      jne SHORT $L1225
<      ; Line 49
---
>      mov eax, DWORD PTR _argc$[ebp]
>      mov DWORD PTR -8+[ebp], eax
>      cmp DWORD PTR -8+[ebp], 100000
>      jg  SHORT $L1207
>      cmp DWORD PTR -8+[ebp], 100000
>      je  $L1199
>      cmp DWORD PTR -8+[ebp], 100
>      jg  SHORT $L1208
>      cmp DWORD PTR -8+[ebp], 100
>      je  SHORT $L1196
>      cmp DWORD PTR -8+[ebp], 1
>      je  SHORT $L1194
>      cmp DWORD PTR -8+[ebp], 10
>      je  SHORT $L1195
>      jmp $L1191
>  $L1208:
>      cmp DWORD PTR -8+[ebp], 1000
>      je  SHORT $L1197
>      cmp DWORD PTR -8+[ebp], 10000
>      je  SHORT $L1198
>      jmp SHORT $L1191
>  $L1207:
>      cmp DWORD PTR -8+[ebp], 100000000
>      jg  SHORT $L1209
>      cmp DWORD PTR -8+[ebp], 100000000
>      je  SHORT $L1202
>      cmp DWORD PTR -8+[ebp], 1000000
>      je  SHORT $L1200
>      cmp DWORD PTR -8+[ebp], 10000000
>      je  SHORT $L1201
>      jmp SHORT $L1191
>  $L1209:
>      cmp DWORD PTR -8+[ebp], 1000000000
>      je  SHORT $L1203
>      jmp SHORT $L1191
```

```
>  $L1194:
>  ; Line 13
44,54c69,72
<  ; Line 53
<    xor eax, eax
<  ; Line 54
<    ret 0
<  $L1243:
<  ; Line 11
<    cmp eax, 1000
<    je  SHORT $L1228
<    cmp eax, 10000
<    jne SHORT $L1225
<  ; Line 49
---
>  ; Line 14
>    jmp SHORT $L1191
>  $L1195:
>  ; Line 17
56,69c74,77
<  ; Line 53
<    xor eax, eax
<  ; Line 54
<    ret 0
<  $L1242:
<  ; Line 11
<    cmp eax, 100000000
<    jg  SHORT $L1244
<    je  SHORT $L1228
<    cmp eax, 1000000
<    je  SHORT $L1228
<    cmp eax, 10000000
<    jne SHORT $L1225
<  ; Line 49
---
>  ; Line 18
>    jmp SHORT $L1191
>  $L1196:
>  ; Line 21
71,79c79,111
<  ; Line 53
<    xor eax, eax
<  ; Line 54
<    ret 0
<  $L1244:
<  ; Line 11
<    cmp eax, 1000000000
<    jne SHORT $L1225
<  $L1228:
---
>  ; Line 22
>    jmp SHORT $L1191
>  $L1197:
>  ; Line 25
>    call    _f
```

```
> ; Line 26
>     jmp SHORT $L1191
> $L1198:
> ; Line 29
>     call    _f
> ; Line 30
>     jmp SHORT $L1191
> $L1199:
> ; Line 33
>     call    _f
> ; Line 34
>     jmp SHORT $L1191
> $L1200:
> ; Line 37
>     call    _f
> ; Line 38
>     jmp SHORT $L1191
> $L1201:
> ; Line 41
>     call    _f
> ; Line 42
>     jmp SHORT $L1191
> $L1202:
> ; Line 45
>     call    _f
> ; Line 46
>     jmp SHORT $L1191
> $L1203:
82c114
< $L1225:
---
> $L1191:
85a118,119
>     mov esp, ebp
>     pop ebp
```

Unfortunately, because nearly every line is marked as either an insertion or deletion, diff's output is more difficult to interpret than manually comparing the two assembly language output files.

A differencing program like diff (or better yet, the differencing facility built into many advanced programming editors) is useful for comparing two different outputs for a given HLL source file when you've made a small change to the source file. In the current example, if the statement case 1000: was changed to case 1001:, a diff of the resulting assembly file against the original will produce the following output:

```
50c50
< cmp eax, 1000

---

> cmp eax, 1001
```

As long as you are comfortable reading diff output, this isn't too bad (though the differencing feature found in advanced programming editors, or a utility like Beyond Compare or Araxis Merge, will still do a better job).

6.6.2 *Manual Comparison*

For nontrivial differences, the best way to compare compiler output is manually. Set the two listings side by side (either on paper or on your monitor), and start analyzing the two. In the current C example, if you compare the two different outputs from the C compiler (without optimization and with the /02 optimization option), you'll discover that both versions use a binary search algorithm to compare the switch value against a list of widely varying constants. The main difference between the optimized and unoptimized versions has to do with code duplication. In the unoptimized version, you see separate calls to the function f throughout the assembly listing. For example:

```
$L1198:
; Line 29
    call    _f
; Line 30
    jmp     SHORT $L1191
$L1199:
; Line 33
    call    _f
; Line 34
    jmp     SHORT $L1191
$L1200:
; Line 37
    call    _f
; Line 38
    jmp     SHORT $L1191
```

The version of this code produced with the /02 optimization command-line option recognizes that these code sequences are semantically identical and folds many of them into the same sequence:

```
$L534:
; Line 45
    call    _f
$L531:
; Line 49
    xor     eax, eax
; Line 50
    ret     0
```

The compiler doesn't combine them all into a single section because the /O2 compiler option tells Microsoft's VC++ to optimize for speed, even at the expense of space. If you specify the /O1 command-line option, VC++ will optimize for space (even at the expense of speed), and it will fold all of the calls to function f() into a single instruction sequence.

Of course, in order to properly compare two assembly listings that a compiler produces, you're going to need to learn how to interpret the assembly language code that the compiler emits and connect certain assembly language sequences with the statements in your HLL code. That's the purpose of many of the following chapters in this book—to teach you how to interpret the machine language output from your compilers.

6.7 For More Information

Your compiler's manual is the first place to look when you're trying to figure out how to view the machine code the compiler produces. Many compilers produce assembly language output as an option, and that's the best way to view code produced by your compiler. If your compiler does not provide an option to emit assembly code, a debugging tool built into the compiler's IDE (if available) is another good choice. See your compiler's or IDE's documentation for details.

Tools like objdump.exe and dumpbin.exe are also useful for examining compiler output. Check the Microsoft or FSF/GNU documentation for details on using these programs. If you decide to use an external debugger, such as OllyDbg or GDB, check out the software's user documentation, or visit the author's support web page (e.g., http://home.t-online.de/home/Ollydbg for the OllyDbg debugger).

7

CONSTANTS AND HIGH-LEVEL LANGUAGES

Some programmers may not realize it, but many CPUs do not treat constant and variable data identically at the machine-code level. Most CPUs provide a special *immediate addressing mode* that lets a language translator incorporate a constant value directly into a machine instruction rather than storing that constant's value in a memory location and accessing it as a variable. However, the ability to represent constant data efficiently varies by CPU and, in fact, by the type of the data. By understanding how a CPU represents constants at the machine-code level, you can appropriately represent constants in your HLL source code to produce smaller and faster executable programs. To that end, this chapter discusses the following topics:

- How to use literal constants properly to improve the efficiency of your programs
- The difference between a literal constant and a manifest constant
- How compilers process compile-time constant expressions to reduce program size and avoid runtime calculations

- The difference between a compile-time constant and read-only data kept in memory
- How compilers represent noninteger constants, such as enumerated data types, Boolean data types, floating-point constants, and string constants
- How compilers represent composite data type constants, such as array constants and record/struct constants.

By the time you finish this chapter, you should have a clear understanding of how the use of various constants can affect the efficiency of the machine code your compiler produces.

NOTE *If you've already read* Write Great Code, Volume 1: Understanding the Machine, *you may want to skim through this chapter, which for the sake of completeness repeats some of the information from Chapters 6 and 7 of Volume 1.*

7.1 Literal Constants and Program Efficiency

High-level programming languages and most modern CPUs allow you to specify constant values just about anywhere you can legally read the value of a memory variable. Consider the following Visual Basic and HLA statements that assign the constant 1,000 to the variable i:

```
i = 1000

mov( 1000, i );
```

The 80x86, like most CPUs, encodes the constant representation for 1,000 directly into the machine instruction. This provides a compact and efficient way to work with constants at the machine level. Therefore, statements that use literal constants in this manner are often more efficient that those that assign constant values to some variable and then reference that variable later in the code. Consider the following Visual Basic code sequence:

```
oneThousand = 1000
    .
    .
    .
x = x + oneThousand 'Using "oneThousand" rather than
                    ' a literal constant.
y = y + 1000        'Using a literal constant.
```

Now consider the 80x86 assembly code you would probably write for these last two statements. For the first statement, you must use two instructions because you cannot directly add the value of one memory location to another:

```
mov( oneThousand, eax ); // x = x + oneThousand
add( eax, x );
```

But you can add a constant to a memory location, so the second Visual Basic statement translates to a single machine instruction:

```
add( 1000, y ); // y = y + 1000
```

As you can see, using a literal constant, rather than a variable, is more efficient. You should not, however, get the impression that every processor operates more efficiently using literal constants, or that every CPU operates more efficiently no matter what the value of the constant. Some very old CPUs don't provide the ability to embed literal constants within a machine instruction. Many RISC processors, such as the PowerPC, provide this facility only for smaller 8-bit or 16-bit constants. Even those CPUs that allow you to load any integer constant may not support literal floating-point constants; the ubiquitous 80x86 processor provides an example of such a CPU. Few CPUs provide the ability to encode large data structures (such as an array, record, or string) as part of a machine instruction. For example, consider the following C code:

```
#include <stdlib.h>
#include <stdio.h >
int main( int argc, char **argv, char **envp )
{
  int i,j,k;

  i = 1;
  j = 16000;
  k = 100000;
  printf( "%d, %d, %d\n", i, j, k );

}
```

Its compilation to PowerPC assembly by the GCC compiler looks like this (edited to remove the code of no interest to this example):

```
L1$pb:
    mflr r31
    stw r3,120(r30)
    stw r4,124(r30)
    stw r5,128(r30)

; The following two instructions copy the value 1 into the variable "i"

    li r0,1
    stw r0,64(r30)

; The following two instructions copy the value 16,000 into the variable "j"

    li r0,16000
    stw r0,68(r30)

; It takes three instructions to copy the value 100,000 into variable "k"
```

```
lis r0,0x1
ori r0,r0,34464
stw r0,72(r30)

; The following code sets up and calls the printf function:

addis r3,r31,ha16(LC0-L1$pb)
la r3,lo16(LC0-L1$pb)(r3)
lwz r4,64(r30)
lwz r5,68(r30)
lwz r6,72(r30)
bl L_printf$stub
mr r3,r0
lwz r1,0(r1)
lwz r0,8(r1)
mtlr r0
lmw r30,-8(r1)
blr
```

The PowerPC CPU allows only 16-bit immediate constants in a single instruction. In order to load a larger value into a register, the program has to first use the lis instruction to load the HO 16 bits of a 32-bit register and then merge in the LO 16 bits using the ori instruction. The exact operation of these instructions isn't too important. What you should note is that the compiler emits three instructions for large constants and only two for smaller constants. Therefore, using 16-bit constant values on the PowerPC produces shorter and faster machine code.

Even though CISC processors like the 80x86 can usually encode any constant (up to the register's maximum size) in a single instruction, don't get the impression that the program's efficiency is independent of the sizes of the constants you use in your programs. CISC processors often use different encodings for machine instructions that have large or small immediate operands, allowing the program to use less memory for smaller constants. For example, consider the following two 80x86/HLA machine instructions:

```
add( 5, ebx );
add( 500_000, ebx );
```

On the 80x86 an assembler can encode the first instruction in 3 bytes: 2 bytes for the opcode and addressing mode information, and 1 byte to hold the small immediate constant. The second instruction, on the other hand, requires 6 bytes to encode: 2 bytes for the opcode and addressing mode information, and 4 bytes to hold the constant 500,000. Certainly the second instruction is larger, and in some cases it may even run a little slower.

7.2 Literal Constants Versus Manifest Constants

A *manifest constant* is a constant value associated with a symbolic name. A language translator can directly substitute the value everywhere the name appears within the source code. Manifest constants allow programmers to attach meaningful names to constant values so you can create easy-to-read and easily maintained programs. The proper use of manifest constants is a good indication of professionally written code.

Declaring manifest constants is easy in many programming languages:

- Pascal programmers use the `const` section.
- HLA programmers can use the `const` or the `val` declaration sections.
- C/C++ programmers can use the `#define` macro facility.

Here is a Pascal code fragment that demonstrates an appropriate use of manifest constants in a program:

```
const
    maxIndex = 9;

var
    a :array[0..maxIndex] of integer;
        .
        .
        .
    for i := 0 to maxIndex do
        a[i] := 0;
```

This code is much easier to read and maintain than code that uses literal constants. By changing a single statement in this program (the `maxIndex` constant declaration) and recompiling the source file, you can easily set the number of elements and the program will continue to function properly.

Because the compiler substitutes the literal numeric constant in place of the symbolic name for the manifest constant, there is no performance penalty when using manifest constants. Because manifest constants improve the readability of your programs without any loss in efficiency, they are an important component of great code. Use them.

7.3 Constant Expressions

Many compilers have the ability to compute the value of a constant expression during compilation. A *constant expression* is one whose component values are all known at compile time, so the compiler can compute the result of the expression and substitute its value at compile time rather than computing its value at runtime. Support for compile-time constant expressions is an important tool that you can use to write readable and maintainable code, without any runtime efficiency loss.

For example, consider the following C code:

```
#define smArraySize 128
#define bigArraySize (smArraySize * 8)
        .
        .
        .
char name[ smArraySize ];
int  values[ bigArraySize ];
```

These two array declarations expand to the following:

```
char name[ 128 ];
int  values[ (smArraySize * 8) ];
```

The C preprocessor further expands this to

```
char name[ 128 ];
int  values[ (128 * 8) ];
```

C compilers allow the use of constant expressions anywhere a simple constant is legal. The compiler will compute an expression like 128 * 8 at compile time and substitute the result (1,024) for the expression.

Although the C language definition supports constant expressions, this feature is not available in every language. You will have to check the language reference manual for your particular compiler to determine whether it supports compile-time constant expression evaluation. The Pascal language definition, for example, says nothing about constant expressions. Some Pascal implementations support compile-time constant expression calculations, but others do not.

Modern optimizing compilers are capable of computing constant subexpressions within arithmetic expressions at compile time, thereby saving the expense of computing fixed values at runtime. Consider the following Pascal code:

```
var
    i   :integer;
        .
        .
        .
    i := j + ( 5 * 2 - 3 );
```

Any decent Pascal implementation is going to recognize that the subexpression 5 * 2 - 3 is a constant expression, compute the value for this expression during compilation (7), and substitute the result at compile time. In other words, a good Pascal compiler generally emits machine code that is equivalent to the following statement:

```
    i := j + 7;
```

If your particular compiler fully supports constant expressions, you can use this feature to help you write better source code. It may seem somewhat of a paradox, but often writing out a full expression at some point in your program can sometimes make that particular piece of code easier to read and understand. This is because the person reading your code can see exactly how you calculated a value in the first place (rather than having to figure out how you arrived at some "magic" number). For example, in the context

of an invoicing or timesheet routine, the expression 5 * 2 - 3 might better
describe the computation "two men working for five hours, minus three man-
hours provided for the job" better than the literal constant 7.

Here is some sample C code and the PowerPC output produced by the
GCC compiler that demonstrates constant expression optimization in action:

```c
#include <stdlib.h>
int main( int argc, char **argv, char **envp )
{
  int j;

  j = argc + 2 * 5 + 1;
  printf( "%d\n", j, argc );

}
```

GCC output (PowerPC assembly language):

```
_main:
    mflr r0
    mr r4,r3            // Register r3 holds the ARGC value upon entry
    bcl 20,31,L1$pb
L1$pb:
    mr r5,r4            // R5 now contains the ARGC value.
    mflr r10
    addi r4,r4,11       // R4 contains argc + 2 * 5 + 1
                        // (i.e., argc + 11)
    mtlr r0             // Code that calls the printf function.
    addis r3,r10,ha16(LC0-L1$pb)
    la r3,lo16(LC0-L1$pb)(r3)
    b L_printf$stub
```

As you can see in this example, GCC has replaced the constant expression
2 * 5 + 1 with the constant 11.

Making your code more readable is definitely a good thing to do and
a major component of writing great code; however, do keep in mind that
some compilers may not support the computation of constant expressions
at compile time but instead emit code to compute the constant value at
runtime. Obviously, this will affect the size and execution speed of your
resulting program. Knowing what your compiler can do will help you
decide whether to use constant expressions or precompute expressions to
increase efficiency at the cost of readability.

7.4 Manifest Constants Versus Read-Only Memory Objects

C++ programmers may have noticed that the previous section did not discuss
the use of C++ const declarations. This is because symbols you declare in a
C++ const statement aren't necessarily manifest constants. That is, C++ does
not always substitute the value for a symbol wherever it appears in a source

file. Instead, C++ compilers may store that const value in memory and then reference the const object as it would a static variable. The only difference, then, between that const object and a static variable is that the C++ compiler doesn't allow you to assign a value to the const object at runtime.

C++ sometimes treats constants you declare in const statements as read-only variables for a very good reason—it allows you to create local constants within a function that can actually have a different value each time the function executes (although while the function is executing, the value remains fixed). Therefore, you cannot always use such "constants" within constant expressions in C++ and expect the C++ compiler to precompute the expression's value.

Most C++ compilers will accept this:

```
const int arraySize = 128;
    .
    .
    .
int anArray[ arraySize ];
```

They will not, however, accept this sequence:

```
const int arraySizes[2] = {128,256}; //This is legal
const int arraySize = arraySizes[0]; // This is also legal

int array[ arraySize ]; // This is not legal
```

arraySize and arraySizes are both constants. Yet the C++ compiler will not allow you to use the arraySizes constant, or anything based on arraySizes, as an array bound. This is because arraySizes[0] is actually a runtime memory location and, therefore, arraySize must also be a runtime memory location. In theory, you'd think the compiler would be smart enough to figure out that arraySize is computable at compile time (128) and just substitute that value. The C++ language, however, doesn't allow this.

7.5 Enumerated Types

Well-written programs often use a set of names to represent real-world quantities that don't have an explicit numeric representation. An example of such a set of names might be various display technologies, like *crt, lcd, led,* and *plasma.* Even though the real world doesn't associate numeric values with these concepts, you must encode the values numerically if you're going to represent them in a computer system. The internal value associated with each symbol is generally arbitrary, as long as we associate a unique value with each symbol. Many computer languages provide a facility known as the *enumerated data type* that will automatically associate a unique value with each name in a list. By using enumerated data types in your programs, you can assign meaningful names to your data rather than using "magic" numbers such as 0, 1, 2, etc.

For example, in early versions of the C language, you would create a sequence of identifiers, each with a unique value, using a sequence like the following:

```
/*
   Define a set of symbols representing the
   different display technologies
*/

#define crt 0
#define lcd (crt + 1)
#define led (lcd + 1)
#define plasma (led + 1)
```

By assigning consecutive values to each of these symbolic constants, you ensure that they each have a unique value. Another advantage to this approach is that it orders the values: crt < lcd < led < plasma. Unfortunately, creating manifest constants this way is laborious and error-prone.

Fortunately, most languages provide *enumerated constants* to solve this problem. To "enumerate" means to count, that is exactly what the compiler does—it numbers each symbol. Therefore, the compiler handles the book-keeping details of assigning values to enumerated constants.

Most modern programming languages provide support for declaring enumerated types and constants. Here are some examples from C/C++, Pascal, and HLA:

```
typedef displays enum{crt, lcd, led, plasma}; // C++
type displays = (crt, lcd, led, plasma);       // Pascal
type displays :enum{crt, lcd, led, plasma};    // HLA
```

These three examples associate 0 with crt, 1 with lcd, 2 with led, and 3 with plasma. In theory, the exact internal representation is irrelevant (as long as each value is unique) because the only purpose of the value is to differentiate the enumerated objects.

Most languages assign *monotonically increasing values* (each successive value is greater than all previous values) to symbols appearing in an enumerated list. Therefore, in these examples, the following relations exist:

```
crt < lcd < led < plasma
```

Although a compiler will assign a unique value to each symbol appearing in a given enumeration list, don't get the impression that all enumerated constants appearing in a single program have a unique internal representation. Most compilers assign a value of zero to the first member in an enumeration list you create, a value of one to the second, and so on. For example, consider the following Pascal type declarations:

```
type
    colors = (red, green, blue);
    fasteners = (bolt, nut, screw, rivet);
```

Most Pascal compilers would use the value zero as the internal representation for both red and bolt; they would use one as the internal representation for green and nut; and so on. In languages (like Pascal) that enforce type checking, you generally cannot use symbols of type colors and fasteners in the same expression. Therefore, the fact that these symbols share the same internal representation is not an issue because the compiler's type-checking facilities preclude a possible confusion. Some languages, like C/C++ and assembly, do not provide strong type checking and so this kind of confusion is possible. It is the programmer's responsibility to avoid mixing different types of enumeration constants in an expression in such languages.

Most compilers will allocate the smallest unit of memory the CPU can efficiently access in order to represent an enumerated type. Because most enumerated type declarations define fewer than 256 symbols, compilers on machines that can efficiently access byte data will usually allocate a byte for any variable whose type is an enumerated data type. Compilers on many RISC machines can allocate a double word (or more) simply because it's faster to access such blocks of data. The exact representation is language and compiler/implementation dependent; you'll have to check your compiler's reference manual for the details.

7.6 Boolean Constants

Many high-level programming languages provide *Boolean* or *logical* constants that let you represent the values True and False. Because there are only two possible Boolean values, their representation requires only a single bit. However, because most CPUs do not allow you to allocate a single bit of storage, most programming languages use a whole byte or even a larger object to represent a Boolean value. What happens to any leftover bits in a Boolean object? Unfortunately, the answer varies by language.

Many languages treat the Boolean data type as an enumerated type. For example, in Pascal, the Boolean type is defined this way:

```
type
    boolean = (false, true);
```

This declaration associates the internal value zero with false and one with true. This association has a couple of desirable attributes:

- Most of the Boolean functions and operators behave as expected—for example, (True and True) = True, (True and False) = False, and so on.

- False is less than True when comparing the two values, an intuitive result.

Unfortunately, associating zero with False and one with True isn't always the best solution. Here are some reasons why:

- Certain Boolean operations, applied to a bit string, do not produce expected results. For example, you might expect (not False) to be equal to True. However, if you store a Boolean variable in an 8-bit object, then (not False) is equal to $FF, which is not equal to True (one).

- Many CPUs provide instructions that easily test for zero or nonzero after an operation; few CPUs provide an implicit test for one.

Many languages, such as C, C++, C#, and Java, treat zero as False and anything else as True. This has a couple of advantages:

- CPUs that provide easy checks for zero/nonzero can easily test a Boolean result.
- The zero/nonzero representation is valid regardless of the size of the object holding a Boolean variable.

Unfortunately, this scheme also has some drawbacks:

- Many bitwise logical operations produce incorrect results when applied to zero/nonzero Boolean values. For example $A5 (True/nonzero) AND $5A (True/nonzero) is equal to zero (False). Logically ANDing True and True should not produce False. Similarly, (NOT $A5) produces $5A. Generally, you'd expect (NOT True) to produce False rather than True ($5A).
- When a bit string is treated as a two's-complement signed-integer value, it is possible for certain values of True to be less than zero (e.g., the 8-bit value $FF is equivalent to –1, which is less than zero). So, in some cases, the intuitive result that False is less than True may not be correct.

Unless you are working in assembly language (where you get to define the values for True and False), you'll have to live with whatever scheme your HLL uses to represent True and False as explained in its language reference manual.

Knowing how your language represents Boolean values can help you write high-level source code that produces better machine code. For example, suppose you are writing C/C++ code. In these languages, False is zero and True is anything else. Consider the following statement in C:

```
int i, j, k;
    .
    .
    .
  i = j && k;
```

The machine code produced for this assignment statement by many compilers is absolutely horrid. It often looks like the following (Visual C++ output):

```
        mov     eax, DWORD PTR _j$[esp-4]
        test    eax, eax
        je      SHORT $L966
        mov     eax, DWORD PTR _k$[esp-4]
        test    eax, eax
        je      SHORT $L966
        mov     eax, 1
$L966:  mov     DWORD PTR _i$[esp-4], eax
```

Now, suppose that you always ensure that you use the values zero for False and one for True (with no possibility of any other value). Under these conditions, you could write the previous statement this way:

```
i = j & k;   /* Notice the bitwise AND operator */
```

Here's the code that Visual C++ generates for the statement above:

```
mov     eax, DWORD PTR _j$[esp-4]
and     eax, DWORD PTR _k$[esp-4]
mov     DWORD PTR _i$[esp-4], eax
```

As you can see, this code is significantly better. Provided that you always use one for True and zero for False, you can get away with using the bitwise AND (&) and OR (|) operators in place of the logical operators. As noted earlier, you cannot use the bitwise NOT operator and get consistent results, but you can do the following to produce correct results for a logical NOT operation:

```
i = ~j & 1; /* "~" is C's bitwise not operator */
```

This short sequence inverts all the bits in j and then clears all bits except bit zero.

The bottom line is that you should be intimately aware of how your particular compiler represents Boolean constants. If you're given a choice (such as any nonzero value) of what values you can use for True and False, then you can pick appropriate values to help your compiler emit better code.

7.7 Floating-Point Constants

Floating-point constants are special cases on most computer architectures. Because floating-point representations can consume a large number of bits, few CPUs provide an immediate addressing mode to load a constant into a floating-point register. This is true even for small (32-bit) floating-point constants. It is even true on many CISC processors such as the 80x86. Therefore, compilers often have to place floating-point constants in memory and then have the program read them from memory, just as though they were variables. Consider, for example, the following C program:

```
#include <stdlib.h>
#include <stdio.h >
int main( int argc, char **argv, char **envp )
{
  static int j;
  static double i = 1.0;
  static double a[8] = {0,1,2,3,4,5,6,7};

  j = 0;
```

```
    a[j] = i + 1.0;


}
```

Now consider the PowerPC code that GCC generates for this program with the -02 option:

```
.lcomm _j.0,4,2
.data

// This is the variable i.
// As it is a static object, GCC emits the data directly
// for the variable in memory. Note that "1072693248" is
// the HO 32 bits of the double-precision floating-point
// value 1.0, 0 is the LO 32 bits of this value (in integer
// form).

    .align 3
_i.1:
    .long       1072693248
    .long       0

// Here is the "a" array. Each pair of double words below
// holds one element of the array. The funny integer values
// are the integer (bitwise) representation of the values
// 0.0, 1.0, 2.0, 3.0, ..., 7.0.

    .align 3
_a.2:
    .long       0
    .long       0
    .long       1072693248
    .long       0
    .long       1073741824
    .long       0
    .long       1074266112
    .long       0
    .long       1074790400
    .long       0
    .long       1075052544
    .long       0
    .long       1075314688
    .long       0
    .long       1075576832
    .long       0

// The following is a memory location that GCC uses to represent
// the literal constant 1.0. Note that these 64 bits match the
// same value as a[1] in the _a.2 array. GCC uses this memory
// location whenever it needs the constant 1.0 in the program.

.literal8
```

```
        .align 3
LC0:
        .long      1072693248
        .long      0
```

// Here's the start of the main program:

```
.text
    .align 2
    .globl _main
_main:
```

// This code sets up the static pointer register (R10), used to
// access the static variables in this program.

```
    mflr r0
    bcl 20,31,L1$pb
L1$pb:
    mflr r10
    mtlr r0
```

```
    // Load floating-point register F13 with the value
    // in variable "i":

    addis r9,r10,ha16(_i.1-L1$pb)  // Point R9 at i
    li r0,0
    lfd f13,lo16(_i.1-L1$pb)(r9)   // Load F13 with i's value.

    // Load floating-point register F0 with the constant 1.0
    // (which is held in "variable" LC0:

    addis r9,r10,ha16(LC0-L1$pb)  // Load R9 with the
                                  //  address of LC0
    lfd f0,lo16(LC0-L1$pb)(r9)    // Load F0 with the value
                                  //  of LC0 (1.0).

    addis r9,r10,ha16(_j.0-L1$pb)  // Load R9 with j's address
    stw r0,lo16(_j.0-L1$pb)(r9)    // Store a zero into j.

    addis r9,r10,ha16(_a.2-L1$pb)  // Load a[j]'s address into R9

    fadd f13,f13,f0               // Compute i + 1.0

    stfd f13,lo16(_a.2-L1$pb)(r9) // Store sum into a[j]
    blr                          // Return to caller
```

Because the PowerPC processor is a RISC CPU, the code that GCC generates for this simple sequence is rather convoluted. For comparison with a CISC equivalent, consider the following HLA code for the 80x86; it is a line-by-line translation of the C code:

```
program main;
static
    j:int32;
```

```
    i:real64 := 1.0;
    a:real64[8] := [0,1,2,3,4,5,6,7];

readonly
    OnePointZero : real64 := 1.0;

begin main;

    mov( 0, j );  // j = 0;

    // push i onto the floating-point stack

    fld( i );

    // push the value 1.0 onto the floating-point stack

    fld( OnePointZero );

    // pop i and 1.0, add them, push sum onto the FP stack

    fadd();

    // use j as an index

    mov( j, ebx );

    // Pop item off FP stack and store into a[j].

    fstp( a[ ebx*8 ] );

end main;
```

This code is much easier to follow than the PowerPC code (this is one advantage of CISC code over RISC code). You'll note that like the PowerPC, the 80x86 does not support an immediate addressing mode for floating-point operands. Therefore, as on the PowerPC, you have to place a copy of the constant 1.0 in some memory location and access that memory location whenever you want to work with the value 1.0.[1]

Because most modern CPUs do not support an immediate addressing mode for floating-point constants, using such constants in your programs is equivalent to accessing variables initialized with those constants. Don't forget that accessing memory can be very slow if the locations you're referencing are not in the data cache. Therefore, using floating-point constants can be very slow, compared with accessing integer or other constant values that fit within a register.

On 32-bit processors, a CPU can often do simple 32-bit floating-point operations using integer registers and the immediate addressing mode. For example, assigning a 32-bit single-precision floating-point value to a variable

---

[1] Actually, HLA does allow you to specify an instruction like fld(1.0);. However, this is not a real CPU instruction. HLA will simply create a constant for you in the read-only data section and load a copy of that value from memory when you execute the fld instruction.

is easily accomplished by loading a 32-bit integer register with the bit pattern for that number and then storing the integer register into the floating-point variable. Consider the following code:

```
#include <stdlib.h>
#include <stdio.h >
int main( int argc, char **argv, char **envp )
{

  static float i;

  i = 1.0;


}
```

Here's the PowerPC code that GCC generates for this sequence:

```
.lcomm _i.0,4,2 // Allocate storage for float variable i

.text
    .align 2
    .globl _main
_main:

    // Set up the static data pointer in R10:

    mflr r0
    bcl 20,31,L1$pb
L1$pb:
    mflr r10
    mtlr r0

    // Load the address of i into R9:

    addis r9,r10,ha16(_i.0-L1$pb)

    // Load R0 with the floating-point representation of 1.0
    // (note that 1.0 is equal to 0x3f800000):

    lis r0,0x3f80 // Puts 0x3f80 in HO 16 bits, 0 in LO bits

    // Store 1.0 into variable i:

    stw r0,lo16(_i.0-L1$pb)(r9)

    // Return to whomever called this code:

    blr
```

The 80x86, being a CISC processor, makes this task trivial in assembly language. Here's the HLA code that does the same job:

```
program main;
static
    i:real32;
begin main;

    mov( $3f80_0000, i ); // i = 1.0;
    // (note that 1.0 is equal to $3f80_0000)

end main;
```

Simple assignments of single-precision floating-point constants to floating-point variables can often use a CPU's immediate addressing mode, thereby sparing the program the expense of accessing memory (whose data might not be in the cache). Unfortunately, compilers don't always take advantage of this trick for assigning a floating-point constant to a double-precision variable. GCC on the PowerPC, for example, reverts to keeping a copy of the constant in memory and copying that memory location's value when assigning the constant to a floating-point variable.

Most optimizing compilers are smart enough to maintain a table of constants they've created in memory. Therefore, if you reference the constant 1.0 (or any other floating-point constant) multiple times in your source file, the compiler will allocate only one memory object for that constant. Keep in mind, however, that this optimization only works within the same source file. If you reference the same constant value, but in different source files, the compiler will probably create multiple copies of that constant.

It's certainly true that having multiple copies of the data wastes storage, but given the amount of memory in most modern systems, this is a minor concern. A bigger problem is that the program usually accesses these constants in a random fashion, so they're rarely sitting in cache and, in fact, they often evict some other more-frequently used data from cache.

One solution to this problem is to manage the floating-point constants yourself. Because these constants are effectively variables as far as the program is concerned, you can take charge of this process and place the floating-point constants you'll need in initialized static variables. For example:

```
#include <stdlib.h>
#include <stdio.h >

static double OnePointZero_c = 1.0;

int main( int argc, char **argv, char **envp )
{
```

```
    static double i;

    i = OnePointZero_c;
}
```

In this example, of course, you gain absolutely nothing by treating the floating-point constants as static variables. However, in more complex situations where you have several floating-point constants, you can analyze your program to determine which constants you access often and place the variables for those constants at adjacent memory locations. Because of the way most CPUs handle spatial locality of reference (that is, accessing nearby variables; see *Write Great Code, Volume 1*), when you access one of these constant objects, the cache line will be filled with the values of the adjacent objects as well. Therefore, when you access those other objects within a short period of time, it's likely that their values will be in the cache. Another advantage to managing these constants yourself is that you can create a global set of constants that you can reference from different compilation units (source files), so the program only accesses a single memory object for a given constant rather the multiple memory objects (one for each compilation unit). Compilers generally aren't smart enough to make decisions like this concerning your data.

7.8   String Constants

Like floating-point constants, string constants cannot be processed efficiently by most compilers (even if they are literal or manifest constants). Understanding when you should use manifest constants and when you should replace such constants with memory references can help you guide the compiler to produce better machine code. For example, most CPUs are not capable of encoding a string constant as part of an instruction. Using a manifest string constant may actually make your program less efficient. Consider the following C code:

```
#define strConst "A string constant"
        .
        .
        .
    printf( "string: %s\n", strConst );
        .
        .
        .
    sptr = strConst;
        .
        .
        .
    result = strcmp( s, strConst );
        .
        .
        .
```

The compiler (actually, the C preprocessor) expands the macro strConst to the string literal A string constant everywhere the identifier strConst appears in the source file, so this code is actually equivalent to:

```
        .
        .
        .
printf( "string: %s\n", "A string constant" );
        .
        .
        .
sptr = "A string constant";
        .
        .
        .
result = strcmp( s, "A string constant" );
```

The problem with this code is that the same string constant appears at different places throughout the program. In C/C++, the compiler places the string constant in memory and substitutes a pointer to the string. A non-optimizing compiler might wind up making three separate copies of the string in memory, thereby wasting space because the data is exactly the same in all three cases. (Remember that I am talking about "constant" strings here.)

Compiler writers discovered this problem a few decades ago and modified their compilers to keep track of the strings in a given source file. If a program used the same string literal two or more times, the compiler would not allocate storage for a second copy of the string. Instead, it would simply use the address of the earlier string. Such optimization (*constant folding*) could reduce the size of the code if the same string appeared throughout a source file.

Unfortunately, this optimization doesn't always work properly. A problem with this approach is that many older C programs assign a string literal constant to a character pointer variable and then proceed to change the characters in that literal string. For example:

```
sptr = "A String Constant";
        .
        .
        .
*(sptr+2) = 's';
        .
        .
        .
/* The following displays "string: 'A string Constant'" */

printf( "string: '%s'\n", sptr );
        .
        .
        .
/* This prints "A string Constant"! */

printf( "A String Constant" );
```

Compilers that reuse the same string constant fail if the user stores data into the string object, as this code demonstrates. Although this is bad programming practice, it occurred frequently enough in older C programs that compiler vendors could not use the same storage for multiple copies of the same string literal. Even if the compiler vendor were to place the string literal constant into write-protected memory to prevent this problem, there are other semantic issues that this optimization raise. Consider the following C/C++ code:

```
sptr1 = "A String Constant";
sptr2 = "A String Constant";
s1EQs2 = sptr1 == sptr2;
```

Will s1EQs2 contain True (1) or False (0) after executing this instruction sequence? In programs written before C compilers had good optimizers available, this sequence of statements would leave False in s1EQs2. This was because the compiler created two different copies of the same string data and placed those strings at different addresses in memory (so the addresses the program assigns to sptr1 and sptr2 would be different). In a later compiler, that kept only a single copy of the string data in memory, this code sequence would leave True sitting in s1EQs2 because both sptr1 and sptr2 would be pointing at the same memory address. This difference exists regardless of whether or not the string data appears in write-protected memory.

To solve this dilemma, many compiler vendors provide an option to give the programmer the ability to determine whether the compiler should emit a single copy of each string or one copy for each occurrence of the string. If you don't compare the addresses of string literal constants and you don't write data into string literal constants, then you can disable this option to reduce the size of your programs. If you have old code that requires separate copies of the string data (hopefully, you won't write new code that requires this), then you can enable this option.

A problem is that many programmers are completely unaware of this option, and the default condition (which is the safest assumption) is generally to make multiple copies of the string data. If you're using C/C++ or some other language that manipulates strings via pointers to the character data, you should investigate whether the compiler provides an option to merge identical strings, and if this is not the default, you should activate that feature in your compiler.

If your (C/C++) compiler does not have this string-merging optimization available, you can implement this optimization manually. To do so, just create a char array variable in your program and initialize it with the address of the string. Then use the name of that array variable exactly as you would a manifest constant throughout your program. For example:

```
char strconst[] = "A String Constant";
    .
    .
    .
```

```
sptr = strconst; // Rather than sptr = "A String Constant"
    .
    .
    .
printf( strconst ); // Rather than printf( "A String Constant" );
    .
    .
    .
// Rather than strcmp( someString, "A String Constant"):
if( strcmp( someString, strconst ) == 0 ) {
    .
    .
    .
}
```

This code will maintain only a single copy of the string literal constant in memory, even if the compiler doesn't directly support the string optimization. Even if your compiler directly supports this optimization, there are several good reasons why you should use this trick rather than relying on your compiler's optimization facilities to do the work for you.

- In the future you might have to port your code to a different compiler that doesn't support this optimization.

- By handling the optimization manually, you don't have to worry about it.

- By using a pointer variable rather than a string literal constant, you have the option of easily changing the string whose address this pointer contains under program control

- In the future you might want to modify the program to switch (natural) languages under program control.

This string optimization discussion assumes that your programming language manipulates strings by reference (that is, by using a pointer to the actual string data). Although this is certainly true for C/C++ programs, it is not true of all languages. Pascal implementations that support strings (e.g., Turbo Pascal) typically manipulate strings by value rather than by reference. Any time you assign a string value to a string variable, the compiler makes a copy of the string data and places that copy in the storage reserved for the string variable. This copying process can be expensive and is unnecessary if your program never changes the data in the string variable. Worse still, if the (Pascal) program assigns a string literal to a string variable, the program will have two copies of the string floating around (the string literal constant appearing somewhere in memory and the copy that the program made for the string variable). If the program never again changes the string (which is not at all uncommon), then the program will waste memory by maintaining two copies of the string when one would suffice. These reasons (space and speed) are probably why

Borland went to a much more sophisticated string format when it created Delphi 4.0 and abandoned the string format in earlier versions of Delphi and Turbo Pascal.[2]

7.9 Composite Data Type Constants

Many languages support other composite constant types in addition to strings (e.g., arrays, structures/records, and sets). Usually, the languages use such constants to statically initialize variables prior to the program's execution. For example, consider the following C/C++ code:

```
static int arrayOfInts[8] = {1,2,3,4,5,6,7,8};
```

Note that arrayOfInts is not a constant. Rather, it is the initializer that completes this variable declaration that constitutes the array constant (i.e., {1,2,3,4,5,6,7,8}). In the executable file, most C compilers will simply overlay the eight integers at the address associated with arrayOfInts with these eight numeric values.

For example, here's what GCC emits for this variable:

```
LC0:            // LC0 is the internal label associated
                //  with arrayOfInts
    .long    1
    .long    2
    .long    3
    .long    4
    .long    5
    .long    6
    .long    7
    .long    8
```

There is no extra space consumed to hold the constant data, assuming that arrayOfInts is a static object in C.

The rules change, however, if the variable you're initializing is not a statically allocated object. Consider the following short C sequence:

```
int f()
{
  int arrayOfInts[8] = {1,2,3,4,5,6,7,8};
    .
    .
    .
} // end f()
```

In this example, arrayOfInts is an *automatic* variable, meaning that the program allocates storage on the stack for the variable each time the program calls function f(). For this reason, the compiler cannot simply initialize the array with the constant data when the program loads into memory.

---

[2] "Abandoning" is probably too strong a word here. Borland continued to support the old format by using a different name for the short string data type.

The arrayOfInts object could actually lie at a different address on each activation of the function. In order to obey the semantics of the C programming language, the compiler will have to make a copy of the array constant data and then physically copy that constant data into the arrayOfInts variable whenever the program calls the function. Therefore, using an array constant in this fashion consumes extra space (to hold a copy of the array constant) and extra time (to copy the data). Sometimes the semantics of your algorithm requires a fresh copy of the data upon each new activation of the function f. However, you need to realize when this is necessary (and when the extra space and time are necessary) rather than blowing memory and CPU cycles due to ignorance.

If your program doesn't modify the array's data, you can use a static object that the compiler can initialize once when it loads the program into memory:

```
int f()
{
    static int arrayOfInts[8] = {1,2,3,4,5,6,7,8};
    .
    .
    .
} // end f
```

The C/C++ languages also support struct constants. The same space and speed considerations we've seen for arrays when initializing automatic variables also apply to struct constants.

Borland's Delphi programming language also supports structured constants, though the term *constant* is a bit misleading here. Borland calls these constants "typed constants," and you declare them in the Delphi const section like this:

```
const
    ary: array[0..7] of integer := (1,2,3,4,5,6,7,8);
```

Although these declarations appear in an Object Pascal (Delphi) const section, the truth is that Delphi treats this declaration as a variable declaration. It is unfortunate that Borland chose to use the const section to declare variable objects in this manner, but that's simply a poor programming language design choice. From the perspective of the programmer who wants to create structured constants, this mechanism works fine even if it is a little strange. Like the C/C++ examples in this section, it's important to remember that the constant in this example is actually the (1,2,3,4,5,6,7,8) object, not the ary variable.

Borland's Delphi (along with most modern Pascals) supports several other composite constant types as well. Set constants are good examples. Whenever you create a set of objects, the Pascal compiler will generally initialize some memory location with a *powerset* (bitmap) representation of the set's data. Wherever you refer to that set constant in your program, the Pascal compiler will generate a memory reference to the set's constant data in memory.

7.10 For More Information

To fully appreciate how a CPU encodes constants in machine instructions and how compilers generate code to process those constants, you need to look at the low-level encoding of machine instructions. Most CPU manufacturers provide documentation for their CPU's that discusses this topic. Studying assembly language is another good way to learn how CPUs deal with constant data. My book *The Art of Assembly Language* (No Starch Press, 2003), is a good one to read. Of course, *Write Great Code, Volume 1* also provides a wealth of information on this subject.

8

VARIABLES IN A HIGH-LEVEL LANGUAGE

This chapter will explore the low-level implementation of variables found in high-level languages. Although assembly language programmers usually have a good feel for the connection between variables and memory locations, high-level languages add sufficient abstraction to obscure this relationship. This chapter will cover the following topics:

- The runtime memory organization typical for most compilers
- How the compiler breaks up memory into different sections and how the compiler places variables into each of those sections
- The attributes that differentiate variables from other objects
- The difference between static, automatic, and dynamic variables
- How compilers organize automatic variables in a stack frame
- The primitive data types that hardware provides for variables
- How machine instructions encode the address of a variable

When you finish reading this chapter, you should have a good understanding of how to declare variables in your program to use the least amount of memory and produce fast-running code.

8.1 Runtime Memory Organization

An operating system like Linux or Windows puts different types of data into different areas (*sections* or *segments*) of main memory. Although it is possible to control the memory organization by running a linker and specifying various command-line parameters, by default Windows loads a typical program into memory using the organization appearing in Figure 8-1 (Linux is similar, although it rearranges some of the sections).

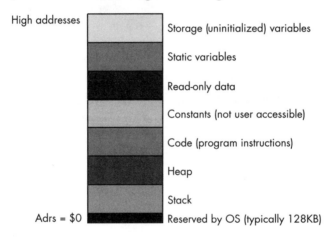

Figure 8-1: Typical runtime memory organization for Windows

The operating system reserves the lowest memory addresses. Generally, your application cannot access data (or execute instructions) at the lowest addresses in memory. One reason the OS reserves this space is to help detect NULL pointer references. Programmers often initialize pointers with NULL (zero) to indicate that the pointer is not valid. Should you attempt to access memory location zero under such an operating system, the OS will generate a *general protection fault* to indicate that you've accessed an invalid memory location.

The remaining six areas in the memory map hold different types of data associated with your program. These sections of memory include the stack section, the heap section, the code section, the constant section, the initialized static-object section, and the uninitialized data section. Each of these memory sections corresponds to some type of data you can create in your programs.

Most of the time, a given application can live with the default layouts chosen for these sections by the compiler and linker/loader. In some cases, however, knowing the memory layout can allow you to develop shorter programs. For example, because the code section is usually read-only, it might be possible to combine the code, constant, and read-only data sections into a single section, thereby saving any padding space that the compiler/linker may place between these sections. Although for large applications this is probably insignificant, for small programs it can have a big impact on the size of the executable.

The following sections discuss each of these sections in detail.

8.1.1 The Code, Constant, and Read-Only Sections

The code section in memory contains the machine instructions for a program. Your compiler translates each statement you write into a sequence of one or more byte values (machine instruction opcodes). The CPU interprets these opcode values during program execution.

Most compilers also attach a program's read-only data and *constant pool* (constant table) sections to the code section because, like the code instructions, the read-only data is already write-protected. However, it is perfectly possible under Windows, Linux, and many other operating systems to create a separate section in the executable file and mark it as read-only. As a result, some compilers do support a separate *read-only* data section, and some compilers even create a different section (the constant pool) for the constants that the compiler emits. Such sections contain initialized data, tables, and other objects that the program should not change during program execution.

Many compilers will generate multiple code sections and leave it up to the linker to combine those sections into a single code segment prior to execution. To understand why a compiler might do this, consider the following short Pascal code fragment:

```
if( SomeBooleanExpression ) then begin

    << Some code that executes 99.9% of the time >>

end
else begin

    << Some code that executes 0.1% of the time >>

end;
```

Without worrying about how it does so, assume that the compiler can figure out that the then section of this if statement executes far more often than the else section. An assembly programmer, wanting to write the fastest possible code, might encode this sequence as follows:

```
<< evaluate Boolean expression, leave True/False in EAX >>
test( eax, eax );
jz exprWasFalse;
<< Some code that executes 99.9% of the time >>
rtnLabel:
<< Code normally following the last END in the
        Pascal example >>
```

```
          .
          .
          .
// somewhere else in the code, not in the direct execution path
// of the above:

exprWasFalse:
    << Some code that executes 0.1% of the time >>

    jmp rtnLabel;
```

This assembly code might seem a bit convoluted, but keep in mind that any control transfer instruction is probably going to consume a lot of time because of pipelined operation on modern CPUs (see *Write Great Code, Volume 1,* for the details). Code that executes without branching (or that *falls straight through*) executes the fastest. In the previous example, the common case falls straight through 99.9 percent of the time. The rare case winds up executing two branches (one to transfer to the else section and one to return back to the normal control flow). But because this code rarely executes, it can afford to take longer to execute.

Many compilers use a little trick to move sections of code around like this in the machine code they generate—they simply emit the code in a sequential fashion, but they place the else code in a separate section. Here's some MASM code that demonstrates this principle in action:

```
    << evaluate Boolean expression, leave True/False in EAX >>
    test eax, eax
    jz exprWasFalse
    << Some code that executes 99.9% of the time >>
alternateCode segment

    << Some code that executes 0.1% of the time >>

    jmp rtnLabel;
alternateCode ends

rtnLabel:
    << Code normally following the last END in the Pascal example >>
```

Even though the else section code appears to immediately follow the then section's code, placing it in a different segment tells the assembler/linker to move this code and combine it with other code in the alternateCode segment. This little trick, which relies upon the assembler or linker to do the code movement, can simplify HLL compilers. GCC, for example, uses this trick to move code around in the assembly language file it emits. As a result, you'll see this trick being used on occasion. Therefore, expect some compilers to produce multiple code segments.

8.1.2 The Static Variables Section

Many languages provide the ability to initialize a global variable during the compilation phase. For example, in the C/C++ language, you could use statements like the following to provide initial values for these static objects:

```
static int i = 10;
static char ch[] = ( 'a', 'b', 'c', 'd' };
```

In C/C++ and other languages, the compiler will place these initial values in the executable file. When you execute the application, the operating system will load the portion of the executable file that contains these static variables into memory so that the values appear at the addresses associated those variables. Therefore, when the program first begins execution, i and ch will magically have these values bound to them.

The static section is often called the DATA or _DATA segment in the assembly listings that most compilers produce. As an example, consider the following C code fragment and the TASM assembly code that the Borland C++ compiler produces for it:

```
#include <stdlib.h>
#include <stdio.h>

static char *c = NULL;
static int i = 0;
static int j = 1;
static double array[4] = {0.0, 1.0, 2.0, 3.0};

int main( void )
{

        .
        .
        .
```

And here's the assembly code emitted by the Borland C++ compiler for the declarations in this C example:

```
_DATA   segment dword public use32 'DATA'
        align   4
_c      label   dword
        dd      0
        align   4
_i      label   dword
        dd      0
        align   4
_j      label   dword
        dd      1
        align   4
```

```
_array    label    qword
          db       0,0,0,0,0,0,0,0
          db       0,0,0,0,0,0,240,63
          db       0,0,0,0,0,0,0,64
          db       0,0,0,0,0,0,8,64
_DATA     ends
```

As you can see in this example, Borland's C++ compiler places these variables in the _DATA segment.

8.1.3   The BSS Section

Most operating systems will *zero out* memory prior to program execution. Therefore, if an initial value of zero is suitable, you don't need to waste any disk space with the static object's initial value. Generally, however, compilers treat uninitialized variables in a static section as though you've initialized them with zero, thereby consuming disk space. Some operating systems provide another section type, the *BSS section,* to avoid this waste of disk space.

The BSS section is where compilers typically put static objects that don't have an explicit initial value. BSS stands for *block started by a symbol,* and it is an old assembly language term describing a pseudo-opcode you would use to allocate storage for an uninitialized static array. In modern operating systems like Windows and Linux, the OS allows the compiler/linker to put all uninitialized variables into a BSS section that simply tells the OS how many bytes to set aside for that section. When the operating system loads the program into memory, it reserves sufficient memory for all the objects in the BSS section and fills this range of memory with zeros. It is important to note that the BSS section in the executable file doesn't contain any actual data. For this reason, programs that declare large uninitialized static arrays in a BSS section will consume less disk space. The following is the C/C++ example from the previous section, modified to remove the initializers so that the compiler will place the variables in the BSS section:

```
#include <stdlib.h>
#include <stdio.h>

static char *c;
static int i;
static int j;
static double array[4];

int main( void )
{
        .
        .
        .
```

Here is the Borland C++ output:

```
_BSS    segment dword public use32 'BSS'
        align   4
_c      label   dword
        db      4       dup(?)
        align   4
_i      label   dword
        db      4       dup(?)
        align   4
_j      label   dword
        db      4       dup(?)
        align   4
_array  label   qword
        db      32      dup(?)
_BSS    ends
```

Not all compilers use a BSS section. Many Microsoft languages and linkers, for example, simply combine the uninitialized objects with the static/data section and explicitly give them an initial value of zero. Although Microsoft claims that this scheme is faster, it certainly makes executable files larger if your code has large, uninitialized arrays (because each byte of the array winds up in the executable file, something that would not happen if the compiler were to place the array in a BSS section). Note, however, that this is a default condition and you can change this by setting the appropriate linker flags.

8.1.4   The Stack Section

The *stack* is a data structure that expands and contracts in response to procedure invocations and returns, among other things. At runtime, the system places all automatic variables (nonstatic local variables), subroutine parameters, temporary values, and other objects in the stack section of memory in a special data structure called the *activation record* (the activation record is aptly named because the system creates an activation record when a subroutine first begins execution and deallocates the activation record when the subroutine returns to its caller). Therefore, the stack section in memory is very busy.

Many CPUs implement the stack using a special-purpose register called the *stack pointer*. Other CPUs (particularly RISC) don't provide an explicit stack pointer and, instead, use a general-purpose register for this purpose. If a CPU provides an explicit stack pointer register, we say that the CPU supports a hardware stack; if a program uses a general-purpose register for this purpose, then we say that the CPU uses a software-implemented stack. The 80x86 is a good example of a CPU that provides a hardware stack—the PowerPC family is a good example of a CPU family that implements the stack in software (most PowerPC programs use R1 as the stack pointer register). Systems that provide hardware stacks can generally manipulate data on the stack using fewer instructions than systems that implement the stack in software. On the other hand, RISC CPU designers who've chosen to use a software stack implementation feel that the presence of a hardware stack actually slows down all instructions the CPU executes. In theory, you could argue that the RISC designers are right; in practice, the 80x86 family includes some of the fastest CPUs around, providing ample proof that having a hardware stack doesn't necessarily mean you'll wind up with a slow CPU.

8.1.5   The Heap Section and Dynamic Memory Allocation

Although simple programs may only need static and automatic variables, sophisticated programs need the ability to allocate and deallocate storage dynamically (at runtime) under program control. In the C and High-Level Assembler (HLA) languages, you would use the malloc and free functions for this purpose. C++ provides the new and delete operators. Pascal uses new and dispose. Other languages provide comparable routines. These memory-allocation routines share a few things in common:

- They let the programmer request how many bytes of storage to allocate.

- They return a *pointer* to the newly allocated storage (that is, the address of that storage).

- They provide a facility for returning the storage space to the system once it is no longer needed so the system can reuse it in a future allocation call.

Dynamic memory allocation takes place in a section of memory known as the *heap*. Generally, an application refers to data on the heap using pointer variables, either implicitly or explicitly; some languages, like Java, implicitly use pointers behind the programmer's back. As such, these objects in heap memory are usually referred to as *anonymous variables* because they are referred to by their memory address (via pointers) rather than by a name.

The OS and application create the heap section in memory after the program begins execution; the heap is never a part of the executable file. Generally, the operating system and language runtime libraries maintain the heap for an application. Despite the variations in memory management implementations, it's still a good idea for you to have a basic idea of how heap allocation and deallocation operate because an inappropriate use of the heap management facilities will have a very negative impact on the performance of your applications.

8.2   What Is a Variable?

If you consider the word *variable*, it should be obvious that it describes something that *varies*. But exactly what is it that varies? To most programmers the answer will seem obvious: it's the value that can vary during program execution. In fact, there are several things that can vary, so before attempting to describe what a variable is, it is probably a good idea to discuss some attributes that variables (and other objects) may possess. To do this, I must first define *attribute, binding, static objects, dynamic objects, scope,* and *lifetime.*

8.2.1 Attributes

An *attribute* is some feature that is associated with an object. For example, common attributes of a variable include that variable's name, its memory address, its runtime value, a data type associated with that value, and the size (in bytes) of that variable. Different objects may have different sets of attributes. For example, a *data type* is an object that possesses attributes such as a name and size, but it won't usually have a value or memory location associated with it. A *constant* can have attributes such as a value and a data type, but it does not have a memory location and it might not have a name (for example, if it is a literal constant). A *variable* may possess all of these attributes. Indeed, the attribute list usually determines whether an object is a constant, data type, variable, or something else.

8.2.2 Binding

Binding is the process of associating an attribute with an object. For example, when a value is assigned to a variable, the value is *bound* to that variable at the point of the assignment. The value remains bound to the variable until some other value is bound to it (via another assignment operation). Likewise, if you allocate memory for a variable while the program is running, the variable is *bound* to the memory address at that point. The variable and address are bound until you associate a different address with the variable. Binding needn't occur at runtime. For example, values are bound to constant objects during compilation, and such bindings cannot change while the program is running. Similarly, some variables can have their address bound to them at compile time, and the memory address cannot change during program execution.

8.2.3 Static Objects

Static objects have an attribute bound to them prior to the execution of the application. Constants are good examples of static objects; they have the same value bound to them throughout the execution of the application. Global (program-level) variables in programming languages like Pascal, C/C++, and Ada are also examples of static objects because they have the same memory address bound to them throughout the program's lifetime. The system binds attributes to a static object before the program begins execution (usually during compilation or during the linking phase, though it is possible to bind values even earlier).

8.2.4 Dynamic Objects

Dynamic objects have some attribute bound to them during program execution. The program may choose to change that attribute (*dynamically*) while the program is running. Dynamic attributes usually cannot be determined at compile time. Examples of dynamic attributes include values bound to variables at runtime and memory addresses bound to certain variables at runtime (e.g., via a *malloc* or other memory allocation function call).

8.2.5 Scope

The *scope* of an identifier is that section of the program where the identifier's name is bound to the object. Because names in most compiled languages exist only during compilation, scope is usually a static attribute (although in some languages it is possible for scope to be a dynamic attribute). By controlling where a name is bound to an object, it is possible to reuse that name elsewhere in the program.

Most modern imperative programming languages (e.g., C/C++/C#, Java, Pascal, and Ada) support the concept of *local* and *global* variables. A local variable's name is bound to a particular object only within a given section of a program (for example, within a particular function). Outside the scope of that object, the name can be bound to a different object. This allows a global and a local object to share the same name without any ambiguity. This may seem potentially confusing, but being able to reuse variable names like i or j throughout a project can spare the programmer from having to dream up equally meaningless unique variable names for loop indexes and other uses in the program. The scope of the object's declaration determines where the name applies to a given object.

In interpretive languages, where the interpreter maintains the identifier names during program execution, scope can be a dynamic attribute. For example, in various versions of the BASIC programming language, the dim statement is an executable statement. Prior to the execution of dim, the name you define might have a completely different meaning than it does after executing dim. SNOBOL4 is another language that supports dynamic scope. Generally, most programming languages avoid dynamic scope because using it can result in difficult-to-understand programs—but the fact that most languages avoid dynamic scope doesn't mean it doesn't exist.

In general, scope can apply to any attribute, not just names. In this book, however, I'll only use the term scope to describe where a name is associated with a given variable.

8.2.6 Lifetime

The *lifetime* of an attribute extends from the point when you first bind an attribute to an object to the point you break that bond, perhaps by binding a different attribute to the object. If the program associates some attribute with an object and never breaks that bond, the lifetime of the attribute is from the point of association to the point the program terminates. For example, the lifetime of a variable is from the time you first allocate memory for the variable to the moment you deallocate that variable's storage. As a program binds static objects prior to execution (and such attributes do not change during program execution), the lifetime of a static object extends from when the program begins execution to when the application terminates.

8.2.7   So What Is a Variable?

A variable is an object that can have a value bound to it dynamically. That is, the program can change the variable's value attribute at runtime. Note the operative word *can*. It is only necessary for the program to be able to change a variable's value at runtime; it doesn't *have* to bind multiple values in order to consider the object a variable.

Dynamic binding of a value to an object is the defining attribute of a variable, though other attributes may be dynamic or static. For example, the memory address of a variable can be statically bound to the variable at compile time or dynamically bound at runtime. Likewise, variables in some languages have dynamic types that change during program execution, while other variables have static types that remain fixed over the execution of a given program. Only the binding of the value determines whether the object is a variable or something else (such as a constant).

8.3   Variable Storage

Values must be stored in and retrieved from memory. To do this, a compiler must bind a variable to one or more memory locations. The variable's type determines the amount of storage it requires. Character variables may require as little as a single byte of storage, while large arrays or records can require thousands or millions of bytes of storage. To associate a variable with some memory, a compiler (or runtime system) binds the address of that memory location to that variable. When a variable requires two or more memory locations, the system will usually bind the address of the first memory location to the variable and assume that the contiguous locations following that address are also bound to the variable at runtime.

Three types of bindings are possible between variables and memory locations: static binding, pseudo-static (automatic) binding, and dynamic binding. Variables are generally classified as *static, automatic*, or *dynamic* based upon how the variable is bound to its memory location.

8.3.1   Static Binding and Static Variables

Static binding occurs prior to runtime, at one of four possible times: at language-design time, at compile time, at link time, or when the system loads the application into memory (but prior to execution). Binding at language design time is not all that common, but it does occur in some languages (especially assembly languages). Binding at compile time is common in assemblers and compilers that directly produce executable code. Binding at link time is fairly common (for example, some Windows compilers do this). Binding at load time, when the operating system copies the executable into memory, is probably the most common for static variables.

8.3.1.1 Binding at Language-Design Time

An address can be assigned at language-design time when a language designer associates a language-defined variable with a specific hardware address (for example, an I/O device or a special kind of memory), and that address never changes in any program. Such objects are common in embedded systems and rarely found in applications on general-purpose computer systems. For example, on an 8051 microcontroller, many C compilers and assemblers automatically associate certain names with fixed locations in the 128 bytes of data space found on the CPU. CPU register references in assembly language are good example of variables bound to some location at language-design time.

8.3.1.2 Binding at Compile Time

An address can be assigned at compile-time when the compiler knows the memory region where it can place static variables at runtime. Generally, such compilers generate absolute machine code that must be loaded at a specific address in memory prior to execution. Most modern compilers generate relocatable code and, therefore, don't fall into this category. Nevertheless, lower-end compilers, high-speed student compilers, and compilers for embedded systems often use this binding technique.

8.3.1.3 Binding at Link Time

Certain linkers (and related tools) have the ability to link together various relocatable object modules of an application and create an absolute load module. So while the compiler produces relocatable code, the linker binds memory addresses to the variables (and machine instructions). Usually, the programmer specifies (via command-line parameters or a linker script file) the base address of all the static variables in the program; the linker will bind the static variables to consecutive addresses starting at the base address. Programmers who are placing their applications in ROM memory (such as a BIOS ROM for a PC) often employ this scheme.

8.3.1.4 Binding at Load Time

The most common form of static binding occurs at load time. Executable formats such as Microsoft's PE/COFF and Linux's ELF usually contain relocation information embedded in the executable file. The operating system, when it loads the application into memory, will decide where to place the block of static variable objects and will then patch all the addresses within instructions that reference those static objects. This allows the loader (for example, the operating system) to assign a different address to a static object each time it loads it into memory.

8.3.1.5 Static Variable Binding

A *static variable* is one that has a memory address bound to it prior to program execution. Static variables enjoy a couple of advantages over other variable types. Because the compiler knows the address of the variable prior to runtime, the compiler can often use an *absolute addressing mode* or some other simple addressing mode to access that variable. Static variable access is often more efficient than other variable accesses because no additional setup is needed to access a static variable.[1]

Another feature of static variables is that they retain any value bound to them until you explicitly bind another value or until the program terminates. This means that static variables retain values while other events (such as procedure activation and deactivation) occur. Different threads in a multi-threaded application can also share data using static variables.

Static variables also have a few disadvantages worth mentioning. First of all, because the lifetime of a static variable matches that of the program, static variables consume memory the entire time the program is running. This is true even if the program no longer requires the value held by the static object. Another disadvantage to static variables (particularly when using the absolute addressing mode) is that the entire absolute address must usually be encoded as part of the instruction, making the instruction much larger. Indeed, on most RISC processors an absolute addressing mode isn't even available because you cannot encode an absolute address in a single instruction.

Another disadvantage to using static variables is that code that uses static objects is not *reentrant* (meaning two threads or processes can be concurrently executing the same code sequence); more effort is required to use that code in a multithreaded environment (where two copies of a section of code could be executing simultaneously, both accessing the same static object). However, multithreaded operation introduces a lot of complexity that I don't want to get into here, so I'll ignore this issue for now. See any good textbook on operating system design or concurrent programming for more details concerning the use of static objects. *Foundations of Multithreaded, Parallel, and Distributed Programming* by Gregory R. Andrews (Addison-Wesley, 1999) is a good place to start.

The following example demonstrates the use of static variables in a C program and shows the 80x86 code that the Borland C++ compiler generates to access those variables:

```
#include <stdio.h>

static int i = 5;
static int j = 6;

int main( int argc, char **argv )
{

    i = j + 3;
    j = i + 2;
    printf( "%d %d", i, j );
    return 0;
```

---

[1] At least, on an 80x86 CPU or some other CPU that supports absolute addresses. Some RISC processors do not support absolute addressing, so the program must set up a "static frame pointer" or "global frame register" when the program first begins execution, but this only has to be done once, so we can ignore the performance issues associated with this.

```
        }


        ; Following are the memory declarations
        ; for the 'i' and 'j' variables. Note that
        ; these are declared in the global '_DATA'
        ; section.

_DATA   segment dword public use32 'DATA'
        align   4
_i      label   dword
        dd      5
        align   4
_j      label   dword
        dd      6
_DATA   ends

_TEXT   segment dword public use32 'CODE'
_main   proc    near
?live1@0:
    ;
    ;       int main( int argc, char **argv )
    ;
        push    ebp
        mov     ebp,esp
    ;
    ;       {
    ;
    ;               i = j + 3;
    ;
@1:
        ; Load the EAX register with the
        ; current value of the global _j
        ; variable using the displacement-only
        ; addressing mode, add three to the
        ; value, and store into '_i':

        mov     eax,dword ptr [_j]
        add     eax,3
        mov     dword ptr [_i],eax
    ;
    ;               j = i + 2;
    ;
        ; Load the EDX register with the
        ; current value of the '_i' global
        ; variable using the displacement-
        ; only addressing mode, add two to
        ; this value, and store into
        ; '_j':

        mov     edx,dword ptr [_i]
        add     edx,2
        mov     dword ptr [_j],edx
```

```
;
;               printf( "%d %d", i, j );
;
        push        dword ptr [_j]
        push        dword ptr [_i]
        push        offset s@
        call        _printf
        add         esp,12
;
;               return 0;
;
        ; xor eax, eax sets the main function
        ; return value to zero.

        xor         eax,eax
;
;       }
;
@3:
@2:
        pop         ebp
        ret
_main   endp
_TEXT   ends
_DATA   segment dword public use32 'DATA'

; s@ is a string used by the printf function:

s@      label       byte
        ;           s@+0:
        db          "%d %d",0
        align       4
_DATA   ends
```

As the comments point out, the assembly language code the compiler
emits uses the displacement-only addressing mode to access all the static
variables.

8.3.2   Pseudo-Static Binding and Automatic Variables

Automatic variables have an address bound to them when a procedure or
other block of code begins execution. The program releases that storage
when the block or procedure completes execution. Such objects are called
automatic variables because the runtime code automatically allocates and
deallocates storage for them, as needed.

In most programming languages, automatic variables use a combination
of static and dynamic binding known as *pseudo-static binding*. The compiler
assigns an offset from a base address to a variable name during compilation.
At runtime the offset always remains fixed, but the base address can vary.
For example, a procedure or function allocates storage for a block of local
variables and then accesses the local variables at fixed offsets from the start

of that block of storage. Although the compiler cannot determine the final memory address of the variable at runtime, it can select an offset that never changes during program execution, hence the name *pseudo-static*.

Some programming languages use the term *local variables* in place of automatic variables. A local variable is one whose name is statically bound to a given procedure or block (that is, the scope of the name is limited to that procedure or block of code). Therefore, *local* is a static attribute in this context. It's easy to see why the terms *local variable* and *automatic variable* are often confused. In some programming languages, such as Pascal, local variables are always automatic variables and vice versa. Nonetheless, always keep in mind that the *local* attribute is a static attribute, while the *automatic* attribute is a dynamic one.

Automatic variables have a couple of important advantages. First, they only consume storage while the procedure or block containing them is executing. This allows multiple blocks and procedures to share the same pool of memory for their automatic variable needs. Although some extra code must execute in order to manage automatic variables (in a memory structure known as an *activation record*), this only requires a few machine instructions on most CPUs and only has to be done once for each procedure/ block entry and exit. While in certain circumstances, the cost can be significant, the extra time and space needed to set up and tear down the activation record is usually inconsequential. Another advantage of automatic variables is that they often use a base-plus-offset addressing mode, where the base of the activation record is kept in a register and the offsets into the activation record are small (often 256 bytes or fewer). Therefore, CPUs don't have to encode a full 32-bit or 64-bit address as part of the machine instruction— just an 8-bit (or other small) displacement, yielding shorter instructions. It's also worth noting that automatic variables are "thread-safe," and code that uses automatic variables can be reentrant. This is because each thread maintains its own stack space (or similar data structure) where compilers maintain automatic variables; therefore, each thread will have its own copy of any automatic variables the program uses.

Automatic variables do have some disadvantages. If you want to initialize an automatic variable, you have to use machine instructions to do so. You cannot initialize an automatic variable, as you can static variables, when the program loads into memory. Also, any values maintained in automatic variables are lost whenever you exit the block or procedure containing them. As noted in the previous paragraph, automatic variables require a small amount of overhead; some machine instructions must execute in order to build and destroy the activation record containing those variables.

Here's a short C example that uses automatic variables and the 80x86 assembly code that the Microsoft Visual C++ compiler produces for it:

```c
#include <stdio.h>


int main( int argc, char **argv )
{
```

```
    int i;
    int j;

    j = 1;
    i = j + 3;
    j = i + 2;
    printf( "%d %d", i, j );
    return 0;
}
```

Assembly code emitted for the previous C code:

```
; Data emitted for the string constant
; in the printf function call:

_DATA   SEGMENT
$SG790  DB      '%d %d', OOH
_DATA   ENDS


PUBLIC  _main
EXTRN   _printf:NEAR
; Function compile flags: /Ods

_TEXT   SEGMENT
_j$ = -8
_i$ = -4
_argc$ = 8
_argv$ = 12
_main   PROC NEAR
; File g:\t.c
; Line 7
;
; Build the "activation record" that
; holds the automatic (local) variables:

        push    ebp
        mov     ebp, esp
        push    ecx ; Storage for _i on stack
        push    ecx ; Storage for _j on stack

; Line 13 // j = 1;

        mov     DWORD PTR _j$[ebp], 1

; Line 14 // i = j + 3;

        mov     eax, DWORD PTR _j$[ebp]
        add     eax, 3
        mov     DWORD PTR _i$[ebp], eax

; Line 15 // j = i + 2;
```

```
        mov     eax, DWORD PTR _i$[ebp]
        inc     eax
        inc     eax
        mov     DWORD PTR _j$[ebp], eax

; Line 16 // printf function call

        push    DWORD PTR _j$[ebp]
        push    DWORD PTR _i$[ebp]
        push    OFFSET FLAT:$SG790
        call    _printf
        add     esp, 12    ; 0000000cH

; Line 17 // Return zero as function result.

        xor     eax, eax

; Line 18 // Deallocates activation record

        leave

; Returns from main.

        ret     0
_main   ENDP
_TEXT   ENDS
```

Note that when accessing automatic variables, the assembly code uses a base-plus-displacement addressing mode (for example, _j$[ebp]). This addressing mode is often shorter than the displacement-only addressing mode that static variables use (assuming, of course, that the offset to the automatic object is within 127 bytes of the base address held in EBP).

8.3.3   Dynamic Binding and Dynamic Variables

A *dynamic variable* is one that has storage bound to it at runtime. In some languages, the application programmer is completely responsible for binding addresses to dynamic objects; in other languages, the runtime system automatically allocates and deallocates storage for a dynamic variable.

Dynamic variables are generally those allocated on the heap via a memory allocation function such as malloc or new. The compiler has no way of determining the runtime address of a dynamic object. Therefore, the program must always refer to a dynamic object indirectly by using a pointer.

The big advantage to dynamic variables is that the application controls their lifetimes. Dynamic variables consume storage only as long as necessary, and the runtime system can reclaim that storage when the variable no longer requires it. Unlike automatic variables, the lifetime of a dynamic variable is not tied to the lifetime of some other object, such as a procedure or code block entry and exit. Memory is bound to a dynamic variable at the point the variable first needs it, and the memory can be released at the point the variable no longer needs it.[2] For variables that require considerable storage, dynamic allocation can make efficient use of memory as dynamically allocated variables hold onto the memory only as long as necessary.

Another advantage to dynamic variables is that most code references dynamic objects using a pointer. If that pointer value is already sitting in a CPU register, the program can usually reference that data using a short machine instruction, requiring no extra bits to encode an offset or address.

Dynamic variables have several disadvantages. First, usually some storage overhead is necessary to maintain dynamic variables. Static and automatic objects usually don't require extra storage associated with each such variable appearing in a program; the runtime system, on the other hand, often requires some number of bytes to keep track of each dynamic variable present in the system. This overhead ranges anywhere from 4 or 8 bytes to many dozens of bytes (in an extreme case) and keeps track of things like the current memory address of the object, the size of the object, and its type. If you're allocating small objects, like integers or characters, the amount of storage required for bookkeeping purposes could exceed the storage that the actual data requires. Also, most languages reference dynamic objects using pointer variables; as such, some additional storage is required by the pointer variable above and beyond the actual storage for the dynamic data.

Another problem with dynamic variables is performance. Because dynamic data is usually found in memory, the CPU has to access memory (which is slower than cached memory) on nearly every dynamic variable access.[3] Even worse, accessing dynamic data often requires two memory accesses—one to fetch the pointer's value and one to fetch the dynamic data, indirectly through the pointer. Another problem is that managing the *heap*, the place where the runtime system keeps the dynamic data, can also be expensive. Whenever an application requests storage for a dynamic object, the runtime system has to search for a contiguous block of free memory large enough to satisfy the request. This search operation can be expensive, depending on the organization of the runtime heap (which affects the amount of overhead storage associated with each dynamic variable). Furthermore, when releasing a dynamic object, the runtime system may need to execute some code in order to make that storage available for use by other dynamic objects. These runtime heap allocation and deallocation operations are usually far more expensive than allocating and deallocating a block of automatic variables during procedure entry/exit.

Another problem with dynamic variables that should be considered here is that some languages (e.g., Pascal and C/C++) require the application programmer to explicitly allocate and deallocate storage for dynamic variables. Because the allocation and deallocation is not automatic, defects can creep into the code because of errors made by the application programmer. This is

---

[2] In practice, many runtime systems will not bother breaking the address binding until the system actually needs the storage for another purpose, but this issue is not important here.

[3] Some compilers are smart enough to keep some dynamic data in registers, avoiding memory in certain cases, but in many cases the runtime code will have to access main memory when referencing dynamic data.

why languages such as C# attempt to handle dynamic allocation automatically for the programmer, even though this can be more expensive (slower). Here's a short example in C that demonstrates the kind of code that the Microsoft Visual C++ compiler will generate in order to access dynamic objects allocated with malloc.

```c
#include <stdlib.h>
#include <stdio.h>


int main( int argc, char **argv )
{

    int *i;
    int *j;


    i = malloc( sizeof( int ) );
    j = malloc( sizeof( int ) );
    *i = 1;
    *j = 2;
    printf( "%d %d", *i, *j );
    free( i );
    free( j );
    return 0;
}
```

Here's the machine code the compiler generates, including manually inserted comments that describe the extra work needed to access dynamically allocated objects:

```asm
_DATA   SEGMENT
$SG1139 DB        '%d %d', 00H
_DATA   ENDS
PUBLIC  _main
EXTRN   _free:NEAR
EXTRN   _malloc:NEAR
EXTRN   _printf:NEAR
; Function compile flags: /Ods
_TEXT   SEGMENT
_j$ = -8
_i$ = -4
_argc$ = 8
_argv$ = 12
_main   PROC NEAR
; File g:\t.c

; Line 8 // Construct the activation record

        push    ebp
        mov     ebp, esp
        push    ecx ; Allocates storge for
        push    ecx ; _i and _j.
```

```
; Line 14
; Call malloc and store the returned
; pointer value into the _i variable:

        push    4
        call    _malloc
        pop     ecx
        mov     DWORD PTR _i$[ebp], eax

; Line 15
; Call malloc and store the returned
; pointer value into the _j variable:

        push    4
        call    _malloc
        pop     ecx
        mov     DWORD PTR _j$[ebp], eax

; Line 16
; Store 1 into the dynamic variable pointed
; at by _i. Note that this requires two
; instructions.

        mov     eax, DWORD PTR _i$[ebp]
        mov     DWORD PTR [eax], 1

; Line 17
; Store 2 into the dynamic variable pointed
; at by _j. This also requires two instructions.

        mov     eax, DWORD PTR _j$[ebp]
        mov     DWORD PTR [eax], 2

; Line 18
; Call printf to print the dynamic variables'
; values:

        mov     eax, DWORD PTR _j$[ebp]
        push    DWORD PTR [eax]
        mov     eax, DWORD PTR _i$[ebp]
        push    DWORD PTR [eax]
        push    OFFSET FLAT:$SG1139
        call    _printf
        add     esp, 12

; Free the two variables
;
; Line 19
        push    DWORD PTR _i$[ebp]
        call    _free
        pop     ecx
; Line 20
        push    DWORD PTR _j$[ebp]
        call    _free
```

```
        pop     ecx


; Line 21
; Return a function result of zero:

        xor     eax, eax

; Line 22
; Deallocate the activation record and
; return from main.

        leave
        ret     0
_main   ENDP
_TEXT   ENDS
END
```

As you can see, a lot of extra work is needed to access dynamically allocated variables via a pointer.

8.4　Common Primitive Data Types

Computer data always has a data type attribute that describes how the program interprets that data. The data type also determines the size (in bytes) of the data in memory. Data types can be divided into two classes: those that the CPU can hold in a CPU register and operate upon directly and those that are composed of the following smaller data types. I'll use the term *primitive data type* to describe atomic objects upon which the CPU may operate directly, and I'll use the term *composite data types* to describe those aggregate objects made up of smaller, primitive data types. In the following sections we'll review (from *Volume 1*) the primitive data types found on most modern CPUs, and in the next chapter I'll begin discussing composite data types.

8.4.1　Integer Variables

Most programming languages provide some mechanism for storing integer values in memory variables. In general, a programming language uses either unsigned binary representation, two's-complement representation, or binary-coded decimal representation (or a combination of these) to represent integer values.

Perhaps the most fundamental property of an integer variable in a programming language is the number of bits allocated to represent that integer value. In most modern programming languages, the number of bits used to represent an integer value is usually 8, 16, 32, 64, or some other power of 2. Many languages only provide a single size for representing integers, but some languages let you select from one of several different sizes. You choose the size based on the range of values you want to represent, the amount of memory you want the variable to consume, and the performance of arithmetic operations involving that value. Table 8-1 lists some common sizes and ranges for various signed, unsigned, and decimal integer variables.

Table 8-1: Common Integer Sizes and Their Ranges

Size, in Bits	Representation	Unsigned Range
8	Unsigned	0..255
	Signed	−128..+127
	Decimal	0..99
16	Unsigned	0..65,535
	Signed	−32768..+32,767
	Decimal	0..9999
32	Unsigned	0..4,294,967,295
	Signed	−2,147,483,648..+2,147,483,647
	Decimal	0..99999999
64	Unsigned	0..18,446,744,073,709,551,615
	Signed	−9,223,372,036,854,775,808..+9,223,372,036,854,775,807
	Decimal	0..9999999999999999
128	Unsigned	0..340,282,366,920,938,463,463,374,607,431,768,211,455
	Signed	−170,141,183,460,469,231,731,687,303,715,884,105,728 .. +170,141,183,460,469,231,731,687,303,715,884,105,727
	Decimal	0..99,999,999,999,999,999,999,999,999,999

Not all languages will support all of these different sizes (indeed, to support all of these different sizes in the same program, you would probably have to use assembly language). As noted earlier, some languages provide only a single size, which is usually the processor's native integer size (that is, the size of a CPU general-purpose integer register).

Languages that do provide multiple integer sizes often don't give you an explicit choice of sizes from which to choose. For example, the C programming language provides up to four different integer sizes: char (which is always 1 byte), short, int, and long. With the exception of the char type, C does not specify the sizes of these integer types other than to state that short integers are less than or equal to int objects in size, and int objects are less than or equal to long integers in size. (In fact, all three could be the same size.) C programs that depend on integers being a certain size may fail when compiled with different compilers that don't use the same sizes as the first compiler.

While it may seem inconvenient that various programming languages avoid providing an exact specification of the size of an integer variable in the language definition, keep in mind that this ambiguity is intentional. When one declares an "integer" variable in a given programming language, the language leaves it up to the compiler's implementer to choose the *best* size for that integer, based on performance and other considerations. The definition of "best" may change based on the CPU for which the compiler generates code. For example, a compiler for a 16-bit processor may choose to implement 16-bit integers because the CPU processes them most efficiently. A compiler for a 32-bit processor, however, may choose to implement 32-bit integers (for the same reason). Languages that specify the exact size of various integer formats (such as Java) can suffer as processor technology marches along and it becomes more efficient to process larger data objects. For example, when the world switched from 16-bit processors to 32-bit processors in general-purpose computer systems, it was actually faster to do 32-bit arithmetic on most of the newer processors. Therefore, compiler writers redefined "integer" to mean "32-bit integer" in order to maximize the performance of programs employing integer arithmetic.

Some programming languages provide support for unsigned integer variables as well as signed integers. At first glance, it might seem that the whole purpose behind supporting unsigned integers is to provide twice the number of positive values when negative values aren't required. In fact, there are many other reasons why great programmers might choose unsigned over signed integers when writing efficient code.

On some CPUs, unsigned integer multiplication and division are faster than their signed counterparts. Comparing values within the range $0..n$ can be done more efficiently using unsigned integers rather than signed integer (requiring only a single comparison against n in the unsigned case); this is especially important when checking bounds of array indices when the array's element indexes begin at zero.

Many programming languages will allow you to include variables of different sizes within the same arithmetic expression. The compiler will automatically sign-extend or zero-extend operands to the larger size within an expression as needed to compute the final result. The problem with this automatic conversion is that it hides the fact that extra work is required when processing the expression, and the expressions themselves don't explicitly show this. An assignment statement such as

```
x = y + z - t;
```

could be a short sequence of machine instructions if the operands are all the same size, or it could require some additional instructions if the operands have different sizes. For example, consider the following C code:

```
#include <stdio.h>

static char c;
static short s;
static long l;

static long a;
static long b;
static long d;

int main( int argc, char **argv )
{

    l = l + s + c;
    printf( "%ld %ld %ld", l, s, c );

    a = a + b + d;
```

```
        printf( "%ld %ld %ld", a, b, d );

    return 0;
}
```

Compiled with the Borland C++ compiler, you get the following two assembly language sequences for the two assignment statements:

```
;               l = l + s + c;
;
@1:
        movsx       eax,word ptr [_s]
        add         eax,dword ptr [_l]
        movsx       edx,byte ptr [_c]
        add         eax,edx
        mov         dword ptr [_l],eax


;               a = a + b + d;
;
        mov         edx,dword ptr [_a]
        add         edx,dword ptr [_b]
        add         edx,dword ptr [_d]
        mov         dword ptr [_a],edx
```

As you can see, the statement that operates on variables whose sizes are all the same uses fewer instructions than the one that mixes operand sizes in the expression.

Another thing to note, when using different-sized integers in an expression, is that not all CPUs support all operand sizes as efficiently. While it should be fairly obvious that using an integer size that is larger than the CPU's general-purpose integer registers will produce inefficient code, it might not be quite as obvious that using *smaller* integer values can be inefficient as well. Many RISC CPUs only work on operands that are exactly the same size as the general-purpose registers. Smaller operands must first be zero-extended or sign-extended to the size of a general-purpose register prior to any calculations involving those values. Even on CISC processors, such as the 80x86, that have hardware support for different sizes of integers, using certain sizes can be more expensive. For example, under 32-bit operating systems, instructions that manipulate 16-bit operands require an extra *opcode prefix byte* and are, therefore, larger than instructions that operate on 8-bit or 32-bit operands.

8.4.2   Floating-Point/Real Variables

Like integers, many HLLs provide multiple floating-point variable sizes. Most languages provide at least two different sizes, a 32-bit single-precision floating-point format and a 64-bit double-precision floating-point format, based on the IEEE 754 floating-point standard. A few languages provide 80-bit floating-point variables, based on Intel's 80-bit extended-precision floating-point format, but such usage is becoming rare.

Different floating-point formats trade off space and performance for precision. Calculations involving smaller floating-point formats are usually quicker than calculations involving the larger formats. However, you give up precision to achieve improved performance and size savings (see *Write Great Code, Volume 1*, Chapter 4 for details).

As with expressions involving integer arithmetic, you should avoid mixing different-sized floating-point operands in an expression. The CPU (or FPU) must convert all floating-point values to the same format before using them. This can involve additional instructions (consuming more memory) and additional time. Therefore, you should try to use the same floating-point types throughout an expression, wherever possible.

Conversion between integer and floating-point formats is another expensive operation you should avoid. Modern HLLs attempt to keep variables' values in registers as much as possible. Unfortunately, on most modern CPUs it is impossible to move data between the integer and floating-point registers without first copying that data to memory (which is expensive, because memory access is slow compared with register access). Furthermore, conversion between integer and floating-point numbers often involves several specialized instructions. All of this consumes time and memory. Whenever possible, avoid these conversions.

8.4.3 Character Variables

Standard character data in most modern HLLs consumes one byte per character. On CPUs that support byte addressing, such as the Intel 80x86 processor, a compiler can reserve a single byte of storage for each character variable and efficiently access that character variable in memory. Some RISC CPUs, however, cannot access data in memory except in 32-bit chunks (or some other size other than 8 bits).

For CPUs that cannot address individual bytes in memory, HLL compilers usually reserve 32 bits for a character variable and only use the LO byte of that double-word variable for the character data. Because few programs have a large number of scalar character variables,[4] the amount of space wasted is hardly an issue in most systems. However, if you have an unpacked array of characters, the wasted space can become significant. I'll return to this issue in Chapter 9.

Modern programming languages support the Unicode character set. Unicode characters require 2 bytes of memory to hold the character's data value. On CPUs that support byte or word addressing, HLL compilers generally reserve only 2 bytes for a Unicode character variable. On CPUs that cannot efficiently access objects smaller than 32 bits, HLL compilers usually reserve 32 bits and use only the LO 16 bits for the Unicode character data.

Lately, because 16 bits cannot encode a sufficient number of characters to represent all the world's different alphabets and symbol sets, applications have begun using multibyte character sets such as UTF-8. These encode individual characters using a variable-length string of 1 to 5 characters (see Chapter 10).

---

[4] *Scalar*, in this context, means "not an array of characters."

8.4.4   Boolean Variables

A Boolean variable requires only a single bit to represent the two values *True* or *False*. HLLs will usually reserve the smallest amount of memory possible for such variables (a byte on machines that support byte addressing, and a larger amount of memory on those CPUs that can only address words or double words).

Although most HLL compilers usually reserve the smallest amount of addressable memory possible for a Boolean variable, this isn't always the case. Some languages (like FORTRAN) allow you to create multibyte Boolean variables (for example, the FORTRAN LOGICAL*4 data type).

Some languages (C for example) don't support an explicit Boolean data type. They use an integer data type to represent Boolean values. In such languages, you get to choose the size of your Boolean variables by choosing the size of the integer you use to hold the Boolean value. For example, in a typical 32-bit implementation of the C/C++ languages, you can define 1-byte, 2-byte, or 4-byte Boolean values as shown here:[5]

C Integer Data Type	Size of Boolean Object
char	1 byte
short int	2 bytes
long int	4 bytes

Some languages, under certain circumstances, will use only a single bit of storage for a Boolean variable when that variable is a field of a record or an element of an array. I'll return to this discussion in Chapter 9 when considering composite data structures.

8.5   Variable Addresses and High-level Languages

The organization, class, and type of variables in your programs can affect the efficiency of the code that a compiler produces. Additionally, issues like the order of declaration, the size of the object, and the placement of the object in memory can have a big impact on the running time of your programs. In this section, I'll describe how you can organize your variable declarations to produce efficient code.

As for immediate constants encoded in machine instructions, many CPUs provide specialized addressing modes that access memory more efficiently than other, more general, addressing modes. Just as you can reduce the size and improve the speed of your programs by carefully selecting the constants you use, you can make your programs more efficient by carefully choosing how you declare variables. But whereas with constants you are primarily concerned with their values, with variables you must consider the address in memory where the compiler places those variables.

---

[5] Assuming, of course, that your C/C++ compiler uses 16-bit integers for short integers and 32-bit integers for long integers.

The 80x86 is a typical example of a CISC processor that provides multiple address sizes. When running on a modern 32-bit operating system like Linux or Windows, the 80x86 CPU supports three address sizes: 0-bit, 8-bit, and 32-bit. The 80x86 uses 0-bit displacements for register-indirect addressing modes. I'll ignore the 0-bit displacement addressing for the time being because 80x86 compilers generally don't use this particular addressing mode to access variables you explicitly declare in your code. The 8-bit and 32-bit displacement addressing modes are the more interesting ones for the current discussion.

8.5.1 Storage Allocation for Global and Static Variables

The 32-bit displacement is, perhaps, the easiest to understand. Variables you declare in your program, which the compiler allocates in memory rather than in a register, have to appear somewhere in memory. On most 32-bit processors, the address bus is 32 bits wide, so it takes a 32-bit address to access a variable at an arbitrary location in memory. An instruction that encodes this 32-bit address as part of the instruction can access any memory variable. The 80x86 provides the *displacement-only* addressing mode whose effective address is exactly the 32-bit constant embedded in the instruction.

A problem with 32-bit addresses (one that gets even worse as we move to 64-bit processors with a 64-bit address) is that the address winds up consuming the largest portion of the instruction's encoding. Certain forms of the displacement-only addressing mode on the 80x86, for example, have a 1-byte opcode and a 4-byte address. Therefore, 80 percent of the instruction's size is consumed by the address. On typical RISC processors, the situation is even worse. Because the instructions are uniformly 32 bits long on a typical RISC CPU, you cannot encode a 32-bit address as part of the instruction. In order to access a variable at an arbitrary 32-bit address in memory, you need to load the 32-bit address of that variable into a register and then use the register indirect addressing mode to access the memory variable. This could require three 32-bit instructions as Figure 8-2 demonstrates; that's expensive in terms of both speed and space.

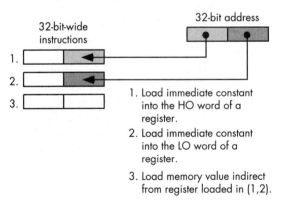

Figure 8-2: RISC CPU access of an absolute address

Because RISC CPUs don't run horribly slower than CISC processors, it should be obvious that compilers rarely generate code this bad. In reality, programs running on RISC CPUs often keep base addresses to blocks of objects in registers, so they can efficiently access variables in those blocks using short offsets from the base register. But how do compilers deal with arbitrary addresses in memory?

8.5.2 Using Automatic Variables to Reduce Offset Sizes

One way to avoid large instruction sizes with large displacements is to use an addressing mode with a smaller displacement. The 80x86, for example, provides an 8-bit displacement form for the base-plus-indexed addressing mode. This form allows you to access data at an offset of –128 through +127 bytes around a base address contained in a 32-bit register. RISC processors have similar features, although the number of displacement bits is usually larger (16 bits), allowing a greater range of addresses.

By pointing a 32-bit register at some base address in memory and placing your variables near that base address, you can use the shorter forms of these instructions so your program will be smaller and will run more quickly. Obviously, this isn't too difficult if you're working in assembly language and you have direct access to the CPU's registers. However, if you're working in an HLL, you may not have direct access to the CPU's registers and even if you did, you probably couldn't convince the compiler to allocate your variables at convenient addresses. How do you take advantage of this small-displacement addressing mode in your HLL programs? The answer is that you don't explicitly specify the use of this addressing mode, the compiler does it for you automatically.

Consider the following trivial function in Pascal:

```
function trivial( i:integer; j:integer ):integer;
var
    k:integer;
begin

    k := i + j;
    trivial := k;

end;
```

Upon entry into this function, the compiled code constructs an *activation record* (sometimes called a *stack frame*). An activation record is a data structure in memory where the system keeps the local data associated with a function or procedure. The activation record includes parameter data, automatic variables, the return address, temporary variables that the compiler allocates, and machine-state information (for example, saved register values). The runtime system allocates storage for an activation record on the fly and, in fact, two different calls to the procedure or function may place the activation record at different addresses in memory. In order to access the data in an activation record, most HLLs point a register (usually called the *frame pointer*) at the activation record, and then the procedure or function references automatic variables and parameters at some offset from this frame pointer. Unless you have many automatic variables and parameters or your local variables[6] and parameters are quite large, these variables generally appear in memory at an offset that is near the base address. This means that the CPU can use a small offset when referencing variables near the base address held in the frame pointer. In the Pascal example given earlier, parameters i and j and the local variable k would most likely be within a few bytes of the frame pointer's address, so the compiler can encode these instructions using a small displacement rather than a large displacement. If your compiler allocates local variables and parameters in an activation record, all you have to do is arrange your variables in the activation record so that they appear near the base address of the activation record. But how do you do that?

Construction of an activation record begins in the code that calls a procedure. The caller places the parameter data (if any) in the activation record. Then the execution of an assembly language call instruction adds the return address to the activation record. At this point, construction of the activation record continues within the procedure itself. The procedure copies the register values and other important state information and then makes room in the activation record for local variables. The procedure must also update the frame-pointer register (e.g., EBP on the 80x86) so that it points at the base address of the activation record.

To see what a typical activation record looks like, consider the following HLA procedure declaration:

```
procedure ARDemo( i:uns32; j:int32; k:dword ); @nodisplay;
var
    a:int32;
    r:real32;
    c:char;
    b:boolean;
    w:word;
begin ARDemo;
    .
    .
    .
end ARDemo;
```

Whenever an HLA program calls this ARDemo procedure, it builds the activation record by pushing the data for the parameters onto the stack. The calling code for this procedure will push the parameters onto the stack in the order they appear in the parameter list, from left to right. Therefore, the calling code first pushes the value for the i parameter, then pushes the value for the j parameter, and finally pushes the data for the k parameter. After pushing the parameters, the program calls the ARDemo procedure. Immediately upon entry into the ARDemo procedure, the stack contains these four items arranged as shown in Figure 8-3, assuming the stack grows from high memory addresses to low memory addresses (as it does on most processors).

---

[6] Remember, in Pascal local variables are always automatic variables, so this discussion will use the two terms interchangeably.

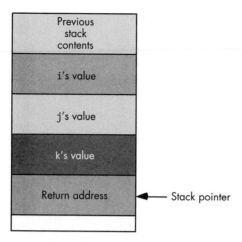

Figure 8-3: Stack organization immediately upon entry into ARDemo

The first few instructions in `ARDemo` will push the current value of the frame-pointer register (e.g., EBP on the 80x86) onto the stack and then copy the value of stack pointer (ESP on the 80x86) into the frame-pointer register. Next, the code drops the stack pointer down in memory to make room for the local variables. This produces the stack organization shown in Figure 8-4 on the 80x86 CPU.

To access objects in the activation record you must use offsets from the frame-pointer register (EBP in Figure 8-4) to the desired object.

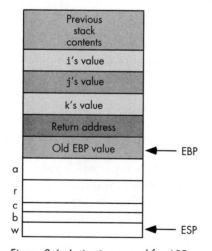

Figure 8-4: Activation record for ARDemo

The two items of immediate interest are the parameters and the local variables. You can access the parameters at positive offsets from the frame-pointer register; you can access the local variables at negative offsets from the frame-pointer register, as Figure 8-5 shows.

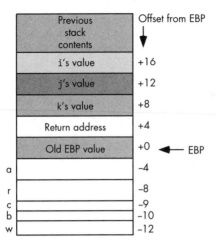

		Offset from EBP
	Previous stack contents	↓
	i's value	+16
	j's value	+12
	k's value	+8
	Return address	+4
	Old EBP value	+0 ◄── EBP
a		-4
r		-8
c		-9
b		-10
w		-12

Figure 8-5: Offsets of objects in the ARDemo activation record on the 80x86

Intel specifically reserves the EBP (extended base pointer) to point at the base of the activation record. Therefore, compilers will typically use this register as the frame-pointer register when allocating activation records on the stack. Some compilers attempt to use the 80x86 ESP (stack pointer) register as the pointer to the activation record because this reduces the number of instructions in the program. Whether the compiler uses EBP, ESP, or some other register, the bottom line is that the compiler typically points some register at the activation record, and most of the local variables and parameters are near the base address of the activation record. That is the important issue for the discussion that follows.

As you can see in Figure 8-5, all the local variables and parameters in the ARDemo procedure are within 127 bytes of the frame-pointer register (EBP). This means that on the 80x86 CPU, an instruction that references one of these variables or parameters will be able to encode the offset from EBP using a single byte. Because of the way the program builds the activation record, parameters will appear at positive offsets from the frame-pointer register, and local variables will appear at negative offsets from the frame-pointer register.

For procedures that have only a few parameters and local variables, the CPU will be able to access all parameters and local variables using a small offset (that is, 8 bits on the 80x86, 16 bits on various RISC processors). Consider, however, the following C/C++ function:

```
int BigLocals( int i, int j );
{
    int array[256];
    int k;

        .
        .
        .

}
```

The activation record for this function appears in Figure 8-6. One difference you'll notice between this activation record and the ones for the Pascal and HLA functions is that C pushes its parameters on the stack in the reverse order (that is, it pushes the last parameter first, and it pushes the first parameter last). This difference, however, does not impact our discussion.

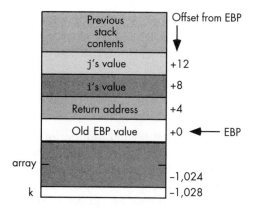

Figure 8-6: Activation record for BigLocals function

The important thing to note in Figure 8-6 is that the local variables array and k have large negative offsets. With offsets of –1,024 and –1,028 (assuming an integer is 32 bits), the displacements from EBP to array and k are well outside the range that the compiler can encode into a single byte on the 80x86. Therefore, the compiler will have no choice but to encode these displacements using a 32-bit value. Of course, this will make accessing these local variables in the function quite a bit more expensive.

Nothing can be done about the array variable in this example (no matter where you put it, the offset to the base address of the array will be at least 1,024 bytes from the activation record's base address). However, consider the activation record appearing in Figure 8-7.

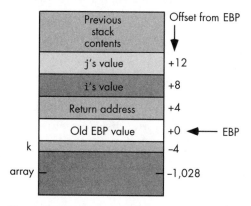

Figure 8-7: Another possible activation record layout for the BigLocals function

In this figure, the compiler has rearranged the local variables in the activation record. Although it will still take a 32-bit displacement to access the array variable, accessing k now uses an 8-bit displacement (on the 80x86) because k's offset is –4. You can produce these offsets with the following code:

```
int BigLocals( int i, int j );
{
    int k;
    int array[256];
        .
        .
        .

}
```

In theory, this isn't a terribly difficult optimization for a compiler to do (rearranging the order of the variables in the activation record), so you'd expect the compiler to make this modification for you so that it can access as many local variables as possible using small displacements. In practice, not all compilers actually do this optimization for various technical and practical reasons (specifically, it can break some poorly written code that makes assumptions about the placement of variables in the activation record).

If you want to ensure that the maximum number of local variables in your procedure have the smallest possible displacements, the solution is trivial: declare all your 1-byte variables first, your 2-byte variables second, your 4-byte variables next, and so on up to the largest local variable in your function. Generally, though, you're probably more interested in reducing the size of the maximum number of instructions in your function rather than reducing the size of the offsets required by the maximum number of variables in your function. For example, if you have 128 1-byte variables and you declare these variables first, you'll only need a single byte displacement if you access them. However, if you never access these variables, the fact that they have a 1-byte displacement rather than a 4-byte displacement saves you nothing. The only time you save any space is when you actually access that variable's value in memory via some machine instruction that is using a 1-byte displacement rather than a 4-byte displacement. Therefore, to reduce your function's object code size, you want to maximize the number of instructions that use a small displacement. If you refer to a 100-byte array far more often than any other variable in your function, you're probably better off declaring that array first, even if it only leaves 28 bytes of storage (on the 80x86) for other variables that will use the shorter displacement.

RISC processors typically use a 16-bit offset to access fields of the activation record. Therefore, you have more latitude with your declarations when using a RISC chip (which is good, because when you do exceed the 16-bit limitation, accessing a local variable gets *really expensive*). Unless you're declaring one or more arrays that consume more than 32,768 bytes (combined), the typical compiler for a RISC chip is going to generate decent code.

This same argument applies to parameters as well as local variables. However, it's rare to find code passing a large data structure (by value) to a function because of the expense involved.

8.5.3 Storage Allocation for Intermediate Variables

Intermediate variables are those that are local to one procedure/function but global to another. You'll find intermediate variables in block-structured languages like Pascal/Delphi/Kylix, Ada, Modula-2, and HLA that support nested procedures. Consider the following example program in Pascal:

```
program nestedProcedures;
var
    globalVariable: integer;

    procedure procOne;
    var
        intermediateVariable: integer;

        procedure procTwo;
        var
            localVariable:integer;
        begin

            localVariable := intermediateVariable +
                                    globalVariable;
                .
                .
                .

        end; (* procTwo *)

    begin (* procOne *)
        .
        .
        .
    end; (* procOne *)

begin (* main program *)
    .
    .
    .
end. (* main program*)
```

As you can see in this code fragment, nested procedures can access variables found in the main program (that is, global variables) as well as variables found in procedures containing the nested procedure (that is, the intermediate variables). As you've seen, local variable access is inexpensive compared to global variable access (because you always have to use a larger offset to access global objects within a procedure). Intermediate variable access, as is done in the procTwo procedure, is expensive. The difference between local and global variable accesses is the size of the offset/displacement coded into the instruction—with local variables typically using a shorter offset than is possible for global objects. Intermediate accesses, on the other hand, typically require several machine instructions. This makes the instruction sequence that accesses an intermediate variable several times slower and several times larger than accessing a local (or even global) variable.

The problem with using intermediate variables is that the compiler must maintain either a linked list of activation records or a table of pointers to the activation records (this table is called the *display*) in order to reference intermediate objects. To access an intermediate variable, the procTwo procedure must either follow a chain of links (there would be only one link in this example) or it would have to do a table lookup in order to get a pointer to procOne's activation record. Worse still, maintaining the display of this linked list of pointers isn't exactly cheap. The work needed to maintain these objects has to be done on every procedure/function entry and exit, even when the procedure or function doesn't access any intermediate variables on a particular call. Although there are, arguably, some software engineering benefits to using intermediate variables (having to do with information hiding) versus a global variable, keep in mind that access to intermediate objects is expensive.

8.5.4   Storage Allocation for Dynamic Variables and Pointers

Pointer access in an HLL provides another opportunity for optimization in your code. Pointers can be expensive to use but, under certain circumstances, they can actually make your programs more efficient by reducing displacement sizes.

A pointer is simply a memory variable whose value is the address of some other memory object (therefore, pointers are the same size as an address on the machine). Because most modern CPUs only support indirection via a machine register, indirectly accessing an object is typically a two-step process: First the code has to load the value of the pointer variable into a register and then the program has to refer (indirectly) to the object through that register.

Consider the following C/C++ code fragment and the corresponding HLA assembly code:

```
int *pi;
    .
    .
    .
i = *pi;    // Assume pi is initialized with a
            //  reasonable address at this point.
```

And here is the corresponding 80x86/HLA assembly code:

```
pi: pointer to int32;
    .
    .
    .
mov( pi, ebx );    // Again, assume pi has
mov( [ebx], eax ); //  been properly initialized
mov( eax, i );
```

Had pi been a regular variable rather than pointer object, this code could have dispensed with the mov([ebx], eax); instruction. Therefore, the use of this pointer variable has both increased the size of the program and reduced the execution speed by inserting an extra instruction into the code sequence that the compiler generates.

Note that if you indirectly refer to an object several times in close succession, then the compiler may be able to reuse the pointer value it has loaded into the register, thus amortizing the cost of the extra instruction across several different instructions. Consider the following C/C++ code sequence and the corresponding HLA code. Here is the C/C++ source code:

```
int *pi;
    .
    .   // Assume code in this area
    .   //  initializes pi appropriately.
    .
*pi = i;
*pi = *pi + 2;
*pi = *pi + *pi;
printf( "pi = %d\n", *pi );
```

Here's the corresponding 80x86/HLA code:

```
pi: pointer to int32;
    .
    . // Assume code in this area
    . //  initializes pi appropriately.
    .
// Extra instruction that we need to initialize EBX

mov( pi, ebx );

mov( i, eax );
mov( eax, [ebx] );  // This code can clearly be optimized;
mov( [ebx], eax );  //  we'll ignore that fact for the
add( 2, eax );      //  sake of the discussion here.
mov( eax, [ebx] );
mov( [ebx], eax );
add( [ebx], eax );
mov( eax [ebx] );
stdout.put( "pi = ", (type int32 [ebx]), nl );
```

Note that this code loads the actual pointer value into EBX only once. From that point forward the code will simply use the pointer value contained in EBX to reference the object at which pi is pointing. Of course, any compiler that can do this optimization can probably eliminate five redundant memory loads and stores from this assembly language sequence, but I'll assume that they aren't redundant for the time being. The first thing about this code you should note is that it didn't have to reload EBX with the value of pi every time it wanted to access the object at which pi points. Therefore, we only have one instruction of overhead (mov(pi, ebx);) amortized across six of these instructions. That's not too bad at all.

Indeed, a good argument could be made that this code is more optimal than accessing a local or global variable directly. An instruction of the form

```
mov( [ebx], eax );
```

uses a 0-bit displacement encoded into the instruction. Therefore, this move instruction is only 2 bytes long rather than 3, 5, or even 6 bytes long. If pi is a local variable, then it's quite possible that the original instruction that copies pi into EBX is only 3 bytes long (a 2-byte opcode and a 1-byte displacement). Because instructions of the form mov([ebx], eax); are only 2 bytes long, it only takes three instructions to "break even" on the byte count using indirection rather than an 8-bit displacement. After the third instruction that references whatever pi points at, the code involving the pointer is actually shorter.

You can even use indirection to provide efficient access to a block of global variables. As noted earlier, the compiler generally cannot determine the address of a global object while it is compiling your program. Therefore, it has to assume the worst case and allow for the largest possible displacement/offset when generating machine code to access a global variable. Of course, you've just seen that you can reduce the size of the displacement value from 32 bits down to 0 bits by using a pointer to the object rather than accessing the object directly. Therefore, you could take the address of the global object (with the C/C++ & operator, for example) and then use indirection to access the variable. The problem with this approach is that it requires a register (a precious commodity on any processor, but especially on the 80x86 that has only six general-purpose registers to utilize). If you access the same variable many times in rapid succession, then this 0-bit displacement trick can make your code more efficient. However, it's somewhat rare to access the same variable a large number of times in a short sequence of code without also needing to access several other variables. Therefore, the compiler may have to flush the pointer from the register and reload the pointer value later (thereby reducing the efficiency of this approach). If you're working on a RISC chip with many registers, you can probably employ this trick to your advantage. On a processor with a limited number of registers, you won't be able to employ this trick as often.

8.5.5   Using Records/Structures to Reduce Instruction Offset Sizes

There is a trick that you can use to gain access to several variables with a single pointer: put all those variables into a structure, and then use the address of the structure. By accessing the fields of the structure via the pointer, you can get away with using smaller instructions to access the objects. This works almost exactly as you've seen for activation records (indeed, activation records are, literally, records that the program references indirectly via the *frame-pointer register*). About the only difference between accessing objects indirectly in a user-defined record/structure and accessing objects in the activation record is that most compilers won't let you refer to fields in a user structure/record using negative offsets. Therefore, you're limited to about half the number of bytes that are normally accessible in an activation record. For example, on the 80x86 you can access the object at offset zero from a pointer using a 0-bit displacement and objects at offsets 1..+127 using a single byte displacement. Consider the following C/C++ example that uses this trick:

```c
typedef struct vars
{
    int i;
    int j;
    char *s;
    char name[20];
    short t;
};

static vars v;
vars *pv = &v;  // Initialize pv with the address of v.
    .
    .
    .
    pv->i = 0;
    pv->j = 5;
    pv->s = &pv->name;
    pv->t = 0;
    strcpy( pv->name, "Write Great Code!" );
    .
    .
    .
```

A well-designed compiler will load the value of pv into a register exactly once for this code fragment. Because all the fields of the vars structure are within 127 bytes of the base address of the structure in memory, an 80x86 compiler can emit a sequence of instructions that require only 1-byte offsets, even though the v variable itself is a static/global object. Note, by the way, that the first field in the vars structure is special. Because this is at offset zero in the structure, this allows the use of a 0-bit displacement when accessing this field. Therefore, it's a good idea to put your most-often-referenced field first in a structure if you're going to refer to that structure indirectly.

Using indirection in your code does come at a cost. On a limited-register CPU such as the 80x86, using this trick will tie up a register for some period and that may, effectively cause the compiler to generate worse code. If the compiler must constantly reload the register with the address of the structure in memory, you can watch the savings that this trick buys you evaporate rather quickly. When using this trick, you should look at the assembly code the compiler generates and verify that you're actually saving something. Tricks such as using pointers to structures vary in effectiveness across different processors (and different compilers for the same processor). Therefore, it's a really good idea to look at the code generated by your compiler when using a trick such as this in order to make sure that your trick is actually saving you something rather than costing you something.

8.5.6 Register Variables

While on the subject of registers, it's worthwhile to point out one other 0-bit displacement way to access variables in your programs. You can also access your variables by keeping them in machine registers. Machine registers are always the most efficient place to keep variables and parameters. Unfortunately, only in assembly language and, to a limited extent, C/C++, do you have any control over whether the compiler should keep a variable or parameter in a register. In some respects, this is not bad. Good compilers do a much better job of register allocation than the casual programmer does. However, an expert programmer can do a better job of register allocation than a compiler because the expert programmer understands the data the program will be processing and the frequency of access to a particular memory location. (And of course, the expert programmer can first look at what the compiler is doing, whereas the compiler doesn't have the benefit of first looking at what the expert programmer has done.)

Some languages, such as Delphi and Kylix, provide limited support for programmer-directed register allocation. In particular, the Delphi/Kylix compilers provide a compiler option that you can use to tell the compiler to pass the first three (ordinal) parameters for a function or procedure in the EAX, EDX, and ECX registers. This is known as the *fastcall calling convention* and several C/C++ compilers support it as well (e.g., Borland's C++ and C++Builder compilers).

In Delphi/Kylix and certain other languages, control of the fastcall parameter passing convention is the only control you get. The C/C++ language, however, provides the `register` keyword, a storage specifier (much like the `const`, `static`, and `auto` keywords) that tells the compiler that the programmer expects to use the variable frequently and the compiler should attempt to keep the variable in a register. Note that the compiler can choose to ignore the `register` keyword (in which case the compiler reserves variable storage using automatic allocation). Many compilers ignore the `register` keyword altogether because the compiler's authors feel that they can do a better job of register allocation than any programmer (a somewhat arrogant assumption). Of course, on some register-starved machines such as the 80x86, there are so few registers to work with that it might not even be possible to allocate a variable to a register throughout the execution of some function. Nevertheless, some compilers do respect the programmer's wishes and *will* allocate a few variables in registers if you request that they do so.

Most RISC compilers reserve several registers for passing parameters and several registers for local variables. Therefore, it's a good idea (if possible) to place the parameters you access most frequently first in the parameter declaration because they're probably the ones that the compiler would allocate in a register.[7] The same is true for local variable declarations. Always declare frequently used local variables first because many compilers may allocate those (ordinal) variables in registers.

---

[7] Many optimizing compilers are smart enough to choose which variables they keep in registers based on how the program uses those variables.

One problem with compiler register allocation is that it is static. That is, the compiler determines which variables to place in registers based on an analysis of your source code during compilation, not during runtime. Compilers often make assumptions (that are usually correct) like "this function references variable xyz far more often than any other variable, so it's a good candidate for a register variable." Indeed, by placing the variable in a register, the compiler will certainly reduce the *size* of the program. However, it could also be the case that all those references to xyz sit in code that rarely, if ever, executes. Although the compiler might save some space (by emitting smaller instructions to access registers rather than memory), the code won't run appreciably faster. After all, if the code rarely or never executes, then making that code run faster does not contribute much to the execution time of the program. On the other hand, it's also quite possible to bury a single reference to some variable in a deeply nested loop that executes many times. With only one reference in the entire function, the compiler's optimizer may overlook the fact that the executing program references the variable frequently. Although compilers have gotten smarter about handling variables inside loops, the fact is that no compiler can predict how many times an arbitrary loop will execute at runtime. Human beings are much better at predicting this sort of behavior (or, at least, measuring it with a profiler); therefore, humans are the best ones to make better decisions concerning variable allocation in registers.

8.6 Variable Alignment in Memory

On many processors (particularly RISC), there is another efficiency concern you must take into consideration. Many modern processors will not let you access data at an arbitrary address in memory. Instead, all accesses must take place on some native boundary (usually 4 bytes) that the CPU supports. Even when a CISC processor allows memory accesses at arbitrary byte boundaries, it's often more efficient to access primitive objects (bytes, words, and double words) on a boundary that is a multiple of the object's size (see Figure 8-8).

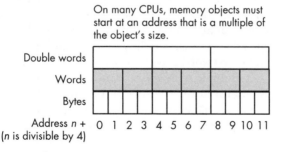

Figure 8-8: Variable alignment in memory

If the CPU supports unaligned accesses—that is, if the CPU allows you to access a memory object on a boundary that is not a multiple of the object's primitive size—then it should be possible to pack the variables into the activation record. This way, you would obtain the maximum number of variables having a short offset. However, because unaligned accesses are sometimes slower than aligned accesses, many optimizing compilers will insert *padding bytes* into the activation record in order to ensure that all variables are aligned on a reasonable boundary for their native size (see Figure 8-9). This trades off slightly better performance for a slightly larger program.

```
char oneByte ;
short twoBytes ;
char oneByte2 ;
int fourBytes ;
```

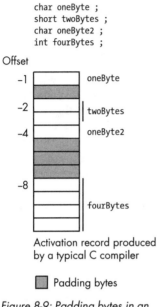

Activation record produced by a typical C compiler

▓ Padding bytes

Figure 8-9: Padding bytes in an activation record

However, if you put all your double-word declarations first, your word declarations second, your byte declarations third, and your array/ structure declarations last, you can improve both the speed and size of your code. The compiler will usually ensure that the first local variable you declare appears at a reasonable boundary (typically a double-word boundary). By declaring all your double-word variables first, you ensure that all such variables appear at an address that is a multiple of 4 (because compilers usually allocate adjacent variables in your declarations in adjacent locations in memory). The first word-sized object you declare will also appear at an address that is a multiple of 4, and that means its address is also a multiple of 2 (which is best for word accesses). By declaring all your word variables together, you ensure that each word variable appears at an address that is a multiple of 2. On processors that allow byte access to memory, the placement of the byte variables (with respect to efficiently accessing the byte data) is irrelevant. By declaring all your local byte variables last in a procedure or function, you generally ensure that such declarations do not impact the performance of the double-word and word variables you also use in the function. Figure 8-10 shows what a typical activation record will look like if you declare your variables as in the following function.

```
int someFunction( void )
{
    int d1;    // Assume ints are 32-bit objects
    int d2;
    int d3;
    short w1; // Assume shorts are 16-bit objects
    short w2;
    char b1;  // Assume chars are 8-bit objects
    char b2;
    char b3;
        .
        .
        .
} // end someFunction
```

Note in Figure 8-10 how all the double-word variables (d1, d2, and d3) begin at addresses that are multiples of 4 (–4, –8, and –12). Also, notice how all the word-sized variables (w1 and w2) begin at addresses that are multiples of 2 (–14 and –16). The byte variables (b1, b2, and b3) begin at arbitrary addresses in memory (both even and odd addresses).

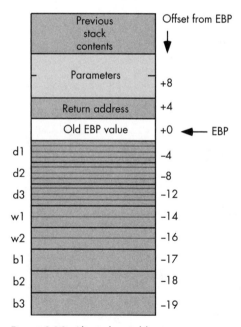

Figure 8-10: Aligned variables in an activation record

Now consider the following function that has arbitrary (unordered) variable declarations and the corresponding activation record (appearing in Figure 8-11):

```
int someFunction2( void )
{
```

```
char b1;   // Assume chars are 8-bit objects
int d1;    // Assume ints are 32-bit objects
short w1;  // Assume shorts are 16-bit objects
int d2;
short w2;
char b2;
int d3;
char b3;
    .
    .
    .
} // end someFunction2
```

As you can see in Figure 8-11, every variable except the byte variables appear at an address that is inappropriate for the object. On processors that allow memory accesses at arbitrary addresses, it may take more time to access a variable that is not aligned on an appropriate boundary.

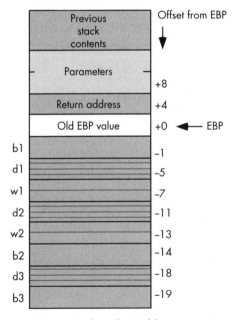

Figure 8-11: Unaligned variables in an activation record

Some processors do not allow a program to access an object at an unaligned address. Most RISC processors, for example, cannot access memory except at 32-bit address boundaries. To access a short or byte value, some RISC processors require the software to read a 32-bit value and extract the 16-bit or 8-bit value (that is, the CPU forces the software to treat bytes and words as packed data). The extra instructions and memory accesses needed to pack and unpack this data reduce the speed of memory access by a considerable amount (that is, two or more instructions—usually more—may be needed to fetch a byte or word from memory). Writing data to memory is even worse because the CPU must first fetch the data from memory, merge the new data with the old data, and then write the result back to memory. Therefore, most RISC compilers won't create an activation record similar to the one in Figure 8-11. Instead, they will add padding bytes so that every memory object begins at an address boundary that is a multiple of four bytes (see Figure 8-12).

In Figure 8-12 notice that all of the variables are at addresses that are multiples of 32 bits. Therefore, a RISC processor has no problems accessing any of these variables. The cost, of course, is that the activation record is quite a bit larger (the local variables consume 32 bytes rather than 19 bytes).

Although the example in Figure 8-12 is typical for RISC-based compilers, don't get the impression that compilers for CISC CPUs won't do this as well. Many compilers for the 80x86, for example, will also build this activation record in order to improve performance of the code the compiler generates. Although declaring your variables in a misaligned fashion may not slow down your code on a CISC CPU, it may result in additional memory usage.

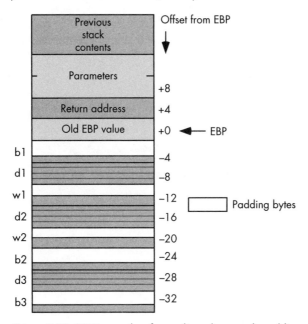

Figure 8-12: RISC compilers force aligned access by adding padding bytes

Of course, if you work in assembly language, it is generally up to you to declare your variables in a manner that is appropriate or efficient for your particular processor. In HLA (on the 80x86), for example, the following two procedure declarations result in the activation records appearing in Figures 8-10, 8-11, and 8-12:

```
procedure someFunction; @nodisplay; @noalignstack;
var
    d1  :dword;
    d2  :dword;
    d3  :dword;
```

```
    w1   :word;
    w2   :word;
    b1   :byte;
    b2   :byte;
    b3   :byte;
begin someFunction;
       .

       .

       .

end someFunction;


procedure someFunction2; @nodisplay; @noalignstack;
var
    b1   :byte;
    d1   :dword;
    w1   :word;
    d2   :dword;
    w2   :word;
    b2   :byte;
    d3   :dword;
    b3   :byte;
begin someFunction2;
       .

       .

       .

end someFunction2;


procedure someFunction3; @nodisplay; @noalignstack;
var
    // HLA align directive forces alignment of the next declaration.

    align(4);
    b1   :byte;
    align(4);
    d1   :dword;
    align(4);
    w1   :word;
    align(4);
    d2   :dword;
    align(4);
    w2   :word;
    align(4);
    b2   :byte;
    align(4);
    d3   :dword;
    align(4);
    b3   :byte;
begin someFunction3;
       .

       .

       .

end someFunction3;
```

HLA procedures someFunction and someFunction3 will produce the fastest-running code on any 80x86 processor because all variables are aligned on an appropriate boundary. HLA procedures someFunction and someFunction2 will produce the most compact activation records on an 80x86 CPU because there is no padding between variables in the activation record. If you're working in assembly language on a RISC CPU, then you'll probably want to choose the equivalent of someFunction or someFunction3 to make it easier to access the variables in memory.

8.6.1 Records and Alignment

Records/structures in HLLs also have alignment issues about which you should worry. Recently, CPU manufacturers have been promoting *Application Binary Interface (ABI)* standards to promote interoperability between different programming languages and implementations of those languages. Although not all languages and compilers adhere to these suggestions, many of the newer compilers do. Among other things, these ABI specifications describe how the compilers should organize fields within a record or structure object in memory. Although the rules vary by CPU, a generic description that is applicable to most ABIs is that a compiler should align a record/structure field at an offset that is a multiple of the object's size. If two adjacent fields in the record or structure have different sizes, and the placement of the first field in the structure would cause the second field to appear at an offset that is not a multiple of that second field's native size, then the compiler will insert some padding bytes to push the second field to a higher offset that is appropriate for that second object's size.

In actual practice, ABIs for different CPUs have minor differences based on the CPUs' ability to access objects at different addresses in memory. Intel, for example, suggests that compiler writers align bytes at any offset, words at even offsets, and everything else at offsets that are a multiple of 4. Some ABIs recommend placing 64-bit objects at 8-byte boundaries within a record. Some CPUs, which have a difficult time accessing objects smaller than 32 bits, may suggest a minimum alignment of 32 bits for all objects in a record/structure. The rules vary depending on the CPU and whether the manufacturer wants to promote faster executing code (the usual case) or smaller data structures.

If you are writing code for a single CPU (e.g., an Intel-based PC) with a single compiler, you should learn that compiler's rules for padding fields and adjust your declarations for maximum performance and minimal waste. However, if you ever need to compile your code using several different compilers, particularly compilers for several different CPUs, following one set of rules will work fine on one machine and produce less efficient code on several others. Fortunately, there are some rules that can help reduce the inefficiencies created by recompiling for a different ABI.

From a performance/memory usage standpoint, the best solution is the same rule we saw earlier for activation records: When declaring fields in a record, group all like-sized objects together and put all the larger (scalar) objects first and the smaller objects last in the record/structure.[8] This scheme will produce the least amount of waste (padding bytes) and provide the highest performance across most of the ABIs in existence. The only drawback to this approach is that you have to organize the fields by their native size rather than by their logical relationship to one another. However, because all fields of a record/structure are logically related insofar as they are all members of that same record/structure, this problem isn't as bad as employing this organization for all of a particular function's local variables.

Many programmers try to add padding fields themselves to a structure. For example, the following type of code is common in the Linux kernel and other bits and pieces of overly hacked software:

```
typedef struct IveAligned
{
    char byteValue;
    char padding0[3];
    int  dwordValue;
    short wordValue;
    char padding1[2];
    unsigned long dwordValue2;
        .
        .
        .
};
```

The padding0 and padding1 fields in this structure were added to manually align the dwordValue and dwordValue2 fields at offsets that are even multiples of 4.

While this padding is not unreasonable, if you're using a compiler that doesn't automatically align the fields, keep in mind that an attempt to compile this code in a different machine can produce unexpected results. For example, if a compiler aligns all fields on a 32-bit boundary, regardless of size, then this structure declaration will consume two extra double words to hold the two paddingX arrays. This winds up wasting space for no good reason. So, keep this fact in mind if you decide to manually add the padding fields yourself.

Many compilers that automatically align fields in a structure provide an option to turn off this facility. This is particularly true for compilers generating code for CPUs where the alignment is optional and the compiler only does this to achieve a slight performance boost. If you're going to manually add padding fields to your record/structure, you obviously need to specify this option so that the compiler doesn't realign the fields after you've manually aligned them.

In theory, a compiler is free to rearrange the offsets of local variables within an activation record. However, it would be extremely rare for a compiler to rearrange the fields of a user-defined record or structure. Too many external programs and data structures depend on the fields of a record appearing in the same order as they are declared. This is particularly true

---

[8] Generally, arrays and records/structures appearing as fields wind up at the end of the list of fields, though you could group arrays with the objects whose size matches the array's element size as well.

when passing record/structure data between code written in two separate languages (for example, when calling a function written in assembly language).

In assembly language, the amount of effort needed to align fields varies from pure manual labor to a rich set of features capable of automatically handling almost any ABI. Some (low-end) assemblers don't even provide record or structure data types. In such systems, the assembly programmer has to manually specify the offsets into a record structure (typically by declaring, as constants, the numeric offsets into the structure). Other assemblers (e.g., NASM) provide macros that automatically generate the equates for you. In such systems as these, the programmer has to manually provide padding fields to align certain fields on a given boundary. Some assemblers, such as MASM and TASM, provide simple alignment facilities. You can specify the value 1, 2, or 4 when declaring a struct in MASM or TASM, and the assembler will align all fields on either the alignment value you specify or at an offset that is a multiple of the object's size, whichever is smaller. It accomplishes this by automatically adding padding bytes to the structure. Also, note that MASM (and TASM) will add a sufficient number of padding bytes to the end of the structure so that the whole structure's length is a multiple of the alignment size. Consider the following struct declaration in MASM:

```
Student   struct  2
score     word    ?   ;offset 0
id        byte    ?   ;offset 2, one byte of padding appears after this field
year      dword   ?   ;offset 4
id2       byte    ?   ;offset 8
Student   ends
```

In this example, MASM will add an extra byte of padding to the end of the structure so that the structure's length is a multiple of 2 bytes.

MASM and TASM also let you control the alignment of individual fields within a structure by using the align directive. The following structure declaration is equivalent to the current example (note the absence of the alignment value operand in the struct operand field):

```
Student   struct
score     word    ?   ;offset 0
id        byte    ?   ;offset 2
          align   2   ;Injects one byte of padding.
year      dword   ?   ;offset 4
id2       byte    ?   ;offset 8
          align   2   ;Adds one byte of padding to the end of the struct.
Student   ends
```

The default field alignment for MASM/TASM structures is unaligned. That is, a field begins at the next available offset within the structure, regardless of the field's (and the previous field's) size.

The High-Level Assembler (HLA) probably provides the greatest control (both automatic and manual) over record field alignment. Like MASM, the default record alignment is unaligned. Also, like MASM, you can use HLA's align directive to manually align fields in an HLA record. The following is the HLA version of the previous MASM example:

```
type
    Student :record
        score :word;
        id    :byte;
        align(2);
        year  :dword;
        id2   :byte;
        align(2);
    endrecord;
```

HLA also lets you specify an automatic alignment for all fields in a record. For example:

```
type
    Student :record[2]   //This tells HLA to align all
                         // fields on a word boundary
        score :word;
        id    :byte;
        year  :dword;
        id2   :byte;
    endrecord;
```

There is a subtle difference between this HLA record and the earlier MASM structure (with automatic alignment). When you specify a directive of the form Student struct 2 MASM will align all fields on a boundary that is an multiple of 2 or a multiple of the object's size, *whichever is smaller*. HLA, on the other hand, will always align all fields on a 2-byte boundary using this declaration, even if the field is a byte.

The fact that you can force field alignment to a minimum size is a nice feature if you're working with data structures generated on a different machine (or compiler) that forces this kind of alignment. However, this type of alignment can unnecessarily waste space in a record for certain declarations if you only want the fields to be aligned on their natural boundaries (which is what MASM is doing). Fortunately, HLA provides another syntax for record declarations that let you specify both the maximum and minimum alignment that HLA will apply to a field. That syntax takes the following form:

```
recordID: record[ maxAlign : minAlign ]
    <<fields>>
endrecord;
```

The maxAlign item specifies the largest alignment that HLA will use within the record. HLA will align any object whose native size is larger than maxAlign on a boundary of maxAlign bytes. Similarly, HLA will align any object whose size is smaller than minAlign on a boundary of at least minAlign bytes. HLA will align objects whose native size is between `minAlign` and `maxAlign` on a boundary that is a multiple of that object's size. The following HLA and MASM record/struct declarations are equivalent. Here's MASM code:

```
Student  struct  4
score    word    ?    ;offset:0
id       byte    ?    ;offset 2

    ; One byte of padding appears here

year     dword   ?    ;offset 4
id2      byte    ?    ;offset:8

    ; 3 padding bytes appear here

courses  dword   ?    ;offset:12
Student  ends
```

Here's the HLA code:

```
type
    // Align on 4-byte offset, or object's size, whichever
    //  is the smaller of the two. Also, make sure that the
    //  entire record is a multiple of 4 bytes long.

    Student  :record[4:1]
        score    :word;
        id       :byte;
        year     :dword
        id2      :byte;
      courses    :dword;
    endrecord;
```

Although few HLLs provide facilities within the language's design to control the alignment of fields within records (or other data structures), many compilers do provide extensions to those languages, in the form of compiler *pragmas*, that let programmers specifying default variable and field alignment. Because there are no standards for this, you'll have to check your particular compiler's reference manual. Although such extensions are nonstandard, they are often quite useful, especially when linking code compiled by different languages or if you're trying to squeeze the last bit of performance out of a system.

8.7 For More Information

One of the best places to look for more information on how HLLs implement variables is a programming language textbook. Dozens of decent programming design textbooks are available, for example:

- *Programming Languages, Design and Implementation*, Terrence Pratt and Marvin Zelkowitz (Prentice Hall, 2001)

- *Programming Languages, Principles and Practice*, Kenneth Louden (Course Technology, 2002)
- *Concepts of Programming Languages*, Robert Sebesta (Addison-Wesley, 2003)
- *Programming Languages, Structures and Models*, Herbert Dershem and Michael Jipping (Wadsworth, 1990)
- *The Programming Language Landscape*, Henry Ledgard and Michael Marcotty (SRA, 1986)
- *Programming Language Concepts*, Carlo Ghezzi and Jehdi Jazayeri (Wiley, 1997)

Of course, any textbook on compiler design and construction can be a source of information about implementating variables in an HLL. Here are a few examples of compiler-construction textbooks you may want to consider looking at:

- *Compilers, Principles, Techniques, and Tools*, Alfred Aho, Ravi Sethi, and Jeffrey Ullman (Addison-Wesley, 1986)
- *Compiler Construction: Theory and Practice*, William Barret and John Couch (SRA, 1986)
- *A Retargetable C Compiler: Design and Implementation*, Christopher Fraser and David Hansen (Addison-Wesley Professional, 1995)
- *Introduction to Compiler Design*, Thomas Parsons (W. H. Freeman, 1992)
- *Compiler Construction, Principles and Practice*, Kenneth Louden (Course Technology, 1997)

CPU manufacturers' literature, data sheets, and books are also quite useful for determining how compilers will often implement variables. For example, *The PowerPC Compiler Writer's Guide*, edited by Steve Hoxey, Faraydon Karim, Bill Hay, and Hank Warren,[9] is a great reference for programmers writing code to run on a PowerPC processor; most PowerPC compiler writers have used this reference to help them decide how to generate code for the PowerPC processor. Similarly, many compiler writers have used Intel's Pentium manual set (including their *Optimization Guide*) to help them write code generators for their compilers. These manuals may prove handy to someone who wants to understand how 80x86-based compilers generate code.

Of course, the ultimate suggestion is to learn assembly language. If you become an expert assembly language programmer, someone who knows the intricacies of all the machine instructions for a particular processor, then you'll have a much better understanding of how a compiler will generate code for that processor. If you're interested in learning 80x86 assembly language, you might consider *The Art of Assembly Language* (No Starch Press, 2003).

---

[9] This document is available in PDF format on IBM's website (www.ibm.com).

9

ARRAY DATA TYPES

High-level language abstractions hide how the machine deals with *composite data types* (a complex data type built from, or composed of, smaller data objects). Although these abstractions are often convenient, if you don't understand the details behind them you might inadvertently use some construct that generates unnecessary code or runs slower than is necessary. In this chapter, I'll take a look at one of the most important composite data types: the array. I'll consider the following topics:

- The definition of an array
- How to declare arrays in various languages
- The memory representation of arrays
- Accessing elements of arrays
- Multidimensional arrays: their declaration, representation, and access
- Row-major and column-major multidimensional array access

- Dynamic versus static arrays
- How your use of arrays can impact the performance and size of your applications

Arrays are very common in modern applications. Therefore, you should have a solid understand of how programs implement and use arrays in memory in order to write efficient code. This chapter will teach you all about arrays so you can use them more efficiently in your programs.

9.1 What Is an Array?

Arrays are one of the most common *composite data types.* Yet, few programmers fully understand how arrays operate and know about their efficiency trade-offs. Programmers frequently view arrays from a completely different perspective once they understand how arrays operate at the machine level.

Abstractly, an array is an aggregate data type whose members (*elements*) are all of the same type. A member from the array is selected by specifying the member's array index with an integer (or with some value whose underlying representation is integer, such as character, enumerated, and Boolean types). In this chapter, I'll assume that all of the integer indexes of an array are numerically contiguous. That is, if both x and y are valid indexes of the array, and if x < y, then all i such that x < i < y are also valid indexes. I will also assume that array elements occupy contiguous locations in memory, although this is not required by the general definition of an array. An array with five elements appears in memory as shown in Figure 9-1.

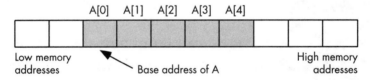

Figure 9-1: Array layout in memory

The *base address* of an array is the address of the first element of the array, and it is at the lowest memory location. The second array element directly follows the first in memory, the third element follows the second, and so on. Note that the indexes do not have to start at zero. They may start with any number as long as they are contiguous. However, discussing array access is easier if the first index is zero. So for this discussion, I'll generally begin most arrays at index zero unless there is a good reason to do otherwise.

Whenever you apply the indexing operator to an array, the result is the unique array element specified by that index. For example, A[i] chooses the ith element from array A.

9.1.1 Array Declarations

Array declarations are very similar across many high-level languages. In this section I'll look at some examples in several languages.

9.1.1.1 Declaring Arrays in C, C++, and Java

C, C++, and Java all let you declare an array by specifying the total number of elements in it. The syntax for an array declaration in these languages is

```
data_type  array_name [ number_of_elements ];
```

Here are some sample C/C++ array declarations:

```
char CharArray[ 128 ];
int intArray[ 8 ];
unsigned char ByteArray[ 10 ];
int *PtrArray[ 4 ];
```

If these arrays are declared as automatic variables, C/C++ "initializes" them with whatever bit patterns happen to be present in memory. If, on the other hand, you declare these arrays as static objects, then C/C++ zeros out (sets to zero) each array element. If you want to initialize an array yourself, then you can use the following C/C++ syntax:

```
data_type array_name[ number_of_elements ] = {element_list};
```

Here's a typical example:

```
int intArray[8] = {0,1,2,3,4,5,6,7};
```

The C/C++ compiler will store these initial array values in the object code file and the operating system will load these values into the memory locations assocated with intArray when the OS loads the program into memory. To see how this works, consider the following C/C++ program:

```
static int intArray[8] = {1,2,3,4,5,6,7,8};
static int array2[8];

int main( int argc, char **argv )
{
    int i;
    for(i = 0; i < 8; ++i )
    {
        array2[i] = intArray[i];
    }
    for(i = 7; i >= 0; --i )
    {
        printf( "%d\n", array2[i] );
    }
    return 0;
}
```

Here is the 80x86 assembly code that Microsoft's Visual C++ compiler emits for the two array declarations:

```
_DATA       SEGMENT
_intArray DD        01H
      DD    02H
      DD    03H
      DD    04H
      DD    05H
      DD    06H
      DD    07H
      DD    08H
_DATA       ENDS

_BSS        SEGMENT
_array2     DD      08H DUP (?)
_BSS        ENDS
```

The DD *(define double word)* statement reserves 4 bytes of storage each, and the operand specifies their initial value when the operating system loads the program into memory. The intArray declaration appears in the _DATA segment, which in the Microsoft memory model can contain initialized data. The array2 variable, on the other hand, is declared inside the BSS segment, where MSVC++ places uninitialized variables (the ? character appearing in the operand field tells the assembler that the data is uninitialized; the 8 dup (?) operand tells the assembler to duplicate the declaration eight times). When the operating system loads the BSS segment into memory, it simply zeros out all the memory associated with the BSS segment. In both of these cases (initialized or uninitialized), you can see that the compiler allocates all eight elements of these arrays in sequential memory locations.

9.1.1.2 Declaring Arrays in HLA

HLA's array declaration syntax takes the following form, which is semantically equivalent to the C/C++ declaration:

array_name : *data_type* [*number_of_elements*];

Here are some examples of HLA array declarations that allocate storage for uninitialized arrays (the second example assumes that you have defined the integer data type in a type section of the HLA program):

```
static

// Character array with elements 0..127.

CharArray: char[128];

// "integer" array with elements 0..7.

IntArray: integer[8];
```

```
// Byte array with elements 0..9.

ByteArray: byte[10];

// Double-word array with elements 0..3.

PtrArray: dword[4];
```

You can also initialize the array elements using declarations like the following:

```
RealArray: real32[8] :=
    [ 0.0, 1.0, 2.0, 3.0, 4.0, 5.0, 6.0, 7.0 ];

IntegerAry: integer[8] :=
    [ 8, 9, 10, 11, 12, 13, 14, 15 ];
```

Both of these definitions create arrays with eight elements. The first definition initializes each 4-byte real32 array element with one of the values in the range 0.0..7.0. The second declaration initializes each integer array element with one of the values in the range 8..15.

9.1.1.3 Declaring Arrays in Pascal, Delphi, and Kylix

Pascal/Delphi/Kylix uses the following syntax to declare an array:

```
array_name : array[ lower_bound..upper_bound ] of data_type;
```

As in the previous examples, array_name is the identifier and data_type is the type of each element in this array. In Pascal/Delphi/Kylix (unlike C/C++, Java, and HLA) you specify the upper and lower bounds of the array rather than the array's size. The following are typical array declarations in Pascal:

```
type
    ptrToChar = ^char;
var
    CharArray: array[0..127] of char;     // 128 elements
    IntArray: array[0..7] of integer;     // 8 elements
    ByteArray: array[0..9] of char;       // 10 elements
    PtrArray: array[0..3] of ptrToChar;   // 4 elements
```

Although these Pascal examples start their indexes at zero, Pascal does not require a starting index of zero. The following is a perfectly valid array declaration in Pascal:

```
var
    ProfitsByYear : array[ 1998..2009 ] of real; // 12 elements
```

The program that declares this array would use indexes 1,998 through 2,009 when accessing elements of this array, not 0 through 11.

Many Pascal compilers provide an extra feature to help you locate defects in your programs. Whenever you access an element of an array, these compilers automatically insert code that will verify that the array index is within the bounds specified by the declaration. This extra code will stop the program if the index is out of range. For example, if an index into ProfitsByYear is outside the range 1,998..2,009 the program will abort with an error. This is a very useful feature that helps verify the correctness of your program.[1]

9.1.1.4   Declaring Arrays with Noninteger Index Values

Generally, array indexes are integer values, although some languages allow other *ordinal types* (data types that use an underlying integer representation). For example, Pascal allows char and boolean array indexes. In Pascal, it's perfectly reasonable and useful to declare an array as follows:

```
alphaCnt : array[ 'A'..'Z' ] of integer;
```

You access elements of alphaCnt using a character expression as the array index. For example, consider the following Pascal code that initializes each element of alphaCnt to zero:

```
for ch := 'A' to 'Z' do
    alphaCnt[ ch ] := 0;
```

Assembly language and C/C++ treat most ordinal values as special instances of integer values, so they are certainly legal array indexes. Most implementations of BASIC allow a floating-point number as an array index, although BASIC always truncates the value to an integer before using it as an index (BASIC allows you to use floating-point values as array indexes because the original BASIC language did not provide support for integer expressions; it only provided real and string values).

9.1.2   Array Representation in Memory

Abstractly, an *array* is a collection of variables that you access using an index. Semantically, you can define an array any way you please as long as it maps distinct indexes to distinct objects in memory and always maps the same index to the same object. In practice, however, most languages utilize a few common algorithms that provide efficient access to the array data.

The most common implementation of arrays is to store array elements in consecutive memory locations. Most programming languages store the first element of an array at a low memory address and then store the following elements in successively higher memory locations.

---

[1] Many Pascal compilers provide an option to turn off this array index range checking once your program is fully tested. Turning off the bounds checking improves the efficiency of the resulting program.

Consider the following C program and the PowerPC assembly code that GCC emits for it:

```
#include <stdio.h>

static char array[8] = {0,1,2,3,4,5,6,7};


int main( void )
{

    printf( "%d\n", array[0] );
}
```

Here is the PowerPC assembly code that corresponds to the array declaration:

```
        .align 2
_array:
        .byte   0   ;Note that the assembler stores the byte
        .byte   1   ; values on successive lines into
        .byte   2   ; contiguous memory locations.
        .byte   3
        .byte   4
        .byte   5
        .byte   6
        .byte   7
```

The number of bytes an array consumes is the number of elements multiplied by the number of bytes per element. In the previous example, each array element is a single byte, so the array consumes the same number of bytes as it has elements. However, for arrays with larger elements, the entire array would consume the product of the number of elements and the element size. Consider the following C code and the corresponding GCC assembly language output:

```
#include <stdio.h>

static int array[8] = {0,0,0,0,0,0,0,1};


int main( void )
{
    printf( "%d\n", array[0] );
}
```

Consider the conversion to PowerPC assembly language by GCC:

```
        .align 2
_array:
        .long  0
        .long  0
        .long  0
        .long  0
        .long  0
        .long  0
        .long  0
        .long  1
```

Many languages also add a few additional bytes of padding at the end of an array so that the total length of the array will be a multiple of a convenient value like 2 or 4 (making it easy to compute indexes into the array using shifts; see *Write Great Code, Volume 1*, for details). However, a program must *not* access the extra padding bytes because they may or may not be present. Some compilers put them in, some will not, and some will only put them in depending on the type of object that immediately follows the array in memory.

Many optimizing compilers try to start an array at a memory address that is a multiple of a common size like 2, 4, or 8 bytes. This, effectively, adds padding bytes before the beginning of the array or, if you prefer to think of it this way, it adds padding bytes to the end of the previous object in memory (see Figure 9-2).

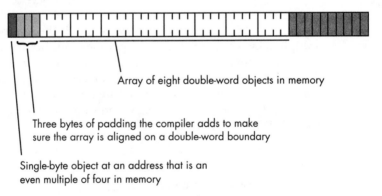

Array of eight double-word objects in memory

Three bytes of padding the compiler adds to make sure the array is aligned on a double-word boundary

Single-byte object at an address that is an even multiple of four in memory

Figure 9-2: Adding padding bytes before an array

On machines that do not support byte-addressable memory, compilers that attempt to place the first element of an array on an easily accessed boundary will allocate storage for an array on whatever boundary the machine supports. In the previous example, the .align 2 directive precedes the _array declaration. In Gas syntax, the .align directive tells the assembler to adjust the memory address of the next object declared in the source file so that it starts at an address that is a multiple of some power of 2 (specified by

.align's operand). In this example, the .align 2 directive tells the assembler to align the first element of _array on an address boundary that is a multiple of 4 (that is, 2^2).

If the size of each array element is less than the minimum-sized memory object the CPU supports, then the compiler implementer has two options:

- Allocate the smallest accessible memory object for each element of the array
- Pack multiple array elements into a single memory cell

Option 1 has the advantage of being fast, but it wastes memory because each array element carries some extra storage that it doesn't need. The following C example creates an array of structures (I'll look at C structures in a later chapter) in order to allocate storage for an array whose element size is 5 bytes (each array element is a structure object consisting of a 4-byte long object and a 1-byte char object). When GCC compiles this code to run on a PowerPC processor that requires double-word alignment for long objects, the compiler automatically inserts 3 bytes of padding between each element. Here's the sample C code that demonstrates this:

```
#include <stdio.h>

typedef struct
{
    long a;
    char b;
} FiveBytes;

static FiveBytes shortArray[2] = {{2,3}, {4,5}};


int main( void )
{
    printf( "%d\n", shortArray[0].a );
}
```

Here is the pertinent PowerPC assembly code that GCC generates for the FiveBytes array declaration:

```
.data
        .align 2    ;Ensure that _shortArray begins on an
                    ; address boundary that is a multiple
                    ; of four.
_shortArray:
        .long   2   ;shortArray[0].a
        .byte   3   ;shortArray[0].b
        .space 3    ;Padding, to align next element to 4 bytes
        .long   4   ;shortArray[1].a
        .byte   5   ;shortArray[1].b
        .space 3    ;Padding, at end of array.
```

Option 2 is compact, but it requires extra instructions to pack and unpack data when accessing array elements, which means that accessing elements is slower. Compilers on such machines often provide an option that lets you specify whether you want the data packed or unpacked so you can choose between space and speed. Keep in mind that if you're working on a byte-addressable machine (like the 80x86) then you probably don't have to worry about this issue. However, if you're using a high-level language and your code might wind up running on a different machine at some point in the future, you should choose an array organization that is efficient on all machines (that is, choose an organization that pads each element of the array with extra bytes).

9.1.3 Accessing Elements of an Array

If you allocate all the storage for an array in contiguous memory locations and the first index of the array is zero, then accessing an element of a single-dimensional array is simple. You can compute the byte address of any given element of an array using the following formula:

```
Element_Address = Base_Address + ( index * Element_Size )
```

The Element_Size item is the number of bytes that each array element occupies. Therefore, if the array contains elements of type byte, the Element_Size field is 1 and the computation is very simple. If each element of the array is a word (or other 2-byte type) then Element_Size is 2, and so on. Consider the following Pascal array declaration:

```
var  SixteenInts : array[ 0..15 ] of integer;
```

To access an element of the SixteenInts on a byte-addressable machine, assuming 4-byte integers, you'd use this calculation:

```
Element_Address = AddressOf( SixteenInts ) + index * 4
```

In assembly language (where you would actually have to do this calculation manually rather than having the compiler do the work for you), you'd use code like the following to access array element SixteenInts[index]:

```
mov( index, ebx );
mov( SixteenInts[ ebx*4 ], eax );
```

To demonstrate this in action, consider the following Pascal/Delphi program and the resulting 80x86 code (obtained by disassembling the EXE output from the Delphi compiler and pasting the result back into the original Pascal code):

```
program x(input,output);
var
    i :integer;
```

```
sixteenInts :array[0..15] of integer;

function changei(i:integer):integer;
begin
    changei := 15 - i;
end;

// changei          proc near
//                  mov    edx, 0Fh
//                  sub    edx, eax
//                  mov    eax, edx
//                  retn
// changei          endp


begin

for i := 0 to 15 do
    sixteenInts[ changei(i) ] := i;

//                  xor    ebx, ebx
//
// loc_403AA7:
//                  mov    eax, ebx
//                  call   changei
//
// Note the use of the scaled-indexed addressing mode
// to multiply the array index by four prior to accessing
// elements of the array:
//
//                  mov    ds:sixteenInts[eax*4], ebx
//                  inc    ebx
//                  cmp    ebx, 10h
//                  jnz    short loc_403AA7

end.
```

As in the HLA example, the Delphi compiler uses the 80x86 scaled-indexed addressing mode to multiply the index into the array by the element size (4 bytes). The 80x86 provides four different scaling values for the scaled-indexed addressing mode: 1, 2, 4, or 8 bytes. If the array's element size is not one of these four values, the machine code must explicitly multiply the index by the array element's size. The following Delphi/Pascal code (and corresponding 80x86 code from the disassembly) demonstrates this using a record that has 9 bytes of active data (Delphi rounds this up to the next multiple of 4 bytes, so Delphi actually allocates 12 bytes for each element of the array of records).

```
program x(input,output);
type
    NineBytes=
        record
            FourBytes       :integer;
```

```
                    FourMoreBytes    :integer;
                    OneByte          :char;
                end;

var
    i                   :integer;
    NineByteArray       :array[0..15] of NineBytes;

    function changei(i:integer):integer;
    begin
        changei := 15 - i;
    end;

    // changei          proc near
    //                  mov     edx, 0Fh
    //                  sub     edx, eax
    //                  mov     eax, edx
    //                  retn
    // changei          endp


begin

    for i:= 0 to 15 do
        NineByteArray[ changei(i) ].FourBytes := i;

//                      xor     ebx, ebx
//
//  loc_403AA7:
//                      mov     eax, ebx
//                      call    changei
//
//                      // Compute EAX = EAX * 3
//
//                      lea     eax, [eax+eax*2]
//
//                  // Actual index used is index * 12 ((EAX * 3) * 4)
//
//                      mov     ds:NineByteArray[eax*4], ebx
//                      inc     ebx
//                      cmp     ebx, 10h
//                      jnz     short loc_403AA7


end.
```

Microsoft and Borland C/C++ compilers emit comparable code (also allocating 12 bytes for each element of the array of records).

9.1.4   *Padding Versus Packing*

These Pascal examples demonstrate an important issue: compilers generally pad each array element to a multiple of 4 bytes, or whatever size is most convenient for the machine's architecture. Compilers do this in order to improve access to array elements (and record fields) by ensuring that those elements are always aligned on a memory boundary that is reasonable for the array element. Some compilers give you the option of eliminating the padding at the end of each array element, so that successive array elements immediately follow the previous element in memory. In Pascal/Delphi, for example, you can achieve this by using the packed keyword:

```
program x(input,output);

// Note the use of the "packed" keyword.
// This tells Delphi to pack each record
// into nine consecutive bytes, without
// any padding at the end of the record.

type
    NineBytes=
        packed record
            FourBytes        :integer;
            FourMoreBytes    :integer;
            OneByte          :char;
        end;

var
    i                   :integer;
    NineByteArray    :array[0..15] of NineBytes;

    function changei(i:integer):integer;
    begin
        changei := 15 - i;
    end;

// changei         proc near
//                 mov     edx, 0Fh
//                 sub     edx, eax
//                 mov     eax, edx
//                 retn
// changei         endp


begin

    for i := 0 to 15 do
        NineByteArray[ changei(i) ].FourBytes := i;

//                 xor     ebx, ebx
//
// loc_403AA7:
//                 mov     eax, ebx
//                 call    changei
//
//      // Compute index (eax) = index * 9
//      // (computed as index = index + index * 8):
//
//                 lea     eax, [eax+eax*8]
```

```
//
//                 mov        ds:NineBytes[eax], ebx
//                 inc        ebx
//                 cmp        ebx, 10h
//                 jnz        short loc_403AA7
```

end.

Note that the packed reserved word is just a hint to a Pascal compiler. A generic Pascal compiler can choose to ignore this keyword—the Pascal standard does not make any explicit claims about its impact on a compiler's code generation. Borland's Pascal products (including Delphi and Kylix) use the packed keyword to tell the compiler to pack array (and record) elements on a byte boundary rather than a 4-byte boundary. Other Pascal compilers actually use this keyword to align objects on *bit* boundaries. See your compiler's documentation for more information about the packed keyword. Few other languages provide a way, within the generic language definition, to pack data into a given boundary. In the C/C++ languages, for example, many compilers provide pragmas or command-line switches to control array element padding, but these facilities are almost always specific to a particular compiler.

In general, choosing between packed and padded array elements (when the choice is possible) is usually a trade-off between speed and space. Packed array elements let you save a small amount of space for each array element at the expense of slower access to those elements (for example, when accessing a double-word object at an odd address in memory). Furthermore, computing the index into an array whose element size is not a convenient multiple of 2 (or better yet, a power of 2) can require more instructions, thereby reducing the speed of programs that access elements of such arrays.

Of course, some machine architectures don't allow misaligned data access, so if you're writing portable code that must compile and run on different CPUs, you shouldn't count on the fact that array elements can be tightly packed into memory. Some compilers may not give you this option.

Before closing this discussion, it's worthwhile to point out that the best array element sizes are those that are some power of 2. Generally, it will take only a single instruction to multiply any array index by a power of 2 (that single instruction is a shift-left instruction). Consider the following C program and the assembly output produced by Borland's C++ compiler; this compiler uses arrays that have 32-byte elements:

```
typedef struct
{
    double EightBytes;
    double EightMoreBytes;
    float  SixteenBytes[4];
} PowerOfTwoBytes;

int i;
```

```
PowerOfTwoBytes ThirtyTwoBytes[16];

int changei(int i)
{
    return 15 - i;
}


int main( int argc, char **argv )
{
    for( i = 0; i < 16; ++i )
    {
        ThirtyTwoBytes[ changei(i) ].EightBytes = 0.0;
    }

    // @5:
    //   push       ebx
    //   call       _changei
    //   pop        ecx             // Remove parameter
    //
    // Multiply index (in EAX) by 32.
    // Note that (eax << 5) = eax * 32
    //
    //   shl        eax,5
    //
    // Eight bytes of zeros are the coding for
    // (double) 0.0:
    //
    //   xor        edx,edx
    //   mov        dword ptr [eax+_ThirtyTwoBytes],edx
    //   mov        dword ptr [eax+_ThirtyTwoBytes+4],edx
    //
    // Finish the for loop here:
    //
    //   inc        dword ptr [esi]   ;ESI points at i.
    // @6:
    //   mov        ebx,dword ptr [esi]
    //   cmp        ebx,16
    //   jl         short @5

    return 0;
}
```

As you can see in this code, the Borland C++ compiler emits a `shl` instruction to multiply the index by 32.

9.1.5 Multidimensional Arrays

A *multidimensional* array is one that lets you select an element of the array using two or more independent index values. A classic example is a two-dimensional data structure (array) that tracks product sales versus date. One index into the table could be the date; the other index into the table would be the product value. The element of the array selected by these two indexes would be the total sales of that product on a given date. A three-dimensional extension of this example could be sales of products by date and by country. Again, a combination of product value, date value, and country value would address an element in the array to give you the sales of that product within that country on the specified date.

Most CPUs can easily handle single-dimensional arrays using an indexed addressing mode. Unfortunately, there is no magic addressing mode that lets you easily access the elements of multidimensional arrays. That's going to take some work and several machine instructions.

9.1.5.1 Declaring Multidimensional Arrays

If you have an *m*-by-*n* array, it will have m × n elements and require m × n × Element_Size bytes of storage. With single-dimensional arrays, the syntax that the different HLLs employ is very similar. However, their syntax starts to differ when you consider multidimensional arrays.

In C, C++, and Java, you would use the following syntax to declare a multidimensional array:

```
data_type array_name [dim₁][dim₂]...[dimₙ];
```

Here is a concrete example of a three-dimensional array declaration in C/C++:

```
int threeDInts[ 4 ][ 2 ][ 8 ];
```

This example creates an array with 64 elements organized with a depth of 4 by 2 rows by 8 columns. Assuming each int object requires 4 bytes, this array consumes 256 bytes of storage.

Pascal's syntax actually supports two equivalent ways of declaring multidimensional arrays. The following example demonstrates both of these two forms:

```
var
    threeDInts:
        array[0..3] of array[0..1] of array[0..7] of integer;

    threeDInts2: array[0..3, 0..1, 0..7] of integer;
```

Semantically, there are only two major differences in the way different languages handle multidimensional arrays. The first difference is whether the array declaration specifies the overall size of each array dimension or whether it specifies the upper and lower bounds. The second difference is whether the starting index is zero, one, or a user-specified value.

9.1.5.2 Mapping Multidimensional Array Elements to Memory

Now that you've seen some example array declarations, you need to figure out how to implement them in memory. The first problem is learning to store a multidimensional object into a one-dimensional memory space.

Consider for a moment a Pascal array of the following form:

```
A:array[0..3,0..3] of char;
```

This array contains 16 bytes organized as four rows of four characters. Somehow, you have to draw a correspondence between each of the 16 bytes in this array and each of the 16 contiguous bytes in main memory. Figure 9-3 shows one way to do this.

The actual mapping of positions within the array grid to memory addresses can be done in different ways as long as two things occur:

- No two entries in the array occupy the same memory location.

- Each element in the array always maps to the same memory location.

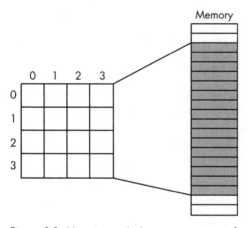

Figure 9-3: Mapping a 4×4 array to sequential memory locations

Therefore, what you really need is a function with two input parameters (one for a row and one for a column value) that produces an offset into a contiguous block of 16 memory locations.

Now any old function that satisfies these two constraints will work fine. However, what you really want is a mapping function that is efficient to compute at runtime and works for arrays with any number of dimensions and any bounds on those dimensions. While there are a large number of possible functions that fit this bill, most HLLs use one of two different organizations: row-major ordering and column-major ordering.

9.1.5.3 Row-Major Ordering

Row-major ordering assigns array elements to successive memory locations by moving across the rows and then down the columns. Figure 9-4 demonstrates this mapping.

Row-major ordering is the method employed by most high-level programming languages including Pascal, C/C++/C#, Java, Ada, and Modula-2. It is very easy to implement and is easy to use in machine language. The conversion from a two-dimensional structure to a linear sequence is very intuitive. Figure 9-5 provides another view of the ordering of a 4×4 array.

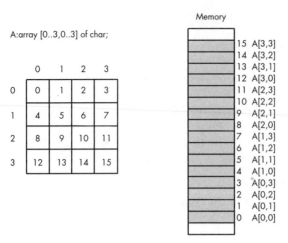

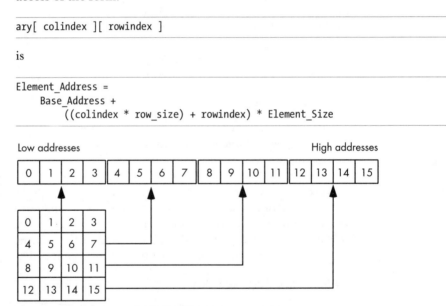

Figure 9-4: Row-major array element ordering

The function that converts the set of multidimensional array indexes into a single offset is a slight modification of the formula for computing the address of an element of a single-dimensional array. The generic formula to compute the offset into a two-dimensional row-major ordered array given an access of the form:

```
ary[ colindex ][ rowindex ]
```

is

```
Element_Address =
    Base_Address +
        ((colindex * row_size) + rowindex) * Element_Size
```

Figure 9-5: Another view of row-major ordering for a 4×4 array

As usual, Base_Address is the address of the first element of the array (A[0][0] in this case), and Element_Size is the size of an individual element of the array, in bytes. Row_size is the number of elements in one row of the array (4, in this case, because each row has four elements). Assuming Element_Size is 1 and row_size is 4, this formula computes the following offsets from the base address.

Column Index	Row Index	Offset into Array
0	0	0
0	1	1
0	2	2
0	3	3
1	0	4
1	1	5
1	2	6
1	3	7
2	0	8
2	1	9
2	2	10
2	3	11
3	0	12
3	1	13
3	2	14
3	3	15

For a three-dimensional array, the formula to compute the offset into memory is only slightly more complex. Consider a C/C++ array declaration given as follows:

```
someType array[depth_size][col_size][row_size];
```

If you have an array access similar to `array[depth_index][col_index][row_index]`, then the computation that yields the offset into memory is the following:

```
Address =
    Base +
        ((((depth_index * col_size) + col_index) *
            row_size) + row_index) * Element_Size
```

`Element_size` is the size, in bytes, of a single array element.

For a four-dimensional array, declared in C/C++ as *type* `A[bounds0]` `[bounds1]` `[bounds2]` `[bounds3]`; the formula for computing the address of an array element when accessing element `A[i][j][k][m]` is

```
Address =
    Base +
        ((((((i * bounds1) + j) * bounds2) + k) * row_size) + bounds3) *
            Element_Size
```

If you have an *n*-dimensional array declared in C/C++ as follows:

```
dataType array[b_{n-1}][b_{n-2}]...[b_0];
```

and you want to access the following element of this array

```
array[a_{n-1}][a_{n-2}]...[a_1][a_0]
```

then you can compute the address of a particular array element using the following algorithm:

```
Address := an - 1
for i := n - 2 downto 0 do
    Address := Address * bi + ai
Address := Base_Address + Address * Element_Size
```

It would be very rare for a compiler to actually execute a loop such as this one in order to compute an array index. Usually, there is a small number of dimensions and the compiler will typically unroll the loop, thereby avoiding the overhead of the loop control instructions.

9.1.5.4   Column-Major Ordering

Column-major ordering is the other common array-element address function. FORTRAN and various dialects of BASIC (such as older versions of Microsoft BASIC) use this scheme to index arrays. Pictorially, a column-major ordered array is organized as shown in Figure 9-6.

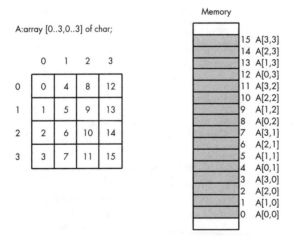

Figure 9-6: Column-major array element ordering

The formulae for computing the address of an array element when using column-major ordering is very similar to that for row-major ordering. The difference is that you reverse the order of the index and size variables in the computation. That is, rather than working from the leftmost index to the rightmost, you operate on the indexes from the rightmost toward the leftmost.

For a two-dimensional column-major array:

```
Element_Address =
    Base_Address +
        ((rowindex * col_size) + colindex) *
            Element_Size
```

For a three-dimensional column-major array:

```
Element_Address =
    Base_Address +
        ((((rowindex * col_size) + colindex) *
            depth_size) + depthindex) *
                Element_Size
```

And so on. Other than using these new formulae, accessing elements of an array using column-major ordering is identical to accessing arrays using row-major ordering.

9.1.5.5 Accessing Elements of a Multidimensional Array

Accessing an element of a multidimensional array in an HLL is so easy that a typical programmer will do so without considering the associated cost. In this section, I'll look at some of the assembly language sequences compilers commonly generate to access elements of a multidimensional array to give you a clearer picture of these costs. Because arrays are one of the more common data structures found in modern applications, and multidimensional arrays are also quite common, compiler designers have put a lot of work into ensuring that they compute array indexes as efficiently as possible. Given a declaration such as:

```
int ThreeDInts[ 8 ][ 2 ][ 4 ];
```

and an array reference like the following:

```
ThreeDInts[ i ][ j ][ k ] = n;
```

accessing the array element requires the computation of the following:

```
Element_Address =
    Base_Address +
        ((((rowindex * col_size) + colindex) *
            depth_size) + depthindex) *
                Element_Size
```

which in brute-force assembly code might be:

```
intmul( 2, i, ebx );    // EBX = 2 * i
add( j, ebx );          // EBX = 2 * i + j
intmul( 4, ebx );       // EBX = (2 * i + j) * 4
```

```
add( k, ebx );          // EBX = (2 * i + j) * 4 + k
mov( n, eax );
mov( eax, ThreeDInts[ebx*4] );  // ThreeDInts[i][j][k] = n
```

In practice, however, compiler authors avoid using the 80x86 intmul (imul) instruction because it is so slow. Many different machine idioms can be used to simulate multiplication using a short sequence of addition, shift, and "load effective address" instructions. Most optimizing compilers use sequences that compute the array element address rather than the brute-force code that uses a multiply instruction.

Consider the following C program that initializes the 16 elements of a 4×4 array:

```
int i, j;
int TwoByTwo[4][4];

int main( int argc, char **argv )
{
    for( j = 0; j < 4; ++j )
    {
        for( i = 0; i < 4; ++i )
        {
            TwoByTwo[i][j] = i + j;
        }
    }
    return 0;
}
```

Now consider the assembly code that the Borland C++ compiler emits for the for loop in this example:

```
        mov       ecx,offset _i
        mov       ebx,offset _j

;
;    {
;           for( j = 0; j < 4; ++j )
;
?live1@16: ; ECX = &i, EBX = &j
        xor       eax,eax
        mov       dword ptr [ebx],eax ;i = 0
        jmp       short @3
;
;       {
;              for( i = 0; i < 4; ++i )
;
@2:
        xor       edx,edx
        mov       dword ptr [ecx],edx ; j = 0

; Compute the index to the start of the
; current column of the array as
; base( TwoByTwo ) + eax*4. Leave this
```

```
; "column base address" in EDX:

    mov         eax,dword ptr [ebx]
    lea         edx,dword ptr [_TwoByTwo+4*eax]
    jmp         short @5
    ;
    ;               {
    ;                   TwoByTwo[i][j] = i + j;
    ;
?live1@48: ; EAX = @temp0, EDX = @temp1, ECX = &i, EBX = &j
@4:

    ;
    mov         esi,eax                 ;Compute i + j
    add         esi,dword ptr [ebx]     ;EBX points at j's value

    shl         eax,4                   ;Multiply row index by 16

; Store the sum (held in ESI) into the specified array element.
; Note that EDX contains the base address plus the column
; offset into the array. EAX contains the row offset into the
; array. Their sum produces the address of the desired array
; element.

    mov         dword ptr [edx+eax],esi  ;Store sum into element

    inc         dword ptr [ecx]     ;increment i by one
@5:
    mov         eax,dword ptr [ecx] ;Fetch i's value
    cmp         eax,4               ;Is i less than four?
    jl          short @4            ;If so, repeat inner loop
    inc         dword ptr [ebx]     ;Increment j by one
@3:
    cmp         dword ptr [ebx],4   ;Is j less than four?
    jl          short @2            ;If so, repeat outer loop.
    ;


        .
        .
        .

; Storage for the 4x4 (x4 bytes) two-dimensional array:
; Total = 4 * 4 * 4 = 64 bytes:

    align   4
_TwoByTwo   label   dword
    db  64  dup(?)
```

In this example, the computation rowIndex * 4 + columnIndex is handled by the following four instructions (which also store the array element, by the way):

```
; EDX = base address + columnIndex * 4

    mov         eax,dword ptr [ebx]
```

```
            lea       edx,dword ptr [_TwoByTwo+4*eax]
                    .
                    .
                    .
; EAX = rowIndex, ESI = i + j
            shl       eax,4                    ;Multiply row index by 16
            mov       dword ptr [edx+eax],esi  ;Store sum into element
```

Note that this code sequence used the scaled-indexed addressing mode (along with the lea instruction) and the shl instruction to do the necessary multiplications. Because multiplication tends to be an expensive operation, most compilers avoid using it when calculating indexes into multidimensional arrays. Nevertheless, by comparing this code against the examples given for single-dimensional array access, you can see that two-dimensional array access is a bit more expensive in terms of the number of machine instructions you must use to compute the index into the array.

Three-dimensional array access is even worse than two-dimensional array access. Here is a C/C++ program and the Visual C++ assembly language output that initializes the elements of a three-dimensional array:

```
#include <stdlib.h>
int i, j, k;
int ThreeByThree[3][3][3];

int main( int argc, char **argv )
{
    for( j = 0; j < 4; ++j )
    {
        for( i = 0; i < 4; ++i )
        {
            for( k = 0; k < 3; ++k )
            {
                // Initialize the 27 array elements
                // with a set of random values:

                ThreeByThree[i][j][k] = rand();
            }
        }
    }
    return 0;
}
```

Here is the 80x86 assembly language output that the Microsoft Visual C++ compiler produces:

```
; Line 8
    xor ebx, ebx
    push    esi
    push    edi
    mov DWORD PTR _j, ebx ;Initialize j = 0
```

```
$L836:
; Line 10
    mov DWORD PTR _i, ebx ;Initialize i = 0
$L839:
; Line 12
    mov DWORD PTR _k, ebx ;Initialize k = 0
$L842:
; Line 14
    call    _rand  ;Get a random value into EAX

    mov esi, DWORD PTR _i
    mov edi, DWORD PTR _j

; Compute ecx = ESI * 3 + EDI  (i * 3 + j):

    mov ecx, esi
    lea edx, DWORD PTR [edi+esi * 2]
    add ecx, edx

; compute ebp = ecx * 3 + EDX (above * 3 + k):

    mov edx, DWORD PTR _k
    lea ebp, DWORD PTR [edx+ecx*2]
    add ecx, ebp

; ECX now contains the (dword) index into the array.

    inc edx          ;++k
    cmp edx, 3       ;exceed for loop bounds?
    mov DWORD PTR _k, edx ;Save away ++k

; Store away the random value into array location
; ThreeByThree[i][j][k]:

    mov DWORD PTR _ThreeByThree[ecx*4], eax

; Repeat loop if k < 4:

    jl  SHORT $L842

; Bump up i by one and see if i >= 4, repeat loop if i < 4:

    inc esi
    cmp esi, 4
    mov DWORD PTR _i, esi
    jl  SHORT $L839

; Bump up j by one and see if j >= 4, repeat loop if j < 4:

    inc edi
    cmp edi, 4
    mov DWORD PTR _j, edi
    jl  SHORT $L836
```

If you are interested, you can write your own short HLL programs and analyze the assembly code emitted for *n*-dimensional arrays (*n* being greater than or equal to 4).

9.1.5.6 Emulating Column-Major or Row-Major Ordering

The choice of column-major or row-major array ordering is generally dictated by your compiler, if not by the programming language definition. No compiler I'm aware of will let you choose which array ordering you prefer on an array-by-array basis (or even across a whole program, for that matter). However, there really is no need to do this, as you can easily simulate either storage mechanism by simply changing the definitions of "rows" and "columns" in your programs.

Consider the following C/C++ array declaration:

```
int array[ NumRows ][ NumCols ];
```

Normally, you'd access an element of this array using a reference like this:

```
element = array[ rowIndex ][ colIndex ]
```

If you increment through all the column index values for each row index value (that you also increment), then you'll access sequential memory locations when accessing elements of this array. That is, the following C for loop initializes sequential locations in memory with zero:

```
for( row = 0; row < NumRows; ++row )
{
    for( col = 0; col < NumCols; ++col )
    {
        array[ row ][ col ] = 0;
    }
}
```

If NumRows and NumCols are the same value, then accessing the array elements in column-major rather than row-major order is trivial—just swap the indexes in the previous code fragment to obtain:

```
for( row = 0; row < NumRows; ++row )
{
    for( col = 0; col < NumCols; ++col )
    {
        array[ col ][ row ] = 0;
    }
}
```

If NumCols and NumRows are not the same value, you're going to have to manually compute the index into the column-major array yourself, and you'll have to allocate the storage in a single-dimensional array, as follows:

```c
int columnMajor[ NumCols * NumRows ]; // Allocate storage
    .
    .
    .
for( row = 0; row < NumRows; ++row)
{
    for( col = 0; col < NumCols; ++col )
    {
        columnMajor[ col * NumRows + row ] = 0;
    }
}
```

Although it is possible to access arrays using a column-major organization, if your application requires it, you should exercise extreme caution when accessing arrays in a manner other than the language's default scheme. Many optimizing compilers are smart enough to recognize when you're accessing arrays in the default manner, and they generate far better code in those circumstances. Indeed, the examples presented so far have explicitly accessed arrays in uncommon ways in order to thwart the compilers' optimizers. Consider the following C code and the Visual C++ output (with optimization enabled):

```c
#include <stdlib.h>
int i, j, k;
int ThreeByThreeByThree[3][3][3];

int main( int argc, char **argv )
{
    // The important difference to note here is how
    // the loops are arranged with the indexes i, j, and k
    // used so that i changes the slowest and k changes
    // most rapidly (corresponding to row-major ordering).

    for( i = 0; i < 3; ++i )
    {
        for( j = 0; j < 3; ++j )
        {
            for( k = 0; k < 3; ++k )
            {
                ThreeByThreeByThree[i][j][k] = 0;
            }
        }
    }
    return 0;
}
```

Here is the Visual C++ assembly language output for the for loops in the previous code. In particular, note how the compiler substituted an 80x86 stosd instruction in place of the three loops:

```
    push    edi
;
; The following code zeros out the 27 (3 * 3 * 3) elements
; of the ThreeByThreeByThree array.

    mov ecx, 27                ; 0000001bH
    xor eax, eax
    mov edi, OFFSET FLAT:_ThreeByThreeByThree
    rep stosd
```

If you rearrange your indexes so that you're not storing zeros into consecutive memory locations, then Visual C++ will not compile to the stosd instruction. Even if the end result is the zeroing of the entire array, the compiler believes that the semantics of stosd are different. (Imagine, if you will, two concurrent threads in a program that are both reading and writing ThreeByThreeByThree array elements concurrently; the program's behavior could be different based on the order of the writes to the array.)

In addition to compiler semantics, there are also good hardware reasons why you shouldn't change the default array ordering. Modern CPU performance is highly dependent on the effectiveness of the CPU's cache. Because cache performance depends on the temporal and spatial locality[2] of the data present in the cache, you want to be careful about accessing data in such a way that disturbs temporality. In particular, accessing array elements in a manner that is inconsistent with their storage order will dramatically impact spatial locality, thereby hurting the performance of your applications. The moral of the story is: "Adopt the compiler's array organization and don't play around unless you *really* know what you're doing."

9.1.5.7   Improving Array Access Efficiency in Your Applications

You should follow these rules when you're using arrays in your applications:

- Never use a multidimensional array when a single-dimensional array will work. This is not to suggest that you should simulate multidimensional arrays by manually computing a row-major (or column-major) index into a single-dimensional array, but if you can express an algorithm using a single-dimensional array rather than a multidimensional array, do so.

- When you must use multidimensional arrays in your application, try to use array bounds that are powers of 2 or, at least, multiples of 4. Compilers can compute indexes into such arrays much more efficiently than arrays whose elements' size is an arbitrary number of bytes.

---

[2] Quickly, termporal locality concerns accessing the same varaible multiple times during a short time period and spatial locality means accessing adjacent variables in memory. See *Write Great Code, Volume 1* for more details.

- When accessing elements of a multidimensional array, try to do so in a manner than supports sequential memory access. For row-major ordered arrays, this implies sequencing through the rightmost index the fastest and the leftmost index the slowest (and just the opposite for column-major ordered arrays).

- If your language supports operations on entire rows (or columns), or other large pieces of the array, with a single operation, use those facilities rather than accessing individual elements using nested loops. Often, the loop overhead, amortized over each array element you access, is greater than the cost of the index calculation and element access. This is particularly important when the array operation is the only thing taking place in the loop(s).

- Always keep in mind the issues of spatial and temporal locality when accessing array elements. Accessing a large number of array elements in a random (or non–cache-friendly) fashion can cause thrashing in the cache and virtual memory subsystem.[3]

The last point is particularly important. Consider the following HLA program:

```
program slow;
#include ( "stdlib.hhf" )
begin slow;

    // A dynamically allocated array accessed as follows:
    // array [12][1000][1000]

    malloc( 12_000_000 ); // Allocate 12,000,000 bytes
    mov( eax, esi );

    // Initialize each byte of the array to zero:

    for( mov( 0, ecx ); ecx < 1000; inc( ecx )) do

        for( mov( 0, edx ); edx < 1000; inc( edx )) do

            for( mov( 0, ebx ); ebx < 12; inc( ebx )) do

                // Compute the index into the array
                // as EBX*1_000_000 + EDX*1_000 + ECX

                intmul( 1_000_000, ebx, eax );
                intmul( 1_000, edx, edi );
                add( edi, eax );
                add( ecx, eax );
                mov( 0, (type byte [esi+eax]));

            endfor;
```

---

[3] See *Write Great Code, Volume 1* for a discussion of thrashing.

```
        endfor;

    endfor;

end slow;
```

By simply swapping the loops around so that the EBX loop is the outer-most loop and the ECX loop is the innermost loop, this program can run up to ten times faster. The reason for the speed difference is that the program, as it is currently written, accesses an array stored in row-major order in a non-sequential fashion. By changing the rightmost index (ECX) most frequently and the leftmost index (EBX) least frequently, this program will access memory sequentially. This allows the cache to work better and dramatically improves program performance.

9.1.6   Dynamic Versus Static Arrays

Some languages provide the ability to declare arrays whose size isn't known until the program is running. Such arrays are quite useful because many programs cannot predict how much space they will need for a data structure until the program receives input from a user. For example, consider a program that reads a text file from disk, line by line, into an array of strings. Until the program actually reads the file and counts the number of lines in the file, it doesn't know how many elements it will need for the array of strings. The programmer had no way of knowing how large the array would need to be when the program was being written. Languages that provide support for such arrays generally call them dynamic arrays. In this section, I'll explore the issues surrounding dynamic (and static) arrays.

I'll begin our exploration with some definitions for static and dynamic arrays.

Static array (or "pure static array")
A pure static array is an array whose size the program knows during compilation and the compiler/linker/operating system can allocate storage for the array before the program begins execution.

Pseudo-static array
A pseudo-static array is one whose size is known to the compiler, but the program doesn't actually allocate storage for the array until runtime. Automatic variables (i.e., nonstatic local variables in a function or procedure) are good examples of pseudo-static objects. The compiler knows their exact size while compiling the program, but the program doesn't actually allocate storage for the array in memory until the function or procedure containing the declaration executes.

Pseudo-dynamic array
A pseudo-dynamic array is one whose size the compiler cannot determine prior to program execution. Typically, the program determines the size of the array at runtime as a result of user input or as part of some other calculation. Once the program allocates storage for a pseudo-dynamic

array, however, the size of the array remains fixed until the program either terminates or deallocates storage for that array. In particular, you cannot change the size of a pseudo-dynamic array to add or delete selected elements (without completely deallocating the storage for the whole array).

Dynamic array (or "pure dynamic array")
A pure dynamic array is one whose size the compiler cannot determine until the program runs and, indeed, cannot even be sure of once it creates the array. A program may change the size of a dynamic array at any time, adding or deleting elements, without affecting the values already present in the array (of course, if you delete some array elements, their values are lost).

Static and pseudo-static arrays are examples of the usual static and automatic objects I've discussed elsewhere in this book, and there is really no need to discuss their storage semantics any further in this section. See Chapter 8 if you have any questions about static or automatic variables.

9.1.6.1   Single-Dimensional Pseudo-Dynamic Arrays

Most languages that claim support for dynamic arrays generally support pseudo-dynamic arrays rather than true dynamic arrays. That is, you may specify the size of an array when you first create it, but once you've specified the size of the array, you cannot easily change the array's size without first deallocating the original storage for the array. Consider the following Visual Basic statement:

```
dim dynamicArray[ i * 2 ]
```

Assuming i is an integer variable that you've assigned some value prior to the execution of this statement, Visual Basic will create an array with i×2 elements upon encountering this statement. In languages that do support dynamic arrays, array declarations are usually executable statements, whereas in languages that don't support dynamic arrays, such as C and Pascal, array declarations are not executable statements. They are simply declarations that the compiler processes for bookkeeping reasons, but for which the compiler generates no machine code.

Although standard C/C++ does not support pseudo-dynamic arrays, the GNU C/C++ implementation does. Therefore, it's legal to write a function like the following in GNU C/C++:

```
void usesPDArray( int aSize )
{
    int array[ aSize ];
       .
       .
       .
} /* end of function usesPDArray */
```

Of course, if you use this feature in GCC, you'll only be able to compile your programs with GCC. Therefore, you won't see many C/C++ programmers using this type of code in their programs.

If you're using a language like C/C++ that doesn't support pseudo-dynamic arrays, but does provide a generic memory allocation function, then you can easily create arrays that act just like single-dimension pseudo-dynamic arrays. This is particularly easy in languages that don't check the range of array indexes, like C/C++. Consider the following code:

```
void usesPDArray( int aSize )
{
    int *array;

    array = malloc( aSize * sizeof( int ));
        .
        .
        .
    free( array );

} /* end of function usesPDArray */
```

Of course, one issue with using a memory allocation function like `malloc` is that you must remember to explicitly free the storage prior to returning from the function (as the `free` call does in this code fragment). Some versions of the C standard library include a `talloc` function that allocates dynamic storage on the stack. Calls to `talloc` are much faster than calls to `malloc`/`free` and the function automatically frees up the storage when you return (without an explicit call to `free`).

9.1.6.2 Multidimensional Pseudo-Dynamic Arrays

If you want to create pseudo-dynamic multidimensional arrays, that's another problem altogether. When creating a single-dimensional pseudo-dynamic array, the program really doesn't need to keep track of the array bounds for any reason but to verify that the array index is valid. For multi-dimensional arrays, however, the program must maintain additional information about the upper and lower bounds of each dimension of the array. This is necessary because the code needs to use that size information when computing the offset of an array element from a list of array indexes, as you saw in the discussion of static multidimensional arrays. So in addition to maintaining a pointer containing the address of the base element of the array, the code that uses pseudo-dynamic arrays must also keep track of the array bounds.[4] This collection of information (the base address, number of dimensions, and the bounds for each dimension) is known as a *dope vector*. In a language like HLA, C/C++, or Pascal, you'd typically create a struct or

---

[4] Technically, the code doesn't need to maintain the size of the last array dimension if the program doesn't bother to check the validity of array indexes applied to the array. In general, however, most languages that support pseudo-dynamic arrays maintain all the information.

record to maintain the dope vector (see Chapter 12 for more information about structs and records). Here's an example of a dope vector you might create for a two-dimensional integer array using HLA:

```
type
    dopeVector2D :
        record
            ptrToArray :pointer to int32;
            bounds :uns32[2];
        endrecord;
```

Here's the HLA code you would use to read the bounds of a two-dimensional array from the user and allocate storage for the pseudo-dynamic array using this dope vector:

```
var
    pdArray :dopVector2D;
        .
        .
        .
stdout.put( "Enter array dimension #1:" );
stdin.get( pdArray.bounds[0] );
stdout.put( "Enter array dimension #2:" );
stdin.get( pdArray.bounds[4] );  //Remember, '4' is a
                                 // byte offset into bounds.

// To allocate storage for the array, we must
// allocate bounds[0]*bounds[4]*4 bytes:

mov( pdArray.bounds[0], eax );

// bounds[0]*bounds[4] -> EAX

intmul( pdArray.bounds[4], eax );

// EAX := EAX * 4 (4=size of int32).

shl( 2, eax );

// Allocate the bytes for the array.

malloc( eax );

// Save away base address.

mov( eax, pdArray.ptrToArray );
```

This example emphasizes that the program must compute the size of the array as the product of the array dimensions and the element size. When processing static arrays, the compiler can compute this product during compilation. When working with dynamic arrays, the compiler must emit machine instructions to compute this product at runtime, which means your program will be slightly larger and slightly slower than if you had used a static array.

If a language doesn't directly support pseudo-dynamic arrays, you will have to translate a list of indexes into a single offset using the row-major function (or something comparable). This is true in HLLs as well as assembly language. Consider the following C++ example that uses row-major ordering to access an element of a pseudo-dynamic array:

```
typedef struct dopeVector2D
{
    int *ptrtoArray;
    int bounds[2];
};

dopeVector2D pdArray;
        .
        .
        .
    // Allocate storage for the pseudo-dynamic array:

    cout << "Enter array dimension #1:";
    cin >> pdArray.bounds[0];
    cout << "Enter array dimension #2:" ;
    cin >> pdArray.bounds[1];
    pdArray.ptrtoArray =
        new int[ pdArray.bounds[0] * pdArray.bounds[1] ];
        .
        .
        .
    // Set all the elements of this dynamic array to
    //   successive integer values:

    k = 0;
    for( i = 0; i < pdArray.bounds[0]; ++i );
    {
        for( j = 0; j < pdArray.bounds[1]; ++j )
        {
            // Use row-major ordering to access
            //   element [i][j]:

            *(pdArray.ptrtoArray + i * pdArray.bounds[1] + j) = k;
            ++k;
        }
    }
```

As for single-dimensional pseudo-dynamic arrays, memory allocation and deallocation can be more expensive than the actual array access—particularly if you allocate and deallocate many small arrays.

A big problem with multidimensional dynamic arrays is that the compiler doesn't know the array bounds at compile time, so it cannot generate array access code that is as efficient as is possible for pseudo-static and static arrays. As an example, consider the following C code:

```
#include <stdlib.h>

int main( int argc, char **argv )
{

    // Allocate storage for a 3x3x3 dynamic array:

    int *iptr = (int*) malloc( 3 * 3 * 3 * 4 );
    int depthIndex;
    int rowIndex;
    int colIndex;

    // A pseudo-static 3x3x3 array for comparison:

    int ssArray[3][3][3];

    // The following nested for loops initialize all
    // the elements of the dynamic 3x3x3 array with
    // zeros:

    for( depthIndex = 0; depthIndex < 3; ++depthIndex )
    {
        for( rowIndex = 0; rowIndex < 3; ++rowIndex )
        {
            for( colIndex = 0; colIndex < 3; ++colIndex )
            {
                iptr
                [
                    // Row-major order computation:

                    ((depthIndex * 3) + rowIndex) * 3
                    + colIndex

                ] = 0;
            }
        }
    }

    // The following three nested loops are comparable
    // to the above, but they initialize the elements
    // of a pseudo-static array. Because the compiler
    // knows the array bounds at compile time, it can
    // generate better code for this sequence.

    for( depthIndex = 0; depthIndex < 3; ++depthIndex )
```

```
    {
        for( rowIndex = 0; rowIndex < 3; ++rowIndex )
        {
            for( colIndex = 0; colIndex < 3; ++colIndex )
            {
                ssArray[depthIndex][rowIndex][colIndex] = 0;
            }
        }
    }

    return 0;
}
```

Here's the pertinent portion of the PowerPC code that GCC emits for this C program (manually annotated). The important thing to notice here is that the dynamic array code is forced to use an expensive multiply instruction, whereas the pseudo-static array code doesn't need this instruction.

```
    .section __TEXT,__text,regular,pure_instructions

_main:

// Allocate storage for local variables
// (192 bytes, includes the ssArray,
// loop control variables, other stuff,
// and padding to 64 bytes):

    mflr r0
    stw r0,8(r1)
    stwu r1,-192(r1)

// Allocate 108 bytes of storage for
// the 3x3x3 array of 4-byte ints.
// This call to  malloc leaves the
// pointer to the array in R3:

    li r3,108
    bl L_malloc$stub

    li r8,0     // R8= depthIndex
    li r0,0

    // R10 counts off the number of
    // elements in rows we've processed:

    li r10,0

// Top of the outermost for loop

L16:
    // Compute the number of bytes
    // from the beginning of the
    // array to the start of the
    // row we are about to process.
```

```
          // Each row contains 12 bytes and
          // R10 contains the number of rows
          // processed thus far. The product
          // of 12 by R10 gives us the number
          // of bytes to the start of the
          // current row. This value is put
          // into R9:

          mulli r9,r10,12

          li r11,0     // R11 = rowIndex

// Top of the middle for loop

L15:
          li r6,3      // R6/CTR = colIndex

          // R3 is the base address of the array.
          // R9 is the index to the start of the
          // current row, computed by the MULLI
          // instruction, above. R2 will now
          // contain the base address of the
          // current row in the array.

          add r2,r9,r3

          // CTR = 3

          mtctr r6

          // Repeat the following loop
          // once for each element in
          // the current row of the array:

L45:
          stw r0,0(r2)    // Zero out current element
          addi r2,r2,4    // Move on to next element
          bdnz L45        // Repeat loop CTR times

          addi r11,r11,1  // Bump up RowIndex by one
          addi r9,r9,12   // Index of next row in array
          cmpwi cr7,r11,2 // Repeat for RowIndex=0..2
          ble+ cr7,L15

          addi r8,r8,1    // Bump up depthIndex by one
          addi r10,r10,3  // Bump up element cnt by three
          cmpwi cr7,r8,2  // Repeat for depthIndex=0..2
          ble+ cr7,L16

/////////////////////////////////////////////////////////
//
// Here's the code that initializes the pseudo-static
// array:

          li r8,0         // DepthIndex = 0
```

```
    addi r10,r1,64   // Compute base address of ssArray
    li r0,0
    li r7,0          // R7 is index to current row
L31:
    li r11,0         // RowIndex = 0
    slwi r9,r7,2     // Convert row/int index to
                     //   row/byte index (int_index*4)
L30:
    li r6,3          // # iterations for colIndex
    add r2,r9,r10    // Base + row_index = row address
    mtctr r6         // CTR = 3

// Repeat innermost loop three times:

L44:
    stw r0,0(r2)     // Zero out current element
    addi r2,r2,4     // Bump up to next element
    bdnz L44         // Repeat CTR times

    addi r11,r11,1   // Bump up RowIndex by one
    addi r9,r9,12    // R9 = Adrs of start of next row
    cmpwi cr7,r11,2  // Repeat until RowIndex >= 3
    ble+ cr7,L30

    addi r8,r8,1     // Bump up depthIndex by one
    addi r7,r7,9     // Index of next depth in array
    cmpwi cr7,r8,2
    ble+ cr7,L31

    lwz r0,200(r1)
    li r3,0
    addi r1,r1,192
    mtlr r0
    blr
```

Different compilers and different optimization levels will handle dynamic array access and pseudo-static array access in different ways. Some compilers will generate the same code for both sequences, many will not. But the bottom line is that multidimensional dynamic array access is never faster than pseudo-static multidimensional array access, and it is sometimes slower.

9.1.6.3   Pure Dynamic Arrays

Pure dynamic arrays are even more difficult to manage. You'll rarely find pure dynamic arrays outside of very high-level languages like APL, SNOBOL4, Lisp, and Prolog. Most languages that support pure dynamic arrays don't force you to explicitly declare or allocate storage for an array. Instead, you just use elements of an array and if that element isn't currently present in the array, the language will automatically create it for you. So, what happens if you currently have an array with elements 0 through 9 and you decide to use element 100? Well, the result is language dependent. Some languages that support pure dynamic arrays will automatically create array elements 10 through 100 and initialize elements 10 through 99 with 0 (or some other default value). Other languages may allocate only element 100 and keep track of the fact that the other elements are not yet present in the array. Regardless, the extra bookkeeping that is necessary for each access to the array can be quite expensive. That is why languages that support pure dynamic arrays aren't more popular—they tend to execute programs slowly.

If you're using a language that supports dynamic arrays, just keep in mind the costs associated with array access in that language. If you're using a language that doesn't support dynamic arrays, but does support memory allocation/deallocation (e.g., C/C++, Java, or assembly), you can implement dynamic arrays yourself. You'll be painfully aware of the costs of using such arrays because you're probably going to have to write all the code that manipulates the array's elements, although this is not an altogether bad thing. If you're using C++, you can even overload the array index operator ([ ]) to hide the complexity of dynamic array element access. Generally, though, programmers who need the true semantics of dynamic arrays will usually choose a language that directly supports them. Just be aware of the costs if you choose to go this route.

9.2   For More Information

This chapter dealt with the low-level implementation of arrays. For more information on data types, you can head off in two directions at this point: lower or higher. To learn more about the low-level implementation of various data types, you'll probably want to start learning and mastering assembly language. *The Art of Assembly Language* (No Starch Press, 2003) is a good place to begin that journey. Higher-level data structure information is available in just about any decent college textbook on data structures and algorithm design. There are, literally, hundreds of these books available covering a wide range of subjects. For those interested in a combination of low-level and high-level concepts, a good choice is Donald Knuth's *The Art of Computer Programming, Volume 1* (Third Edition, Addison-Wesley Professional, 1997) This text is available in almost every bookstore that carries technical books.

As noted in the previous chapter, textbooks on programming language design and compiler design and implementation are good sources of information about the low-level implementation of data types, including composite data types. See the last section of the previous chapter for more details.

10

STRING DATA TYPES

After integers, character strings are probably the most common data type used in modern programs; they are also the second most commonly used composite data type (arrays are the most commonly used composite data type). A *string* is a sequence of objects. Most often, the term *string* describes a sequence of character values, but it's quite possible to have strings of integers, real values, Boolean values, and so on. I've already discussed bit strings in this book and in *Write Great Code, Volume 1*. Nevertheless, in this section I'll stick to the common use of the term string and use it to refer to character strings.

In general, a *character string* is a sequence of characters that possesses two main attributes: a *length* and some *character data*. Character strings can also possess other attributes, such as the *maximum length* allowable for that particular variable or a *reference count* that specifies how many different string variables refer to the same character string. I'll look at these attributes and how programs can use them in the following sections that describe various string formats and some of the possible string operations. This chapter discusses the following topics:

- Character string formats including zero-terminated strings, length-prefixed strings, HLA strings, and 7-bit strings
- When to use (and when not to use) standard library string processing functions
- Static, pseudo-dynamic, and dynamic strings
- Reference counting and strings
- Unicode and UTF-8 character data in strings

String manipulation consumes a fair amount of CPU time in today's applications. Therefore, understanding how programming languages represent and operate on character strings is important if you want to write efficient code that manipulates those strings. This chapter provides the basic information you'll need to write great code that manipulates character string data.

10.1 Character String Formats

Different languages use different data structures to represent strings. Some string formats use less memory, others allow faster processing, some are more convenient to use, some are easy for the compiler writers to implement, and some provide additional functionality for the programmer and operating system.

Although their internal representations vary, every string format has one thing in common: the character data. This is a sequence of zero or more bytes (the term *sequence* implies that the order of the characters is important). How a program references this sequence of characters varies by format. In some string formats, the sequence of characters is kept in an array of characters; in other string formats the program maintains a pointer to the sequence of characters elsewhere in memory.

All character string formats share the length attribute. However, different string formats use a lot of different ways to represent the length of a string. Some string formats use a special *sentinel character* to mark the end of the string. Other formats precede the character data with a numeric value that specifies the number of characters in the sequence. Still other string formats encode the length as a numeric value in a variable that is not connected to the character sequence. Some character string formats use a special bit (set or cleared) to mark the end of a string. Some string formats use a combination of these methods. How a particular string format determines the length of a string can have a big impact on the performance of the functions that manipulate those strings. This method can also affect how much extra storage is needed to represent string data.

Some string formats provide additional attributes such as a maximum length and reference count values that certain string functions can use to operate on string data more efficiently. These extra attributes are optional insofar as they aren't strictly necessary to define a string value. They do, however, allow string manipulation functions to provide certain tests for correctness or to work more efficiently than had these attributes not been present.

To help you better understand the reasoning behind the design of character strings, I'll look at some common string representations popularized by various languages.

10.1.1   Zero-Terminated Strings

Without question, *zero-terminated strings* (see Figure 10-1) are probably the most common string representation in use today because this is the native string format for C, C++, Java, and several other languages. In addition, you'll find zero-terminated strings used in programs written in languages that don't have a specific native string format, such as assembly language.

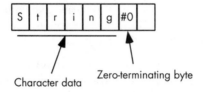

Figure 10-1: Zero-terminated string format

A zero-terminated ASCII string (also called an *ASCIIz* string or a *zstring*) is a sequence containing zero or more 8-bit character codes and ending with a byte containing zero (or, in the case of Unicode [UTF-16], a sequence containing zero or more 16-bit character codes ending with a 16-bit word containing zero). For example, in C/C++, the ASCIIz string abc requires 4 bytes: 1 byte for each of the 3 characters a, b, and c, followed by a zero byte.

Zero-terminated strings have several advantages over other string formats:

- Zero-terminated strings can represent strings of any practical length with only 1 byte of overhead (2 bytes in Unicode).

- Given the popularity of the C/C++ programming languages, high-performance string processing libraries are available that work well with zero-terminated strings.

- Zero-terminated strings are easy to implement. Indeed, except for dealing with string literal constants, the C/C++ programming languages don't provide native string support. As far as the C and C++ languages are concerned, strings are just arrays of characters. That's probably why C's designers chose this format in the first place—so they wouldn't have to clutter up the language with string operators.

- This format allows you to easily represent zero-terminated strings in any language that provides the ability to create an array of characters.

However, despite these advantages, zero-terminated strings also have disadvantages—they are not always the best choice for representing character string data. These disadvantages are as follows:

- String functions often aren't very efficient when operating on zero-terminated strings. Many string operations need to know the length of the string before working on the string data. The only reasonable way to compute the length of a zero-terminated string is to scan the string from the beginning to the end. The longer your strings are, the slower this function runs. Therefore, the zero-terminated string format isn't the best choice if you need to process long strings.

- Although this is a minor problem, you cannot easily represent the character code zero (such as the ASCII NUL character) with the zero-terminated string format.

- With zero-terminated strings no information is contained within the string data itself that tells you how long a string can grow beyond the terminating zero byte. Therefore, some string functions, like concatenation, can only extend the length of an existing string variable and check for overflow if the caller explicitly passes the maximum length.

One nice feature of zero-terminated strings is that you can easily implement them using pointers and arrays of characters. This is probably the main reason the C programming language originally adopted them—they are easy to implement. Consider the following C/C++ statement:

```
someCharPtrVar = "Hello World";
```

If you look at the code a compiler generates for this statement, it will probably look like the following (emitted by the Borland C++ compiler):

```
;       char *someCharPtrVar;
  ;         someCharPtrVar = "Hello World";
  ;
@1:
; "offset" means "take the address of" and "s@" is
; the compiler-generated label where the string
; "Hello World" can be found.

    mov        eax,offset s@
       .
       .
       .
_DATA   segment dword public use32 'DATA'
;       s@+0:
; Zero-terminated sequence of characters
; emitted for the literal string "Hello World":

s@      label   byte
        db      "Hello World",0

_DATA   ends
```

The Borland C++ compiler simply emits the literal string Hello World to the global data segment in memory and then loads the someCharPtrVar variable with the address of the first character of this string literal in the data segment. From that point forward, the program can refer to the string data indirectly via this pointer. This is a very convenient scheme from the compiler writer's point of view.

When using zero-terminated strings in a language like C, C++, C#, Java, or any of a dozen other languages that have adopted C's string format, you can improve the performance of your string-handling code sequences by keeping a few points in mind:

- Try to use the language's runtime library functions rather than attempting to code comparable functions yourself. Most compiler vendors provide highly optimized versions of their string functions that will run many times faster than code you would probably write yourself.

- Once you are forced to compute the length of a string by scanning the entire string, save that length for future use (rather than recomputing the length every time you need it).

- Avoid copying string data from one string variable to another. Copying string data from one place to another in memory is one of the more expensive costs (after length computation) in applications using zero-terminated strings.

I'll consider each of these points, in turn, in the following subsections.

10.1.1.1   Utilize C Standard Library String Functions

Some programmers, especially assembly language programmers, find it hard to believe that someone else could write faster or higher-quality code. When it comes to replicating standard library functions, avoid the temptation to replace the standard library code with code of your own choosing. Unless the library code you're considering is especially bad, chances are pretty good you won't come close to duplicating the efficiency of the existing library code. This is especially true for string functions that handle zero-terminated strings in languages like C and C++.

Standard libraries are generally better than the code you might write yourself for three main reasons: experience, maturity, and inline substitution.

The first reason you should avoid writing your own string functions is experience—your lack of experience with string-handling functions compared to the experience of the typical programmer who writes compiler runtime libraries. New compilers often have notoriously inefficent libraries accompanying them. However, as time passes, the compiler vendor's programming staff gains considerable experience writing those library routines and they figure out how to do a good job writing various string-handling functions. Unless you've spent considerable time writing those same types of routines, chances are pretty good that you'll write inferior code. Many compiler vendors purchase their standard library code from some other party that specializes in writing library code, so even if the compiler you're using is fairly new, it may have a good library accompanying it. Today, few commercial compilers contain horribly inefficient library code. For the most part, only research or "hobby" compilers contain library code that is so bad you can easily improve on it by rewriting that code. Consider a simple example—the C standard library strlen (string length) function. Here's a typical implementation of strlen that an inexperienced programmer might write:

```c
#include <stdlib.h>

int myStrlen( char *s )
{
    char *start;

    start = s;
    while( *s != 0 )
    {
        ++s;
    }
    return s - start;
}

int main( int argc, char **argv )
{


    printf( "myStrlen = %d", myStrlen( "Hello World" ));
    return 0;
}
```

The 80x86 machine code that Microsoft's Visual C++ compiler generates for myStrlen is probably what any assembly programmer would expect:

```asm
_myStrlen PROC NEAR
; File t.c
; Line 7
        mov     eax, DWORD PTR _s$[esp-4]
        mov     ecx, eax
; Line 8
        cmp     BYTE PTR [eax], 0
        je      SHORT $L833
$L832:
        mov     dl, BYTE PTR [eax+1]
; Line 10
        inc     eax
        test    dl, dl
        jne     SHORT $L832
$L833:
; Line 12
        sub     eax, ecx
; Line 13
        ret     0
_myStrlen ENDP
```

No doubt, an experienced assembly language programmer could rearrange these particular instructions to speed them up a bit. Indeed, even an average 80x86 assembly language programmer could point out that the 80x86 scasb instruction does most of the work found in this code sequence.[1] Although this code is fairly short and easy to understand, by no means will it run as fast as possible. An expert assembly language programmer might note that this loop repeats one iteration for each character in the string and accesses the characters in memory 1 byte at a time. The performance of this string function could be improved by unrolling the loop and processing more than one character per loop iteration. For example, consider the following HLA standard library str.zlen function that computes the length of a zero-terminated string by processing four characters at a time:

```
unit stringUnit;

#include( "strings.hhf" );


/*
 * zlen-
 *
 * Returns the current length of the z-string
 * passed as a parameter.
 *                                                      */

procedure str.zlen( var zstr:byte );
    @noalignstack;
    @nodisplay;
    @noframe;
const
    zstrp    :text := "[esp+8]";

begin zlen;

    push( esi );
    mov( zstrp, esi );

    // We need to get ESI dword-aligned before proceeding.
    // If the L.O. two bits of ESI contain zeros, then
    // the address in ESI is a multiple of four. If they
    // are not both zero, then we need to check the one,
    // two, or three bytes starting at ESI to see if they
    // contain a zero-terminator byte.

    test( 3, esi );
    jz ESIisAligned;

    // Does the byte at ESI contain zero?
    // If so, we're done.
```

---

[1] Of course, a really good assembly programmer also knows that the scasb instruction is usually slower than the discrete set of instructions that accomplish the same task.

```
        cmp( (type char [esi]), #0 );
        je SetESI;

        // If not, move on to the next byte and
        // see if ESI is now dword-aligned:

        inc( esi );
        test( 3, esi );
        jz ESIisAligned;

        // If we're still not dword-aligned,
        // check this byte to see if it contains
        // a zero (marking the end of the string):

        cmp( (type char [esi]), #0 );
        je SetESI;

        // Okay, still not at the end of the string,
        // bump up ESI by one and try again:

        inc( esi );
        test( 3, esi );
        jz ESIisAligned;

        // Check the third byte to see if it
        // is the zero-terminating byte.

        cmp( (type char [esi]), #0 );
        je SetESI;

        inc( esi );

        // At this point, we have to be
        // dword-aligned.


        // The following loops process 32 bytes
        // at a time (it is unrolled to help
        // reduce loop overhead cost).

    ESIisAligned:

            // To counteract add immediately below.

            sub( 32, esi );

    ZeroLoop:

            // Skip the chars this loop just processed.

            add( 32, esi );
```

```
ZeroLoop2:

            // The following code grabs
            // four bytes and does a quick
            // check to see if any of these
            // bytes might be zero.

            mov( [esi], eax );

            // Clear H.O. bit (note:$80->$00!)

            and( $7f7f7f7f, eax );

            // $00 and $80->$FF,
            // all others have pos val.

            sub( $01010101, eax );

            // Test all H.O. bits.
            // If any are set, then
            // we've got a $00 or $80 byte.

            and( $80808080, eax );
            jnz MightBeZero0;

            // The following are all
            // inline expansions of the above
            // (we'll process 32 bytes on
            // each iteration of this loop).

            mov( [esi+4], eax );
            and( $7f7f7f7f, eax );
            sub( $01010101, eax );
            and( $80808080, eax );
            jnz MightBeZero4;

            mov( [esi+8], eax );
            and( $7f7f7f7f, eax );
            sub( $01010101, eax );
            and( $80808080, eax );
            jnz MightBeZero8;

            mov( [esi+12], eax );
            and( $7f7f7f7f, eax );
            sub( $01010101, eax );
            and( $80808080, eax );
            jnz MightBeZero12;

            mov( [esi+16], eax );
            and( $7f7f7f7f, eax );
            sub( $01010101, eax );
            and( $80808080, eax );
            jnz MightBeZero16;
```

```
            mov( [esi+20], eax );
            and( $7f7f7f7f, eax );
            sub( $01010101, eax );
            and( $80808080, eax );
            jnz MightBeZero20;

            mov( [esi+24], eax );
            and( $7f7f7f7f, eax );
            sub( $01010101, eax );
            and( $80808080, eax );
            jnz MightBeZero24;

            mov( [esi+28], eax );
            and( $7f7f7f7f, eax );
            sub( $01010101, eax );
            and( $80808080, eax );
            jz ZeroLoop;
```

```
// The following code handles the case where we
// found a $80 or a $00 byte.  We need to determine
// whether it was a 0 byte and the exact position
// of the 0 byte.  If it was a $80 byte, then
// we've got to continue processing characters
// in the string.
```

```
// Okay, we've found a $00 or $80 byte in positions
// 28..31.  Check for the location of the 0 byte,
// if any.

    add( 28, esi );
    jmp MightBeZero0;
```

```
// If we get to this point, we've found a 0 byte in
// positions 4..7:

MightBeZero4:
    add( 4, esi );
    jmp MightBeZero0;
```

```
// If we get to this point, we've found a 0 byte in
// positions 8..11:

MightBeZero8:
    add( 8, esi );
    jmp MightBeZero0;
```

```
// If we get to this point, we've found a 0 byte in
// positions 12..15:

MightBeZero12:
    add( 12, esi );
    jmp MightBeZero0;
```

```
        // If we get to this point, we've found a 0 byte in
        // positions 16..19:

MightBeZero16:
        add( 16, esi );
        jmp MightBeZero0;

        // If we get to this point, we've found a 0 byte in
        // positions 20..23:

MightBeZero20:
        add( 20, esi );
        jmp MightBeZero0;

        // If we get to this point, we've found a 0 byte in
        // positions 24..27:

MightBeZero24:
        add( 24, esi );

        // If we get to this point, we've found a 0 byte in
        // positions 0..3 or we've branched here from one of
        // the above conditions

MightBeZero0:

            // Get the original 4 bytes.

            mov( [esi], eax );

            // See if the first byte contained a 0.

            cmp( al, 0 );
            je SetESI;

            // See if the second byte contained a 0.

            cmp( ah, 0 );
            je SetESI1;

            // See if the third byte contained a 0.

            test( $FF_0000, eax );
            je SetESI2;

            // See if the H.O. byte contained a 0.

            test( $FF00_0000, eax );
            je SetESI3;

        // Well, it must have been a $80 byte we encountered.
        // (Fortunately, they are rare in ASCII strings, so
        // all this extra computation rarely occurs).  Jump
        // back into the zero loop and continue processing.
```

```
        add( 4, esi );   // Skip bytes we just processed.
        jmp ZeroLoop2;   // Don't add 32 in the ZeroLoop!

    // The following computes the length of the string by
    // subtracting the current ESI value from the original
    // value and then adding zero, one, two, or three,
    // depending on where we branched out of the
    // MightBeZero0 sequence above.

SetESI3:

    // Compute length +3 since it was in the H.O. byte.

    sub( zstrp, esi );
    lea( eax, [esi+3] );
    pop( esi );
    ret(4);

    // Compute length +2 since zero was in the third byte.

SetESI2:
    sub( zstrp, esi );
    lea( eax, [esi+2] );
    pop( esi );
    ret(4);

    // Compute length +1 since zero was in the second byte.

SetESI1:
    sub( zstrp, esi );
    lea( eax, [esi+1] );
    pop( esi );
    ret(4);

    // Compute length. No extra addition
    // because zero was in the L.O. byte.

SetESI:
    mov( esi, eax );
    sub( zstrp, eax );
    pop( esi );
    ret(4);

end zlen;

end stringUnit;
```

Even though this function is much longer and much more complex than the simple example given earlier, it manages to run faster because it executes far fewer loop iterations because it processes four characters per loop iteration rather than one. Also, this code reduces loop overhead by "unrolling" eight copies of the loop (that is, expanding eight copies of the loop body inline), thereby saving the execution of 87 percent of the loop control instructions. As a result, this code runs anywhere from two to six times faster than the code given earlier; the exact savings depend upon the length of the string.[2]

The second reason that writing your own library functions is a bad idea is due to the maturity of the code. Most popular optimizing compilers available today have been around for a while. This time has allowed the compiler vendors to use their routines, determine where the bottlenecks lie, and optimize their code. When you write your own version of a standard library string-handling function, chances are pretty good you won't have the time to dedicate to optimizing that particular function—you've got your entire application to worry about. Because of project time limitations, chances are pretty good you will never go back and rewrite that string function to improve its performance. Even if there is a slight performance advantage to your routine, don't forget that the compiler vendor may very well update their library in the future, and you could take advantage of those improvements by simply relinking the new code with your project. However, if you write the library code yourself, it will never improve unless you explicitly improve it yourself. Of course, most people are too busy working on new projects to go back and clean up their old code, so the likelihood of improving self-written string functions in the future is quite low.

The third reason for using standard library string functions in a language like C or C++ is the most important: inline expansion. Many compilers recognize certain standard library function names expand them inline to efficient machine code in place of the function call. This inline expansion can be many times faster than an explicit function call, especially if the function call contains several parameters. As a simple example, consider the following (almost trivial) C program:

```
#include <stdlib.h>

int main( int argc, char **argv )
{
    char localStr[256];

    strcpy( localStr, "Hello World" );
    printf( localStr );
    return 0;
}
```

The 80x86 assembly code that Visual C++ produces is quite interesting:

```
; Storage for the literal string appearing in the
; strcpy invocation:

_DATA   SEGMENT
??_C@_0M@FEIK@Hello?5World?$AA@ DB 'Hello World', 00H
```

---

[2] It is worth pointing that this code is not an exact replacement for the simplistic C code given in this section. The HLA code assumes that all strings are padded to a multiple of 4 bytes in length (a reasonable assumption in HLA). This isn't necessarily true for standard C strings.

```
_DATA    ENDS


_TEXT    SEGMENT
_localStr$ = -256
_main    PROC NEAR

; Allocate storage for the localStr variable on the stack:

    sub esp, 256

; strcpy( localStr, "Hello World" );
;
; Note how this code directly copies the 12 bytes
; (11 characters plus a zero byte) in the string
; literal object to localStr.

    mov eax, DWORD PTR ??_C@_OM@FEIK@Hello?5World?$AA@
    mov ecx, DWORD PTR ??_C@_OM@FEIK@Hello?5World?$AA@+4
    mov edx, DWORD PTR ??_C@_OM@FEIK@Hello?5World?$AA@+8
    mov DWORD PTR _localStr$[esp+256], eax
    mov DWORD PTR _localStr$[esp+260], ecx
    mov DWORD PTR _localStr$[esp+268], edx

; printf( localStr );

    lea eax, DWORD PTR _localStr$[esp+256]
    push    eax
    call    _printf

; return 0;

    xor eax, eax
    add esp, 260
    ret 0
_main    ENDP
```

The impressive thing to note here is how the compiler recognizes what is going on and substitutes six inline instructions that copy the 12 bytes of the string from the literal constant in memory to the localStr variable. The overhead of a call and return to an actual strcpy function is going to be more expensive than this (and that's without considering the work needed to copy the string data). This example demonstrates quite well why you should usually call standard library functions rather than writing your own "optimized" functions to do the same job.

10.1.1.2 When Not to Use Standard Library Functions

Although it is usually better to call a standard library routine rather than to write your own version of the routine, there are some special situations when you should write your own code rather than rely on one or more library functions in the standard library.

Library functions work great when they perform exactly the function you need—no more and no less. One area where programmers get into trouble is when they misuse a library function and call it to do something that the function wasn't really intended to do, or the programmer only needs part of the work done that the function provides. For example, consider the C standard library strcspn function:

```
size_t strcspn( char *source, char *cset );
```

This function scans for the first character in source that is not found in the set of characters specified in the cset string. This function returns the number of characters in source up to the first character it finds that is present (somewhere) in the cset string. It is not at all uncommon to see calls to this function that look like this:

```
len = strcspn( SomeString, "a" );
```

The intent here is to return the number of characters in SomeString before the first occurrence of an a character in that string. That is, to do something like the following:

```
len = 0;
while
(
        SomeString[ len ] != '\0'
    && SomeString[ len ] != 'a'
){
    ++len;
}
```

Unfortunately, the call to the strcspn function is probably a lot slower than this simple while loop implementation. That's because strcspn actually does a lot more work than search for a single character within a string. It looks for any character from a set of characters within the source string. The generic implementation of this function might be something like:

```
len = 0;
for(;;) // Infinite loop
{
    ch = SomeStr[ len ];
    if( ch == '\0' ) break;
    for( i=0; i<strlen( cset ); ++i )
    {
        if( ch == cset[i] ) break;
    }
    if( ch == cset[i] ) break;
    ++len;
}
```

With a little analysis (and noting that we have a pair of nested loops here), it should be pretty obvious that this code is slower than the code given earlier, even if you pass in a cset string containing a single character. This is a classic example of calling a function that is more general than you need (it searches for any of several termination characters rather than the special case of a single terminating character). When a function does *exactly* what you want, using the standard library's version of that function is a good idea. However, when it does more than you need to do, using the standard library function can be more trouble than it's worth from a program efficiency point of view.

10.1.1.3 Avoid Recomputing Data

The last example in the previous section demonstrates a common C programming mistake. Consider the coded fragment:

```
for( i = 0; i < strlen( cset ); ++i )
{
    if( ch == cset[i] ) break;
}
```

On each iteration of this loop, the code tests the loop index to see if it is less than the length of the cset string. Because this loop body does not modify the cset string (and because, presumably, this is not a multithreaded application with another thread modifying the cset string), there really is no need to recompute the string length on each iteration of this loop. Look at the code that the Microsoft Visual C++ compiler emits for this code fragment:

```
; (EAX = src)

    mov eax, DWORD PTR _src$[esp-4]

;    len = 0;

    xor ebp, ebp

;    for( ;; )
;    {
;        ch = src[ len ];

    mov bl, BYTE PTR [eax]

;        if( ch == '\0' ) break;

    test    bl, bl
    je  SHORT $L872

; (ESI = cset )

    mov esi, DWORD PTR _cset$[esp+12]

;        for( i = 0; i < strlen( cset ); ++i )
;        {
```

```
$L836:

; i = 0

    xor edx, edx

;strlen( cset )

    mov edi, esi    ;Scan through cset
    or  ecx, -1     ;Scan all chars
    xor eax, eax    ;Scan for 0 byte
    repne scasb
    not ecx         ;Compute strlen
    dec ecx
    je  SHORT $L867

$L839:

;           if( ch == cset[i] ) break;

    cmp bl, BYTE PTR [edx+esi]
    je  SHORT $L872

; ++i;

    inc edx

; Note: The compiler unrolled the
; while test down here; this is another
; copy of the strlen function call.
;
; ** IMPORTANT **
;
; Note how the program executes this
; strlen "function" on each iteration
; of the loop.

    mov edi, esi
    or  ecx, -1
    xor eax, eax
    repne scasb
    not ecx
    dec ecx
    cmp edx, ecx
    jb  SHORT $L839

$L867:

;       if( ch == cset[i] ) break;

    cmp bl, BYTE PTR [edx+esi]
    je  SHORT $L872
```

```
;        ch = src[ len ];

    mov ecx, DWORD PTR _src$[esp+12]

;        ++len;

    inc ebp

; The following is the first if statement
; in the "for(;;)" loop that the compiler
; has copied down here for efficiency
; reasons:
;
;        if( ch == '\0' ) break;

    mov bl, BYTE PTR [ecx+ebp]
    test    bl, bl
    jne SHORT $L836

; } // end for(;;)
```

As mentioned in the comments, the important thing to note is that the machine code will recompute the string's length on each and every iteration of the innermost for loop. Because the cset string's length never changes, it is not necessary to recompute this value on each iteration of the loop. This problem can be easily rectified by rewriting the code fragment this way:

```
slen = strlen( cset );
len = 0;
for(;;) // Infinite loop
{
    ch = SomeStr[ len ];
    if( ch == '\0' ) break;
    for( i = 0; i < slen; ++i )
    {
        if( ch == cset[i] ) break;
    }
    if( ch == cset[i] ) break;
    ++len;
}
```

A fair number of string operations require the string's length before operations on the string are possible. Consider the strdup function commonly found in many C libraries.[3] The following code is a common implementation of this function:

```
char *strdup( char *src )
{
    char *result;
```

---

[3] strdup is not defined in the original C standard library, but it is very common for vendors to include this function as an extension to the C standard library.

```
    result = malloc( strlen( src ) + 1 );
    assert( result != NULL ); // Check malloc check
    strcpy( result, src );
    return result;
}
```

Fundamentally, nothing is wrong with this implementation of strdup. If you know absolutely nothing about the string object you're passing as a parameter, then you must compute the string's length so you know how much memory to allocate for a copy of that string. Consider, however, the following code sequence that calls strdup:

```
len = strlen( someStr );
if( len == 0 )
{
    newStr = NULL;
}
else
{
    newStr = strdup( someStr );
}
```

The problem here is that you wind up calling strlen twice: once for the explicit call to strlen in this code fragment, and once for the call buried in the strdup function. The worst part of this problem is that it isn't obvious that you're calling strlen twice, so it's not even clear that you're wasting CPU cycles in this code. This is another example of calling a function that is more general than you need, causing the recomputation of the string's length (an inefficient process). One solution is to provide a less general version of strdup, say strduplen, that lets you pass it the length of the string you've already computed. You could implement strduplen as follows:

```
char *strduplen( char *src, size_t len)
{
    char *result;

    // Allocate storage for new string:

    result = malloc( len + 1 );
    assert( result != NULL );

    // Copy the source string and
    // zero byte to the new string:

    memcpy( result, src, len+1 );
    return result;
}
```

Notice the use of memcpy rather than strcpy (or, better yet, strncpy). Again, we already know the length of the string, there is no need to execute any code looking for the zero-terminating byte (as both strcpy and strncpy will do).

Of course, this function implementation assumes that the caller passes the correct length, but that's a standard C assumption for most string and array operations.

10.1.1.4 Avoid Copying Data

Copying strings, especially long strings, can be a time-consuming process on a computer. Keep in mind that most programs maintain string data in memory and memory is much slower than the CPU (often by an order of magnitude, or more). Although cache memory can help mitigate this problem, processing a lot of string data can eliminate other data from the cache and lead to thrashing problems if you don't frequently reuse all the string data you move through the cache. Although it isn't always possible to avoid moving string data around, many programs needlessly copy data—and that can have a detrimental impact on program performance.

A better solution is to pass around *pointers* to zero-terminated strings rather than copying those strings from string variable to string variable. Pointers to zero-terminated strings can fit in registers and don't consume much memory when you use memory variables to hold them. Therefore, passing pointers has far less impact on cache and CPU performance than copying string data amongst string variables.

10.1.1.5 A Final Comment on Zero-Terminated Strings

Zero-terminated string functions are generally less efficient than functions that manipulate other types of strings. Furthermore, programs that utilize zero-terminated strings tend to make mistakes, such as calling strlen multiple times or abusing generic functions to achieve specific goals. Fortunately, designing and using a more efficient string format is easy enough in languages whose native string format is the zero-terminated string.

10.1.2 Length-Prefixed Strings

A second common string format, *length-prefixed strings*, overcomes some of the problems with zero-terminated strings. Length-prefixed strings are common in languages like Pascal; they generally consist of a single byte that specifies the length of the string, followed by zero or more 8-bit character codes (see Figure 10-2). In a length-prefixed scheme, the string abc would consist of 4 bytes: the length byte ($03) followed by the characters a, b, and c.

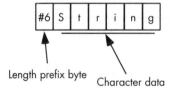

Length prefix byte   Character data

Figure 10-2: Length-prefixed string format

Length-prefixed strings solve two of the problems associated with zero-terminated strings.

- NUL characters can be represented in length-prefixed strings
- String operations are more efficient.

Another advantage to length-prefixed strings is that the length is usually sitting at position zero in the string (when viewing the string as an array of characters), so the first character of the string begins at index one in the array representation of the string. For many string functions, having a 1-based index into the character data is much more convenient than a 0-based index (which zero-terminated strings use).

Length-prefixed strings do suffer from their own drawbacks, the principal drawback being that they are limited to a maximum of 255 characters in length (assuming a 1-byte length prefix). You can remove this limitation by using a 2- or 4-byte length value, but doing so increases the amount of overhead data from 1 to 2 or 4 bytes. However, extending the length field to 2 or 4 bytes also changes the starting index of the string from 1 to either 2 or 4, eliminating the 1-based index feature. While there are ways to overcome this problem, they entail extra overhead.

Many string functions are much more efficient when using length-prefixed strings. Obviously, computing the length of a string is a trivial operation; it's just a memory access. Other string functions that ultimately need the string's length (such as concatenation and assignment) are usually more efficient than similar functions for zero-terminated strings. Furthermore, you don't have to worry about recomputing the string's length every time you call a string function that is built into the language's standard library.

Although length-prefixed string functions are generally faster than the comparable functions you'd find in a zero-terminated string package, don't get the impression that programs using length-prefixed string functions are always going to be efficient. You can still waste many CPU cycles by needlessly copying data. And as with zero-terminated strings, if you only use a subset of a string function's capabilities, you can waste lots of CPU cycles performing unnecessary tasks.

As with zero-terminated strings, you should keep the following points in mind:

- Try to use the language's runtime library functions rather than attempting to code comparable functions yourself. Most compiler vendors provide highly optimized versions of their string functions that will run many times faster than code you would probably write yourself.
- Although computing the string length when using the length-prefixed string format is fairly trivial, many (Pascal) compilers will actually emit a function call to extract the length value from the string's data. The function call and return is far more expensive than retrieving the length value from a variable. So once you compute the string's length, you might want to save that length in a local variable if you intend to use that

same value again. Of course, if a compiler is smart enough to replace a call to the length function with a simple data fetch from the string's data structure, this "optimization" won't buy you much.

- Avoid copying string data from one string variable to another. Copying string data from one memory location to another in an application is one of the more expensive costs in programs using length-prefixed strings.

10.1.3 7-Bit Strings

The *7-bit string format* is an interesting string format that works for 7-bit encodings like ASCII. It uses the (normally unused) HO bit of the characters in the string to indicate the end of the string. All but the last character code in the string has its HO bit clear, and the last character in the string would have its HO bit set (see Figure 10-3).

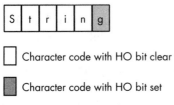

☐ Character code with HO bit clear

■ Character code with HO bit set

Figure 10-3: 7-bit string format

This 7-bit string format has several disadvantages:

- You have to scan the entire string in order to determine the length of the string.
- You cannot have 0-length strings in this format.
- Few languages provide literal string constants for 7-bit strings.
- You are limited to a maximum of 128 character codes, although this is fine when you are using plain ASCII.

However, the big advantage of 7-bit strings is that they don't require any overhead bytes to encode the length. Assembly language (using a macro to create literal string constants) is probably the best language to use when dealing with 7-bit strings. The advantage of 7-bit strings is their compactness, and assembly language programmers tend to be the ones who worry most about compactness, so this is a good match. Here's an HLA macro that will convert a literal string constant to a 7-bit string:

```
#macro sbs( s );

    // Grab all but the last character of the string:

    (@substr( s, 0, @length(s) - 1) +

        // Concatenate the last character
```

```
                       // with its HO bit set:

                       char
                       (
                           uns8
                           (
                               char( @substr( s, @length(s) - 1, 1))
                           ) | $80
                       )
                   )

               #endmacro
                   .
                   .
                   .
               byte sbs( "Hello World" );
```

Because few languages provide support for 7-bit strings, the first suggestion that applied to zero-terminated and length-prefixed strings doesn't apply to 7-bit strings: You're probably going to have to write your own string-handling functions. Standard libraries generally don't provide support for 7-bit strings. Computing lengths and copying data are still expensive operations, even with 7-bit strings, so these two suggestions do apply:

- Once you are forced to compute the length of a string by scanning the entire string, save that length for future use (rather than recomputing the length every time you need it).

- Avoid copying string data from one string variable to another. Copying string data from one memory location to another in an application is one of the more expensive costs (after length computation) in programs using 7-bit strings.

10.1.4   HLA Strings

As long as you're not too concerned about a few extra bytes of overhead per string, it's quite possible to create a string format that combines the advantages of both length-prefixed and zero-terminated strings without their disadvantages. The HLA language has done this with its native string format.[4]

The biggest drawback to the HLA character string format is the amount of overhead required for each string (which can be significant, percentage-wise, if you're in a memory-constrained environment and you process many small strings). HLA strings contain a length prefix and a zero-terminating byte, as well as some other information, that cost 9 bytes of overhead per string.[5]

---

[4] Note that HLA is an assembly language, so it's perfectly possible, and easy in fact, to support any reasonable string format. HLA's native string format is the one it uses for literal string constants, and this is the format that most of the routines in the HLA standard library support.

[5] Actually, because of memory alignment restrictions, there can be up to 12 bytes of overhead, depending on the string.

The HLA string format uses a 4-byte length prefix, allowing character strings to be just over 4 billion characters long (obviously, this is far more than any practical application will use). HLA also sticks a zero byte at the end of the character string data, so HLA strings are compatible with string functions that reference (but do not change the length of) zero-terminated strings. The remaining 4 bytes of overhead in an HLA string contain the maximum legal length for that string. Having this extra field allows HLA string functions to check for string overflow, if necessary. In memory, HLA strings take the form shown in Figure 10-4.

The 4 bytes immediately before the first character of the string contain the current string length. The 4 bytes preceding the current string length contain the maximum string length. Immediately following the character data is a zero byte. Finally, HLA always ensures that the string data structure's length is a multiple of 4 bytes (for performance reasons). There may be up to 3 additional bytes of padding at the end of the object in memory (note that the string appearing in Figure 10-4 only requires 1 byte of padding to ensure that the data structure is a multiple of 4 bytes in length).

Figure 10-4: HLA string format

HLA string variables are actually pointers that contain the byte address of the first character in the string. To access the length fields, you would load the value of the string pointer into a 32-bit register. You'd access the Length field at offset −4 from the base register and the MaxLength field at offset −8 from the base register. Here's an example:

```
static
    s :string := "Hello World";
      .
      .
      .

// Move the address of 'H' in
//   "Hello World" into esi.

mov( s, esi );

// Puts length of string
// (11 for "Hello World") into ECX.

mov( [esi-4], ecx );
      .
      .
      .
mov( s, esi );

// See if value in EAX exceeds the
// maximum string length.
```

```
cmp( eax, [esi-8] );
ja StringOverflow;
```

As noted earlier, the amount of memory reserved to hold an HLA string's character data is always a multiple of 4 bytes. Therefore, you're always guaranteed that you can move data from one HLA string to another by copying double words rather than individual bytes. This allows string copy routines to run up to four times faster, because you execute one-fourth the number of loop iterations copying a string of double words as you would copying the string a byte at a time. For example, here is the highly modified version of the pertinent code in the HLA str.cpy function that copies one string to another:

```
// Get the source string pointer into ESI,
// and the destination pointer into EDI:

    mov( dest, edi );
    mov( src, esi );

// Get the length of the source string
// and make sure that the source string
// will fit in the destination string.

    mov( [esi-4], ecx );

// Save as the length of the destination string.

    mov( ecx, [edi-4] );


// Add one byte to the length so we will
// copy the zero byte. Also compute the
// number of dwords to copy (rather than bytes).
// Then copy the data.

    add( 4, ecx );   // Adds one, after division by 4.
    shr( 2, ecx );   // Divides length by four
    rep.movsd();     // Moves length/4 dwords
```

The HLA str.cpy function also checks for string overflows and NULL pointer references (for clarity, that code does not appear in this example). However, the important thing to see in this example is that HLA copies the strings as double words in order to improve performance.

One nice thing about HLA string variables is that (as read-only objects) HLA strings are compatible with zero-terminated strings. For example, if you have a function written in C or some other language that expects you to pass a zero-terminated string to it, you can call that function and pass an HLA string variable to it, like this:

```
someCFunc( hlaStringVar );
```

The only catch is that the C function must not make any changes to the string that would affect its length (because the C code won't update the Length field of the HLA string). Of course, you can always call a C strlen function upon returning to update the length field yourself, but generally, it's best not to pass HLA strings to a function that modifies zero-terminated strings.

The comments on length-prefixed strings generally apply to HLA strings, specifically:

- Try to use the HLA standard library functions rather than attempting to code comparable functions yourself. Although you might want to check out the library function's source code (available with HLA), most of the string functions do a good job on generic string data.

- Although, in theory, you shouldn't count on the explicit length field appearing in the HLA string data format, most programs simply grab the length from the 4 bytes immediately preceding the string data, so there generally is no need to save the length. Careful HLA programmers will actually call the strlen function in the HLA standard library and simply save this value in a local variable for future use. However, accessing the length directly is probably a safe thing to do.

- Avoid copying string data from one string variable to another. Copying string data from one memory to another in an application is one of the more expensive costs in programs using HLA strings.

10.1.5 Descriptor-Based Strings

The string formats I've considered up to this point have kept the attribute information (the lengths and terminating bytes) for a string in memory along with the character data. Perhaps a slightly more flexible scheme is to maintain information like the maximum and current lengths of a string in a record structure that also contains a pointer to the character data (see Figure 10-5). Such records are called *descriptors*. Consider the following Pascal/Delphi/Kylix data structure:

```
type
    dString :record
        curLength  :integer;
        strData    :^char;
    end;
```

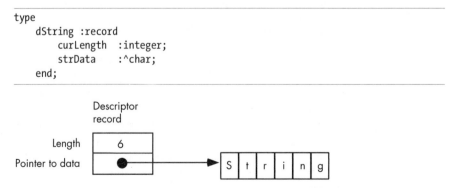

Figure 10-5: String descriptors

Note that this data structure does not hold the actual character data. Instead, the strData pointer contains the address of the first character of the string. The curLength field specifies the current length of the string. Of course, you could add any other fields you like to this record, such as a maximum length field, although a maximum length isn't usually necessary because most string formats employing a descriptor are *dynamic* (as will be discussed in the next section). Most string formats employing a descriptor just maintain the length field.

An interesting attribute of a descriptor-based string system is that the actual character data associated with a string could be part of a larger string. Because no length or terminating bytes are in the actual character data, it is possible to have the character data for two strings overlap. For example, take a look at Figure 10-6. In this example, there are two strings: one representing the string Hello World and the second representing World. Notice that the two strings overlap. This can save memory and make certain functions (like substring) very efficient. Of course, when strings overlap as these do, you cannot modify the string data because that could wipe out part of some other string.

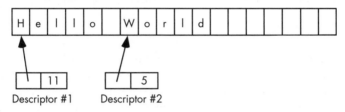

Figure 10-6: Overlapping strings using descriptors

The suggestions given for other string formats don't apply as strongly to descriptor-based strings as they do to the other formats. Certainly, if standard libraries are available, you should call those functions because they're probably better than the ones you would write yourself. There is no need to save the length, because extracting the length field from the string's descriptor is usually a minor task. Also, many descriptor-based string systems use *copy on write* (see Volume 1 for a discussion of copy on write) to reduce string copy overhead. In a string descriptor system, you should avoid making changes to a string because the copy-on-write semantics generally require the system to make a complete copy of the string whenever you change a single character (something that isn't necessary with other string formats).

10.2 Static, Pseudo-Dynamic, and Dynamic Strings

So far, I've discussed the various string data formats. Now it is time to consider where to store string data in memory. Strings can be classified according to when (and where) the system allocates storage for the string. This set has three members: static strings, pseudo-dynamic strings, and dynamic strings.

10.2.1 Static Strings

Pure *static strings* are those whose maximum size a programmer chooses when writing the program. Pascal strings and Delphi *short strings* fall into this category. Arrays of characters that you will use to hold zero-terminated strings in C/C++ also fall into this category as do fixed-length arrays of characters. Consider the following declaration in Pascal:

```
(* Pascal static string example *)

var
    //Max length will always be 255 characters.

    pascalString :string(255);
```

And here's an example in C/C++:

```
// C/C++ static string example:

//Max length will always be 255 characters (plus zero byte).

char cString[256];
```

While the program is running, there is no way to increase the maximum sizes of these static strings or to reduce the storage they will use. These string objects will consume 256 bytes at runtime, period. One advantage to pure static strings is that the compiler can determine their maximum length at compile time and implicitly pass this information to a string function so it can test for bounds violations at runtime.

10.2.2 Pseudo-Dynamic Strings

Pseudo-dynamic strings are those whose length the system sets at runtime by calling a memory-management function like malloc to allocate storage for the string. However, once the system allocates storage for the string, the maximum length of the string is fixed. HLA strings generally operate in this manner.[6] An HLA programmer would typically call the stralloc function to allocate storage for a string variable. Once created via stralloc, however, that particular string object has a fixed length that cannot change.[7]

10.2.3 Dynamic Strings

Dynamic string systems, which typically use a descriptor-based format, will automatically allocate sufficient storage for a string object whenever you create a new string or otherwise do something that affects an existing string.

---

[6] Though, being assembly language, of course it's possible to create static strings and pure dynamic strings in HLA, as well.

[7] Actually, you could call strrealloc to change the size of an HLA string, but dynamic string systems generally do this automatically, something that the existing HLA string functions will not do for you if they detect a string overflow.

Operations like string assignment and substring extraction are relatively trivial in dynamic string systems—generally they copy only the string descriptor data, so such operations are fast. However, as noted in the section on descriptor strings, when using strings this way, you cannot store data back into a string object, because it could modify data that is part of other string objects in the system.

The solution to this problem is to use a technique known as *copy on write*. Whenever a string function needs to change some characters in a dynamic string, the function first makes a copy of the string and then makes whatever modifications are necessary to the copy of the data. Research with typical programs suggests that copy-on-write semantics can improve the performance of many applications because operations like string assignment and substring extraction (which is just a *partial string assignment*) are far more common than the modification of character data within strings. The only drawback to this mechanism is that after several modifications to string data in memory, there may be sections of the string heap area that contain character data that is no longer in use. To avoid a *memory leak*, dynamic string systems employing copy on write usually provide *garbage collection code* that scans through the string area looking for *stale* character data in order to recover that memory for other purposes. Unfortunately, depending on the algorithms in use, garbage collection can be quite slow.

10.3 Reference Counting for Strings

Consider the case where you have two string descriptors (or just pointers) pointing at the same string data in memory. Clearly, you can't deallocate (that is, reuse for a different purpose) the storage associated with one of these pointers while the program is still using the other pointer to access the same data. One common solution is to make the programmer responsible for keeping track of such details. Unfortunately, as applications become more complex, relying on the programmer to keep track of such details often leads to dangling pointers, memory leaks, and other pointer-related problems in the software. A better solution is to allow the programmer to deallocate the storage for the character data in the string and to have the deallocation process hold off on the actual deallocation until the programmer releases the last pointer referencing the character data for the string. To accomplish this, a string system can use *reference counters* to track the pointers and their associated data.

A reference counter is an integer that counts the number of pointers that reference a string's character data in memory. Every time you assign the address of the string to some pointer, you increment the reference counter by one. Likewise, whenever you want to deallocate the storage associated with the character data for the string, you decrement the reference counter. Deallocation of the storage for the actual character data doesn't happen until the reference counter decrements to zero.

Reference counting works great when the language handles the details of string assignment automatically for you. If you try to implement reference counting manually, the only difficulty is ensuring that you always increment the reference counter when you assign a string pointer to some other pointer variable. The best way to do this is to never assign pointers directly but handle all string assignments via some function (or macro) call that updates the reference counters in addition to copying the pointer data. If your code fails to update the reference counter properly, you'll wind up with dangling pointers or memory leaks.

10.4 Delphi/Kylix Strings

Although Delphi and Kylix provide a "short string" format that is compatible with the length-prefixed strings in earlier versions of Delphi and Turbo Pascal, later versions of Delphi (v4.0 and later) and Kylix use dynamic strings for their native string format. Although this string format is unpublished (therefore, subject to change), experiments with Delphi at the time of this writing indicate that Delphi's string format is very similar to HLA's. Delphi uses a zero-terminated sequence of characters with a leading string length and a reference counter (rather than a maximum length as HLA uses). Figure 10-7 shows the layout of a Delphi/Kylix string in memory.

Figure 10-7: Delphi/Kylix string data format

Just like HLA, Delphi/Kylix string variables are pointers that point to the first character of the actual string data. To access the length and reference-counter fields, the Delphi/Kylix string routines use a negative offset of −4 and −8 from the character data's base address. However, because this string format is not published, applications should never access the length or reference counter fields directly. Delphi/Kylix provides a length function that extracts the string length for you, and there really is no need for your applications to access the reference counter field because the Delphi/Kylix string functions maintain this field automatically.

10.5 Using Strings in a High-Level Language

Strings are a very common data type found in high-level programming languages. Because applications often make extensive use of string data, many HLLs provide libraries with lots of complex string manipulation routines that hide considerable complexity from the programmer. Unfortunately, it is easy to forget the amount of work involved in a typical string operation when you execute a statement like:

```
aLengthPrefixedString := 'Hello World';
```

In a typical Pascal implementation, this assignment statement calls a function that winds up copying each character from the string literal to the storage reserved for the aLengthPrefixedString variable. That is, this statement roughly expands to the following:

```
(* Copy the characters in the string *)

for i := 1 to length( HelloWorldLiteralString ) do begin

    aLengthPrefixedString[ i ] :=
        HelloWorldLiteralString[ i ];

end;

(* Set the string's length *)

aLengthPrefixedString[0] :=
    char( length( HelloWorldLiteralString ));
```

This code doesn't even include the overhead of the procedure call, return, and parameter passing. Copying string data is one of the more expensive operations programs commonly do. This is why many HLLs have switched to dynamic strings and copy-on-write semantics—string assignments are far more efficient when you only copy a pointer rather than all of the character data. This is not to suggest that copy on write is always better. But for many string operations, such as assignment, substring, and other operations that do not change the string's character data, copy on write can be very efficient.

Although few programming languages give you the option of choosing which string format you want to use, many programming languages do let you create pointers to strings, so you can manually support copy on write. If you're willing to write your own string-handling functions, you can create some very efficient programs by avoiding the use of your language's built-in string-handling capabilities. For example, the substring operation in C is usually handled by the strncpy function and is often implemented in a fashion similar to the following:[8]

```
char *
strncpy( char* dest, char *src, int max )
{
    char *result = dest;
    while( max > 0 )
    {
        *dest = *src++;
        if( *dest++ == '\0) break;
```

---

[8] Most real-world strncpy routines are often more efficient than this example; indeed, many are written in assembly language, but we will ignore that here.

```
        --max;
    }
    return result;
}
```

A typical "substring" operation might use strncpy as follows:

```
strncpy( substring, fullString+start, length );
substring[ length ] = '\0';
```

where substring is the destination string object, fullString is the source string, start is the starting index of the substring to copy, and length is the length of the substring to copy.

If you create a descriptor-based string format in C using a struct, similar to the HLA record in Section 10.1.5, "Descriptor-Based Strings," you could do a substring operation with the following two statements in C:

```
// Assumption: ".strData" field is char*

    substring.strData = fullString.strData + start;
    substring.curLength = length;
```

This code executes much faster than the strncpy version.

Sometimes, a particular programming language won't provide access to the underlying string data representation that the language supports, and you will have to live with the performance loss, switch languages, or write your own string-handling code in assembly language. Generally, though, there are alternatives to copying string data in your applications. The example just given, using a string descriptor, demonstrates a common way that programs can avoid copying data when performing string functions.

10.6 Character Data in Strings

To this point, this chapter has made the tacit assumption that each character in a string consumes exactly 1 byte of storage. This chapter has also explicitly assumed the use of the 7-bit ASCII character set when discussing the character data appearing in a string. Traditionally, this has been the way programming languages have represented a string's character data. Today, however, the ASCII character set is too limited for worldwide use and several new character sets have risen in popularity including Unicode (or UTF-16), UTF-32, UTF-8, and UTF-7. Because these character formats can have a big impact on the efficiency of string functions that operate upon them, I'll spend a few moments discussing them.

The original Unicode character format was devised as a way of representing all the possible characters in use in the world, something that was not possible with 7-bit ASCII characters. The thought at the time was that 65,536 different character codes would prove sufficient. This turned out to be incorrect, as there were far more than 65,536 different characters that people needed to represent, and this hobbled the acceptance of 16-bit Unicode (UTF-16) as a universal standard. Still, Windows and Windows CE use UTF-16 internally, so this is an important character set on that basis alone.

The big advantage to the UTF-16 encoding is that it is very easy to compute the number of characters in a string based on the amount of memory the string consumes (and vice versa; it's easy to compute the memory requirements based on the string's length). Because each character consumes exactly 2 bytes, you can compute the memory requirements for a string by multiplying that string's length by 2. There are four main disadvantages to the UTF-16 format. The first is pretty obvious: character strings consume twice as much storage as their 7-bit ASCII counterparts. The second limitation was the incorrect assumption that 65,536 different values would be sufficient to handle all the world's different characters. The third limitation has to do with data transmission of a UTF-16 string; if you drop a byte along the way, there is no way to resynchronize the transmission stream. A final problem with UTF-16 encoding is that Unicode strings are completely incompatible with all ASCII string functions and formats that operate on single byte values.

UTF-8 (UTF stands for *Unicode Transformational Format,* though it's often called the *Unix Transformational Format,* too) addressed many of the major issues with Unicode/UTF-16. The advantages of UTF-8 include:

- Characters from the 7-bit ASCII character set require only 1 byte of storage and use the existing ASCII format. Therefore, existing ASCII strings are compatible with UTF-8.

- UTF-8 supports up to 31 bits for character code values, certainly enough to represent all characters found in modern languages.

- UTF-8 strings are self-synchronizing. If you drop a character during transmission, you can resynchronize within no more than five characters.

- Although UTF-8 does require special string functions, many existing ASCII string functions will operate properly on UTF-8 strings, thus reducing the number of functions that need to be rewritten.

UTF-8 does offer some additional advantages; see www.unicode.org or http://czyborra.com/utf/#UTF-8 for details.

UTF-8 does have one big disadvantage: it is a *multibyte character set.* This means that some character values will require 2 or more bytes (up to 6 bytes in the current definition) to represent a single character. This makes the computation of certain string functions (such as string length) quite difficult because you cannot simply "count bytes" as is possible with ASCII strings. Because the number of bytes in a string is not equal to the number of characters in a string, string functions that use the formats discussed in this chapter will have to manually scan each character of the string to compute the number of characters in that string. Certainly, it is possible to create a string format that encodes both the number of bytes and the number of characters in the string, although none of the string formats this chapter describes do that.

UTF-32 is an attempt to create a character format that can represent all possible characters found on the planet today, and to do so using a character format that allows a simple conversion between the number of characters in a string and the number of bytes within a string. The problem, of course, is that if a program manipulates a large amount of string data, the 32-bit UTF-32 consumes considerable memory. Given that most programs simply manipulate 7-bit ASCII characters, this can be quite wasteful. Nevertheless, for internal computations it may be more convenient to convert Unicode strings in UTF-16 or UTF-8 to UTF-32 prior to a long series of operations.

The UTF-8 format is upward compatible with the 7-bit ASCII character set, but it redefines some 8-bit codes commonly used for some accented Latin characters. UTF-7 (or, technically, UTF-7.5) modifies UTF-8 slightly in order to maintain certain ANSI character codes for those Latin characters. Note that in exchange for supporting single-byte Latin characters, UTF-7 extends some other character representations from 2 to 3 bytes. So UTF-7 can save memory if you use the extra Latin characters it encodes in a single byte, but it can waste some memory (compared with UTF-8) when using other character sets.

As this book is being written, Unicode and UTF support in HLLs is still in its infancy. Many compilers will support UTF strings and even provide some library routines to manipulate those strings. However, the support for these non-ASCII character sets is still not as mature as the support for ASCII character strings. You'll have to evaluate the support your compiler provides to determine the quality of its implementation.

10.7 For More Information

This chapter dealt with the low-level implementation of strings that you'll find in various languages. For more information on strings and string functions, a good place to start is with a book on assembly language, such as *The Art of Assembly Language* (No Starch Press, 2003). If you have access to the library source code for any compilers you own, perusing the sources for its string functions might be a good idea. For more information on the evolving Unicode character sets, you'll definitely want to visit the Unicode website at www.unicode.org.

11

POINTER DATA TYPES

Pointers are the data type equivalent of a goto statement. Used carelessly, they can reduce a well-written program to unreadable junk; they can turn a robust and efficient program into a buggy and inefficient junk pile. Unlike gotos, however, pointers and their use can be difficult to avoid in many common programming languages. There are no "pointers considered harmful" papers in academic journals like the "Gotos Considered Harmful" paper. Although many languages attempt to do away with explicit control of pointers (e.g., Java), the truth is that great programmers need to be able to deal with pointers because too many popular languages still use them. In this chapter, I'll discuss:

- The memory representation of pointers
- How high-level languages implement pointers
- Dynamic memory allocation and its relationship to pointers
- Pointer arithmetic

- How memory allocators work
- Garbage collection
- Common pointer problems

By understanding the low-level implementation and use of pointers, you will be able to write better high-level code that is more efficient, safer, and more readable. Although pointer abuse could be considered harmful in your programs, knowing how to properly use pointers can help you avoid all the problems people normally associate with their use. This chapter will provide the information you need to use pointers appropriately.

11.1 Defining and Demystifying Pointers

You probably experienced pointers firsthand in Pascal, C/C++, or some other high-level language, and you may feel a little anxious right now. HLL programmers generally rely on the high degree of abstraction provided by the language because they don't want to know what's going on behind the scenes. They just want a "black box" that produces predictable results. In the case of pointers, the abstraction may be too effective; pointers seem intimidating and opaque to many programmers. Well, fear not! Pointers are actually *easy* to deal with.

Exactly what is a pointer? A *pointer* is a variable whose value refers to some other object. OK, but what does that mean? High-level languages like Pascal and C/C++ hide the simplicity of pointers behind a wall of abstraction. This added complexity tends to frighten programmers because *they don't understand what's going on behind the scenes*. However, a little knowledge can erase all such fears.

To understand how pointers work, I'll use the array data type as an example. Consider the following array declaration in Pascal:

```
M: array [0..1023] of integer;
```

Even if you don't know Pascal, the concept here is easy to understand. M is an array of 1,024 integers, indexed from M[0] to M[1023]. Each of these array elements can hold an independent integer value. In other words, this array gives you 1,024 different integer variables, each of which you access via an array index (the variable's sequential position within the array) rather than by name.

You can probably figure out what the statement M[0] := 100; is doing. It stores the value 100 into the first element of the array M. Now consider the following two statements:

```
    i := 0; (* assume "i" is an integer variable *)
    M [i] := 100;
```

Clearly, these two statements do the same thing as M[0] := 100;. Indeed, you'll probably agree that you can use any integer expression producing a value in the range 0..1,023 as an index into this array. The following statements *still* perform the same operation as our earlier statements:

```
i := 5;          (* assume all variables are integers *)
j := 10;
k := 50;
m [i * j - k] := 100;
```

But now look at the following:

```
M [1] := 0;
M [ M [1] ] := 100;
```

At first glance these statements might seem confusing. However, you should agree that these two instructions perform the same operation I've been considering. The first statement stores 0 into array element M[1]. The second statement fetches the value of M[1], which is 0, and uses that value to determine where it stores the value 100.

If you think this example is reasonable—perhaps bizarre, but usable nonetheless—then you'll have no problems with pointers—*because M[1] is a pointer!* Well, not really, but if you were to change M to "memory" and treat each element of this array as a separate memory location, then it would meet the definition of a pointer. That is, a pointer is a memory variable whose value is the address of some other memory object.

11.2 Pointer Implementation in High-Level Languages

Although most languages implement pointers using memory addresses, a pointer is actually an abstraction of a memory address. Therefore, a language could define a pointer using any mechanism that maps the value of the pointer to the address of some object in memory. Some implementations of Pascal, for example, use offsets from a fixed memory address as pointer values. Some languages (e.g., dynamic languages like Lisp or even Java) might actually implement pointers by using double indirection. That is, the pointer object contains the address of some memory variable whose value is the address of the object to access. This double indirection may seem somewhat convoluted, but it does offer certain advantages when using a complex memory management system, making it easier and more efficient to reuse blocks of memory. However, this chapter will assume that a pointer is a variable whose value is the address of some other object in memory. This is a safe assumption for many of the high-performance HLLs you're likely to encounter, such as C, C++, C#, and Delphi/Kylix.

You can indirectly access an object using a pointer with two 80x86 machine instructions, as follows:

```
// Load the pointer variable into a register.

mov( PointerVariable, ebx );
```

```
// Use register indirect mode to access data.

mov( [ebx], eax );
```

Now consider the double-indirect pointer implementation described earlier. Access to data via double indirection is less efficient than the straight pointer implementation because it takes an extra machine instruction to fetch the data from memory. This isn't obvious even in an HLL like C/C++ or Pascal, where using double indirection is explicit:

```
i = **cDblPtr;      // C/C++
i := ^^pDblPtr;     (* Pascal/Delphi *)
```

This is syntactically similar to single indirection. In assembly language, however, you'll see the extra work involved:

```
mov( hDblPtr, ebx );  // Get the pointer to a pointer
mov( [ebx], ebx );    // Get the pointer to the value
mov( [ebx], eax );    // Get the value.
```

Contrast this with the two assembly instructions (given earlier) needed to access an object using single indirection. Because double indirection requires 50 percent more code (and twice as many slow memory accesses) than single indirection, you can see why many languages implement pointers using single indirection. To verify this, consider the machine code produced by a couple of different compilers when processing to the following C code:

```
static int i;
static int j;
static int *cSnglPtr;
static int **cDblPtr;

int main( void )
{
        .
        .
        .
    j = *cSnglPtr;
    i = **cDblPtr;
```

Here's the GCC output for the PowerPC processor.

```
; j = *cSnglPtr;

        addis  r11,r31,ha16(_j-L1$pb)
        la     r11,lo16(_j-L1$pb)(r11)
        addis  r9,r31,ha16(_cSnglPtr-L1$pb)
```

```
        la    r9,lo16(_cSnglPtr-L1$pb)(r9)
        lwz   r9,0(r9) // Get the ptr into register R9
        lwz   r0,0(r9) // Get the data at the pointer
        stw   r0,0(r11) // Store into j

; i = **cDblPtr;
;
; Begin by getting the address of cDblPtr into R9:

        addis r11,r31,ha16(_i-L1$pb)
        la    r11,lo16(_i-L1$pb)(r11)
        addis r9,r31,ha16(_cDblPtr-L1$pb)
        la    r9,lo16(_cDblPtr-L1$pb)(r9)

        lwz   r9,0(r9) // Get the dbl ptr into R9
        lwz   r9,0(r9) // Get the ptr into R9
        lwz   r0,0(r9) // Get the value into R9
        stw   r0,0(r11) // Store value into i
```

As you can see in this PowerPC example, fetching the value using double indirection takes one more instruction than it does using single indirection. Of course, the total number of instructions is rather large here, so this extra instruction doesn't contribute as much to the execution time as it does on the 80x86 where fewer instructions are involved. Consider the following GCC code output for the 80x86:

```
; j = *cSnglPtr;

        movl   cSnglPtr, %eax
        movl   (%eax), %eax
        movl   %eax, j

; i = **cDblPtr;

        movl   cDblPtr, %eax
        movl   (%eax), %eax
        movl   (%eax), %eax
        movl   %eax, i
```

As we saw with the PowerPC code, double indirection requires extra machine instructions, so programs using double indirection will be larger and slower.

As a side issue, note that the PowerPC instruction sequences are twice as long as the 80x86 instruction sequences.[1] One positive way of viewing this is to realize that double indirection has less impact on the execution time of the PowerPC code than it does on the 80x86 code. That is, the extra instruction represents only 13 percent of the total, versus 25 percent of the

---

[1] This, by the way, is not a general rule concerning PowerPC versus 80x86 code. Memory references on the PowerPC are very costly, that's why the PowerPC code here is so long. However, the PowerPC has four times as many registers, so in real applications the code isn't always larger.

total in the 80x86 code.[2] This little example should help demonstrate that execution time and code space are not processor independent. And bad coding practices (such as using double indirection when it's not required) can have more impact on some processors than with others.

11.3 Pointers and Dynamic Memory Allocation

Pointers typically reference anonymous variables that you allocate on the *heap* (a region in memory reserved for dynamic storage allocation) using memory allocation/deallocation functions like *malloc/free, new/dispose*, and *new/delete*. Objects that you allocate on the heap are known as *anonymous variables* because you refer to them by their address; you do not associate a name with them. True, the pointer variable may have a name, but that name applies to the pointer's data (an address), not the object referenced by this address.

Dynamic languages automatically handle memory allocation and deallocation operations in a transparent, automatic fashion. That is, the application simply uses the dynamic data and leaves it up to the runtime system to allocate memory as needed and reuse storage for a different purpose when it is no longer needed. Without the need to explicitly allocate and deallocate memory for pointer variables, applications written in dynamic languages (such as AWK or Perl) are usually much easier to program and often contain far fewer errors. But this comes at the cost of efficiency—programs written in dynamic languages often run much slower than programs written in other languages. Conversely, traditional languages (such as C/C++) that require the programmer to explicitly manage memory often produce more efficient applications, although the memory management code the programmer writes often contains a higher percentage of defects due to the additional complexity of that code.

11.4 Pointer Operations and Pointer Arithmetic

Most HLLs that provide a pointer data type let you assign addresses to pointer variables, compare pointer values for equality or inequality, and indirectly reference an object via a pointer. Some languages also allow additional operations; we're going to look at the possibilities in this section.

Many programming languages provide the ability to do limited arithmetic with pointers. At the very least, these languages will provide the ability to add an integer constant to a pointer or subtract an integer constant from a pointer. To understand the purpose of these two arithmetic operations, recall the syntax of the malloc function in the C standard library:

```
ptrVar = malloc( bytes_to_allocate );
```

---

[2] Do keep in mind, however, that memory accesses are very slow if the data is not sitting in the cache. If the data is not sitting in the cache, the majority of the time spent in this code will be waiting for memory, not executing instructions, so the two code sequences will have more comparable execution times, all other things being equal.

The parameter you pass `malloc` specifies the number of bytes of storage to allocate. A good C programmer will generally supply an expression like `sizeof(int)` as the parameter to `malloc`. The `sizeof` function returns the number of bytes needed by its single parameter. Therefore, `sizeof( int )` tells `malloc` to allocate at least enough storage for an `int` variable. Now consider the following call to `malloc`:

```
ptrVar = malloc( sizeof( int ) * 8 );
```

If the size of an integer is 4 bytes, this call to `malloc` will allocate storage for 32 bytes. The `malloc` function allocates these 32 bytes at consecutive addresses in memory (see Figure 11-1).

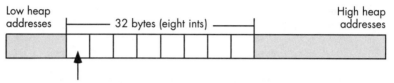

Pointer (address) that `malloc( sizeof( int ) * 8 )` returns

Figure 11-1: Memory allocation via `malloc( sizeof( int ) * 8 )`

The pointer that `malloc` returns contains the address of the first integer in this set, so the C program will only be able to directly access the very first of these eight integers. To access the individual addresses of the other seven integers, you will need to add an integer offset to that *base* address. On machines that support byte-addressable memory (such as the 80x86), the address of each successive integer in memory is the address of the previous integer plus the size of an integer. For example, if a call to the C standard library `malloc` routine returns the memory address $0300_1000, then the eight integers that `malloc` allocates will reside at the following memory addresses:

Integer	Memory address
First	$0300_1000..$0300_1003
Second	$0300_1004..$0300..1007
Third	$0300_1008..$0300_100b
Fourth	$0300_100c..$0300_100f
Fifth	$0300_1010..$0300_1013
Sixth	$0300_1014..$0300..1017
Seventh	$0300_1018..$0300_101b
Eighth	$0300_101c..$0300_101f

11.4.1 Adding an Integer to a Pointer

Because the eight integers in the previous section are exactly 4 bytes apart, you only need to add 4 bytes to the address of the first integer to obtain the address of the second integer. Likewise, the address of the third integer is the address of the second integer plus 4 bytes, and so on. In assembly language, you could access these eight integers using code like the following:

```
// malloc returns storage for eight
//  int32 objects in EAX.

malloc( @size( int32 ) * 8 );

mov( 0, ecx );
mov( ecx, [eax] );       // Zero out the 32 bytes (four
mov( ecx, [eax+4] );     // bytes at a time).
mov( ecx, [eax+8] );
mov( ecx, [eax+12] );
mov( ecx, [eax+16] );
mov( ecx, [eax+20] );
mov( ecx, [eax+24] );
mov( ecx, [eax+28] );
```

Notice the use of the 80x86 indexed addressing mode to access the eight integers that malloc allocates. The EAX register maintains the base address (first address) of the eight integers that this code allocates, and the constant appearing in the addressing mode of the mov instruction specifies the offset of the specific integer from this base address.

Most CPUs use byte addresses for memory objects. Therefore, when allocating multiple copies of some *n*-byte object in memory, the objects will not begin at consecutive memory addresses; instead, they will appear in memory at addresses that are *n* bytes apart. Some machines, however, do not allow a program to access memory at any arbitrary address; they require that applications access data on address boundaries that are a multiple of a word, a double word, or even a quad word. Any attempt to access memory on some other boundary will raise an exception and (possibly) halt the application. If an HLL supports pointer arithmetic, it must take this fact into consideration and provide a generic pointer arithmetic scheme that is portable across different CPU architectures. The most common solution that HLLs use when adding an integer offset to a pointer is to multiply that offset by the size of the object that the pointer references. That is, if you have a pointer p to a 16-byte object in memory, then p + 1 points 16 bytes beyond where p points. Likewise, p + 2 points 32 bytes beyond the address contained in the pointer p. As long as the size of the data object is a multiple of the required alignment size (which the compiler can enforce by adding padding bytes, if necessary), this scheme avoids problems on those architectures that require aligned data access.

Consider, for example, the following C/C++ code:

```
int *intPtr;
    .
    .
    .
// Allocate storage for eight integers:

intPtr = malloc( sizeof( int ) * 8 );

// Initialize each of these integer values:

*(inPtr+0) = 0;
*(intPtr+1) = 1;
*(intPtr+2) = 2;
*(intPtr+3) = 3;
*(intPtr+4) = 4;
*(intPtr+5) = 5;
*(intPtr+6) = 6;
*(intPtr+7) = 7;
```

This example demonstrates how C/C++ uses pointer arithmetic to specify an integer-sized offset, rather than a byte offset, from the base pointer address.

An important thing to realize is that the addition operator only makes sense between a pointer and an integer value. For example, in the C/C++ language, you can indirectly access objects in memory using an expression like *(p + i) (where p is a pointer to an object and i is an integer value). It doesn't make any sense to add two pointers together. Similarly, it isn't reasonable to add other data types with a pointer. For example, adding a floating-point value to a pointer makes no sense. What does it mean to reference the data at some base address plus 1.5612? Operations on pointers involving strings, characters, and other data types don't make much sense, either. Integers (signed and unsigned) are the only reasonable values to add to a pointer.

On the other hand, not only can you add an integer to a pointer, but you can add a pointer to an integer and the result is still a pointer (both p + i and i + p are legal). This is because addition is commutative; in other words, the order of the operands does not affect the result.

11.4.2   Subtracting an Integer from a Pointer

Another reasonable pointer arithmetic operation is subtraction. Subtracting an integer from a pointer references a memory location immediately before the base address held in the pointer. However, subtraction is not commutative and subtracting a pointer from an integer is not a legal operation (p - i is legal, but i - p is not).

In C/C++, *(p - i) accesses the ith object immediately before the object at which p points. In 80x86 assembly language, as in assembly on many processors, you can also specify a negative constant offset when using an indexed addressing mode. For example:

```
mov( [ebx-4], eax );
```

Keep in mind that 80x86 assembly language uses byte offsets, not object offsets (as C/C++ does). Therefore, this statement loads into EAX the double word in memory immediately preceding the memory address in EBX.

11.4.3 Subtracting a Pointer from a Pointer

Unlike addition, it actually makes sense to subtract the value of one pointer variable from another. Consider the following C/C++ code that marches through a string of characters looking for the first e character that follows the first a that it finds (you could use the result of such a calculation, for example, to extract a substring):

```
int distance;
char *aPtr;
char *ePtr;
    .
    .
    .

aPtr = someString;  // Get ptr to start of string in aPtr.

// While we're not at the end of the string
// and the current char isn't 'a':

while( *aPtr != '\0' && *aPtr != 'a' )
{
    // Move on to the next character pointed at by aPtr.

    aPtr = aPtr + 1;
}

// while we're not at the end of the string
// and the current characters isn't 'e'
//
// Start at the 'a' char (or end of string if no 'a').

ePtr = aPtr;
while( *ePtr != '\0' && *ePtr != 'e' )
{
    // Move on to the next character pointed at by ePtr.
    ePtr = ePtr + 1;
}

// Now compute the number of characters between
// the 'a' and the 'e' (counting the 'a' but not
// counting the 'e'):

distance = (ePtr - aPtr);
```

The subtraction of these two pointers produces the number of data objects that exist between the two pointers (in this case, ePtr and aPtr point at characters, so this subtraction produces the number of characters, or bytes if 1-byte characters, between the two pointers).

The subtraction of two pointer values makes sense only if the two pointers reference the same data structure (e.g., an array, string, or record) in memory. Although assembly language will allow you to subtract two pointers that point at completely different objects in memory, their difference will probably have very little meaning.

When using pointer subtraction in C/C++ the base types of the two pointers must be identical (that is, the two pointers must contain the address of two objects whose types are identical). This restriction exists because pointer subtraction in C/C++ produces the number of objects between the two pointers, not the number of bytes. Computing the number of objects between a byte in memory and a double word in memory wouldn't make any sense. The result would be neither a byte count nor a double-word count.

The subtraction of two pointers can return a negative number if the left pointer operand is at a lower memory address than the right pointer operand. Depending on your language and its implementation, you might need to take the absolute value of the result if you're only interested in the distance between the two pointers and you don't care which pointer contains the greater address.

11.4.4 Comparing Pointers

Comparisons are another set of operations that make sense for pointers. Almost every language (that supports pointers) will let you compare two pointers to see if they are equal or not equal. A pointer comparison will tell you whether the pointers reference the same object in memory. Some languages (e.g., assembly and C/C++) will also let you compare two pointers to see if one pointer is less than or greater than another. Like subtraction of two pointers, comparing two pointers only makes sense if the pointers have the same base type and point into the same data structure. If one pointer is less than another, this tells you that the pointer references an object within the data structure that appears before the object whose address the second pointer contains. The converse is equally true for the greater-than comparison. Here is a short example in C that demonstrates pointer comparison:

```
#include <stdio.h>

int iArray[256];
int *ltPtr;
int *gtPtr;



int main( int argc, char **argv )
{
    int lt;
    int gt;

    // Put the address of the "argc" element
    // of iArray into ltPtr. This is done
    // so that the optimizer doesn't completely
```

```
            // eliminate the following code (as would
            // happen if we just specified a constant
            // index):

            ltPtr = &iArray[argc];

            // Put the address of the eighth array
            // element into gtPtr.

            gtPtr = &iArray[7];

            // Assuming you don't type seven or more
            // command-line parameters when running
            // this program, the following two
            // assignments should set lt and gt to 1 (True).

            lt = ltPtr < gtPtr;
            gt = gtPtr > ltPtr;
            printf( "lt:%d, gt:%d\n", lt, gt );
            return 0;
}
```

At the (80x86) machine-language level, addresses are simply 32-bit quantities so the machine code can compare these pointers as though they were 32-bit integer values. Here's the 80x86 assembly code that MSVC emits for this example:

```
; Line 23
;
; Grab ARGC (passed to the program on the stack), use
; it as an index into iArray (four bytes per element,
; hence the "*4" in the scaled-indexed addressing mode),
; compute the address of this array element (using the
; LEA -- load effective address -- instruction), and
; store the resulting address into ltPtr:

    mov eax, DWORD PTR _argc$[esp-4]
    lea eax, DWORD PTR _iArray[eax*4]
    mov DWORD PTR _ltPtr, eax

; Line 28
;
; Put the address of iArray[7] into gtPtr. Because
; the compiler computes the address of iArray[7]
; at compile time (base address of the static variable
; iArray + 7 * 4), this instruction sequence is much
; simpler than the above (which had a variable index
; into the array):

    mov DWORD PTR _gtPtr, OFFSET FLAT:_iArray+28
```

```
; Line 36
;
; Set ECX to 1 if the address of iArray[argc] (held
; in EAX) is less than the address of iArray[7].
;
; Note that "sbb ecx, ecx" and "neg ecx" is a
; sneaky way of setting ECX to 0 or 1 depending
; on whether EAX is less than the address of
; iArray[7] after the comparison.

    cmp eax, OFFSET FLAT:_iArray + 28
    sbb ecx, ecx
    neg ecx

; Line 37
; As above. It is interesting to note that
; the compiler (MSVC) failed to notice that
; it is recomputing exactly the same value as
; the above instruction sequence. Oh well,
; compilers aren't perfect (a good example
; of why human programmers can still beat
; compilers in some instances):

    cmp eax, OFFSET FLAT:_iArray + 28
    sbb edx, edx
    neg edx

    push    ecx
    push    edx
    push    OFFSET FLAT:FormatString
    call    _printf
```

Other than the trickery behind computing True (1) or False (0) after comparing the two addresses, this code is a very straightforward compilation to machine code.

11.4.5   Logical AND/OR and Pointers

On byte-addressable machines, it makes sense to logically AND an address with a bit string value because masking off the low-order (LO) bits in an address is an easy way to align an address on a boundary that is a power of 2. For example, if the 80x86 EBX register contains an arbitrary address, then the following assembly language statement rounds the pointer in EBX down to an address that is a multiple of 4 bytes:

```
and( $FFFF_FFFC, ebx );
```

This is a very useful operation when you want to ensure that memory is accessed on a nice memory boundary. For example, suppose that you have a memory-allocation function that can return a pointer to a block of memory that begins at an arbitrary byte boundary. If you want to ensure that the data structure the pointer points to begins on a double-word boundary, you can use (assembly) code like the following:

```
// # of bytes to allocate

mov( nBytes, eax );

// Provide a "cushion" for rounding.

add( 3, eax );

// Allocate the memory (returns pointer in EAX).

memAlloc( eax );

// Round up to the next-higher dword, if not dword-aligned.

add( 3, eax );

// Make the address a multiple of four.

and( $ffff_fffc, eax );
```

This code allocates an extra 3 bytes when calling memAlloc so that it can add 0, 1, or 3 to the address that memAlloc returns (in order to align the object on a double-word address). On return from memAlloc, this code adds 3 to the address and if it was not already a multiple of four, this will cause it to cross the next double-word boundary. Using the AND instruction reduces the address back to the previous double-word boundary (either the next double-word boundary, or the original address if it was already double-word aligned).

11.4.6   Other Operations with Pointers

Beyond addition, subtraction, comparisons, and possibly AND or OR, very few arithmetic operations make sense with pointer operands. What does it mean to multiply a pointer by some integer value (or another pointer)? What does division of pointers mean? What do you get when you shift a pointer to the left by one bit position? You could make up some sort of definition for these operations, but considering the original arithmetic definitions, these operations just don't make much sense for pointers.

Several languages (including C/C++ and Pascal) restrict the operations possible on a pointer. There are several good reasons for limiting what a programmer can do with a pointer. Here are some of those reasons:

- Code involving pointers is notoriously difficult to optimize. By limiting the number of pointer operations, the compiler can make assumptions about the code it would not otherwise be able to make. This allows the compiler (in theory) to produce better machine code.

- Code containing pointer manipulations is more likely to be defective. Limiting the programmer's options in this area helps prevent pointer abuse and produces more robust code.

NOTE *Section 11.9, "Common Pointer Problems," describes the most serious of these errors and ways to avoid them in your code.*

- Some pointer operations are not portable across CPU architectures (particularly certain arithmetic operations). For example, on some segmented architectures (such as the original 16-bit 80x86), subtracting the values of two pointers may not produce an expected result.

- Although the proper use of pointers can help create efficient programs, the improper use of pointers can destroy program efficiency. By limiting the number of pointer operations that a language supports, that language helps prevent gratuitous use of pointers that often lead to inefficiencies in the code.

The major problem with these "good reasons" for limiting pointer operations is that most exist to protect programmers from themselves. Many programmers (especially beginning programmers) benefit from the discipline these restrictions enforce. However, for the careful programmer who does not abuse pointers, the restrictions on pointer use may eliminate some opportunities that would otherwise be present for writing some great code. Therefore, languages that provide a rich set of pointer operations, like C/C++ and assembly language, are popular with advanced programmers who need absolute control over the use of pointers in their programs.

11.5 A Simple Memory Allocator Example

To help you understand the performance and memory costs of using dynamically allocated memory and pointers to such memory, this section presents a simple memory-allocation/deallocation system. By considering the operations associated with memory allocation and deallocation, you'll be aware of the costs of using these facilities, and you will be better able to use them in an appropriate fashion.

An extremely simple (and fast) memory-allocation scheme would maintain a single variable that forms a pointer into the heap region of memory. Whenever a memory-allocation request comes along, the system makes a copy of this heap pointer to return to the application. The heap management routines add the size of the memory request to the address held in the pointer variable and verify that the memory request won't try to use more memory than is available in the heap region. (Some memory managers return an error indication, like a NULL pointer, when the memory request is too great; others raise an exception.) The problem with this simple memory management scheme is that it wastes memory because there is no mechanism to allow the application to free the memory so that the application can reuse that freed memory later. One of the main purposes of a heap management system is to perform *garbage collection*, that is, reclaim unused memory when an application finishes using that memory.

The only catch is that supporting garbage collection requires some overhead. The memory management code will need to be more sophisticated, will take longer to execute, and will require some additional memory to maintain internal data structures the heap management system uses. Consider an easy implementation of a heap manager that supports garbage collection. This simple system maintains a (linked) list of free memory blocks. Each free memory block in the list will require two double-word values: one double-word value specifies the size of the free block, and the other double-word value contains the address of the next free block in the list (i.e., the link), see Figure 11-2.

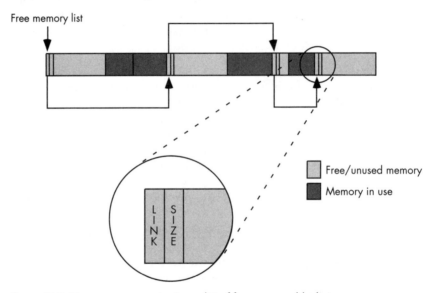

Free memory list

Free/unused memory

Memory in use

Figure 11-2: Heap management using a list of free memory blocks

The system initializes the heap with a NULL link pointer, and the size field contains the size of the entire free space of the heap. When a memory request comes along, the heap manager first determines if a sufficiently large block is available for the allocation request. To do this, the heap manager has to search through the list to find a free block with enough memory to satisfy the request. One of the defining characteristics of a heap manager is how it searches through the list of free blocks to satisfy the request. Some common search algorithms are *first-fit search* and *best-fit search*. The first-fit search, as its name suggests, scans through the list of blocks until it finds the first block of memory large enough to satisfy the allocation request. The best-fit algorithm scans through the entire list and finds the smallest block large enough to satisfy the request. The advantage of the best-fit algorithm is that it tends to preserve larger blocks better than the first-fit algorithm, thereby allowing the system to handle larger subsequent allocation requests when they arrive, though using more time to find the best-fit block. The first-fit algorithm, on the other hand, just grabs the first sufficiently large block it finds, even if there is a smaller block that would satisfy the request. As a result, the first-fit algorithm may reduce the number of large free blocks in the system that could satisfy large memory requests.

The first-fit algorithm does have a couple of advantages over the best-fit algorithm. The most obvious advantage is that the first-fit algorithm is usually faster. The best-fit algorithm has to scan through every block in the free block list in order to find the smallest block large enough to satisfy the allocation request (unless, of course, it finds a perfectly sized block along the way). The first-fit algorithm, on the other hand, can stop once it finds a block large enough to satisfy the request.

Another advantage to the first-fit algorithm is that it tends to suffer less from a degenerate condition known as *external fragmentation*. Fragmentation occurs after a long sequence of allocation and deallocation requests. Remember, when the heap manager satisfies a memory-allocation request it usually creates two blocks of memory—one in-use block for the request and one free block that contains the remaining bytes in the original block (assuming the request did not exactly match the block size). After operating for a while, the best-fit algorithm may wind up producing lots of smaller, leftover blocks of memory that are too small to satisfy an average memory request (because the best-fit algorithm also produces the smallest leftover blocks as a result of its behavior). As a result, the heap manager will probably never allocate these small blocks; hence they are effectively unusable. Although each individual fragment may be small, as multiple fragments accumulate throughout the heap they can wind up consuming a fair amount of memory. This can lead to a situation where the heap doesn't have a sufficiently large block to satisfy a memory-allocation request even though there is enough free memory available (spread throughout the heap). See Figure 11-3 for an example of this condition.

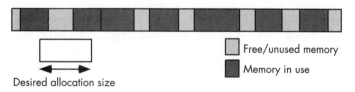

Desired allocation size

▭ Free/unused memory

■ Memory in use

Figure 11-3: Memory fragmentation

In addition to the first-fit and best-fit search algorithms, other memory-allocation strategies exist. Some execute faster, some have less (memory) overhead, some are easy to understand (and some are very complex), some produce less fragmentation, and some have the ability to combine and use noncontiguous blocks of free memory. Memory/heap management is one of the more heavily studied subjects in computer science. A considerable amount of literature exists that explains the benefits of one scheme over another. For more information on memory-allocation strategies, check out a good book on operating system design.

11.6 Garbage Collection

Memory allocation is only half of the story. In addition to a memory-allocation routine, the heap manager has to provide a call that allows an application to free memory it no longer needs for future reuse. In C and HLA, for example, an application accomplishes this by calling the free function. At first blush, free might seem to be a very simple function to write. All it has to do is append the previously allocated and now unused block onto the end of the free list, right? The problem with this trivial implementation of free is that it almost guarantees that the heap will become fragmented and unusable in very short order. Consider the situation in Figure 11-4.

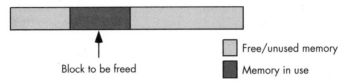

Block to be freed

■ Free/unused memory

■ Memory in use

Figure 11-4: Freeing a memory block

If a trivial implementation of free simply takes the block to be freed and appends it to the free list, the memory organization in Figure 11-4 produces three free blocks. However, because these three blocks are all contiguous, the heap manager should really coalesce these three blocks into a single free block, so that it will be able to satisfy a larger request. Unfortunately, this coalescing operation would require our simple heap manager to scan through the free block list to determine if there are any free blocks adjacent to the block the system is freeing. While it is possible to come up with a data structure that makes it easier to coalesce adjacent free blocks, such schemes generally involve the use of additional overhead bytes (usually 8 or more) with each block on the heap. Whether this is a reasonable trade-off depends on the average size of a memory allocation. If the applications that use the heap manager tend to allocate small objects, the extra overhead for each memory block could wind up consuming a large percentage of the heap space. However, if most allocations are large, then the few bytes of overhead will be of little consequence.

11.7 The OS and Memory Allocation

The performance of the algorithms and data structures that the heap manager uses are only a part of the performance problem. Ultimately, the heap manager needs to request blocks of memory from the operating system. At one extreme, the operating system handles all memory-allocation requests. At the other extreme, the heap manager is a runtime library routine that links with your application; the heap manager first requests large blocks of memory from the operating system and then doles out pieces of this block as memory requests arrive from the application.

The problem with making direct memory-allocation requests to the operating system is that OS API calls are often very slow. If an application calls the operating system for every memory request it makes, the performance of the application will probably suffer if the application makes several memory-allocation and deallocation calls. OS API calls are very slow because they generally involve switching between kernel mode and user mode on the CPU (which is not fast). Therefore, a heap manager that the operating system implements directly will not perform well if your application makes frequent calls to the memory-allocation and deallocation routines.

Because of the high overhead of an operating system call, most languages implement their own versions of malloc and free (or whatever they call them) within the language's runtime library. On the very first memory allocation, the malloc routine will request a large block of memory from the operating system, and then the application's malloc and free routines will manage this block of memory themselves. If an allocation request comes along that the malloc function cannot fulfill in the block it originally created, then malloc will request another large block (generally much larger than the request) from the operating system and add that block to the end of its free list. Because the calls to the application's malloc and free routines only call the operating system on an occasional basis, this dramatically reduces the overhead associated with OS calls.

However, you should keep in mind that the procedure illustrated in the previous paragraph is very implementation and language specific; it's dangerous for you to assume that malloc and free are relatively efficient when writing software that requires high-performance components. The only portable way to ensure a high-performance heap manager is to develop your own application-specific set of routines.

Most standard heap-management functions perform reasonably well for a typical program. For your specific application, however, you might be able to write a specialized set of functions that are much faster or have less memory overhead. If your application's allocation routines effectively handle the program's memory-allocation patterns, the allocation/deallocation functions may be able to handle the application's requests in a more efficient manner. Writing such routines is beyond the scope of this book (see an operating system textbook for more details), but you should be aware of this possibility.

11.8 Heap Memory Overhead

A heap manager often exhibits two types of overhead: performance (speed) and memory (space). Until now, this discussion has mainly dealt with the performance characteristics of a heap manager, now it's time to turn our attention to the memory overhead associated with the heap manager.

Each block the system allocates is going to require some amount of overhead above and beyond the storage the application requests. At the very least, each block the heap manager allocates requires a few bytes to keep track of the block's size. Fancier (higher-performance) schemes may require additional bytes, but typically the number of overhead bytes will be between 4 and 16. The heap manager can keep this information in a separate internal table or it can attach the block size and other memory-management information directly to the block it allocates.

Saving this information in an internal table has a couple of advantages. First, it is difficult for the application to accidentally overwrite the information stored there; attaching the data to the heap memory blocks themselves doesn't provide as much protection against the application wiping out this control information (thereby corrupting the memory manager's data structures). Second, putting memory management information in an internal data structure allows the memory manager to easily determine if a given pointer is valid (one that points at some block of memory that the heap manager believes it has allocated).

Attaching the control information to each block that the heap manager allocates makes it very easy to locate this information, which is an advantage. When the heap manager maintains this information in an internal table, a search operation of some sort might be required in order to locate the information.

Another issue that affects the overhead associated with the heap manager is the allocation *granularity*. Although most heap managers allow you to request an allocation as small as 1 byte, they may actually allocate some minimum number of bytes greater than 1. The minimum amount is the *allocation granularity* that the heap manager supports. Generally, the engineer designing the memory-allocation functions chooses a granularity that will guarantee that any object allocated on the heap will begin at a reasonably aligned memory address for that object. As such, most heap managers allocate memory blocks on a 4-, 8-, or 16-byte boundary. For performance reasons, many heap managers begin each allocation on a cache-line boundary (see *Write Great Code, Volume 1*, for details on cache lines), usually 16, 32, or 64 bytes. Whatever the granularity, if the application requests some number of bytes that is less than the heap manager's granularity or is not a multiple of the granularity value, the heap manager will allocate extra bytes of storage. Therefore, a few unrequested bytes may be tacked on to each request to fill out the minimum-sized block the heap manager allocates (see Figure 11-5). Of course, this amount varies by heap manager (and possibly even by version of a specific heap manager), so an application should never assume that it has more memory available than it requests. Doing so would be silly, because the application could have requested more memory in the initial allocation call.

The extra memory the heap manager allocates to ensure that the request is a multiple of the granularity size results in another form of fragmentation called *internal fragmentation* (see Figure 11-5). Like external fragmentation, internal fragmentation results in the loss of small amounts of memory throughout the system that cannot satisfy future allocation requests. Assuming random-sized memory allocations, the average amount of internal fragmentation that will occur on each allocation is one-half the granularity size. Fortunately, the granularity size is quite small for most memory managers (typically 16 bytes or less), so after thousands and thousands of memory allocations you'll only lose a couple dozen or so kilobytes to internal fragmentation.

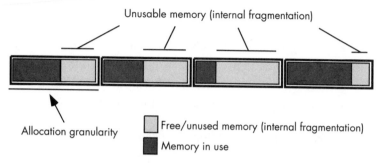

Figure 11-5: Allocation granularity and internal fragmentation

Between the costs associated with allocation granularity and the memory control information, a typical memory request may require between 4 and 16 bytes plus whatever the application requests. If you are making large memory-allocation requests (hundreds or thousands of bytes), the overhead bytes won't consume a large percentage of memory on the heap. However, if you allocate lots of small objects, the memory consumed by internal fragmentation and control information may represent a significant portion of your heap area. For example, consider a simple memory manager that always allocates blocks of data on 4-byte boundaries and requires a single 4-byte length value that it attaches to each allocation request for control purposes. This means that the minimum amount of storage the heap manager will require for each allocation is 8 bytes. If you make a series of malloc calls to allocate a single byte, the application will not be able to use almost 88 percent of the memory it allocates. Even if you allocate 4-byte values on each allocation request, the heap manager consumes two-thirds of the memory for overhead purposes. However, if your average allocation is a block of 256 bytes, the overhead only requires about 2 percent of the total memory allocation. The moral of the story is, "The larger your allocation request, the less impact the control information and internal fragmentation will have on your heap."

Many software engineering studies in computer science journals have found that memory-allocation/deallocation requests cause a significant loss of performance. In such studies, the authors often obtained performance improvements of 100 percent or better by simply implementing their own simplified, application-specific, memory-management algorithms rather than calling the standard runtime library or OS kernel memory-allocation code. Hopefully, this section has made you aware of this potential problem in your own code.

11.9 Common Pointer Problems

Programmers make five common mistakes when using pointers. Some of these mistakes will immediately stop a program with a diagnostic message. Others are subtler, yielding incorrect results without otherwise reporting an error. Still others simply negatively affect the program's performance. Needless to say, programmers who write great code are always aware of these problems when using pointers and avoid them. These five mistakes are:

- Using an uninitialized pointer
- Using a pointer that contains an illegal value like NULL
- Continuing to use storage after it has been freed
- Failing to free storage once the program is done using it
- Accessing indirect data using the wrong data type

11.9.1   Using an Uninitialized Pointer

Using a pointer variable before you have assigned a valid memory address to the pointer is a very common problem. Beginning programmers often don't realize that declaring a pointer variable only reserves storage for the pointer itself; it does not reserve storage for the data that the pointer references. The following short C/C++ program demonstrates this problem:

```
int main()
{
    static int *pointer;

    *pointer = 0;
}
```

Although static variables you declare are, technically, initialized with zero (i.e., NULL), static initialization doesn't initialize the pointer with a valid address. Therefore, when this program executes, the variable pointer will not contain a valid address, and the program will fail. To avoid this problem, you should ensure that all pointer variables contain a valid address prior to dereferencing those pointers. For example:

```
int main()
{
    static int i;
    static int *pointer = &i;

    *pointer = 0;
}
```

Of course, there is no such thing as a truly uninitialized variable on most CPUs.[3] Variables are initialized in two different ways:

- The programmer explicitly gives them an initial value.
- They inherit whatever bit pattern happens to be in memory when the system binds storage to the variable.

---

[3] There are a few CPUs that have special *tag bits* to denote uninitialized values; however, few mainstream CPUs support this feature.

Much of the time, garbage bit patterns laying around in memory don't correspond to a valid memory address. Attempting to *dereference* such an invalid pointer (that is, access the data in memory at which it points) raises a *Memory Access Violation* exception, assuming that your operating system is capable of trapping this exception.

Sometimes, however, those random bits in memory just happen to correspond to a valid memory location you can access. In this situation, the CPU will access the specified memory location without aborting the program. A naive programmer might think that accessing random memory is preferable to aborting a program. However, ignoring the error is far worse because your defective program continues to run without alerting you. If you store data using an uninitialized pointer, you may very well overwrite the values of other important variables in memory. This can produce some problems that are very difficult to locate.

11.9.2 Using a Pointer That Contains an Illegal Value

The second problem programmers have with pointers is assigning them invalid values (invalid in the sense of not containing the address of an actual object in memory). This can be considered a more general case of the first problem; without initialization, the garbage bits in memory supply the invalid address. The effects are the same. If you attempt to dereference a pointer containing an invalid address, either you will get a Memory Access Violation exception or you will access an unexpected memory location. Therefore, you must be careful when dereferencing a pointer variable and make sure that you've assigned a valid address to the pointer before using it.

11.9.3 Continuing to Use Storage After It Has Been Freed

The third problem is also known as the *dangling pointer problem*. To understand this problem, consider the following Pascal code fragment:

```
(* Allocate storage for a new object of type p  *)

new( p );

(* Use the pointer *)

p^ := 0;
 .
 . (* Code that uses the storage associated with p *)
 .

(* free the storage associated with pointer p *)

dispose( p );


 .
 . (* Code that doesn't reference p *)
 .
```

```
(* Dangling pointer                              *)

p^ := 5;
```

In this example, you will note that the program allocates some storage and saves the address of that storage in the p variable. The code uses the storage for a while and then frees it, returning it to the system for other uses. Note that calling dispose doesn't change any data in the allocated memory. It doesn't change the value of p in any way; p still points at the block of memory allocated earlier by new. However, note that the call to dispose does tell the system that the program no longer needs this block of memory and that the system can use this region of memory for other purposes. The dispose function cannot enforce the fact that you will never access this data again. You are simply promising that you won't. Of course, this code fragment breaks that promise. The last statement in the program stores the value 4 at the address pointed to by p in memory.

The biggest problem with dangling pointers is that sometimes you can get away with using them, so you won't immediately know there is a problem. As long as the system doesn't reuse the storage you've freed, using a dangling pointer produces no ill effects in your program. However, with each additional call to new, the system may decide to reuse the memory released by that previous call to dispose. When it does reuse the memory, any subsequent attempt to dereference the dangling pointer may produce some unintended consequences. The problems can include reading data that has been overwritten, overwriting the new data, and (in the worst case) overwriting system heap management pointers (doing so will probably cause your program to crash). The solution is clear: *Never use a pointer value once you free the storage associated with that pointer.*

11.9.4   Failing to Free Storage When Done with It

Of all these problems, failing to free allocated storage will probably have the least impact on the proper operation of your program. The following C code fragment demonstrates this problem:

```
// Pointer to storage in "ptr" variable.

ptr = malloc( 256 );
    .
    . // Code that doesn't free "ptr"
    .
ptr = malloc( 512 );

// At this point, there is no way to reference the
// original block of 256 bytes allocated by malloc.
```

In this example, the program allocates 256 bytes of storage and references this storage using the ptr variable. Later, the program allocates another block of 512 bytes and overwrites the value in ptr with the address of this new block. The former address value in ptr is lost. And because the program has overwritten this former value, there is no way to pass the address of the first 256 bytes to the free function. As a result, these 256 bytes of memory are no longer available to your program.

While making 256 bytes of memory inaccessible to your program might not seem like a big deal, imagine that this code executes within a loop. With each iteration of the loop, the program will lose another 256 bytes of memory. After a sufficient number of repetitions, the program will exhaust the memory available on the heap. This problem is often called a *memory leak* because the effect is as if the memory bits were leaking out of your computer during program execution.

Memory leaks are less of a problem than dangling pointers. Indeed, there are only two problems with memory leaks:

- The danger of running out of heap space (which, ultimately, may cause the program to abort, though this is rare)

- Performance problems due to virtual memory page swapping

Nevertheless, you should develop the habit of freeing all of the storage you allocate.

NOTE *When your program quits, the operating system will reclaim all of the storage, including the data lost via memory leaks. Therefore, memory lost via a leak is only lost to your program, not the whole system.*

11.9.5 Accessing Indirect Data Using the Wrong Data Type

The last problem with pointers is that their lack of type-safe access makes it easy to accidentally use the wrong data type. Some languages, like assembly, cannot and do not enforce pointer type checking. Others, like C/C++, make it very easy to override the type of the object a pointer references. For example, consider the following C/C++ program fragment:

```
char *pc;
    .
    .
    .
pc = malloc( sizeof( char ) );
    .
    .
    .
// Type-cast pc to be a pointer to an integer
// rather than a pointer to a character:

*((int *) pc) = 5000;
```

Generally, if you attempt to assign the value 5000 to the object pointed to by pc, the compiler will complain bitterly. The value 5000 won't fit in the amount of storage associated with a character (char) object, which is 1 byte. This example, however, uses *type casting* (or *coercion*) to tell the compiler that pc really contains a pointer to an integer rather than a pointer to a character. Therefore, the compiler will assume that this assignment is legal.

Of course, if pc doesn't actually point at an integer object, then the last statement in this sequence can be disastrous. Characters are 1 byte long and integers are usually larger. If the integer is larger than 1 byte, this assignment will overwrite some number of bytes beyond the 1 byte of storage that malloc allocated. Whether or not this is a problem depends upon what data immediately follows the character object in memory.

11.10 For More Information

This chapter dealt with the low-level implementation of pointers. For more information on pointers, you'll probably want to start learning and mastering assembly language. *The Art of Assembly Language* (No Starch Press, 2003) is a good place to begin that journey. There are a number of books that deal with the problems of errant pointers in C and C++; Steve Oualline's *How Not to Program in C++* (No Starch Press, 2003) is an example. Any title that describes common C/C++ programming mistakes should pay proper respect to pointer problems.

12

RECORD, UNION, AND CLASS DATA TYPES

Records, unions, and classes are popular composite data types found in many modern programming languages. Incorrectly used, these data types can have a very negative impact on the performance of your software. Correctly used, they can actually improve the performance of your applications (compared with using alternative data structures). In this chapter we will explore the implementation of these data types so that you can understand how to use them to maximize the efficiency of your programs and make the most of these data structures. The topics this chapter covers include:

- Definitions for the record, union, and class data types
- Declaration syntax for records, unions, and classes in various languages
- Record variables and instantiation
- Compile-time initialization of records
- Memory representation of record, union, and class data

- Using records to improve runtime memory performance
- Dynamic record types
- Namespaces
- Variant data types and their implementation as a union
- Virtual method tables for classes and their implementation
- Inheritance and polymorphism in classes
- The performance cost associated with classes and objects

By properly using composite data types such as unions, records, and classes in your applications, you can produce code that is more efficient and easier to read and maintain. This chapter introduces the basic concepts you will need to effectively use these data types in your applications.

12.1   Records

The Pascal *record* and the C/C++ *structure* are terms used to describe comparable composite data structures. Language design textbooks sometimes refer to these types as *cartesian products* or *tuples*. The Pascal terminology is probably better because it avoids confusion with the term *data structure*. Therefore, I'll adopt the term *record* here. Regardless of what you call these data types, records are a great tool for organizing data in an application, and a good understanding of how languages implement records can help you write more efficient code.

An array is homogeneous, meaning that its elements are all of the same type. A record, on the other hand, is heterogeneous, and its elements can have differing types. The purpose of a record is to let you encapsulate logically related values into a single object.

Arrays let you select a particular element via an integer index. With records, you must select an element, known as a *field*, by the field's name. Each of the field names within the record must be unique. That is, the same name may not be used more than once in the same record. However, all field names are local to their record, and you may reuse those names elsewhere in the program.[1]

12.1.1   Record Declarations in Various Languages

Before discussing how various languages implement record data types, I need to provide a quick look at the declaration syntax for some of these languages. The following subsections provide quick glimpses at the declaration syntax for Pascal, C/C++, and HLA.

---

[1] Technically, nested records may reuse field names within the nested records but those are different record structures so the basic rule remains true.

12.1.1.1　Records in Pascal/Delphi

Here's a typical record declaration for a "student" data type in Pascal/Delphi/Kylix:

```
type
    student =
        record
            Name:      string [64];
            Major:     smallint;    // 2-byte integer in Delphi
            SSN:       string[11];
            Mid1:      smallint;
            Midt:      smallint;
            Final:     smallint;
            Homework:  smallint;
            Projects:  smallint;
        end;
```

A record declaration consists of the keyword record followed by a sequence of *field declarations*, ending with the keyword *end*. The field declarations are syntactically identical to variable declarations in the Pascal language.

Many Pascal compilers allocate all of the fields in contiguous memory locations. This means that Pascal will reserve the first 65 bytes for the name,[2] the next 2 bytes for the major code, the next 12 bytes for the Social Security number, and so on.

12.1.1.2　Records in C/C++

Here's the same declaration in C/C++:

```
typedef
    struct
    {
        // Room for a 64-character zero-terminated string:

        char Name[65];

        // Typically a 2-byte integer in C/C++:

        short Major;

        // Room for an 11-character zero-terminated string:

        char SSN[12];
```

---

[2] Pascal strings usually require an extra byte, in addition to all the characters in the string, to encode the length.

```
        short Mid1;
        short Mid2;
        short Final;
        short Homework;
        short Projects

} student;
```

Record declarations in C/C++ begin with the keyword typedef, which is followed by the struct keyword, a set of *field declarations* enclosed by a pair of braces, and a structure name (note that C++ allows an alternative syntax, which I will ignore here as it is totally equivalent for the purposes of discussion). As for Pascal, most C/C++ compilers will assign memory offsets to the fields in the order of their declaration in the record.

12.1.1.3 Records in HLA

In HLA, you can create record types using the record/endrecord declaration. You would encode the record from the previous sections as follows:

```
type
    student:
        record
            Name:      char[65];
            Major:     int16;
            SSN:       char[12];
            Mid1:      int16;
            Mid2:      int16;
            Final:     int16;
            Homework:  int16;
            Projects:  int16;
        endrecord;
```

As you can see, the HLA declaration is very similar to the Pascal declaration. Note that, to stay consistent with the Pascal declaration, this example uses character arrays rather than strings for the Name and SSN (Social Security number) fields. In a typical HLA record declaration you'd probably use a string type for at least the Name field (keeping in mind that a string variable is only a 4-byte pointer).

12.1.2 Instantiation of a Record

Generally, record declations do not reserve storage for a record object. A record declaration specifies a data type that you can use as a template when declaring record variables. *Instantiation* is the process of using a record template, or type, to create a record variable.

Consider the HLA type declaration for student from the following section. This type declaration does not allocate any storage for a record variable. It simply provides the structure for the record object to use. To create an actual student variable, you must set aside some storage for the record variable, either at compile time or at runtime. In HLA, for example, you can set aside storage for a student object at compile time by using variable declarations such as:

```
var
    automaticStudent :student;

static
    staticStudent :student;
```

The var declaration tells HLA to reserve sufficient storage for a student object in the current activation record when the program enters the current procedure. The second statement tells HLA to reserve sufficient storage for a student object in the static data section; this is done at compilation time.

You can also allocate storage for a record object dynamically using memory allocation functions. For example, in the C language you can use the malloc function to allocate storage for a student object thusly:

```
student *ptrToStudent;
    .
    .
    .
    ptrToStudent = malloc( sizeof( student ));
```

A record is simply a collection of (otherwise) unrelated variables. You might wonder why records are really necessary. Why not just create separate variables? In C, for example, why not just write:

```
// Room for a 64-character zero-terminated string:

char someStudent_Name[65];

// Typically a 2-byte integer in C/C++:

short someStudent_Major;

// Room for an 11-character zero-terminated string:

char someStudent_SSN[12];

short someStudent_Mid1;
short someStudent_Mid2;
short someStudent_Final;
short someStudent_Homework;
short someStudent_Projects
```

There are several reasons why this approach fails. On the software engineering side of things, there are maintenance issues to consider. For example, what happens if you create several sets of "student" variables and then decide you want to add a field? Now you've got to go back and edit every set of declarations you've created—not a pretty sight. With struct/record declarations, however, you only need to make a single change to the type declaration and all the variable declarations automatically get the new field. Also, consider what happens if you want to create an array of "student" objects.

Software engineering issues aside, collecting disparate fields into a record is a good idea for efficiency reasons. Many compilers allow you to treat a whole record as a single object for the purposes of assignment, parameter passing, and so on. In Pascal, for example, if you have two variables, s1 and s2, of type student, you can assign all the values of one student object to the other with a single assignment statement like this:

```
s2 := s1;
```

Not only is this more convenient than assigning the individual fields, but the compiler can often generate better code by using a block move operation. Consider the following C++ code and associated x86 assembly language output:

```
#include <stdlib.h>

// A good-sized, but otherwise arbitrary structure, that
// demonstrates how a C++ compiler can handle structure
// assignments.

typedef struct
{
    int x;
    int y;
    char *z;
    int a[16];
}aStruct;


int main( int argc, char **argv )
{
    static aStruct s1;
    aStruct s2;
    int i;

    // Give s1 some nonzero values so
    // that the optimizer doesn't simply
    // substitute zeros everywhere fields
    // of s1 are referenced:

    s1.x = 5;
    s1.y = argc;
    s1.z = *argv;

    // Do a whole structure assignment
    // (legal in C++!)
```

```
    s2 = s1;

    // Make an arbitrary change to S2
    // so that the compiler's optimizer
    // won't eliminate the code to build
    // s2 and just use s1 because s1 and
    // s2 have the same values.

    s2.a[2] = 2;

    // The following loop exists, once again,
    // to thwart the optimizer from eliminating
    // s2 from the code:

    for( i = 0; i < 16; ++i)
    {
        printf( "%d\n", s2.a[i] );
    }

    // Now demonstrate a field-by-field assignment
    // so we can see the code the compiler generates:

    s1.y = s2.y;
    s1.x = s2.x;
    s1.z = s2.z;
    for( i = 0; i < 16; ++i )
    {
        s1.a[i] = s2.a[i];
    }
    for( i = 0; i < 16; ++i)
    {
        printf( "%d\n", s2.a[i] );
    }
    return 0;
}
```

Here's the relevant portion of the 80x86 assembly code that Microsoft's Visual C++ compiler produces (with the /02 optimization option):

```
;Storage for the s1 array in the BSS segment:

_BSS    SEGMENT
_?s1@?1??main@@9@9 DB  04cH DUP (?)
_BSS    ENDS


_main   PROC NEAR
; Line 14
;
; Allocate storage for the local variables
; (including s2):

    sub esp, 76
```

```
; Line 25
;
; Get argc value passed on the stack into EAX:

    mov eax, DWORD PTR _argc$[esp+72]

; Line 26
;
; Get argv value passed on stack into ECX:

    mov ecx, DWORD PTR _argv$[esp+72]

; Initialize fields of the s1 struct:

    push    esi

    ; s1.x = 5;

    mov DWORD PTR _?s1@?1??main@@9@9, 5

    ; s2.y = argc;

    mov DWORD PTR _?s1@?1??main@@9@9+4, eax

    ; s2.z = *argv;

    mov edx, DWORD PTR [ecx]
    mov DWORD PTR _?s1@?1??main@@9@9+8, edx
    push    edi


; Line 31
;
; s2 = s1;
; Note how the compiler copies the entire structure
; using a block move operation (movsd).

    mov ecx, 19                     ; 00000013H
    mov esi, OFFSET FLAT:_?s1@?1??main@@9@9
    lea edi, DWORD PTR _s2$[esp+84]
    rep movsd


; Line 39
;
; s2.a[2] = 2;

    mov DWORD PTR _s2$[esp+104], 2

; For loop to print the 16 values in s2.a in
; order to thwart the optimizer from eliminating
; s2 altogether:
```

```
    lea esi, DWORD PTR _s2$[esp+96]
    mov edi, 16                      ; 00000010H
$L52953:
; Line 47
    mov eax, DWORD PTR [esi]
    push    eax
    push    OFFSET FLAT:??_C@_03HMFC@?$CFd?6?$AA@   ; 'string'
    call    _printf
    add esp, 8
    add esi, 4
    dec edi
    jne SHORT $L52953


; Line 53
;   s1.y = s2.y;

    mov ecx, DWORD PTR _s2$[esp+88]
    mov DWORD PTR _?s1@?1??main@@9@9+4, ecx

; Line 54
;   s1.x = s2.x;

    mov edx, DWORD PTR _s2$[esp+84]
    mov DWORD PTR _?s1@?1??main@@9@9, edx

; Line 55
;   s1.z = s2.z;

    mov eax, DWORD PTR _s2$[esp+92]
    mov DWORD PTR _?s1@?1??main@@9@9+8, eax

; Line 58
;
; For loop that copies s2.a to s1.a (note how
; the optimizer converts this to a block move,
; too.

    mov ecx, 16
    lea esi, DWORD PTR _s2$[esp+96]
    mov edi, OFFSET FLAT:_?s1@?1??main@@9@9+12
    rep movsd


; Line 60
;
; For loop that prints out the 16 values in
; s1.a (to thwart the optimizer):

    lea esi, DWORD PTR _s2$[esp+96]
    mov edi, 16
$L52961:
```

```
; Line 62
    mov ecx, DWORD PTR [esi]
    push    ecx
    push    OFFSET FLAT:??_C@_03HMFC@?$CFd?6?$AA@    ; 'string'
    call    _printf
    add esp, 8
    add esi, 4
    dec edi
    jne SHORT $L52961
```

The important thing to see in this example is that the MSVC compiler emits a block copy instruction sequence (movsd) whenever you assign whole structures, but may degenerate to a sequence of individual mov instructions for each of the fields when you do a field-by-field assignment of two structures. Likewise, if you had not encapsulated all the fields into a struct, assignment of the variables associated with your struct via a block copy operation would not have been possible.

Combining fields together into a record has many advantages. Some of these advantages are listed here:

- It is much easier to maintain the record structure (that is, add, remove, rename, and change fields).

- Compilers can do additional type and semantic checking on records, thereby helping catch logic errors in your programs when you use a record improperly.

- Compilers can treat records as monolithic objects, generating more efficient code (for example, movsd instructions) than they can when working with individual field variables.

- Most compilers respect the order of declaration in a record, allocating successive fields to consecutive memory locations. This is important when interfacing data structures from two different languages. There is no guarantee for the organization of separate variables in memory in most languages.

- As you'll soon see, you can use records to improve cache memory performance and reduce virtual memory thrashing.

- Records can contain pointer fields that contain the address of other (like-typed) record objects. This isn't possible when using bulk variables in memory.

You'll certainly see some other advantages of records in the following sections.

12.1.3   Initialization of Record Data at Compile Time

Some languages, for example C/C++ and HLA, allow you to initialize record variables at compile time. For static objects, this spares your application the code and time needed to manually initialize each field of a record. For example, consider the following C code. This example provides initializers for both static and automatic struct variables.

```
#include <stdlib.h>

// Arbitrary structure that consumes a nontrivial
// amount of space:

typedef struct
{
    int x;
    int y;
    char *z;
    int a[4];
}initStruct;

// The following exists just to thwart
// the optimizer and make it think that
// all the fields of the structure are
// needed.

extern thwartOpt( initStruct *i );

int main( int argc, char **argv )
{
    static initStruct staticStruct = {1,2,"Hello", {3,4,5,6}};
    initStruct autoStruct = {7,8,"World",{9,10,11,12}};

    thwartOpt( &staticStruct );
    thwartOpt( &autoStruct );
    return 0;

}
```

Compiled with MSVC using the /O2 and /Fa command-line options, the following 80x86 machine code (edited manually to eliminate irrelevant output) is obtained:

```
; Static structure declaration.
; Note how each of the fields are
; initialized with the initial values
; specified in the C source file:


_DATA    SEGMENT
_?staticStruct@?1??main@@9@9 DD 01H   ;x field
      DD  02H                  ;y field
      DD  FLAT:$SG52954        ;z field
      DD  03H                  ;a[0] field
      DD  04H                  ;a[1] field
      DD  05H                  ;a[2] field
      DD  06H                  ;a[3] field


$SG52954 DB 'Hello', 00H   ;String constant used above.
     ORG $+2
```

```
$SG52956 DB  'World', 00H
     ORG $+2
$SG52957 DB  'World', 00H   ;Used by autoStruct
_DATA   ENDS

_TEXT   SEGMENT
_autoStruct$ = -28
_main   PROC NEAR
; File t.c
; Line 20
    push    ebp
    mov ebp, esp

    sub esp, 28 ;Allocate storage for autoStruct

; Line 24
;
; Programmatically initialize all the fields of the
; autoStruct variable:

    mov DWORD PTR _autoStruct$[ebp], 7
    mov DWORD PTR _autoStruct$[ebp+4], 8
    mov DWORD PTR _autoStruct$[ebp+8], OFFSET FLAT:$SG52957
    mov DWORD PTR _autoStruct$[ebp+12], 9
    mov DWORD PTR _autoStruct$[ebp+16], 10  ; 0000000aH
    mov DWORD PTR _autoStruct$[ebp+20], 11  ; 0000000bH
    mov DWORD PTR _autoStruct$[ebp+24], 12  ; 0000000cH

; Calls to thwart:

    push    OFFSET FLAT:_?staticStruct@?1??main@@9@9
    call    _thwartOpt
; Line 25
    lea eax, DWORD PTR _autoStruct$[ebp]
    push    eax
    call    _thwartOpt
```

Look carefully at the machine code the compiler emits for the initialization of the autoStruct variable. Unlike static initialization, the compiler cannot initialize memory at compile time because it doesn't know the addresses of the various fields of the automatic record that the system allocates at runtime. Sadly, this particular compiler generates a field-by-field sequence of assignments to initialize the fields of the structure. While this is relatively fast, it can consume quite a bit of memory, especially if you've got a large structure. If you want to reduce the size of the automatic structure variable initialization, one possibility is to create an initialized static structure and assign that structure to the automatic variable upon each entry into the function in which you've declared the automatic variable. Consider the following C++ and 80x86 assembly code:

```
#include <stdlib.h>
typedef struct
{
```

```
    int x;
    int y;
    char *z;
    int a[4];
}initStruct;

// The following exists just to thwart
// the optimizer and make it think that
// all the fields of the structure are
// needed.

extern thwartOpt( initStruct *i );

int main( int argc, char **argv )
{
    static initStruct staticStruct = {1,2,"Hello", {3,4,5,6}};

    // initAuto is a "readonly" structure used to initialize
    // autoStruct upon entry into this function:

    static initStruct initAuto = {7,8,"World",{9,10,11,12}};

    // Allocate autoStruct on the stack and assign the initial
    // values kept in initAuto to this new structure:

    initStruct autoStruct = initAuto;

    thwartOpt( &staticStruct );
    thwartOpt( &autoStruct );
    return 0;

}
```

Here's the corresponding 80x86 assembly code that MSVC emits:

```
_DATA   SEGMENT

; Static initialized data for the staticStruct structure:

_?staticStruct@?1??main@@9@9 DD 01H
    DD  02H
    DD  FLAT:??_C@_05DPEH@Hello?$AA@
    DD  03H
    DD  04H
    DD  05H
    DD  06H

; Static initialized data for the initAuto structure:

    ORG $+4
_?initAuto@?1??main@@9@9 DD 07H
    DD  08H
    DD  FLAT:??_C@_05MKFP@World?$AA@
    DD  09H
```

```
        DD    0aH
        DD    0bH
        DD    0cH

; Initial string data:

??_C@_05DPEH@Hello?$AA@ DB 'Hello', 00H


??_C@_05MKFP@World?$AA@ DB 'World', 00H

_DATA   ENDS



_TEXT   SEGMENT
_autoStruct$ = -28
_main   PROC NEAR
;
; Allocate storage for the autoStruc structure:

    sub esp, 28

; Line 31
;
; Initialize autoStruct by copying the data from
; initAuto to autoStruct (using a block move
; operation):

    mov ecx, 7
    push    esi
    push    edi
    mov esi, OFFSET FLAT:_?initAuto@?1??main@@9@9
    lea edi, DWORD PTR _autoStruct$[esp+36]
    rep movsd


; Line 33
    push      OFFSET FLAT:_?staticStruct@?1??main@@9@9
    call      _thwartOpt

; Line 34
    lea eax, DWORD PTR _autoStruct$[esp+40]
    push      eax
    call      _thwartOpt
```

As you can see in this assembly code, it only takes a six-instruction sequence to copy the data from the statically initialized record into the automatically allocated record. This code is quite a bit shorter. Note, however, that it isn't necessarily faster. Copying data from one structure to another involves memory-to-memory moves, which can be quite slow if all the memory locations are not currently cached. Moving immediate constants directly to the individual fields will often be faster, though it may take many instructions to accomplish this.

Of course, this example should remind you that if you attach an initializer to an automatic variable, the compiler is going to have to emit some code to handle that initialization at runtime. Unless your variables need to be re-initialized on each entry to your function, you should consider using static record objects instead.

12.1.4 Memory Storage of Records

The following Pascal example demonstrates a typical student record variable declaration:

```
var
    John: Student;
```

Given the earlier declaration for the Pascal Student data type, this allocates 81 bytes of storage laid out in memory as shown in Figure 12-1. If the label John corresponds to the *base address* of this record, then the Name field is at offset John+0, the Major field is at offset John+65, the SSN field is at offset John+67, and so on.

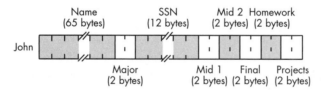

Figure 12-1: Student data structure storage in memory

Most programming languages let you refer to a record field by its name rather than by its numeric offset into the record (indeed, only a few low-end assemblers require that you reference fields by numeric offset; it's safe to say that such assemblers don't really support records). The typical syntax for a field access uses the *dot operator* to select a field from a record variable. Given the variable John from the previous example, here's how you could access various fields in this record:

```
John.Mid1 = 80;          // C/C++ example
John.Final := 93;        (* Pascal Example *)
mov( 75, John.Projects ); // HLA example
```

Figure 12-1 suggests that all fields of a record appear in memory in the order of their declaration. In theory, a compiler can freely place the fields anywhere in memory that it chooses. In practice, almost every compiler places the fields in memory in the same order they appear within the record declaration. The first field usually appears at the lowest address in the record, the second field appears at the next-highest address, the third field follows the second field in memory, and so on.

Figure 12-1 also suggests that compilers pack the fields into adjacent memory locations with no gaps between the fields. While this is true for many languages, this certainly isn't the most common memory organization for a record. For performance reasons, most compilers will actually align the fields of a record on appropriate memory boundaries. The exact details vary by language, compiler implementation, and CPU, but a typical compiler will place fields at an offset within the record's storage area that is "natural" for that particular field's data type. On the 80x86, for example, compilers that follow the Intel ABI (Application Binary Interface) will allocate single-byte objects at any offset within the record, words only at even offsets, and double-word or larger objects on double-word boundaries. Although not all 80x86 compilers support the Intel ABI, most do, which allows records to be shared among functions and procedures written in different languages on the 80x86. Other CPU manufacturers provide their own ABI for their processors and programs that adhere to an ABI can share binary data at runtime with other programs that adhere to the same ABI.

In addition to aligning the fields of a record at reasonable offset boundaries, most compilers will also ensure that the length of the entire record is a multiple of 2, 4, or 8 bytes. They accomplish this by adding padding bytes at the end of the record to fill out the record's size. The reason that compilers pad the size of a record is to ensure that the record's length is a multiple of the largest scalar (non-array/non-record) object in the record.[3] For example, if a record has fields whose lengths are 1, 2, 4, and 8 bytes long, then an 80x86 compiler will generally pad the record's length so that it is a multiple of 8. This allows you to create an array of records and be assured that each record in the array starts at a reasonable address in memory.

Although some CPUs don't allow access to objects in memory at misaligned addresses, many compilers allow you to disable the automatic alignment of fields within a record. Generally, the compiler will have an option you can use to globally disable this feature. Many of these compilers also provide a *pragma* or a packed keyword of some sort that lets you turn off field alignment on a record-by-record basis. Disabling the automatic field alignment feature may allow you to save some memory by eliminating the padding bytes between the fields (and at the end of the record), provided that field misalignment is acceptable on your CPU. The cost, of course, is that the program may run a little more slowly when it needs to access misaligned values in memory.

One reason to use a packed record is to gain manual control over the alignment of the fields within the record. For example, suppose you have a couple of functions written in two different languages, and both of these functions need to access some data in a record. Further, suppose that the two

---

[3] Or a multiple of the CPU's maximum boundary size, if it is smaller than the size of the largest field in the record.

compilers for these functions do not use the same field alignment algorithm. A record declaration like the following (in Pascal) may not be compatible with the way both functions access the record data:

```
type
    aRecord: record

        (* assume Pascal compiler supports a
        ** byte, word, and dword type
        *)

        bField : byte;
        wField : word;
        dField : dword;

    end; (* record *)
```

The problem here is that the first compiler could use the offsets 0, 2, and 4 for the bField, wField, and dField fields, respectively, while the second compiler might use offsets 0, 4, and 8.

Suppose, however, that the first compiler allows you to specify the packed keyword before the record keyword, causing the compiler to store each field immediately following the previous one. Although using the packed keyword will not make the records compatible with both functions, it will allow you to manually add padding fields to the record declaration, as follows:

```
type
    aRecord: packed record
        bField   :byte;

        (* add padding to dword align wField *)

        padding0 :array[0..2] of byte;

        wField   :word;

        (* add padding to dword align dField *)

        padding1 :word;

        dField   :dword;

    end; (* record *)
```

Maintaining code where you've handled the padding in a manual fashion can be a real chore. However, if incompatible compilers need to share data, this trick is worth knowing because it can make data sharing possible. For the exact details concerning packed records, you'll have to consult your language's reference manual.

12.1.5 Using Records to Improve Memory Performance

From the perspective of someone who wants to write great code, records offer an important capability: the ability to control variable placement in memory. By controlling the placement of variables in memory, you can better control cache usage by those variables. This can help you write code that executes much faster.

Consider, for a moment, the following C global/static variable declarations:

```
int i;
int j = 5;
int cnt = 0;
char a = 'a';
char b;
```

You might think that the compiler would allocate storage for these variables in consecutive memory locations. However, few if any languages guarantee this. C certainly doesn't and, in fact, C compilers like Microsoft's Visual C++ compiler don't allocate these variables in sequential memory locations. Consider the MSVC assembly language output for the variable declarations above:

```
PUBLIC   _j
PUBLIC   _cnt
PUBLIC   _a

_DATA    SEGMENT
COMM     _i:DWORD
_DATA    ENDS

_BSS     SEGMENT
_cnt     DD       01H DUP (?)
_BSS     ENDS

_DATA    SEGMENT
COMM     _b:BYTE
_j       DD       05H
_a       DB       061H
_DATA    ENDS
```

Even if you don't understand the purpose of all the directives here, it's pretty obvious that MSVC has rearranged all the variable declarations in memory. Therefore, you cannot count on adjacent declarations in your source file yielding adjacent storage cells in memory. Indeed, there is nothing to stop the compiler from allocating one or more variables in a machine register.

Of course, you might question why you would be concerned about the placement of variables in memory. After all, one of the main reasons for using named variables as an abstraction for memory is to avoid having to think about low-level memory allocation strategies. There are times, however, when being able to control the placement of variables in memory is important. For example, if you want to maximize program performance, you should try to place sets of variables that you access together in adjacent memory locations. This way, those variables will tend to sit in the same cache line, and you won't pay a heavy latency cost for accessing variables not currently held in cache. Furthermore, by placing variables you use together adjacent to one another in memory, you'll use fewer cache lines and, therefore, have less thrashing.

Universally, programming languages that support the traditional notion of records maintain the fields of their records in adjacent memory locations. Therefore, if you have some reason to keep different variables in adjacent memory locations (so that they share cache lines as much as possible), putting your variables into a record is a reasonable approach.

12.1.6   Dynamic Record Types and Databases

As stated in the previous section, "Universally, programming languages that support the traditional notion of records maintain the fields of their records in adjacent memory locations." The key word here is *traditional.* Some dynamic languages employ a *dynamic type system,* and object types can change at run-time. I'll discuss dynamic types a little later in this chapter, but suffice to say that if your language uses a dynamic type record structure, then all bets are off concerning the placement of fields in memory. Chances are pretty good that the fields will *not* be sitting in adjacent memory locations. Then again, if you're using a dynamic language, the fact that you're sacrificing a little performace because you're not getting maximal benefit from your cache will be the least of your worries.

A classical example of a dynamic record is the data you read from a database engine. The engine itself has no preconceived (that is, compile-time) notion of what structure the database records will take. Instead, the database itself provides *metadata* that tells the database the record structure. The database engine reads this metadata from the database and uses it to organize the field data into a single record prior to returning this data to the database application. In a dynamic language, the actual field data is typically spread out across memory, and the database application references that data indirectly.

Of course, if you're using a dynamic language, you have much greater concerns about performance than the placement or organization of your record fields in memory. Dynamic languages, such as database engines, execute many instructions processing the metadata (or otherwise determining the type of their data operands), so losing a few cycles to cache thrashing here and there is going to be the least of your worries. For more information about the overhead associated with a dynamic typing system, see Section 12.6, "Variant Types."

12.2 Discriminant Unions

A *discriminant union* (or just *union*) is very similar to a record. A discriminant is something that distinguishes or separates items in a quantity. In the case of a discriminant union, the term means that different field names are used to distinguish the various ways that a given memory location's data type can be interpreted.

Like records, unions in typical languages that support them have fields that you access using dot notation. In fact, in many languages, about the only syntactical difference between records and unions is the use of the keyword union rather than record. Semantically, however, there is a big difference between a record and a union. In a record, each field has its own offset from the base address of the record, and the fields do not overlap. In a union, however, all fields have the same offset, 0, and all the fields of the union overlap. As a result, the size of a record is the sum of the sizes of all the fields (plus, possibly, some padding bytes), whereas a union's size is the size of its largest field (plus, possibly, some padding bytes at the end).

Because the fields of a union overlap, you might think that a union has little use in a real-world program. After all, if all the fields overlap, then changing the value of one field changes the values of all the other fields as well. This generally means that the use of a union's field is *mutually exclusive*—that is, you can use only one field at any given time. This observation is generally correct, but although this means that unions aren't as generally applicable as records, they still have many uses. As you'll see later in this chapter, you can use unions to save memory by reusing memory for different values, to coerce data types, and to create variant data types. For the most part, though, programs use unions to share memory between different variable objects whose use never overlaps (that is, the variables' use is mutually exclusive).

For example, imagine that you have a 32-bit dword variable, and you find yourself constantly extracting out the LO or the HO 16-bit word. In most HLLs, this would require a 32-bit read and then a mask to AND out the unwanted word. If that wasn't enough, if you want the HO word, you have to then shift the result to the right 16 bits. With a union, you can declare memory addresses to the 32-bit double word and to each 16-bit word and not have to do the mask or possible shift. I explain how to do this later in this chapter (see Section 12.5, "Other Uses of Unions").

12.3 Union Declarations in Various Languages

Before discussing how various languages implement union data types, I need to provide a quick look at the declaration syntax for some of these languages. The following subsections provide quick glimpses at the declaration syntax for Pascal, C/C++, and HLA.

12.3.1   Union Declarations in C/C++

Here's an example of a union declaration in C/C++:

```
typedef union
{
    unsigned int  i;
    float         r;
    unsigned char c[4];

} unionType;
```

Assuming the C/C++ compiler in use allocates 4 bytes for unsigned integers, the size of a `unionType` object will be 4 bytes (because all three fields are 4-byte objects).

12.3.2   Union Declarations in Pascal/Delphi/Kylix

Pascal, Delphi, and Kylix use *case-variant records* to create a discriminant union. The syntax for a case-variant record is the following:

```
type
    typeName =
        record

            <<non-variant/union record fields go here>>

            case tag of
                const1:( field_declaration );
                const2:( field_declaration );
                    .
                    .
                    .
                constn:( field_declaration )

        end;
```

The `tag` item can be either a type identifier (e.g., `boolean`, `char`, or some user-defined type), or it can be a field declaration of the form `identifier:type`. If the `tag` item takes the latter form, then `identifier` becomes another field of the record (and not a member of the variant section) and has the specified type. When using the second form, the Pascal compiler could generate code that raises an exception whenever the application attempts to access any of the variant fields except the one specified by the value of the tag field. In practice, almost no Pascal compilers do this. Still, keep in mind that the Pascal language standard suggests that compilers should do this, so some compilers might actually do this check.

Here's an example of two different case-variant record declarations in Pascal:

```
type
    noTagRecord=
        record
            someField: integer;
            case boolean of
                true:( i:integer );
                false:( b:array[0..3] of char)
        end; (* record *)

    hasTagRecord=
        record
            case which:(0..2) of
                0:( i:integer );
                1:( r:real );
                2:( c:array[0..3] of char )
        end; (* record *)
```

As you can see in the hasTagRecord union, a Pascal case-variant record does not require any normal record fields. This is true even if you do not have a tag field.

12.3.3 Union Declarations in HLA

HLA supports unions as well. Here's a typical union declaration in HLA:

```
type
    unionType:
        union
            i: int32;
            r: real32;
            c: char[4];
        endunion;
```

12.4 Memory Storage of Unions

Remember that the big difference between a union and a record is the fact that records allocate storage for each field at different offsets, whereas unions overlay each of the fields at the same offset in memory. For example, consider the following HLA record and union declarations:

```
type
    numericRec:
        record
            i: int32;
            u: uns32;
            r: real64;
        endrecord;
```

```
numericUnion:
    union
          i: int32;
          u: uns32;
          r: real64;
    endunion;
```

If you declare a variable, say n, of type numericRec, you access the fields as n.i, n.u, and n.r, exactly as though you had declared the n variable to be type numericUnion. However, the size of a numericRec object is 16 bytes because the record contains two double-word fields and a quad-word (real64) field. The size of a numericUnion variable, however, is 8 bytes. Figure 12-2 shows the memory arrangement of the i, u, and r fields in both the record and union.

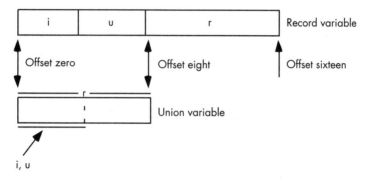

Figure 12-2: Layout of a union versus a record variable

12.5 Other Uses of Unions

In addition to conserving memory, programmers often use unions to create *aliases* in their code. As you may recall, an alias is a different name for the same memory object. Although aliases are often a source of confusion in a program and should be used sparingly, using an alias can sometimes be convenient. For example, in some section of your program you might need to constantly use type coercion to refer to a particular object. One way to avoid this is to use a union variable with each field representing one of the different types you want to use for the object. As an example, consider the following HLA code fragment:

```
type
    CharOrUns:
        union
            c:char;
            u:uns32;
        endunion;

static
    v:CharOrUns;
```

With a declaration like this one, you can manipulate an uns32 object by accessing v.u. If, at some point, you need to treat the LO byte of this uns32 variable as a character, you can do so by simply accessing the v.c variable, as follows:

```
mov( eax, v.u );
stdout.put( "v, as a character, is '", v.c, "'" nl );
```

Another common practice is to use unions to disassemble a larger object into its constituent bytes. Consider the following C/C++ code fragment:

```
typedef union
{
    unsigned int u;
    unsigned char bytes[4];
} asBytes;

asBytes composite;
        .
        .
        .
    composite.u = 1234576890;
    printf
    (
        "HO byte of composite.u is %u, LO byte is %u\n",
        composite.u[3],
        composite.u[0]
    );
```

Although composing and decomposing data types using unions is a useful trick every now and then, be aware that this code is not portable. Remember that the HO and LO bytes of a multibyte object appear at different addresses on big endian versus little endian machines. This code fragment works fine on little endian machines, but fails to display the correct bytes on big endian CPUs. Any time you use unions to decompose larger objects, you should be aware that the code might not be portable across different machines. Still, disassembling larger values into the corresponding bytes, or assembling a larger value from bytes, is usually much more efficient that using shift lefts, shift rights, and AND operations. Therefore, you'll see this trick used quite a bit.

12.6 Variant Types

A *variant* object is one whose type is dynamic—that is, the object's type can vary at runtime. This spares the programmer from having to decide on a data type when designing the program and allows the end user to enter whatever data they like as the program operates. Programs written in a dynamically typed language are typically far more compact than languages written in a traditional statically typed language. This makes dynamically typed languages very popular for rapid prototyping, interpretive, and very high-level languages. A few mainstream languages (including Visual Basic and Delphi/Kylix) also support variant types. In this section, I'll show how compilers implement variant types and the efficiency costs associated with them.

To implement a variant type, most languages use a union to reserve storage for all the different types the variant supports. This means that variant objects will consume at least as much space as the largest primitive data type the variant type supports. In addition to the storage required to keep the variant's value, the variant data structure will also need some additional storage to keep track of the object's current type. And if the language allows variants to assume an array type, additional storage may be necessary to specify how many elements are in the array (or the bounds on each dimension if the language allows multidimensional variant arrays). The bottom line is that a variant will consume a fair amount of memory, even if the actual data only consumes a single byte.

Perhaps the best way to illustrate how variant data types work is to implement a variant type manually. Consider the following Delphi case-variant record declaration:

```
type
    dataTypes =
        (
            vBoolean, paBoolean, vChar, paChar,
            vInteger, paInteger, vReal, paReal,
            vString, paString
        );

    varType =
        record
            elements : integer;
            case theType: varType of
                vBoolean:  ( b:boolean );
                paBoolean: ( pb:^boolean[0..0] );
                vChar:     ( c:char );
                paChar:    ( pc:^char[0..0] );
                vInteger:  ( i:integer );
                paInteger: ( pi:^integer[0..0] );
                vReal:     ( r:real );
                paReal:    ( pr:&real[0..0] );
                vString:   ( s:string );
                paString:  ( ps:^string[0..0] )
        end;
```

In this record, elements will contain the number of elements in the array if the object is a single-dimensional array (this particular data structure does not support multidimensional arrays). If, on the other hand, the object is a scalar variable, then the elements value will be irrelevant. The theType field specifies the current type of the object. If this tag field contains one of the enumerated constants vBoolean, vChar, vInteger, vReal, or vString, then the object is a scalar variable, and if this field contains one of the constants paBoolean, paChar, paInteger, paReal, or paString then the object is a single-dimensional array of the specified type.

The fields in the case-variant section of the Pascal record hold the variant's value if it is a scalar object, or they hold a pointer to an array of objects if the variant is an array object. Technically, Pascal requires that you specify the bounds of the array in its declaration. But fortunately, Delphi lets you turn off bound checking (as well as allowing you to allocate memory for an array of arbitrary size), hence the dummy array bounds in this example.

Manipulating two variant objects that have the same type is easy. For example, suppose you want to add two variant values together. First, you'd determine the current type of both objects and whether the addition operation even makes sense for the data types.[4] Once you've decided that the addition operation is reasonable, it's easy enough to use a case (or switch) statement based on the tag field of the two variant types:

```
// Handle the addition operation:

// Load variable theType with either left.theType
// or right.theType  (which, presumably, contain
// the same value at this point).

case( theType ) of

    vBoolean: writeln( "Cannot add two Boolean values!" );
    vChar: writeln( "Cannot add two character values!" );
    vString: writeln( "Cannot add two string values!" );
    vInteger: intResult := left.vInteger + right.vInteger;
    vReal: realResult := left.vReal + right.vReal;
    paBoolean: writeln( "Cannot add two Boolean arrays!" );
    paChar: writeln( "Cannot add two character arrays!" );
    paInteger: writeln( "Cannot add two integer arrays!" );
    paReal: writeln( "Cannot add two real arrays!" );
    paString: writeln( "Cannot add two Boolean arrays!" );

end;
```

If the left and right operands are not the same type, then the operation is a bit more complex. Some mixed-type operations are legal. For example, adding an integer operand and a real operand together is reasonable (it produces a real type result in most languages). Other operations may be legal only if the values of the operands can be added. For example, it's reasonable to add a string and an integer together if the string happens to contain a string of digits that could be converted to an integer prior to the addition (likewise for string and real operands). What is needed here is a two-dimensional case/switch statement. Unfortunately, outside of assembly language, you won't find such a creature (you won't really find it in assembly language,

---

[4] For example, you can't add two Boolean values together.

either, but you can easily write assembly code that does the same thing as a two-dimensional switch/case statement). However, you can simulate one easily enough by nesting case/switch statements:

```
case( left.theType ) of

    vInteger:
        case( right.theType ) of
            vInteger:
                (* code to handle integer+integer operands *)
            vReal:
                (* code to handle integer+real operands *)
            vBoolean:
                (* code to handle integer+boolean operands *)
            vChar:
                (* code to handle integer+char operands *)
            vString:
                (* code to handle integer+string operands *)
            paInteger:
                (* code to handle integer+intArray operands *)
            paReal:
                (* code to handle integer+realArray operands *)
            paBoolean:
                (* code to handle integer+booleanArray operands *)
            paChar:
                (* code to handle integer+charArray operands *)
            paString:
                (* code to handle integer+stringArray operands *)
        end;

    vReal:
        case( right.theType ) of
            (* cases for each of the right operand types
                REAL + type *)
        end;

    Boolean:
        case( right.theType ) of
            (* cases for each of the right operand types:
                BOOLEAN + type *)
        end;

    vChar:
        case( right.theType ) of
            (* cases for each of the right operand types:
                CHAR + type *)
        end;

    vString:
        case( right.theType ) of
            (* cases for each of the right operand types:
                STRING + type *)
        end;
```

```
paInteger:
    case( right.theType ) of
        (* cases for each of the right operand types:
            intArray + type *)
    end;

paReal:
    case( right.theType ) of
        (* cases for each of the right operand types:
            realArray + type *)
    end;

paBoolean:
    case( right.theType ) of
        (* cases for each of the right operand types:
            booleanArray + type *)
    end;

paChar:
    case( right.theType ) of
        (* cases for each of the right operand types:
            charArray + type *)
    end;

paString:
    case( right.theType ) of
        (* cases for each of the right operand types:
            stringArray + type *)
    end;

end;
```

Once you expand all the code alluded to in these comments, you can see that this will be quite a few statements. And this is just for one operator! Obviously, it is going to take considerable work to implement all the basic arithmetic, string, character, and Boolean operations. Clearly, expanding this code inline whenever you need to add two variant values together is out of the question. Generally, you'd write a function like vAdd that would accept two variant parameters and produce a variant result (or raise some sort of exception if the addition of the operands is illegal).

The important thing to note by looking at this code is not that the code to do a variant addition is long. The real problem is performance. It's not at all unreasonable to expect a variant addition operation to require dozens, if not hundreds, of machine instructions to accomplish. By contrast, it only takes two or three machine instructions to add two integer or floating-point values together. Therefore, you can expect operations involving variant objects to run approximately one to two orders of magnitude slower than the standard operations. This, in fact, is one of the major reasons "typeless" languages (usually very high-level languages) are so slow. When you truly need a variant type, the performance is often just as good (or even better) than the alternative code you'd have to write to get around using the variant type. However, if you're using variant objects to hold values whose type you know when you first write the program, you're going to pay a heavy performance penalty for not using typed objects.

12.7 Namespaces

As your programs become larger, and particularly as these large programs use third-party software libraries to reduce development time, the more likely it is that name conflicts will develop in your source files. A name conflict occurs when you want to use a specific identifier at one point in your program, but that name is already in use elsewhere (for example, in some library you're using). At some point in a very large project you may find yourself dreaming up a new name to resolve a naming conflict only to discover that the new name is also already in use. Software engineers call this the *namespace pollution* problem. Like environmental pollution, the problem is easy to live with when it's small and localized. As your programs get larger, however, dealing with the fact that "all the good identifiers are already used up" gets to be a real problem.

At first blush, it might seem that the namespace pollution problem is a synthetic problem. After all, a programmer can always dream up a different name: the global namespace, the set of all possible names, is huge. However, programmers who write great code often adhere to certain naming conventions so that their source code is consistent and easy to read (I'll come back to this subject in Volume 3 of the Write Great Code series). Constantly dreaming up new names, even if those new names aren't all that bad, tends to produce inconsistencies in the source code that make programs a little harder to read. It would be nice to choose whatever name you like for your identifiers and not have to worry about conflicts with other code or libraries. Namespaces provide just this ability.

A namespace is a mechanism by which you can associate a set of identifiers with a namespace identifier. In many respects, a namespace is like a record declaration. Indeed, you can use a record declaration as a poor man's namespace in languages that don't support namespaces directly (with a few major restrictions). For example, consider the following Pascal variable declarations:

```
var
    myNameSpace:
        record
            i: integer;
            j: integer;
            name: string(64);
            date: string(10);
            grayCode: integer;
        end;

    yourNameSpace:
        record
            i: integer;
```

```
        j: integer;
        profits: real;
        weekday: integer;
    end;
```

It should be obvious from what you learned earlier that the i and j fields in these two records are distinct variables. There will never be a naming conflict because the program must qualify these two field names with the record variable name. That is, you refer to these variables using the following names:

```
myNameSpace.i, myNameSpace.j,
yourNameSpace.i, yourNameSpace.j
```

The record variable that prefixes the fields uniquely identifies each of these field names. This is obvious to anyone who has ever written code that uses a record or structure. Therefore, in languages that don't support namespaces, you can use records in their place.

There is one major problem with creating namespaces by using records or structures: most languages let you declare only variables within a record. Namespace declarations (like those available in C++ and HLA) specifically allow you to include other types of objects as well. In HLA, for example, a namespace declaration takes the following form:

```
namespace nsIdentifier;

    << constant, type, variable, procedure,
            and other declarations >>

end nsIdentifier;
```

Namespaces are a declaration section unto themselves. In particular, they do not have to go in a var or static (or any other) section. You can create constants, types, variables, static objects, procedures, and so on, all within a namespace.

Access to namespace objects in HLA uses the familiar dot notation that records, classes, and unions use. As long as the namespace identifier is unique and all the fields within the namespace are unique to that namespace, you won't have any problems. By carefully partitioning a project into various namespaces, you can easily avoid most of the problems that occur because of namespace pollution.

Another interesting aspect to namespaces is that they are extensible. For example, consider the following declarations in C++:

```
namespace aNS
{
    int i;
    int j;
}
```

```
int i;  // Outside the namespace, so this is unique.
int j;  // ditto.

namespace aNS
{
    int k;
}
```

This example code is perfectly legal. The second declaration of aNS does not conflict with the first; it extends the aNS namespace to include identifier k as well as i and j. This feature is very handy when, for example, you want to extend a set of library routines and header files without modifying the original header files for that library (assuming the library names all appear within a namespace).

From an implementation point of view, there really is no difference between a namespace and a set of declarations appearing outside a namespace. The compiler typically deals with both types of declarations in a nearly identical fashion with the only difference being that the program prefixes all objects located within the namespace with the namespace's identifier.

12.8 Classes and Objects

The *class* data type is the bedrock of modern object-oriented programming. In most object-oriented programming languages the class is closely related to the record or structure. However, unlike records (which have a surprisingly uniform implementation across most languages), class implementations tend to vary. Nevertheless, many contemporary object-oriented languages achieve their results using similar approaches, so this section will use a few concrete examples from C++. HLA and Delphi users will find that these languages work in a similar manner.

12.8.1 Classes Versus Objects

Many programmers often confuse the terms *object* and *class*. A class is a data type. It is a template for how the compiler organizes memory with respect to the class's fields. An object is an *instantiation* of a class—that is, an object is a variable of some class type that has memory allocated to hold the data associated with the class's fields. For a given class, there is only one class definition. You may, however, have several objects (variables) of that class type.

12.8.2 Simple Class Declarations in C++

Structs and classes are syntactically and semantically similar in C++. Indeed, there is only one syntactical difference between a struct and a class in C++: the use of the class keyword versus the struct keyword. Consider the following two valid type declarations in C++:

```
struct student
{
```

```
        // Room for a 64-character zero-terminated string:

        char Name[65];

        // Typically a 2-byte integer in C/C++:

        short Major;

        // Room for an 11-character zero-terminated string:

        char SSN[12];

        // Each of the following is typically a 2-byte integer

        short Mid1;
        short Mid2;
        short Final;
        short Homework;
        short Projects
};


class myClass
{
public:

// Room for a 64-character zero-terminated string:

        char Name[65];

        // Typically a 2-byte integer in C/C++:

        short Major;

        // Room for an 11-character zero-terminated string:

        char SSN[12];

        // Each of the following is typically a 2-byte integer

        short Mid1;
        short Mid2;
        short Final;
        short Homework;
        short Projects
};
```

Although these two data structures both contain the same fields, and you would access those fields the same way, their memory implementation is slightly different. Figure 12-3 compares the memory layout for the struct with the memory layout for the class (in Figure 12-4).

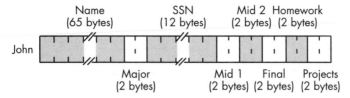

Figure 12-3: Student struct storage in memory

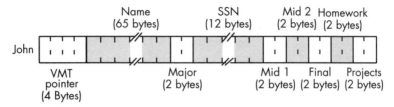

Figure 12-4: Student class storage in memory

12.8.3 Virtual Method Tables

If you look at these two figures, you can see that the difference between them is the VMT field that is present in the class definition and absent from the struct. VMT stands for *virtual method table*, and these 4 bytes contain a pointer to an array of "method pointers" for the class. Virtual methods (also known as *virtual member functions* in C++) are special class-related functions that you declare as fields in the class. In the current student example, the class doesn't actually have any virtual methods, so some C++ compilers might eliminate the VMT field, but most object-oriented languages will still allocate storage for the VMT pointer within the class.

Here's a little C++ class that actually has a virtual member function and, therefore, also has a virtual method table:

```
class myclass
{
    public:
        int a;
        int b;
        virtual int f( void );
};
```

When C++ calls a standard function, it directly calls that function. Virtual member functions are another story altogether. Each object in the system carries a pointer to a virtual method table which is an array of pointers to all the member functions (methods) appearing within the object's class (see Figure 12-5).

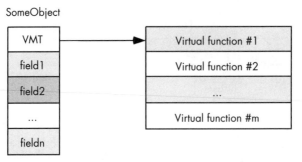

SomeObject

VMT
field1
field2
...
fieldn

Virtual function #1
Virtual function #2
...
Virtual function #m

Figure 12-5: A virtual method table (VMT)

Calling a virtual member function requires *two* indirect accesses. First, the program has to fetch the VMT pointer from the class object and use that to indirectly fetch a particular virtual function address from the VMT. Then the program has to make an indirect call to the virtual member function via the pointer it retrieved from the VMT. As an example, consider the following C++ function and the corresponding 80x86 assembly code that Visual C++ generates for it:

```
#include <stdlib.h>

// A C++ class with two trivial
// member functions (so the VMT
// will have two entries).

class myclass
{
    public:
        int a;
        int b;
        virtual int f( void );
        virtual int g( void );
};

// Some trivial member functions,
// We're really only interested
// in looking at the calls, so
// these functions will suffice
// for now.

int myclass::f( void )
{
    return b;
}

int myclass::g( void )
{
    return a;
}
```

```
// A main function that creates
// a new instance of myclass and
// then calls the two member functions

int main( int argc, char **argv )
{
    myclass *c;

    // Create a new object:

    c = new myclass;

    // Call both member functions:

    c->a = c->f() + c->g();
    return 0;

}
```

Here's the 80x86 assembly code the MSVC generates:

```
CONST    SEGMENT

; Here is the VMT for myclass. It contains
; two entries, a pointer to the myclass::f
; member function and a pointer to the
; myclass::g member function.

??_7myclass@@6B@ DD FLAT:?f@myclass@@UAEHXZ ;myclass::f
    DD   FLAT:?g@myclass@@UAEHXZ      ;myclass::g

CONST    ENDS

    .
    .
    .


; Line 23
;
; Allocate storage for a new instance of myclass:

    push   12      ;12 bytes (two 4-byte fields+VMT)
    call   ??2@YAPAXI@Z    ; operator new
    add esp, 4     ;Remove parameter from NEW call.

    test   eax, eax    ;Did NEW FAIL (returning NULL)?
    je  SHORT $L628

    ;Initialize VMT field with the address of the VMT:

    mov DWORD PTR [eax], OFFSET FLAT:??_7myclass@@6B@
    mov esi, eax
    jmp SHORT $L629
```

```
$L628:
    xor esi, esi    ;For failure, put NULL in esi
$L629:

; At this point, ESI contains the "THIS" pointer
; that refers to the object in question. In this
; particular code sequence, "THIS" is the address
; of the object whose storage we allocated above.

; Line 25
;
; Get the VMT into EAX (first indirect access
; needed to make a virtual member function call)

    mov eax, DWORD PTR [esi]

; Member function expects us to pass THIS in
; the ECX register, so move it there.

    mov ecx, esi

; Call the virtual member function indirectly
; through the VMT pointer (remember, EAX
; holds the pointer to the VMT). This particular
; instruction is calling the myclass:g member
; function, whose address appears at VMT+4, above.

    call    DWORD PTR [eax+4]
    mov edi, eax    ;Save g's return result

; Okay, now let's call the myclass:f member
; function. ESI still contains a copy of THIS.
; VMT+0 holds the pointer to myclass::f.
; Again, a double-indirect fetch is required
; to call this virtual member function:

    mov edx, DWORD PTR [esi]
    mov ecx, esi    ;Pass THIS in ECX.
    call    DWORD PTR [edx]

; Compute c->f() + c->g()

    add edi, eax

; Line 26
; Store the sum into c->b.

    mov DWORD PTR [esi+4], edi
```

This example amply demonstrates why object-oriented programs generally run a little more slowly than standard procedural programs—extra indirection that you don't have when calling functions at a fixed address in memory is associated with each virtual member function. C++

attempts to address this inefficiency by providing *static member functions*, but static member functions lose many of the benefits of virtual member functions that make object-oriented programming possible.

12.8.4   Sharing VMTs

For a given class there is only one copy of the VMT in memory. This is a static object so all objects of a given class type share the same VMT. This is reasonable because all objects of the same class type have exactly the same member functions (see Figure 12-6).

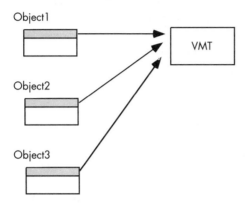

Note: Objects are all the same class type

Figure 12-6: Objects sharing the same VMT

Because the addresses in a virtual method table never change during program execution, most languages place the VMT in a constant (write-protected) section in memory. In the previous example of the last section the compiler places the myclass VMT in the CONST segment.

12.8.5   Inheritance in Classes

Inheritance is one of the fundamental ideas behind object-oriented programming. The basic idea is that a class inherits, or copies, all the fields from some existing class and then possibly expands the number of fields in the new class data type. For example, suppose you created a data type point which describes a point in the planar (two-dimensional) space. The class for this point might look like the following:

```
class point
{
    public:
        float x;
        float y;

        virtual float distance( void );
};
```

The distance member function would probably compute the distance from the origin (0,0) to the coordinate specified by the (x,y) fields of the object.

Here's a typical implementation of this member function:

```
float point::distance( void )
{
    return sqrt( x*x + y*y );
}
```

Inheritance allows you to extend an existing class by adding new fields or replacing existing fields. For example, suppose you want to extend the two-dimensional point definition to a third spatial dimension. You can easily do this with the following C++ class definition:

```
class point3D :public point
{
    public:
        float z;

        virtual void rotate( float angle1, float angle2 );
};
```

The point3D class inherits the x and y fields, as well as the distance member function. Of course, distance does not compute the proper result for a point in three-dimensional space, but I'll address that in just a moment. By *inherits*, I mean that point3D objects can find their x and y fields at exactly the same offsets in the object as for point objects (see Figure 12-7).

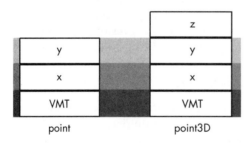

Derived (child) classes locate their inherited fields at the same offsets as those fields in the base class.

Figure 12-7: Inheritance in classes

As you've probably noticed, there were actually two items added to the point3D class—a new data field (z) and a new member function (rotate). If you look at Figure 12-7 you'll discover that adding the rotate virtual member function has had no impact at all on the layout of a point3D object. This is because virtual member functions' addresses appear in the VMT, not in the object itself. Although both `point` and `point3D` contain a field named *VMT*, these fields do not point at the same table in memory. Every class has its own unique VMT (see Figure 12-8). That VMT consists of an array of pointers to all of the member functions (inherited or explicitly declared) for the class.

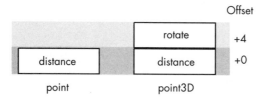

Figure 12-8: Virtual method tables for inherited classes

All the objects for a given class share the same VMT, but this is not true for objects of different classes. Because `point` and `point3D` are different classes, their objects' VMT fields will point at different VMTs in memory (see Figure 12-9).

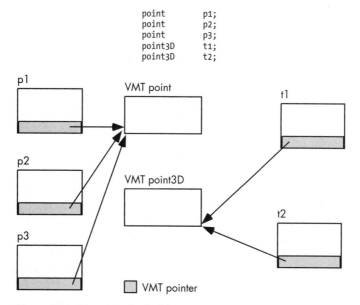

Figure 12-9: Virtual method table access

One problem with the `point3D` definition given thus far is that it inherits the distance function from the `point` class. By default, if a class inherits member functions from some other class, the entries in the VMT corresponding to those inherited functions will point at the functions associated with the base class. If you have an object pointer variable of type `point3D`, let's say "p3D," and you invoke the member function `p3D->distance()`, you will not get a correct result. Because `point3D` inherits the distance function from class `point`, `p3->distance()` will compute the distance to the projection of (x,y,z) onto the two-dimensional plane rather than the correct value. In C++ you can overcome this problem by *overloading* the inherited function and writing a new, point3D-specific member function, as shown here:

```
class point3D :public point
{
    public:
        float z;

        virtual void distance( void );
        virtual void rotate( float angle1, float angle2 );
};


float point3D::distance( void )
{
    return sqrt( x*x + y*y + z*z );
}
```

Creating an overloaded member function does not change the layout of the class's data nor does it change the layout of the point3D virtual method table. The only change this function evokes is that the C++ compiler initializes the distance entry in the point3D VMT with the address of the point3D::distance function rather than the address of the point::distance function.

12.8.6   Polymorphism in Classes

Inheritance and overloading are two of the essential components needed for object-oriented programming; polymorphism is the other anchor upon which object-oriented programming is based. Polymorphism literally means "many-faced" (or translated a little better, "many forms" or "many shapes") and the concept describes how a single instance of a function call in your program, such as x->distance(), could wind up calling different functions (in the examples from the previous section, this could be point::distance or point3D::distance). The trick that makes this possible is the fact that C++ relaxes its type-checking facilities a bit when dealing with derived (inherited) classes.

Normally, a C++ compiler will generate an error if you try to assign the address of some item to a pointer whose base type doesn't match the type of that item. For example, consider the following code fragment:

```
float f;
int *i;

    .

    .

    .
i = &f; // C++ isn't going to allow this.
```

When you are assigning addresses to a pointer, the type of the object whose address you're taking must exactly match the base type of the pointer variable to which you're assigning the address, well, with one major exception. C++ relaxes this restriction so you can assign the address of some object to a pointer as long as the base type of the pointer is the same as the object or the base type is an ancestor of that object's type (an *ancestor class* is one from which some other class type is derived, directly or indirectly, via inheritance). That is, something like the following code is legal:

```
point *p;
point3d t;
point generic;

    p = new point;
    t = new point3D;
        .
        .
        .
    generic = t;
```

If you're wondering how this could be legitimate, take another look at Figure 12-7. If generic's base type is point, then the C++ compiler will allow access to a VMT at offset 0 in the object, an x field at offset 4 in the object, and a y field at offset 8 in the object. Similarly, any attempt to invoke the distance member function is going to access the function pointer at offset 0 into the virtual method table pointed at by the object's VMT field. If generic points at an object of type point, of course, all of these requirements are satisified. *This is also true if generic points at any derived class of point* (that is, any class that inherits the fields from point). Of course, none of the extra fields in the derived class (point3D) will be accessible via the generic pointer, but that's to be expected because generic's base class is point.

A crucial thing to note, however, is that when you invoke the distance member function, you're calling the one pointed at by the point3D VMT, not the one pointed at by the point VMT. This fact is the complete basis for polymorphism in an object-oriented programming language such as C++. The code a compiler emits is exactly the same code it would emit if generic contained the address of an object of type point. All of the "magic" occurs because the compiler allows the programmer to load the address of a point3D object into generic.

12.8.7 Classes, Objects, and Performance

As you saw in the sample code earlier in this chapter, the direct cost associated with object-oriented programming isn't terribly significant. Calls to member functions (methods) are a bit more expensive because of the double indirection that takes place; however, the added expense is a small price to pay for the flexibility you'll obtain when doing object-oriented programming. The extra instructions and memory accesses will probably only cost about 10 percent of your application's total performance. And some languages, like C++ and HLA, support the notion of a *static member function* that allows direct calls to member functions when polymorphism is unnecessary.

The big problem that object-oriented programmers sometimes have is that they tend to take things to an extreme. Rather than directly accessing the fields of an object, they write accessor functions to read and write those field values. Unless the compiler does a *very* good job of inlining such accessor functions, the cost of accessing the object's fields increases by about an order of magnitude. These are the types of applications whose performance suffers because of the overuse of the object-oriented programming paradigms. There may be good reasons for doing things the "object-oriented way" (such as using accessor functions to access all fields of an object), but keep in mind that these costs add up rather quickly. Unless you absolutely need the facilities provided by using such techniques, your programs may wind up running considerably slower (and taking up a whole lot more space) than necessary.

Another common problem with many object-oriented programs is *overgeneralization*. This typically occurs when a programmer uses a lot of class libraries, often extending classes through inheritance in order to solve some problem with as little programming effort as possible. While saving programming effort is generally a good idea, extending class libraries often leads to situations where you need some little task done and you call a library routine that does everything you want. The only problem is that in object-oriented systems, library routines tend to be highly layered. That is, you need some work done, so you invoke some member function from a class you've inherited. That function probably does a little bit of work on the data you pass it and then it calls a member function in a class that *it* inherits. And then that function massages the data a little and calls a member function it inherits, and so on down the line. Before too long, the CPU spends more time calling and returning from functions than it does doing any useful work. While this same situation could occur in standard (non–object-oriented) libraries, it's far more common in object-oriented applications.

Carefully designed object-oriented programs needn't run significantly slower than comparable procedural-oriented programs. Just be careful not to make a lot of expensive function calls to do trivial little tasks.

12.9 For More Information

This chapter dealt with the low-level implementation of common data structures you'll find in various programming languages. It concludes our exploration of composite data types that began in Chapter 9. For more information on data types, you can head off in two directions from this point. To learn more about the low-level implementation of various data types, you'll probably want to start learning and mastering assembly language. *The Art of Assembly Language* (No Starch Press, 2003) is a good place to begin that journey. If you want to learn high-level implementations, you can find a wealth of information. Higher-level data structure information is available in just about any decent college textbook on data structures and algorithm design. There are, literally, hundreds of these books available covering a wide range of subjects. If you are interested in a combination of low-level and high-level concepts, Donald Knuth's *The Art of Computer Programming, Volume I* (Addison-Wesley Professional, 1997) is a good choice. This text is available in nearly every bookstore that carries technical books.

As noted in the previous chapter, textbooks on programming language design and compiler design and implementation are another good source of information about the low-level implementation of data types, including composite data types such as records, unions, and classes. Some good books to consider on this subject include:

- *Programming Languages, Design and Implementation,* Terrence Pratt and Marvin Zelkowitz (Prentice Hall, 2001)

- *Programming Languages, Principles and Practice,* Kenneth Louden (Course Technology, 2002)

- *Concepts of Programming Languages,* Robert Sebesta (Addison-Wesley, 2003)

- *Programming Languages, Structures and Models,* Herbert Dershem and Michael Jipping (Wadsworth, 1990)

- *The Programming Language Landscape,* Henry Ledgard and Michael Marcotty (SRA, 1986)

- *Programming Language Concepts,* Carlo Ghezzi and Jehdi Jazayeri (Wiley, 1997)

13

ARITHMETIC AND LOGICAL EXPRESSIONS

One of the major advances that high-level languages provide over low-level languages is the use of algebraic arithmetic and logical expressions (from now on, I'll just refer to them as *arithmetic expressions*). High-level language arithmetic expressions are an order of magnitude more readable than the sequence of machine instructions the compiler produces. However, the conversion process (from arithmetic expressions into machine code) is also one of the more difficult transformations to do efficiently, and a fair percentage of a typical compiler's optimization phase is dedicated to handling the transformation. Because of the difficulty with translation, this is one area where you can help the compiler. In this chapter, I'll briefly describe:

- How computer architecture affects the computation of arithmetic expressions
- The optimization of arithmetic expressions
- Side effects of arithmetic expressions

- Sequence points in arithmetic expressions
- Order of evaluation in arithmetic expression
- Short-circuit and complete evaluation of arithmetic expressions
- The computational cost of arithmetic expressions

Armed with this information, you should be able to write more efficient and more robust applications.

13.1 Arithmetic Expressions and Computer Architecture

With respect to arithmetic expressions, we can classify traditional computer architectures into three basic types: stack-based machines, register-based machines, and accumulator-based machines. The major difference between these architectural types has to do with where the CPUs keep the operands for the arithmetic operations. Once the CPU fetches the data from these operands, the data is passed along to the arithmetic and logical unit where the actual arithmetic or logical calculation occurs.[1] I'll explore each of these architectures in the following sections.

13.1.1 Stack-Based Machines

Stack-based machines use memory for most calculations, employing a stack in memory to hold all operands and results. Computer systems employing a stack architecture offer some important advantages over other architectures:

- The instructions are often smaller (each consuming fewer bytes) than those found in other architectures because the instructions generally don't have to specify any operands.

- It is generally easier to write compilers for stack architectures than for other machines because converting arithmetic expressions to a sequence of stack operations is very easy.

- Temporary variables are rarely needed in a stack architecture, because the stack itself serves that purpose.

Unfortunately, stack machines also suffer from some serious disadvantages:

- Almost every instruction references memory (which is slow on modern machines). Though caches can help mitigate this problem, memory performance is still a major problem on stack machines.

- Even though conversion from HLLs to a stack machine is very easy, there is less opportunity for optimization than there is with other architectures.

---

[1] As it turns out, all calculations are logical in nature. Even arithmetic operations such as addition and subtraction are "logical" in the sense that the CPU computes their result based on a series of Boolean expressions. For our purposes, therefore, the phrases "logical expression" and "arithmetic expression" are synonymous. Please see *Write Great Code, Volume 1* for more details concerning Boolean expressions and low-level arithmetic.

- Because stack machines are constantly accessing the same data elements (that is, data on the *top of the stack*), pipelining and instruction parallelism is difficult to achieve (see *Write Great Code, Volume 1* for details on pipelining and instruction parallelism).

A *stack* is a data structure that allows operations only on a few limited elements of the stack (often called the *top of stack* and *next on stack*). With a stack you generally do one of three things: push new data onto the stack, pop data from the stack, or operate on the data that is currently sitting on the top of the stack (and possibly the data immediately below it).

13.1.1.1 Basic Stack Machine Organization

I'll create a hypothetical stack machine to help demonstrate how stack machines operate. A typical stack machine will maintain a couple of registers inside the CPU (see Figure 13-1). In particular, you can expect to find a *program counter register* (like the 80x86's EIP register) and a *stack pointer register* (like the 80x86 ESP register).

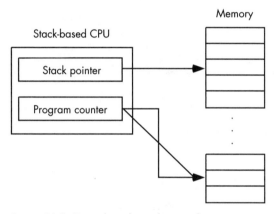

Figure 13-1: Typical stack machine architecture

The stack pointer register contains the memory address of the current *top-of-stack* element in memory. The CPU increments or decrements the stack pointer register whenever a program places data onto the stack or removes data from the stack. On some architectures the stack expands from higher memory locations to lower memory locations; on other architectures the stack grows from lower memory locations toward higher memory locations. Fundamentally, the direction of stack growth is irrelevant; all this really determines is whether the machine decrements the stack pointer register when placing data on the stack (if the stack grows toward lower memory addresses) or increments the stack pointer register (when the stack grows toward higher memory addresses).

13.1.1.2 Pushing Data onto a Stack

A typical machine instruction used to place data on the stack is a push instruction. This instruction typically takes a single operand that specifies the value to push onto the stack and a typical syntax for a push instruction might be:

```
push <<memory or constant operand>>
```

Here are a couple of concrete examples:

```
push 10 ;Pushes the constant 10 onto the stack
push mem ;Pushes the contents of memory location mem
```

A push operation will typically increase the value of the stack pointer register by the size of its operand in bytes and then copy that operand to the memory location the stack pointer now specifies. For example, Figure 13-2 and Figure 13-3 illustrate what the stack looks like before and after a push 10 operation.

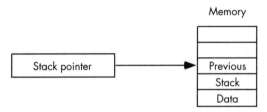

Figure 13-2: Before a push 10 operation

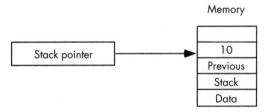

Figure 13-3: After a push 10 operation

13.1.1.3 Popping Data from a Stack

To remove a data item from the top of a stack, most stack machines use a pop or pull instruction. I'll use the term "pop" in this book; just be aware that some architectures use the term "pull" instead. A typical pop instruction might use syntax like the following:

```
pop <<memory location>>
```

Note that you cannot pop data into a constant. The pop operand must be a memory location.

The pop instruction makes a copy of the data pointed at by the stack pointer and stores it into the destination memory location. Then it decrements the stack pointer register to point at the next-lower item on the stack (see Figures 13-4 and 13-5). The value in stack memory that the pop instruction removes from the stack is still physical present in memory above the new top of stack. However, the next time the program pushes data onto the stack it will overwrite this value with the new value.

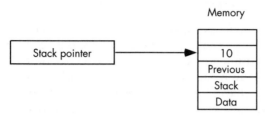

Figure 13-4: Before a pop mem operation

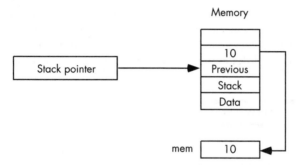

Figure 13-5: After a pop mem operation

13.1.1.4 Arithmetic Operations on a Stack Machine

The arithmetic and logical instructions found on a stack machine generally do not allow any operands. This is why stack machines are often called *zero-address machines*; the arithmetic instructions themselves do not encode any operand addresses. For example, consider an add instruction on a typical stack machine. This instruction will pop two values from the stack (top of stack and next on stack), compute, and push the sum back onto the stack (see Figures 13-6 and 13-7).

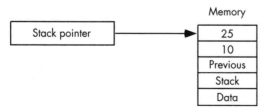

Figure 13-6: Before an add operation

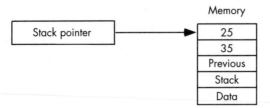

Figure 13-7: After an add operation

Because arithmetic expressions are recursive in nature, and recursion requires a stack for proper implementation, it should come as no surprise that converting arithmetic expressions to a sequence of stack-machine instructions is relatively simple. Arithmetic expressions found in common programming languages use an *infix notation* where the operator appears between two operands. For example, a + b and c - d are examples of infix notation because the operators (+ and -) appear between the operands ([a, b] and [c, d]). If we convert these infix expressions into *postfix notation* (also known as *reverse polish notation*), where the operator immediately follows the operands to which the operator applies, converting the (postfix) notation to a sequence of stack machine instructions is a simple process. For example, the previous two infix expressions would have these corresponding postfix forms:

Infix Form	Postfix Form
a + b	a b +
c - d	c d -

Once you have an expression in postfix form, converting it to a sequence of stack machine instructions is very easy. You simply emit a push instruction for each operand and the corresponding arithmetic instruction for the operators. For example, a b + becomes:

```
push a
push b
add
```

and c d - becomes:

```
push c
push d
sub
```

assuming, of course, that add adds the top two items on the stack and sub subtracts the top of stack from the value immediately below it on the stack.

13.1.1.5 Real-World Stack Machines

A big advantage of the stack architecture is that it is easy to write a compiler for such a machine. It's also very easy to write an emulator for a stack-based machine. For these reasons, stack architectures are popular in *virtual machines* (VMs) such as the Java Virtual Machine and the Microsoft Visual Basic p-code interpreter. A few real-world stack-based CPUs do exist, such as a hardware implementation of the Java VM; however, they are not very popular because of the performance limitations of memory access. Nonetheless, understanding the basics of a stack architecture is important because many compilers translate HLL source code into a stack-based form prior to translating to actual machine code. Indeed, in the worst case (though rare), compilers are forced to emit code that emulates a stack-based machine when compiling complex arithmetic expressions.

13.1.2 Accumulator-Based Machines

The simplicity of a stack machine-instruction sequence hides an enormous amount of complexity. Consider the following stack-based instruction from the previous section:

```
add
```

This instruction looks simple, but it actually specifies a large number of operations:

- Fetch an operand from the memory location pointed to by the stack pointer.
- Send the stack pointer's value to the ALU (arithmetic/logical unit).
- Instruct the ALU to decrement the stack pointer's value just sent to it.
- Route the ALU's value back to the stack pointer.
- Fetch the operand from the memory location pointed to by the stack pointer.
- Send the values from the previous step and the first step to the ALU.
- Instruct the ALU to add those values.
- Store the sum away in the memory location pointed to by the stack pointer.

The organization of a typical stack machine prevents many parallel operations that are possible with pipelining (see *Write Great Code, Volume 1* for more details on pipelining). So stack architectures are hit twice: typical instructions require many steps to complete, and those steps are difficult to execute in parallel with other operations.

One big problem with the stack architecture is that it goes to memory for just about everything. In particular, if you simply want to compute the sum of two variables and store this sum in a third variable, you have to fetch the two variables and write them to the stack (four memory operations), then you have to fetch the two values from the stack, add them, and write their sum back to the stack (three memory operations), and finally, you have to pop the item from the stack and store the result into the destination memory location (two memory operations). That's a total of nine memory operations. When memory access is slow, this is an expensive way to compute the sum of two numbers.

One way to avoid this large number of memory accesses is to provide a general-purpose arithmetic register within the CPU. The idea behind an accumulator-based machine is that you provide a single accumulator register, where the CPU computes temporary results, rather than computing temporary values in memory (on the stack). Accumulator-based machines are also known as *one-address* or *single-address machines* because most instructions that operate on two operands use the accumulator as the default destination operand and require a single memory or constant operand to use as the source operand for the computation. A typical example of an accumulator machine is the 6502 that includes the following instructions:

```
LDA <<constant or memory>> ;Load accumulator register
STA <<memory>>             ;Store accumulator register
ADD <<constant or memory>> ;Add operand to accumulator
SUB <<constant or memory>> ;Subtract operand from accumulator
```

Because one-address instructions require an operand that is not present in many of the zero-address instructions, individual instructions found on an accumulator-based machine tend to be larger than those found on a typical stack-based machine (because you have to encode the operand address as part of the instruction, see *Write Great Code Volume 1* for details). In practice, however, programs are often smaller because fewer instructions are needed to do the same thing. Suppose, for example, you want to compute x = y + z;. On a stack machine, you might use an instruction sequence like the following:

```
push y
push z
add
pop x
```

On an accumulator machine, you might use a sequence like this:

```
lda y
add z
sta x
```

Assuming that the push and pop instructions are roughly the same size as the accumulator machine's lda, add, and sta instructions (a good assumption), it should be fairly obvious that the stack machine's instruction sequence is actually longer (because it requires more instructions). Furthermore, assuming all other things are equal, the accumulator machine will probably execute the code faster (even ignoring the extra instruction) because the accumulator machine only requires three memory accesses (to fetch y and z and to store x), compared with the nine memory accesses the stack machine will require. Furthermore, the accumulator machine doesn't waste any time manipulating the stack pointer register during computation.

Even though accumulator-based machines generally have higher performance than stack-based machines (for reasons you've just seen), they are not without their own problems. Having only one general-purpose register available for arithmetic operations creates a bottleneck in the system, resulting in *data hazards* (see *Write Great Code, Volume 1,* for a discussion of data hazards). Many calculations result in the production of temporary results that the application must write to memory in order to compute other components of the expression. This results in extra memory accesses that could be avoided if the CPU provided additional accumulator registers.

Accumulator-based architectures were popular in early computer systems when the manufacturing process limited the number of features within the CPU, but today you rarely see accumulator-based architectures outside of low-cost embedded microcontrollers.

13.1.3 Register-Based Machines

Of the three architectures I am discussing here, register-based machines are the most prevalent today because they offer the highest performance. By providing a fair number of on-CPU registers, this architecture spares the CPU from expensive memory accesses during the computation of complex expressions.

In theory, a register-based machine could have as few as two general-purpose (arithmetic-capable) registers. In practice, about the only machines that fall into this category (include only two general-purpose registers) are the Motorola 680x processors, and most people consider them to be a special case of the accumulator architecture with two separate accumulators. Register machines generally contain at least eight "general-purpose" registers (this number isn't arbitrary; it's the number of general-purpose registers found on the 80x86 CPU, the 8080 CPU, and the Z80 CPU, which are probably the minimalist examples of what a computer architect would call a "register-based" machine).

Although some register-based machines (e.g., the 80x86) have a small number of registers available, a general principle is "the more, the better." Typical RISC machines (such as the PowerPC) have at least 32 general-purpose registers. Intel's Itanium processor, for example, provides 128 general-purpose integer registers. IBM's CELL processor provides 128 registers in each of the processing units found on the device (each processing unit is a mini-CPU capable of certain operations); a typical CELL processor contains eight such processing units along with a PowerPC CPU core.

The main reason for having as many general-purpose registers as possible is to be able to avoid memory access. In an accumulator-based machine, the accumulator register is a transient register used for calculations, but you cannot keep a variable's value in the accumulator for long periods of time because you'll need the accumulator for other purposes. In a register machine with a large number of registers, it's possible to keep certain (often-used) variables in registers so you don't have to access memory at all when using those variables. Consider the assignment statement x = y + z;. On a register-based machine (such as the 80x86), we could compute this result using the following HLA code:

```
// Note: Assume x is held in EBX, y is held in ECX,
// and z is held in EDX:

mov( ecx, ebx );
add( edx, ebx );
```

Only two instructions and no memory accesses (for the variables) are required here. This is quite a bit more efficient than the accumulator or stack architectures. From this example, you can see why the register architecture has become prevalent in modern computer systems.

As you will see in the following sections, register machines are often described as either two-address machines or three-address machines, depending on the particular CPU's architecture.

13.1.4 Typical Forms of Arithmetic Expressions

Computer architects have made extensive studies of typical source files, and one thing they've discovered is that a large percentage of assignment statements in such programs take one of the following forms:

```
var = var2;
var = constant;
var = op var2;
var = var op var2;
var = var2 op var3;
```

Although other assignments do exist, the set of statements in a program that takes one of these forms is generally larger than any other group of assignment statements. Therefore, computer architects usually optimize their CPUs to efficiently handle these forms.

13.1.5 Three-Address Architectures

Many machines use what is known as a *three-address architecture*. This means
that an arithmetic statement supports three operands: two source operands
and a destination operand. For example, most RISC CPUs offer an add
instruction that will add together the values of two operands and store the
result into a third operand:

```
add source1, source2, dest
```

On such architectures, the operands are usually machine registers
(or small constants), so typically you would write this instruction as follows
(assuming you use the names R0, R1, ..., Rn to denote registers):

```
add r0, r1, r2    ;computes r2 := r0 + r1
```

Because RISC compilers attempt to keep variables in registers, this single
instruction handles the last assignment statement given in the previous
section:

```
var = var2 op var3;
```

Handling an assignment of the form:

```
var = var op var2;
```

is also relatively easy—just use the destination register as one of the source
operands. For example:

```
add r0, r1, r0  ; computes r0 := r0 + r1
```

The drawback to a three-address architecture is that you must encode all
three operands into each instruction that supports three operands. This is why
three-operand instructions generally operate only upon register operands—
encoding three separate memory addresses can be quite expensive. (Just ask
any VAX programmer. The DEC VAX computer system is a good example of
a three-address CISC machine; instructions are up to 150 bytes long on VAX
machines, because one could arbitrarily encode memory operands in an
instruction.)

13.1.6 Two-Address Architectures

The 80x86 architecture is known as a *two-address machine*. In a two-address
machine, one of the source operands is also the destination operand. Consider the following 80x86/HLA add instruction:

```
add( ebx, eax );  ; computes eax := eax + ebx;
```

Two-address machines, such as the 80x86, can handle the first four forms of the assignment statement given earlier with a single instruction. The last form, however, requires two or more instructions and a temporary register. For example, to compute

```
var1 = var2 + var3;
```

you would need to use the following code (assuming var2 and var3 are memory variables and the compiler is keeping var1 in the EAX register):

```
mov( var2, eax );
add( var3, eax );  //Result (var1) is in EAX.
```

13.1.7 Architectural Differences and Your Code

One-address, two-address, and three-address architectures form the following hierarchy:

$$1\text{Address} \subset 2\text{Address} \subset 3\text{Address}$$

That is, two-address machines are capable of doing anything a one-address machine is capable of, and three-address machines are capable of doing anything one-address or two-address machines are capable of doing. The proof is trivial:[2]

- To show that a two-address machine is capable of anything a one-address machine is, simply choose one register on the two-address machine and use it as the "accumulator" when simulating a one-address architecture.

- To show that a three-address machine is capable of anything a two-address machine can do, simply use the same register for one of the source operands and the destination operand, thereby limiting yourself to two registers (operands/addresses) for all operations.

Given this hierarchy, you might think that if you limit the code you write so that it runs well on a one-address machine, you'll get good results on all machines. In reality, most general-purpose CPUs available today are two-address or three-address machines, so writing your code to favor a one-address machine may limit the optimizations that are possible on a two-address or three-address machine. Furthermore, there is such a difference in the optimization quality among compilers that backing up an assertion such as this one would be very difficult. You should probably try to create expressions that take one of the five forms given earlier if you want your compiler to produce the best possible code. Because most modern programs run on two-address or three-address machines, the remainder of this chapter will assume that environment.

---

[2] Technically, we must also show that you can do things with a two-address machine that cannot be done with a one-address machine and that you can do things with a three-address machine that cannot be done with a two-address machine to complete this proof. I'll leave that as an exercise to the reader. It's still a fairly trivial proof.

13.1.8 Handling Complex Expressions

Once your expressions get more complex than the five forms given earlier, the compiler will have to generate a sequence of two or more instructions to evaluate the expression. When compiling the code, most compilers will internally translate complex expressions into a sequence of "three-address statements" that are semantically equivalent to the more complex expression. The following is an example of a complex expression and a sequence of three-address instructions that a typical compiler might produce:

```
// complex = ( a + b ) * ( c - d ) - e / f;

temp1 = a + b;
temp2 = c - d;
temp1 = temp1 * temp2;
temp2 = e / f;
complex = temp1 - temp2;
```

If you study these five statements, you should be able to determine that they are semantically equivalent to the complex expression appearing in the comment. The major difference in the computation is the introduction of two temporary values (temp1 and temp2). Most compilers will attempt to use machine registers to maintain these temporary values.

Because the compiler will internally translate a complex instruction into a sequence of three-address statements, you may wonder if you can help the compiler by manually converting complex expressions into three address forms. Well, it depends on your compiler. For many (good) compilers, breaking a complex calculation into smaller pieces may, in fact, thwart the compiler's ability to optimize certain sequences. So, most of the time you should do your job (write the code as clearly as possible) and let the compiler do its job (optimize the result) when it comes to arithmetic expressions. However, if you can specify a calculation using a form that naturally converts to a two-address or three-address form, by all means do so. At the very least it, will have no effect on the code the compiler generates. It could, however, help the compiler produce better code under some special circumstances. Not to mention that the resulting code will probably be easier to read and maintain if it is less complex.

13.2 Optimization of Arithmetic Statements

Because HLL compilers were originally designed to let programmers use algebraic-like expressions in their source code, this is one area in computer science that has been well researched. Most modern compilers that provide a reasonable optimizer will do a decent job of translating arithmetic expressions into machine code. You can usually assume that the compiler you're using doesn't need a whole lot of help with optimizing arithmetic expressions (and if it does, perhaps you should consider switching to a better compiler before worrying about how to manually optimize the code).

To help you appreciate the job the compiler is doing for you, I'll discuss some of the typical optimizations you can expect from modern optimizing compilers. By understanding what a (decent) compiler will do for you, you can avoid hand-optimizing those things that the compiler can deal with just fine.

13.2.1 Constant Folding

Constant folding is an optimization that computes the value of constant expressions or subexpressions at compile time rather than emitting code to compute their result at runtime. For example, a Pascal compiler that supports this optimization would translate a statement of the form i := 5 + 6; to i := 11; prior to generating machine code for the statement. This, obviously, saves the emission of an add instruction that would have to execute at runtime. As another example, suppose that you want to allocate an array containing 16MB of storage. One way to do this is as follows:

```
char bigArray[ 16777216 ]; // 16MB of storage
```

The only problem with this approach is that 16,777,216 is a *magic number*. It represents the value 2^{24} and not some other arbitrary value. Now consider the following C/C++ declaration:

```
char bigArray[ 16*1024*1024 ]; // 16MB of storage
```

Most programmers realize that 1,024 times 1,024 is a *binary million,* and 16 times this value corresponds to 16 mega-somethings. Yes, you need to recognize that the subexpression 16*1024*1024 is equivalent to 16,777,216. But this pattern is easier to recognize as 16MB (at least, when used within a character array) than 1677216 is (or was it 16777214?). In both cases the amount of storage the compiler allocates is exactly the same, but the second case is, arguably, more readable. Hence, it is better code.

Variable declarations aren't the only place a compiler can use this optimization. Any arithmetic expression (or subexpression) containing constant operands is a candidate for constant folding optimization. Therefore, if an arithmetic expression can be written more clearly by using constant expressions rather than computing the results by hand, you should definitely go for the more readable version and leave it up to the compiler to handle the constant calculation at compile time.

If your compiler doesn't support constant folding you can certainly simulate it by performing all constant calculations manually. However, you should do this only as a last resort. Finding a better compiler is almost always a better choice.

Some good optimizing compilers may take some extreme steps when folding constants. For example, some compilers with a sufficiently high optimization level enabled will replace certain function calls, with constant parameters, to the corresponding constant value. For example, a compiler might translate a C/C++ statement of the form sineR = sin(0); to sineR = 0;

during compilation (as the sine of zero radians is zero). This type of constant folding, however, is not all that common and you usually have to enable a special compiler mode to get it.

13.2.2 Constant Propagation

Constant propagation is an optimization a compiler uses to replace a variable access with a constant value if the compiler determines that this is possible. For example, a compiler that supports constant propagation will make the following optimization:

```
// original code:

    variable = 1234;
    result = f( variable );

// code after constant propagation optimization

    variable = 1234;
    result = f( 1234 );
```

In object code, manipulating immediate constants is more efficient than manipulating variables; therefore, constant propagation often produces much better code. In some cases, constant propagation also allows the compiler to eliminate certain variables and statements altogether (in this example, the compiler could remove variable = 1234; from the code if there are no later references to the variable object in the source code).

In some cases, well-written compilers can do some outrageous optimizations involving constant folding. Consider the following C code and the 80x86 output that GCC produces with the -O3 (maximum) optimization option:

```
#include <stdio.h>
static int rtn3( void )
{
    return 3;
}

int main( void )
{
    printf( "%d", rtn3() + 2 );
    return( 0 );
}
```

Here's the 80x86 code emitted by GCC:

```
.LC0:
        .string "%d"
        .text
        .p2align 2,,3
.globl main
```

```
        .type   main,@function
main:
        ;Build main's activation record:

        pushl   %ebp
        movl    %esp, %ebp
        subl    $8, %esp
        andl    $-16, %esp
        subl    $8, %esp

        ;Print the result of "rtn3()+5":

        pushl   $5        ;Via constant propagation/folding!
        pushl   $.LC0
        call    printf
        xorl    %eax, %eax
        leave
        ret
```

A quick glance shows that the rtn3 function is nowhere to be found. With the -03 command-line option enabled, GCC figured out that rtn3 simply returns a constant and it propagates that constant return result everywhere you call rtn3. In the case of the printf function call, the combination of constant propagation and constant folding yielded a single constant (5) that the code passes on to the printf function.

As with constant folding, if your compiler doesn't support constant propagation you can certainly simulate it manually. However, you should only do this as a last resort. Finding a better compiler is almost always a better choice.

13.2.3   Dead Code Elimination

Dead code elimination is the removal of the object code associated with a particular source code statement if the program never again uses the result of that statement. Often, this is a result of a programming error. (Why would someone compute a value and not use it?) If a compiler encounters dead code in the source file, it may warn you to check the logic of your code. In some cases, however, earlier optimizations can produce dead code. For example, the constant propagation for the value variable in the former example could result in the statement variable = 1234; being dead. Compilers that support dead code elimination will quietly remove the object code for this statement from the object file.

As an example of dead code elimination, consider the following C program and the 80x86 assembly code that GCC emits when supplied the -03 command-line option:

```
static int rtn3( void )
{
    return 3;
}
```

```
int main( void )
{
    int i = rtn3() + 2;

    // Note that this program
    //  never again uses the value of i.

    return( 0 );
}
```

Here's the 80x86 code emitted by GCC:

```
.file    "t.c"
        .text
        .p2align 2,,3
.globl main
        .type    main,@function
main:
        ;Build main's activation record:

        pushl    %ebp
        movl     %esp, %ebp
        subl     $8, %esp
        andl     $-16, %esp

        ;Notice that there is no
        ; assignment to i here.

        ;Return zero as main's function result.

        xorl     %eax, %eax
        leave
        ret
```

Now consider the 80x86 output from GCC when optimization is not enabled:

```
.file    "t.c"
        .text
        .type    rtn3,@function
rtn3:
        pushl    %ebp
        movl     %esp, %ebp
        movl     $3, %eax
        leave
        ret
.Lfe1:
        .size    rtn3,.Lfe1-rtn3
.globl main
        .type    main,@function
main:
        pushl    %ebp
        movl     %esp, %ebp
```

```
        subl    $8, %esp
        andl    $-16, %esp
        movl    $0, %eax
        subl    %eax, %esp

        ;Note the call and computation:

        call    rtn3
        addl    $2, %eax
        movl    %eax, -4(%ebp)

        ;Return zero as the function result.

        movl    $0, %eax
        leave
        ret
```

In fact, one of the main reasons that program examples throughout this book call a function like printf to display various values is to explicitly use those variables' values to prevent dead code elimination from erasing the code under study from the assembly output file. If you remove the final printf from the C program in many of these examples, most of the assembly code will disappear because of dead code elimination.

13.2.4 Common Subexpression Elimination

Often, a small (or even a large) portion of some expressions may appear elsewhere in the current function. If there are no changes to the values of the variables appearing in this subexpression, the program does not need to compute the value of the expression twice. Instead, the program can save the value of the subexpression on the first evaluation and then use that value everywhere the subexpression appears again. For example, consider the following Pascal code:

```
complex := ( a + b ) * ( c - d ) - ( e div f );
lessSo  := ( a + b ) - ( e div f );
quotient := e div f;
```

A decent compiler might translate these to the following sequence of three-address statements:

```
temp1 := a + b;
temp2 := c - d;
temp3 := e div f;
complex := temp1 * temp2;
complex := complex - temp3;
lessSo := temp1 - temp3;
quotient := temp3;
```

Although the former statements use the subexpression (a + b) twice and the subexpression (e div f) three times, the three-address code sequence only computes these subexpressions once, and it uses their values when the common subexpressions appear later.

As another example, consider the following C/C++ code:

```c
#include <stdio.h>

static int i, j, k, m, n;
static int expr1, expr2, expr3;

extern int someFunc( void );

int main( void )
{
    // The following is a trick to
    // confuse the optimizer. When we call
    // an external function, the optimizer
    // knows nothing about the value this
    // function returns, so it cannot optimize
    // the values away. This is done to demonstrate
    // the optimizations that this example is
    // trying to show (that is, the compiler
    // would normally optimize away everything
    // and we wouldn't see the code the optimizer
    // would produce in a real-world example without
    // the following trick).

    i = someFunc();
    j = someFunc();
    k = someFunc();
    m = someFunc();
    n = someFunc();

    expr1 = (i + j) * (k * m + n);
    expr2 = (i + j);
    expr3 = (k * m + n);

    printf( "%d %d %d", expr1, expr2, expr3 );
    return( 0 );
}
```

Here's the 80x86 assembly file that GCC generates (with the -03 option) for the above C code:

```asm
.file   "t.c"
        .section        .rodata.str1.1,"aMS",@progbits,1
.LC0:
        .string "%d %d %d"
        .text
```

```
        .p2align 2,,3
.globl main
        .type   main,@function
main:
        ;Build the activation record:

        pushl   %ebp
        movl    %esp, %ebp
        subl    $8, %esp
        andl    $-16, %esp

        ;Initialize i, j, k, m, and n:

        call    someFunc
        movl    %eax, i
        call    someFunc
        movl    %eax, j
        call    someFunc
        movl    %eax, k
        call    someFunc
        movl    %eax, m
        call    someFunc ;n's value is in EAX.

        ;Compute EDX = k*m+n
        ; and ECX = i+j

        movl    m, %edx
        movl    j, %ecx
        imull   k, %edx
        addl    %eax, %edx
        addl    i, %ecx

        ;EDX is expr3, so push it
        ; on the stack for printf

        pushl   %edx

        ; Save away n's value:

        movl    %eax, n
        movl    %ecx, %eax

        ;ECX is expr2, so push it onto
        ; the stack for printf:

        pushl   %ecx

        ;expr1 is the product of the
        ; two subexpressions (currently
        ; held in EDX and EAX), so compute
        ; their product and push the result
        ; for printf.
```

```
imull    %edx, %eax
pushl    %eax

;Push the address of the format string
; for printf:

pushl    $.LC0

;Save the variable's values and then
; call printf to print the values
; previously pushed on the stack:

movl     %eax, expr1
movl     %ecx, expr2
movl     %edx, expr3
call     printf

;Return zero as the main function's result:

xorl     %eax, %eax
leave
ret
```

Note how the compiler maintains the results of the common subexpressions in various registers (see the comments in the assembly output for details).

If the compiler you're using doesn't support common subexpression optimizations (you can determine this by examining the assembly output), chances are pretty good that the compiler's optimizer is subpar, and you should consider using a different compiler. However, if you are forced to use a compiler that doesn't perform this common optimization, you can always explicitly code this optimization yourself. Consider the following version of the former C code, which manually computes common subexpressions:

```
#include <stdio.h>

static int i, j, k, m, n;
static int expr1, expr2, expr3;
static int ijExpr, kmnExpr;

extern int someFunc( void );

int main( void )
{
    // The following is a trick to
    // confuse the optimizer. By calling
    // an external function, the optimizer
    // knows nothing about the value this
    // function returns, so it cannot optimize
    // the values away because of constant propagation.
```

```
        i = someFunc();
        j = someFunc();
        k = someFunc();
        m = someFunc();
        n = someFunc();

        ijExpr = i + j;
        kmnExpr = (k * m + n);
        expr1 = ij * kmn;
        expr2 = ij;
        expr3 = kmn;

        printf( "%d %d %d", expr1, expr2, expr3 );
        return( 0 );
}
```

Of course, there was no reason to create the ijExpr and kmnExpr variables because we could have simply used the expr2 and expr3 variables for this purpose. However, this code was written to make the changes to the original program as obvious as possible.

13.2.5 Strength Reduction

Often, the CPU can directly compute some value using a different operator than the source code specifies, thereby replacing a more complex (or stronger) instruction with a simpler instruction. For example, a shift operation can implement multiplication or division by a constant that is a power of 2 and certain modulo (remainder) operations are possible using a bitwise and instruction (the shift and and instructions generally execute much faster than multiply and divide instructions). Most compiler optimizers are good at recognizing such operations and replacing the more expensive computation with a less expensive sequence of machine instructions. Here is some C code and 80x86 GCC output that shows strength reduction in action:

```
#include <stdio.h>

unsigned i, j, k, m, n;

extern unsigned someFunc( void );
extern void preventOptimization( unsigned arg1, ... );

int main( void )
{
    // The following is a trick to
    // confuse the optimizer. By calling
    // an external function, the optimizer
    // knows nothing about the value this
    // function returns, so it cannot optimize
    // the values away.

    i = someFunc();
    j = i * 2;
```

```
k = i % 32;
m = i / 4;
n = i * 8;

// The following call to "preventOptimization" is done
// to trick the compiler into believing the above results
// are used somewhere else (GCC will eliminate all the
// code above if you don't actually use the computed result,
// and that would defeat the purpose of this example).

preventOptimization( i,j,k,m,n );
return( 0 );
}
```

Here's the resulting 80x86 code generated by GCC:

```
.file   "t.c"
        .text
        .p2align 2,,3
.globl main
        .type   main,@function
main:
        ;Build main's activation record:

        pushl   %ebp
        movl    %esp, %ebp
        pushl   %esi
        pushl   %ebx
        andl    $-16, %esp

        ;Get i's value into EAX:

        call    someFunc

        ;compute i * 8 using the scaled
        ; indexed addressing mode and
        ; the LEA instruction (leave
        ; n's value in EDX):

        leal    0(,%eax,8), %edx

        ;Adjust stack for call to
        ; preventOptimization:

        subl    $12, %esp

        movl    %eax, %ecx      ;ECX = i
        pushl   %edx            ;Push n for call
        movl    %eax, %ebx      ;Save i in k
        shrl    $2, %ecx        ;ECX = i / 4 (m)
        pushl   %ecx            ;Push m for call

        andl    $31, %ebx       ;EBX = i%32
        leal    (%eax,%eax), %esi ;j = i * 2
```

```
        pushl    %ebx              ;Push k for call
        pushl    %esi              ;Push j for call
        pushl    %eax              ;Push i for call
        movl     %eax, i           ;Save values in memory
        movl     %esi, j           ; variables.
        movl     %ebx, k
        movl     %ecx, m
        movl     %edx, n
        call     preventOptimization

        ;Clean up the stack and return
        ; zero as main's result:

        leal     -8(%ebp), %esp
        popl     %ebx
        xorl     %eax, %eax
        popl     %esi
        leave
        ret
.Lfe1:
        .size    main,.Lfe1-main
        .comm    i,4,4
        .comm    j,4,4
        .comm    k,4,4
        .comm    m,4,4
        .comm    n,4,4
```

The important thing to note in this 80x86 code is that GCC never emitted a multiplication or division instruction, even though the C code used these two operators extensively. GCC replaced each of these (expensive) operations with less expensive address calculations, shifts, and logical AND operations.

This C example declared its variables as unsigned rather than as int. There is a very good reason for this modification: strength reduction produces more efficient code for certain unsigned operands than it does for signed operands. This is a very important point! If you can choose between using either signed or unsigned integer operands, you should always try to use unsigned values because compilers can often generate better code when processing unsigned operands. To show the difference, I'll rewrite the previous C code using signed integers and take a look at GCC's 80x86 output:

```
#include <stdio.h>

// Change from unsigned to int:

int i, j, k, m, n;

extern int someFunc( void );
extern void preventOptimization( int arg1, ... );

// The remainder of the code is the same as the earlier C program...
```

Here is GCC's 80x86 assembly output for this modification to the C code:

```
.file    "t.c"
        .text
        .p2align 2,,3
        .globl main
        .type   main,@function
main:
        ;Build main's activation record:

        pushl   %ebp
        movl    %esp, %ebp
        pushl   %esi
        pushl   %ebx
        andl    $-16, %esp

        ; Call someFunc to get i's value:

        call    someFunc
        leal    (%eax,%eax), %esi ;j = i * 2
        testl   %eax, %eax        ;Test i's sign
        movl    %eax, %ecx
        movl    %eax, i
        movl    %esi, j
        js      .L4

; Here's the code we execute if i is non-negative:

.L2:
        andl    $-32, %eax        ;MOD operation
        movl    %ecx, %ebx
        subl    %eax, %ebx
        testl   %ecx, %ecx        ;Test i's sign
        movl    %ebx, k
        movl    %ecx, %eax
        js      .L5
.L3:
        subl    $12, %esp
        movl    %eax, %edx
        leal    0(,%ecx,8), %eax ;i * 8
        pushl   %eax
        sarl    $2, %edx          ;Signed div by 4
        pushl   %edx
        pushl   %ebx
        pushl   %esi
        pushl   %ecx
        movl    %eax, n
        movl    %edx, m
        call    preventOptimization
        leal    -8(%ebp), %esp
        popl    %ebx
        xorl    %eax, %eax
        popl    %esi
```

```
        leave
        ret
        .p2align 2,,3

; For signed division by four,
;   using a sarl operation, we need
;   to add 3 to i's value if i was
;   negative.

.L5:
        leal    3(%ecx), %eax
        jmp     .L3
        .p2align 2,,3

; For signed % operation, we need to
;   first add 31 to i's value if it was
;   negative to begin with:

.L4:
        leal    31(%eax), %eax
        jmp     .L2
```

The difference in these two coding examples demonstrates why you should try to use unsigned integers (rather than signed integers) whenever you don't absolutely need to deal with negative numbers.

Attempting strength reduction manually is risky. While certain operations (like division) are almost always slower than others (like shifting to the right) on most CPUs, many strength reduction optimizations are not portable across CPUs. That is, substituting a left shift operation for multiplication may not always produce faster code when you compile for different CPUs. Some older C programs contain manual strength reductions that were originally added to improve performance. Today, those strength reductions can actually cause the programs to run slower than they should. Be very careful about incorporating strength reductions directly into your HLL code. This is one area where you should let the compiler do its job.

13.2.6 Induction

In many expressions, particularly those appearing within a loop, the value of one variable in the expression is completely dependent on some other variable. As an example, consider the following for loop in Pascal:

```
for i := 0 to 15 do begin

    j := i * 2;
    vector[ j ] := j;
    vector[ j + 1 ] := j + 0.5;

end;
```

A compiler's optimizer may recognize that j is completely dependent on the value of i and rewrite this code as follows:

```
ij := 0;  {ij is the combination of i and j from the previous code}
while( ij < 30 ) do

    vector[ ij ] := j;
    vector[ ij + 1 ] := ij + 0.5;
    ij := ij + 2;

end;
```

This optimization saves some work in the loop (specifically, the computation of j := i * 2;).

As another example, consider the following C code and the MASM output that Microsoft's Visual C++ compiler produces:

```
extern unsigned vector[16];

extern void someFunc( unsigned v[] );
extern void preventOptimization( int arg1, ... );

int main( void )
{

    unsigned i, j;

    // "Initialize" vector (or, at least,
    //   make the compiler believe this is
    //   what's going on):

    someFunc( vector );

    // For loop to demonstrate induction:

    for( i = 0; i < 16; ++i )
    {
        j = i * 2;
        vector[ j ] = j;
        vector[ j + 1 ] = j + 1;
    }

    // The following prevents dead code elimination
    // of the former calculations:

    preventOptimization( vector[0], vector[15] );
    return( 0 );
}
```

Here's the MASM (80x86) output from Visual C++:

```
_main   PROC NEAR ; COMDAT
; File t.c
```

```
; Line 19 -- call someFunc to initialize vector:

        push    OFFSET FLAT:_vector
        call    _someFunc
        add     esp, 4

        ;ECX is roughly "j".
        ;EAX points at the current vector element.

        xor     ecx, ecx
        mov     eax, OFFSET FLAT:_vector+4

;This is what the for loop translates to:

$L403:
; Line 23
        ;vector[j] = j;

        mov     DWORD PTR [eax-4], ecx
; Line 24
        ;vector[ j + 1 ] = j + 1;

        lea     edx, DWORD PTR [ecx+1]
        mov     DWORD PTR [eax], edx

        ;Advance EAX (pointer to vector
        ; element) past two elements:

        add     eax, 8

        ;Bump up j by two:

        add     ecx, 2

        ;Repeat for each element of the array
        ; that we process:

        cmp     eax, OFFSET FLAT:_vector+132
        jl      SHORT $L403


; Line 26 - call preventOptimization:

        mov     eax, DWORD PTR _vector+60
        mov     ecx, DWORD PTR _vector
        push    eax
        push    ecx
        call    _preventOptimization
        add     esp, 8
; Line 27
        xor     eax, eax
; Line 28
        ret     0
_main   ENDP
```

As you can see in this MASM output, the Visual C++ compiler recognizes that i is not used in this loop. There are no calculations involving i, and it is completely optimized away. Furthermore, there is no j = i * 2 computation. Instead, the compiler uses induction to determine that j increases by 2 on each iteration, and the compiler emits the code to do this rather than computing j's value from i. Finally, note that the compiler doesn't index into the vector array. Instead it marches a pointer through the array on each iteration of the loop—once again using induction to produce a faster and shorter code sequence than you'd get without this optimization.

As for common subexpressions, you can manually incorporate induction optimization into your programs. The result is almost always harder to read and understand, but if your compiler's optimizer fails to produce good machine code in a section of your program, you can always resort to a manual optimization.

13.2.7   Loop Invariants

The optimizations I've shown so far have all been techniques a compiler can use to improve code that is already well written. Handling loop invariants, by contrast, is a compiler optimization for fixing bad code. A loop invariant is an expression that does not change on each iteration of some loop. The following Basic code demonstrates a trivial loop-invariant calculation:

```
i = 5;
for j = 1 to 10
    k = i * 2
next j
```

The value of k does not change during the execution of this loop. Once the loop completes execution, k's value is exactly the same as if the calculation of k had been moved before or after the loop. For example:

```
i = 5;
k = i * 2
for j = 1 to 10
next j
' At this point, k will contain the same
' value as in the previous example
```

The difference between these two code fragments, of course, is that the second example computes the value k = i * 2 only once rather than on each iteration of the loop.

Many compilers' optimizers are smart enough to discover whenever a loop invariant calculation occurs and use *code motion* to move the invariant calculation outside the loop. As an example of this operation, consider the following example C program and the output that the Microsoft Visual C++ compiler produces:

```
extern unsigned someFunc( void );
extern void preventOptimization( unsigned arg1, ... );
```

```
int main( void )
{
    unsigned i, j, k, m;

    k = someFunc();
    m = k;
    for( i = 0; i < k; ++i )
    {
        j = k + 2;      // Loop-invariant calculation
        m += j + i;
    }
    preventOptimization( m, j, k, i );
    return( 0 );
}
```

Here's the 80x86 MASM code emitted by Visual C++:

```
_main   PROC NEAR ; COMDAT
; File t.c
; Line 5
        push    ecx
        push    esi
; Line 8
        call    _someFunc
; Line 10
        xor     ecx, ecx  ; i = 0
        test    eax, eax  ; see if k == 0
        mov     edx, eax  ; m = k
        jbe     SHORT $L108
        push    edi

; Line 12
; Compute j = k + 2, but only execute this
; once (code was moved out of the loop):

        lea     esi, DWORD PTR [eax+2] ;j = k + 2

; Here's the loop the above code was moved
;   out of:

$L99:
; Line 13
        ;m(edi) = j(esi) + i(ecx)

        lea     edi, DWORD PTR [esi+ecx]
        add     edx, edi

        ; ++i
        inc     ecx

        ;While i < k, repeat:
```

```
        cmp     ecx, eax
        jb      SHORT $L99

        pop     edi
; Line 15
;
; This is the code after the loop body:

        push    ecx
        push    eax
        push    esi
        push    edx
        call    _preventOptimization
        add     esp, 16                              ; 00000010H
; Line 16
        xor     eax, eax
        pop     esi
; Line 17
        pop     ecx
        ret     0
$L108:
; Line 10
        mov     esi, DWORD PTR _j$[esp+8]
; Line 15
        push    ecx
        push    eax
        push    esi
        push    edx
        call    _preventOptimization
        add     esp, 16                              ; 00000010H
; Line 16
        xor     eax, eax
        pop     esi
; Line 17
        pop     ecx
        ret     0
_main   ENDP
```

As you can see by reading the comments in the assembly code, the loop-invariant expression j = k + 2 was moved out of the loop and executed prior to the start of the loop's code, thereby saving some execution time on each iteration of the loop.

Unlike most optimizations, which you should leave up to the compiler if possible, you should try to move all loop-invariant calculations out of a loop unless there is a justifiable reason for leaving them in the loop. Loop-invariant calculations raise questions in the mind of someone reading your code (e.g., "Isn't this supposed to change in the loop?"), and their presence actually makes the code harder to read and understand. Therefore, you should move the code out of the loop. If, for some reason, you want to leave the invariant code in the loop, be sure to comment your reasoning so that the next person to look at your code won't question your sanity.

13.2.8 Optimizers and Programmers

One can divide HLL programmers into three groups based on their understanding of these compiler optimizations:

- The first group of HLL programmers is unaware of how compiler optimizations work, and they write their code without considering the effect that their code organization will have on the optimizer.

- The second group understands how compiler optimizations work; these programmers write their code to be more readable. They assume that the optimizer will handle issues such as converting multiplication and division to shifts (where appropriate) and preprocessing constant expressions. This second group places a fair amount of faith in the compiler's ability to correctly optimize their code.

- The third group of programmers is also aware of the general types of optimizations that compilers can do, but they don't trust the compilers to do the optimization for them. Instead, they manually incorporate those optimizations into their code.

Interestingly enough, compiler optimizers are actually designed for the first group of programmers who are ignorant of how the compiler operates. Therefore, a good compiler will usually produce roughly the same quality of code for all three types of programmers (at least, with respect to arithmetic expressions). This is particularly true when compiling the same program across different compilers. However, do keep in mind that this assertion is only valid for compilers that have decent optimization capabilities. If you have to compile your code on a large number of compilers and you can't be assured that all of them have good optimizers, manual optimization may be one way to achieve consistently good performance across all compilers.

Of course, the real question is, "Which compilers are good, and which are not?" It would be nice to provide a table or chart in this book that describes the optimization capabilities of all the different compilers you might encounter. Unfortunately, the rankings change as compiler vendors improve their products, so anything appearing in this book would rapidly become obsolete. Fortunately, there are several websites that try to keep up-to-date comparisons of different compilers. For example, by searching with Google using the phrase "C C++ compiler benchmarks Visual Watcom Intel GCC," I found www.willus.com/ccomp_benchmark.shtml, which does an excellent job of benchmarking PC compilers. (The Google search listed several other sites. Of course, with a more generic search request, you can obtain information about other compilers as well.)

13.3 Side Effects in Arithmetic Expressions

You will definitely want to give a compiler some guidance with respect to *side effects* that may occur in an expression. If you do not understand how compilers deal with side effects in arithmetic expressions, you may write code that doesn't always produce correct results, particularly when moving source code between different compilers. Wanting to write the fastest or the smallest possible code is all well and good, but if it doesn't produce the correct answer, any optimizations you make on the code are all for naught. Therefore, learning how compilers deal with side effects in an expression is important because ignorance in this area may lead you to write incorrect code.

A side effect is any modification to the global state of a program outside the immediate result a piece of code is producing. The primary purpose of an arithmetic expression is to produce the expression's result. Any other change to the system's state in an expression is a side effect. The C, C++, C#, Java, and other C-based languages are especially guilty of allowing side effects in an arithmetic expression. For example, consider the following C code fragment:

```
i = i + *pi++ + (j = 2) * --k
```

This expression exhibits four separate side effects:

- The decrement of k at the end of the expression
- The assignment to j prior to using j's value
- The increment of the pointer pi after dereferencing pi
- The assignment to i[3]

Although few non–C-based languages provide as many ways to create side effects in arithmetic expressions as C does, most languages do allow the creation of side effects within an expression via a function call.[4] Side effects in functions are useful, for example, when you need to return more than a single value as a function result. Consider the following Pascal code fragment:

```
var
    k:integer;
    m:integer;
    n:integer;

function hasSideEffect( i:integer; var j:integer ):integer;
begin

    k := k + 1;
    hasSideEffect := i + j;
    j = i;

end;
        .
        .
        .
    m := hasSideEffect( 5, n );
```

---

[3] Generally, if this expression is converted to a stand-alone statement by placing a semicolon after the expression, we consider the assignment to i to be the purpose of the statement, not a side effect.

[4] There are some languages that prohibit side effects within an expression. The advantage of such languages is that the compiler can do a much better job of optimizing code when there is no possibility of a side effect in the program. However, side effects are sometimes useful in real-world applications, so most languages allow them.

In this example, the call to the hasSideEffect function produces two different side effects:

- The modification of the global variable k
- The modification of the pass by reference parameter j (the actual parameter is n in this code fragment).

The real purpose of the function is to compute the function's return result; any modification of global values or reference parameters constitutes a side effect of that function, hence the invocation of such a function within an expression produces side effects. Obviously, any language that allows the modification of global values (either directly or through parameters) from a function is capable of producing side effects within an expression; this concept is not limited to Pascal programs.

The problem with side effects in an expression is that most languages do not guarantee the order of evaluation of the components that make up an expression. Many naive programmers (incorrectly) assume that when they write an expression such as the following:

```
i := f(x) + g(x);
```

the compiler will emit code that first calls function f and then calls function g. Very few programming languages, however, require this order of execution. That is, some compilers will indeed call f, then call g, and then add their return results together. Some other compilers, however, will call g first, then f, and then compute the sum of the function return results. That is, the compiler could translate this expression into either of the following simplified code sequences before actually generating native machine code:

```
{ Conversion #1 for "i := f(x) + g(x);" }

    temp1 := f(x);
    temp2 := g(x);
    i := temp1 + temp2;

{ Conversion #2 for "i := f(x) + g(x);" }

    temp1 := g(x);
    temp2 := f(x);
    i := temp2 + temp1;
```

These two different function call sequences could produce completely different results if f or g produce a side effect. For example, if function f modifies the value of the x parameter you pass to it, the preceding sequence could produce different results.

Note that issues such as precedence, associativity, and commutativity have no bearing on whether the compiler evaluates one subcomponent of an expression before another.

For example, consider the following arithmetic expression and several possible intermediate forms for the expression:

```
j := f(x) - g(x) * h(x);
```

```
{ Conversion #1 for this expression: }

    temp1 := f(x);
    temp2 := g(x);
    temp3 := h(x);
    temp4 := temp2 * temp3
    j := temp1 - temp4;
```

```
{ Conversion #2 for this expression: }

    temp2 := g(x);
    temp3 := h(x);
    temp1 := f(x);
    temp4 := temp2 * temp3
    j := temp1 - temp4;
```

```
{ Conversion #3 for this expression: }

    temp3 := h(x);
    temp1 := f(x);
    temp2 := g(x);
    temp4 := temp2 * temp3
    j := temp1 - temp4;
```

Other combinations are also possible.

The specifications for most programming languages explicitly leave the order of evaluation undefined. This may seem somewhat bizarre, but there is a good reason for it: Sometimes the compiler can produce better machine code by rearranging the order it uses to evaluate certain subexpressions within an expression. Any attempt on the part of the language designer to force a particular order of evaluation on a compiler's implementer could limit the range of optimizations possible. Therefore, few languages explicitly state the order of evaluation for an arbitrary expression.

There are, of course, certain rules that most languages do enforce. Although the rules vary by language, there are some obvious rules that most languages (and their implementations) always follow because intuition suggests the behavior. Probably the most common rule you can count on is that all side effects within an expression will occur prior to the completion of that statement's execution. For example, if the function f modifies the global variable x, then the following statements will always print the value of x after f modifies it:

```
i := f(x);
writeln( "x=", x );
```

Another rule you can count on is that the assignment to a variable on the left-hand side of an assignment statement does not occur prior to the use of that same variable on the right-hand side of the expression. That is, the following code will not write the result of the expression into variable n until it uses the previous value of n within the expression:

```
n := f(x) + g(x) - n;
```

Because the order of the production of side effects within an expression is undefined in most languages, the result of the following code is generally undefined (in Pascal):

```
function incN:integer;
begin
    incN := n;
    n := n + 1;
end;
        .
        .
        .
    n := 2;
    writeln( incN + n * 2 );
```

The compiler is free to first call the incN function (so n will contain 3 prior to executing the subexpression n * 2) or the compiler is allowed to first compute n * 2 and then call the incN function. As a result, one compilation of this statement could produce the output 8, while a different compilation might produce 6. In both cases, n would contain 3 after the writeln statement is executed, but the order of computation of the expression in the writeln statement could vary.

Don't make the mistake of thinking you can run some experiments to determine the order of evaluation. At the very best, such experiments will tell you only the order a particular compiler uses. A different compiler may well compute subexpressions in a different order. Indeed, the same compiler might also compute the components of a subexpression differently based on the context of that subexpression. This means that a compiler might compute the result using one ordering at one point in the program and using a different ordering somewhere else *in the same program.* Therefore, it is dangerous to "determine" the ordering your particular compiler uses and rely on that ordering. Even if the compiler is consistent in the ordering of the computation of side effects, the compiler vendor could change the ordering in a later version. If you must depend upon the order of evaluation, you need to break the computation down into to a sequence of simpler statements, whose computational order you can control. For example, if you really need to have your program call f before g in the statement

```
i := f(x) + g(x);
```

then you should write the code this way:

```
temp1 := f(x);
temp2 := g(x);
i := temp1 + temp2;
```

If you must control the order of evaluation within an expression, take special care when doing so in order to ensure that all side effects are computed at the appropriate time. To see how to do this, you need to learn about *sequence points.*

13.4 Containing Side Effects: Sequence Points

As noted earlier, most languages guarantee that the computation of side effects completes before certain points in your program's execution. For example, almost every language guarantees the completion of all side effects by the time the statement containing the expression completes execution. The point at which a compiler guarantees that the computation of a side effect is completed is called a *sequence point.* The end of a statement is an example of a sequence point.

The C programming language provides several important sequence points within expressions, in addition to the semicolon at the end of a statement. C defines sequence points between each of the following operators:

```
expression1, expression2                      (comma operator in an expression)
expression1 && expression2                    (logical AND operator)
expression1 || expression2                    (logical OR operator)
expression1 ? expression2 : expression3   (conditional expression operator)
```

C[5] guarantees that all side effects in expression1 are completed before the computation of expression2 or expression3 in these examples. Note that for the conditional expression, C only evaluates one of expression2 or expression3, so the side effects of only one of these subexpressions ever occurs on a given execution of the conditional expression.

To understand how side effects and sequence points can affect the operation of your program, consider the following example in C:

```
int array[6] = {0, 0, 0, 0, 0, 0};
int i;
    .
    .
    .
i = 0;
array[i] = i++;
```

---

[5] C++ compilers generally provide the same sequence points as C, although the original C++ standard did not define any sequence points.

Note that C does not define a sequence point across the assignment operator. Therefore, the C language makes no guarantees about the value of the expression i it uses as an index. The compiler can choose to use the value of i before or after indexing into array. That the ++ operator is a post-increment operation only implies that i++ returns the value of i prior to the increment; this does not guarantee that the compiler will use the pre-increment value of i anywhere else in the expression. The bottom line is that the last statement in this example could be semantically equivalent to either of the following statements:

```
    array[0] = i++;
-or-
    array[1] = i++;
```

The C language definition allows either form, and does not require the first form simply because the array index appears in the expression before the post-increment operator.

To control the assignment to array in this example, you will have to ensure that no part of the expression depends upon the side effects of some other part of the expression. That is, you cannot both use the value of i at one point in the expression and apply the post-increment operator to i in another part of the expression unless there is a sequence point between the two uses. Because no such sequence point exists between the two uses of i in this statement, the result is undefined by the C language standard.

To guarantee that a side effect occurs at an appropriate point, you must have a sequence point between two subexpressions. For example, if you'd like to use the value of i prior to the increment as the index into the array, you could write the following code:

```
    array [i] = i; //<-semicolon marks a sequence point
    ++i;
```

To use the value of i after the increment operation as the array index, you could use code such as the following:

```
    ++i;                //<-semicolon marks a sequence point.
    array[ i ] = i - 1;
```

Note, by the way, that a decent compiler will not increment i and then compute i - 1. A reasonable compiler will recognize the symmetry here, grab the value of i prior to the increment, and use that value as the index into array. This is an example of where someone who is familiar with the optimizations found in typical compilers could take advantage of this behavior to write code that is more readable. A programmer who inherently mistrusts compilers and their ability to optimize well might write code such as the following:

```
    j = i;
    ++i;                //<-semicolon marks a sequence point.
    array[ i ] = j;
```

An important distinction to make is that a sequence point does not specify when a computation will take place. A sequence point tells you that any outstanding side effects will be computed before crossing the sequence point. The computation of the side effect could have actually taken place much earlier in the code, at any point between the previous sequence point and the current sequence point. Another important fact to remember is that sequence points do not force the compiler to complete some computations between a pair of sequence points if that computation does not produce any side effects. The optimization of eliminating common subexpressions, for example, would be far less useful if the compiler could only use the result of common subexpression computations between sequence points. The compiler is free to compute the result of a subexpression as far ahead as necessary as long as that subexpression produces no side effects. Similarly, a compiler can compute the result of a subexpression as late as it cares to, as long as that result doesn't become part of a side effect.

Because statement endings (i.e., the semicolons) are a sequence point in most languages, one way to control the computation of side effects is to manually break a complex expression down into a sequence of three-address-like statements. For example, rather than relying on the Pascal compiler to translate an earlier example into three-address code using its own rules, you can explicitly write the code using whichever set of semantics you prefer. For example:

```
{ Statement with an undefined result in Pascal }

    i := f(x) + g(x);

{ Corresponding statement with well-defined semantics }

    temp1 := f(x);
    temp2 := g(x);
    i := temp1 + temp2;

{ Another version, also with well-defined but different semantics }

    temp1 := g(x);
    temp2 := f(x);
    i := temp2 + temp1;
```

Again, operator precedence and associativity do not control when a computation takes place in an expression. Even though addition is left associative, the compiler may compute the value of the addition operator's right operand before it computes the value of the addition operator's left operand. Precedence and associativity control how the compiler arranges the computation to produce the result. They do not control when the program computes the subcomponents of the expression. As long as the final computation produces the results one would expect based on precedence and associativity, the compiler is free to compute the subcomponents in any order and at any time it pleases.

Thus far, this section has given the impression that a compiler will always compute the value of an assignment statement and complete that assignment (and any other side effects) upon encountering the semicolon at the end of the statement. Strictly speaking, this isn't true. What many compilers will do is ensure that all side effects occur between a sequence point and the next reference of the object changed by the side effect. For example, consider the following two statements:

```
j = i++;
k = m * n + 2;
```

Although the first statement in this code fragment has a side effect, some compilers may compute the value (or portions thereof) of the second statement before completing the execution of the first statement. For example, many compilers will rearrange various machine instructions to avoid data hazards and other execution dependencies in the code that might result in lower performance (for details on data hazards, see *Write Great Code, Volume 1*). The semicolon sitting between these two statements does not guarantee that all computations for the first statement are complete before the CPU begins any new computation. Its presence only guarantees that the program computes any side effects occurring before the first semicolon prior to the execution of any code that depends on those side effects. Because the second statement does not depend upon the values of j or i, the compiler may freely start the computation of the second assignment prior to the completion of the first statement.

Sequence points act as barriers. A code sequence must complete its execution before following code affected by the side effect can execute. A compiler cannot compute the value of a side effect before some other code that appears before the previous sequence point in the program.

Consider the following two code fragments:

```
// Code fragment #1:

    i = j + k;
    m = ++k;

// Code fragment #2:

    i = j + k;
    m = ++n;
```

In the first example, the compiler must not rearrange the code so that it produces the side effect ++k prior to using k in the previous statement. The end-of-statement sequence point guarantees that the first statement in this example uses the value of k prior to any side effects produced in subsequent statements. In code fragment 2, however, the result of the side effect that ++n produces does not affect anything in the i = j + k; statement, so the compiler is free to move the ++n operation into the code that computes i's value if doing so is more convenient or more efficient.

13.5 Avoiding Problems Caused by Side Effects

Because it is often difficult to see the impact side effects have in your code, it's a good idea to try to limit your program's exposure to problems with side effects. Of course, the best way to do this is to eliminate side effects altogether in your programs. Unfortunately, that isn't a realistic option. Many algorithms depend upon side effects for proper operation (functions returning multiple results via reference parameters or even global variables are good examples). You may, however, reduce unintended consequences of side effects by observing a few simple rules. Here are a few suggestions:

- Avoid placing side effects in Boolean expressions within program flow-control statements such as if, while, do..until, and so on.
- If a side effect exists on the right side of an assignment operator, try moving the side effect into its own statement before or after the assignment (depending on whether the assignment statement uses the value of the object before or after it applies the side effect).
- Avoid multiple assignments in the same statement; break them into separate statements.
- Avoid calling more than one function (that might produce a side effect) in the same expression.
- Avoid modifications to global objects (e.g., side effects) when writing functions.
- Always document side effects thoroughly. For functions, you should document the side effect in the function's documentation, and you should document the side effect on every call to that function as well.

13.6 Forcing a Particular Order of Evaluation

As noted earlier, operator precedence and associativity do not control when a compiler may compute subexpressions. For example, if X, Y, and Z are each subexpressions (which could be anything from a single constant or variable reference to a complex expression in and of themselves), then an expression of the form X / Y * Z does not imply that the compiler computes the value for X before it computes the value for Y and Z. In fact, the compiler is free to compute the value for Z first, then Y, and finally X. All that operator precedence and associativity require is that the compiler must compute the value of X and Y (in any order) before computing X / Y, and the compile must compute the value of the subexpression X / Y before computing (X / Y) * Z. Of course, compilers are free to transform expressions via applicable algebraic transformations, but compilers are generally careful about this because not all standard algebraic transformations apply when using limited-precision arithmetic.

Although compilers are free to compute subexpressions in any order they choose (which is why side effects can create obscure problems), compilers generally avoid rearranging the order of actual computations. For example, mathematically, the following two expressions are equivalent following the standard rules of algebra (versus limited precision computer arithmetic):

```
X / Y * Z
Z * X / Y
```

In standard mathematics, this identity exists because the multiplication operator is commutative. That is, A * B is equal to B * A. Indeed, these two expressions will generally produce the same result as long as they are computed as follows:

```
(X / Y) * Z
Z * (X / Y)
```

The parentheses exist here not to show precedence, but to group calculations that the CPU must perform as a unit. That is, the statements are equivalent to:

```
A = X / Y;
B = Z
C = A * B
D = B * A
```

In most systems, C and D should have the same value. To understand why the former examples are not equivalent, consider what happens when X, Y, and Z are all integer objects with the values 5, 2, and 3, respectively:

```
    X / Y * Z
=   5 / 2 * 3
=   2 * 3
=   6

    Z * X / Y
=   3 * 5 / 2
=   15 / 2
=   7
```

For this reason, compilers are careful about algebraically rearranging expressions.

Any competent programmer understands the rules of integer arithmetic and, in fact, many algorithms depend upon the truncation that integer division produces in order to obtain a correct answer. Most programmers realize that X * (Y / Z) is not the same thing as (X * Y) / Z. Most compilers realize this too. In theory, a compiler should translate an expression of the form X * Y / Z as though it were (X * Y) / Z because the multiplication and division operators have the same precedence and are left associative. However, good programmers never rely on the rules of associativity to guarantee this. Although most compilers will correctly translate this expression as intended, the next engineer who comes along might not realize what's going on. Therefore, explicitly including the parentheses to make the intended evaluation clear is a good idea. Better still, treat integer truncation as a side effect and break the expression down into its constituent computations (using three-address–like expressions) to ensure the proper order of evaluation.

Integer arithmetic obviously obeys its own rules, and the rules of real algebra don't always apply. However, don't get the impression that floating-point arithmetic doesn't suffer from the same set of problems. Any time you're doing limited-precision arithmetic involving the possibility of rounding, truncation, overflow, or underflow, standard real-arithmetic algebraic transformations may not be legal. Because floating-point arithmetic is still a limited-precision format and suffers from rounding, truncation, underflow, and overflow, applying arbitrary real-arithmetic transformations to a floating-point expression can introduce inaccuracies in the computation. Therefore, a good compiler will not perform these types of transformations on real expressions. Unfortunately, some compilers apply the rules of real arithmetic to floating-point operations. Most of the time, the results they produce are reasonably correct (within the limitations of the floating-point representation); in some special cases, however, the assumption that real arithmetic and floating-point arithmetic are the same can produce especially bad results.

In general, if you must control the order of evaluation and when the program computes subcomponents of an expression, your only choice is to use assembly language. Subject to minor issues such as *out-of-order instruction execution*, you can specify exactly when your software will compute various components of an expression when implementing the expression in assembly code. For very accurate computations, when the order of evaluation can affect the results you obtain, assembly language may be the safest approach. Although fewer programmers are capable of reading and understanding assembly language code, there is no question that you can exactly specify the semantics of an arithmetic expression in assembly language—what you read is what you get without any modification by the assembler. This simply isn't true for most HLL systems.

13.7   Short-Circuit Evaluation

Certain arithmetic and logical operators exhibit the property that if one component of the expression has a certain value, the value for the whole expression is automatically known regardless of the values of the remaining components that make up the expression. A classic example is the multiplication operator. If you have an expression A * B and you know that either A or B is zero, there is no need to compute the other component because the result is already zero. If the cost of computing the subexpressions is rather expensive relative to the cost of a comparison, then a program can save some time by testing the first component to determine if it needs to bother computing the second component of the expression. This optimization is known as *short-circuit evaluation* because the program skips over ("short-circuits" in electronics terminology) the computation of the remainder of the expression.

Although a couple of arithmetic operations could employ short-circuit evaluation, the cost of checking for short-circuit evaluation is usually more expensive than completing the computation. Multiplication, for example, could use short-circuit evaluation to avoid multiplication by zero. However, in real programs, multiplication by zero occurs so infrequently that the cost of the comparison against zero in all the other cases generally overwhelms any savings achieved by avoiding multiplication by zero. Therefore, you'll rarely see a language system that supports short-circuit evaluation for arithmetic operations.

13.7.1 Short-Circuit Evaluation and Boolean Expressions

One type of expression that can benefit from short-circuit evaluation is a Boolean/logical expression. Boolean expressions are good candidates for short-circuit evaluation for three reasons:

- Boolean expressions only produce two results, True and False; therefore it's highly likely (50-50 chance assuming random distribution) that one of the short-circuit "trigger" values will appear.
- Boolean expressions tend to be complex.
- Boolean expressions occur frequently in programs.

Therefore, you'll find that many compilers use short-circuit evaluation when processing Boolean expressions.

Consider the following two C statements:

```
A = B && C;
D = E || F;
```

Note that if B is False, then A will be False regardless of C's value. Similarly, if E is True, then D will be True regardless of F's value. We can, therefore, compute the values for A and D as follows:

```
A = B;
if( A )
{
    A = C;
}

D = E;
if( !D )
{
    D = F;
}
```

Now this might seem like a whole lot of extra work (it certainly is more typing), but if C and F represent complex Boolean expressions, then this code sequence could possibly run much faster if B is usually False and E is usually

True. Of course, if your compiler fully supports short-circuit evaluation, you would never type this code; the compiler would generate the equivalent code for you.

By the way, the converse of short-circuit evaluation is *complete Boolean evaluation*. In complete Boolean evaluation, the compiler emits code that always computes each subcomponent of a Boolean expression. Some languages (such as C, C++, C#, and Java) specify the use of short-circuit evaluation. A few languages (such as Ada) let the programmer specify whether to use short-circuit or complete Boolean evaluation. Most languages (such as Pascal) don't define whether expressions will use short-circuit or complete Boolean evaluation—the language leaves it up to the implementer to decide which to use. Indeed, the same compiler could use complete Boolean evaluation for one instance of an expression and use short-circuit evaluation for another occurrence of that same expression in the same program. Unless you're using a language that strictly defines the type of Boolean evaluation, you will have to check with your specific compiler's documentation to determine how it processes Boolean expressions. Of course, you should avoid compiler-specific mechanisms if there is a chance you'll have to compile your code with a different compiler at some point in the future.

Look again at the expansions of the earlier Boolean expressions. It should be easy to see that the program will not evaluate C and F if A is False and D is True. Therefore, the left-hand side of a conjunction (&&) or disjunction (||) operator can act as a gate, preventing the execution of the right-hand side of the expression. This is an important fact and, indeed, many algorithms depend on this property for correct operation. Consider the following (very common) C statement:

```
if( ptr != NULL && *ptr != '\0' )
{
    << process current character in string pointed at by ptr >>
}
```

This example could fail if it used complete Boolean evaluation. Consider the case where the ptr variable contains NULL. With short-circuit evaluation, the program will not compute the subexpression *ptr != '\0'; because the program realizes the result is always false. As such, control immediately transfers to the first statement beyond the ending bracket (}) in this if statement. Consider, however, what would happen if this compiler utilized complete Boolean evaluation rather than short-circuit evaluation. After determining that ptr contains NULL, the program would still attempt to dereference ptr. Unfortunately, such an attempt would probably produce a runtime error. Therefore, complete Boolean evaluation would cause this program to fail, even though it dutifully checks to make sure that access via pointer is legal.

Another semantic difference between complete and short-circuit Boolean evaluation has to do with side effects. In particular, if a subexpression does not execute because of short-circuit evaluation, then that subexpression doesn't produce any side effects. This behavior is incredibly useful but inherently dangerous. It is useful insofar as some algorithms absolutely depend upon short-circuit evaluation. It is dangerous because some algorithms also expect all the side effects to occur, even if the expression evaluates to False at some point. As an example, consider the following bizarre (but absolutely legal) C statement that advances a "cursor" pointer to the next 8-byte boundary in a string, or the end of the string (whichever comes first):

```
*++ptr && *++ptr && *++ptr && *++ptr && *++ptr && *++ptr && *++ptr && *++ptr;
```

For the benefit of those who don't immediately see how this statement works (and that covers the majority of C programmers, so don't feel bad), this statement begins by incrementing a pointer and then fetching a byte from memory (pointed to by ptr). If the byte fetched was zero, then execution of this expression/statement immediately stops as the entire expression evaluates to False at that point. If the character fetched is not zero, then the process repeats up to seven more times. At the end of this sequence, either ptr points at a zero byte or it points 8 bytes beyond the original position. The trick here (involving short-circuit Boolean evaluation) is that the expression immediately terminates upon reaching the end of the string rather than blindly skipping beyond that point.

Of course, there are complementary examples that demonstrate desirable behavior when side effects occur in Boolean expressions involving complete Boolean evaluation. The important thing to note is that no one scheme is correct and the other scheme incorrect. In different situations, a given algorithm may require the use of short-circuit Boolean evaluation or complete Boolean evaluation to produce correct results. Only a few programming languages (such as Ada) provide a standardized way to select either scheme under program control. Some languages (such as C, C++, C#, and Java) specify one form or the other. Most languages, however, leave it up to the compiler implementation to determine which scheme to use. If the definition of the language you're using doesn't explicitly specify which form, or you want to use the other form (such as complete Boolean evaluation in C), then you have to write your code in such a fashion so that it forces the evaluation scheme you desire.

13.7.2   Forcing Short-Circuit or Complete Boolean Evaluation

Forcing complete Boolean evaluation in a language where short-circuit evaluation is used (or may be used) is relatively easy. All you have to do is break the expression into individual statements, place the result of each subexpression into a variable, and then apply the conjunction and disjunction operators to these temporary variables. For example, consider the following conversion:

```
// Complex expression:

if( (a < f(x)) && (b != g(y)) || predicate( a + b ))
```

```
{
    <<stmts to execute if this expression is True>>
}

// Translation to a form that uses complete Boolean evaluation:

temp1 = a < f(x);
temp2 = b != g(y);
temp3 = predicate( a + b );
if( temp1 && temp2 || temp3 )
{
    <<stmts to execute if this expression is True>>
}
```

The Boolean expression appearing within the if statement still uses short-circuit evaluation. However, because this code evaluates the sub-expressions prior to the if statement, this code ensures that all of the side effects that the f, g, and predicate functions produce will occur.

Suppose you want to go the other way? That is, what if your language only supports complete Boolean evaluation (or doesn't specify the evaluation type), and you want to force short-circuit evaluation? This direction is a little more work than forcing complete Boolean evaluation, but it is still not difficult.

Consider the following Pascal code:[6]

```
if( ((a < f(x)) and (b <> g(y))) or predicate( a + b )) then begin

    <<stmts to execute if the expression is True>>

end; (*if*)
```

To force short-circuit Boolean evaluation, you need to test the value of the first subexpression and evaluate the second subexpression (and the conjunction of the two expressions) only if the first subexpression evaluates to True. You can do this with the following code:

```
boolResult := a < f(x);
if( boolResult ) then
    boolResult := b <> g(y);

if( not boolResult ) then
    boolResult := predicate( a + b );

if( boolResult ) then begin

    <<stmts to execute if the IF's expression is True>>

end; (*if*)
```

----

[6] The standard definition for Pascal doesn't specify whether the compiler uses complete or short-circuit Boolean evaluation. Most Pascal compilers, however, implement complete Boolean evaluation.

This code simulates short-circuit evaluation by using if statements to block (or force) execution of the g and predicate functions based on the current state of the Boolean expression (kept in the boolResult variable).

Converting an expression to force short-circuit evaluation or complete Boolean evaluation looks as though it requires far more code than the original forms. If you're concerned about the efficiency of this translation (and you should be), relax. Internally, the compiler translates those Boolean expressions to three-address code that is similar to the translation that you did manually.

13.7.3 Efficiency Issues

Don't infer from the preceding discussion that complete Boolean evaluation and short-circuit evaluation have equivalent efficiencies. If you're processing complex Boolean expressions or the cost of some of your subexpressions is rather high, then short-circuit evaluation is generally faster than complete Boolean evaluation. As to which form produces less object code, they're roughly equivalent, and the exact difference will depend entirely upon the expression you're evaluating.

To understand the efficiency issues surrounding complete versus short-circuit Boolean evaluation, look at some assembly code that implements the examples discussed in this section. The following HLA code implements this Boolean expression using both forms:[7]

```
// Complex expression:

//   if( (a < f(x)) && (b != g(y)) || predicate( a + b ))
//   {
//       <<stmts to execute if the IF's expression is True>>
//   }
//
// Translation to a form that uses complete
//   Boolean evaluation:
//
//   temp1 = a < f(x);
//   temp2 = b != g(y);
//   temp3 = predicate( a + b );
//   if( temp1 && temp2 || temp3 )
//   {
//       <<stmts to execute if the expression evaluates to True>>
//   }
//
//
// Translation into 80x86 assembly language code,
//   assuming all variables and return results are
//   unsigned 32-bit integers:
```

---

[7] HLA, of course, supports an if statement with short-circuit Boolean evaluation. We won't use that feature here because the whole purpose of this exercise is to avoid the high-level abstractions of an if statement.

```
        f(x);            // Assume f returns its result in EAX
        cmp( a, eax );   // Compare a with f(x)'s return result.
        setb( bl );      // bl = a < f(x)
        g(y);            // Assume g returns its result in EAX
        cmp( b, eax );   // Compare b with g(y)'s return result
        setne( bh );     // bh = b != g(y)
        mov( a, eax );   // Compute a + b to pass along to the
        add( b, eax );   //   predicate function.
        predicate( eax );// al holds predicate's result (0/1)
        and( bh, bl );   // bl = temp1 && temp2
        or( bl, al );    // al = (temp1 && temp2) || temp3
        jz skipStmts;    // Zero if false, not zero if true.

        <<stmts to execute if the condition is True>>

skipStmts:
```

Here's the same expression using short-circuit Boolean evaluation:

```
//  if( (a < f(x)) && (b != g(y)) || predicate( a + b ))
//  {
//       <<stmts to execute if the IF's expression evaluates to True>>
//  }

        f(x);
        cmp( a, eax );
        jnb TryOR;       // If a is not less than f(x), try the OR clause
        g(y);
        cmp( b, eax );
        jne DoStmts      // If b is not equal g(y) [and a < f(x)], then do
                         // the body.

TryOR:
        mov( a, eax );
        add( b, eax );
        predicate( eax );
        test( eax, eax );  // EAX = 0?
        jz SkipStmts;

DoStmts:
        <<stmts to execute if the condition is True>>
SkipStmts:
```

As you can see by simply counting statements, the version using short-circuit evaluation is slightly shorter (11 instructions versus 12). However, the short-circuit version will probably run much faster because half the time the code will only evaluate two of the three expressions. This code evaluates all three subexpressions only when the first subexpression (a < f(x)) evaluates to True and the second expression (b != g(y)) evaluates to False. If the outcomes of these Boolean expressions are equally probable, then this code will test all three subexpressions 25 percent of the time. The remainder of the time it only has to test two subexpressions (50 percent of the time it will test a < f(x) and predicate(a + b), 25 percent of the time it will test a < f(x) and b != g(y), and the remaining 25 percent of the time it will need to test all three conditions).

The interesting thing to note about these two assembly language sequences is that complete Boolean evaluation tends to maintain the state of the expression (True or False) in an actual variable, whereas short-circuit evaluation maintains the current state of the expression by the program's position in the code. Take another look at the short-circuit example. Note that it does not maintain the Boolean results from each of the subexpressions anywhere other than the position in the code. For example, if you get to the TryOR label in this code, you know that the subexpression involving conjunction (logical AND) is False. Likewise, if the program executes the call to g(y), you know that the first subexpression in the example [a < f(x)] has evaluated to True. When you make it to the DoStmts label, you know that the entire expression has evaluated to True.

If the time needed to execute the functions f, g, and predicate is roughly the same in the current example, you can greatly improve the performance of this code with a nearly trivial modification. Consider the following modification to the previous example:

```
//   if( predicate( a + b ) || (a < f(x)) && (b != g(y)))
//   {
//       <<stmts to execute if the expression evaluates to True>>
//   }

        mov( a, eax );
        add( b, eax );
        predicate( eax );
        test( eax, eax );    // EAX = True (nonzero)?
        jnz DoStmts;

        f(x);
        cmp( a, eax );
        jnb SkipStmts;       // If a is not less than f(x), try the OR clause
        g(y);
        cmp( b, eax );
        je SkipStmts;        // If b is not equal g(y) (and a < f(x)), then
                             // do the body.

DoStmts:
        <<stmts to execute if the condition is true>>
SkipStmts:
```

Again, if you assume that the outcome of each subexpression is random and evenly distributed (that is, there is a 50-50 chance that each subexpression produces True), then this code will, on the average, run about 50 percent faster than the previous version. Why? By moving the test for predicate to the beginning of the code fragment the code can now determine with one test whether it needs to execute the body. Because 50 percent of the time predicate returns True, you can determine if you're going to execute the loop body with a single test about half the time. In the earlier example, it always took at least two tests to determine if we were going to execute the loop body.

The two assumptions here (that the Boolean expressions are equally likely to produce True or False and that the costs of computing each of the subexpressions are equal) rarely hold in practice. However, this means that you have an even greater opportunity to optimize your code, not less. For example, if the cost of calling the predicate function is high (relative to the computation of the remainder of the expression), then you'll want to arrange the expression so that it only calls predicate when it absolutely must. Conversely, if the cost of calling predicate is low compared to the cost of computing the other subexpressions, then you'll want to call it first. A similar situation exists for the f and g functions. Because the logical AND operation is commutative, the following two expressions are semantically equivalent (in the absence of side effects):

```
a < f(x) && b != g(y)
b != g(y) && a < f(x)
```

When the compiler uses short-circuit evaluation, the first expression executes faster than the second if the cost of calling function f is less than the cost of calling function g. Conversely, if calling f is more expensive than calling g, then the second expression usually executes faster.

Another factor that affects the performance of short-circuit Boolean expression evaluation is the likelihood that a given Boolean expression will return the same value on each call. Consider the following two templates:

```
expr1 && expr2
expr3 || expr4
```

When working with conjunctions, you should try to place the expression that is more likely to return True on the right-hand side of the conjunction operator (&&). Remember, for the logical AND operation, if the first operand is False, a Boolean system employing short-circuit evaluation will not bother to evaluate the second operand. For performance reasons, you want to place the operand that is most likely to return False on the left-hand side of the expression. This will avoid the computation of the second operand more often than had you reversed the operands.

The situation is reversed for disjunction (||). In this case, you'd arrange your operands so that expr3 is more likely to return True than expr4. By organizing your disjunction operations this way, you'll skip the execution of the right-hand expression more often than if you had switched the operands.

It goes without saying that you cannot arbitrarily reorder Boolean expression operands if those expressions produce side effects. The proper computation of those side effects may depend upon the exact order of the subexpressions. Rearranging the subexpressions may cause a side effect to happen that wouldn't otherwise occur. So, be cognizant of this when you are trying to improve performance by rearranging operands in a Boolean expression.

13.8 The Relative Cost of Arithmetic Operations

Most algorithm analysis methodologies use a simplifying assumption that all operations take the same amount of time.[8] This assumption is rarely correct because some arithmetic operations are two orders of magnitude slower than other computations. For example, a simple integer addition is often much faster than an integer multiplication. Similarly, integer operations are usually much faster than the corresponding floating-point operations. For algorithm analysis purposes, it may be okay to ignore the fact that one operation may be n times faster than some other operation. For someone interested in writing great code, however, knowing which operators are the most efficient is important, especially when you have the option of choosing among them.

Unfortunately, we can't create a table of operators that lists their relative speeds. The performance of a given arithmetic operator is going to vary by CPU. Even within the same CPU family, you see a wide variance in performance for the same arithmetic operation. For example, shift and rotate operations are relatively fast on a Pentium III (relative, say, to an addition operation). On a Pentium 4, however, they're considerably slower. So an operator such as the C/C++ << or >> can be fast or slow, relative to an addition operation, depending upon which CPU it executes.

Although I can't summarize at a glance the relative performances of various arithmetic operations in most major programming languages, I can provide some general guidelines. For example, on most CPUs the addition operation is one of the most efficient arithmetic and logical operations around. Few CPUs support faster arithmetic or logical operations than addition. Therefore, it's useful to group various operations into classes based on their performance relative to an operation like addition. Table 13-1 provides an attempt to estimate relative performance.

Table 13-1: Relative Performances of Arithmetic Operations (Guidelines)

Relative Performance	Operations
Fastest	Integer addition, subtraction, negation, logical AND, logical OR, logical XOR, logical NOT, and comparisons
	Logical shifts
	Logical rotates
	Multiplication
	Division
	Floating-point comparisons and negation
	Floating-point addition and subtraction
	Floating-point multiplication
Slowest	Floating-point division

---

[8] Actually, to be technically correct, these methodologies assume that different arithmetic operations vary by a constant amount and that they ignore constant multiplicative differences.

The estimates in Table 13-1 are not accurate for all CPUs, but they do provide a "first approximation" from which you can work until you gain more experience with a particular processor. On many processors you'll find anywhere between two and three orders of magnitude difference in the performances between the fastest and slowest operations. In particular, division tends to be quite slow on most processors (floating-point division is even slower). Multiplication is usually slower than addition, but the exact variance differs greatly between processors.

Of course, if you absolutely need to do floating-point division, there is little you can do to improve your application's performance by using a different operation. However, note that many integer arithmetic calculations can be computed using different algorithms. For example, a left shift is often less expensive than multiplication by two. While most compilers will automatically handle such "operator conversions" for you, compilers aren't omniscient and can't always figure out the best way to calculate some result. However, if you manually do the "operator conversion" yourself, you don't have to rely on the compiler to get this right for you.

13.9 For More Information

There are many textbooks on compiler design and implementation that spend a fair amount of time discussing code generation for arithmetic expressions and the optimization of the code for those expressions. Here are a few compiler-construction textbooks you may want to investigate:

- *Compilers, Principles, Techniques, and Tools*, Alfred Aho, Ravi Sethi, and Jeffrey Ullman (Addison-Wesley, 1986)
- *Compiler Construction: Theory and Practice*, William Barret and John Couch (SRA, 1986)
- *A Retargetable C Compiler: Design and Implementation*, Christopher Fraser and David Hansen (Addison-Wesley Professional, 1995)
- *Introduction to Compiler Design*, Thomas Parsons (W. H. Freeman, 1992)
- *Compiler Construction: Principles and Practice*, Kenneth Louden (Course Technology, 1997)

One of the best ways to learn how to write better HLL code that generates good machine code is to learn assembly language programming. *The Art of Assembly Language* (No Starch Press, 2003) is a great resource for learning more about how to evaluate arithmetic expression in assembly language.

For more information about compiler benchmarks and compiler optimizer capabilities, you'll want to visit the Willus.com compiler benchmark page at www.willus.com/ccomp_benchmark.shtml.

14

CONTROL STRUCTURES AND PROGRAMMATIC DECISIONS

Control structures are the bread and butter of high-level language programming. The ability to make decisions based on the evaluation of stated conditions is fundamental to practically every kind of automation that computers provide. The translation of HLL control structures into machine code has, perhaps, the largest impact on program performance and size. Knowing which control structures to use in a given situation is the key to writing great code. This chapter discusses the conversion of high-level control structures into machine code so that you can choose the best HLL statements to produce the best machine code. In particular, this chapter describes the machine implementation of control structures related to decision making and unconditional flow control, including:

- if statements
- switch and case statements
- goto and related statements

The following two chapters will expand this discussion to loop control structures and procedure/function calls and returns.

14.1 Control Structures Are Slower Than Computations!

A fair percentage of the machine instructions in a program control the execution path through that program. Because control transfer instructions often flush the instruction pipeline (see *Write Great Code, Volume 1*), they tend to be slower than instructions that perform simple calculations. To produce effficient programs, you should reduce the number of control transfer instructions or, if this is not possible, choose the fastest ones.

The exact set of instructions that CPUs use to control program flow varies across processors. Nevertheless, many CPUs (including the two families covered in this book) control program flow using the compare and jump paradigm; that is, after a compare or another instruction that modifies the CPU flags, a conditional jump instruction transfers control to another location based on the CPU flag settings. Some CPUs can do all this with a single instruction; some require two, three, or more instructions to achieve this. Some CPUs allow you to compare two values for a large range of different conditions; some allow only a few tests. Regardless of the mechanism, HLL statements that map to a given sequence on one CPU will map to a comparable sequence on a second CPU. Therefore, if you understand the basic conversion for one CPU, you'll have a good idea how the compiler works across all CPUs.

14.2 Introduction to Low-Level Control Structures

Most CPUs use a two-step process to make a programmatic decision. First, the program will compare two values and save the result of the comparison in a machine register or flag. Then the program will execute a second instruction that tests the result of that comparison and transfers control to one of two locations based on the result of the comparison. With little more than this *compare and conditional branch* sequence, it is possible to synthesize most of the major HLL control structures.

Even within the compare and conditional branch paradigm, CPUs commonly implement conditional code sequences using two different approaches. One technique, especially common on stack-based architectures (such as the Java Virtual Machine), is to have different forms of the compare instruction that test for specific conditions. For example, you might have *compare if equal, compare if not equal, compare if less than, compare if greater than*, and so on. The result of each is a Boolean value. Then a pair of conditional branch instructions, *branch if true* and *branch if false*, can test the result of the comparison and transfer control to some other location depending on the sense of the branch.

The second, and historically more popular approach, is for the CPU's instruction set to contain a single comparison instruction that sets (or clears) several bits in the CPU's *program status* or *flags* register. Then the program uses one of several more specific conditional branch instructions to transfer control to some other location. These conditional branch instructions might have names such as *jump if equal, jump if not equal, jump if less than,* or *jump if greater than.* Because this "compare and jump" technique is the one the 80x86 and PowerPC use, I'll employ this approach in the examples appearing in this chapter; however, conversion to the multiple comparisons/jump true/jump false paradigm is easy.

Conditional branches are typically two-way branches. That is, they transfer control to one location in the program if the condition they're testing is true and a different location if the condition is false. To reduce the size of the instruction, the conditional branches on most CPUs only encode the address of one of the two possible branch locations, and they use an implied address for the opposite condition. Specifically, most conditional branches transfer control to some target location if the condition is true and they fall through to the next instruction if the condition is false. For example, consider the following 80x86 je (jump if equal) instruction sequence:

```
// Compare the value in EAX to the value in EBX

        cmp( eax, ebx );

// Branch to label EAXequalsEBX if EAX==EBX

        je EAXequalsEBX;

        mov( 4, ebx );        // Drop down here if EAX != EBX
            .
            .
            .
EAXequalsEBX:
```

This instruction sequence begins by comparing the value in the EAX register against the value in EBX (the cmp instruction); this sets the *condition-code bits* in the 80x86 EFLAGS register. In particular, this instruction sets the 80x86 *zero flag* to 1 if the value in EAX is equal to the value in EBX. The je instruction tests the zero flag to see if it is set; if it is set, the je instruction transfers control to the machine instruction immediately following the EAX-equalsEBX label in this code example. If the value in EAX is not equal to EBX, then the cmp instruction clears the zero flag, and the je instruction falls through to the mov instruction rather than transferring control to the destination label.

In Volume 1 of this series, you learned that certain machine instructions that access data can be smaller (and faster) if the memory location the machine instruction accesses is near the base address of the activation record containing that variable. This rule also applies to conditional jump instructions. The 80x86 provides two forms of the conditional jump instructions. One form is only 2 bytes long (1 byte for an opcode and 1 byte for a signed displacement in the range −128...+127). The other form is 6 bytes long (2 bytes for the opcode and 4 bytes for a signed displacement in the range

−2 billion...+2 billion). The displacement value specifies how far (in bytes) the program must jump to reach the target location. To transfer control to a nearby location, the program can use the short form of the branch. Because 80x86 instructions are between 1 and 15 bytes long (and are typically around 3 or 4 bytes long), the short forms of the conditional jump instructions can usually skip over about 32 to 40 machine instructions. Once the target location is out of the plus or minus 127-byte range, the 6-byte version of these conditional jump instructions extends the range to 2 billion bytes around the current instruction. Obviously, if you're interested in writing the most efficient code, you'll want to use the 2-byte form as often as possible.

Branching is an expensive operation in a modern (pipelined) CPU because a branch may require the CPU to flush the pipeline and reload it (see *Write Great Code, Volume 1* for more details). For conditional branches, this cost occurs only if the branch is taken. If the conditional branch instruction falls through to the next instruction, then the CPU will continue to use the instructions found in the pipeline without flushing them. Therefore, on many systems the *branch that falls through to the next instruction is* is faster than the *branch that is taken*. Note, however, that some CPUs (like the PowerPC) support a feature known as *branch prediction* that tells the CPU to begin fetching instructions for the pipeline from the branch's target location rather than from the instructions that immediately follow the conditional jump. Unfortunately, branch prediction algorithms vary from processor to processor (even within the 80x86 CPU family), so it's difficult to predict, in general, how branch prediction will affect your HLL code. Probably the safest thing to assume, unless you're writing code for a specific processor, is that falling through to the next instruction is more efficient than taking the jump.

Although the compare and conditional branch paradigm is the most common control structure found in machine code programs, there are other ways to transfer control another location in memory based on some computed result. Without question, the indirect jump (especially via a table of addresses) is the most common alternative form. Consider the following 80x86 jmp instruction:

```
readonly
    jmpTable: dword[4] := [&label1, &label2, &label3, &label4];
        .
        .
        .
        jmp( jmpTable[ ebx*4 ] );
```

This jmp instruction fetches the double-word value at the index specified by the value in EBX in the jmpTable array. That is, the instruction transfers control to one of four different locations based upon the value (0..3) in EBX. For example, if EBX contains zero then the jmp instruction fetches the double word at index 0 in jmpTable (the address of the instruction prefixed by label1). Likewise, if EBX contains 2, then this jmp instruction fetches the third double word from this table (which is the address of label3 in the program). This is roughly equivalent to, but usually shorter than, the following sequence of instructions:

```
cmp( ebx, 0 );
je label1;
cmp( ebx, 1 );
je label2;
cmp( ebx, 2 );
je label 3;
cmp( ebx, 3 );
je label4;

// Results are undefined if EBX <> 0, 1, 2, or 3
```

A few other conditional control transfer mechanisms are available on various CPUs, but these two mechanisms (compare/conditional branch and indirect jump) are the mechanisms most HLL compilers will use to implement standard control structures in the HLL.

14.3 The goto Statement

The goto statement is, perhaps, the most fundamental low-level control structure. Since the wave of "structured programming" in the late 1960s and 1970s, the use of the goto statement in HLL code has diminished. Indeed, some modern high-level programming languages don't even provide an unstructured (traditional) goto statement. Even in those languages where an unrestricted goto is available, programming style guidelines usually restrict the use of the goto statement to special circumstances. Combined with the fact that student programmers have been religiously taught to avoid goto statements in their programs since the middle 1970s, it's now rare to find many goto statements in a modern program. From a readability point of view, this is a good thing (and if you don't believe this, try reading some 1960s-era FORTRAN programs to get an idea of how hard-to-read code can be when it's peppered with goto statements). Nevertheless, some programmers believe that they can write code that is more efficient by using goto statements in their code. While this is sometimes true, the resulting efficiency gains are rarely worth the loss of readability that ultimately occurs.

One of the big efficiency arguments that is made for the goto statement is that it helps avoid duplicate code. Consider the following trivial C/C++ example:

```
if( a == b || c < d )
{
    << execute some number of statements >>

    if( x == y )
    {
        << execute some statements if x == y >>
```

```
    }
    else
    {
        << execute some statements if x != y >>
    }
}
else
{
    << execute the same sequence of statements
       that the code executes if x != y in the
       previous else section >>
}
```

A programmer who is constantly looking for ways to make programs more efficient will immediately notice all the duplicated code and might be tempted to rewrite the code as follows:

```
if( a == b || c < d )
{
    << execute some number of statements >>

    if( x != y ) goto DuplicatedCode;

    << execute some statements if x == y >>
}
else
{
DuplicatedCode:
    << execute the same sequence of statements
       if x != y or the original
       Boolean expression is false >>
}
```

There are, of course, several software engineering problems with this code, including the fact that it is a little bit harder to read, modify, and maintain than the original example. However, you could argue that it's actually a little easier to maintain, because you no longer have duplicated code and you only have to fix defects in the common code at one spot in this example. However, there is no denying that there is less code in this example. Or is there?

The optimizers in many modern compilers will actually look for code sequences similar to the former example and generate code that is identical to what you would expect to get for the second example. Therefore, a *good* compiler will avoid generating duplicate machine code even when the source file contains duplication, as in the first example appearing here.

Consider the following C/C++ example compiled to PowerPC code by GCC:

```
#include <stdio.h>

static int a;
```

```
static int b;

extern int x;
extern int y;
extern int f( int );
extern int g( int );

int main( void )
{
    if( a==f(x))
    {
        if( b==g(y))
        {
            a = 0;
        }
        else
        {
            printf( "%d %d\n", a, b );
            a = 1;
            b = 0;
        }
    }
    else
    {
        printf( "%d %d\n", a, b );
        a = 1;
        b = 0;
    }

    return( 0 );
}
```

Here's the compilation of the if sequence to PowerPC code by GCC:

```
        ; f(x):

        lwz r3,0(r9)
        bl L_f$stub

        ; Compute a==f(x), jump to L2 if false

        lwz r4,0(r30)
        cmpw cr0,r4,r3
        bne+ cr0,L2

        ; g(y):

        addis r9,r31,ha16(L_y$non_lazy_ptr-L1$pb)
        addis r29,r31,ha16(_b-L1$pb)
        lwz r9,lo16(L_y$non_lazy_ptr-L1$pb)(r9)
        la r29,lo16(_b-L1$pb)(r29)
        lwz r3,0(r9)
        bl L_g$stub
```

```
                  ; Compute b==g(y), jump to L3 if false:

                  lwz  r5,0(r29)
                  cmpw cr0,r5,r3
                  bne- cr0,L3


                  ; a = 0

                  li   r0,0
                  stw  r0,0(r30)
                  b    L5

                  ;Set up a and b parameters if
                  ; a==f(x) but b != g(y):

L3:
                  lwz  r4,0(r30)
                  addis r3,r31,ha16(LC0-L1$pb)
                  b    L6

                  ; Set up parameters if a != f(x):
L2:
                  addis r29,r31,ha16(_b-L1$pb)
                  addis r3,r31,ha16(LC0-L1$pb)
                  la   r29,lo16(_b-L1$pb)(r29)
                  lwz  r5,0(r29)

                  ; Common code shared by both
                  ; ELSE sections:
L6:
                  la   r3,lo16(LC0-L1$pb)(r3) ;Call printf
                  bl   L_printf$stub
                  li   r9,1                  ;a = 1
                  li   r0,0                  ;b = 0
                  stw  r9,0(r30)             ;Store a
                  stw  r0,0(r29)             ;Store b
L5:
```

Of course, not every compiler has an optimizer that will recognize the duplicated code. So if you want to write a program that compiles to efficient machine code regardless of the compiler, you might be tempted to go ahead and use the version of the code that employs the goto statement. Indeed, a strong software engineering argument could be made that having duplicate code in a source file makes the program harder to read and harder to maintain. (If you fix a defect in one copy of the code, chances are that you'll forget to correct the defect in the other copies of the code.) While this is definitely true, if you make changes to the code at the target label it's not immediately obvious that the change is appropriate for each and every section of code that jumps to the target label. And it's not immediately obvious how many different goto statements transfer control to the same target label when you're reading through the source code.

The traditional software engineering approach is to put the common code into a procedure or function and simply call that function. However, the overhead of a function call and return can be rather large (especially if there isn't much duplicated code), so from a performance point of view, using a procedure or function may not be satisfactory. For short sequences of common code, creating a macro or an inline function is probably the best solution. To complicate the issue, you might need a change that only affects one instance of the duplicated code (that is, it would no longer be a duplicate). The bottom line is that using a goto statement to gain efficiency in this manner should be your last resort.

Another common use for goto statements is for exceptional conditions. When you find yourself nested deeply in several statements and you encounter a situation where you need to exit all those statements, the common consensus is that a goto is acceptable if restructuring the code would not make it more readable. However, jumps out of nested blocks may thwart the optimizer's ability to generate decent code for the entire procedure or function. The use of the goto statement may save a few bytes or processor cycles in the code immediately affected by the goto, but the presence of the goto could have some detrimental effects on the rest of the function, resulting in less efficient code overall. Therefore, take care when inserting goto statements into your code. They could make your source code harder to read, and they might wind up making it less efficient, as well.

14.4 break, continue, next, return, and Other Limited Forms of the goto Statement

In an effort to support structured *goto-less* programming, many programming languages have added restricted forms of the goto statement that allow a programmer to immediately exit some control structure such as a loop or a procedure or function. Typical statements include break/exit, which jump out of an enclosing loop; continue/cycle/next, which restart an enclosing loop; and return/exit, which immediately return from an enclosing procedure/function. These statements are more *structured* than a standard goto because the programmer doesn't choose the destination; instead, control transfers to a fixed location based upon whatever control statement (or function/procedure) encloses the statement.

Almost every one of these statements compiles into a single jmp instruction. The statements that jump out of some loop (e.g., break) compile into a single jmp instruction that transfers control to the first statement beyond the bottom of the loop. The statements that restart a loop (e.g., continue, next, or cycle) also compile into a single jmp instruction; that jmp transfers control to the loop termination test (in the case of while or repeat..until/do..while) or to the top of the loop (in the case of most other loops).

Although these statements typically compile to a single machine instruction (jmp), don't get the impression that they are efficient to use. Even ignoring the fact that a jmp can be somewhat expensive (because it forces the CPU to flush the instruction pipeline), statements that branch out of a loop can have a serious impact on the compiler's optimizer, dramatically reducing the opportunity to generate high quality code. Therefore, you should attempt to use these statements as sparingly as possible.

14.5 The if Statement

Perhaps the most basic high-level control structure is the if statement. Indeed, with nothing more than an if and a goto statement, you can (semantically) implement all other control structures.[1] I'll use this fact when discussing other control structures, but for now I'll show how a typical compiler will convert an if statement into machine code.

For a simple if statement that compares two values and executes the body if the condition is true, you can easily implement the if statement with a single compare and a conditional branch instruction. Consider the following Pascal if statement and its 80x86 conversion:

```
if( EAX = EBX ) then begin

    writeln( "EAX is equal to EBX" );
    i := i + 1;

end;
```

Here's the conversion to 80x86/HLA assembly language code:

```
    cmp( EAX, EBX );
    jne skipIfBody;
    stdout.put( "EAX is equal to EBX", nl );
    inc( i );
skipIfBody:
```

In this Pascal source code, the body of the if statement executes if the value of EAX is equal to EBX. In the resulting assembly code, the program compares EAX with EBX and then branches over the statements that correspond to the if statement's body if EAX does not equal EBX. This is the "boilerplate" conversion of an HLL if statement into machine code: Test some condition and branch over the if statement's body if the condition turns out to be false.

The implementation of an if..then..else statement is only slightly more complicated than the basic if statement. An if..then..else statement typically employs syntax and semantics such as the following:

```
if( some_boolean_expression ) then

    << Statements to execute if the expression is true >>

else
```

---

[1] Doing so isn't a good idea for reasons of maintainability, but it's certainly possible.

```
    << Statements to execute if the expression is false >>

endif
```

To implement this code sequence in machine code requires only a single machine instruction beyond what a simple if statement requires. Consider this example C/C++ code:

```
if( EAX == EBX )
{
    printf( "EAX is equal to EBX\n" );
    ++i;
}
else
{
    printf( "EAX is not equal to EBX\n" );
}
```

Here is the conversion to 80x86/HLA assembly language code:

```
cmp( EAX, EBX );        // See if EAX == EBX
jne doElse;             // Branch around "Then" code
stdout.put( "EAX is equal to EBX", nl );
inc( i );
jmp skipElseBody        // Skip over "else" section.

// if they are not equal.

doElse:
    stdout.put( "EAX is not equal to EBX", nl );

skipElseBody:
```

You should note two things about this code. First, if the condition evaluates to False, the code transfers to the first statement of the else block rather than the first statement following the (entire) if statement. The second thing to note is the jmp instruction at the end of the true clause skips the else block.

Some languages, including HLA, support an elseif clause in their if statement to evaluate a second condition if the first one fails. This is a straightforward extension of the code generation of the if statement I've shown. Consider the following HLA if..elseif..else..endif statements and the corresponding *pure* machine code that HLA compiles it to. Here's the HLA source code:

```
if( EAX = EBX ) then

    stdout.put( "EAX is equal to EBX" nl );
    inc( i );

elseif( EAX = ECX ) then
```

```
        stdout.put( "EAX is equal to ECX" nl );

    else

        stdout.put( "EAX is not equal to EBX or ECX" nl);

    endif;
```

And here's the conversion to pure 80x86/HLA assembly language code:

```
// Test to see if EAX = EBX

    cmp( eax, ebx );
    jne tryElseif; // Skip "then" section if not equal

// Start of the "then" section

    stdout.put( "EAX is equal to EBX", nl );
    inc( i );
    jmp skipElseBody // End of "then" section, skip
                     // over the elseif clause.
tryElseif:
    cmp( eax, ecx ); // ELSEIF test for EAX = ECX
    jne doElse;      // Skip "then" clause if not equal

    // ELSEIF "then" clause

    stdout.put( "EAX is equal to ECX", nl );
    jmp skipElseBody; // Skip over the "else" section

doElse: // ELSE clause begins here
    stdout.put( "EAX is not equal to EBX or ECX", nl );

skipElseBody:
```

As you can see in this pure machine code version, the translation of the elseif clause is very straightforward; the machine code for the elseif clause is identical to an if statement. The only thing to note here is how the compiler emits a jmp instruction at the end of the if..then clause to skip around the Boolean test emitted for the elseif clause.

14.5.1   Improving the Efficiency of Certain if/else Statements

From an efficiency point of view, the important thing to note about the if..else statement is that there is no path through the statement that doesn't involve a transfer of control (unlike the simple if statement, that simply falls through if the conditional expression is true). As this chapter points out repeatedly, branches are bad because they often flush the CPU's instruction pipeline and it takes several CPU cycles to refill the pipeline. If either outcome of the Boolean expression (True or False) is equally likely, there is little you can do to improve the performance of your code by rearranging the `if..else` statement. For most `if` statements, however, one outcome is often more likely—perhaps much more likely—than the other. Assembly coders who understand the likelihood of one comparison over another will often encode their `if..else` statements as follows:

```
// if( eax == ebx ) then
//    //<likely case>
//    stdout.put( "EAX is equal to EBX", nl );
// else
//    // unlikely case
//    stdout.put( "EAX is not equal to EBX" nl );
// endif;

    cmp( EAX, EBX );
    jne goDoElse;
    stdout.put( "EAX is equal to EBX", nl );
backFromElse:
        .
        .
        .
// Somewhere else in the code:

doElse:
    stdout.put( "EAX is not equal to EBX", nl );
    jmp backFromElse
```

Note that in the most common case (where the expression evaluates to True), the code falls through to the then section, which then falls straight through to the code that follows the entire `if` statement. Therefore, if the Boolean expression (EAX == EBX) is true most of the time, then this code executes straight through without any branches. In the rare case when EAX does not equal EBX, the program actually has to execute two branches, one to transfer control to the section of code that handles the `else` clause and one to return control back to the first statement following the `if`. As long as this occurs less than half of the time, the software sees an overall performance boost. You can achieve this same result in an HLL such as C using goto statements. For example:

```
if( eax != ebx ) goto doElseStuff;

    // << body of the if statement goes here>>
    // (statements between THEN and ELSE)

endOfIF:
// << statements following the IF..ENDIF statement >>
    .
    .
    .
doElseStuff:
    << Code to do if the expression is false >>
    goto endOfIF;
```

Of course, the drawback to this scheme is that it produces *spaghetti code* that becomes unreadable once you add more than a few of these kludges to your code. Assembly language programmers get away with this type of code because most assembly language code is, by definition, spaghetti code.[2] For HLL code, however, this type of coding is generally unacceptable programming style and you should use it only when necessary. (See Section 14.3, "The goto Statement.")

The following generic if statement is common in programs written in HLLs such as C:

```
if( eax == ebx )
{
    // Set i to some value along this execution path.

    i = j + 5;
}
else
{
    // Set i to a different value along this path

    i = 0;
}
```

Here's the conversion of this C code into 80x86/HLA assembly code:

```
        cmp( eax, ebx );
        jne doElse;
        mov( j, edx );
        add( 5, edx );
        mov( edx, i );
        jmp ifDone;

doElse:
        mov( 0, i );
ifDone:
```

As you've seen in previous examples, the if..then..else statement conversion to assembly language requires two transfer of control instructions:

- The jne instruction that tests the comparison between EAX and EBX

- The unconditional jmp instruction that skips over the else section of the if statement

Regardless of which path the program takes (through the then or the else section), the CPU executes a slow branch instruction that winds up flushing the instruction pipeline. Consider the following code that does not have this problem:

```
i = 0;
if( eax == ebx )
```

---

[2] Though it is quite easy to write structured code with an assembler such as HLA.

```
    {
        i = j + 5;
    }
```

Here is its conversion to pure 80x86 assembly code:

```
        mov( 0, i );
        cmp( eax, ebx );
        jne skipIf;
        mov( j, edx );
        add( 5, edx );
        mov( edx, i );
skipIf:
```

As you can see, if the expression evaluates to True, then the CPU
executes no transfer of control statements at all. True, the CPU will execute
an extra mov instruction whose result is immediately overwritten (so the
execution of the first mov instruction is wasted); however, the execution of
this extra mov instruction happens much more rapidly than the execution of
the jmp instruction. This trick is a prime example of why it's a good idea to
know some assembly language code (and know how compilers generate
machine code from high-level code). It's not at all obvious that the second
sequence is better than the first. Beginning programmers, in fact, would
probably believe it to be inferior because the program "wastes" an assignment to i when the expression evaluates to True (and no such assignment
is made in the first version). This is a prime example of why this chapter
exists—to make sure you understand the costs associated with using high-
level control structures.

14.5.2 Forcing Complete Boolean Evaluation in an if Statement

Because complete Boolean evaluation and short-circuit Boolean evaluation
can produce different results (see Section 13.7, "Short-Circuit Evaluation"),
there are times when you will need to ensure that your code uses one form or
the other when computing the result of a Boolean expression. In this
section, I'll discuss how to force complete Boolean evaluation even if the
language doesn't guarantee this form of computation.

The general way to force complete Boolean evaluation is to evaluate
each subcomponent of the expression and store the subresult into temporary variables. Then you can combine the temporary results after their
computation to produce the complete result. For example, consider the
following Pascal code fragment:

```
if( i < g(y) and k > f(x) ) then begin

    i := 0;

end;
```

Because Pascal does not guarantee complete Boolean evaluation, function f might not be called in this expression [if i is less than g(y)], and any side effects produced by the call to f might not occur. (See Section 13.3, "Side Effects in Arithmetic Expressions," to learn more about side effects.) If the logic of the application depends on any side effects produced by the calls to f and g, then you must ensure that this application calls both functions. Note that simply swapping the two subexpressions around the AND operator is insufficient to solve this problem; with that change the application might not call g.

One way to solve this problem is to compute the Boolean results of the two subexpressions using separate assignment statements and then compute the logical AND of the two results within the if expression:

```
lexpr := i < g(y);
rexpr := k > f(x);
if( lexpr AND rexpr ) then begin

    i := 0;

end;
```

Don't be too concerned about the efficiency loss that could occur because of the use of these temporary variables. Any compiler that provides optimization facilities is going to put these values into registers and not bother using actual memory locations (and if your compiler doesn't do this, then the efficiency loss associated with these two temporary variables is going to be the least of your concerns). Consider the following variant of the previous Pascal program written in C and compiled with the Borland C++ compiler:

```
#include <stdio.h>

static int i;
static int k;

extern int x;
extern int y;
extern int f( int );
extern int g( int );

int main( void )
{
    int lExpr;
    int rExpr;

    lExpr = i < g(y);
    rExpr = k > f(x);
    if( lExpr && rExpr )
    {
        printf( "Hello" );
    }
```

```
        return( 0 );
}
```

Here's the conversion to TASM code by Borland C++ compiler:

```
_main   proc    near
?live1@0:
    ;
    ;   int main( void )
    ;
@1:
    push        ebx
    ;
    ;   {
    ;           int lExpr;
    ;           int rExpr;
    ;
    ;           lExpr = i < g(y);
    ;
    mov         eax,dword ptr [_y]
    push        eax
    call        _g
    pop         ecx
    cmp         eax,dword ptr [_i]
    setg        bl
    and         ebx,1
    ;
    ;           rExpr = k > f(x);
    ;
?live1@32: ; EBX = lExpr
    mov         eax,dword ptr [_x]
    push        eax
    call        _f
    pop         ecx
    cmp         eax,dword ptr [_k]
    setl        al
    and         eax,1
    ;
    ;           if( lExpr && rExpr )
    ;
?live1@48: ; EBX = lExpr, EAX = rExpr
    test        ebx,ebx
    je          short @2
    test        eax,eax
    je          short @2
    ;
    ;           {
    ;               printf( "Hello" );
    ;
?live1@64: ;
    push        offset s@
    call        _printf
    pop         ecx
```

```
    ;
    ;          }
    ;
    ;          return( 0 );
    ;
@2:
    xor        eax,eax
    ;
    ;    }
    ;
@4:
@3:
    pop        ebx
    ret
_main    endp
```

If you scan through the assembly code, you'll see that this code fragment always executes the calls to both f and g. Contrast this with the following C code and assembly output:

```
#include <stdio.h>

static int i;
static int k;

extern int x;
extern int y;
extern int f( int );
extern int g( int );

int main( void )
{
    if( i < g(y) && k > f(x) )
    {
        printf( "Hello" );
    }

    return( 0 );
}
```

Here's the TASM assembly output:

```
_main    proc    near
?live1@0:
    ;
    ;    int main( void )
    ;    {
    ;        if( i < g(y) && k > f(x) )
    ;
@1:
    mov        eax,dword ptr [_y]
    push       eax
    call       _g
```

```
        pop     ecx
        cmp     eax,dword ptr [_i]
        jle     short @2

; Note that the branch above may cause this code
; sequence to skip the call to the _f function.

        mov     edx,dword ptr [_x]
        push    edx
        call    _f
        pop     ecx
        cmp     eax,dword ptr [_k]
        jge     short @2
;
;               {
;                   printf( "Hello" );
;
        push    offset s@
        call    _printf
        pop     ecx
;
;               }
;
;           return( 0 );
;
@2:
        xor     eax,eax
;
;       }
;
@4:
@3:
        ret
_main   endp
```

In the C programming language, you can use another trick to force complete Boolean evaluation in *any* Boolean expression. The C bitwise operators do not support short-circuit Boolean evaluation. If your subexpressions in a Boolean expression always produce 0 or 1, the bitwise Boolean conjunction and disjunction operators (i.e., & and |) produce identical results to the logical Boolean operators (&& and ||). Consider the following C code and the TASM code that Borland's C++ compiler produces:

```
#include <stdio.h>

static int i;
static int k;

extern int x;
extern int y;
extern int f( int );
extern int g( int );
```

```
int main( void )
{
    if(( i < g(y)) & k > f(x) )
    {
        printf( "Hello" );
    }
    return( 0 );
}
```

Here's the TASM code produced by Borland's C++ compiler:

```
_main     proc     near
?live1@0:
    ;
    ;       int main( void )
    ;
@1:
        push      ebx
    ;
    ;       {
    ;               if( i < g(y) & k > f(x) )
    ;
        mov       eax,dword ptr [_y]
        push      eax
        call      _g
        pop       ecx
        cmp       eax,dword ptr [_i]
        setg      bl
        and       ebx,1
        mov       eax,dword ptr [_x]
        push      eax
        call      _f
        pop       ecx
        cmp       eax,dword ptr [_k]
        setl      dl
        and       edx,1
        and       ebx,edx
        je        short @2
    ;
    ;               {
    ;                       printf( "Hello" );
    ;
        push      offset s@
        call      _printf
        pop       ecx
    ;
    ;               }
    ;
    ;               return( 0 );
    ;
@2:
        xor       eax,eax
    ;
    ;       }
```

```
        ;
@4:
@3:
        pop     ebx
        ret
_main   endp
```

Note how the use of the bitwise operators produces comparable code to the earlier sequence that used temporary variables. This creates less clutter in your original C source file.

Do keep in mind, however, that C's bitwise operators only produce the same results as the logical operators if the operands are 0 and 1. Fortunately, you can use a little C trick to convert any zero/nonzero logical value to 0 and 1. Just write !!(expr) and C will convert the result to 0 or 1 if the expression's value is zero or nonzero. To see this in action, consider the following C/C++ code fragment:

```
#include <stdlib.h>
#include <math.h>
#include <stdio.h>

int main( int argc, char **argv )
{
    int boolResult;

    boolResult = !!argc;
    printf( "!!(argc) = %d\n", boolResult );
    return 0;
}
```

Here's the 80x86 assembly code that Microsoft's Visual C++ compiler produces for this short program:

```
; Line 9
;
; ECX = argc

    mov ecx, DWORD PTR _argc$[esp-4]

; EAX (32 bits) = 0;

    xor eax, eax

; Is ARGC (ECX) zero or nonzero?
; Set zero flag if it is, clear zero
; flag if it is not.

    test    ecx, ecx

; Set AL (and, therefore, EAX) to zero
; if ARGC (ECX) was zero, set AL (EAX)
; to one if ARGC was nonzero:
```

```
        setne   al

; Line 10
; print the value of boolResult (in EAX):

        push    eax
        push    OFFSET FLAT:formatString
        call    _printf
        add esp, 8
```

As you can see in the 80x86 assembly output, only three machine instructions (involving no expensive branches) are needed to convert "zero/nonzero" to 0/1.

14.5.3 Forcing Short-Circuit Boolean Evaluation in an if Statement

Although being able to force complete Boolean evaluation on occasion is important, the need for short-circuit evaluation is probably more common. Consider the following Pascal statement:

```
if( ptrVar <> NIL AND ptrVar^ < 0 ) then begin

    ptrVar^ := 0;

end;
```

The Pascal language definition leaves it up to whomever writes the compiler to decide whether to use complete Boolean evaluation or short-circuit evaluation. In fact, the compiler's author is free to use both schemes whenever they feel like it. So it's quite possible that the same compiler could use complete Boolean evaluation for the statement above in one section of the code and short-circuit evaluation in another. Running a few tests on your Pascal compiler does not provide any guarantees about how that compiler will operate.

It should be clear that this Boolean expression will fail if ptrVar contains the NIL pointer value and if the compiler uses complete Boolean evaluation. The only way for this statement to work properly is by using short-circuit Boolean evaluation.

Simulating short-circuit Boolean evaluation with the AND operator is actually quite simple. All you have to do is create a pair of nested if statements and place each subexpression in each one. For example, you could guarantee short-circuit Boolean evaluation in the current Pascal example by rewriting it as follows:

```
if( ptrVar <> NIL ) then begin

    if( ptrVar^ < 0 ) then begin

        ptrVar^ := 0;
```

```
              end;

       end;
```

This statement is semantically identical to the previous one. It should be clear that the second subexpression will not execute if the first expression evaluates to False. Even though this approach clutters up the source file a little bit, it does guarantee short-circuit evaluation regardless of whether the compiler supports this.

Handling the logical OR operation is a little more difficult. Guaranteeing that the right operand of a logical OR does not execute if the left operand evaluates to True requires an extra test. Consider the following C code (remember that C supports short-circuit evaluation by default):

```c
#include <stdio.h>

static int i;
static int k;

extern int x;
extern int y;
extern int f( int );
extern int g( int );

int main( void )
{
    if( i < g(y) || k > f(x) )
    {
        printf( "Hello" );
    }

    return( 0 );
}
```

Here's the machine code that the Microsoft Visual C++ compiler produces for this C code:

```asm
_main   PROC NEAR                                          ; COMDAT
; File t.c
; Line 13
;
; if( i < g(y)

        mov     eax, DWORD PTR _y
        push    eax
        call    _g
        mov     ecx, DWORD PTR _i
        add     esp, 4
        cmp     ecx, eax
        jl      SHORT $L403
```

```
;       || k > f(x) )

        mov     ecx, DWORD PTR _x
        push    ecx
        call    _f
        mov     ecx, DWORD PTR _k
        add     esp, 4
        cmp     ecx, eax
        jle     SHORT $L410

; {
;    printf( "Hello" );
;
$L403:
; Line 15
        push    OFFSET FLAT:??_C@_05DPEH@Hello?$AA@ ; 'string'
        call    _printf
        add     esp, 4
$L410:
; Line 18
        xor     eax, eax
; Line 19
        ret     0
_main   ENDP
```

Here's a version of the C program that implements short-circuit evaluation without relying on the C compiler to do this (not that this is necessary for C, as the C language definition guarantees short-circuit evaluation, but this code does demonstrate the approach you could use in any language):

```
#include <stdio.h>

static int i;
static int k;

extern int x;
extern int y;
extern int f( int );
extern int g( int );

int main( void )
{
    int temp;

        // Compute left subexpression and
        // save.

    temp = i < g(y);

        // If the left subexpression
        // evaluates to False, then try
        // the right subexpression.

    if( !temp )
```

```
    {
        temp = k > f(x);
    }

        // If either subexpression evaluates
        // to True, then print "Hello"

        if( temp )
    {
        printf( "Hello" );
    }

    return( 0 );
}
```

Here's the corresponding MASM code emitted by the Microsoft Visual C++ compiler:

```
_main    PROC NEAR                                    ; COMDAT
; File t.c
; Line 15:
;
;  temp = i < g(y); // EAX is used to hold temp.

        mov     eax, DWORD PTR _y
        push    eax
        call    _g
        mov     edx, DWORD PTR _i
        add     esp, 4
        xor     ecx, ecx
        cmp     edx, eax
        setl    cl
        mov     eax, ecx


; Line 16
;
;  if( !temp )
;  {
        test    eax, eax
        jne     SHORT $L411

; Line 18
;
;     temp = k > f(x);  // EAX (ultimately) is temp.

        mov     edx, DWORD PTR _x
        push    edx
        call    _f
        mov     edx, DWORD PTR _k
        add     esp, 4
        xor     ecx, ecx
        cmp     edx, eax
        setg    cl
        mov     eax, ecx
```

```
; Line 20
;
; if( temp )
; {

        test    eax, eax
        je      SHORT $L412
$L411:
; Line 22
;
;     printf( "Hello" );

        push    OFFSET FLAT:??_C@_05DPEH@Hello?$AA@ ; 'string'
        call    _printf
        add     esp, 4

; }
$L412:
; Line 25
;
; return 0;
        xor     eax, eax
; Line 26
        ret     0
_main   ENDP
```

As you can see in this example, the code the compiler emits for the second version of the routine, which manually forces short-circuit evaluation, isn't quite as good as that emitted by the C compiler for the first example. However, if you need the semantics for short-circuit evaluation so the program will execute correctly, you'll have to live with possibly less-efficient code than you'd get if the compiler supported this facility directly.

If speed, minimal size, and short-circuit evaluation are all three necessary, and you're willing to sacrifice a little readability and maintainability in your code to achieve them, then you can destructure the code and create something that is comparable to what the C compiler produces using short-circuit evaluation. Consider the following C code and the output of the Microsoft Visual C++ compiler:

```
#include <stdio.h>

static int i;
static int k;

extern int x;
extern int y;
extern int f( int );
extern int g( int );

int main( void )
```

```
{
    if( i < g(y)) goto IntoIF;
    if( k > f(x) )
    {
      IntoIF:

        printf( "Hello" );
    }

    return( 0 );
}
```

Here's the MASM output from Visual C++:

```
_main   PROC NEAR
; File t.c
; Line 13
        mov     eax, DWORD PTR _y
        push    eax
        call    _g
        mov     ecx, DWORD PTR _i
        add     esp, 4
        cmp     ecx, eax
        jl      SHORT $IntoIF$403
; Line 14
        mov     ecx, DWORD PTR _x
        push    ecx
        call    _f
        mov     ecx, DWORD PTR _k
        add     esp, 4
        cmp     ecx, eax
        jle     SHORT $L411
$IntoIF$403:
; Line 18
        push    OFFSET FLAT:formatString
        call    _printf
        add     esp, 4
$L411:
; Line 21
        xor     eax, eax
; Line 22
        ret     0
_main   ENDP
```

If you compare this code to the MASM output for the original C example
(that relies on short-circuit evaluation), you'll see that this code is just as
efficient. This is a classic example of why there was considerable resistance to
structured programming in the 1970s—sometimes the structured programming approach leads to less-efficient code. Of course, readability and maintainability are usually more important than a few bytes or machine cycles.
But never forget that if performance is paramount for a small section of
code, destructuring that code can improve efficiency in some special cases.

14.6 The switch/case Statement

The switch (or case) high-level control statement is another conditional statement found in HLLs. An if statement tests a Boolean expression and executes one of two different paths in the code based on the result of the expression. A switch/case statement, on the other hand, can branch to one of several different points in the code based on the result of an ordinal (integer) expression. The following examples demonstrate the switch and case statements in C/C++, Pascal, and HLA. First, the C/C++ switch statement:

```
switch( expression )
{
  case 0:
    << statements to execute if the
        expression evaluates to zero >>
    break;

  case 1:
    << statements to execute if the
        expression evaluates to one >>
    break;

  case 2:
    << statements to execute if the
        expression evaluates to two >>
    break;

  <<etc>>

  default:
    << statements to execute if the expression is
        not equal to any of these cases >>
}
```

Here is an example of a Pascal case statement:

```
case ( expression ) of
  0: begin
    << statements to execute if the
        expression evaluates to zero >>
    end;

  1: begin
    << statements to execute if the
        expression evaluates to one >>
    end;

  2: begin
    << statements to execute if the
        expression evaluates to two >>
    end;
```

```
    <<etc>>

end; (* case *)
```

And finally, here is the HLA switch statement:

```
switch( REG32 )

  case( 0 )
    << statements to execute if
        EAX contains zero >>

  case( 1 )
    << statements to execute
        REG32 contains one >>

  case( 2 )
    << statements to execute if
        REG32 contains two >>

  <<etc>>

  default
    << statements to execute if
        REG32 is not equal to any of these cases >>

endswitch;
```

As you can tell by these examples, these statement all share a similar syntax.

14.6.1   Semantics of a switch/case Statement

In most beginning programming classes and textbooks, the semantics of the switch/case statement are taught by comparing this statement with a chain of if..else..if statements. This is done in order to introduce the switch/case statement using a concept the student already understands. To see why this approach can be misleading, consider the following code, which an introductory book on Pascal programming might claim is equivalent to our Pascal case statement:

```
if( expression = 0 ) then begin

  << statements to execute if expression is zero >>

end
else if( expression = 1 ) then begin

  << statements to execute if expression is one >>

end
else if( expression = 2 ) then begin
```

```
        << statements to execute if expression is two >>

    end;
```

Although this particular sequence will achieve the same result as the case statement, there are several fundamental differences between the if..then..elseif sequence and the case implementation. First, the case labels in a case statement must all be constants, in an if..then.elseif chain you can actually compare variables and other nonconstant values against the control variable. Another limitation of the switch/case statement is that you may only compare the value of a single expression against a set of constants; you cannot compare one expression against a constant for one case and a separate expression against a second constant as you can with an if..then..elseif chain. The reason for these limitations will become clear in a moment, but the important thing to note is that an if..then..elseif chain is semantically different from a switch/case statement (and more powerful).

14.6.2 Jump Tables Versus Chained Comparisons

Although a switch/case statement is arguably more readable and convenient than an if..then..elseif chain, this type of statement was orginally added to an HLL for efficiency, not readability or convenience. Consider an if..then..elseif chain with ten separate expressions to test. If all the cases are mutually exclusive and equally likely, then on the average the program will execute five comparisons before encountering an expression that evaluates to True. In assembly language, it's possible to transfer control to one of several different locations in a fixed amount of time, independent of the number of cases, by using a table lookup and an indirect jump. Effectively, such code uses the value of the switch/case expression as an index into a table of addresses and then jumps (indirectly) to the statement specified by the table entry. When you have more than about three or four cases, this scheme is typically faster and consumes less memory than the corresponding if..then..elseif chain. Consider the following simple implementation of a switch/case statement in assembly language:

```
// Conversion of
//    switch(i)
//    { case 0:...case 1:...case 2:...case 3:...}
// into assembly

static
  jmpTable: dword[4] :=
    { &label0, &label1, &label2, &label3 };
        .
        .
        .
```

```
    // jmps to address specified by jmpTable[i]

    mov( i, eax );
    jmp( jmpTable[ eax*4 ] );

label0:
    << code to execute if i = 0 >>
    jmp switchDone;

label1:
    << code to execute if i = 1 >>
    jmp switchDone;

label2:
    << code to execute if i = 2 >>
    jmp switchDone;

label3:
    << code to execute if i = 3 >>

switchDone:
    << Code that follows the switch statement >>
```

To see how this code operates, I'll describe its operation one instruction at a time. The jmpTable declaration defines an array of four double-word pointers, one pointer for each case in our switch statement emulation. Entry 0 holds the address of the statement to jump to when the switch expression evaluates to 0, entry 1 of this array contains the address of the statement to execute with the switch expression evaluates to 1, and so on. Note that the array must have one element whose index matches each of the possible cases in the switch statement (0 through 3 in this particular example).

The first machine instruction in this example code loads the value of the switch expression (variable i's value) into the EAX register. Because this code uses the value of the switch expression as an index into the jmpTable array, this value must be an ordinal (integer) value in an 80x86 32-bit register. The next instruction (jmp) does the real work of the switch statement emulation: It jumps to the address specified by the entry found in the jmpTable array, indexed by EAX. If EAX contains 0 upon execution of this jmp statement, the program fetches the double word from jmpTable[0] and transfers control to that address; this is the address of the first instruction following the label0 label in the program code. If EAX contains 1, then the jmp instruction fetches the double word at address jmpTable + 4 in memory (note that the *4 scaled-indexed addressing mode is in use in this code; see Section 3.6.5, "Indexed Addressing Mode," for more details). Likewise, if EAX contains 2 or 3, then the jmp instruction transfers control to the double-word address held at jmpTable + 8 or jmpTable + 12 (respectively). Because the jmpTable array is initialized with the addresses of label0, label1, label2, and label3, at respective offsets 0, 4, 8, and 12, this particular indirect jmp instruction will transfer control to the statement at the label corresponding to i's value (label0, label1, label2, or label3, respectively).

The first thing of interest to note about this switch statement emulation is that it only requires two machine instructions (and a jump table) to transfer control to any of the four possible cases. Contrast this with an if..then..elseif implementation that will require at least two machine instructions for each case. Indeed, as you add additional cases to the if..then..elseif implementation, the number of compare and conditional branch instructions increases, yet the number of machine instructions for the jump table implementation remains fixed at two (even though the size of the jump table increases by one entry for each case). As such, the if..then..elseif implementation gets progressively slower as you add more cases while the jump table implementation takes a constant amount of time to execute (regardless of the number of cases). Assuming your HLL compiler uses a jump table implementation for switch statements, a switch statement will typically be much faster than an if..then..elseif sequence if there are a large number of cases.

The jump table implementation of switch statements does have a couple of drawbacks. First, because the jump table is an array in memory and accessing (noncached) memory can be slow, accessing the jump table array could possibly impair system performance.

Another problem with the jump table implementation is that you must have one entry in the table for every possible case between the largest and the smallest case values, including those values for which you haven't actually supplied an explicit case. In the example up to this point, this hasn't been an issue because the case values started with 0 and were contiguous through 3. However, consider the following Pascal case statement:

```
case( i ) of

    0: begin
        << statements to execute if i = 0 >>
       end;

    1: begin
        << statements to execute if i = 1 >>
       end;

    5: begin
        << statements to execute if i = 5 >>
       end;

    8: begin
        << statements to execute if i = 8 >>
       end;

end; (* case *)
```

We cannot implement this case statement with a jump table containing four entries. If the value of i were 0 or 1, then it would fetch the correct address. However, for case five, the index into the jump table would be 20 (5*4), not 8. If the jump table contained only four entries (16 bytes), indexing into the jump table using the value 20 (5*4) would grab an address beyond the end of the table and would likely crash the application. This is exactly why in the original definition of Pascal, the results were undefined if the program supplied a case value that was not present in the set of labels for a particular case statement.

To solve this problem in assembly language, a programmer should make sure there are entries for each of the possible case labels as well as all values in between the case labels. In the current example, the jump table would need nine entries to handle all the possible case values 0 through 8:

```
// Conversion of
//    switch(i)
//    { case 0:...case 1:...case 5:...case 8:}
// into assembly

static
  jmpTable: dword[9] :=
          {
            &label0, &label1, &switchDone,
            &switchDone, &switchDone,
            &label5, &switchDone, &switchDone,
            &label8
          };
       .
       .
       .

    // jumps to address specified by jmpTable[i]

    mov( i, eax );
    jmp( jmpTable[ eax*4 ] );

label0:
    << code to execute if i = 0 >>
    jmp switchDone;

label1:
    << code to execute if i = 1 >>
    jmp switchDone;

label5:
    << code to execute if i = 5 >>
    jmp switchDone;

label8:
    << code to execute if i = 8 >>

switchDone:
  << Code that follows the switch statement >>
```

Notice that if i is equal to 2, 3, 4, 6, or 7, then this code transfers control to the first statement beyond the switch statement (e.g., the standard semantics for C's switch statement and the case statement in most modern variants of Pascal). Of course, C will also transfer control to this point in the code if the switch/case expression value is greater than the largest case value. Most compilers implement this feature with a comparison and conditional branch immediately before the indirect jump. For example:

```
// Conversion of
//    switch(i)
//    { case 0:...case 1:...case 5:...case 8:}
// into assembly, that automatically
// handles values greater than eight.

static
  jmpTable: dword[9] :=
          {
            &label0, &label1, &switchDone,
            &switchDone, &switchDone,
            &label5, &switchDone, &switchDone,
            &label8
          };
          .
          .
          .

    // Check to see if the value is outside the range
    //  of values allowed by this switch/case stmt.

    mov( i, eax );
    cmp( eax, 8 );
    ja switchDone;

    // jmps to address specified by jmpTable[i]

    jmp( jmpTable[ eax*4 ] );

          .
          .
          .


switchDone:
  << Code that follows the switch statement >>
```

You may have noticed another assumption that this code is making—that the case values start at zero. Modifying the code to handle an arbitrary range of case values is simple. Consider the following code:

```
// Conversion of
//    switch(i)
//    { case 10:...case 11:...case 12:...case 15:...case 16:}
// into assembly, that automatically handles values
// greater than 16 and values less than 10.

static
  jmpTable: dword[7] :=
          {
            &label10, &label11, &label12,
```

```
                    &switchDone, &switchDone,
                    &label15, &label16
                 };

             .
             .
             .

        // Check to see if the value is outside the
        //   range 10..16.

        mov( i, eax );
        cmp( eax, 10 );
        jb switchDone;
        cmp( eax, 16 );
        ja switchDone;

        // The "- 10*4" part of the following expression
        // adjusts for the fact that EAX starts at 10
        // rather than zero, we still need a zero-based
        // index into our array.

        jmp( jmpTable[ eax*4 - 10*4] );

             .
             .
             .


switchDone:
   << Code that follows the switch statement >>
```

There are two differences between this example and the previous one. First, of course, this one compares the value in EAX against the range 10..16 and branches to the switchDone label if the value in EAX falls outside this range (in other words, there is no case label for the value in EAX). The second difference you will notice is that the jmpTable index has been modified to be [eax*4 - 10*4]. Arrays at the machine level always begin at index 0; the - 10*4 component of this expression adjusts for the fact that EAX actually contains a value starting at 10 rather than 0. Effectively, this expression makes jmpTable start 40 bytes earlier in memory than its declaration states. Because EAX is always 10 or greater (40 bytes or greater because of the eax*4 component), this code begins accessing table at its declared beginning location. Note that HLA subtracts this offset from the address of jmpTable; the CPU doesn't actually perform this subtraction at runtime. Hence, there is no additional efficiency loss to create this zero-based index.

You'll notice that a fully generalized switch/case statement actually requires six instructions to implement: the original two instructions plus four instructions to test the range.[3] This, plus the fact that an indirect jump is slightly more expensive to execute than a conditional branch, is why the break-even point for a switch/case statement (versus an if..then..elseif chain) is around three to four cases.

---

[3] Actually, with a little assembly language trickery, a good programmer or compiler can reduce this from four to three machine instructions.

One serious drawback to the jump table implementation of the switch/case statement is the fact that you must have one table entry for every possible value between the smallest case and the largest case. Consider the following C/C++ switch statement:

```
switch( i )
{
  case 0:
      << statements to execute if i == 0 >>
      break;

  case 1:
      << statements to execute if i == 1 >>
      break;

  case 10:
      << statements to execute if i == 10 >>
      break;

  case 100:
      << statements to execute if i == 100 >>
      break;

  case 1000:
      << statements to execute if i == 1000 >>
      break;

  case 10000:
      << statements to execute if i == 10000 >>
      break;
}
```

If the C/C++ compiler implements this switch statement using a jump table, that table will require 10,001 entries (i.e., 40,004 bytes of memory). That's quite a chunk of memory for such a simple statement! Although the wide separation of the cases has a major effect on memory usage, it has only a minor effect on the execution speed of the switch statement. The program executes the same four instructions it would execute if the values were all contiguous (only four instructions are necessary because the cases start at zero, so there is no need to check the switch expression against a lower bound). Indeed, the only reason there is a performance difference at all is because of the effects of the table size on the cache (it's less likely you will find a particular table entry in the cache when the table is large). Speed issues aside, the memory usage by the jump table is difficult to justify for most applications. Therefore, if you know that your particular compiler emits a jump table for all switch/case statements (by looking at the code it produces), then you should be careful about creating switch/case statements whose cases are widely separated.

14.6.3 Other Implementations of switch/case

Because of the issue with jump table sizes, some HLL compilers do not implement switch/case statements using jump tables. Some compilers will simply convert a switch/case statement into the corresponding if..then..elseif chain. Obviously, such compilers tend to produce low-quality code (from a speed point of view) whenever a jump table would be appropriate. Many modern compilers are relatively smart about their code generation. They'll determine the number of cases in a switch/case statement and also determine the spread of the case values. Then the compiler will choose a jump table or if..then..elseif implementation based on some threshold criteria (code size versus speed). Some compilers might even use a combination of techniques. For example, consider the following Pascal case statement:

```
case( i ) of
  0: begin
      << statements to execute if i = 0 >>
     end;

  1: begin
      << statements to execute if i = 1 >>
     end;

  2: begin
      << statements to execute if i = 2 >>
     end;

  3: begin
      << statements to execute if i = 3 >>
     end;

  4: begin
      << statements to execute if i = 4 >>
     end;

  1000: begin
      << statements to execute if i = 1000 >>
        end;
end; (* case *)
```

A good compiler will recognize that the majority of the cases work well in a jump table with only one (or a few) cases proving to be the exception. Such a compiler will translate this to a sequence of instructions that is a combination of the if..then and jump table implementation. For example:

```
mov( i, eax );
cmp( eax, 4 );
ja try1000;
jmp( jmpTable[ eax*4 ] );
   .
   .
   .
```

```
try1000:
    cmp( eax, 1000 );
    jne switchDone;
    << code to do if i = 1000 >>
switchDone:
```

Although the switch/case statement was originally created to allow the use of an efficient jump table transfer mechanism in an HLL, there are few language definitions that require a specific implementation for a control structure. Therefore, unless you stick with a specific compiler and you know how that compiler generates code under all circumstances, there is absolutely no guarantee that your switch/case statements will compile to a jump table, an if..then..elseif chain, some combination of the two, or something else entirely. For example, consider the following short C program and the 80x86 assembly output that the Borland C++ compiler emits for it:

```
extern void f( void );
extern void g( void );
extern void h( void );
int main( int argc, char **argv )
{
    int boolResult;

    switch( argc )
    {
        case 1:
            f();
            break;

        case 2:
            g();
            break;

        case 10:
            h();
            break;

        case 11:
            f();
            break;

    }
    return 0;
}
```

Here's the 80x86 output from the Borland C++ compiler:

```
_main   proc    near
?live1@0:
    ;
    ;   int main( int argc, char **argv )
    ;
```

```
@1:
    push        ebp
    mov         ebp,esp
    ;
    ;       {
    ;           int boolResult;
    ;
    ;           switch( argc )
    ;

; Is ARGC == 1?

    mov         eax,dword ptr [ebp+8]
    dec         eax
    je          short @7

; Is ARGC == 2?

    dec         eax
    je          short @6

; Is ARGC == 10?

    sub         eax,8
    je          short @5

; Is ARGC == 11?

    dec         eax
    je          short @4

; If none of the above

    jmp         short @2
    ;
    ;           {
    ;               case 1:
    ;                   f();
    ;
@7:
    call        _f
    ;
    ;                   break;
    ;
    jmp         short @8
    ;
    ;
    ;               case 2:
    ;                   g();
    ;
@6:
    call        _g
    ;
    ;                   break;
    ;
```

```
        jmp     short @8
    ;
    ;
    ;           case 10:
    ;               h();
    ;
@5:
    call    _h
    ;
    ;               break;
    ;
        jmp     short @8
    ;
    ;
    ;           case 11:
    ;               f();
    ;
@4:
    call    _f
    ;
    ;               break;
    ;
    ;       }
    ;           return 0;
    ;
@2:
@8:
    xor     eax,eax
    ;
    ;   }
    ;
@10:
@9:
    pop     ebp
    ret
_main   endp
```

As you can see at the beginning of the main program, this code compares the value in argc against the four values (1, 2, 10, and 11) in a sequential fashion. For a switch statement as small as this one, this isn't a bad implementation.

Many modern optimizing compilers will generate a binary search tree to test the cases when there are a fair number of cases and a jump table would be too large. For example, consider the following C program and the output from the MSVC compiler:

```
#include <stdio.h>

extern void f( void );
int main( int argc, char **argv )
{
    int boolResult;
```

```c
    switch( argc )
    {
        case 1:
            f();
            break;

        case 10:
            f();
            break;

        case 100:
            f();
            break;

        case 1000:
            f();
            break;

        case 10000:
            f();
            break;

        case 100000:
            f();
            break;

        case 1000000:
            f();
            break;

        case 10000000:
            f();
            break;

        case 100000000:
            f();
            break;

        case 1000000000:
            f();
            break;

    }
    return 0;
}
```

Here's the MASM output from the MSVC compiler. Note how Microsoft's compiler generates a binary search through each of the ten cases:

```asm
_main   PROC NEAR                    ; COMDAT
; File t.c
; Line 11
;
; Binary search. Is argc less or greater than 100,000?
```

```
      mov eax, DWORD PTR _argc$[esp-4]
      cmp eax, 100000              ; 000186a0H
      jg  SHORT $L1242
      je  SHORT $L1228

; Binary search: is argc less than 100 or
; greater than 100 (but less than 100,000)

      cmp eax, 100                 ; 00000064H
      jg  SHORT $L1243
      je  SHORT $L1228

; Is argc == 1?

      dec eax
      je  SHORT $L1228

; is argc == 10? If not, branch to default
; case.

      sub eax, 9
      jne SHORT $L1225

; argc == 10 at this point.
;
; Line 49
      call     _f
; Line 53
      xor eax, eax
; Line 54
      ret 0

; Cases where argc is greater than 100
; but less than 100,000 (1,000 & 10,000)

$L1243:
; Line 11
      cmp eax, 1000
      je  SHORT $L1228
      cmp eax, 10000
      jne SHORT $L1225     ;Default case
; Line 49
      call     _f
; Line 53
      xor eax, eax
; Line 54
      ret 0

;Cases where argc is greater than 100,000

$L1242:
```

```
; Line 11
; Above or below 100,000,000?

    cmp eax, 100000000
    jg  SHORT $L1244
    je  SHORT $L1228    ;100,000,000

; Below 100,000,000 and above 10,000

    cmp eax, 1000000    ;1,000,000
    je  SHORT $L1228
    cmp eax, 10000000   ;10,000,000
    jne SHORT $L1225    ;Default case

; Line 49
    call    _f
; Line 53
    xor eax, eax
; Line 54
    ret 0

; Handle the case where it's 1,000,000,000
$L1244:
; Line 11
    cmp eax, 1000000000
    jne SHORT $L1225
$L1228:
; Line 49
    call    _f

; Default case and BREAK come down here:

$L1225:
; Line 53
    xor eax, eax
; Line 54
    ret 0
_main   ENDP
_TEXT   ENDS
END
```

Borland's compiler also generates a binary search for this example.

Some compilers, especially those for some microcontroller devices, will generate a table of 2-tuples (records/structures) with one element of the tuple being the value of the case and the second element being the address to jump to if the value matches. Then the compiler emits a loop that scans through this little table searching for the current switch/case expression value. If this is a linear search, then this implementation is even slower than the if..then..elseif chain. If the compiler emits a binary search, then the code may be faster than an if..then.elseif chain (although probably not as fast as a jump table implementation).

Sometimes, compilers will resort to some code tricks to generate marginally better code under certain circumstances. Consider again the short switch statement that led the Borland compiler to produce a linear search:

```
switch( argc )
    {
        case 1:
            f();
            break;

        case 2:
            g();
            break;

        case 10:
            h();
            break;

        case 11:
            f();
            break;

    }
```

Here's the code that the Microsoft Visual C++ compiler generates for this switch statement:

```
; File t.c
; Line 13
;
; Use ARGC as an index into the $L1240 table,
; which returns an offset into the $L1241 table:

    mov eax, DWORD PTR _argc$[esp-4]
    dec eax         ;--argc, 1 = 0, 2 = 1, 10 = 9, 11 = 10
    cmp eax, 10     ;Out of range of cases?
    ja  SHORT $L1229
    xor ecx, ecx
    mov cl, BYTE PTR $L1240[eax]
    jmp DWORD PTR $L1241[ecx*4]

    npad    3
$L1241:
    DD  $L1232   ;cases that call f
    DD  $L1233   ;cases that call g
    DD  $L1234   ;cases that call h
    DD  $L1229   ;Default case

$L1240:
    DB  0    ;case 1 calls f
    DB  1    ;case 2 calls g
    DB  3    ;default
```

```
        DB  3    ;default
        DB  3    ;default
        DB  3    ;default
        DB  3    ;default
        DB  3    ;default
        DB  3    ;default
        DB  2    ;case 10 calls h
        DB  0    ;case 11 calls f

; Here is the code for the various cases:

$L1233:
; Line 19
    call    _g
; Line 31
    xor eax, eax
; Line 32
    ret 0


$L1234:
; Line 23
    call    _h
; Line 31
    xor eax, eax
; Line 32
    ret 0


$L1232:
; Line 27
    call    _f
$L1229:
; Line 31
    xor eax, eax
; Line 32
    ret 0
```

The trick in this 80x86 code is that MSVC first does a table lookup to make an argc value in the range 1..11 to a value in the range 0..3 (that corresponds to the three different code bodies appearing in the cases, plus a default case). This code is shorter than a jump table (with the corresponding double-word entries mapping to the default case), although it is a little slower than the jump table because it needs to access two different tables in memory. As for how the speed of this code compares with a binary search or linear search, that research is left up to you (the answer will probably vary by processor).

Few compilers give you the option of explicitly specifying how the compiler will translate a specific switch/case statement. For example, if you really want the switch statement with cases 0, 1, 10, 100, 1,000, and 10,000 given earlier to generate a jump table, you'll have to write the code in assembly language or use a specific compiler whose code generation traits you understand. Certainly, any HLL code you've written that depends on the compiler generating a jump table is not going to be portable to other compilers because few languages specify the actual machine-code implementation of high-level control structures.

Of course, you don't have to totally rely on the compiler to generate decent code for a switch/case statement. Assuming your compiler uses the jump table implementation for all switch/case statements, you can help the compiler produce better code when modifications to your HLL source code would generate a huge jump table. For example, consider the switch statement given earlier with the cases 0, 1, 2, 3, 4, and 1,000. If your compiler generates a jump table with 1,001 entries (consuming a little more than 4KB of memory), you can help the compiler generate better code by writing the following Pascal code:

```
if( i = 1000 ) then begin

   << statements to execute if i = 1000 >>

end
else begin

  case( i ) of
    0: begin
        << statements to execute if i = 0 >>
       end;

    1: begin
        << statements to execute if i = 1 >>
       end;

    2: begin
        << statements to execute if i = 2 >>
       end;

    3: begin
        << statements to execute if i = 3 >>
       end;

    4: begin
        << statements to execute if i = 4 >>
       end;
  end; (* case *)
end; (* if *)
```

By handling case value 1,000 outside the switch statement, the compiler can produce a short jump table for the main cases, which are contiguous.

Another possibility (which is arguably easier to read) is the following C/C++ code:

```
switch( i )
{
   case 0:
```

```
        << statements to execute if i == 0 >>
        break;

    case 1:
        << statements to execute if i == 1 >>
        break;

    case 2:
        << statements to execute if i == 2 >>
        break;

    case 3:
        << statements to execute if i == 3 >>
        break;

    case 4:
        << statements to execute if i == 4 >>
      break;

    default:
      if( i == 1000 )
      {
        << statements to execute if i == 1000 >>
      }
      else
      {
        << Statements to execute if none of the cases match >>
      }
  }
```

The difference that makes this code slightly easier to read is that the code for the case when i is equal to 1,000 has been moved into the switch statement (thanks to the default clause), so it doesn't appear to be separate from all the tests taking place in the switch.

Some compilers simply won't generate a jump table for a switch/case statement. Obviously, there is little you can do (short of dropping into assembly language) if you're using such a compiler and you want to generate a jump table. On the other hand, if your compiler does not generate jump tables for switch/case statements, chances are good that this is one of the least of your optimization problems (i.e., the compiler probably generates poor code for other statements as well).

Although jump table implementations of switch/case statements are generally efficient when you have a fair number of cases and each case is equally likely, do keep in mind that an if..then..elseif chain can be faster if one or two cases are far more likely than the other cases. For example, if some variable has the value 15 more than half the time, the value 20 about a quarter of the time, and one of several other different values the remaining 25 percent of the time, it's probably more efficient to implement the multi-way test using an if..then..elseif chain (or a combination of if..then..elseif and a switch/case statement). By testing the most common case(s) first, you can often reduce the average time the multiway statement needs to execute. For example:

```
if( i == 15 )
{
  // If i = 15 better than 50% of the time,
  // then we only execute a single test
  // better than 50% of the time:
}
else if( i == 20 )
{
  // if i == 20 better than 25% of the time,
  // then we only execute one or
  // two comparisons 75% of the time.
}
else if etc....
```

If i is equal to 15 more often than not, then most of the time this code sequence will execute the body of the first if statement after executing only two instructions. Even in the best switch statement implementation, you're going to need more instructions than this.

14.6.4   Compiler Output for switch Statements

Before you run off to "help" your compiler produce better code for switch statements, you might want to examine the actual code your compiler produces. This chapter described several of the techniques that various compilers use for implementing switch/case statements at the machine-code level, but you can rest assured that there are several additional implementations that this book has not covered (nor could cover). Although you cannot assume that a compiler will always generate the same code for a switch/case statement, observing the code the compiler produces can help demonstrate the different implementations that compiler authors use.

14.7   For More Information

One of the best places to look for more information on how HLLs implement control statements is a programming language design textbook. There are dozens of decent programming design textbooks available. Here are some examples:

- *Programming Languages: Design and Implementation*, Terrence Pratt and Marvin Zelkowitz (Prentice Hall, 2001)

- *Programming Languages: Principles and Practice*, Kenneth Louden (Course Technology, 2002)

- *Concepts of Programming Languages*, Robert Sebesta (Addison-Wesley, 2003)

- *Programming Languages: Structures and Models*, Herbert Dershem and Michael Jipping (Wadsworth Publishing, 1990)

- *The Programming Language Landscape*, Henry Ledgard and Michael Marcotty (SRA, 1986)

- *Programming Language Concepts*, Carlo Ghezzi and Jehdi Jazayeri (Wiley, 1997)

Of course, another source of information about the implementation of control structures in an HLL is any textbook on compiler design and construction. Here are a few compiler-construction textbooks you may want to investigate:

- *Compilers, Principles, Techniques, and Tools*, Alfred Aho, Ravi Sethi, and Jeffrey Ullman (Addison-Wesley, 1986)

- *Compiler Construction: Theory and Practice*, William Barret and John Couch (SRA, 1986)

- *A Retargetable C Compiler: Design and Implementation*, Christopher Fraser and David Hansen (Addison-Wesley Professional, 1995)

- *Introduction to Compiler Design*, Thomas Parsons (W. H. Freeman, 1992)

- *Compiler Construction: Principles and Practice*, Kenneth Louden (Course Technology, 1997)

CPU manufacturers' literature, data sheets, and books are also quite useful for determining how compilers will often implement variables. For example, *The PowerPC Compiler Writer's Guide*, edited by Steve Hoxey, Faraydon Karim, Bill Hay, and Hank Warren[4] is a great reference for those programmers writing code to run on a PowerPC processor; most PowerPC compiler writers have used this reference. Similarly, many compiler writers have used Intel's Pentium manual set (including their *Optimization Guide*) to help them when writing code generators for their compilers. These manuals may prove handy to someone wanting to understand how 80x86-based compilers generate code.

Of course, the ultimate suggestion is to learn assembly language. If you become an expert assembly language programmer, someone who knows the intricacies of all the machine instructions for a particular processor, then you'll have a much better understanding of how a compiler will generate code for that processor. If you're interested in learning 80x86 assembly language, you might consider *The Art of Assembly Language* (No Starch Press, 2003).

---

[4] This document is available in PDF format on IBM's website at www.ibm.com.

15

ITERATIVE CONTROL STRUCTURES

Most programs spend the majority of their time executing program instructions within a loop. Therefore, if you want to improve the execution speed of your applications, you should first look to see if you can improve the performance of the loops that execute in your code. In this chapter, I'll describe the following varieties of loops:

- while loops
- repeat..until/do..while loops
- forever (infinite) loops
- for (definite) loops

15.1 The while Loop

The while loop is, perhaps, the most general-purpose iterative statement that HLLs provide. For this reason, compilers generally work hard at emitting optimal code for while loops. The while loop tests a Boolean expression at the top of a loop body and executes the loop body if the expression evaluates to True. When the loop body completes execution, control transfers back to the test and the process repeats. When the Boolean control expression evaluates to False, the program transfers control to the first statement beyond the loop's body. Note that if the Boolean expression evaluates to False when the program first encounters the while statement, the program immediately skips over all statements in the loop's body without executing any of them. The following example demonstrates a Pascal while loop:

```
while( a < b ) do begin

    << statements to execute if a is less than b,
       presumably, these statements modify the value
       of either a or b so that this loop ultimately
       terminates >>

end; (* while *)
<< statements that execute when a is not less than b >>
```

It is easy to simulate a while loop in an HLL by using an if statement and a goto statement. Consider the following C/C++ while loop and the (semantically) equivalent code that uses an if and a goto:

```
// While loop:

while( x < y )
{
    array[x] = y;
    ++x;
}

// Conversion to an if and a goto:

whlLabel:
if( x < y )
{
    array[x] = y;
    ++x;
    goto whlLabel;
}
```

Tracing through the if/goto implementation should convince you that this code is semantically equivalent to the former while loop. Assume for the sake of this example that x is less than y when the if/goto combination first executes. This being the case, the "body" of the loop (the then portion of the if statement) will execute. At the bottom of the "loop body" a goto statement transfers control to just before the if statement. This means that the code will test the expression again, just as the while loop does. Whenever the if expression evaluates to False, control will transfer to the first statement after the if (and this transfers control beyond the goto statement in this code).

Although the if/goto arrangement is semantically identical to the while loop, don't get the impression that the if/goto scheme presented here is more efficient than what a typical compiler would generate. It's not. The following assembly code shows what you'd get from a mediocre compiler for the previous while loop:

```
// while( x < y )

whlLabel:
    mov( x, eax );
    cmp( eax, y );
    jnl exitWhile;   // jump to exitWhile label if
                     // x is not less than y

    mov( y, edx );
    mov( edx, array[ eax*4 ] );
    inc( x );
    jmp whlLabel;
exitWhile:
```

A decent compiler will improve upon this slightly by using a technique known as code movement (or expression rotation). Consider the following implementation of the previous while loop that is slightly more efficient:

```
// while( x < y )

    // Skip over the while loop's body.

    jmp testExpr;

whlLabel:
    // This is the body of the while loop (same as
    //  before, except moved up a few instructions).

    mov( y, edx );
    mov( edx, array[ eax*4 ] );
    inc( x );

// Here is where we test the expression to
// determine if we should repeat the loop body.

testExpr:
    mov( x, eax );
    cmp( eax, y );
    jl whlLabel;     // Transfer control to loop body if x < y.
```

You'll notice that this example has exactly the same number of machine instructions as the previous example, but the test for loop termination has been moved to the bottom of the loop. To preserve the semantics of a while loop (so that we don't execute the loop body if the expression evaluates to False upon first encountering the loop), the first statement in this sequence is a `jmp` statement that transfers control down to the code that tests the loop termination expression. If that test evaluates to True, this code transfers control to the body of the `while` loop (immediately after `whlLabel`).

Although this code has the same number of statements as the previous example, there is a subtle difference between these two implementations. In this latter example, the initial `jmp` instruction executes only once, the very first time the loop executes. For each iteration thereafter, the code skips the execution of this statement. In the original example, the corresponding `jmp` statement is at the bottom of the loop's body and it executes on each iteration of the loop. Therefore, if the loop body executes more than once, the second version runs faster (on the other hand, if the `while` loop rarely executes the loop body even once, then the former implementation is slightly more efficient). If your compiler does not generate the best code for a `while` statement, you should consider getting a different compiler. Attempting to write optimal code in an HLL by using `if` and `goto` statements will produce difficult-to-read spaghetti code and, more often than not, the presence of `goto`s in your code will actually impair the compiler's ability to produce decent code. When this chapter discusses the `repeat..until/do..while` loop, you'll see an alternative to the `if..goto` scheme that will produce more structured code that the compiler may be able to handle. Still, if your compiler cannot make a simple transformation like this one, chances are the efficiency of the compiled `while` loops are among the least of your problems.

Compilers that do a decent job of optimizing `while` loops typically make certain assumptions about the loop. Probably the biggest assumption that an optimizer will make is that the loop has exactly one entry point and one exit point. Many languages provide statements that allow the premature exit of a loop (e.g., `break`, as discussed in Section 14.4, "break, continue, next, return, and Other Limited Forms of the goto Statement"). Of course, many languages provide some form of the `goto` statement that will allow you to enter or exit the loop at an arbitrary point. However, keep in mind that the use of such statements, while probably legal, may severely affect the compiler's ability to optimize the code. So use them with caution.[1] The `while` loop is one area where you should let the compiler do its job and not try to manually optimize the code yourself (actually, this statement is true for all loops; compilers generally do a good job of optimizing loops).

15.1.1   Forcing Complete Boolean Evaluation in a while Loop

The execution of a `while` statement depends upon the semantics of Boolean expression evaluation. As with the `if` statement, sometimes the correct execution of a `while` loop may depend upon whether the Boolean expression uses complete evaluation or short-circuit evaluation. In this section I'll describe ways to force a `while` loop to use full Boolean evaluation. In the following section, I'll demonstrate ways to force short-circuit evaluation.

---

[1] It is a paradox that many programmers will attempt to use multiple entries or exits within a loop in order to optimize their code, yet their hard work often destroys the very thing they are trying to achieve.

Without thinking too much about the problem, you might guess that forcing complete Boolean evaluation in a while loop is done the same way as in an if statement. However, if you look back at the solutions given for the if statement earlier (see Section 14.5.2, "Forcing Complete Boolean Evaluation in an if Statement"), you'll discover that the approaches we used for the if statement (nesting ifs and temporary calculations) won't work for a while statement. A different approach will be necessary.

15.1.1.1 The Easy but Inefficient Approach

One easy way to force complete Boolean evaluation is to write a function that computes the result of the Boolean expression and use complete Boolean evaluation within that function. Consider the following C code that implements this idea:

```c
#include <stdio.h>

static int i;
static int k;

extern int x;
extern int y;
extern int f( int );
extern int g( int );

/*
** Complete Boolean evaluation
** for the expression:
** i < g(y) || k > f(x)
*/

int func( void )
{
    int temp;
    int temp2;

    temp = i < g(y);
    temp2 = k > f(x);
    return temp || temp2;
}

int main( void )
{
    /*
    ** The following while loop
    ** uses complete Boolean evaluation
    */

    while( func() )
    {
      IntoIF:

        printf( "Hello" );
```

```
        }

        return( 0 );
}
```

Here's the code that GCC (x86) emits for this C code:

```
func:
        pushl    %ebp
        movl     %esp, %ebp
        pushl    %ebx
        subl     $16, %esp
        pushl    y
        call     g
        popl     %edx
        xorl     %ebx, %ebx
        pushl    x
        cmpl     %eax, i
        setl     %bl
        call     f
        addl     $16, %esp
        cmpl     %eax, k
        setg     %al
        xorl     %edx, %edx
        testl    %ebx, %ebx
        movzbl   %al, %eax
        jne      .L3
        testl    %eax, %eax
        je       .L2
.L3:
        movl     $1, %edx
.L2:
        movl     %edx, %eax
        movl     -4(%ebp), %ebx
        leave
        ret
.Lfe1:
        .size    func,.Lfe1-func
        .section         .rodata.str1.1,"aMS",@progbits,1
.LC0:
        .string "Hello"
        .text
        .p2align 2,,3
.globl main
        .type    main,@function
main:
        pushl    %ebp
        movl     %esp, %ebp
        subl     $8, %esp
        andl     $-16, %esp
        .p2align 2,,3
.L5:
        call     func
```

```
        testl   %eax, %eax
        je      .L10
.L8:
        subl    $12, %esp
        pushl   $.LC0
        call    printf
        addl    $16, %esp
        jmp     .L5
.L10:
        xorl    %eax, %eax
        leave
        ret
```

As the assembly code demonstrates, the problem with this approach is that this code must make a function call and return (both of which are slow operations) in order to compute the value of the expression. For many expressions, the overhead of the call and return is more expensive than the actual computation of the expression's value.

15.1.1.2 Using Inline Functions

The big problem with this code is that the use of the function introduces considerable overhead, both in terms of space and speed. It's definitely not the greatest code you could obtain. If your compiler supports inline functions, then you can produce a much better result by inlining func in this example:

```
#include <stdio.h>

static int i;
static int k;

extern int x;
extern int y;
extern int f( int );
extern int g( int );

inline int func( void )
{
    int temp;
    int temp2;

    temp = i < g(y);
    temp2 = k > f(x);
    return temp || temp2;
}

int main( void )
{
    while( func() )
    {
      IntoIF:

        printf( "Hello" );
```

```
        }

        return( 0 );
}
```

Here's the conversion to Gas assembly by the GCC compiler:

```
main:
        pushl   %ebp
        movl    %esp, %ebp
        pushl   %ebx
        pushl   %ecx
        andl    $-16, %esp
        .p2align 2,,3
.L2:
        subl    $12, %esp

; while( i < g(y) || k > f(x) )
;
; Compute g(y) into %EAX:

        pushl   y
        call    g
        popl    %edx
        xorl    %ebx, %ebx
        pushl   x

; See if i < g(y) and leave Boolean result
; in %EBX:

        cmpl    %eax, i
        setl    %bl

; Compute f(x) and leave result in %EAX:

        call    f           ; Note that we call f, even if the
        addl    $16, %esp   ; above evaluates to True

; Compute k > f(x), leaving the result in %EAX.

        cmpl    %eax, k
        setg    %al

; Compute the logical OR of the above two expressions.

        xorl    %edx, %edx
        testl   %ebx, %ebx
        movzbl  %al, %eax
        jne     .L6
        testl   %eax, %eax
        je      .L7
.L6:
        movl    $1, %edx
.L7:
```

```
        testl   %edx, %edx
        je      .L10
.L8:

; Loop body:

        subl    $12, %esp
        pushl   $.LC0
        call    printf
        addl    $16, %esp
        jmp     .L2
.L10:
        xorl    %eax, %eax
        movl    -4(%ebp), %ebx
        leave
        ret
```

As this example demonstrates, GCC compiles the function directly into the while loop's test, sparing this program the overhead associated with the function call and return.

15.1.1.3   Using Bitwise Logical Operations

In the C programming language, which supports Boolean operations on bits (also called *bitwise logical operations* in C), you can use the same trick employed for the if statement to force complete Boolean evaluation—just use the bitwise operators. In the special case where the left and right operands of the && or || operators are always 0 or 1, you can use code like the following to force complete Boolean evaluation:

```
#include <stdio.h>

static int i;
static int k;

extern int x;
extern int y;
extern int f( int );
extern int g( int );

int main( void )
{
    // Use "|" rather than "||"
    // to force complete Boolean
    // evaluation here.

    while( i < g(y) | k > f(x) )
    {
        printf( "Hello" );
    }

    return( 0 );
}
```

Here's the assembly code that Borland C++ generates for this C source code:

```
_main    proc    near
?live1@0:
    ;
    ;       int main( void )
    ;
@1:
        push      ebx
        jmp       short @3 ;Skip to expr test.

    ;
    ;       {
    ;               while( i < g(y) | k > f(x) )
    ;               {
    ;                       printf( "Hello" );
    ;
@2:
        ;Loop body.

        push      offset s@
        call      _printf
        pop       ecx

; Here's where the test of the expression
; begins:

@3:
        ; Compute "i < g(y)" into ebx:

        mov       eax,dword ptr [_y]
        push      eax
        call      _g
        pop       ecx
        cmp       eax,dword ptr [_i]
        setg      bl
        and       ebx,1

        ;  Compute "k > f(x)" into EDX:

        mov       eax,dword ptr [_x]
        push      eax
        call      _f
        pop       ecx
        cmp       eax,dword ptr [_k]
        setl      dl
        and       edx,1

        ; Compute the logical OR of
        ; the two results above:

        or        ebx,edx

        ; Repeat loop body if true:
```

```
        jne        short @2
;
;                  }
;
;                  return( 0 );
;
        xor        eax,eax
;
;       }
;
@5:
@4:
        pop        ebx
        ret
_main   endp
```

As you can see in this 80x86 output, the compiler generates semantically equivalent code when using the bitwise logical operators. Just keep in mind that this code is valid only if you use 0/1 for the Boolean values False/True.

15.1.1.4 Using Unstructured Code

If you don't have inline function capability or if bitwise logical operators aren't available, you can use unstructured code to force complete Boolean evaluation as a last resort. The basic idea is to create an infinite loop and then write code to explicitly exit the loop if the condition fails. Generally, you'd use a goto statement (or a limited form of the goto statement like C's break or continue statements) to control loop termination. Consider the following example in C:

```c
#include <stdio.h>

static int i;
static int k;

extern int x;
extern int y;
extern int f( int );
extern int g( int );

int main( void )
{
    int temp;
    int temp2;

    for( ;; )                   //Infinite loop in C/C++
    {
        temp = i < g(y);
        temp2 = k > f(x);
        if( !temp && !temp2 ) break;
        printf( "Hello" );
    }
```

```
        return( 0 );
}
```

By using an infinite loop with an explicit break, we were able to compute
the two components of the Boolean expression using separate C statements
(hence, forcing the compiler to execute both subexpressions). Here's the
TASM code that Borland's C++ compiler produces for this C code:

```
_main   proc    near
?live1@0:
    ;
    ;       int main( void )
    ;
@1:
        push        ebx

    ;
    ;       {
    ;               int temp;
    ;               int temp2;
    ;
    ;               for( ;; )
    ;               {
    ;                       temp = i < g(y);
    ;
@2:
        mov         eax,dword ptr [_y]
        push        eax
        call        _g
        pop         ecx
        cmp         eax,dword ptr [_i]
        setg        bl
        and         ebx,1

    ;
    ;                       temp2 = k > f(x);
    ;
?live1@32: ; EBX = temp
        mov         eax,dword ptr [_x]
        push        eax
        call        _f
        pop         ecx
        cmp         eax,dword ptr [_k]
        setl        al
        and         eax,1

    ;
    ;                       if( !temp && !temp2 ) break;
    ;
?live1@48: ; EBX = temp, EAX = temp2
        test        ebx,ebx
        jne         short @3
        test        eax,eax
        je          short @4

    ;
    ;                       printf( "Hello" );
```

```
        ;
?live1@64: ;
@3:
        push        offset s@
        call        _printf
        pop         ecx
        jmp         short @2
    ;
    ;           }
    ;
    ;           return( 0 );
    ;
@4:
        xor         eax,eax
    ;
    ;       }
    ;
@7:
@6:
        pop         ebx
        ret
_main   endp
```

As you can see by studying the assembly code, this program always evaluates both parts of the original Boolean expression (that is, you get complete Boolean evaluation).

You should be careful using unstructured code in this fashion. Not only is the result harder to read, but it's difficult to coerce the compiler into producing the code you want when using this approach. Furthermore, you can automatically assume that code sequences that produce good code on one compiler will not produce comparable code with other compilers.

If your particular language doesn't support a statement like break, you can always use a goto statement to break out of the loop and achieve the same result. Of course, injecting gotos into your code is not a great idea. However, if you need complete Boolean evaluation semantics and using a goto is the only way to accomplish this in your language, you have no choice.

15.1.2   Forcing Short-Circuit Boolean Evaluation in a while Loop

Sometimes you need to guarantee short-circuit evaluation of the Boolean expression in a while statement even if the language (such as BASIC or Pascal) doesn't implement short-circuit evaluation. As for the if statement, you can achieve this in your program by rearranging the way you compute the loop-control expression. Unlike the if statement, you cannot use nested while statements or preface your while loop with other statements to achieve this, but it is still possible to do in most programming languages.

Consider the following C code fragment:

```
while( ptr != NULL && ptr->data != 0 )
{
    << loop body >>
```

```
    ptr = ptr->Next; // Step through a linked list.
}
```

This code could fail if C didn't guarantee short-circuit evaluation of the Boolean expression.

As with forcing complete Boolean evaluation, the easiest way to do this in a language like Pascal is to write a function that computes and returns the Boolean result using short-circuit Boolean evaluation. However, this scheme is relatively slow because of the high overhead of a function call. Consider the following Pascal example, compiled with the Borland Delphi compiler:[2]

```
program shortcircuit;
{$APPTYPE CONSOLE}
uses SysUtils;
var
    ptr     :Pchar;

    function shortCir( thePtr:Pchar ):boolean;
    begin

        shortCir := false;
        if( thePtr <> NIL ) then begin

            shortCir := thePtr^ <> #0;

        end; //if

    end;  // shortCircuit

begin

    ptr := 'Hello world';
    while( shortCir( ptr )) do begin

        write( ptr^ );
        inc( ptr );

    end; // while

end.
```

And then consider this 80x86 assembly code produced by Borland's Delphi compiler (and disassembled with IDAPro):

```
; function shortCir( thePtr:Pchar ):boolean
;
; Note: thePtr is passed into this function in
; the EAX register.
```

---

[2] Note that Delphi provides the ability to choose short-circuit or complete Boolean evaluation, so you wouldn't need to use this scheme with Delphi. However, Delphi will compile this code, hence the use of the Delphi compiler for this example.

```
sub_408570  proc near

            ;EDX holds function return
            ; result (assume false).
            ;
            ; shortCir := false;

            xor     edx, edx

            ;if( thePtr <> NIL ) then begin

            test    eax, eax
            jz      short loc_40857C    ;branch if NIL

            ; shortCir := thePtr^ <> #0;

            cmp     byte ptr [eax], 0
            setnz   dl   ;DL = 1 if not #0

loc_40857C:

            ;Return result in EAX:

            mov     eax, edx
            retn
sub_408570  endp



; Main Program (pertinent section):
;
; Load EBX with the address of the global "ptr" variable and
; then enter the "WHILE" loop (Delphi moves the test for the
; while loop to the physical end of the loop's body):

            mov     ebx, offset loc_408628
            jmp     short loc_408617
; ----------------------------------------------------------

loc_408600:
            ; Print the current character whose address
            ; "ptr" contains:

            mov     eax, ds:off_4092EC  ;ptr pointer
            mov     dl, [ebx]                ;fetch char
            call    sub_404523               ;print char
            call    sub_404391
            call    sub_402600

            inc     ebx              ;inc( ptr )

; while( shortCir( ptr )) do ...

loc_408617:
            mov     eax, ebx         ;Pass ptr in EAX
```

```
call    sub_408570      ;shortCir
test    al, al          ;Returns True/False
jnz     short loc_408600 ;branch if true
```

The sub_408570 procedure contains the function that will compute the short-circuit Boolean evaluation of an expression similar to the one appearing in the earlier C code. As you can see (by reading through that function), the code that dereferences thePtr never executes if thePtr contains NIL (zero).

If a function call is out of the question, then about the only reasonable solution is to use an unstructured approach. The following is a Pascal version of the while loop in the earlier C code that forces short-circuit Boolean evaluation:

```
while( true ) do begin

    if( ptr = NIL ) then goto 2;
    if( ptr^.data = 0 ) then goto 2;
    << loop body >>
    ptr = ptr^.Next;

end;
2:
```

Again, producing unstructured code, like the code appearing in this example, is something that should only be done as a last resort. But if the language (or compiler) you're using doesn't guarantee short-circuit evaluation and you need those semantics, unstructured code, or inefficient code (using a function call), might be the only solution.

15.2 The repeat..until (do..until/do..while) Loop

Another common loop appearing in most modern programming languages is the repeat..until loop. The repeat..until loop tests for its terminating condition at the bottom of the loop. This means that the body of the loop always executes at least once, even if the Boolean control expression evaluates to False on the first iteration of the loop. Although the repeat..until loop is a little less broadly applicable than the while loop, and you won't use it anywhere near as often as a while loop, there are many situations where the repeat..until loop is the best choice of control structure for the job. Perhaps the classic example is reading input from the user until the user inputs a certain value. The following Pascal code fragment is very typical:

```
repeat

    write( 'Enter a value (negative quits): ' );
    readln( i );
    // do something with i's value

until( i < 0 );
```

This loop always executes the body once. Which, of course, is necessary because you must execute the loop's body to read the value from the user that the program checks to determine when loop execution is complete.

The repeat..until loop terminates when its Boolean control expression evaluates to True (rather than False, as for the while loop). This makes sense, because the phrase "until" suggests that the loop terminates when the control expression evaluates to True. Note, however, that this is a minor syntactical issue, the C/C++/Java languages (and many languages that share a C heritage) provide a do..while loop that repeats the execution of the loop's body as long as the loop condition evaluates to True. From an efficiency point of view, there is absolutely no difference between these two loops, and you can easily convert one loop termination condition to the other by simply using your language's logical NOT operator. The following examples demonstrate the syntax of the Pascal, HLA, and C/C++ repeat..until and do..while loops. Here's the Pascal repeat..until loop example:

```
repeat

    (* Read a raw character from the "input" file, which in this case is
the keyboard *)

    ch := rawInput( input );

    (* Save the character away. *)

    inputArray[ i ] := ch;
    i := i + 1;

    (* Repeat until the user hits the enter key    *)

until( ch = chr( 13 ));
```

Now here's the C/C++ do..while version of the same loop:

```
do
{
    /* Read a raw character from the "input" file, which in this case is
the keyboard */

    ch = getKbd();

    /* Save the character away. */

    inputArray[ i++ ] = ch;

    /* Repeat until the user hits the enter key    */
}
while( ch != '\r' );
```

And here is the HLA repeat..until loop:

```
repeat

    // Read a character from the standard input device.

    stdin.getc();

    // Save the character away.

    mov( al, inputArray[ ebx ] );
    inc( ebx );

    // Repeat until the user hits the enter key.

until( al = stdin.cr );
```

Converting the repeat..until (or do..while) loop into assembly language is relatively easy and straightforward. All the compiler needs to do is substitute code for the Boolean loop-control expression and branch back to the beginning of the loop's body if the expression evaluates affirmative (False for repeat..until or True for do..while). Here's the straightforward pure assembly implementation of the HLA repeat..until loop appearing earlier (compilers for C/C++ and Pascal would generate nearly identical code for the other examples):

```
rptLoop:

    // Read a character from the standard input.

    call stdin.getc;

    // Store away the character.

    mov( al, inputArray[ ebx ] );
    inc( ebx );

    // Repeat the loop if the user did not hit
    //   the enter key.

    cmp( al, stdio.cr );
    jne rptLoop;
```

As you can see, the code that a typical compiler generates for a repeat..until (or do..while) loop is usually a tiny bit more efficient than the code you'll get for a regular while loop.

Because a compiler can often generate slightly more efficient code for a repeat..until/do..while loop (than a while loop), you should consider using the repeat..until/do..while form if semantically possible. In many programs, the Boolean control expression always evaluates to True on the first iteration of some loop constructs. For example, it's not that uncommon to find a loop like the following in an application:

```
i = 0;
while( i < 100 )
{
    printf( "i: %d\n", i );
    i = i * 2 + 1;
    if( i < 50 )
    {
        i += j;
    }
}
```

This while loop is easily converted to a do..while loop as follows:

```
i = 0;
do
{
    printf( "i: %d\n", i );
    i = i * 2 + 1;
    if( i < 50 )
    {
        i += j;
    }
} while( i < 100 );
```

This conversion is possible because we know that i's initial value (zero) is less than 100, so the loop's body always executes at least once.

You can help the compiler generate better code by using the more appropriate repeat..until/do..while loop rather than a regular while loop. Note that the efficiency gain is small, so be careful about sacrificing readability or maintainability when doing this. The bottom line is this: Always use the most logically appropriate loop construct. If the body of the loop always executes at least once, you should use a repeat..until/do..while loop, even if a while loop would work equally well.

15.2.1   Forcing Complete Boolean Evaluation in a repeat..until Loop

Because the test for loop termination occurs at the bottom of the loop on a repeat..until (or do..while) loop, forcing complete Boolean evaluation in a repeat..until loop is done in a similar manner to forcing complete Boolean evaluation in an if statement. Consider the following C/C++ code:

```
extern int x;
extern int y;
extern int f( int );
extern int g( int );

int main( void )
{
```

```
do
    {
        ++a;
        --b;
    }while( a < f(x) && b > g(y));

    return( 0 );
}
```

Here's the GCC output for the PowerPC (using short-circuit evaluation, standard for C) for the do..while loop:

```
L2:
        // ++a
        // --b

        lwz r9,0(r30)   ; get a
        lwz r11,0(r29)  ; get b
        addi r9,r9,-1    ; --a
        lwz r3,0(r27)    ; Set up x parm for f
        stw r9,0(r30)    ; store back into a
        addi r11,r11,1  ; ++b
        stw r11,0(r29)  ; store back into b

        ; compute f(x)

        bl L_f$stub      ; call f, result to R3

        ; is a >= f(x)? If so, quit loop

        lwz r0,0(r29)   ; get a
        cmpw cr0,r0,r3  ; Compare a with f's value
        bge- cr0,L3

        lwz r3,0(r28)    ; Set up y parm for g
        bl L_g$stub      ; call g

        lwz r0,0(r30)   ; get b
        cmpw cr0,r0,r3  ; Compare b with g's value
        bgt+ cr0,L2      ; Repeat if b > g's value
L3:
```

As you can see in this code example, the program skips over the test for b > g(y) to label L3 if the expression a < f(x) is False (that is, if a >= f(x)). To force complete Boolean evaluation in this situation, our C source code needs to compute the subcomponents of the Boolean expression just prior to the while clause (keeping the results of the subexpressions in temporary variables) and then test only the results in the while clause:

```
static int a;
static int b;
```

```
extern int x;
extern int y;
extern int f( int );
extern int g( int );

int main( void )
{
    int temp1;
    int temp2;

    do
        {
            ++a;
            --b;
            temp1 = a < f(x);
            temp2 = b > g(y);
        }while( temp1 && temp2 );

    return( 0 );
}
```

Here's the conversion to PowerPC code by GCC:

```
L2:
        lwz r9,0(r30)       ;r9 = b
        li r28,1            ;temp1 = True
        lwz r11,0(r29)      ;r11 = a
        addi r9,r9,-1       ;--b
        lwz r3,0(r26)       ;r3 = x (set up f's parm)
        stw r9,0(r30)       ;Save b
        addi r11,r11,1      ;++a
        stw r11,0(r29)      ;Save a
        bl L_f$stub         ;Call f
        lwz r0,0(r29)       ;Fetch a
        cmpw cr0,r0,r3      ;Compute temp1 = a < f(x)
        blt- cr0,L5         ;Leave temp1 true if a < f(x)
        li r28,0            ;temp1 = false
L5:
        lwz r3,0(r27)       ;r3 = y, set up g's parm
        bl L_g$stub         ;Call g
        li r9,1             ;temp2 = True
        lwz r0,0(r30)       ;Fetch b
        cmpw cr0,r0,r3      ;Compute b > g(y)
        bgt- cr0,L4         ;Leave temp2 true if b > g(y)
        li r9,0             ;Else set temp2 false
L4:
        ;Here's the actual termination test in
        ;the while clause:

        cmpwi cr0,r28,0
        beq- cr0,L3
        cmpwi cr0,r9,0
        bne+ cr0,L2
L3:
```

You'll note, of course, that the actual Boolean expression (temp1 && temp2) still uses short-circuit evaluation. However, this short-circuit evaluation only involves the temporary variables created. The loop computes both of the original subexpressions regardless of the result of the first one.

15.2.2 Forcing Short-Circuit Boolean Evaluation in a repeat..until Loop

If your programming language provides a facility to break out of a repeat..until loop, such as C's break statement, then forcing short-circuit evaluation is fairly easy. Consider the C do..while loop from the previous section that forces complete Boolean evaluation:

```
do
{
    ++a;
    --b;
    temp1 = a < f(x);
    temp2 = b > g(y);

}while( temp1 && temp2 );
```

The following shows one way to convert this code so that it evaluates the termination expression using short-circuit Boolean evaluation:

```
static int a;
static int b;

extern int x;
extern int y;
extern int f( int );
extern int g( int );

int main( void )
{
    do
    {
        ++a;
        --b;

        if( !( a < f(x) )) break;
    }while( b > g(y) );

    return( 0 );
}
```

Here's the code that GCC emits for the PowerPC for the do..while loop in this code sequence:

```
L2:
        lwz r9,0(r30)    ;r9 = b
        lwz r11,0(r29)   ;r11 = a
```

```
          addi r9,r9,-1    ;--b
          lwz r3,0(r27)    ;Set up f(x) parm
          stw r9,0(r30)    ;Save b
          addi r11,r11,1   ;++a
          stw r11,0(r29)   ;Save a
          bl L_f$stub      ;Call f

          ; break if a < f(x):

          lwz r0,0(r29)
          cmpw cr0,r0,r3
          bge- cr0,L3

          ; while( b > g(y) ):

          lwz r3,0(r28)    ;Set up y parm
          bl L_g$stub      ;Call g
          lwz r0,0(r30)    ;Compute b > g(y)
          cmpw cr0,r0,r3
          bgt+ cr0,L2      ;Branch if true
L3:
```

If a is less than the value that f(x) returns, this code immediately breaks out of the loop (at label L3) without testing to see if b is greater than the value g(y) returns. Hence, this code simulates short-circuit Boolean evaluation of the expression a < f(x) && b > g(y).

If the compiler you're using doesn't support a statement equivalent to C/C++'s break statement, you'll have to use slightly more sophisticated logic. One way to do that might be as follows:

```
static int a;
static int b;

extern int x;
extern int y;
extern int f( int );
extern int g( int );

int main( void )
{
    int temp;

    do
    {
        ++a;
        --b;

        temp = a < f(x);
        if( temp )
        {
            temp = b > g(y);
        };
    }while( temp );
```

```
       return( 0 );
}
```

Here is the PowerPC code that GCC produces for this example:

```
L2:
        lwz r9,0(r30)    ;r9 = b
        lwz r11,0(r29)   ;r11 = a
        addi r9,r9,-1    ;--b
        lwz r3,0(r27)    ;Set up f(x) parm
        stw r9,0(r30)    ;Save b
        addi r11,r11,1   ;++a
        stw r11,0(r29)   ;Save a
        bl L_f$stub      ;Call f
        li r9,1          ;Assume temp is True
        lwz r0,0(r29)    ;Set temp false if
        cmpw cr0,r0,r3   ;a < f(x)
        blt- cr0,L5
        li r9,0
L5:
        cmpwi cr0,r9,0   ;If !(a < f(x)) then bail
        beq- cr0,L10     ; on the do..while loop
        lwz r3,0(r28)    ;Compute temp = b > f(y)
        bl L_g$stub      ; using a code sequence
        li r9,1          ; that is comparable to
        lwz r0,0(r30)    ; the above.
        cmpw cr0,r0,r3
        bgt- cr0,L9
        li r9,0
L9:
        ; Test the while termination expression:

        cmpwi cr0,r9,0
        bne+ cr0,L2
L10:
```

Even though these examples have been using the conjunction operation (logical AND), using the disjunction operator (logical OR) is just as easy. To close off this section, here's a Pascal sequence and its conversion for your consideration:

```
repeat

    a := a + 1;
    b := b - 1;

until( a < f(x) OR b > g(y) );
```

Here's the conversion to force complete Boolean evaluation:

```
repeat

    a := a + 1;
```

```
        b := b - 1;
        temp := a < f(x);
        if( not temp ) then begin

            temp := b > g(y);

        end;
    until( temp );
```

Here's the code that Borland's Delphi produces for the two loops (assuming you select *complete Boolean evaluation* in the compiler's options):

```
;    repeat
;
;        a := a + 1;
;        b := b - 1;
;
;    until( (a < f(x)) or (b > g(y)));

loc_4085F8:
            inc     ebx         ; a := a + 1;
            dec     esi         ; b := b - 1;
            mov     eax, [edi]  ;EDI points at x
            call    locret_408570
            cmp     ebx, eax    ;Set AL to 1 if
            setl    al          ; a < f(x)
            push    eax             ;Save Boolean result.

            mov     eax, ds:dword_409288    ;y
            call    locret_408574           ;g(6)

            cmp     esi, eax    ;Set AL to 1 if
            setnle  al          ; b > g(y)
            pop     edx             ;Retrieve last value.
            or      dl, al      ;Compute their OR
            jz      short loc_4085F8 ;Repeat if false.

;    repeat
;
;        a := a + 1;
;        b := b - 1;
;        temp := a < f(x);
;        if( not temp ) then begin
;
;            temp := b > g(y);
;
;        end;
;
;    until( temp );

loc_40861B:
            inc     ebx     ;a := a + 1;
            dec     esi     ;b := b - 1;
            mov     eax, [edi] ;Fetch x
```

```
        call    locret_408570 ;call f
        cmp     ebx, eax    ;is a < f(x)?
        setl    al              ;Set AL to 1 if so.

    ; If the result of the above calculation is
    ; True, then don't bother with the second
    ; test (i.e., short-circuit evaluation)

        test    al, al
        jnz     short loc_40863C

    ;Now check to see if b > g(y)

        mov     eax, ds:dword_409288
        call    locret_408574

    ;Set AL = 1 if b > g(y):

        cmp     esi, eax
        setnle  al

; Repeat loop if both conditions were false:

loc_40863C:
        test    al, al
        jz      short loc_40861B
```

The code that the Delphi compiler generates for this forced short-circuit evaluation is nowhere near as good as the code it would generate if you allowed the compiler to do this job for you (by not selecting *complete Boolean evaluation* in the Delphi compiler options). Here's the Delphi code with complete Boolean evaluation unselected (that is, instructing Delphi to use short-circuit evaluation):

```
loc_4085F8:
        inc     ebx
        dec     esi
        mov     eax, [edi]
        call    nullsub_1 ;f
        cmp     ebx, eax
        jl      short loc_408613
        mov     eax, ds:dword_409288
        call    nullsub_2 ;g
        cmp     esi, eax
        jle     short loc_4085F8
```

While this trick is useful for forcing short-circuit evaluation when the compiler does not support that facility, this latter Delphi example amply demonstrates that you should use the compiler's facilities if at all possible—you will generally get better machine code.

15.3 The forever..endfor Loop

The while loop tests for loop termination at the beginning (top) of the loop. The repeat..until loop tests for loop termination at the end (bottom) of the loop. The only place left to test for loop termination is somewhere in the middle of the loop's body. The forever..endfor loop, along with some special loop-termination statements, handles this case.

Most modern programming languages provide a while loop and a repeat..until loop (or loops that are equivalent to these). Interestingly enough, only a few modern imperative programming languages (that is, languages like C/C++, Java, Pascal, BASIC, and Ada) provide an explicit forever..endfor loop. Ada provides one—so do C and C++ (the for(;;) loop)—but this loop is missing in many other languages. This is especially surprising, because the forever..endfor loop (along with a loop-termination test) is actually the most general of the three forms. You can easily synthesize a while loop or a repeat..until loop from a single forever..endfor loop.

Of course, it is easy to create a simple forever..endfor loop in any language that provides a while loop or a repeat..until/do..while loop. All you need do is supply a Boolean control expression that always evaluates to False for repeat..until or True for do..while. In Pascal, for example, you could use code such as the following:

```
const
    forever := true;
        .
        .
        .
    while( forever ) do begin

        << code to execute in an infinite loop >>

    end;
```

The big problem with (standard) Pascal is that it doesn't provide a mechanism for explicitly breaking out of a loop (other than a generic goto statement). Fortunately, many modern Pascals (e.g., Delphi) provide a statement like break to immediately exit the current loop.

Although the C/C++ language does not provide an explicit statement that creates a forever loop, the syntactically bizarre for(;;) statement has served this purpose since the very first C compiler was written. Therefore, C/C++ programmers can create a forever..endfor loop as follows:

```
for(;;)
{
    << code to execute in an infinite loop >>
}
```

C/C++ programmers can use C's break statement (along with an if statement) to place a loop-terminate condition in the middle of a loop. For example:

```
for(;;)
{
    << Code to execute (at least once)
       prior to the termination test >>

    if( termination_expression ) break;

    << Code to execute after the loop-termination test >>
}
```

The HLA language provides an explicit (high-level) forever..endfor statement (along with a break and a breakif statement) that lets you terminate the loop somewhere in the middle. Here is an example of an HLA forever..endfor loop that tests for loop termination in the middle of the loop:

```
forever

    << Code to execute (at least once) prior to
       the termination test >>

    breakif( termination_expression );

    << Code to execute after the loop-termination test >>

endfor;
```

Converting a forever..endfor loop into pure assembly language is a trivial matter. All you need is a single jmp instruction that can transfer control from the bottom of the loop back to the top of the loop. The implementation of the break statement is just as trivial, it's just a jump (or conditional jump) to the first statement following the loop. The following two code fragments demonstrate an HLA forever..endfor loop (along with a breakif) and the corresponding "pure" assembly code:

```
// High-level forever statement in HLA:

forever

    stdout.put
    (
     "Enter an unsigned integer less than five:"
    );
    stdin.get( u );
    breakif( u < 5);
    stdout.put
    (
        "Error: the value must be between zero and five" nl
```

```
          );

    endfor;

    // Low-level coding of the forever loop in HLA:

    foreverLabel:
        stdout.put
        (
          "Enter an unsigned integer less than five:"
        );
        stdin.get( u );
        cmp( u, 5 );
        jbe endForeverLabel;
        stdout.put
        (
          "Error: the value must be between zero and five" nl
        );
        jmp foreverLabel;

    endForeverLabel:
```

Of course, you can also rotate this code to create a slightly more efficient version:

```
// Low-level coding of the forever loop in HLA
// using code rotation:

jmp foreverEnter;
foreverLabel:
        stdout.put
        (
          "Error: the value must be between zero and five"
          nl
        );
    foreverEnter:
        stdout.put
        (
          "Enter an unsigned integer less "
          "than five:"
        );
        stdin.get( u );
        cmp( u, 5 );
        ja foreverLabel;
```

If the language you're using doesn't support a forever..endfor loop, any decent compiler will convert a while(true) statement into a single jump instruction. For reasons you'll soon see, you shouldn't try to create the forever..endfor loop using a goto statement. If your compiler doesn't translate while(true) into a single jump instruction, then it does a poor job of optimization, and any attempts to manually optimize the code are a lost cause.

15.3.1   Forcing Complete Boolean Evaluation in a forever Loop

Because you exit from a forever loop using an if statement, the techniques for forcing complete Boolean evaluation when exiting a forever loop are the same you use with an if statement. See Section 14.5.2, "Forcing Complete Boolean Evaluation in an if Statement," for details.

15.3.2   Forcing Short-Circuit Boolean Evaluation in a forever Loop

Likewise, because you exit from a forever loop using an if statement, the techniques for forcing short-circuit Boolean evaluation when exiting a forever loop are the same you use with an if statement. See Section 15.2.2, "Forcing Short-Circuit Boolean Evaluation in a repeat..until Loop," for details.

15.4   The Definite Loop (for Loops)

The forever..endfor loop is an *infinite* loop (assuming you don't break out of the loop via a break statement). The while and repeat..until loops are examples of *indefinite* loops. They are known as indefinite loops because, in general, the program cannot determine how many iterations the loop will execute when the program first encounters the loop. A *definite* loop, on the other hand, is one for which the program can determine exactly how many iterations the loop will repeat prior to executing the first statement of the loop's body. The Pascal for loop is a good example of a definite loop in a traditional HLL, and it uses the following syntax:

```
for <<variable>> := <<expr1>> to <<expr2>> do
     <<statement>>
```

which iterates over the range expr1..expr2 if expr1 is less than or equal to expr2, or

```
for <<variable>> := <<expr1>> downto <<expr2>> do
     <<statement>>
```

which iterates over the range expr1..expr2 if expr1 is greater than or equal to expr2. Here is a typical example of a Pascal for loop:

```
for i := 1 to 10 do
    writeln( "hello world" );
```

This loop always executes exactly ten times (obviously); hence it's a definite loop. However, don't get the impression that a compiler has to be able to determine the number of loop iterations at compile time. Definite loops also allow the use of expressions that force the program to determine the number of iterations at runtime. For example:

```
write( "Enter an integer:" );
readln( cnt );
```

```
for i := 1 to cnt do
    writeln( "Hello World" );
```

The Pascal compiler cannot determine the number of iterations this loop will execute. Indeed, because the number of iterations is dependent upon user input, the exact number of iterations could vary each time this loop executes in a single execution of the enclosing program. However, the program can determine exactly how many iterations the loop will execute whenever the program encounters this loop (specifically, the value in the cnt variable determines the number of iterations in this example). Note that Pascal (like most languages that support definite loops) expressly forbids code such as the following:

```
for i := 1 to j do begin

    << some statements >>
    i := <<some value>>;
    << some other statements >>

end;
```

You are not allowed to the change the value of the loop control variable during the execution of the loop's body. A high-quality Pascal compiler will detect an attempt to change the for loop's control variable and report an error should you try this. Also, a definite loop computes the starting and ending values only once. Therefore, if the for loop modifies a variable that appears as the second expression, the for loop does not reevaluate the expression on each iteration of the loop. For example, if the body of the for loop in the previous example modifies the value of j, this will not affect the number of iterations of the for loop.[3]

Definite loops have certain special properties that allow a (good) compiler to generate better machine code. In particular, because the compiler can determine how many iterations the loop will execute prior to executing the first statement of the loop's body, the compiler can often dispense with complex tests for loop termination and simply decrement a register down to zero to control the number of loop iterations. The compiler can also use induction to optimize access to the loop control variable in a definite loop (see the description of induction in Section 13.2, "Optimization of Arithmetic Statements").

C/C++/Java users should note that the for loop appearing in these languages is not a true definite loop; rather, it is a special case of the indefinite while loop. Most good C/C++ compilers will attempt to determine if a for loop is a definite loop and generate decent code if the compiler can determine beforehand that the loop is a definite loop.

---

[3] Of course, some compilers might actually recompute this on each iteration, but the Pascal language standard doesn't require this; indeed, the standard suggests that these values shouldn't change during the execution of the loop body.

To help the compiler generate good code for your C/C++ for loops, you should ensure the following:

- Your C/C++ for loops should use the same semantics as the definite (for) loops in languages such as Pascal. That is, the for loop should initialize a single loop control variable, test for loop termination when that value is less than or greater than some ending value, and increment or decrement the loop control variable by one.

- Your C/C++ for loops do not modify the value of the loop control variable within the loop.

- The test for loop termination remains static over the execution of the loop's body. That is, the loop body should not be able to change the termination condition (which, by definition, would make the loop an indefinite loop). For example, if the loop termination condition is $i < j$, the loop body should not modify the value of i or j.

- The loop body does not pass the loop control variable or any variable appearing in the loop termination condition by reference to a function if that function modifies the actual parameter.

15.5 For More Information

Section 14.7, "For More Information," applies to this chapter as well. Please see that section for more details.

16

FUNCTIONS AND PROCEDURES

Since the beginning of the structured programming revolution in the 1970s, subroutines (procedures and functions) have been one of the primary tools software engineers use to organize, modularize, and otherwise structure their programs. Because programmers use procedure and function calls so frequently in their code, CPU manufacturers have responded by attempting to make these calls as efficient as possible. Nevertheless, a procedure or function call (and the associated return) has costs that many programmers don't consider when creating functions. The inappropriate use of procedures and functions within a program can yield a huge increase in size and execution time. In this chapter, I'll discuss those costs and how to avoid them. I'll cover the following subjects:

- Function and procedure calls
- Macros and inline functions
- Parameter passing and calling conventions

- Activation records and local variables
- Function return results

By understanding these topics, you can avoid the efficiency pitfalls that are common in modern programs that make heavy use of procedures and functions.

16.1   Simple Function and Procedure Calls

A *function* is a section of code that computes and returns some value (the function result); a *procedure* (or *void function*, in C/C++ terminology) simply accomplishes some action. Function calls generally appear within an arithmetic or logical expression; procedure calls look like statements in the programming language. For the purpose of discussion in this section, you can generally assume that a procedure call and a function call are the same and simply use the terms *function* and *procedure* interchangeably. For the most part, a compiler implements procedure and function calls identically.

NOTE *There are, however, some differences. At the end of the chapter I'll consider some efficiency issues related to function results. (See Section 16.7, "Function Return Values.")*

With most CPUs, you invoke procedures via an instruction similar to the 80x86 call and use the ret (return) instruction for a return back to the caller. The call instruction performs three discrete operations:

- It determines the address of the instruction to execute upon returning from the procedure (this is usually the instruction immediately following the call instruction).

- It saves this address (commonly known as the *return address* or the *link address*) into a known location.

- It transfers control (via a jump mechanism) to the first instruction of the procedure.

Execution starts with the first instruction of the procedure and continues until the CPU encounters a ret (return) instruction. The ret instruction fetches the return address and transfers control to the machine instruction at that address. Consider the following C function and the corresponding 80x86 and PowerPC code produced by GCC. Here's the C source code:

```
#include <stdio.h>

void func( void )
{
    return;
}

int main( void )
{
    func();
```

```
        return( 0 );
}
```

Here's the conversion to PowerPC Code by GCC:

```
.text

; void func( void )

        .align 2
        .globl _func
_func:
        ; Set up activation record for function.
        ; Note R1 is used as the stack pointer by
        ; the PowerPC ABI (Application Binary
        ; Interface, defined by IBM).

        stmw r30,-8(r1)
        stwu r1,-48(r1)
        mr r30,r1

        ; Clean up activation record prior to the return

        lwz r1,0(r1)
        lmw r30,-8(r1)

        ; Return to caller (branch to address
        ; in the link register):

        blr

        .align 2
        .globl _main
_main:
        ; Save return address from
        ; main program (so we can
        ; return to the OS):

        mflr r0
        stmw r30,-8(r1) ;Preserve r30/31
        stw r0,8(r1)    ;Save rtn adrs
        stwu r1,-80(r1) ;Update stack for func()
        mr r30,r1       ;Set up frame pointer

        ; Call func:

        bl _func

        ; Return zero as the main
        ; function result:

        li r0,0
        mr r3,r0
        lwz r1,0(r1)
```

```
        lwz  r0,8(r1)
        mtlr r0
        lmw  r30,-8(r1)
        blr
```

And here's the conversion of the same source code to 80x86 code by GCC:

```
.file   "t.c"
        .text
        .p2align 2,,3

; Conversion of void func( void )

        .globl func
        .type  func,@function
func:
        ; Construct activation record:

        pushl   %ebp
        movl    %esp, %ebp

        ; Clean up activation record:

        leave

        ; Return to main program:

        ret


        .globl main
        .type  main,@function
main:
        ; Build activation record for
        ; the main program.

        pushl   %ebp
        movl    %esp, %ebp
        subl    $8, %esp
        andl    $-16, %esp

        ; call func():

        call    func

        ; Return zero as the main
        ; function's result:

        xorl    %eax, %eax
        leave
        ret
```

As you can see, both the 80x86 and the PowerPC devote considerable effort building and managing activation records (see Section 8.1.4, "The Stack Section"). The important things to see in these two assembly language sequences are the bl _func and blr instructions in the PowerPC code and the call func and ret instructions in the 80x86 code. These are the instructions that call the function and return from it.

16.1.1   Storing the Return Address

But where, exactly, does the CPU store the return address? In the absence of recursion and certain other program control constructs, the CPU could store the return address in any arbitrary location that is large enough to hold the address and that will still contain that address when the procedure returns to its caller. For example, the program could choose to store the return address in a machine register (in which case the return operation would consist of an indirect jump to the address contained in that register). One problem with using registers, however, is that CPUs generally have a limited number of them. Every register that holds a return address is unavailable for other purposes. For this reason, on CPUs that save the return address in a register the applications usually moves the return address to memory so they can reuse that register for other purposes.

Consider the PowerPC bl (branch then link) instruction. This instruction transfers control to the target address specified by its operand and copies the address of the instruction following bl into the LINK register. Inside a procedure, if no code modifies the value of the LINK register, the procedure can return to its caller by executing a blr (branch to LINK register) instruction. In our trivial example, the func() function does not execute any code that modifies the value of the LINK register, so this is exactly how func returns to its caller. However, if this function had used the LINK register for some other purpose, it would have been the procedure's responsibility to save the return address so that it could restore the value prior to returning via a blr instruction at the end of the function call.

A more common place to keep return addresses is in memory. Although accessing memory on most modern processors is much slower than accessing a CPU register, keeping return addresses in memory allows a program to have a large number of nested procedure calls. Most CPUs actually use a *stack* to hold return addresses. For example, the 80x86 call instruction *pushes* the return address onto a stack data structure in memory and the ret instruction *pops* this return address off the stack. Using a stack of memory locations to hold return addresses offers several advantages:

- Stacks, because of their *last-in, first-out (LIFO)* organization, fully support nested procedure calls and returns as well as recursive procedure calls and returns.

- Stacks are memory efficient because they reuse the same memory locations for different procedure return addresses (rather than requiring a separate memory location to hold each procedure's return address).

- Even though stack access is slower than register access, the CPU can generally access memory locations on the stack faster than separate return addresses elsewhere because the CPU frequently accesses the stack, and the stack contents tend to remain in the cache.

- As discussed in Chapter 8, stacks are also great places to store activation records (e.g., parameters, local variables, and other procedure state information).

The use of a stack does incur a few penalties as well. Most importantly, maintaining a stack generally requires dedicating a CPU register to keep track of the stack in memory. This could be a register that the CPU explicitly dedicates for this purpose (e.g., the ESP register on the 80x86) or a general-purpose register on a CPU that doesn't provide explicit hardware stack support (for example, applications running on the PowerPC processor family typically use R1 for this purpose).

On CPUs that provide a hardware stack implementation and a call/ret instruction pair, making a procedure call is easy. As shown earlier in the 80x86 GCC example output, the program simply executes a call instruction to transfer control to the beginning of the procedure and then executes a ret instruction to return from the procedure.

The PowerPC approach, using a "branch then link" instruction might seem less efficient than the call/ret mechanism. While it is certainly the case that the "branch then link" approach requires a little more code, it is not so clear that the "branch then link" approach is slower than the call/ret approach. A call instruction is a complex instruction (accomplishing several independent tasks with a single instruction). As a result, a typical call instruction requires several CPU clock cycles to execute. The execution of the ret instruction is similar. Whether the extra overhead is more costly than maintaining a software stack varies by CPU and compiler. However, a "branch then link" instruction and an indirect jump through the link address, without the overhead of maintaining the software stack, is usually faster than the corresponding call/ret instruction pair. If a procedure does not call any other procedures and it can maintain parameters and local variables in machine registers, then it's possible to skip the software stack maintenance instructions altogether. For example, the call to func() in the previous example is probably more efficient on the PowerPC than on the 80x86 because func() doesn't need to save the LINK register's value into memory—it simply leaves that value in LINK throughout the execution of the function.

Because many procedures are short and have few parameters and local variables, a good RISC compiler can often dispense with the software stack maintenance entirely. Therefore, for many common procedures, this RISC approach is faster than the CISC (call/ret) approach. However, don't get the impression that the RISC approach is always better. The brief example in this section is a very special case. In our simple demonstration program the function that this code calls, via the bl instruction, is near the bl instruction. In a complete application, func might be *very* far away, and the compiler would not be able to encode the target address as part of the instruction. That's because RISC processors (like the PowerPC) must encode their entire instruction within a single 32-bit value (which must include both the opcode and the displacement to the function). If func is farther away than can be encoded in the remaining displacement bits (24, in the case of the PowerPC bl instruction), the compiler has to emit a sequence of instructions that will compute the address of the target routine and indirectly transfer control through that indirect address. Most of the time, this shouldn't be a problem. After all, few programs are so large that the functions would be outside this range (64MB, in the case of the PowerPC). However, there is a very common case where GCC (and other compilers, presumably) must generate this type of code—when the compiler doesn't know the target address of the function because it's an external symbol that the linker must merge in after compilation is complete. Because the compiler doesn't know where the routine will be sitting in memory (and also because most linkers only work with 32-bit addresses, not 24-bit displacement fields), the compiler must assume that the function's address is out of range and emit the long version of the function call. Consider the following slight modification to the earlier example:

```
#include <stdio.h>

extern void func( void );

int main( void )
{
    func();

    return( 0 );
}
```

I've declared func() to be an external function. Now look at the PowerPC code that GCC produces and compare it with the earlier code:

```
.text
        .align 2
        .globl _main
_main:
        ; Set up main's activation record:

        mflr r0
        stw r0,8(r1)
        stwu r1,-80(r1)

        ; Call a "stub" routine that will
        ; do the real call to func():

        bl L_func$stub

        ; Return zero as Main's function
        ; result:

        lwz r0,88(r1)
```

```
        li r3,0
        addi r1,r1,80
        mtlr r0
        blr


; The following is a stub that calls the
; real "func" function, wherever it is in
; memory.

        .data
        .picsymbol_stub
L_func$stub:
        .indirect_symbol _func

        ; Begin by saving the LINK register
        ; value in R0 so we can restore it
        ; later.

        mflr r0

        ; The following code sequence gets
        ; the address of the L_func$lazy_ptr
        ; pointer object into R12:

        bcl 20,31,L0$_func        ; R11<-adrs(L0$func)
L0$_func:
        mflr r11
        addis r11,r11,ha16(L_func$lazy_ptr-L0$_func)

        ; Restore the LINK register (used by the
        ; preceeding code) from R0:

        mtlr r0

        ; Compute the address of func and move it
        ; into the PowerPC COUNT register:

        lwz r12,lo16(L_func$lazy_ptr-L0$_func)(r11)
        mtctr r12

        ; Set up R11 with an environment pointer:

        addi r11,r11,lo16(L_func$lazy_ptr-L0$_func)

        ; Branch to address held in the COUNT
        ; register (that is, to func):

        bctr

; The linker will initialize the following
; dword (.long) value with the address of
; the actual "func" function:

        .data
```

```
        .lazy_symbol_pointer
L_func$lazy_ptr:
        .indirect_symbol _func
        .long dyld_stub_binding_helper
```

This code effectively winds up calling two functions in order to call func. First, it calls a stub function (L_func$stub), which then transfers control to the actual func routine. Clearly there is considerable overhead here. Without actually benchmarking the PowerPC code against the 80x86 code, it's probably a safe bet that the 80x86 solution is a bit more efficient. (The 80x86 version of the GCC compiler emits the same code for the main program as in the earlier example, even when compiling in the external reference.) You'll soon see that the PowerPC also generates stub functions for things other than external functions. Therefore, the CISC solution often is more efficient than the RISC solution (presumably, RISC CPUs make up the difference in performance in other areas).

16.1.2   Other Sources of Overhead

Of course, there is additional overhead to a typical procedure call and return beyond the execution of the actual procedure call and return instructions. Prior to calling the procedure, the calling code must compute and pass any parameters to the procedure. Upon entry into the procedure, it may also need to complete the construction of the *activation record* (that is, allocate space for local variables). The costs of these operations vary by CPU and compiler. For example, if the calling code can pass parameters in registers rather than on the stack (or some other memory location) this is usually more efficient. Similarly, if the procedure can keep all its local variables in registers rather than in the activation record on the stack, accessing those local variables is much more efficient. This is one area where RISC processors have a considerable advantage over CISC processors. A typical RISC compiler can reserve eight or so registers for passing parameters and eight or so registers for local variables (RISC processors typically have 32 or more general-purpose registers so setting aside 16 registers for this purpose is not entirely outrageous). For procedures that don't call any other procedures (known as *leaf* procedures, as discussed in the next section), there is no need to preserve these register values, so parameter and local variable access is very efficient. On CPUs with a limited number of registers (e.g., the 80x86), it is still possible to pass a small number of parameters in registers or maintain a few local variables in registers. Many 80x86 compilers, for example, will keep up to three values (parameters or local variables) in the registers. Clearly, though, the RISC processors have an advantage in this regard.[1]

---

[1] The 80x86's saving grace is that, paradoxically, the CPU runs so much faster than typical RISC devices, so it can afford to execute a few more instructions or execute instructions that take multiple clock cycles, and it will still run faster than contemporary RISC CPUs. This is a paradox because the whole purpose of RISC design in the first place was to create a CPU that could run at a higher clock frequency, even if it took more instructions to accomplish the same thing as a CISC CPU.

Armed with this knowledge, along with the discussion of activation records and stack frames appearing earlier in this book (see Section 8.1.4, "The Stack Section"), we can now discuss how to write procedures and functions that operate as efficiently as possible. The exact rules are highly dependent upon your CPU and the compiler you're using, but some of the concepts are generic enough to apply to all programs. As usual, the following sections assume that you're writing for an 80x86 or PowerPC CPU (as most of the world's software runs on one of these two CPUs).

16.2 Leaf Functions and Procedures

Compilers can often generate better code for *leaf* procedures and functions. The metaphor comes from a graphical representation of procedure/function invocations known as a *call tree*. A call tree consists of a set of circles (called *nodes*) that represent the functions and procedures in a program. An arrow from one node to another implies that the first node contains a call to the second. Figure 16-1 illustrates a typical call tree. In this example, the main program directly calls procedure prc1 and functions fnc1 and fnc2. Function fnc1 directly calls procedure prc2. Function fnc2 directly calls procedures prc2 and prc3 as well as function fnc3. The leaf procedures and functions in this call tree are prc1, prc2, fnc3, and prc3, which do not call any other procedures or functions. With this in mind, remember that leaf procedures and functions don't further call other procedures or functions.

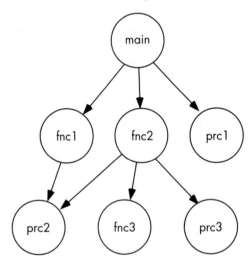

Figure 16-1: A call tree

Working with leaf procedures and functions has an advantage. They do not need save parameters passed to them in registers or preserve the values of local variables they maintain in registers. For example, if main passes two parameters to fnc1 in the EAX and EDX registers, and fnc1 passes a different pair of parameters to prc2 in EAX and EDX, then fnc1 must first save the values it found in EAX and EDX before calling prc2. The prc2 procedure, on the other hand, doesn't have to save the values in EAX and EDX prior to some procedure or function call, because it doesn't make such calls. In a similar vein, if fnc1 allocates any local variables in registers, then fnc1 will need to preserve those registers across a call to prc2 because prc2 can use the registers for its own purposes. By contrast, if prc2 uses a register for a local variable, it never has to save the value of that variable if it were to make another procedure or function call because it never makes such a call. Therefore, good compilers tend to generate better code for leaf procedures and functions because they don't have to preserve the register values.

One way to *flatten the call* tree is to take the code associated with procedures and functions appearing in interior nodes of the call tree and inlining that code into functions higher in the call tree. In Figure 16-1, for example, if it is practical to move the code for fnc1 into main, you don't need to save and restore registers (among other operations). Keep in mind, however, that you should not sacrifice readability and maintainability when flattening the call tree. You want to avoid writing procedures and functions that simply call other procedures and functions without doing any work on their own, but you don't want to destroy the modularity of your application's design by expanding function and procedure calls throughout your code.

You've already seen that having a leaf function is handy when you're using a RISC processor, like the PowerPC, that uses a "branch then link" instruction to make a subroutine call. The PowerPC LINK register is a perfect example of a register that you have to preserve across procedure calls. Because a leaf procedure does not (normally) modify the value in the LINK register, no extra code is necessary in a leaf procedure to preserve the LINK register's value. To see the benefits of calling leaf functions on a RISC CPU, consider the following C code:

```c
void g( void )
{
    return;
}

void f( void )
{
    g();
    g();
    return;
}

int main( void )
{
    f();
    return( 0 );
}
```

GCC emits the following PowerPC assembly code:

```
.text

; g's function code:
```

```
            .align 2
            .globl _g
_g:
            ;Set up g's environment
            ; (set up activation record):

            stmw r30,-8(r1)
            stwu r1,-48(r1)
            mr r30,r1

            ;Tear down the activation
            ; record.

            lwz r1,0(r1)
            lmw r30,-8(r1)

            ; Return to caller via LINK:

            blr

; f's function code:

            .align 2
            .globl _f
_f:
            ;Set up activation record,
            ; including saving the value
            ; of the LINK register:

            mflr r0           ;R0 = LINK
            stmw r30,-8(r1)
            stw r0,8(r1)      ;Save LINK
            stwu r1,-80(r1)
            mr r30,r1

            ; Call g (twice):

            bl _g
            bl _g

            ;Restore LINK from the
            ; activation record and
            ; then clean up activation
            ; record:

            lwz r1,0(r1)
            lwz r0,8(r1)      ;R0 = saved adrs
            mtlr r0           ;LINK = R0
            lmw r30,-8(r1)

            ; Return to main function:

            blr
```

```
; Main function code:

        .align 2
        .globl _main
_main:
        ;Save main's return
        ; address into main's
        ; activation record:

        mflr r0
        stmw r30,-8(r1)
        stw r0,8(r1)
        stwu r1,-80(r1)
        mr r30,r1

        ; Call the f function:

        bl _f

        ;Return zero to whomever
        ; called main:

        li r0,0
        mr r3,r0
        lwz r1,0(r1)
        lwz r0,8(r1)    ;Move saved return
        mtlr r0         ; address to LINK
        lmw r30,-8(r1)

        ;Return to caller:

        blr
```

You'll note an important difference between the implementations of the f and g functions in this PowerPC code—f has to preserve the value of the LINK register, whereas g does not. Note that not only does this involve extra instructions, but it also involves accessing memory, which can be slow.

Another advantage to using leaf procedures, which isn't obvious from the call tree, is that you can reduce the amount of work needed to construct the activation record for such procedures and functions. On the 80x86, for example, a good compiler doesn't have to preserve the value of the EBP register, load EBP with the address of the activation record, and then restore the original value by accessing local objects via the stack pointer register (ESP). On RISC processors, which maintain the stack manually, this can be a significant difference. For such procedures, the overhead of the procedure call/return and activation record maintenance is greater than the actual work done by the procedure. Therefore, eliminating the activation record maintenance code could nearly double the speed of the procedure. For these and other reasons, you should try to keep your call trees as shallow as possible. The more leaf procedures your program uses, the more efficient it may become when you compile the program with a decent compiler.

16.3 Macros and Inline Functions

One offshoot of the structured programming revolution was that computer programmers were taught to write small, modular, and logically coherent functions. A function that is logically coherent does one thing well. All of the statements in such a procedure or function are dedicated to doing the task at hand without producing any side computations or doing any extraneous operations. Years of software engineering research indicate that decomposing a problem into small components and implementing those small components in code produces programs that are easier to read, maintain, and modify. Unfortunately, it is easy to get carried away with this process and produce functions similar to the following Pascal example:

```
function sum( a:integer; b:integer ):integer;
begin

        (* returns sum of a & b as function result *)

        sum := a + b;

end;
    .
    .
    .
sum( aParam, bParam );
```

On the 80x86, it would probably take about three instructions to compute the sum of two values and store that sum into a memory variable somewhere. For example:

```
        mov( aParam, eax );
        add( bParam, eax );
        mov( eax, destVariable );
```

Contrast this with the code necessary to simply *call* the function sum:

```
        push( aParam );
        push( bParam );
        call sum;
```

Within the procedure sum (assuming a mediocre compiler), you might expect to find code similar to the following HLA sequence:

```
        // Construct the activation record

        push( ebp );
        mov( esp, ebp );

        // Get aParam's value

        mov( [ebp+12], eax );
```

```
// Compute their sum and return in EAX

add( [ebp+8], eax );

// Restore EBP's value

pop( ebp );

// Return to caller, cleaning up
//   the activation record.

ret( 8 );
```

As you can see in this simple example, with a function it takes three times as many instructions to compute the sum of these two objects as the straight-line (no function call) code. Worse still, these nine instructions are generally slower than the three that make up the inline code. The inline code could run five to ten times faster than the code with the function call.

The one redeeming quality about the overhead associated with a function or procedure call is that it's fixed. It takes the same number of instructions to set up the parameters and the activation record (as well as tear them down) if the procedure or function has one machine instruction as its body or 1,000 instructions. Although the percentage of overhead of a procedure call is huge when the procedure's body is small, the overhead associated with a procedure call is inconsequential when the procedure's body is large. There-fore, to reduce the impact of procedure/function call overhead in your programs, you should try to place larger code procedures and functions, and write shorter sequences as inline code.

Finding the optimum balance between the benefits of modular structure and the cost of too-frequent procedure calls can be difficult. Unfortunately, good program design often prevents us from increasing the size of our pro-cedures and functions to the point that the overhead of the call and return reduces to an inconsequential level. Sure, we could combine several functions and procedure calls into a single procedure or function, but this would violate several rules of programming style, so we usually don't want to resort to such tactics when writing great code. (One problem with such programs is that few people can figure out how those programs work in order to optimize them.) However, if you can't make the overhead of a procedure's body trivial by increasing the size of the procedure, you can still improve the overall performance of the procedure by reducing the overhead in other ways. As you've seen, one way to do that is to use leaf procedures and functions. Good compilers emit fewer instructions for leaf nodes in the call tree, thereby reduc-ing the call/return overhead. However, if the procedure's body is short, you need a way to completely eliminate the procedure call/return overhead. Some languages provide a way to do this with *macros*.

A *pure* macro expands the body of a procedure or function in place of the invocation of that procedure/function. Because there is no call and no return to code elsewhere in the program, a macro expansion avoids the over-head associated with the call/ret instructions. Furthermore, macros also save considerable expense by using textual substitution for parameters rather than pushing the parameter data onto the stack or moving the parameter data into registers. The drawback to a macro is that the compiler expands the macro's body for each invocation of the macro. If the macro body is large and you invoke it in many different places, the size of the executable program can grow by a fair amount. Macros represent the classic time/space trade-off—they can produce faster code at the expense of greater size. For this reason, you should only use macros to replace procedures and functions that have a small number of statements (say, between one and five short statements)—except in some rare cases where speed is paramount.

A few languages (e.g., C/C++) provide *inline* functions and procedures. An inline function or procedure is a cross between a true function (or procedure) and a pure macro. Most languages that support inline functions and procedures do not guarantee that the compiler will expand the code inline. Inline expansion or a call to an actual function in memory is done at the compiler's discretion. Most compilers will not expand an inline function if the function's body is too large or if it has an excessive number of parameters. Furthermore, unlike pure macros, which don't have any procedure call overhead associated with them, inline functions may still need to build an activation record in order to handle local variables, temporaries, and other requirements. As such, even if the compiler expands such a function inline, there may still be some overhead that you wouldn't get with a pure macro.

To see the result of function inlining, consider the following C source file prepared for compilation by Microsoft Visual C++:

```c
#include <stdio.h>

// Make geti and getj external functions
// to thwart constant propagation so we
// can see the effects of the following
// code.

extern int geti( void );
extern int getj( void );

// Inline function demonstration. Note
// that "_inline" is the MSVC++ "C" way
// of specifying an inline function (the
// actual "inline" keyword is a C++ feature,
// which this code avoids in order to make
// the assembly output a little more readable).
//
//
// "inlineFunc" is a simple inline function
// that demonstrates how the C/C++ compiler
// does a simple inline macro expansion of
// the function:

_inline int inlineFunc( int a, int b )
{
    return a + b;
```

```c
}

_inline int ilf2( int a, int b )
{
    // Declare some variable that will require
    // an activation record to be built (i.e.,
    // register allocation won't be sufficient):

    int m;
    int c[4];
    int d;

    // Make sure we use the "c" array so that
    // the optimizer doesn't ignore its
    // declaration:

    for( m = 0; m < 4; ++m )
    {
        c[m] = geti();
    }
    d = getj();
    for( m = 0; m < 4; ++m )
    {
        d += c[m];
    }

    // Return a result to the calling program:

    return (a + d) - b;
}


int main( int argc, char **argv )
{
    int i;
    int j;
    int sum;
    int result;

    i = geti();
    j = getj();
    sum = inlineFunc( i, j );
    result = ilf2( i, j );
    printf( "i+j=%d, result=%d\n", sum, result );
    return 0;
}
```

Here's the MASM-compatible assembly language code that MSVC emits when you specify a C compilation (versus a C++ compilation, which produces messier output):

```
_main    PROC NEAR

; Allocate storage for the "c" array declared
```

```
; in the ilf2 function (that gets expanded
; inline in this main program):

    sub     esp, 20

; Preserve the registers as required by
; the caller:

    push    ebx
    push    ebp
    push    esi
    push    edi

;   i = geti();

    call    _geti
    mov     ebx, eax

;   j = getj();

    call    _getj
    mov     ebp, eax

;   sum = inlineFunc( i,j );
;       = i + j (expanded inline)

    lea     eax, DWORD PTR [ebx+ebp]
    mov     DWORD PTR _sum$[esp+36], eax


;   result = ilf2( i, j );
;   Expanded inline to:
;
;   for( m = 0; m < 4; ++m )
;   {
;           c[m] = geti();
;   }


    lea     esi, DWORD PTR _c$874[esp+36]  ; ESI = c[m]
    mov     edi, 4                         ; # of iterations

$L876:
    call    _geti
    mov     DWORD PTR [esi], eax       ;c[m] = geti();

    add     esi, 4                     ;Next element
    dec     edi                        ;Next iteration
    jne     SHORT $L876

;   d = getj();

    call    _getj
```

```
        lea     ecx, DWORD PTR _c$874[esp+36]    ;ECX = c[m]

;   for( m = 0; m < 4; ++m )
;   {
;           d += c[m];
;   }

        mov     edx, 4       ;Loop iterations
$L879:
        mov     esi, DWORD PTR [ecx]
        add     ecx, 4       ;Next element
        add     eax, esi     ;d += c[m]
        dec     edx          ;Next iteration
        jne     SHORT $L879

;   return (a + d) - b;

        mov     ecx, DWORD PTR _sum$[esp+36]
        sub     eax, ebp
        add     eax, ebx

;   printf( "i+j=%d, result=%d\n", sum, result );

        push    eax
        push    ecx
        push    OFFSET FLAT:formatString ; `string'
        call    _printf
        add     esp, 12 ;Pop printf parameters


;   return 0;

        xor     eax, eax
        pop     edi
        pop     esi
        pop     ebp
        pop     ebx
; Line 72
        add     esp, 20 ;Clean up activation record
        ret     0
_main   ENDP
_TEXT   ENDS
END
```

As you can see in this assembly output, there are no function calls to the inlinefunc and ilf2 functions. Instead, the compiler expanded these functions in place in the main function, at the point where the main program calls these functions. You'll also notice that the local variables declared in the ilf2 function were allocated in the main function's activation record. Because of the inline expansion, this program does not incur the overhead of a procedure call and return (as well as building an activation record) for these two functions.

16.4 Passing Parameters to a Function or Procedure

The number and type of parameters can also have a big impact on the efficiency of the code a compiler generates for your procedures and functions. Simply put, the more parameter data you pass, the more expensive the procedure or function call is going to be. Often, programmers call generic functions (or design generic functions) that require you to pass several optional parameters whose values the function won't use. This scheme can make functions more generally applicable to different applications, but as you'll see in this section there is a cost associated with that generality, so you might want to consider using a version of the function specific to your application if space or speed is an issue.

The parameter-passing mechanism (for example, pass-by-reference or pass-by-value) also has an impact on the overhead associated with a procedure call and return. Some languages allow you to pass large data objects by value. (Pascal lets you pass strings, arrays, and records by value and C/C++ allows you to pass structures by value.) Whenever you pass a large data object by value, the compiler must emit machine code that makes a copy of that data into the procedure's activation record. This can be time-consuming (especially when copying large arrays or structures). Furthermore, large objects probably won't fit in the CPU's register set, so accessing such data within a procedure or function is going to be expensive. It is usually more efficient to pass large data objects such as arrays and structures by reference than by value. The extra cost of accessing the data indirectly is usually saved many times over by not having to copy the data into the activation record. Consider the following C code that passes a large structure by value to a C function:

```c
#include <stdio.h>

typedef struct
{
    int array[256];
} a_t;

void f( a_t a )
{
    a.array[0] = 0;
    return;
}

int main( void )
{
    a_t b;

    f( b );
    return( 0 );
}
```

Here's the PowerPC code that GCC emits:

```
.text
        .align 2
        .globl _f
_f:
        li r0,0 ; To set a.array[0] = 0

        ;Note: the PowerPC ABI passes the
        ; first eight dwords of data in
        ; R3..R10. We need to put that
        ; data back into the memory array
        ; here:

        stw r4,28(r1)
        stw r5,32(r1)
        stw r6,36(r1)
        stw r7,40(r1)
        stw r8,44(r1)
        stw r9,48(r1)
        stw r10,52(r1)

        ;Okay, store zero into a.array[0]:

        stw r0,24(r1)

        ;Return to caller:

        blr

; Main function:

        .align 2
        .globl _main
_main:

        ;Set up main's activation record:

        mflr r0
        li r5,992
        stw r0,8(r1)

        ;Allocate storage for a:

        stwu r1,-2096(r1)

        ;Copy all but the first
        ; eight dwords to the
        ; activation record for f:

        addi r3,r1,56
        addi r4,r1,1088
        bl L_memcpy$stub
```

```
        ;Load the first eight dwords
        ; into registers (as per the
        ; PowerPC ABI):

        lwz r9,1080(r1)
        lwz r3,1056(r1)
        lwz r10,1084(r1)
        lwz r4,1060(r1)
        lwz r5,1064(r1)
        lwz r6,1068(r1)
        lwz r7,1072(r1)
        lwz r8,1076(r1)

        ;Call the f function:

        bl _f

        ;Clean up the activation record
        ; and return zero to main's caller:

        lwz r0,2104(r1)
        li r3,0
        addi r1,r1,2096
        mtlr r0
        blr

;Stub function that copies the structure
; data to the activation record for the
; main function (this calls the C standard
; library memcpy function to do the actual copy):

        .data
        .picsymbol_stub
L_memcpy$stub:
        .indirect_symbol _memcpy
        mflr r0
        bcl 20,31,LO$_memcpy
LO$_memcpy:
        mflr r11
        addis r11,r11,ha16(L_memcpy$lazy_ptr-LO$_memcpy)
        mtlr r0
        lwz r12,lo16(L_memcpy$lazy_ptr-LO$_memcpy)(r11)
        mtctr r12
        addi r11,r11,lo16(L_memcpy$lazy_ptr-LO$_memcpy)
        bctr
.data
.lazy_symbol_pointer
L_memcpy$lazy_ptr:
        .indirect_symbol _memcpy
        .long dyld_stub_binding_helper
```

As you can see, the call to function f calls memcpy to transfer a copy of the data from main's local array to f's activation record. Copying memory is a slow process and this code amply demonstrates that you should avoid passing large objects by value. Consider the same code when you pass the structure by reference:

```
#include <stdio.h>

typedef struct
{
    int array[256];
} a_t;

void f( a_t *a )
{
    a->array[0] = 0;
    return;
}

int main( void )
{
    a_t b;

    f( &b );
    return( 0 );
}
```

Here's the conversion of this C source code to PowerPC assembly by GCC:

```
.text
        .align 2
        .globl _f

; function f:

_f:
        li r0,0         ;Store zero into
        stw r0,0(r3)    ; a.array[0]
        blr             ;Return to main

        .align 2
        .globl _main

; The main function:

_main:
        ; Build main's activation record

        mflr r0         ;Save return adrs
        stw r0,8(r1)
        stwu r1,-1104(r1) ;Allocate a

        ;Pass the address of a to f in R3:

        addi r3,r1,64
```

```
;Call f:

bl _f

;Tear down activation record
; and return:

lwz r0,1112(r1)
li r3,0
addi r1,r1,1104
mtlr r0
blr
```

Depending on your CPU and compiler, it may be slightly more efficient to pass small (scalar) data objects by value rather than by reference. For example, if you're using an 80x86 compiler that passes parameters on the stack, two instructions will be needed to pass a memory object by reference but only a single instruction to pass that same object by value. So, although trying to pass large objects by reference is a good idea, the reverse is generally true for small objects. However, this is not a hard and fast rule; its validity varies based on the CPU and compiler you're using.

Some programmers may feel that it's more efficient to pass data to a procedure or function via global variables. After all, if the data is already sitting in a global variable that is accessible to the procedure or function, a call to that procedure or function won't require any extra instructions to pass the data to the subroutine, thus reducing the call overhead. While this seems like a big win, one thing you should consider before doing this is that compilers have a difficult time optimizing programs that make excessive use of global variables. Although using globals may reduce the function/procedure call overhead, doing so may also prevent the compiler from handling other optimizations that would have been otherwise possible. Here's a simple example using Microsoft Visual C++ that demonstrates this problem:

```
#include <stdio.h>

// Make geti an external function
// to thwart constant propagation so we
// can see the effects of the following
// code.

extern int geti( void );

// globalValue is a global variable that
// we use to pass data to the "usesGlobal"
// function:

int globalValue = 0;

// Inline function demonstration. Note
// that "_inline" is the MSVC++ "C" way
// of specifying an inline function (the
```

```
// actual "inline" keyword is a C++ feature,
// which this code avoids in order to make
// the assembly output a little more readable).


_inline int usesGlobal( int plusThis )
{
    return globalValue+plusThis;
}

_inline int usesParm( int plusThis, int globalValue )
{
    return globalValue+plusThis;
}


int main( int argc, char **argv )
{
    int i;
    int sumLocal;
    int sumGlobal;

    // Note: the call to geti inbetween setting globalValue
    // and calling usesGlobal is intentional. The compiler
    // doesn't know that geti doesn't modify the value of
    // globalValue (and neither do we, frankly), therefore,
    // the compiler cannot use constant propagation here.

    globalValue = 1;
    i = geti();
    sumGlobal = usesGlobal( 5 );

    // If we pass the "globalValue" as a parameter rather
    // than setting a global variable, then the compiler
    // can optimize the code away:

    sumLocal = usesParm( 5, 1 );
    printf( "sumGlobal=%d, sumLocal=%d\n", sumGlobal, sumLocal );
    return 0;
}
```

Here's the MASM source code (with manual annotations) that the MSVC++ compiler generates for this code:

```
_main       PROC NEAR

;   globalValue = 1;

    mov     DWORD PTR _globalValue, 1

;   i = geti();
;
; Note that because of dead code elimination,
; MSVC++ doesn't actually store the result
```

```
; away into i, but it must still call geti()
; because geti() could produce side-effects
; (such as modifying globalValue's value).

    call   _geti

;   sumGlobal = usesGlobal( 5 );
;
; Expanded inline to:
;
; globalValue+plusThis

    mov    eax, DWORD PTR _globalValue
    add    eax, 5           ; plusThis = 5

; The compiler uses constant propagation
; to compute:
;   sumLocal = usesParm( 5, 1 );
; at compile time. The result is six, which
; the compiler directly passes to print here:

    push   6

; Here's the result for the usesGlobal expansion,
; computed above:

    push   eax
    push   OFFSET FLAT:formatString ; 'string'
    call   _printf
    add    esp, 12      ;Remove printf parameters

; return 0;

    xor    eax, eax
    ret    0
_main      ENDP
_TEXT      ENDS
END
```

As you can see in this assembly language output, the compiler's ability to optimize around global variables can be easily thwarted by the presence of some seemingly unrelated code. In this example, the compiler cannot determine that the call to the external geti() function doesn't modify the value of the globalValue variable. Therefore, the compiler cannot assume that globalValue still has the value 1 when it computes the inline function result for usesGlobal. Use extreme caution when using global variables to communicate information between a procedure or function and its caller. Code that is unrelated to the task at hand (such as the call to geti(), which probably doesn't affect globalValue's value) can prevent the compiler from optimizing code that uses global variables.

16.5 Activation Records and the Stack

Because of how a stack works, the last procedure activation record the software creates will be the first activation record that the system deallocates. Because activation records hold procedure parameters and local variables, a *last-in, first-out (LIFO)* organization is a very intuitive mechanism for implementing activation records. To see how this works, consider the following (trivial) Pascal program:

```
program ActivationRecordDemo;

    procedure C;
    begin

        (* Stack Snapshot here *)

    end;

    procedure B;
    begin

        C;

    end;

    procedure A;
    begin

        B;

    end;

begin (* Main Program *)

    A;

end.
```

Figure 16-2 shows the stack layout as this program executes. When the program begins execution, it first creates an activation record for the main program. The main program calls the A procedure (step 1 in Figure 16-2). Upon entry into the A procedure, the code completes the construction of the activation record for A; this effectively pushes A's activation record onto the stack. Once inside procedure A, the code calls procedure B (step 2). Note that A is still active while the code calls B, so A's activation record remains on the stack. Upon entry into B, the system builds B's activation record and pushes this activation record onto the top of the stack (step 3). Once inside B, the code calls procedure C and C builds its activation record on the stack. Upon arriving at the comment (* Stack Snapshot here *) the stack looks like that shown at step 4 in Figure 16-2.

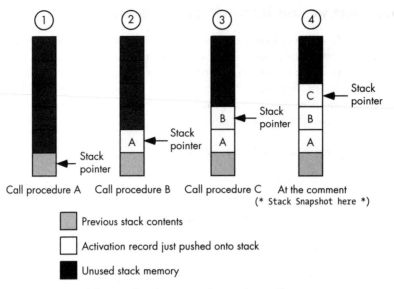

Figure 16-2: Stack layout after three nested procedure calls

Because procedures keep their local variables and parameter values in their activation record, the lifetime of these variables extends from the point the system first creates the activation record until the system deallocates the activation record when the procedure returns to its caller. In the diagram above, you'll notice that A's activation record remains on the stack during the execution of the B and C procedures. Therefore, the lifetime of A's parameters and local variables completely brackets the lifetimes of B's and C's activation records.

Now consider the following C/C++ code with a recursive function:

```
void recursive( int cnt )
{
    if( cnt != 0 )
    {
        recursive( cnt - 1 );
    }
}

int main( int argc; char **argv )
{
    recursive( 2 );
}
```

It should be clear that this program will call the recursive function three times before it begins returning (the main program calls recursive once with the parameter value 2; recursive calls itself twice with the parameter values 1 and 0). Because each recursive call to recursive pushes another activation record before the current call returns, when this program finally hits the if statement in the code above with cnt equal to 0, the stack looks something like that in Figure 16-3.

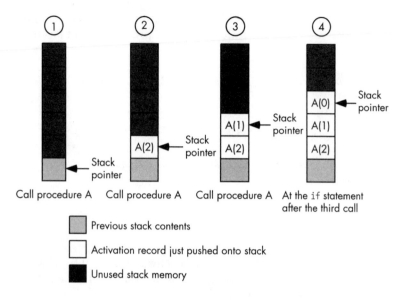

Figure 16-3: Stack layout after three recursive procedure calls

Because each procedure invocation has a separate activation record, each activation of the procedure will have its own copy of the parameters and local variables. While the code for a procedure or function is executing, it will access only those local variables and parameters in the activation record it has most recently created,[2] thus preserving the values from previous calls (as we would expect).

16.5.1   Composition of the Activation Record

Now that you've seen how procedures manipulate activation records on the stack, it's time to take a look at the internal composition of a typical activation record. In this section we'll use a typical activation record layout that you'll see when executing code on an 80x86. Although different languages, different compilers, and different CPUs lay out the activation record differently, these differences, if they exist at all, will be minor.

The 80x86 maintains the stack and activation records using two registers: ESP (the stack pointer) and EBP (the frame-pointer register, which Intel calls the *base pointer* register). The ESP register points at the current top of stack, and the EBP register points at the base address of an activation record.[3] A procedure can access objects within its activation record by using the indexed addressing mode (see Section 3.6.5, "Indexed Addressing Mode") and supplying a positive or negative offset from the value in the EBP register. Generally, a procedure will allocate memory storage for local variables at

---

[2] The only exception occurs when a procedure recursively calls itself and passes one of its local variables or parameters by reference to the new invocation.

[3] Some people call activation records *stack frames* which is where the phrase *frame pointer* comes from. Intel chose the name *base pointer* for the EBP register because it points at the base address of the stack frame.

negative offsets from EBP's value and for parameters at positive offsets from EBP. Consider the following Pascal procedure that has both parameters and local variables:

```
procedure HasBoth( i:integer; j:integer; k:integer );
var
    a  :integer;
    r  :integer;
    c  :char;
    b  :char;
    w  :smallint;  (* smallints are 16 bits *)
begin

    .
    .
    .

end;
```

Figure 16-4 shows a typical activation record for this Pascal procedure (remember, when looking at this diagram, that the stack grows toward lower member on the 80x86).

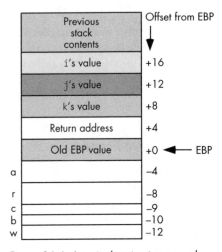

Figure 16-4: A typical activation record

When you see the term *base* associated with a memory object, you probably think that the base address is the lowest address of that object in memory. However, there is no such requirement. The base address is simply the address in memory on which you base the offsets to particular fields of that object. As this activation record demonstrates, 80x86 activation record base addresses are actually in the middle of the record.

Construction of the activation record occurs in two phases. The first phase begins in the code that calls the procedure when that code pushes the parameters for the call onto the stack. For example, consider the following call to HasBoth in the previous example:

```
HasBoth( 5, x, y + 2 );
```

The HLA/x86 assembly code that might correspond to this call is

```
pushd( 5 );
push( x );
mov( y, eax );
add( 2, eax );
push( eax );
call HasBoth;
```

The three push instructions in this code sequence build the first three double words of the activation record, and the call instruction pushes a *return address* onto the stack, thereby creating the fourth double word in the activation record. After the call, execution continues in the HasBoth procedure itself, where the program continues to build the activation record.

The first few instructions of the HasBoth procedure are responsible for finishing the construction of the activation record. Immediately upon entry into HasBoth, the stack takes the form shown in Figure 16-5.

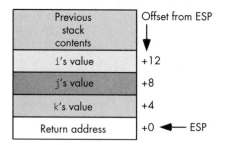

Figure 16-5: Activation record upon entry to HasBoth

The first thing the procedure's code should to do is to preserve the value in the 80x86 EBP register. On entry, EBP probably points at the base address of the caller's activation record. On exit from HasBoth, EBP needs to contain its original value. Therefore, upon entry, HasBoth will need to push the current value of EBP on the stack in order to preserve EBP's value. Next, the HasBoth procedure needs to change EBP so that it points at the base address of HasBoth's activation record. The following HLA/x86 code takes care of these two operations:

```
// Preserve caller's base address.

    push( ebp );

    // ESP points at the value we just saved. Use its address
    //  as the activation record's base address.

    mov( esp, ebp );
```

Finally, the code at the beginning of the HasBoth procedure needs to allocate storage for its local (automatic) variables. As you saw in Figure 16-4, those variables sit below the frame pointer in the activation record. To prevent future pushes from wiping out the values in those local variables, the code has to set ESP to the address of the last double word of local variables in the activation record. This is easily accomplished by simply subtracting the number of bytes of local variables from ESP with the following single machine instruction:

```
sub( 12, esp );
```

The *standard entry sequence* for a procedure like HasBoth consists of the three machine instructions just considered: push(ebp);, mov(esp, ebp);, and sub(12, esp);. These three instructions complete the construction of the activation record inside the procedure. Just before returning, the Pascal procedure is responsible for deallocating the storage associated with the activation record. The *standard exit sequence* usually takes the following form (in HLA) for a Pascal procedure:

```
// Deallocates the local variables
//  by copying EBP to ESP.

mov( ebp, esp );

// Restore original EBP value.

pop( ebp );

// Pops return address and
//  12 parameter bytes (3 dwords)

ret( 12 );
```

The first instruction in this standard exit sequence deallocates storage for the local variables shown in Figure 16-4. Note that EBP is pointing at the old value of EBP; this value is stored at the memory address just above all the local variables. By copying the value in EBP to ESP, we move the stack pointer past all the local variables, effectively deallocating them. After copying the value in EBP to ESP, the stack pointer now points at the old value of EBP on the stack; therefore, the pop instruction in the sequence above restores EBP's original value and leaves ESP pointing at the return address on the stack. The ret instruction in the standard exit sequence does two things: it pops the return address from the stack (and, of course, transfers control to this address), and it also removes 12 bytes of parameters from the stack. Because HasBoth has three double-word parameters, popping 12 bytes from the stack removes those parameters.

16.5.2 Assigning Offsets to Local Variables

This HasBoth example allocates local (automatic) variables in the order the compiler encounters them. A typical compiler maintains a *current offset* into the activation record for local variables (the initial value of current offset will be 0). Whenever the compiler encounters a local variable it simply subtracts the size of that variable from the current offset and then uses the new current offset value as the offset of the local variable (from EBP) in the activation record. For example, upon encountering the declaration for variable a, the compiler subtracts the size of a (4 bytes) from the current offset (0) and uses the result as the offset for a (–4). Next, the compiler encounters variable r (which is also 4 bytes) and sets the current offset to –8 and assigns this offset to variable r. This process repeats for each of the local variables in the procedure. This is a typical way compilers assign offsets to local variables.

Most languages, however, give compiler implementers a free reign with respect to how they allocate local objects. A compiler can rearrange the objects in the activation record if doing so will be more convenient. So while the previous paragraph describes the basic idea, you should not design any algorithms that depend on this allocation scheme because many compilers do it differently.

Many compilers will try to ensure that all local variables you declare have an offset that is a multiple of the object's size. For example, suppose you have the following two declarations in a C function:

```
char c;
int  i;
```

Normally, you'd expect that the compiler would attach an offset like –1 to the c variable and –5 to the (4-byte) int variable i. However, some CPUs (e.g., RISC CPUs) require the compiler to allocate double-word objects on a double-word boundary. Even on CPUs that don't require this (for example, the 80x86), it may be faster to access a double-word variable if the compiler aligns it on a double-word boundary. For this reason, many compilers automatically add padding bytes between local variables so that each variable resides at a *natural* offset in the activation record. In general, bytes may appear at any offset, words are happiest on even address boundaries, and double words should have a memory address that is a multiple of 4.

Although an optimizing compiler might automatically handle this alignment for you, the alignment does extract a certain cost—those extra padding bytes. Although compilers are usually free to rearrange the variables in an activation record as they see fit, most compilers do not always do this. Therefore, if you intertwine the definitions for several byte, word, double-word, and other-sized objects in your local variable declarations, the compiler may wind up inserting several bytes of padding into the activation record. You can minimize this problem in your software by attempting to group as many like-sized objects together as is reasonable in your procedures and functions. Consider the following C/C++ code:

```
char c0;
int  i0;
char c1;
int  i1;
char c2;
int  i2;
```

```
char c3;
int  i3;
```

An optimizing compiler may elect to insert 3 bytes of padding between each of the character variables above and the (4-byte) integer variable that immediately follows. This means that the code above will have about 12 bytes of wasted space (3 bytes for each of the character variables above). Now consider the following declarations in the same C code:

```
char c0;
char c1;
char c2;
char c3;
int  i0;
int  i1;
int  i2;
int  i3;
```

In this example, the compiler will emit no extra padding bytes to the code. Why? Because characters (being 1 byte each) may begin at any address in memory. Therefore, the compiler can place the character variables above at offsets –1, –2, –3, and –4 within the activation record. Because the last character variable appears at an address that is a multiple of four, the compiler does not need to insert any padding bytes between c3 and i0 (i0 will naturally appear at offset –8 in the preceding declarations).

Therefore, you can help the compiler generate better code by arranging your declarations so that all like-sized objects are next to one another. Of course, you shouldn't take this suggestion to an extreme. If such rearrangement would make your program more difficult to read or maintain, you should carefully consider whether this idea is worthwhile in your program. But in the absence of other negative factors, organizing your local variable declarations by size is probably a good idea.

16.5.3   Associating Offsets with Parameters

Compilers are given considerable leeway with respect to how they assign offsets to local (automatic) variables within a procedure. As long as the compiler uses these offsets consistently, the exact allocation algorithm the compiler uses is almost irrelevant; indeed, a compiler could use a different allocation scheme in different procedures of the same program. Note, however, that a procedure doesn't have a free hand when assigning offsets to parameters. The compiler has to live with certain restrictions on the assignment of offsets to parameters because other code outside the procedure accesses those parameters. Specifically, the procedure and the calling code must agree on the layout of the parameters in the activation record because the calling code needs to build the parameter list. Note that the calling code might not be in the same source file. Indeed, the code calling a procedure could be in a different programming language. Therefore, compilers need to adhere to certain *calling conventions* to ensure interoperability between a procedure and whatever code calls that procedure. This section will explore the three common calling conventions for Pascal/Delphi/Kylix and C/C++.

16.5.3.1 The Pascal Calling Convention

In Pascal (including Delphi and Kylix) the standard parameter-passing convention is to push the parameters on the stack in the order of their appearance in the parameter list. Consider, again, the following call to the HasBoth procedure from the earlier example:

```
HasBoth( 5, x, y + 2 );
```

The following assembly code implements this call:

```
// Push the value for parameter i:

pushd( 5 );

// Push x's value for parameter j:

push( x );

// Compute y + 2 in EAX and push this as the value
//   for parameter k:

mov( y, eax );
add( 2, eax );
push( eax );

// Call the HasBoth procedure with these
// three parameter values:

call HasBoth;
```

When assigning offsets to a procedure's formal parameters, the compiler assigns the highest offset to the first parameter and the lowest offset to the last parameter. Because the old value of EBP is at offset 0 in the activation record and the return address is at offset 4, the last parameter in the activation record (when using the Pascal calling convention on the 80x86 CPU) will reside at offset 8 from EBP. Looking back at Figure 16-4 you can see that parameter k is at offset +8, parameter j is at offset +12, and parameter i (the first parameter) is at offset +16 in the activation record.

The Pascal calling convention also stipulates that it is the procedure's responsibility to remove the parameters the caller pushes when the procedure returns to its caller. As you saw earlier, the 80x86 CPU provides a variant of the ret instruction that lets you specify how many bytes of parameters to remove from the stack upon return. Therefore, a procedure that uses the Pascal calling convention will typically supply the number of parameter bytes as an operand to the ret instruction when returning to its caller.

16.5.3.2 The C Calling Convention

The C/C++/Java languages employ another very popular calling convention, generally known as the *cdecl calling convention* (or, simply, the *C calling convention*). There are two major differences between the C and Pascal calling conventions. First, calls to functions that use the C calling convention must push their parameters on the stack in the reverse order. That is, the first parameter must appear at the lowest address on the stack (assuming the stack grows downward), and the last parameter must appear at the highest address in memory. The second difference is that C requires the caller, rather than the function, to remove all parameters from the stack.

Consider the following version of HasBoth written in C instead of Pascal:

```c
void HasBoth( int i, int j, int k )
{
    int a;
    int r;
    char c;
    char b;
    short w;  /* assumption: short ints are 16 bits */
        .
        .
        .
}
```

Figure 16-6 provides the layout for a typical HasBoth activation record (written in C). If you look closely, you'll see the difference between it and Figure 16-4. The positions of the i and k variables are reversed in the activation record (it is only a coincidence that j happens to appear at the same offset in both activation records).

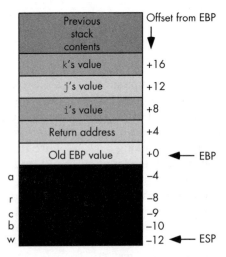

Figure 16-6: HasBoth activation record in C

Because the C calling convention reverses the order of the parameters and it is the caller's responsibility to remove all parameter values from the stack, the calling sequence for HasBoth is a little different in C than in Pascal. Consider the following call to HasBoth and its corresponding assembly code:

```
HasBoth( 5, x, y + 2 );
```

Here's the HLA assembly code for this call:

```
// Compute y + 2 in EAX and push this
//   as the value for parameter k

mov( y, eax );
add( 2, eax );
push( eax );

// Push x's value for parameter j

push( x );

// Push the value for parameter i

pushd( 5 );

// Call the HasBoth procedure with
//   these three parameter values

call HasBoth;

// Remove parameters from the stack.

add( 12, esp );
```

This code differs in two ways with the assembly code for the Pascal implementation; both differences are a result of the use of the C calling convention. First, this assembly code pushes the values of the actual parameters in the opposite order of the Pascal code; that is, it first computes y+2 and pushes that value, then it pushes x and finally it pushes the value 5. The second difference above is the inclusion of the add(12,esp); instruction immediately after the call. This instruction removes 12 bytes of parameters from the stack upon return. The return from HasBoth will use only the ret instruction, not the ret n instruction.

16.5.3.3 Passing Parameters in Registers

As you can see by looking at these examples, a fair amount of code is needed to pass parameters between two procedures or functions when passing parameters on the stack. Good assembly language programmers have long known that it is better to pass parameters in registers. Therefore, several 80x86 compilers following Intel's ABI (Application Binary Interface) rules may attempt to pass as many as three parameters in the EAX, EDX, and ECX registers.[4] Most RISC processors specifically set aside a set of registers for passing parameters between functions and procedures; for example, the PowerPC reserves eight general-purpose registers, R3..R10, to hold parameter values. The only problem with passing parameters in the registers is that both the caller and callee need to agree on which registers and how many registers to use for the parameters. Fortunately, many CPU manufacturers specify a convention (e.g., Intel's 80x86 ABI and IBM's PowerPC ABI), so as long as the compiler follows the convention a small degree of interoperability is possible.

Most CPUs require that the stack pointer remain aligned on some reasonable boundary (for example, a double-word boundary), and CPUs that don't absolutely require this may perform much better if you keep the stack pointer aligned properly. Furthermore, many CPUs (the 80x86 included) cannot easily push certain small-sized objects, like bytes, onto the stack. Therefore, most compilers reserve a minimum number of bytes for a parameter (typically 4), regardless of its actual size. As an example, consider the following HLA procedure fragment:

```
procedure OneByteParm( b:byte ); @nodisplay;
    // local variable declarations
begin OneByteParm;
    .
    .
    .
end OneByteParm;
```

The activation record for this procedure appears in Figure 16-7. As you can see in this diagram, the HLA compiler reserves 4 bytes for the b parameter even though b is only a byte variable. This extra padding ensures that the ESP register will remain aligned on a double-word boundary.[5] We will be able to easily push the value of b onto the stack in the code that calls OneByteParm using a 4-byte push instruction.[6]

Even if your program could access the extra bytes of padding associated with the b parameter, doing so is never a good idea. Unless you've explicitly pushed the parameter onto the stack (e.g., using assembly language code), there is no guarantee about the data values that appear in the padding bytes. In particular, they may not contain 0. Nor should your code assume that the padding is present or that the compiler pads such variables out to 4 bytes. Some 16-bit processors may only require a single byte of padding. Some 64-bit processors may require 7 bytes of padding. Some compilers on the 80x86 may use 1 byte of padding while others use 3 bytes. Unless

---

[4] The number of parameters chosen, three, is not arbitrary. Studies in software engineering strongly suggest that most user-written procedures have three or fewer parameters.

[5] Assuming, of course, it was so aligned prior to appearance of the b parameter on the stack.

[6] The 80x86 does not directly support 1-byte pushes onto the stack, so if the compiler only reserved 1 byte of storage for this parameter, it would take several machine instructions in order to simulate that 1-byte push.

you're willing to live with code that only one compiler can compile (and code that could break when the next version of the compiler comes along), it's best to ignore these padding bytes.

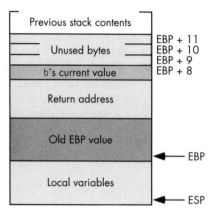

Figure 16-7: OneByteParm activation record

16.5.4 Accessing Parameters and Local Variables

Once a subroutine sets up the activation record, accessing local (automatic) variables and parameters is easy. The machine code simply uses the indexed addressing mode to access such objects. Consider again the activation record in Figure 16-4. The variables in the HasBoth procedure have the offsets found in Table 16-1.

Table 16-1: Offsets to Local Variables and Parameters in HasBoth (Pascal Version)

Variable	Offset	Addressing Mode Example
i	+16	mov([ebp+16], eax);
j	+12	mov([ebp+12], eax);
k	+8	mov([ebp+8], eax);
a	−4	mov([ebp-4], eax);
r	−8	mov([ebp-8], eax);
c	−9	mov([ebp-9], al);
b	−10	mov([ebp-10], al);
w	−12	mov([ebp-12], ax);

The compiler allocates static local variables in a procedure at a fixed address in memory. Static variables do not appear in the activation record. Therefore, the CPU accesses static objects using the direct addressing mode.[7] As you may recall from Chapter 3, in 80x86 assembly language instructions that use the direct address mode need to encode the full 32-bit address as part of the machine instruction. Therefore, instructions that use the direct

---

[7] Assuming the object is a scalar object. If it is an array, for example, the machine code may use the indexed addressing mode to access elements of the static array.

addressing mode are usually at least 5 bytes long (and are often longer). On the 80x86, if the offset from EBP is −128 through +127, then a compiler can encode an instruction of the form [ebp+constant] in as few as 2 or 3 bytes. Such instructions will be more efficient that those that encode a full 32-bit address. The same principle applies on other processors, even if those CPUs provide different addressing modes, address sizes, and so on. Specifically, access to local variables whose offset is relatively small is generally more efficient than accessing static variables or variables with larger offsets.

Because most compilers allocate offsets for local (automatic) variables as the compiler encounters them, the first 128 bytes of local variables will be the ones with the shortest offsets (at least, on the 80x86; this value may be different for other processors).

Consider the following two sets of local variable declarations (presumably appearing with some C function):

```
// Declaration set #1:

char string[256];
int i;
int j;
char c;
```

Here's a second version of the declarations above:

```
// Declaration set #2

int i;
int j;
char c;
char string[256];
```

Although these two declaration's sections are semantically identical, there is a big difference in the code a compiler for the 80x86 generates to access these variables. In the first preceding declaration, the variable string appears at offset −256 within the activation record, i appears at offset −260, j appears at offset −264, and c appears at offset −265. Because these offsets are outside the range −128..+127, the compiler will have to emit machine instructions that encode a 4-byte offset constant rather than a 1-byte constant. As such, the code associated with these declarations will be larger and may run slower.

Now consider the second preceding declaration. In this example the programmer declares the scalar (non-array) objects first. Therefore, the variables have the following offsets: i =- 4, j =- 8, c =- 9, and string =- 265. This turns out to be the optimal configuration for these variables (i, j, and c will use 1-byte offsets; string will require a 4-byte offset).

This example demonstrates another rule you should try to follow when declaring local (automatic) variables: declare smaller, scalar, objects first within a procedure and put all the arrays, structures/records, and other large objects after the smaller objects.

As you may recall from an earlier discussion (Section 16.5.3, "Associating Offsets with Parameters"), if you declare several local objects with differing sizes adjacent to one another, the compiler may need to insert padding bytes to keep the larger objects aligned at an appropriate memory address. While worrying about a few wasted bytes here and there may seem ridiculous on machines with a gigabyte (or more) of RAM, those few extra bytes of padding may be just enough to push the offsets of certain local variables beyond –128. This would cause the compiler to emit 4-byte offsets rather than 2-byte offsets for those variables. So here is one more reason you should try to declare like-sized local variables adjacent to one another.

On RISC processors, such as the PowerPC, the range of possible offsets is usually much greater than plus or minus 128. This is good, because once you exceed the range of the activation record offset that a RISC CPU can encode directly into an instruction, parameter and local variable access gets very expensive. Consider the following C program and PowerPC output (from GCC):

```c
#include <stdio.h>
int main( int argc )
{
    int a;
    int b[256];
    int c;
    int d[16*1024*1024];
    int e;
    int f;

    a = argc;
    b[0] = argc + argc;
    b[255] = a + b[0];
    c = argc + b[1];
    d[0] = argc + a;
    d[4095] = argc + b[255];
    e = a + c;
    printf
    (
        "%d %d %d %d %d ",
        a,
        b[0],
        c,
        d[0],
        e
    );
    return( 0 );
}
```

Here's the PowerPC assembly output from GCC:

```
.data
        .cstring
        .align 2
        LC0:
```

```
            .ascii "%d %d %d %d %d \0"
            .text

; Main function:

            .align 2
            .globl _main
_main:
            ;Set up main's activation record:

            mflr r0
            stmw r30,-8(r1)
            stw r0,8(r1)
            lis r0,0xfbff
            ori r0,r0,64384
            stwux r1,r1,r0
            mr r30,r1
            bcl 20,31,L1$pb
L1$pb:
            mflr r31

            ; The following allocates
            ; 16MB of storage on the
            ; stack (R30 is the stack
            ; pointer here).

            addis r9,r30,0x400
            stw r3,1176(r9)

            ;Fetch the value of argc
            ; into the R0 register:

            addis r11,r30,0x400
            lwz r0,1176(r11)
            stw r0,64(r30)        ;a = argc

            ;Fetch the value of argc
            ; into r9

            addis r11,r30,0x400
            lwz r9,1176(r11)

            ;Fetch the value of argc
            ; into R0:

            addis r11,r30,0x400
            lwz r0,1176(r11)

            ;Compute argc + argc and
            ; store it into b[0]:

            add r0,r9,r0
            stw r0,80(r30)

            ;Add a + b[0] and
```

```
; store into c:

lwz r9,64(r30)
lwz r0,80(r30)
add r0,r9,r0
stw r0,1100(r30)

;Get argc's value, add in
; b[1], and store into c:

addis r11,r30,0x400
lwz r9,1176(r11)
lwz r0,84(r30)
add r0,r9,r0
stw r0,1104(r30)

;Compute argc + a and
; store into d[0]:

addis r11,r30,0x400
lwz r9,1176(r11)
lwz r0,64(r30)
add r0,r9,r0
stw r0,1120(r30)

;Compute argc + b[255] and
; store into d[4095]:

addis r11,r30,0x400
lwz r9,1176(r11)
lwz r0,1100(r30)
add r0,r9,r0
stw r0,17500(r30)

;Compute argc + b[255]:

lwz r9,64(r30)
lwz r0,1104(r30)
add r9,r9,r0
```

; **
```
;Okay, here's where it starts
; to get ugly. We need to compute
; the address of e so we can store
; the result currently held in r9
; into e. But e's offset exceeds
; what we can encode into a single
; instruction, so we have to use
; the following sequence rather
; than a single instruction.

lis r0,0x400
ori r0,r0,1120
stwx r9,r30,r0
```

; **

```
;The following sets up the
; call to printf and calls printf:

addis r3,r31,ha16(LC0-L1$pb)
la r3,lo16(LC0-L1$pb)(r3)
lwz r4,64(r30)
lwz r5,80(r30)
lwz r6,1104(r30)
lwz r7,1120(r30)
lis r0,0x400
ori r0,r0,1120
lwzx r8,r30,r0
bl L_printf$stub
li r0,0
mr r3,r0
lwz r1,0(r1)
lwz r0,8(r1)
mtlr r0
lmw r30,-8(r1)
blr
```

```
; Stub, to call the external printf function:

        .data
        .picsymbol_stub
L_printf$stub:
        .indirect_symbol _printf
        mflr r0
        bcl 20,31,L0$_printf
L0$_printf:
        mflr r11
        addis r11,r11,ha16(L_printf$lazy_ptr-L0$_printf)
        mtlr r0
        lwz r12,lo16(L_printf$lazy_ptr-L0$_printf)(r11)
        mtctr r12
        addi r11,r11,lo16(L_printf$lazy_ptr-L0$_printf)
        bctr
.data
.lazy_symbol_pointer
L_printf$lazy_ptr:
        .indirect_symbol _printf
        .long dyld_stub_binding_helper
```

This compilation was done under GCC without optimization to show what happens when your activation record grows to the point you can no longer encode activation record offsets into the instruction.

To encode the address of e, whose offset is too large, we need these three instructions:

```
lis r0,0x400
ori r0,r0,1120
stwx r9,r30,r0
```

instead of a single instruction that stores R0 into the a variable, such as:

```
stw r0,64(r30)        ;a = argc
```

While two extra instructions in a program of this size might seem insignificant, keep in mind that the compiler will generate these extra instructions for each such access. If you access a local variable with a huge offset frequently, the compiler may generate a significant number of extra instructions throughout your function or procedure.

Of course, in a standard application running on a RISC, this problem rarely occurs because we rarely allocate local storage beyond the range that a single instruction can encode. Also, RISC compilers generally allocate scalar (non-array/non-structure) objects in registers rather than blindly allocating them at the next memory address in the activation record. For example, if you turn on GCC's optimization with the -02 command-line switch, you'll get the following PowerPC output:

```
.globl _main
_main:

; Build main's activation record:

        mflr r0
        stw r31,-4(r1)
        stw r0,8(r1)
        bcl 20,31,L1$pb
L1$pb:
        ;Compute values, set up parameters,
        ; and call printf:

        lis r0,0xfbff
        slwi r9,r3,1
        ori r0,r0,64432
        mflr r31
        stwux r1,r1,r0
        add r11,r3,r9
        mr r4,r3
        mr r0,r3
        lwz r6,68(r1)
        add r0,r0,r11 ;c = argc + b[1]
        stw r0,17468(r1)
        mr r5,r9
        add r6,r3,r6
        stw r9,64(r1)
        addis r3,r31,ha16(LC0-L1$pb)
        stw r11,1084(r1)
        stw r9,1088(r1)
        la r3,lo16(LC0-L1$pb)(r3)
        mr r7,r9
        add r8,r4,r6
        bl L_printf$stub
```

```
; Clean up main's activation
; record and return zero:

        lwz r1,0(r1)
        li r3,0
        lwz r0,8(r1)
        lwz r31,-4(r1)
        mtlr r0
        blr
```

One thing that you'll notice in this version with optimization enabled
is that GCC did not allocate variables in the activation record as they were
encountered. Instead, it placed most of the objects in registers (even array
elements). Keep in mind that an optimizing compiler may very well rearrange
all the local variables you declare.

If you find the optimized PowerPC code a bit hard to follow, consider
the following 80x86 GCC output for the same C program:

```
.file   "t.c"
        .section        .rodata.str1.1,"aMS",@progbits,1
.LC0:
        .string "%d %d %d %d %d "
        .text
        .p2align 2,,3
        .globl main
        .type   main,@function
main:
        ;Build main's activation record:

        pushl   %ebp
        movl    %esp, %ebp
        pushl   %ebx
        subl    $67109892, %esp

        ;Fetch ARGC into ECX:

        movl    8(%ebp), %ecx

        ; EDX = 2*argc:

        leal    (%ecx,%ecx), %edx

        ; EAX = a (ECX) + b[0] (EDX):

        leal    (%edx,%ecx), %eax

        ; c (ebx) = argc (ecx) + b[1]:

        movl    %ecx, %ebx
        addl    -1028(%ebp), %ebx
        movl    %eax, -12(%ebp)

        ;Align stack for printf call:
```

```
        andl    $-16, %esp

        ;d[0] (eax) = argc (ecx) + a (eax);

        leal    (%eax,%ecx), %eax

        ; Make room for printf parameters:

        subl    $8, %esp
        movl    %eax, -67093516(%ebp)

        ; e = a + c

        leal    (%ebx,%ecx), %eax


        pushl   %eax    ;e
        pushl   %edx    ;d[0]
        pushl   %ebx    ;c
        pushl   %edx    ;b[0]
        pushl   %ecx    ;a
        pushl   $.LC0
        movl    %edx, -1032(%ebp)
        movl    %edx, -67109896(%ebp)
        call    printf
        xorl    %eax, %eax
        movl    -4(%ebp), %ebx
        leave
        ret
```

Of course, the 80x86 doesn't have as many registers to use for passing parameters and holding local variables, so the 80x86 code has to allocate more locals in the activation record. Also, the 80x86 only provides an offset range of −128 to +127 bytes around the EBP register, so a larger number of instructions have to use the 4-byte offset rather than the 1-byte offset. Fortunately, the 80x86 does allow you to encode a full 32-bit address as part of the instructions that access memory, so you don't have to execute multiple instructions in order to access a variable stored a long distance away from where EBP points in the stack frame.

16.6 Parameter-Passing Mechanisms

Most high-level languages provide at least two mechanisms for passing actual parameter data to a subroutine: pass-by-value and pass-by-reference.[8] In languages like Visual Basic, Pascal, and C++, declaring and using both types of parameters is so easy that a programmer may conclude that there is little difference in efficiency between the two mechanisms. That's a fallacy this section intends to eradicate.

---

[8] The C language only allows pass-by-value, but it easily lets you take an address of some object so that you can easily simulate pass-by-reference. C++ fully supports pass-by-reference parameters.

NOTE *Before discussing the details of the pass-by-value and pass-by-reference parameter-passing mechanisms, I should briefly mention that there are other parameter-passing mechanisms. FORTRAN and HLA, for example, support a mechanism known as pass-by-value/result (or pass-by-value/returned). Ada and HLA support a pass-by-result parameter-passing mechanism. HLA and Algol support a parameter-passing mechanism known as pass-by-name. There are even some other parameter-passing schemes. This text will not discuss these alternative parameter-passing mechanisms because you probably won't see them very often. To use one of these parameter-passing schemes, consult a good book on programming language design or the HLA documentation.*

16.6.1   Pass-by-Value

Pass-by-value is the easiest parameter-passing mechanism to understand. The code that calls a procedure makes a copy of the parameter's data and passes this copy to the procedure. For small values, passing a parameter by value generally requires little more than a push instruction (or an instruction that moves the value into a register when passing parameters in the registers). Therefore, passing parameters by value is often very efficient.

One big advantage of pass-by-value parameters is that the CPU treats them just like a local variable within the activation record. Because you'll rarely have more than 120 bytes of parameter data that you pass to a procedure, CPUs that provide a shortened displacement with the indexed addressing mode will be able to access most parameter values using a shorter (and, therefore, more efficient) instruction.

The one time when passing a parameter by value can be inefficient is when you need to pass a large data structure such as an array or record. The calling code needs to make a byte-for-byte copy of the actual parameter into the procedure's activation record, as you saw in an earlier example. This can be a very slow process, for example, if you decide to pass a million-element array to a subroutine by value. Therefore, you should avoid passing large objects by value unless absolutely necessary.

16.6.2   Pass-by-Reference

The pass-by-reference mechanism passes the address of an object rather than its value. This has a couple of distinct advantages over pass-by-value. First, regardless of the parameter's size, pass-by-reference parameters always consume the same amount of memory—the size of a pointer (usually a double word). Second, pass-by-reference parameters provide the ability to modify the value of the actual parameter, something that is impossible with pass-by-value parameters.

Pass-by-reference parameters are not without their drawbacks. Usually, accessing a reference parameter within a procedure is more expensive than accessing a value parameter. This is because the subroutine needs to dereference that address on each access of the object. This generally involves loading a register with the pointer in order to dereference the pointer using a register indirect addressing mode.

For example, consider the following Pascal code:

```pascal
procedure RefValue
(
    var dest:integer;
    var passedByRef:integer;
        passedByValue:integer
);
begin

    dest := passedByRef + passedByValue;

end;
```

Here's the HLA/x86 assembly code that is equivalent to this procedure:

```hla
procedure RefValue
(
var     dest:int32;
var     passedByRef:int32;
        passedByValue:int32
); @noframe;
begin RefValue;

    // Standard Entry Sequence (needed because of @noframe).
    // Set up base pointer.
    // Note: don't need SUB(nn,esp) because
    // we don't have any local variables.

    push( ebp );
    mov( esp, ebp );

    // Get pointer to actual value.

    mov( passedByRef, edx );

    // Fetch value pointed at by passedByRef

    mov( [edx], eax );

    // Add in the value parameter.

    add( passedByValue, eax );

    // Get address of destination reference parameter.

    mov( dest, edx );

    // Store sum away into dest.

    mov( eax, [edx] );

    // Exit sequence doesn't need to deallocate any local
    //  variables because there are none.
```

```
        pop( ebp );
        ret( 12 );

end RefValue;
```

If you look closely at this code, you'll notice that it requires two more instructions than a version that uses pass-by-value specifically, the two instructions that load the addresses of dest and passedByRef into the EDX register. In general, only a single instruction is needed to access the value of a pass-by-value parameter. However, two instructions are needed to manipulate the value of a parameter when you pass it by reference (one instruction to fetch the address and one to manipulate the data at that address). Therefore, unless you need the semantics of pass-by-reference, you should try to use pass-by-value rather than pass-by-reference.

The issues with pass-by-reference tend to diminish when your CPU has lots of available registers that it can use to maintain the pointer values. In such situations, the CPU can use a single instruction to fetch or store a value via a pointer that is maintained in the register.

16.7 Function Return Values

Most HLLs return function results in one or more CPU registers. Exactly which register the compiler uses depends on the data type, CPU, and compiler. For the most part, however, functions return their results in registers.

On the 80x86, most functions that return ordinal (integer) values return their function results in the AL, AX, or EAX register. Functions that return 64-bit values (long long int) generally return the function result in the EDX:EAX register pair (with EDX containing the HO double word of the 64-bit value). On 64-bit variants of the 80x86 family, 64-bit compilers return 64-bit results in the RAX register. On the PowerPC, most compilers follow the IBM ABI and return 8-, 16-, and 32-bit values in the R3 register. Compilers for the 32-bit versions of the PowerPC return 64-bit ordinal values in the R4:R3 register pair (with R4 containing the HO word of the function result). Presumably, compilers running on 64-bit variants of the PowerPC can return 64-bit ordinal results directly in R3.

Generally, compilers return floating-point results in one of the CPU's (or FPU's) floating-point registers. On 32-bit variants of the 80x86 CPU family, most compilers return a floating-point result in the 80-bit ST0 floating-point register. Although the 64-bit versions of the 80x86 family also provide the same FPU registers as the 32-bit members, some OSes such as Windows64 typically use one of the SSE registers (XMM0) to return floating-point values. PowerPC systems generally return floating-point function results in the F1 floating-point register. Other CPUs return floating-point results in comparable locations.

Some languages allow a function to return a nonscalar (aggregate) value. The exact mechanism that compilers use to return large function return results varies from compiler to compiler. However, a typical solution is to pass a function the address of some storage where the function can place the return result. As an example, consider the following short C++ program whose func function returns a structure object:

```c
#include <stdio.h>

typedef struct
{
    int a;
    char b;
    short c;
    char d;
} s_t;

s_t func( void )
{
    s_t s;

    s.a = 0;
    s.b = 1;
    s.c = 2;
    s.d = 3;
    return s;
}

int main( void )
{
    s_t t;

    t = func();
    printf( "%d", t.a, func().a );
    return( 0 );
}
```

Here's the PowerPC code that GCC emits for this C++ program:

```
.text
        .align 2
        .globl _func

; func() -- Note: upon entry, this
;           code assumes that R3
;           points at the storage
;           to hold the return result.

_func:
        li r0,1
        li r9,2
        stb r0,-28(r1) ;s.b = 1
        li r0,3
        stb r0,-24(r1) ;s.d = 3
        sth r9,-26(r1) ;s.c = 2
        li r9,0        ;s.a = 0
```

```
            ;Okay, set up the return
            ; result.

            lwz r0,-24(r1) ;r0 = d::c
            stw r9,0(r3)    ;result.a = s.a
            stw r0,8(r3)    ;result.d/c = s.d/c
            lwz r9,-28(r1)
            stw r9,4(r3)    ;result.b = s.b
            blr


            .data
            .cstring
            .align 2
LC0:
            .ascii "%d\0"
            .text
            .align 2
            .globl _main
_main:
            mflr r0
            stw r31,-4(r1)
            stw r0,8(r1)
            bcl 20,31,L1$pb
L1$pb:
            ;Allocate storage for t and
            ; temporary storage for second
            ; call to func:

            stwu r1,-112(r1)

            ; Restore LINK from above:

            mflr r31

            ;Get pointer to destination
            ; storage (t) into R3 and call func:

            addi r3,r1,64
            bl _func

            ;Compute "func().a"

            addi r3,r1,80
            bl _func

            ;Get t.a and func().a values
            ; and print them:

            lwz r4,64(r1)
            lwz r5,80(r1)
            addis r3,r31,ha16(LC0-L1$pb)
            la r3,lo16(LC0-L1$pb)(r3)
            bl L_printf$stub
```

```
        lwz r0,120(r1)
        addi r1,r1,112
        li r3,0
        mtlr r0
        lwz r31,-4(r1)
        blr

;stub for printf function:

        .data
        .picsymbol_stub
L_printf$stub:
        .indirect_symbol _printf
        mflr r0
        bcl 20,31,L0$_printf
L0$_printf:
        mflr r11
        addis r11,r11,ha16(L_printf$lazy_ptr-L0$_printf)
        mtlr r0
        lwz r12,lo16(L_printf$lazy_ptr-L0$_printf)(r11)
        mtctr r12
        addi r11,r11,lo16(L_printf$lazy_ptr-L0$_printf)
        bctr
.data
.lazy_symbol_pointer
L_printf$lazy_ptr:
        .indirect_symbol _printf
        .long dyld_stub_binding_helper
```

Here's the 80x86 code that GCC emits for this same function:

```
.file   "t.c"
        .text
        .p2align 2,,3
        .globl func
        .type   func,@function

;On entry, assume that the address
; of the storage that will hold the
; function's return result is passed
; on the stack immediately above the
; return address.

func:
        pushl   %ebp
        movl    %esp, %ebp
        subl    $24, %esp        ;Allocate storage for s.

        movl    8(%ebp), %eax    ;Get address of result
        movb    $1, -20(%ebp)    ;s.b = 1
        movw    $2, -18(%ebp)    ;s.c = 2
        movb    $3, -16(%ebp)    ;s.d = 3
        movl    $0, (%eax)       ;result.a = 0;
        movl    -20(%ebp), %edx  ;Copy the rest of s
```

```
              movl    %edx, 4(%eax)    ; to the storage for
              movl    -16(%ebp), %edx  ; the return result.
              movl    %edx, 8(%eax)
              leave
              ret     $4
.Lfe1:
              .size   func,.Lfe1-func
              .section        .rodata.str1.1,"aMS",@progbits,1
.LC0:
              .string "%d"

              .text
              .p2align 2,,3
              .globl main
              .type   main,@function
main:
              pushl   %ebp
              movl    %esp, %ebp
              subl    $40, %esp        ;Allocate storage for
              andl    $-16, %esp       ; t and temp result.

              ;Pass the address of t to func:

              leal    -24(%ebp), %eax
              subl    $12, %esp
              pushl   %eax
              call    func

              ;Pass the address of some temporary storage
              ; to func:

              leal    -40(%ebp), %eax
              pushl   %eax
              call    func

              ;Remove junk from stack:

              popl    %eax
              popl    %edx

              ;Call printf to print the two values:

              pushl   -40(%ebp)
              pushl   -24(%ebp)
              pushl   $.LC0
              call    printf
              xorl    %eax, %eax
              leave
              ret
```

The one thing that you should note from these 80x86 and PowerPC examples is that functions returning large objects often copy the function result data just prior to returning. This extra copying can take considerable time, especially if the return result is large. Instead of returning a large structure as a function result, as I've done above, it is usually a better solution to explicitly pass a pointer to some destination storage to a function that returns a large result and let the function do whatever copying is necessary. This often saves some time and code. Consider the following C code that implements this policy:

```c
#include <stdio.h>

typedef struct
{
    int a;
    char b;
    short c;
    char d;
} s_t;

void func( s_t *s )
{
    s->a = 0;
    s->b = 1;
    s->c = 2;
    s->d = 3;
    return;
}

int main( void )
{
    s_t s,t;

    func( &s );
    func( &t );
    printf( "%d", s.a, t.a );
    return( 0 );
}
```

Here's the conversion to 80x86 code by GCC:

```asm
.file   "t.c"
        .text
        .p2align 2,,3
.globl func
        .type   func,@function
func:
        pushl   %ebp
        movl    %esp, %ebp
        movl    8(%ebp), %eax
        movl    $0, (%eax)      ;s->a = 0
        movb    $1, 4(%eax)     ;s->b = 1
        movw    $2, 6(%eax)     ;s->c = 2
        movb    $3, 8(%eax)     ;s->d = 3
        leave
        ret
```

```
.Lfe1:
        .size   func,.Lfe1-func
        .section        .rodata.str1.1,"aMS",@progbits,1
.LC0:
        .string "%d"
        .text
        .p2align 2,,3
.globl main
        .type   main,@function
main:
        ;Build activation record and allocate
        ; storage for s and t:

        pushl   %ebp
        movl    %esp, %ebp
        subl    $40, %esp
        andl    $-16, %esp
        subl    $12, %esp

        ;Pass address of s to func and
        ; call func:

        leal    -24(%ebp), %eax
        pushl   %eax
        call    func

        ;Pass address of t to func and
        ; call func:

        leal    -40(%ebp), %eax
        movl    %eax, (%esp)
        call    func

        ;Remove junk from stack:

        addl    $12, %esp

        ;Print the results:

        pushl   -40(%ebp)
        pushl   -24(%ebp)
        pushl   $.LC0
        call    printf
        xorl    %eax, %eax
        leave
        ret
```

As you can see, this approach is more efficient because the code doesn't have to copy the data twice, once to a local copy of the data and once to the final destination variable.

16.8 For More Information

A good textbook on compiler design and implementation or programming language design is an excellent source of information concerning functions, procedures, and parameters. Many such books were listed in the previous chapters on control structures (Section 14.7, "For More Information"). The HLA programming language supports a wide variety of parameter-passing mechanisms beyond pass-by-value and pass-by-reference. You might check out the HLA reference manual at http://webster.cs.ucr.edu for more details on those parameter types.

ENGINEERING SOFTWARE

The goal of this volume, *Thinking Low-Level, Writing High-Level,* was to get you to consider the impact of your high-level coding techniques on the machine code that the compiler generates for that code. Unless you understand the efficiency trade-offs of statements and data structures in your HLL programs, you won't be able to produce efficient programs consistently. And if you want to write great code, you can't write inefficient programs. However, as noted in Chapter 1 of this book, efficiency isn't the only attribute that great code possesses. The first two volumes of this series, *Understanding the Machine* and *Thinking Low-Level, Writing High-Level,* have addressed some of the efficiency concerns facing modern programmers. The next volume in this series, *Engineering Software,* will head off in a different direction and discuss other attributes that great code possesses.

Write Great Code, Volume 3: Engineering Software begins discussing the *personal software engineering* aspects of programming. The field of *software engineering* is principally concerned with the management of large software systems. Personal software engineering, on the other hand, covers those topics germane to writing great code at a personal level: craftsmanship, art, and pride in workmanship. *Engineering Software* discusses things like coding styles, commenting, code layout, and other coding tasks that make code readable and easy to maintain. No matter how efficient your code is, if it is not readable and maintainable by others, then it's not great code. In *Engineering Software*, I'll begin to describe how to write code so that other people think it's great, too.

Congratulations on your progress thus far toward knowing how to write great code. See you in Volume 3.

A BRIEF COMPARISON OF THE 80X86 AND POWERPC CPU FAMILIES

The CPUs from the Intel/AMD 80x86 and IBM/Motorola PowerPC families are the most popular CPUs found in personal computer systems and game consoles today. As such, more applications are written for these two CPU families than for any other. Although other processor families, such as MIPS and ARM, are quite popular in embedded systems, the majority of software applications are written for 80x86 or PowerPC CPUs. This is the main reason 80x86 and PowerPC examples appear in this book.

Another reason this book's examples use code produced for these two processors is that they provide representative samples of the two fundamental CPU designs in common use today: CISC and RISC. If you understand how to generate good code for one CISC processor, then you can do a decent job on any other CISC processor. The same is true for RISC processors. As the examples in this book demonstrate, however, there are some fundamental differences between RISC and CISC CPUs, so you should understand the differences between these two basic architectures when you write code that might have to run on either technology. The purpose of this appendix is to compare and contrast the 80x86 (CISC) and PowerPC (RISC) families and their impact on high-level language code.

A.1 Architectural Differences Between RISC and CISC

The architectural differences between the two processor families can be grouped into these categories:

- The amount of work accomplished per instruction
- The size of an individual instruction
- The clock speed and clock cycles per instruction
- Their methods of memory access and their addressing modes
- The number of registers they provide, and the way they use those registers
- Their use of immediate (constant) operands
- Their use of the stack

A.1.1 Work Accomplished per Instruction

Perhaps the most fundamental difference between the RISC and CISC philosophies is the amount of work accomplished by a single instruction. Although today's 80x86 CPUs aren't "pure" CISC processors and the PowerPC CPUs aren't "pure" RISC processors, the amount of work accomplished by individual instructions is one of the fundamental differences between these CPU families.

The original CISC philosophy was to do as much work per instruction as possible. Doing more work with fewer instructions meant that writing programs (in assembly language) was easier, and it was easier to write code generators for compilers.

RISC designs, on the other hand, attempt to perform only one operation per instruction. For this reason, it often takes two or more RISC instructions to do the same work as a single CISC instruction. As a result, RISC programs generally execute between 1.5 and 2.5 times as many instructions to do the same work as an equivalent program running on a CISC processor.

If all things were equal (and they are not), the CISC philosophy would win, hands down. In practice, however, there are several problems with designing instructions to do as much work as possible. The main problem is that all this extra work isn't achieved without cost. Instructions that do complex things often take longer to execute than simpler instructions. If you're not fully utilizing all the features of a given instruction, then you're paying an execution-time penalty for all those extra features you're not using. In extreme cases, executing two or more simple instructions that accomplish only what you need may execute quicker than executing a single complex instruction that does more than you require.

As stated, the 80x86 is not a "pure" CISC processor, and the PowerPC is not a "pure" RISC processor. In order to remain competitive, Intel's designers have utilized many RISC design principles in later variants of the

80x86 family. They've provided a *RISC instruction subset* (called the *RISC core*); these instructions execute quickly by avoiding complex operations. Likewise, IBM's designers have "corrupted" the RISC design philosophies in a couple of places in order to improve the CPU's performance for many common operations by doing several operations with a single instruction. By and large, though, the 80x86 is still a representative CISC CPU and the PowerPC follows RISC design philosophies.

A.1.2 Instruction Size

Most CISC designs use a variable instruction length, whereas RISC designs use fixed instruction lengths. Instructions on the 80x86, for example, range in length from 1 byte to 15 bytes. PowerPC instructions, on the other hand, are always 4 bytes long.

From a memory-usage point of view, CISC designs are more efficient than RISC designs. A well-designed CISC instruction set can pack more instructions into the same memory, thereby using less memory to hold the same number of instructions. Combined with the fact that those (smaller) instructions often do more work than individual RISC instructions, CISC processors usually have a big advantage over RISC processors when it comes to instruction density (that is, the number of instructions appearing in a given block of memory).

Because many CISC instructions are greater than 4 bytes in length, you might wonder why CISC programs wouldn't average more instruction bytes per program than a RISC counterpart. The answer is "work per instruction." For example, loading a 32-bit constant into a 32-bit register typically requires a single 5-byte or 6-byte instruction on the 80x86. On the PowerPC, however, all instructions are 4 bytes long, so you cannot load a 32-bit constant into a register using a single instruction. You must leave some bits to hold the instruction's opcode. This is why two (or more) 4-byte instructions are needed to load a 32-bit constant into a register on a typical RISC CPU.

A.1.3 Clock Speed and Clocks per Instruction

So far, it appears that the CISC design philosophy is the outright winner when comparing the two designs. CISC instructions do more work and, on the average, require less memory to do that work. All other things being equal, you might expect that programs running in a CISC processor would run faster than equivalent programs running on a RISC processor.

In fact, this assumption turns out to be false. The implicit assumption here is that all instructions take the same amount of time to execute, regardless of their size and complexity. In the real world, and especially for CISC processors, complex instructions often take far longer to execute than simpler instructions. Indeed, the holy grail of RISC design has always been to reduce instruction execution time to one clock per instruction (CPI) or less. Although contemporary 80x86 designs also attempt to achieve this goal for the "RISC core" instruction set, in reality the RISC CPUs (such as the PowerPC) tend to achieve the goal of one clock per instruction (or less) better than the 80x86.

Another stated goal for RISC design is to achieve higher operating frequencies than comparable CISC designs. By simplifying the instruction set, circuit paths within the CPU are also simplified, allowing the manufacturer to run their CPUs at a higher clock frequency. In practice, CPU clock frequency is dependent upon many things besides the instruction complexity. As this book was being written, the 80x86 was still the champion at the clock frequency competition. However, because 80x86 instructions typically take multiple clocks cycles to execute, the higher clock frequency does not always equate to faster running programs. In the area of clock speed, the 80x86 has the (current) advantage, but RISC CPUs such as the PowerPC still use fewer clocks per instruction, on the average.

A.1.4 Memory Access and Addressing Modes

One of the most fundamental differences between RISC and CISC designs has to do with memory access. RISC CPUs typically utilize a *load/store architecture* that allows memory access only via specialized load and store instructions. No other instructions can access memory. Instead, they must operate on data in registers. CISC processors, on the other hand, allow most instructions to access operands in memory. If a program needs to access an object in memory, then the CISC approach is more efficient—the instruction that needs to access the data can do so directly. On a RISC CPU (such as the PowerPC), the program must first execute an instruction to load the memory value into a register and then operate on the data in that register. This assumes, of course, that a register is available to hold the data (the CISC approach doesn't require an available register, because it can operate directly on the object in memory without first loading it into a register). Worse still, because RISC instructions are generally only 32 bits long, you cannot encode a full static memory address as part of an instruction; instead, RISC CPUs might need to execute two or more instructions to load the address of a memory location into a register prior to accessing that memory location indirectly through the register.

At first blush, the ability to access objects in memory would seem to give CISC processors a big advantage. There are, however, two problems with memory access:

- Memory access is slow. If the memory data is not in cache, the memory access could take one or two orders of magnitude longer than a corresponding register access (and if the data has been paged out to disk by the virtual memory subsystem, access will be even slower).

- Encoding the address of the memory operand in the instruction takes considerable space. Accessing a simple global static object rather than a register, for example, can turn a 2-byte 80x86 instruction into a 6-byte 80x86 instruction.

On modern computer systems, memory access is so slow (compared with register access) that efficient programs tend to minimize memory operations. Therefore, the advantage of superior memory access by CISC CPUs is under-utilized, diminishing this advantage of CISC processors.

A.1.5 Registers

Most CPUs perform intermediate calculations in registers and use registers to hold parameter and local variable values (to avoid accessing memory). The more registers you have, the more data a CPU can manipulate without accessing main memory. This is one area where RISC processors have a huge advantage over CISC processors. A typical RISC CPU, like the PowerPC, pro-vides 32 general-purpose registers, compared to the eight general-purpose registers found on a 32-bit 80x86 CPU.[1] As a result, RISC CPUs do not have to access memory anywhere near as often as the 80x86 CPU does. Because register access is much faster than memor access, having these extra registers helps RISC CPUs overcome the fact that many operations require the exe-cution of two or more RISC instructions to do the same work as one CISC instruction that can directly access memory.

A.1.6 Immediate (Constant) Operands

RISC and CISC CPUs often vary considerably with respect to the type of immediate operands that instructions allow. CISC CPUs support variable-sized instructions that allow a program to specify 8-, 16-, 32-, and even 64-bit constant operands as part of a single instruction.[2] RISC processors only allow a single 32-bit instruction format and, therefore, cannot encode an instruc-tion opcode, destination register operand, and a large immediate constant into a single instruction. RISC CPUs, therefore, have to use two or more instructions to load large constant values into a register. This situation worsens as the instruction operands become larger (e.g., loading a 64-bit constant into a 64-bit variant of the PowerPC).

Although the 80x86 handles immediate integer constants well, you should note that it does not allow the encoding of immediate floating-point, MMX, or SSE values into an instruction. To load such constants into the 80x86, most programmers (or compilers) initialize a memory location with the constant value and load the contents of that memory location into the desired register. Code on the PowerPC CPU often works this same way for floating-point and Altivec constant operands.

A.1.7 Stacks

CISC CPUs generally provide a hardware stack that maintains subroutine return addresses, parameters, local variables, and other temporary values. Machine instructions such as call, ret, push, and pop automatically maintain data on the stack. These are classic examples of CISC instructions that perform

---

[1] The 64-bit variants of the 80x86 provide 16 general-purpose registers.

[2] 64-bit immediate operands are only available on 64-bit variants of the 80x86.

multiple operations. Because of their complexity, you rarely see instructions such as these in a RISC instruction set. As such, RISC processors do not provide a hardware stack—return addresses and other objects that need to be maintained on a stack data structure must be maintained under software control.

Maintaining a stack in software is definitely more expensive than doing it in hardware (in terms of CPU cycles). The main reason PowerPC (and other RISC) function calls aren't considerably slower than 80x86 code is because the PowerPC doesn't use the stack as much as the 80x86 does. The PowerPC, for example, sets aside eight registers to use to pass parameters to a function. Therefore, a PowerPC program can load parameter values into registers (cheap and easy) rather than "pushing" them onto a software-maintained stack (slow and expensive). Similarly, for many short procedures and functions (see Section 16.2, "Leaf Functions and Procedures"), there is no need to copy the return address onto the software stack, you can keep the return address in a register. The PowerPC sets aside eight additional registers to hold local variables for a procedure or function; so if you don't need more than eight local variables, you can avoid using the stack for this purpose as well. A surprising number of procedures on the PowerPC can be coded into machine code that does not manipulate the data on the stack at all. In such cases, the code will execute faster than it would even if a hardware stack were available.

High-quality 80x86 compilers also attempt to maintain parameters and local variables in registers (rather than on the stack). However, because the 80x86 has a very limited number of general-purpose registers available, most compilers only have three registers to use for local variable and parameter objects (compared to a total of 16 registers for locals and parameters on the PowerPC). Clearly, the PowerPC, with its larger register set, is better able to allocate parameters and local variables to registers.

A.2 Compiler and Application Binary Interface Issues

As a general rule, compilers adhere to an *Application Binary Interface (ABI)* when emitting code for a particular machine and operating system. The choice of ABI often places some restrictions on the compiler's code generation capabilities that result in less efficient code than would otherwise be possible. Although a hardware manufacturer typically specifies an ABI in order to create a standard, the truth is that ABIs are computer system– and operating system–specific, not simply CPU-specific. For example, the Linux operating system could use a different ABI than the Windows operating system, even when both are using the same 80x86 processor. Similarly, the Mac OS X operating system places restrictions on the code that might not be present in an embedded PowerPC application. In order to produce high-quality code, you need to understand how an ABI can affect a compiler's code generation strategies and adjust your coding style appropriately.

While there are a wide variety of other operating systems and ABIs we could consider, these two operating systems and ABI provide a good contrast with respect to the things we should consider when writing code.

Global and external objects are two areas where code quality differs dramatically between the PowerPC and 80x86 architectures. The problem is the lack of 32-bit offset encodings on the PowerPC.

A.3   Writing Great Code for Both Architectures

Furndamentally, efficient code possesses three important attributes: (1) it executes as few instructions as possible to do a given job; (2) it accesses memory as infrequently as possible (and tries to access data in the cache when memory accesses are necessary); and (3) it uses as little memory as possible. These facts remain true whether the CPU is a RISC or CISC design. If you are writing code that must exhibit excellent properties on both processor types, you should give priority to RISC optimizations in your code. Optimizations like minimizing constant size, trying to keep offsets to variables short (so you can encode their offsets in a 32-bit instruction format) and so on will only have a small deterimental effect on a CISC compiler's code generation capabilities. However, optimizing for a CISC processor, taking advantage of its ability to easily access memory and deal with large immediate constants, can have a very deterimental effect on the code a RISC compiler generates.

Ultimately, the best solution is to tailor your code for a given CPU architecture. Given the fact that almost all personal computers (including Apple) are using the 80x86 architecture, you would probably be advised to develop your code for the CISC architecture if you're targeting personal computers with your applicaation. On the other hand, as most embedded systems use RISC processors, you would be well-advised to apply RISC optimiations to embedded code.

ONLINE APPENDICES

Write Great Code: Thinking Low-Level, Writing High-Level includes supplimentary materials online at www.writegreatcode.com. These two appendices are published in electronic form to allow them to be kept up to date.

Online Appendix A

The Minimal 80x86 Instruction Set

Online Appendix B

The Minimal PowerPC Instruction Set

Visit www.writegreatcode.com. Under Volume 2, you will find the PDFs of these two resources available for download.

INDEX

Assembler syntax, 22
Assemblers
    See Gas (GNU assembler)
    See HLA (High-Level Assembler)
    See MASM (Microsoft Macro
        Assembler)
    See TASM (Borland Turbo
        Assembler)
    FASM assembler, 22
    GoAsm assembler, 22
    NASM assembler, 22
Assembly language, 1–2
    80x86, 21. *See also* 80x86
    as compiler output, 83
    macro to declare seven-bit
        strings, 302
    operand sizes, 44
    output from a compiler, 84,
        115–116
        from Borland C++, 121
        from a C/C++ compiler, 118
    programming paradigm, 16
Assigning offsets to local variables, 552
Associating offsets with parameters, 554
AST (abstract syntax tree), 69–70
Attributes
    for a token, 68
    of variables and other program
        objects, 196
Automatic disassemblers, 146
Automatic variables, 186, 189, 203
    advantages of, 204
    disadvantages of, 204
    versus local variables, 204
    and offset sizes, 217
Auxiliary carry flag (80x86), 25
Avoiding data copying, 300
Avoiding problems with side
    effects, 425
AWK programming language, 320
AX register (80x86), 24

B

Back end to a compiler, 123
Base address, 550
    of an allocated memory region, 321
    of an array, 242, 322
    of a record, 355
Base of an activation record, 220
Base pointer register, 549

Base register (PowerPC), 56
Base-2 (binary) literal constants, 26
BaseOfCode field in a COFF file, 90
BaseOfData field in a COFF file, 90
Basic blocks, 72–77
BASIC programming language, 7
    and dynamic scoping, 198
    interpreters, 63
bcc32/bcc32i compilers, 123
Benchmarks, 4
Best size of an integer, 211
Best-fit memory allocation, 330
Beyond Compare differencing
    utility, 162
BH register (80x86), 24
Big endian issues when using
    unions, 364
Binary
    constants, 33
    literal constants, 26
        in Gas, 26
        in HLA, 26
        in MASM/TASM, 26
    numbering system, 7
    search, 4
Binary-coded decimal
    representation, 210
Binding
    attributes to objects, 197
    at compile time, 199, 200
    dynamic, 206
    at language design time, 199, 200
    at link time, 199, 200
    at load time, 199, 200
    objects dynamically, 197
    values dynamically, 199
    variables
        pseudo-static, 203
        static, 199–200
BIOS ROM, 200
Bit strings, 281
bits functions
    bits.cnt function, 110
    bits.reverse8 library function, 105
    bits.reverse16 library function, 105
    bits.reverse32 library function, 105
Bitwise logical operations, 176, 497
BL register (80x86), 24
bl instruction (PowerPC), 525
BLOCK alignment option (GNU's ld
    linker), 102

Update register addressing mode (PowerPC), 55–56

User mode (CPU), 333

Usage
of allocated storage after it has been freed, 336
of bitwise logical operations to improve code generation, 176
of a debugger to analyze compiler output, 116, 149
of a disassembler to analyze compiler output, 146
of function calls to force short-circuit Boolean evaluation, 502
of IDE's Debugger to disassemble object code, 149
of inline functions to force complete Boolean evaluation in a while loop, 495
of integer operations to operate on floating-point data, 176
of object code utilities to analyze compiler output, 129
of strings in a high-level language, 310

UTF. *See* Unicode Transformational Format

V

val section in an HLA program, 30

Variables, 196, 199
addresses, 189, 215
alignment in memory, 229
allocation for global and static variables, 216
automatic, 203
and memory consumption, 204
and offset sizes, 217
in basic blocks, 74
Boolean, 215
byte, accessing in assembly language, 42
character, 214
dynamic, 206
efficient access using short offsets, 215
floating-point, 213

FORTRAN LOGICAL*4 variables, 215
global, 223
in high-level languages, 189
integer variables, 210
size and efficiency, 213
intermediate, accessing, 223
local, accessing, 559
offset sizes, reducing by using a pointer, 226
ordering declarations for efficiency, 230
pseudo-static binding, 203–204
real, 213
signed integer, 212
size of an integer, 210
static, 199
memory consumption, 201
static binding, 199
storage, 199
type, 199
unsigned integer, 212

Variant data types, 342

Variant types, 364–365

VC++ (Visual C++), 8, 118
compiler, 118
optimization options, 80
output, 117–119
command-line option, 118

Version number of a COFF format, 89

VHLL (very high-level language), 83

Viewing Delphi-produced object code in a debugger, 151

Virtual (hypothetical) machine language, 65

Virtual machines, 391

Virtual member functions, 373

Virtual method table. *See* VMT

VirtualAddress field in a COFF file, 92

VirtualSize field in a COFF file, 92

Visual Basic, 8
arrays, 271
variant types, 365

Visual C++. *See* VC++

Visual Studio debugger, 149

VLIW (very large instruction word) processors, 48

VM (virtual machine), 391

VMT (virtual method table), 342, 373
  pointers, 373
void function (C/C++), 522
Von Neuman architecture, 23, 49
vstamp field in a COFF file, 89

W

When not to call a standard library
      routine, 294
while loops, 489
  with complete Boolean
      evaluation, 492
  conversion to an if and a goto, 490
Windows runtime memory
      organization, 190
Word (halfword) values (PowerPC), 56
Word count program, 63
Word data (80x86), 39
word declaration (MASM/TASM), 42
Work accomplished per
      instruction, 582
Working set, 99
Worst case performance of an
      optimizer, 71

X

XER register (PowerPC), 49, 51

Z

Z80 CPU, 393
Zero (NULL) address, 190
Zero bit (PowerPC condition code
      register), 50
Zero flag (80x86), 25, 441
Zero/nonzero Boolean
      representation, 175
Zero/one Boolean representation, 174
Zero-address machines, 389
Zero-terminated string (zstring), 283
  advantages, 283
  disadvantages, 284
  implementation, 284
  overhead, 283
zstring (zero-terminated string), 283

WRITE PORTABLE CODE
An Introduction to Developing Software for Multiple Platforms

by BRIAN HOOK

Write Portable Code contains the lessons, patterns, and knowledge for developing cross-platform software that programmers usually must acquire through trial and error. This book is targeted at intermediate- to advanced-level programmers and will be a valuable resource for designers of cross-platform software, programmers looking to extend their skills to additional platforms, and programmers faced with the tricky task of moving code from one platform to another.

JULY 2005, 272 PP., $34.95 ($47.95 CDN)
ISBN 1-59327-056-9

WICKED COOL JAVA
Code Bits, Open-Source Libraries, and Project Ideas

by BRIAN D. EUBANKS

Wicked Cool Java contains 101 fun, interesting, and useful ways to get more out of Java. It is not intended as a Java tutorial—it's targeted at developers and system architects who have some basic Java knowledge but may not be familiar with the wide range of libraries available. Full of example code and ideas for combining it into useful projects, this book is perfect for hobbyists and professionals looking for tips and open-source projects to enhance their code and make their jobs easier.

NOVEMBER 2005, 248 PP., $29.95 ($40.95 CDN)
ISBN 1-59327-061-5

THE BOOK OF™ VISUAL BASIC 2005
.NET Insight for Classic VB Developers

by MATTHEW MACDONALD

The Book of Visual Basic 2005 is a comprehensive introduction to Microsoft's newest programming language, Visual Basic 2005, the next iteration of Visual Basic .NET. A complete revision of the highly-acclaimed *Book of VB .NET*, the book is organized as a series of lightning-fast tours and real-world examples that show developers the VB 2005 way of doing things. Perfect for old-school Visual Basic developers who haven't made the jump to .NET, the book is also useful to developers from other programming backgrounds (like Java) who want to cut to the chase and quickly learn how to program with VB 2005.

APRIL 2006, 528 PP., $39.95 ($51.95 CDN)
ISBN 1-59327-074-7

WRITE GREAT CODE, VOLUME 1
Understanding the Machine

by RANDALL HYDE

Write Great Code, Volume 1 teaches machine organization, including numeric representation; binary arithmetic and bit operations; floating point representation; system and memory organization; character representation; constants and types; digital design; CPU, instruction set, and memory architecture; input and output; and how compilers work.

NOVEMBER 2004, 464 PP., $39.95 ($55.95 CDN)
ISBN 1-59327-003-8

THE ART OF ASSEMBLY LANGUAGE
by RANDALL HYDE

Presents assembly language from the high-level programmer's point of view so programmers can start writing meaningful programs within days. The CD-ROM includes the author's High Level Assembler (HLA), the first assembler that allows programmers to write portable assembly language programs that run under either Linux or Windows with nothing more than a recompile.

SEPTEMBER 2003, 928 PP. W/CD, $59.95 ($89.95 CDN)
ISBN 1-886411-97-2

PHONE:
800.420.7240 OR
415.863.9900
MONDAY THROUGH FRIDAY,
9 A.M. TO 5 P.M. (PST)

FAX:
415.863.9950
24 HOURS A DAY,
7 DAYS A WEEK

EMAIL:
SALES@NOSTARCH.COM

WEB:
HTTP://WWW.NOSTARCH.COM

MAIL:
NO STARCH PRESS
555 DE HARO ST, SUITE 250
SAN FRANCISCO, CA 94107
USA

Electronic Frontier Foundation
Defending Freedom in the Digital World

Free Speech. Privacy. Innovation. Fair Use. Reverse Engineering. **If you care about these rights in the digital world, then you should join the Electronic Frontier Foundation (EFF). EFF was founded in 1990 to protect the rights of users and developers of technology. EFF is the first to identify threats to basic rights online and to advocate on behalf of free expression in the digital age.**

The Electronic Frontier Foundation Defends Your Rights!
Become a Member Today!
http://www.eff.org/support/

Current EFF projects include:

Protecting your fundamental right to vote. Widely publicized security flaws in computerized voting machines show that, though filled with potential, this technology is far from perfect. EFF is defending the open discussion of e-voting problems and is coordinating a national litigation strategy addressing issues arising from use of poorly developed and tested computerized voting machines.

Ensuring that you are not traceable through your things. Libraries, schools, the government and private sector businesses are adopting radio frequency identification tags, or RFIDs – a technology capable of pinpointing the physical location of whatever item the tags are embedded in. While this may seem like a convenient way to track items, it's also a convenient way to do something less benign: track people and their activities through their belongings. EFF is working to ensure that embrace of this technology does not erode your right to privacy.

Stopping the FBI from creating surveillance backdoors on the Internet. EFF is part of a coalition opposing the FBI's expansion of the Communications Assistance for Law Enforcement Act (CALEA), which would require that the wiretap capabilities built into the phone system be extended to the Internet, forcing ISPs to build backdoors for law enforcement.

Providing you with a means by which you can contact key decision-makers on cyber-liberties issues. EFF maintains an action center that provides alerts on technology, civil liberties issues and pending legislation to more than 50,000 subscribers. EFF also generates a weekly online newsletter, EFFector, and a blog that provides up-to-the minute information and commentary.

Defending your right to listen to and copy digital music and movies. The entertainment industry has been overzealous in trying to protect its copyrights, often decimating fair use rights in the process. EFF is standing up to the movie and music industries on several fronts.

Check out all of the things we're working on at http://www.eff.org and join today or make a donation to support the fight to defend freedom online.

ELECTRONIC FRONTIER FOUNDATION · 454 SHOTWELL STREET · SAN FRANCISCO, CA 94110 · 415.436.9333

COLOPHON

Write Great Code: Thinking Low-Level, Writing High-Level was laid out in Adobe FrameMaker. The font families used are New Baskerville for body text, Futura for headings and tables, and Dogma for titles.

The book was printed and bound at Malloy Incorporated in Ann Arbor, Michigan. The paper is Glatfelter Thor 50# Antique, which is made from 50 percent recycled materials, including 30 percent postconsumer content. The book uses a RepKover binding, which allows it to lay flat when open.

UPDATES

Visit **http://www.nostarch.com/greatcode2.htm** for updates, errata, and other information.